Criminal Procedure
and Sentencir

Criminal Procedure and Sentencing provides a comprehensive, engaging and up-to-date guide to each step of criminal procedure, from the arrest of the suspect through to trial, sentencing and appeals. Taking a strong practical focus throughout, it covers all aspects of the process of the criminal courts.

The ninth edition has been fully revised and significantly expanded to include more information about the workings of the criminal courts of England and Wales.

The supporting website offers readers access to regular updates to the law and also a comprehensive set of web links and advice on additional reading and research for those seeking to engage in critical evaluation of the criminal justice system.

This is an ideal text for anyone studying the criminal justice system at a professional or academic level. The author's authoritative yet engaging writing style brings the subject to life and helps to explain complex issues in an easy-to-understand way.

Peter Hungerford-Welch is a Professor of Law and Assistant Dean (Head of Professional Programmes) at the City Law School, City, University of London. He teaches on the Bar Professional Training Course LLM in the areas of Criminal Litigation and Sentencing, Fraud and Economic Crime, and Advanced Criminal Litigation. Peter also teaches *Criminal Justice: The Process of the Criminal Courts*, and *Sentencing: Theory and Practice* on the School's LLM programme.

Criminal Procedure and Sentencing

Ninth Edition

Peter Hungerford-Welch

Routledge
Taylor & Francis Group

LONDON AND NEW YORK

First published 2019
by Routledge
2 Park Square, Milton Park, Abingdon, Oxon OX14 4RN

and by Routledge
52 Vanderbilt Avenue, New York, NY 10017

Routledge is an imprint of the Taylor & Francis Group, an informa business

British Library Cataloguing-in-Publication Data
A catalogue record for this book is available from the British Library

Library of Congress Cataloging-in-Publication Data
Names: Hungerford-Welch, Peter, author.
Title: Criminal procedure and sentencing/by Peter Hungerford-Welch.
Description: 9th edition. | Milton Park, Abingdon, Oxon; New York, NY: Routledge, an imprint of the Taylor & Francis Group, an informa business, 2019. | Includes bibliographical references and index.
Identifiers: LCCN 2018044710| ISBN 9780815376620 (hbk) | ISBN 9780815376637 (pbk) | ISBN 9781351237260 (ebk) | ISBN 9781351237253 (adobe) | ISBN 9781351237246 (epub) | ISBN 9781351237239 (mobipocket)
Subjects: LCSH: Criminal procedure–England. | Sentences (Criminal procedure)–England.
Classification: LCC KD8329.6. H86 2019 | DDC 345.42/05–dc23
LC record available at https://lccn.loc.gov/2018044710

ISBN: 978-0-815-37662-0 (hbk)
ISBN: 978-0-815-37663-7 (pbk)
ISBN: 978-1-351-23726-0 (ebk)

Typeset in Joanna
by Integra Software Services Pvt. Ltd.

Printed and bound in Great Britain by
TJ International Ltd, Padstow, Cornwall

Contents

Contents

Table of Cases

Table of Statutes

Table of Statutory Instruments

Table of European Legislation

Table of Abbreviations

CCRC	Criminal Cases Review Commission
CDA	Crime and Disorder Act
CJA	Criminal Justice Act
CJPOA	Criminal Justice and Public Order Act
CPIA	Criminal Procedure and Investigations Act
CPS	Crown Prosecution Service
CrimPR	Criminal Procedure Rules
DPP	Director of Public Prosecutions
DTO	Detention and Training Order
ECHR	European Convention on Human Rights
ECtHR	European Court of Human Rights
JP	Justice of the Peace
LASPO	Legal Aid, Sentencing and Punishment of Offenders Act
MCA	Magistrates' Courts Act
PACE	Police and Criminal Evidence Act
PII	Public interest immunity
PTPH	Plea and Trial Preparation Hearing
SC	Sentencing Council
SCA	Senior Courts Act
TIC	taken into consideration
VRR	Victim Right to Review
YOT	Youth Offending Team
YRO	Youth Rehabilitation Order

In this chapter, we consider some preliminary matters relating to criminal procedure, including:

- the structure of the criminal courts in England and Wales;
- the overriding objective that governs the criminal process;
- the investigative powers of the police (including powers of stop and search);
- the commencement of criminal proceedings (arrest; written charge and requisition; information and summons);
- alternatives to criminal proceedings; and
- abuse of process

1.1 The structure of the criminal courts in England and Wales

An adult defendant in a criminal case in England and Wales will make his/her first appearance in a magistrates' court. Some cases are tried in the magistrates' court, whereas others are tried in the Crown Court. An offence is a 'summary offence' if it must be tried in a magistrates' court. An offence is an 'indictable offence' if it either may or must be tried in the Crown Court; where an indictable offence *may* be tried by a magistrates' court instead of the Crown Court, it is known as an 'either-way' offence, and where it *must* be tried in the Crown Court it is referred to as an 'indictable-only' offence.

The Crown Court can also hear appeals from a magistrates' court, as can the High Court. Appeals following Crown Court trials are heard by the Court of Appeal (Criminal Division).

1.1.1 Magistrates' courts

A magistrates' court usually comprises three lay justices and a legally qualified 'court legal adviser' (sometimes referred to as the 'clerk'). The lay justices are ordinary members of the public who have put themselves forward to sit as justices of the peace (JPs). They are unpaid, although they can claim reimbursement for travel expenses and loss of earnings. They receive basic training in the law, and in the rules of procedure and evidence which they are likely to encounter. Because they have only very elementary legal training, the lay justices need the help of the court legal adviser, who is legally qualified. When a lay bench is sitting, submissions are addressed to the chair, who is addressed as 'sir' or 'madam', as the case may be.

In some magistrates' courts, especially those in cities, there may be a District Judge (Magistrates' Court). District Judges are legally qualified, and can (and usually do) try cases sitting alone, whereas at least two lay justices must be sitting for a summary trial to take place. A district judge is addressed as 'sir' or 'madam', as the case may be.

Solicitors and barristers both have complete rights of audience in the magistrates' court.

1.1.2 The Crown Court

The Crown Court is always presided over by a judge. Where the Crown Court is trying a case, the judge almost invariably sits with a jury. Very serious offences are usually tried by a High Court judge; most cases, however, will be tried by a circuit judge or by a part-time judge known as a 'recorder'. A circuit judge or recorder is addressed as 'your Honour'; a High Court judge is addressed as 'my Lord' or 'my Lady' as the case may be.

Barristers can appear in Crown Court trials but solicitors can do so only if they have been granted a right of audience in the higher courts.

1.1.3 Public access to the courts

Magistrates' courts and the Crown Court normally sit in open court and there is a strong presumption that they should do. However, any court does have a discretion to sit in private if this is necessary for the administration of justice. Decisions to sit in private are, therefore, taken very rarely (see, generally, *Attorney-General v Leveller Magazine Ltd* [1979] AC 440). Under r.24.2 of the Criminal Procedure Rules, 'the general rule' for trials in magistrates' courts 'is that the hearing must be in public', but the court may exercise its powers to impose reporting restrictions, withhold information from the public, or order a hearing in private; r.25.2 makes the same provision in respect of trials on indictment in the Crown Court.

1.2 The overriding objective of the Criminal Procedure Rules

Section 69 of the Courts Act 2003 made provision for the creation of Criminal Procedure Rules. These rules govern the practice and procedure to be followed in the criminal courts. Under s.69 (4) of the Courts Act 2003, the power to make or alter Criminal Procedure Rules is to be exercised with a view to securing that the criminal justice system is accessible, fair and efficient, and that the rules are both simple and simply expressed.

Rule 1.1(1) of the Criminal Procedure Rules sets out the 'overriding objective'. This requires that 'criminal cases be dealt with justly'. Rule 1.1(2) goes on to explain that dealing with a criminal case justly includes:

(a)   acquitting the innocent and convicting the guilty;

(b)   dealing with the prosecution and the defence fairly;

(c)   recognising the rights of a defendant, particularly those under Article 6 of the European Convention on Human Rights;

(d)   respecting the interests of witnesses, victims and jurors and keeping them informed of the progress of the case;

(e)   dealing with the case efficiently and expeditiously;

(f)   ensuring that appropriate information is available to the court when bail and sentence are considered; and

(g)   dealing with the case in ways that take into account—
    (i)   the gravity of the offence alleged,
    (ii)   the complexity of what is in issue,
    (iii)   the severity of the consequences for the defendant and others affected, and
    (iv)   the needs of other cases.

The presumption of innocence, and the requirement that a defendant should be convicted only if the jury or magistrates are satisfied so that they are sure that the defendant is guilty, are not mentioned explicitly but may be regarded as being subsumed within the defendant's right to a fair trial (para.(c)).

Care must be taken with para.(e), as it is important that the emphasis on speed and efficiency should not be allowed to detract from ensuring that the procedure is fair and, so far as possible, conducive to reaching an accurate determination of the defendant's guilt or innocence.

Paragraph (g) is essentially a requirement of proportionality, and makes it clear the seriousness of the offence is partly a subjective matter, given that the consequences of conviction may vary according to the circumstances of a particular defendant. For example, a conviction for theft would be a very serious matter indeed for a lawyer or an accountant, even if the amount involved was small.

Rule 1.2(1) goes on to provide that each participant (defined as anyone involved in any way with a criminal case) must, in the conduct of each case:

(a) 'prepare and conduct the case in accordance with the overriding objective';

(b) comply with the Criminal Procedure Rules, the Criminal Practice Directions issued by the Lord Chief Justice, and with any directions given by the court in the particular case; and

(c) inform the court and all other parties immediately if there is any 'significant failure' (whether or not that participant is responsible for that failure) to take any procedural step required by the Rules, a Practice Direction or a direction of the court. For this purpose, a failure is to be regarded as significant 'if it might hinder the court in furthering the overriding objective'.

1.2.1 The court's case management powers

One of the ways in which effect is given to the overriding objective is through proactive case management by the court. The court's case management powers are set out in Part 3 of the Rules. Rule 3.2 requires 'active case management' by the court. Rule 3.2(2) says that active case management includes:

(a) the early identification of the real issues;

(b) the early identification of the needs of witnesses;

(c) achieving certainty as to what must be done, by whom, and when, in particular by the early setting of a timetable for the progress of the case;

(d) monitoring the progress of the case and compliance with directions;

(e) ensuring that evidence, whether disputed or not, is presented in the shortest and clearest way;

(f) discouraging delay, dealing with as many aspects of the case as possible on the same occasion, and avoiding unnecessary hearings;

(g) encouraging the participants to co-operate in the progression of the case; and

(h) making use of technology.

Rule 3.2(4) and (5) create a presumption that, where facilities are available, live links or telephones should be used for pre-trial case management hearings.

Rule 3.3(1) requires that each party must actively assist the court in fulfilling its duty under r.3.2. In particular, r.3.3(2) requires communication between the parties and with the court. Rule 3.3(2)(c) states that this communication should establish, among other things:

(i) whether the defendant is likely to plead guilty or not guilty,

(ii) what is agreed and what is likely to be disputed,

(iii) what information, or other material, is required by one part of another, and why, and

(iv) what is to be done, by whom, and when ....

Rule 3.9(1) requires that, at every hearing, if a case cannot be concluded there and then, the court must give directions so that it can be concluded at the next hearing or as soon as possible after that. Under r.3.9(2), the court must, as appropriate:

(a) if the defendant is absent, decide whether to proceed nonetheless;

(b) take the defendant's plea (unless already done) or if no plea can be taken then find out whether the defendant is likely to plead guilty or not guilty;

(c) set, follow or revise a timetable for the progress of the case, which may include a timetable for any hearing including the trial or (in the Crown Court) the appeal;

(d) in giving directions, ensure continuity in relation to the court and to the parties' representatives where that is appropriate and practicable; and

(e) where a direction has not been complied with, find out why, identify who was responsible, and take appropriate action.

Rule 3.9(3) requires the court, in order to prepare for the trial, to take every reasonable step to encourage and to facilitate the attendance of witnesses when they are needed, and to facilitate the participation of other people, including the defendant.

The conduct of criminal trials (and appeals) is governed by r.3.11. This provides that, in order to manage a trial (or appeal), the court:

(a) must establish, with the active assistance of the parties, what are the disputed issues;

(b) must consider setting a timetable that—
    (i) takes account of those issues and of any timetable proposed by a party, and
    (ii) may limit the duration of any stage of the hearing;

(c) may require a party to identify—
    (i) which witnesses that party wants to give evidence in person,
    (ii) the order in which that party wants those witnesses to give their evidence,
    (iii) whether that party requires an order compelling the attendance of a witness,
    (iv) what arrangements are desirable to facilitate the giving of evidence by a witness,
    (v) what arrangements are desirable to facilitate the participation of any other person, including the defendant,
    (vi) what written evidence that party intends to introduce,
    (vii) what other material, if any, that person intends to make available to the court in the presentation of the case, and
    (viii) whether that party intends to raise any point of law that could affect the conduct of the trial or appeal; and

(d) may limit—
    (i) the examination, cross-examination or re-examination of a witness, and
    (ii) the duration of any stage of the hearing.

Robust case management was encouraged by the Court of Appeal in R v Jisl [2004] EWCA Crim 696. Judge LJ (at [116]) said that: 'Active, hands on, case management, both pre-trial and throughout the trial itself, is now regarded as an essential part of the judge's duty'. This was a point that had been emphasised by Judge LJ in the earlier case of R v Chaaban [2003] EWCA Crim 1012, where his Lordship (at [37]) said:

[N]owadays, as part of his responsibility for managing the trial, the judge is expected to control the timetable and to manage the available time. Time is not unlimited. No one should assume that trials can continue to take as long or use up as much time as either or both sides may wish, or think, or assert, they need. The entitlement to a fair trial is not inconsistent with proper judicial control over the use of time ... [E]very trial which takes longer than it reasonably should is wasteful of limited resources. It also results in delays to justice in cases still waiting to be tried, adding to the tension and distress of victims, defendants, particularly those in custody awaiting trial, and witnesses. Most important of all it does nothing to assist the jury to reach a true verdict on the evidence.

The approach required by the overriding objective echoes the words of Auld LJ in R. v *Gleeson* [2003] EWCA Crim 3357; [2004] 1 Cr App R 29 (at [36]), quoting from his *Report of the Criminal Courts Review* (October 2001), Chapter 10, para.154:

> A criminal trial is not a game under which a guilty defendant should be provided with a sporting chance. It is a search for truth in accordance with the twin principles that the prosecution must prove its case and that a defendant is not obliged to inculpate himself, the object being to convict the guilty and acquit the innocent. Requiring a defendant to indicate in advance what he disputes about the prosecution case offends neither of those principle.

For example, R (*Hassani*) v *West London Magistrates' Court* [2017] EWHC 1270 (Admin) concerned the taking of what were regarded as unmeritorious points in a drink-driving case. Echoing the oft-cited words of Auld LJ in *Gleeson*, Irwin LJ said (at [9]):

> The criminal law is not a game to be played in the hope of a lucky outcome, a game to be played as long and in as involved a fashion as the paying client is able or prepared to afford.

His Lordship went to say (at [10]) that the Criminal Procedure Rules "are there to be employed actively so as to preclude game-playing and ensure that the courts only have to address real issues with some substance", adding (at [11]):

> Time wasting, extension of hearings and taking hopeless points in the hope of wearing down an opponent or the court are neither proper nor legitimate ways in which to conduct a case, for a party or for a party's lawyers. Courts must be aware of such behaviour and employ firm case management to prevent it.

Attention is drawn (at [12]) to the effect on the defence of the duty to co-operate in the achievement of the overriding objective:

> If the defence are going to suggest that some document or some piece of service is missing, they must do so early. If they do not, then it is open to the court to find that the point was raised late, and any direction then sought to produce a document or to apply for an adjournment may properly be refused.

1.2.1.1 "Better Case Management"

In January 2015, the *Review of Efficiency in Criminal Proceedings* by Sir Brian Leveson was published. The Review made a number of recommendations based on some 'overarching principles':

● *Getting it right first time*: the police and CPS working to achieve "appropriate charging decisions, based on fair appraisal of sufficient evidence, with proportionate disclosure of material to the defence" (para.25);
● *Case ownership*: 'for each case, in the police, the CPS and for the defence, to maximise the opportunities for case management, there must be one person who is (and is identified to be) responsible for the conduct of the case' (para.26);
● A duty of *direct engagement* between identified representatives who have case ownership responsibilities (para.33); it should be made clear that 'the parties are under a duty to engage at the first available opportunity' (para.34); and 'there is an obligation on any party to justify the need for an interlocutory hearing to take the form of a formal court hearing with all parties present' (para.37);

● *Effective and consistent judicial case management*: 'the court must be prepared robustly to manage its work', and 'all parties must be required to comply with the Criminal Procedure Rules and to work to identify the issues so as to ensure that court time is deployed to maximum effectiveness and efficiency' (para.38).

The Better Case Management ('BCM') project subsequently sought to implement some of the recommendations in the Review. Macur LJ, Senior Presiding Judge for England and Wales, observes the BCM Handbook (January 2018), the key principles of which are:

● a single national process;
● getting it right first time;
● identifiable person responsible for the case;
● serving material on a proportionate basis;
● duty of direct engagement and participation from every participant;
● the earlier resolution of pleas and the identification of the issues in the case;
● reduced number of hearings;
● effective hearings;
● consistent and robust judicial case management;
● compliance with the Criminal Procedure Rules; Criminal Practice Direction and Court Orders;
● digital working.

1.2.1.2 Sanctions for non-compliance

Rule 3.5(6) provides that if a party fails to comply with a rule or a direction, the court may:

(a) fix, postpone, bring forward, extend, cancel or adjourn a hearing;
(b) exercise its powers to make a costs order; and
(c) impose such other sanction as may be appropriate.

The 'other' sanctions include excluding evidence under s.78 of PACE (a sanction available only against the prosecution) or reporting misconduct to a regulatory body such as the Solicitors Regulation Authority or the Bar Standards Board.

It will be noted that these sanctions are comparatively limited in scope. In many cases, all the court will be able to do is to adjourn the case and impose a costs penalty on the party (or their representative) responsible for the delay. In an extreme case where the prosecution have been guilty of egregious misconduct, it might be possible to stay the proceedings as an abuse of process. In the civil courts, a statement of case can be struck out for failure to comply with a rule, practice direction or court order (see r.3.4(2)(c) of the Civil Procedure Rules). However, in the criminal context, dismissing a prosecution would amount to the same as granting a stay for abuse of process, and would carry the disadvantage that there would be no trial, and so no decision 'on the merits': a very unsatisfactory state of affairs both for the alleged victim(s) of the offence and the accused. Not allowing an accused to defend a case because of a failure to comply with the rules would clearly be inappropriate, as it would mean that a person stands convicted of an offence even though the defendant does not admit that offence and the prosecution have not proved that the defendant committed it.

1.3 Investigative powers of the police

The most important rules which govern the investigative stage are to be found in the Police and Criminal Evidence Act 1984 ('PACE'), and in the Codes of Practice issued thereunder:

- Part 1 of PACE and Code A: police powers to search a person or a vehicle without first making an arrest ('stop and search').
- Part 2 of PACE and Code B: the issue and execution of search warrants to enable the police to enter premises and to seize and retain property (these warrants are normally issued by magistrates, but in the case of sensitive material will be issued by Crown Court judges).
- Part 3 of PACE: powers of arrest by police officers and by other people (Code G gives further detail on police powers of arrest).
- Part 4 of PACE: detention of suspects by the police (including limitation of the length of time for which a person can be detained without charge).
- Part 5 of PACE and Code C: questioning of suspects detained by the police (Code E deals with audio recording police interviews with suspects and Code F deals with video recording such interviews).

1.3.1 Power to stop and search

The power to stop and search is contained in s.1 of PACE. Section 1(2) empowers a police officer to search any person or vehicle, or anything which is in or on a vehicle, for 'stolen or prohibited articles', and to detain a person or vehicle for the purpose of such a search. However, under s.1(1), this power may be exercised only in a place where the public has access 'on payment or otherwise, as of right or by virtue of express or implied permission', or where 'people have ready access at the time when he proposes to exercise the power' (so long as it is not a dwelling). Moreover, this power arises only if the officer has 'reasonable grounds for suspecting that he will find stolen or prohibited articles' (s.1(3)).

Section 1(6) confers a power of seizure if, in the course of the search, the officer discovers an article which he has reasonable grounds for suspecting to be a stolen or prohibited article.

The term 'prohibited article' is defined by s.1(7). It encompasses offensive weapons (defined in subs.(9) as articles made or adapted for use for causing injury to persons, or intended by the person having it with him for such use) and articles which are made or adapted for use in the course of or in connection with (or intended by the person having it with him for such use) the offences listed in subs.(8), namely burglary, theft, taking a motor vehicle without authority, fraud, criminal damage.

Sections 2 and 3 of PACE set out detailed rules regarding the procedure to be followed by a police officer when exercising the powers conferred by s.1 and the details that have to be recorded. Failure to comply with these provisions may make an otherwise lawful search unlawful, and thereby deprive police officers who face resistance of the protection afforded by the offence of assaulting a constable acting in the execution of his duty. Section 2(3), for example, requires a constable conducting a search to inform the person to be searched (before the search commences) of his name and police station, the object of the proposed search, and the grounds for making it. Failure to do so renders the search unlawful, and the illegality is not cured by the fact that the search was reasonable (Osman v DPP (1999) 163 JP 725).

Code of Practice A (issued under PACE) sets out detailed rules regulating the exercise of these powers of stop and search.

1.3.2 Searching premises

It may also be necessary for the police to enter and search premises. Usually a search warrant is required, but there are circumstances where the police can proceed without a warrant.

1.3.2.1 Entry with a warrant

Entry with a warrant is governed by s.8 of PACE. Section 8(1) enables a justice of the peace, following an application by a police officer, to grant a warrant authorising the police to enter and search premises if there are reasonable grounds for believing that:

- an indictable offence has been committed (this includes either-way offences);
- there is material on the premises which is likely to be of substantial value to the investigation of the offence;
- the material is likely to be relevant evidence (defined in subs.(4) as 'anything that would be admissible in evidence at a trial for the offence');
- the material does not consist of or include items subject to 'legal privilege', 'excluded material' or 'special procedure material' (see ss.9–14 and sch.1); and
- any of the conditions specified in subs.(3) are satisfied, namely that:
  - ○ it is not practicable to communicate with any person entitled to grant entry to the premises (or to grant access to the evidence); or
  - ○ entry to the premises will not be granted unless a warrant is produced; or
  - ○ the purpose of a search may be frustrated or seriously prejudiced unless the police can secure immediate entry to the premises.

In *Redknapp v Metropolitan Police Commissioner* [2008] EWHC 1177 (Admin); [2009] 1 WLR 2091, it was held that, if the application for the warrant does not identify which of the conditions in s.8 (3) is being relied on, the issue of the warrant will be unlawful.

The importance of complying with the correct procedure was emphasised in R *(AB)* v *Huddersfield Magistrates' Court* [2014] EWHC 1089 (Admin); [2015] 1 WLR 4737. Stuart-Smith LJ (at [13]) said:

> The parties' submissions referred us to a generous selection of the cases over the past few years where the courts have considered the legality of warrants. Most need not be individually cited in this judgment. However, it should by now be clearly appreciated by all who make or decide applications for the issuing of warrants that there is no part of the process that should be regarded as a formality. Each application must be carefully and precisely formulated so as to satisfy both the statutory requirements and the duty of full and frank disclosure; and a decision to issue may only be taken after that level of critical scrutiny that is required when the court is asked to sanction a substantial invasion of fundamental rights. The flow of the authorities tends towards requiring increasing rigour and precision at all stages of the process and nothing we say in this judgment should be taken or interpreted as going against that flow.

Under s.8(1A), the magistrate may grant either a 'specific premises warrant' (authorising the search of one or more sets of premises specified in the application) or an 'all premises warrant' (authorising the search of any premises occupied or controlled by the person specified in the application). Section 8(1B) provides that where the application is for an 'all premises warrant', the magistrate must also be satisfied that the nature of the offence under investigation is such that it is necessary to search premises occupied or controlled by the person in question which are not specified in the application, and that it is not reasonably practicable to specify in the application all the premises which he occupies or controls and which might need to be searched.

Under s.8(1C), the search warrant may authorise entry to, and search of, premises on more than one occasion if the magistrate is satisfied that it is necessary to authorise multiple entries in order to achieve the purpose for which the warrant is issued. If the warrant authorises multiple entries, the number of entries authorised may be unlimited, or limited to a maximum (subs.(1D)). By virtue of s.15(5), a warrant authorises entry on one occasion only unless it specifically authorises multiple entries; if it specifies that it authorises multiple entries, it must also specify whether the number of entries authorised is unlimited, or limited to a specified maximum (s.15(5A)).

Under s.15(2) of PACE, the police officer applying for the warrant has to set out the grounds on which he makes the application, and to identify, so far as is practicable, the material to be sought.

The application for such a search warrant is made *ex parte* and must be supported by an 'information' in writing (subs.(3)). The officer must answer on oath any question that the magistrate hearing the application asks him (subs.(4)).

Section 8(2) empowers the police to seize and retain anything for which a search has been authorised under subs.(1).

This power is supplemented by s.50(1) of the Criminal Justice and Police Act 2001, which empowers a person who is lawfully on the premises, and who is authorised to search for something, to seize anything on those premises which he has reasonable grounds for believing to be something for which he may search and which he is empowered to seize. This enables seizure the item and its removal from the premises for the purpose of determining whether it falls within the ambit of the search. It is a condition of exercise of this power that it is not reasonably practicable to make this determination on the premises.

Rules regarding the execution of the search warrant are set out in s.16 of PACE. Under s.16 (4), entry and search under a warrant 'must be at a reasonable hour unless it appears to the constable executing it that the purpose of a search may be frustrated on an entry at a reasonable hour'. A search under a warrant 'may only be a search to the extent required for the purpose for which the warrant was issued' (subs.(8)).

Section 16(2A) enables any person authorised in the warrant to accompany the police when executing the warrant to search for and seize property. This enables civilians to take an active role in search and seizure operations. However, civilians may exercise those powers only in the company, and under the supervision, of a police officer (s.16(2B)).

If the warrant is an 'all premises' warrant, premises which are not specified in it may be entered or searched only if an officer of at least the rank of Inspector has given written authorisation (subs.(3A)). No premises may be entered or searched for a second or subsequent time under a warrant which authorises multiple entries unless an officer of at least the rank of Inspector has given written authorisation (subs.(3B)).

1.3.2.2 Entry without a warrant

There are also statutory provisions that enable the police to enter premises without a warrant. These provisions include ss.17 and 18 of PACE.

Section 17 of PACE empowers the police to enter and search premises in order to:

(a) execute an arrest warrant;
(b) arrest someone for an indictable offence (this includes either-way offences);
(c) arrest someone for an offence specified in subs.(1)(c);
(d) recapture a person who is unlawfully at large;
(e) save life or limb, or prevent serious damage to property.

As far as the last of these is concerned, in *Syed v DPP* [2010] EWHC 81 (Admin); [2010] 1 Cr App R 34, Collins J (at [11]) said:

> It is plain that Parliament intended that the right of entry by force without any warrant should be limited to cases where there was an apprehension that something serious was otherwise likely to occur, or perhaps had occurred, within the house.

Under s.17(4), the power of search conferred by s.17 is limited to a power 'to search to the extent that is reasonably required for the purpose for which the power of entry is exercised'.

Section 18(1) of PACE allows a police officer to enter and search any premises occupied or controlled by a person who is under arrest for an indictable offence, if the officer has reasonable grounds to suspect that there is on the premises evidence relating to the offence for which the suspect has been arrested, or to some other indictable offence which is 'connected with or similar to that offence'. The officer may seize and retain anything for which he may search under subs.(1), but the scope of the search must be restricted to whatever is 'reasonably required for the purpose of discovering such evidence' (s.18(2), (3)). Premises must be occupied or controlled by the person under arrest for a search under s.18 to be lawful; a reasonable belief that the premises are so occupied or controlled is not sufficient (*Khan v Metropolitan Police Commissioner* [2008] EWCA Civ 723).

Normally, such a search should be authorised in writing by an officer of at least the rank of Inspector (s.18(4)). However, a search may take place without such authorisation and without taking the suspect to the police station first if the suspect's presence at some other place is 'necessary for the effective investigation of the offence' (s.18(5), (5A)).

Section 117 of PACE gives the police the power to use reasonable force, if necessary, when exercising the powers conferred by the Act. It is reasonable, for the purpose of s.117, that police officers executing a search warrant should seek, by no more force than necessary, to restrict the movement of those in occupation of premises while those premises are being searched (*DPP v Meaden* [2003] EWHC 3005; [2004] 1 WLR 945).

Code of Practice B (issued under PACE), sets out detailed rules regulating the exercise of the powers of entry and search.

1.4 Powers of arrest

In this section, we examine the powers of arrest that are vested in the police and in other people.

1.4.1 Arrest without warrant

Arrest without warrant by police officers is governed by s.24 of PACE. Section 24(1) provides that a police officer may arrest without warrant:

- anyone who is about to commit an offence;
- anyone who is in the act of committing an offence;
- anyone whom the officer has reasonable grounds for suspecting to be about to commit an offence;
- anyone whom the officer has reasonable grounds for suspecting to be committing an offence.

Under s.24(2), if the officer has reasonable grounds for suspecting that an offence has been committed, he may arrest without a warrant anyone whom he has reasonable grounds to suspect of being guilty of it.

Under s.24(3), if an offence has been committed, a police officer may arrest without a warrant:

- anyone who is guilty of the offence;
- anyone whom the officer has reasonable grounds for suspecting to be guilty of it.

However, all these powers are subject to the important proviso in s.24(4), that they may be exercised only where the police officer has reasonable grounds for believing that it is 'necessary' to arrest the person in question. An arrest will be necessary only in the circumstances set out in s.24(5):

(a) to enable the name of the person in question to be ascertained (in the case where the constable does not know, and cannot readily ascertain, the person's name, or has reasonable grounds for doubting whether a name given by the person as his name is his real name);

(b)   correspondingly as regards the person's address;

(c)   to prevent the person in question –
   (i)   causing physical injury to himself or any other person;
   (ii)   suffering physical injury;
   (iii) causing loss of or damage to property;
   (iv)   committing an offence against public decency ...; or
   (v)   causing an unlawful obstruction of the highway;

(d)   to protect a child or other vulnerable person from the person in question;

(e)   to allow the prompt and effective investigation of the offence or of the conduct of the person in question;

(f)   to prevent any prosecution for the offence from being hindered by the disappearance of the person in question.

Code G of the Codes of Practice issued pursuant to PACE provides additional guidance on these powers of arrest. Paragraph 2.9 of the Code suggests that condition (e) may include cases such as interviewing the suspect on occasions when their voluntary attendance is not considered to be a practicable alternative to arrest, because (for example), 'it is thought unlikely that the person would attend the police station voluntarily to be interviewed'. The same paragraph says that condition (f) may arise when it is thought that, 'if the person is not arrested they are unlikely to attend court if they are prosecuted' or where the address given by the suspect 'is not a satisfactory address for service of a summons or a written charge and requisition to appear at court'.

In *Hayes v Chief Constable of Merseyside Police* [2011] EWCA Civ 911; [2012] 1 WLR 517, Hughes LJ said (at [40]) that there is a two-stage test to determine whether the necessity test for an arrest is satisfied: firstly, the police officer 'must honestly believe that arrest is necessary, for one or more identified s.24(5) reasons' and, secondly, the officer's 'decision must be one which, objectively reviewed afterwards according to the information known to him at the time, is held to have been made on reasonable grounds'.

1.4.1.1 Meaning of 'reasonable grounds'

In *O'Hara v Chief Constable of the RUC* [1997] AC 286, the House of Lords considered the meaning of 'reasonable grounds' in the context of anti-terrorism legislation, which applied the same test as s.24 of PACE. It was held that, for a police officer to have reasonable grounds to effect an arrest, the question is whether a reasonable person would be of that opinion, having regard to the information which was in the mind of the arresting officer. The test is therefore partly subjective (the officer must have formed a 'genuine suspicion' in his own mind that the suspect has committed the offence in question) and partly objective (there must be reasonable grounds for that suspicion). The House of Lords went on to hold that the information acted on by the officer need not be based on his own observations; he is entitled to form a suspicion on the basis of what he has been told. It is not necessary to prove what was known to the person who gave the information to the police officer or to prove that any facts on which the officer based his suspicion were actually true.

O'Hara was considered in *Metropolitan Police Commissioner v Raissi* [2008] EWCA Civ 1237; [2009] QB 564. Sir Anthony Clarke MR (at [13]) said:

(i)   In order to have a reasonable suspicion the officer need not have evidence amounting to a prima facie case ...

(ii) Hearsay evidence may therefore afford a constable reasonable grounds to arrest. Such information may come from other officers.

(iii) The information which causes the constable to be suspicious of the individual must be in existence to the knowledge of the police officer at the time he makes the arrest.

(iv) The executive 'discretion' to arrest or not ... vests in the constable, who is engaged on the decision whether to arrest or not, and not in his superior officers.

Because the discretion to arrest or not is that of the arresting officer, the mere fact that an arresting officer has been instructed by a superior officer to effect the arrest is not capable of amounting to reasonable grounds for the necessary suspicion. His Lordship observed (at [19]) that it is 'the information actually in the possession of the officer upon which the question whether he had reasonable grounds for suspicion must be judged' and, therefore, 'it does not avail the officer to say that his superior probably had other information justifying arrest but he did not tell him what it was'. That said, 'the threshold for the existence of reasonable grounds for suspicion is low' ([20]).

This test is compatible with the requirements of Art.5 of the European Convention on Human Rights (the right to liberty). In *O'Hara v UK* (2002) 34 EHRR 32 (following *Fox, Campbell and Hartley v UK* (1990) 13 EHRR 157), the European Court of Human Rights held (at [34]) that 'reasonable suspicion' requires 'the existence of some facts or information which would satisfy an objective observer that the person concerned may have committed the offence, though what may be regarded as reasonable will depend on all the circumstances of the case'. The Court went on to observe (at [36]), that the standard imposed by Art.5 'does not presuppose that the police have sufficient evidence to bring charges at the time of arrest'. Rather, the object of questioning during detention is to further the criminal investigation by way of confirming or dispelling the suspicion that gave rise to the arrest. Accordingly, facts that raise a suspicion need not be of the same level as those necessary to justify a conviction, or even the bringing of a charge.

1.4.1.2 Information to be given on arrest

Section 28 of PACE sets out what the accused must be told when he is arrested. It requires that the arrested person must be informed at the time of the arrest, if that is practicable (and if not, as soon as it becomes practicable), that they are under arrest and of the ground for their arrest. This is so even if the reason is obvious (*Abbassy v Metropolitan Police Commissioner* [1990] 1 WLR 385).

Under para.10.5 of Code C, the person arrested must also be cautioned:

You do not have to say anything. But it may harm your defence if you do not mention when questioned something which you later rely on in Court. Anything you do say may be given in evidence.

1.4.1.3 'Citizen's arrest'

Arrest by people other than police officers is governed by s.24A of PACE. Section 24A(1) provides that a person other than a constable may arrest without a warrant:

- anyone who is in the act of committing an indictable offence;
- anyone whom he has reasonable grounds for suspecting to be committing an indictable offence.

Under s.24A(2), where an indictable offence has been committed, a person other than a constable may arrest without a warrant:

- anyone who is guilty of the offence;
- anyone whom he has reasonable grounds for suspecting to be guilty of it.

The scope of this power of arrest is limited not only by the fact that it applies only to indictable offences (that is, offences that may or must be tried in the Crown Court), but also by s.24A(3), which provides that this power may be exercised only if the person making the arrest has reasonable grounds for believing that it is 'necessary' to arrest the person in question, and it appears to the person making the arrest that it is not reasonably practicable for a police officer to make it instead.

Under s.24A(4), an arrest will be necessary only if it is to prevent the person in question:

(a) causing physical injury to himself or any other person;
(b) suffering physical injury;
(c) causing loss of or damage to property; or
(d) making off before a constable can assume responsibility for him.

The police powers of arrest are wider, in that a police officer can arrest for any offence (not just an indictable offence) and only has to have reasonable grounds for suspecting that an offence has been committed before arresting anyone whom he reasonably suspects of committing it. The practical effect of this difference is that, if a member of the public (for example, a store detective) arrests someone whom he reasonably suspects of committing an indictable offence, the arrest will not be valid if an indictable offence has not in fact been committed (*R v Self* [1992] 1 WLR 657). Furthermore, a member of the public cannot arrest someone who is apparently about to commit an offence, whereas a police officer can.

1.4.1.4 Voluntary attendance at a police station

Sometimes, a person will agree to go to a police station to be interviewed by the police without first being arrested. Someone who has not been arrested but who is 'helping the police with their inquiries' is free to leave at any time unless and until he is arrested (s.29 of PACE).

1.4.1.5 Arrest with a warrant

Under s.1 of the Magistrates' Courts Act 1980, a warrant for the suspect's arrest may be issued following the laying of an 'information' if the information is in writing (s.1(3)), and either the offence to which the warrant relates is an indictable offence or is punishable with imprisonment, or the person's address is not sufficiently established for a summons, or written charge and requisition, to be served on him (s.1(4)).

Whereas a magistrate or a justices' clerk may issue a summons, only a magistrate is empowered to issue an arrest warrant. The warrant requires the police to arrest the suspect and take him before the magistrates' court named on the warrant (usually the issuing court).

Where the offence charged is an indictable offence, a warrant may be issued even if a summons or a written charge and requisition have previously been issued (s.1(6)); this would be appropriate if, for example, the documents had been returned by the Royal Mail undelivered.

In practice, it is quite rare for an arrest warrant to be sought as a means of commencing criminal proceedings. The police are able to arrest a suspect for any offence where the criteria in s.24 of PACE are satisfied (so a warrant is unnecessary in the vast majority of cases). In many cases it is preferable to issue a written charge and requisition and, if those documents cannot be served, the police can then apply to the magistrates' court for an arrest warrant. Indeed, under s.1(6A), where the offence charged is an indictable offence and a written charge and requisition have already been issued, an arrest warrant may be issued by a justice of the peace upon a copy of the written charge (rather than an information) being laid before the justice by a public prosecutor.

1.5 Rules governing detention and interviews of suspects

In this section, we examine the rules that govern the pre-charge detention of suspects.

1.5.1 Procedure after arrest

A person who has been arrested will (unless granted 'street bail' – see below) be taken to a 'designated police station' (that is, under s.35 of PACE, one with facilities for the detention of suspects) as soon as practicable after arrest: s.30(1A) of PACE. The suspect will not be taken immediately to the police station if the case is one where the presence of the suspect elsewhere 'is necessary in order to carry out such investigations as it is reasonable to carry out immediately' (s.30(10A)); it may be necessary, for example, to search the suspect's home.

The time of the suspect's arrival at the police station is called the 'relevant time' (s.41(2)). This is the moment from which the length of the suspect's detention starts to be measured. On arrival at the police station, the suspect is taken to the custody officer, who must be an officer of the rank of Sergeant or above (s.36(3)) who is not involved in the investigation of the offence (s.36(5)).

1.5.2 'Street bail'

The requirement that the person must be taken to a police station as soon as practicable after the arrest (s.30(1A)) is subject to s.30A (see s.30(1B)). Sections 30A–30D provide for what has been termed 'street bail'. This empowers police officers to grant bail to persons following their arrest without the need to take them to a police station first. Section 30A(2) provides that a constable may release on bail a person who has been arrested 'at any time before he arrives at a police station'; however, the person released on bail 'must be required to attend a police station' (s.30A(3)).

Under s.30A(4), conditions may be imposed on the grant of street bail only as permitted by s.30A(3A) and (3B). Section 30A(3A) specifically excludes requiring the person to provide security or a surety to guarantee his surrender to custody and also forbids the imposition of a condition of residence in a bail hostel. Section 30A(3B) provides that, subject to these exclusions, the constable may impose any condition which appears necessary to secure that the person surrenders to custody, does not commit an offence while on bail, does not interfere with witnesses or otherwise obstruct the course of justice, or for the person's own protection (or, if he is under 17, his own welfare) or in the person's own interests.

Section 30C(4) provides that a person who has been released on bail under s.30A cannot be rearrested unless, since his release, new evidence has come to light or an examination or analysis of existing evidence has been made which could not reasonably have been made before his release.

Section 30D deals with failure to answer to bail granted under s.30A. A person who fails to attend the police station at the specified time may be arrested without warrant (s.30D(1)). Under s.30D(2A), a person who has been released on conditional street bail may be arrested without warrant by a police officer if the officer has reasonable grounds for suspecting that the person has broken any of the conditions of bail.

Section 30CA(1) enables the person arrested to seek a variation of any conditions imposed on the street bail. The request is made to a custody officer at the police station which the suspect is required to attend. Under s.30CB(1), if the request for a variation of conditions is refused by the police, the suspect may then seek variation of the conditions by a magistrates' court. Under subs.(2), the application to the court must be based on the ground that was relied upon when the request was made to the police; however, the court may also consider different grounds provided that they arise out of a change in circumstances that has occurred since the making of the application to the custody officer.

1.5.3 Arrival at the police station: duties of the custody officer

The main duties of the custody officer include:

- deciding whether there is sufficient evidence for the suspect to be charged or whether to authorise detention without charge (see s.37 of PACE);
- informing the suspect of their rights (for example, the right under s. 56 to have someone informed of their arrest, and the right under s.58 to consult in private with a solicitor); and
- keeping a 'custody record' documenting all that occurs during the suspect's detention (for example, meal breaks and interviews).

1.5.3.1 The right to have someone informed of the arrest

Under s.56 of PACE, a person who has been arrested has the right to have someone informed of their arrest. However, where the offence is an indictable one, the exercise of this right can be delayed for up to 36 hours on the authority of an officer of the rank of Inspector or above. Under s.56(5), an officer may authorise such delay only where he has reasonable grounds for believing that telling the named person of the arrest:

(a) will lead to interference with or harm to evidence connected with an indictable offence or interference with or physical injury to other persons; or

(b) will lead to the alerting of other persons suspected of having committed such an offence but not yet arrested for it; or

(c) will hinder the recovery of any property obtained as a result of such an offence.

In addition, subs.(5A) permits an officer to authorise delay where he has reasonable grounds for believing that the person detained for the indictable offence has benefited from his criminal conduct, and the recovery of the value of the property constituting the benefit will be hindered by telling the named person of the arrest.

1.5.4 Release from custody or detention without charge

Section 37(2) of PACE covers the situation where the custody officer decides that there is insufficient evidence to charge the suspect with the offence for which he was arrested. It requires the custody officer to release the suspect 'without bail unless the pre-conditions for bail are satisfied', or 'on bail if those pre-conditions are satisfied'. In other words, the release must be unconditional unless any of the grounds for making the release subject to bail are satisfied. Those pre-conditions are set out in s.50A:

(a) that the custody officer is satisfied that releasing the person on bail is necessary and proportionate in all the circumstances (having regard, in particular, to any conditions of bail which would be imposed), and

(b) that an officer of the rank of inspector or above authorises the release on bail (having considered any representations made by the person or the person's legal representative).

Police bail prior to charge is subject to an initial limit of 28 days (s.47ZB). However, that period can be extended by three months if there are reasonable grounds for believing that: the suspect is guilty of the offence in question; further time is needed to investigate; the investigation is being conducted diligently and expeditiously; and it is necessary and proportionate for the suspect to remain on police bail (ss.47ZC and 47ZD). Further extensions of time are possible only if permitted by a magistrates' court (s.47ZF). PACE also permits a suspect to be held in police detention prior to being charged with an offence. By virtue of s.37(3), if there are reasonable grounds for believing that 'the person's detention without being charged is necessary to secure or preserve evidence relating to an offence for which the person is under arrest or to obtain such evidence by questioning the person', the custody officer may authorise the person arrested to be kept in police detention.

1.5.4.1 Detention without charge: reviews

If the suspect is detained without charge, the detention is subject to periodic reviews according to the timetable set out in ss.40–44 of PACE.

Under s.40(3), reviews take place as follows:

- the first review must be not later than six hours after the detention was first authorised;
- the second review must be not later than nine hours after the first;
- subsequent reviews must be at intervals of not more than nine hours.

Thus, the first review takes place no later than six hours after detention was first authorised; the second review no later than 15 hours after detention was first authorised; and the third review no later than 24 hours after detention was first authorised.

Under s.40(1)(b), the reviews must be carried out by an officer of at least the rank of Inspector who has not been directly involved in the investigation. At each of these reviews, the review officer has to be satisfied that the conditions of continued detention (s.37(3), as set out above) continue to be satisfied.

Before deciding whether to authorise the continued detention of the suspect, the review officer must give the suspect (unless he is asleep or otherwise unfit by reason of his condition or behaviour), or any solicitor who is representing him and who is available at the time of the review, the opportunity to make representations about the continued detention (s.40(12)).

A review may be postponed if, having regard to the circumstances prevailing at the latest time when that review should take place, it is not practicable to carry out the review then (for example, because the suspect is then being interviewed and it would wreck the interview if it were to be suspended for a review to take place, or because no review officer is readily available at that time). Where a review is postponed, it must take place as soon as practicable after the time it should have taken place, and a reason for the delay must be noted on the custody record (s.40(4), (5), (7)). Importantly, a postponement of one review does not affect the time when subsequent reviews have to take place (s.40(6)).

Section 40A of PACE enables these reviews of detention to be conducted by telephone rather than in person at the police station. The review officer will usually speak to the custody officer, and to the detained person (or their legal representative) if he wishes to exercise the right to make representations about the continuing need for detention. Under s.40A(2) of the 1984 Act, telephone reviews must not be conducted where it is reasonably practicable to carry out the review using live-link facilities.

1.5.4.2 Detention beyond 24 hours

After 24 hours have elapsed from the time when detention was first authorised, the suspect can be detained without charge only if the provisions of ss.42–43 apply (s.41(1)). Otherwise the suspect must be released (on bail if the pre-conditions in s.50A are satisfied (see above), otherwise unconditionally): s.41(7).

If the suspect is released because 24 hours have elapsed, he cannot be re-arrested without a warrant for the offence for which he was previously arrested unless, since his release, 'new evidence has come to light or an examination or analysis of existing evidence has been made which could not reasonably have been made before his release' (s.41(9)). This does not, however, prevent the arrest of the suspect under s.46A of PACE (arrest for failure to answer police bail).

Section 42(1) of PACE enables a suspect to be detained after 24 hours have expired if certain conditions are met. It provides that an officer of the rank of superintendent or above who is responsible for the police station at which a person is detained may authorise the keeping of that person in police detention for a period expiring at or before 36 hours after detention was first authorised by the custody officer, if he has reasonable grounds for believing that:

(a) the detention of that person without charge is necessary to secure or preserve evidence relating to an offence for which he is under arrest or to obtain such evidence by questioning him;
(b) an offence for which he is under arrest is an indictable offence; and
(c) the investigation is being conducted diligently and expeditiously.

It follows that, if the offence in question is a summary offence, the maximum period of detention without charge is 24 hours. If the offence is indictable (whether indictable only or triable either way), a superintendent can authorise the continued detention of the suspect provided that the test originally applied by the custody officer remains satisfied, and the investigating officers are conducting the investigation efficiently.

1.5.4.3 Detention beyond 36 hours

After 36 hours have elapsed since the 'relevant time', the suspect can be detained further without being charged only if this is permitted by a magistrates' court. The court has to be satisfied that there are reasonable grounds for believing that the further detention of the suspect is justified (s.43(1)). The application for a warrant for continued detention is made in private (that is, with the public excluded) before a court that comprises two or more lay justices (s.45(1)). The application has to be made on oath (s.43(1)). The suspect has a right to be present (s.43(2)) and, if he so wishes, to be legally represented at this hearing (s.43(3)).

Section 43(4) provides that a person's further detention is only justified if:

(a) his detention without charge is necessary to secure or preserve evidence relating to an offence for which he is under arrest or to obtain such evidence by questioning him;
(b) an offence for which he is under arrest is an indictable offence; and
(c) the investigation is being conducted diligently and expeditiously.

It should be noted that this is the same test as that applied by the superintendent at the 24-hour point.

Section 43(14) stipulates that any information submitted in support of an application for a warrant of continued detention must state:

● the nature of the offence for which the suspect was arrested;
● the general nature of the evidence on which the suspect was arrested;
● what inquiries relating to the offence have been made by the police and what further inquiries are proposed by them;

- the reasons for believing the continued detention of the suspect to be necessary for the purposes of such further inquiries.

Section 43(5) stipulates that an application for a warrant of further detention may be made at any time before the expiry of 36 hours after the suspect's detention was first authorised. If it is not practicable for the magistrates' court to hear the application before the expiry of that 36-hour period, the court can hear the application during the 6 hours following the end of that period; thereafter, the suspect's continued detention can no longer be authorised and his continued detention is unlawful.

The magistrates can issue a warrant allowing a maximum period of no more than a further 36 hours' detention (s.43(12)). If the police need even more time, they can make a further application to the magistrates, under s.44(1), for continued permission to detain the suspect without charge. However, the magistrates cannot authorise a period of further detention which exceeds 36 hours or which would mean that the suspect is in custody for a total of more than 96 hours from the initial authorisation of his detention (s.44(3)).

Once 96 hours have elapsed from the relevant time, the suspect must either be charged or else released, either unconditionally or, if the preconditions in s.50A are met, on bail (s.43(18)). Following his release, the suspect cannot be rearrested without a warrant for the same offence unless since his release, new evidence has come to light or an examination or analysis of existing evidence has been made which could not reasonably have been made before his release (s.43(19)).

It should be noted that this timetable does not apply to suspects detained under the Prevention of Terrorism legislation (which permits a considerably longer period of detention without charge).

1.5.4.4 Non-compliance with review timetable

Where the suspect's detention is not reviewed in accordance with PACE (and none of the circumstances in s.40 which allow for postponement of the review is applicable), the detention is unlawful from the time when the review should have taken place, giving rise to a potential civil claim for damages for false imprisonment. It is immaterial in such a case that there were grounds to justify the continued detention, and so the suspect's continued detention would have been authorised had a review taken place.

1.5.5 Interviewing suspects

PACE Code of Practice C sets out detailed rules for the detention and questioning of suspects. It requires, for example, that suspects be given two light meals and a main meal each day and that they are given at least eight hours' rest per day (Code C 8.6 and Code C 12.2).

1.5.5.1 The caution

Paragraph 10.1 of Code C, says that:

> A person whom there are grounds to suspect of an offence ... must be cautioned before any questions about an offence, or further questions if the answers provide the grounds for suspicion, are put to them if either the suspect's answers or silence (i.e. failure or refusal to answer or answer satisfactorily) may be given in evidence to a court in a prosecution.

Thus, a person whom there are grounds to suspect of an offence must be cautioned before any questions about it are put to him regarding his involvement or suspected involvement in that offence. This definition of when a caution must be administered excludes preliminary questions, for example, to establish the suspect's identity. However, where the questions amount to an 'interview', a caution must be administered. Paragraph 11.1A defines 'interview' in these terms:

> An interview is the questioning of a person regarding their involvement or suspected involvement in a criminal offence or offences which, under paragraph 10.1, must be carried out under caution.

It follows that if a person is being questioned only as a potential witness, there is no need to caution that person; however, if a person is about to be questioned as a potential suspect, a caution must be administered before that questioning begins.

Under para.10.5, the wording of the caution is the same as the caution given upon arrest, namely 'You do not have to say anything. But it may harm your defence if you do not mention when questioned something which you later rely on in Court. Anything you do say may be given in evidence'. Paragraph 10.7 makes the point that 'minor deviations' from the prescribed words of the caution do not constitute a breach of the Code, provided that the sense of the caution is preserved.

Paragraph 10.8 stipulates that, after any break in questioning under caution, the person being questioned must be made aware they remain under caution. If there is any doubt, the caution should be given again in full when the interview resumes.

When the suspect is charged, the caution is repeated in the same terms except that the word 'now' replaces the words 'when questioned' (Code C 16.2).

Breaches of the provisions of the Codes do not mean that any evidence obtained in breach of the Code in question (for example, a confession) is automatically inadmissible. However, if there have been breaches of the Code, any evidence so obtained may well be ruled inadmissible as a result. For example, in R v Senior [2004] EWCA Crim 454; [2004] 3 All ER 9, where questions had been asked by customs officers to establish the ownership of suspicious baggage prior to administering a caution (even though the passengers were effectively suspects at that stage), the questioning amounted to a breach of para.10.1 of Code C, but the court held that this did not require the evidence to be excluded at the trial.

1.5.5.2 The police interview

Paragraph 11.1 of Code C provides that, except in certain limited instances, an interview may only take place at a police station. The interview should be recorded (either a tape-recording or a video-recording). Code E deals with audio-recording, and Code F dealing with video-recording.

This, of course, means that there is a definitive record of what the suspect said and what was said to him. This protects the suspect from any risk that the police might be tempted to fabricate a confession, and it protects the police from allegations that they have fabricated any confession.

If the interview is not recorded, a written record must be made showing what is said; this should be done during or as soon as practicable after the interview. The record should be signed by the maker, and the person interviewed should be given the opportunity to read and correct the record; see paras 11.7–14.

Under para.11.6, the interview must cease when the officer in charge of the investigation is satisfied that all the questions relevant to obtaining accurate and reliable information about the offence have been put to the suspect (this includes allowing the suspect an opportunity to give an innocent explanation and asking questions to test whether the explanation is accurate and reliable, for example to clear up ambiguities or clarify what the suspect said), or when the custody officer reasonably believes that there is sufficient evidence to provide a 'realistic prospect of conviction' for the offence under investigation (that is the same test as that applied by the Crown Prosecution Service when deciding whether or not to continue a prosecution).

It should be noted that, under s.34 of the Criminal Justice and Public Order Act 1994, where the defendant was questioned under caution and 'failed to mention any fact relied on in his defence in those proceedings':

- the court, in determining whether there is a case to answer; and
- the court or jury, in determining whether the accused is guilty of the offence charged, 'may draw such inferences from the failure as appear proper'.

Sometimes, rather than answering police questions or simply giving a 'no comment' interview, the suspect will produce a prepared statement that is handed to the police instead of answering their questions. In R v *Knight* [2003] EWCA Crim 1977; [2004] 1 WLR 340, Laws LJ (at [11]) said:

> We have come to the clear conclusion that the aim of s.34(1)(a) does not distinctly include police cross-examination of a suspect upon his account over and above the disclosure of that account. Had that been intended, it seems to us that Parliament would have used significantly different language. The relevant failure could readily have been described as a failure 'to answer questions properly put to him under caution by a constable trying to discover whether or by whom the offence had been committed', rather than a failure to mention any facts relied on in his defence. But the point is not merely linguistic. A requirement to submit to police cross-examination (so long as the questions are proper), or at any rate an encouragement to do so on pain of later adverse inferences being drawn, is a significantly greater intrusion into a suspect's general right of silence than is a requirement, or encouragement, upon the suspect to disclose his factual defence. We by no means suggest that such an intrusion could not properly be legislated for without offence to art.6 of the European Convention on Human Rights; but it would, we think, require a much sharper expression of the legislature's will than can be found in the words of the statute as enacted.

However, his Lordship also sounded a cautionary note, at [13]):

> The making of a prepared statement is not of itself an inevitable antidote to later adverse inferences. The prepared statement may be incomplete in comparison with the defendant's later account at trial, or it may be, to whatever degree, inconsistent with that account. One may envisage many situations in which a prepared statement in some form has been put forward, but yet there is a proper case for an adverse inference arising out of the suspect's failure 'on being questioned under caution ... to mention any fact relied on in his defence'. We wish to make it crystal clear that of itself the making of a prepared statement gives no automatic immunity against adverse inferences under s.34.

This necessarily presents something of a challenge to police station advisers, as it requires a prediction of what facts are likely to be relied upon at trial in order to ensure that the prepared statement does not omit significant facts, with the consequential risk of adverse inferences being drawn if those facts are relied on at trial.

1.5.5.3 Access to legal advice

Under s.58(1) of PACE, a person who has been arrested and is being held in police custody is 'entitled, if he so requests, to consult a solicitor privately at any time'. Under subs.(4), a person who makes such a request must be permitted to consult a solicitor as soon as is practicable, except to the extent that delay is permitted by ss.58(6)–(8A). Even if those subsections apply, the suspect must be permitted to consult a solicitor within 36 hours (subs.(5)). Delay in access to legal advice is permissible only where the offence is an indictable one, and the delay is authorised by an officer of at least the rank of Superintendent (s.58(6)). Under s.58(8), the officer may authorise the delay only where he has reasonable grounds for believing that the exercise of the right to consult a solicitor, at the time when the detainee desires to exercise it:

(a) will lead to interference with or harm to evidence connected with an indictable offence or interference with or physical injury to other persons; or

(b) will lead to the alerting of other persons suspected of having committed such an offence but not yet arrested for it; or

(c) will hinder the recovery of any property obtained as a result of such an offence.

Additionally, under s.58(8A), the officer may authorise delay where he has reasonable grounds for believing that the detainee has benefited from criminal conduct, and the recovery of the value of the property constituting the benefit will be hindered by the exercise of the right to consult a solicitor.

Under s.58(11), there may be no further delay in permitting the exercise of the right of access to a solicitor once the reason for authorising delay ceases to subsist.

In R v Samuel [1988] QB 615, it was held that the suspicion must relate to the particular solicitor whom the suspect wishes to see. The police must therefore have grounds to suspect the honesty of that solicitor or else think him particularly naive. Samuel was followed in R v James [2008] EWCA Crim 1869, where the Court of Appeal emphasised (at [35] and [36]) a number of propositions set out in Samuel, namely that the right of access to legal advice is one of the most important and fundamental rights of a citizen; where it is sought to justify denial of the right of access to a solicitor on reasonable grounds, that cannot be done except by reference to specific circumstances; it will only be in rare cases that the officer will genuinely have the requisite belief, namely that the solicitor will act improperly; the grounds put forward must relate to a specific solicitor, not solicitors generally.

Given the importance of the right to legal advice while being detained (and questioned) by the police, and the risk that evidence will be excluded by the court if obtained where this right has been withheld, it is very rare for the police to invoke the power to delay access to a solicitor. There is a substantial risk that any evidence obtained from a suspect who is being denied access to a solicitor will be ruled inadmissible.

1.5.5.4 Wrongful denial of access to legal advice

Should there be wrongful exclusion of a solicitor, any confession obtained by the police may well be held inadmissible at trial under s.78 of PACE, which allows the court to exclude any prosecution evidence which would have an adverse effect on the fairness of the proceedings. The importance of legal advice was reaffirmed in R v Mason [1988] 1 WLR 139, where the police deceived a solicitor into thinking that the case against his client was stronger than it was and, because the legal advice was based on this fact, the suspect had effectively been denied legal advice. The Court of Appeal ruled that his subsequent confession should have been excluded.

Article 6 of the European Convention on Human Rights guarantees the right to legal representation. Denial of access to a solicitor during a police interview may violate this provision, especially if adverse inferences can be drawn from the defendant's failure to answer questions. It is for this reason that s.34(2A) of the Criminal Justice and Public Order Act 1994 provides that where the accused was not allowed an opportunity to consult a solicitor prior to being questioned or charged, as the case may be, no adverse inferences may be drawn from his failure to mention facts that he subsequently relies on in court.

The importance of access to legal advice was also emphasised in Salduz v Turkey (2009) 49 EHRR 19 (at [50]), where the European Court of Human Rights ruled that Art.6 (the right to a fair trial) may be relevant before a case is sent for trial, if and so far as the fairness of the trial is likely to be seriously prejudiced by an initial failure to comply with its provisions. The Court went on (at [55]):

Article 6.1 requires that, as a rule, access to a lawyer should be provided as from the first interrogation of a suspect by the police, unless it is demonstrated in the light of the particular circumstances of each case that there are compelling reasons to restrict this right. Even where compelling reasons may exceptionally justify denial of access to a lawyer, such restriction – whatever its justification – must not unduly prejudice the rights of the accused under Article 6 ... The rights of the defence will in principle be irretrievably prejudiced when incriminating statements made during police interrogation without access to a lawyer are used for a conviction.

This decision was considered in the Scottish case of *Cadder v Her Majesty's Advocate (Scotland)* [2010] UKSC 43; [2010] 1 WLR 2601. Lord Hope said (at [41]) that Art.6(1) permits a departure from the principle that access to a lawyer should be provided as from the first interrogation of a suspect 'only if the facts of the case make it impracticable to adhere to it'. His Lordship went on to say (at [48]) that the *Salduz* principle cannot be confined to admissions made during police questioning; it extends to incriminating evidence obtained from elsewhere as a result of lines of inquiry that the detainee's answers have given rise to. Similarly, Lord Rodger (at [95]) said that the right to legal assistance at the stage when a suspect is to be questioned is 'not absolute and must be subject to exceptions when, in the particular circumstances, there are compelling reasons to restrict it' but that 'even a justified restriction may deprive an accused of a fair hearing and so lead to a violation of Article 6'.

1.5.5.5 Securing access to legal advice

Paragraph 6.1 of Code C provides that (except in those cases where delay in access to a solicitor is authorised under s.58 of PACE), 'all detainees must be informed that they may at any time consult and communicate privately with a solicitor, whether in person, in writing or by telephone, and that free independent legal advice is available'.

A detainee can ask for advice from a solicitor they know, or, if they do not know a solicitor or the solicitor they know cannot be contacted, from the duty solicitor. Note 6B in Code C sets out the mechanism for securing legal advice. When a detainee asks for free legal advice, the Defence Solicitor Call Centre (DSCC) must be informed of the request. Free legal advice is limited to telephone advice provided by Criminal Defence Service Direct (CDSD) if a detainee is detained for a non-imprisonable offence, a drink-driving offence or has been arrested for breach of bail.

To arrange free legal advice, the police should telephone the DSCC. The call centre will decide whether legal advice should be limited to telephone advice from CDSD, or whether a solicitor known to the detainee or the duty solicitor should speak to the detainee. When a detainee wants to pay for legal advice, the DSCC will contact a solicitor of their choice on his/her behalf. Apart from carrying out duties necessary to implement these arrangements, an officer must not advise the suspect about any particular firm of solicitors.

Paragraph 6.4 of Code C says that no police officer should, at any time, do or say anything with the intention of dissuading a detainee from obtaining legal advice. Paragraph 6.5 requires that the custody officer should act without delay to secure the provision of legal advice if it is sought. If the detainee has the right to speak to a solicitor in person but declines to exercise the right, the officer should point out that the right includes the right to speak with a solicitor on the telephone. If the detainee continues to waive this right, or a detainee whose right to free legal advice is limited to telephone advice declines to exercise that right, the officer should ask them why and any reasons should be recorded on the custody record or the interview record.

Under para.6.6, a detainee who wants legal advice may not be interviewed (or continue to be interviewed) until they have received such advice unless the power to delay access to a solicitor under s.58 applies. If the suspect names a particular solicitor but that solicitor cannot be contacted or declines to attend, the detainee must be advised of the Duty Solicitor Scheme; if the suspect declines to ask for the duty solicitor, the interview may start (or continue) without further delay provided an officer of the rank of Inspector or above agrees.

1.5.5.6 The role of the solicitor during police interviews

Under para.6.8 of the Code, a detainee who has been permitted to consult a solicitor in person is entitled to have the solicitor present when he is interviewed, unless the power to delay access to a solicitor under s.58 applies. The solicitor may only be required to leave the interview if his conduct is such that the interviewer is unable properly to put questions to the suspect (para.6.9). If the interviewer considers a solicitor is acting in such a way, the interview will be stopped and the interviewing officer will consult a colleague not below the rank of Superintendent if one is readily available (failing that, an officer not below the rank of Inspector who is not connected with the investigation). After speaking to the solicitor, the officer consulted will decide whether the interview should continue in the presence of that solicitor. If they decide it should not, the suspect will be given the opportunity to consult another solicitor before the interview continues and that solicitor will be given an opportunity to be present at the interview (para.6.10). Paragraph 6.11 makes the point that the removal of a solicitor from an interview is a serious step and, if it occurs, the officer who took the decision should consider whether the incident should be reported to the Solicitors Regulation Authority.

Guidance Note 6D deals with the role of the solicitor during the interview:

> The solicitor's only role in the police station is to protect and advance the legal rights of their client. On occasions this may require the solicitor to give advice which has the effect of the client avoiding giving evidence which strengthens a prosecution case. The solicitor may intervene in order to seek clarification, challenge an improper question to their client or the manner in which it is put, advise their client not to reply to particular questions, or if they wish to give their client further legal advice. Paragraph 6.9 only applies if the solicitor's approach or conduct prevents or unreasonably obstructs proper questions being put to the suspect or the suspect's response being recorded. Examples of unacceptable conduct include answering questions on a suspect's behalf or providing written replies for the suspect to quote.

Thus, a solicitor who is present when a suspect is being interviewed by the police should intervene if (for example) the police officers:

● ask unfair questions;
● ask questions which do not relate to the alleged offence(s);
● misrepresent the law;
● claim to know things but without having any factual basis for that knowledge;
● produce or refer to evidence which has not been shown to the suspect or the solicitor;
● misrepresent information;
● put pressure on the suspect by questioning him in a burdensome manner, by behaving abusively, or by attempting to influence the suspect's decision making.

1.5.5.7 Special rules for interviewing juveniles and persons at risk

Special rules apply to protect juveniles and other vulnerable groups. For example (under para.11.15 of Code C), a juvenile, or someone who is mentally disordered or otherwise mentally vulnerable, must not be interviewed unless an 'appropriate adult' (that is, a parent, guardian, or social worker) is present. Under para.11.17, the appropriate adult must be informed that they are not expected to act simply as an observer and that the purpose of their presence is to:

● advise the person being interviewed;
● observe whether the interview is being conducted properly and fairly;
● facilitate communication with the person being interviewed.

1.6 The decision to prosecute

Under s.3(2)(a) of the Prosecution of Offences Act 1985, it is the duty of the Director of Public Prosecutions (DPP) to take over the conduct of all criminal proceedings, other than specified proceedings, instituted on behalf of a police force. This means that the case will be taken forward by the CPS, and this will include a review of the evidence (by a Crown Prosecutor).

1.6.1 The Full Code Test

The decision to start, or continue, a prosecution is taken in accordance with the Code of Conduct for Crown Prosecutors. This provides that, except in cases where it is proposed to apply to the court to keep the suspect in custody after charge but the evidence required to apply the 'Full Code Test' is not yet available (in which case the 'Threshold Test' applies), prosecutors must only start or continue a prosecution when the case has passed both stages of the Full Code Test: evidential sufficiency and public interest.

The Code provides that there must be 'a realistic prospect of conviction', based on the prosecutor's 'objective assessment of the evidence'. There is a realistic prospect of conviction only if a court (whether a magistrates' court or the Crown Court) is 'more likely than not to convict the defendant of the charge alleged' (para.4.7). In other words, the likelihood of conviction must be 51 per cent or better.

The Code makes it clear that a case which does not pass the evidential stage must not proceed, however serious or sensitive the case may be (para.4.6).

In considering whether this test is satisfied, the prosecutor must consider what the defence case may be, and how it is likely to affect the prospects of conviction. This includes (for example) consideration of what the suspect said when interviewed by the police. The prosecutor also has to consider the quality of the evidence against the suspect (see para.4.8). This requires consideration of:

● The *admissibility* of the evidence (if there is any question over the admissibility of certain evidence, the prosecutor should assess the likelihood of that evidence being held inadmissible by the court and the importance of that evidence in relation to the evidence as a whole);
● The *reliability* of the evidence (whether there are any reasons to question the reliability of the evidence, including its accuracy or integrity); and
● The *credibility* of the evidence (whether there are any reasons to doubt the credibility of the evidence).

The second stage (assuming there is sufficient evidence to justify a prosecution or to offer an out-of-court disposal) is to consider whether it is in the 'public interest' to prosecute the suspect (para.4.9). The Code makes it clear that the fact that the evidential stage is met does not mean that a prosecution has to be brought. Rather, a prosecution will 'usually take place unless the prosecutor is satisfied that there are public interest factors tending against prosecution which outweigh those tending in favour'. In some cases, however, the prosecutor may be satisfied that the public interest can be properly served by offering an out-of-court disposal (i.e. a caution or conditional caution) rather than bringing a prosecution (see para.4.10). Nonetheless, there is, in effect, a presumption in favour of prosecution where there is sufficient evidence against the suspect.

The Code identifies a number of factors that have to be taken into account when deciding whether or not prosecution is in the public interest (see para.4.14):

● The seriousness of the offence (the more serious the offence, the more likely it is that a prosecution is required);
● The culpability of the suspect (the greater the suspect's level of culpability, the more likely it is that a prosecution is required);

- The circumstances of the victim and the harm caused to the victim (both of which are relevant to the seriousness of the offence);
- Whether the suspect was under the age of 18 at the time of the offence (the younger the suspect, the less likely it is that a prosecution is required);
- The impact on the community (the greater the impact of the offending on the community, the more likely it is that a prosecution is required);
- Whether prosecution is a proportionate response (for example, it might be better to prosecute only the main participants in order to avoid excessively long and complex proceedings);
- Whether sources of information require protecting (whether, in cases where public interest immunity does not apply, details might need to be made public that could harm sources of information, international relations or national security).

The Code makes the point that, in most cases, prosecutors should consider whether a prosecution is in the public interest only after considering whether there is sufficient evidence to prosecute. However, 'there will be cases where it is clear, prior to the reviewing all the evidence, that the public interest does not require a prosecution. In these instances, prosecutors may decide that the case should not proceed further' (para.4.4).

1.6.2 The Threshold Test

In certain limited circumstances, where the Full Code Test is not met, the Threshold Test may be applied instead to charge a suspect. The Code states that the seriousness or circumstances of the case must justify the making of an immediate charging decision, and there must be substantial grounds to object to bail (para.5.1).

The Code makes it clear that the Threshold Test may be applied only where five conditions are met:

- there are reasonable grounds to suspect that the person to be charged has committed the offence;
- there are reasonable grounds to believe that further evidence can be obtained to provide a realistic prospect of conviction;
- the seriousness or the circumstances of the case justifies the making of an immediate charging decision;
- there are continuing substantial grounds to object to bail in accordance with the Bail Act 1976 and, in all the circumstances of the case, it is proper to do so; and
- it is in the public interest to charge the suspect (applying the public interest stage of the Full Code Test, based on the information available at the time).

It should be emphasised that the Threshold Test is effectively a temporary measure. The Full Code Test must be applied as soon as is reasonably practicable to decide whether the prosecution should continue (see para.5.11).

1.6.3 Selection of charges

The CPS Code (para.6.1) states that prosecutors should select charges which:

- reflect the seriousness and extent of the offending;
- give the court adequate powers to sentence and impose appropriate post-conviction orders;
- allow a confiscation order to be made in appropriate cases, where a defendant has benefited from criminal conduct; and
- enable the case to be presented in a clear and simple way.

The Code goes on to say that prosecutors should never go ahead with more charges than are necessary just to encourage a defendant to plead guilty to a few, or with a more serious charge just to encourage a defendant to plead guilty to a less serious one (para.6.3), and that they should not change the charge simply because of the decision made by the court or the defendant about where the case will be heard (para.6.4).

1.6.3.1 Accepting guilty pleas

The CPS Code makes it clear that, where defendants wish to plead guilty to some but not all charges, or to plead guilty to a lesser charge, prosecutors should accept the defendant's plea only if they think the court is able to pass a sentence that matches the seriousness of the offending (para.9.2). Prosecutors should ensure that the interests and, where possible, the views of the victim (or, in appropriate cases, the views of the victim's family) are 'taken into account when deciding whether it is in the public interest to accept the plea. However, the decision rests with the prosecutor' (para.9.5).

1.6.4 Reconsidering a prosecution decision

The CPS Code also makes the point that, normally, if the CPS tells a suspect or defendant that there will not be a prosecution, or that the prosecution has been stopped, the case will not start again. However, there will occasionally be reasons why the CPS will overturn a decision not to prosecute or to deal with the case by way of an out-of-court disposal, or when it will restart the prosecution, particularly if the case is serious (para.10.1). Examples of situations in which this course of action might be justified include (see para.10.2):

- cases where review of the original decision shows that it was 'wrong and, in order to maintain confidence in the criminal justice system, a prosecution should be brought despite the earlier decision';
- cases which are stopped so that more evidence, which is likely to become available in the fairly near future, can be collected and prepared (in these cases, the prosecutor will tell the defendant that the prosecution may well start again);
- cases which are not prosecuted or which are stopped because of a lack of evidence but where 'more significant evidence is discovered later'; and
- cases involving a death in which a review takes place after an inquest and concludes that a prosecution should be brought, notwithstanding any earlier decision not to prosecute.

1.6.5 Challenging a decision to prosecute

In R v DPP, ex p Kebilene [2000] 2 AC 326, it was held that, given the availability of a remedy within the criminal process itself, the decision to prosecute is not amenable to judicial review unless there is a claim of dishonesty, bad faith or other exceptional circumstance (per Lord Steyn at p.371). Judicial review will therefore be available only in 'wholly exceptional circumstances' (R (Gjovalin Pepushi) v CPS [2004] EWHC 798 (Admin), per Thomas LJ (at [49])).

A key reason for this reluctance to allow judicial review to be invoked in such cases is the fact that the trial process is usually capable of providing a remedy. In Sharma v Brown-Antoine [2007] 1 WLR 780, the Privy Council ruled that, before allowing judicial review, the court would have to be satisfied that the complaint could not adequately be resolved within the criminal process itself, either at the trial or by way of an application to stay the criminal proceedings as an abuse of process. Similarly, in Moss & Son Ltd v CPS [2012] EWHC 3658 (Admin); (2013) 177 JP 221, Sir John Thomas P said (at [23]) that:

In R v *Grafton* [1993] QB 101, it was held that the decision to discontinue proceedings is entirely a matter for the prosecution; the agreement of the court is not required. This applies both in the magistrates' court and the Crown Court.

The powers of the DPP to discontinue a prosecution under s.23 of the Prosecution of Offences Act may be contrasted with the power of the Attorney General to enter a *nolle prosequi*. This common law power enables the Attorney General to terminate a prosecution at any time after the draft indictment has been signed. This power is exercised only rarely but its exercise cannot be challenged in the courts (*Gouriet v Union of Post Office Workers* [1978] AC 435).

1.7 Commencement of proceedings

There are a number of ways of bringing someone before the criminal courts:

- using a 'written charge' and 'requisition';
- laying of an 'information', followed by the issue of a 'summons';
- charging the suspect following their arrest, whether the arrest was with or without out a warrant.

1.7.1 Written charge and requisition

Under s.29(1) of the Criminal Justice Act (CJA) 2003 a 'relevant' prosecutor may institute criminal proceedings against a person by issuing a 'written charge', which charges that person with an offence. The prosecutor must, at the same time, issue a 'requisition' (s.29(2)), which requires the person to appear before a magistrates' court to answer the written charge (subs. (2A)). The written charge and requisition must be served on the person concerned and a copy of both must be served on the court named in the requisition (s.29(3)). For these purposes, a 'relevant prosecutor' is defined (in s.29(5)) as including (among others) the police, the DPP, the Attorney General, the Serious Fraud Office, and the Director of the National Crime Agency.

The effect of s.29 is that notification of the requirement to attend court is communicated to the accused by the prosecutor, not by the magistrates' court. Indeed, the magistrates' court has no active involvement in the case until the accused makes his first appearance before the court.

1.7.2 Laying an information and issuing a summons

This is a two-stage process: the laying of an 'information' by the prosecutor, followed by the issue and service of a summons by the magistrates' court. It applies only to private prosecutions.

1.7.2.1 Laying an information

Before a summons can be issued to require the suspect to attend court, an application has to be made to a magistrates' court (historically known as 'laying' an 'information'). This may be done before a magistrate or a magistrates' clerk, and it may be done orally (in which case, the informant attends the magistrates' court) or in writing. A written information is 'laid' as soon as it is received in the clerk's office, even if it is not considered by a clerk or a magistrate until later (*R v Manchester Justices ex p Hill* [1983] 1 AC 328).

Rule 7.2(1) provides that a prosecutor who wants the court to issue a summons must:

(a) serve on the court officer a written application [i.e. lay an information]; or
(b) unless other legislation prohibits this, present an application orally to the court, with a written statement of the allegation or allegations made by the prosecutor.

By virtue of r.7.2(5), unless the prosecutor is legally represented or is a public authority (as defined by s.17(6)) of the Prosecution of Offences Act 1985, the application for the summons must (under r.7.2(6)):

(a) concisely outline the grounds for asserting that the defendant has committed the alleged offence or offences;
(b) disclose—
    (i) details of any previous such application by the same applicant in respect of any allegation now made, and
    (ii) details of any current or previous proceedings brought by another prosecutor in respect of any allegation now made; and
(c) include a statement that to the best of the applicant's knowledge, information and belief—
    (i) the allegations contained in the application are substantially true,
    (ii) the evidence on which the applicant relies will be available at the trial,
    (iii) the details given by the applicant under paragraph (6)(b) are true, and
    (iv) the application discloses all the information that is material to what the court must decide.

The importance of the prosecutor's statement is emphasised by the fact that, where the statement required by r.7.2(6)(c) is made orally, it must (unless the court otherwise directs) be made on oath or affirmation (r.7.2(7)).

It should be noted that the duty under r.7.2(6) does not apply where the prosecutor is legally represented or is a public authority. For these purposes, a public authority (as defined by the 1985 Act) includes the police, the CPS, government departments, and local authorities. The point to bear in mind is that an unrepresented non-governmental private prosecutor may struggle to understand that they have a binding duty to comply with the overriding objective of the Criminal Procedure Rules and so cannot strive for a conviction 'at all costs'.

1.7.2.2 Issuing a summons

Once an information has been laid, a summons may then be issued by a magistrate or clerk (usually the latter). In R (*Kay*) v *Leeds Magistrates' Court* [2018] EWHC 1233 (Admin); [2018] 4 WLR 91, the court noted (at [20]) that the decision whether to issue a summons 'is a judicial function involving the exercise of a discretion'. The court reviewed a number of authorities, and summarised their effect (at [22]) by saying that they establish that, when considering whether to issue a summons:

(1) The magistrate must ascertain whether the allegation is an offence known to the law, and if so whether the essential ingredients of the offence are prima facie present; that the offence alleged is not time-barred; that the court has jurisdiction; and whether the informant has the necessary authority to prosecute.
(2) If so, generally the magistrate ought to issue the summons, unless there are compelling reasons not to do so – most obviously that the application is vexatious (which may involve the presence of an improper ulterior purpose and/or long delay); or is an abuse of process; or is otherwise improper.
(3) Hence the magistrate should consider the whole of the relevant circumstances to enable him to satisfy himself that it is a proper case to issue the summons and, even if there is evidence of the offence, should consider whether the application is vexatious, an abuse of process, or otherwise improper.
(4) Whether the applicant has previously approached the police may be a relevant circumstance.

(5) There is no obligation on the magistrate to make enquiries, but he may do so if he thinks it necessary.
(6) A proposed defendant has no right to be heard, but the magistrate has a discretion to:
   (a) Require the proposed defendant to be notified of the application.
   (b) Hear the proposed defendant if he thinks it necessary for the purpose of making a decision.

1.7.3 Contents of the written charge (or information and summons)

Rule 7.3(1) of the Criminal Procedure Rules provides that an allegation of an offence in an application for the issue of a summons or warrant or in a charge must contain:

(a) a statement of the offence that:
   (i) describes the offence in ordinary language; and
   (ii) identifies any legislation that creates it; and
(b) such particulars of the conduct constituting the commission of the offence as to make clear what the prosecutor alleges against the defendant.

By virtue of r.7.3(2):

More than one incident of the commission of the offence may be included in the allegation if those incidents taken together amount to a course of conduct having regard to the time, place or purpose of commission.

Thus, the documentation must set out the substance of the allegation against the accused.

The charge will set out the statutory provision contravened (assuming the offence is a statutory one, as most are), together with a short summary of the facts of the case.

For example, an allegation of careless driving would be set out as follows:

On 26 December 2019, driving a mechanically propelled vehicle, namely, a Ford Focus motor car registration number YZ 69 ABC, on a road, namely, Warmington High Street, without due care and attention, contrary to s.3 of the Road Traffic Act 1988.

In *Nash v RSPCA* [2005] EWHC Admin 338; (2005) 169 JP 157, it was held that the accused is entitled to know what act or omission is alleged against him. However, if the documentation fails to give sufficient information to the accused as to the nature of the charge he faces, that of itself does not render the proceedings a nullity or any resulting conviction unsafe, provided that the requisite information was given to the accused in good time for him to be able fairly to meet the case against him.

Rule 7.4(2) stipulates that a summons or requisition must (among other matters) contain notice of when and where the defendant is required to attend the court and must specify each offence in respect of which it is issued.

1.7.3.1 Service of the requisition or summons

A summons or requisition may be served on an individual:

● by handing it to him (r.4.3(1)(a)); or
● by leaving it at, or sending it by first class post to, an address where it is reasonably believed that he will receive it (r.4.4(1) and (2)(a)).

If the accused is a company, the requisition or summons may be served:

- by handing it to a person holding a senior position in that company (r.4.3(1)(b)); or
- by leaving it at, or sending it by first class post to, its principal office in England and Wales or, if there is no readily identifiable principal office, then any place in England and Wales where it carries on its activities or business (r.4.4(1) and (2)(b)).

1.7.4 Charge after arrest

Section 37(7) of PACE provides that if the custody officer determines that there is sufficient evidence to charge the person arrested with the offence for which he was arrested, the person arrested must be:

- released without charge on bail, pending a charging decision by the CPS under s.37B, provided that the pre-conditions for bail set out in s.50A are satisfied; or
- released without charge and not on bail, pending a charging decision by the CPS under s.37B, if the pre-conditions for bail in s.50A are not satisfied;
- kept in police custody pending a charging decision by the CPS under s.37B; or
- charged.

To charge a suspect, the custody officer simply tells the suspect what offence(s) he is accused of. The suspect is cautioned that he does not have to say anything, that it may harm his defence if he does not mention now something he later relies on in court, and that anything he does say will be written down and may be given in evidence. The suspect is then asked if he has anything to say. Any reply must be noted down.

1.7.4.1 Involvement of the CPS in the charging decision

The prospect of the defendant pleading guilty, or being found guilty, depends in large measure on the defendant being charged with the right offence(s) on the basis of sufficient evidence.

According to para.15 of the DPP's Guidance on Charging (5th edition, May 2013), the police may charge:

- any summary-only offence (including criminal damage where the value of the loss or damage is less than £5,000) irrespective of plea;
- any offence of retail theft (shoplifting) or attempted retail theft irrespective of plea provided it is suitable for sentence in the magistrates' court; and
- any either-way offence anticipated as a guilty plea and suitable for sentence in a magistrates' court (although several offences are excluded, for example: cases involving a death; offences classified as hate crime or domestic violence under CPS Policies; offences of violent disorder or affray, causing grievous bodily harm or wounding, or actual bodily harm; Sexual Offences Act offences committed by or upon a person under 18).

Paragraph 16 goes on to state that prosecutors will make charging decisions in all cases not allocated to the police in para.15.

Section 37B(2) of PACE provides that where a suspect is released (whether on bail or not) without charge, or kept in police detention, for the purpose of enabling the CPS to make a charging decision, the CPS must decide whether there is sufficient evidence to charge the person with an offence. Under subs.(3), if CPS decides that there is sufficient evidence to charge the person with an offence, the prosecutor must decide whether or not the person should be charged and, if so, with what offence(s), or whether the person should be given a caution and, if so, for what offence(s).

Under subs.(6), if the Crown Prosecutor decides that the person should be charged with an offence, or given a caution in respect of an offence, the person must be charged or cautioned accordingly. However, if the decision is that the person should be given a caution but it proves not to be possible to give the person such a caution (as would be the case where the suspect denies the offence), he will instead be charged with the offence (subs.(7)).

Under subs.(8), the charging will be done by a custody officer at the police station if the suspect is still in police detention; if not, he will either be charged by the CPS using the written charge and requisition procedure established by s.29 of the Criminal Justice Act 2003, or else by the police when he returns to the police station to answer his bail.

Under s.37B(5), if the prosecutor decides that there is insufficient evidence to prosecute (or that it would not be in the public interest to prosecute or give a caution), the custody officer has to be informed accordingly. However, subs.(5A) makes it clear that this does not prevent the prosecution of the person for an offence if new evidence comes to light after the notice was given to the custody officer.

The practical effect of these provisions is that, if the offence is one where the police think there is enough evidence to charge, and they do not wish to release the suspect on police bail, the suspect will be held in custody pending a charging decision by the CPS. If, on the other hand, the police believe that there is sufficient evidence to charge the suspect but are content for him to be released pending the charging decision, the suspect will be released (usually on bail), and the CPS will then take the charging decision.

1.7.4.2 Police bail after charge

A suspect who has been charged with an offence must be released on police bail (with the condition that he must attend a specified magistrates' court on a specified date and at a specified time) unless any of the exceptions contained in s.38 of PACE apply. Under s.38(1)(a), bail may be withheld from a person who has been charged only if:

(i) his name or address cannot be ascertained or the custody officer has reasonable grounds for doubting whether a name or address furnished by him as his name or address is his real name or address;

(ii) the custody officer has reasonable grounds for believing that the person arrested will fail to appear in court to answer to bail;

(iii) in the case of a person arrested for an imprisonable offence, the custody officer has reasonable grounds for believing that the detention of the person arrested is necessary to prevent him from committing an offence;[. . .]

(iv) in the case of a person arrested for an offence which is not an imprisonable offence, the custody officer has reasonable grounds for believing that the detention of the person arrested is necessary to prevent him from causing physical injury to any other person or from causing loss of or damage to property;

(v) the custody officer has reasonable grounds for believing that the detention of the person arrested is necessary to prevent him from interfering with the administration of justice or with the investigation of offences or of a particular offence; or

(vi) the custody officer has reasonable grounds for believing that the detention of the person arrested is necessary for his own protection.

A suspect who is not granted bail under s.38 of PACE will be kept in police custody (s.38 (2)), but must then be taken before the magistrates' court 'as soon as is practicable and in any event not later than the first sitting after he is charged with the offence' (s.46(2)). For these purposes, Sundays, Christmas Day and Good Friday are disregarded (s.46(8)). The magistrates will then decide whether or not to grant bail, using the criteria laid down in the Bail Act 1976.

1.7.4.3 Imposition of conditions on police bail after charge

Where a person is released on police bail under s.38 of PACE having been charged with an offence, the custody officer has power (under s.3A of the Bail Act 1976) to impose any condition on the grant of bail which a court could impose (with certain exceptions, such as a requirement of residence in a bail hostel).

Section 3A(5) of the Bail Act 1976 says that, where police bail is granted, no conditions may be imposed unless it appears to the officer granting bail that it is necessary to do so:

(a) for the purpose of preventing that person from failing to surrender to custody; or

(b) for the purpose of preventing that person from committing an offence while on bail; or

(c) for the purpose of preventing that person from interfering with witnesses or otherwise obstructing the course of justice, whether in relation to himself or any other person; or

(d) for that person's own protection or, if he is a child or young person, for his own welfare or in his own interests.

Section 3A(4) of the Bail Act 1976 allows a custody officer, at the request of the accused, to vary the conditions of bail which were imposed when he was charged, and adds that 'in doing so he may impose conditions or more onerous conditions'.

Where conditions have been attached to police bail, the defendant may apply to a magistrates' court to vary those conditions (under s.43B(1) of the Magistrates' Courts Act 1980), although it should be borne in mind that the court also has the power to withhold bail altogether or to 'impose more onerous conditions' (s.43B(2)).

1.7.4.4 Further questioning

Code C 16.5 provides that a suspect who has been charged cannot be asked any further questions about the offence(s) with which they have been charged unless further questions are necessary:

● to prevent or minimise harm or loss to some other person, or the public;

● to clear up an ambiguity in a previous answer or statement;

● in the interests of justice for the detainee to have put to them, and have an opportunity to comment on, information concerning the offence which has come to light since they were charged or informed they might be prosecuted.

1.7.4.5 Release without charge on police bail

Sometimes the police release a suspect without charge but require him to return to the police station at a later date (for example, for further questioning or to give the police or CPS further time in which to decide whether or not to charge him). If the suspect is released on police bail (which is possible only if the preconditions in s.50A are satisfied), conditions may be imposed under s.47(1A) of PACE.

Where a suspect has been released on police bail with the condition that he should return to the police station on a specified date, he may be arrested without a warrant if he fails to attend the police station at the appointed time (s.46A(1) of PACE). He may also be arrested if the police have reasonable grounds for suspecting that he has broken any conditions of bail (s.46A(1A)).

1.7.5 Early administrative hearings

Section 50 of the Crime and Disorder Act 1998 provides for 'early administrative hearings' in the magistrates' court. It provides that where the accused has been charged with an offence at a police station, the magistrates' court before which he appears for the first time may consist of a single magistrate (s.50(1)). At this hearing, the accused must be asked whether he wishes to apply for legal aid (s.50(2)); if necessary, the hearing may be adjourned in order to enable an application to be made (s.50(4A)). The single justice may then remand the accused in custody or on bail (s.50(3)).

1.7.6 Private prosecutions

Section 6 of the Prosecution of Offences Act 1985 provides as follows:

(1) Subject to subsection (2) below, nothing in this Part shall preclude any person from instituting any criminal proceedings or conducting any criminal proceedings to which the Director's duty to take over the conduct of proceedings does not apply.

(2) Where criminal proceedings are instituted in circumstances in which the Director is not under a duty to take over their conduct, he may nevertheless do so at any stage.

Subsection (1) thus confirms the long-established right to institute and conduct private prosecutions, subject to subs.(2). Subsection (2) gives the DPP the right to take over any prosecution that has been initiated privately.

Where a member of the public or an organisation that is not a recognised public prosecutor wishes to commence a 'private prosecution', they may do so by laying an information at a magistrates' court. A private prosecution may be brought for any offence unless the offence is one for which the consent of the Attorney General or the DPP is required before a prosecution can take place (s.6(1) of the Prosecution of Offences Act 1985); such consent is needed for a small number of offences.

It must be remembered that private prosecutors have to comply with the overriding objective of the Criminal Procedure Rules and so cannot strive for a conviction at all costs. In R (Kay) v Leeds Magistrates' Court [2018] EWHC 1233 (Admin); [2018] 4 WLR 91, Sweeney J (at [23]) said:

(1) Whilst the Code for Crown Prosecutors does not apply to private prosecutions, a private prosecutor is subject to the same obligations as a Minister for Justice as are the public prosecuting authorities – including the duty to ensure that all relevant material is made available both for the court and the defence.

(2) Advocates and solicitors who have the conduct of private prosecutions must observe the highest standards of integrity, of regard for the public interest and duty to act as a Minister for Justice in preference to the interests of the client who has instructed them to bring the prosecution – owing a duty to the court to ensure that the proceeding is fair.

One consequence of this (and the fact that an application for a summons is made without the intended defendant being present) is that a prosecutor who seeks a summons owes a 'duty of candour' (see [24]). This includes a duty to disclose any material which is potentially adverse to the application (at [25]), and putting to the court any arguments that the defence would have made in opposition to the application for a summons (see [26]).

The only other way in which a member of the public can commence criminal proceedings is to effect a 'citizen's arrest' under s.24A of PACE. However, following the arrest, the suspect must be handed over to the police (and the CPS will then decide whether or not to charge the suspect).

Section 6(2) of the Prosecution of Offences Act 1985 enables the DPP to take over the conduct of any criminal proceedings. Once the DPP has taken over the conduct of the proceedings, he is free to discontinue them if he thinks it appropriate to do so. The CPS policy on private prosecutions, in the section dealing with taking over private prosecutions in order to discontinue them, states that:

A private prosecution should be taken over and stopped if, upon review of the case papers, either the evidential sufficiency stage or the public interest stage of the Full Code Test is not met ... Furthermore, there may be factors which would be damaging to the interests of justice if the private prosecution was not discontinued.

The guidance goes on to give a number of examples, including cases where the prosecution interferes with the investigation of another criminal offence or the prosecution of another criminal charge; where it can be said that the prosecution is vexatious (within the meaning of s.42 of the Senior Courts Act 1981), or malicious; where the prosecuting authorities (the police, the CPS or any other public prosecutor) have promised the defendant that he will not be prosecuted at all (this is not the same as a mere statement to the defendant that they will not be bringing or continuing proceedings); where the defendant has already (and appropriately) been given either a simple caution or a conditional caution for the offence.

In R (Gujra) v CPS [2012] UKSC 52; [2013] 1 AC 484, the Supreme Court ruled that the approach taken by the CPS to taking over private prosecutions with the intention of discontinuing them, unless the evidential sufficiency and public interest tests (which apply to cases brought by the CPS) are met, was lawful and did not frustrate or emasculate the objects underpinning the right to bring a private prosecution to be found in s.6 of the Prosecution of Offences Act 1985.

The continued existence of private prosecution is seen by some as an anachronism. In *Jones v Whalley* [2006] UKHL 41; [2007] 1 AC 63, Lord Bingham of Cornhill (at [16]) said:

A crime is an offence against the good order of the state. It is for the state by its appropriate agencies to investigate alleged crimes and decide whether offenders should be prosecuted. In times past, with no public prosecution service and ill-organised means of enforcing the law, the prosecution of offenders necessarily depended on the involvement of private individuals, but that is no longer so. The surviving right of private prosecution is of questionable value, and can be exercised in a way damaging to the public interest.

By contrast, Lord Mance (at [39]) noted the 'traditional English view that the right to institute a private prosecution is an important right and safeguard possessed by any aggrieved citizen', adding (at [43]) that it operates 'as a safeguard against wrongful refusal or failure by public prosecuting authorities to institute proceedings'.

The value of private prosecutions was emphasised in R (*Virgin Media Ltd*) v Zinga [2014] EWCA Crim 52; [2014] 1 WLR 2228. Lord Thomas CJ (at [15]) noted that 'private prosecutions by charitable or public interest bodies such as the Royal Society for the Prevention of Cruelty to Animals are common. Furthermore, public bodies such as the Financial Services Authority also rely for their authority to prosecute on the general power of a private individual to prosecute: see R v *Rollins* [2010] 1 WLR 1922'. His Lordship added (at [16]) that it was evident 'commercial organisations regularly undertake private prosecutions. This type of private prosecution is undertaken not only by trade organisations such the Federation Against Copyright Theft (principally the visual media) and the British Music Industry (the music industry) but also ordinary commercial companies'.

1.8 Alternatives to prosecution

The fact that the police or CPS believes that there is sufficient evidence to justify prosecuting someone for an offence does not necessarily mean that the person will be prosecuted; alternatives to prosecution are available for both adult offenders and young offenders.

1.8.1 Cautions

There are two types of caution for adults, non-statutory 'simple' cautions and statutory 'conditional cautions'. For offenders under the age of 18, there are also two types of caution, but both are statutory: 'youth cautions' and 'youth conditional cautions'.

1.8.1.1 Adults: 'simple cautions'

In the case of an adult offender, a 'caution' may be administered instead of the case going to court. This caution should not be confused with the warning given on arrest and before questioning; rather, it is a warning that committing a further offence will result in court action.

There is no statutory basis for these cautions, but s.17 of the Criminal Justice and Courts Act 2015 restricts their use in some cases. Section 17(2) prohibits the police from giving a simple caution to an offender for an indictable-only offence unless there are exceptional circumstances and a Crown Prosecutor agrees that a caution should be given. Under subs.(3), a caution can be administered in respect of specified either-way offences (see the Criminal Justice and Courts Act 2015 (Simple Cautions) (Specification of Either-Way Offences) Order 2015 (SI 2015/790), only if there are exceptional circumstances. Where the offence is a summary one, or an either-way offence that has not been specified under subs.(3), a caution can only be administered in exceptional circumstances if, in the two years before the commission of the present offence, the person has been convicted of, or cautioned for, a similar offence (subs.(4)).

Guidance may be found in *Simple Cautions for Adult Offenders* (Ministry of Justice, April 2015). Paragraph 6 notes that the scheme is designed to provide the police and the CPS with an alternative means for dealing with low-level, mainly first-time, offending. A simple caution must not be offered to a person who has not made a clear and reliable admission to committing the offence (para.20). In deciding whether a simple caution is appropriate the decision-maker must apply the Full Code Test set out in the Code for Crown Prosecutors (para. 24). There must be sufficient evidence to provide a realistic prospect of conviction in respect of the offence if the offender were to be prosecuted. Moreover, a simple caution must not be offered in order to secure an admission of guilt that could then provide sufficient evidence to meet the evidential stage of the Full Code test (para.25). The decision-maker must also be satisfied that it is in the public interest to offer a simple caution in respect of the offence rather than to prosecute (para.26). A simple caution can only be given when the offender agrees to accept it (para.77). The offender must also have had the opportunity of receiving free and independent legal advice before accepting the caution (para.78).

The need for the offender to give informed consent to the administration of a police caution was emphasised in R (Stratton) v Chief Constable of Thames Valley Police [2013] EWHC 1561 (Admin).

A simple caution forms part of an offender's criminal record and a record will be retained by the police on the Police National Computer (para.83).

If a formal caution is administered in breach of these guidelines, then judicial review may be sought to quash the caution and have it deleted from police records (R v Metropolitan Police Commissioner ex p Thompson [1997] 1 WLR 1519).

1.8.1.2 Adults: conditional cautions

Section 22(2) of the Criminal Justice Act 2003 defines a conditional caution as 'a caution which is given in respect of an offence committed by the offender and which has conditions attached to it with which the offender must comply'.

A conditional caution may be administered only if all of the requirements set out in s.23 are satisfied (s.22(1)). Those requirements are:

- the police have evidence that the offender has committed an offence;
- the CPS or the police decide that there is sufficient evidence to charge the offender with the offence, and that a conditional caution should be given to the offender in respect of the offence;

- the offender admits to the police that he committed the offence;
- the police explain the effect of the conditional caution to the offender and warn him that failure to comply with any of the conditions attached to it may result in his being prosecuted for the offence; and
- the offender signs a document containing details of the offence, an admission by him that he committed the offence, his consent to being given the conditional caution, and the conditions attached to the caution.

Section 22(3) says that the conditions which may be attached to a conditional caution are those that have one or more of the following objects:

- facilitating the rehabilitation of the offender;
- ensuring that the offender makes reparation for the offence;
- punishing the offender.

Under s.22(3A), the conditions which may be attached to a conditional caution include a condition that the offender pay a financial penalty, and a condition 'that the offender attend at a specified place at specified times'. The maximum amount of such the financial penalty is prescribed by the Criminal Justice Act 2003 (Conditional Cautions: Financial Penalties) Order 2013 (SI 2013/615):

Summary offence:	£50
Either-way offence:	£100
Indictable-only offence:	£150

These limits do not preclude offenders also being required to pay compensation to victims for the purpose of making reparation for the offence, or to pay a sum of money to a charity by way of indirect reparation to the community.

The sanction for non-compliance with the conditions is set out in s.24(1) of the 2003 Act:

> If the offender fails, without reasonable excuse, to comply with any of the conditions attached to the conditional caution, criminal proceedings may be instituted against the person for the offence in question.

Under s.24A of the 2003 Act, where a police officer has reasonable grounds for believing that the offender has failed, without reasonable excuse, to comply with any of the conditions attached to the conditional caution, the offender may be arrested without warrant.

Further details about adult conditional cautions can be found in the *Code of Practice for Adult Conditional Cautions* (Ministry of Justice, January 2013) and in the *Director's Guidance on Adult Conditional Cautions* (DPP, April 2013).

1.8.1.3 Youth offenders: cautions

Section 66ZA(6) of the Crime and Disorder Act 1998 says that no form of caution other than a youth caution or a youth conditional caution may be given to a child or young person. Section 66ZA(1) provides that a police officer may give a child or young person (that is, a person between the ages of 10 and 17) a caution if:

- the officer decides that there is sufficient evidence to charge the child/young person with an offence;
- the child/young person admits committing the offence; and
- the officer does not consider that the child/young person should be prosecuted or given a youth conditional caution in respect of the offence.

The caution must be given in the presence of an appropriate adult (subs.(2)).

Where the police have administered a youth caution, they must, as soon as practicable, refer the child/young person to a youth offending team (s.66ZB(1)). The youth offending team must, unless they consider it inappropriate to do so, arrange for the child/young person to participate in a rehabilitation programme (subs.(2)).

Youth cautions (and a report on any failure to participate in a rehabilitation programme) may be cited in subsequent criminal proceedings (s.66ZB(7)).

1.8.1.4 Young offenders: conditional cautions

A youth conditional caution is defined by s.66A(2) of the Crime and Disorder Act 1998 as 'a caution which is given in respect of an offence committed by the offender and which has conditions attached to it with which the offender must comply'.

Under s.66A(1), a youth conditional caution may be given to a child or young person who has not previously been convicted of an offence, if each of the five requirements in s.66B is satisfied: these requirements are the same as those applicable to adult conditions cautions under s.23 of the Criminal Justice Act 2003 (see above).

As with adults, the conditions must have the object of facilitating the rehabilitation of the offender, ensuring that the offender makes reparation for the offence, and/or punishing the offender (s.66A(3)).

The conditions that may be imposed include payment of a financial penalty. The Crime and Disorder Act 1998 (Youth Conditional Cautions: Financial Penalties) Order 2013 (SI 2013/608) specifies the maximum amount which may be specified in a financial penalty condition.

As with adults, s.66E(1) provides that if the offender fails, without reasonable excuse, to comply with any of the conditions, proceedings may be instituted against the child/young person for the offence in question.

Further details may be found in the *Code of Practice for Youth Conditional Cautions* (Ministry of Justice, March 2013) and the *Director's Guidance on Youth Conditional Cautions* (DPP, January 2015).

1.8.2 Fixed penalty notices

Fixed penalty notices are a familiar feature of road traffic law. Section 54 of the Road Traffic Offenders Act 1988 provides that where a uniformed police officer has reason to believe that a person is committing, or has on that occasion committed, a fixed penalty offence, the officer may give him a fixed penalty notice in respect of the offence.

However, such notices are not confined to road traffic law. Sections 1 and 2 of the Criminal Justice and Police Act 2001 make provision for fixed penalty notices for a large number of offences related to public order, drugs and alcohol; ss.43–44 of the Anti-Social Behaviour Act 2003 make similar provision for a number of offences relating to damage to property. There are also a number of statutory provisions for fixed penalty notices in environmental protection legislation (for example, s.88 of the Environmental Protection Act 1990, fixed penalty for leaving litter).

Further information about fixed penalty notices for disorder may be found in *Penalty Notices for Disorder* (Ministry of Justice, June 2014).

1.9 Abuse of process

Where proceedings would amount to an abuse of process, the court may order that those proceedings be 'stayed'. The usual effect of a stay is that the case against the accused is stopped permanently.

In R v *Beckford* [1996] 1 Cr App R 94, Neill LJ said (at p.100) that the 'constitutional principle which underlies the jurisdiction to stay proceedings is that the courts have the power and the duty to protect the law by protecting its own purposes and functions'. His Lordship quoted the words of Lord Devlin in *Connelly v DPP* [1964] AC 1254 at p.1354, that the courts have 'an inescapable duty to secure fair treatment for those who come or are brought before them'.

In R v *Maxwell* [2010] UKSC 48; [2011] 4 All ER 941 (at [13]), cited in *Warren v A-G for Jersey* [2011] UKPC 10; [2012] 1 AC 22 (at [22]), Lord Dyson set out the two categories of case in which the court has the power to stay proceedings for abuse of process:

> It is well established that the court has the power to stay proceedings in two categories of case, namely (i) where it will be impossible to give the accused a fair trial, and (ii) where it offends the court's sense of justice and propriety to be asked to try the accused in the particular circumstances of the case. In the first category of case, if the court concludes that an accused cannot receive a fair trial, it will stay the proceedings without more. No question of the balancing of competing interests arises. In the second category of case, the court is concerned to protect the integrity of the criminal justice system. Here a stay will be granted where the court concludes that in all the circumstances a trial will offend the court's sense of justice and propriety (per Lord Lowry in R v Horseferry Road Magistrates' Court, ex p Bennett [1994] 1 AC 42 (at 74G)), or will undermine public confidence in the criminal justice system and bring it into disrepute (per Lord Steyn in Latif [1996] 1 WLR 104 (at 112F)).

In R v *Crawley* [2014] EWCA Crim 1028; [2014] 2 Cr App R 16, Sir Brian Leveson P summarised the scope of abuse of process thus (at [17]–[18]):

> [T]here are two categories of case in which the court has the power to stay proceedings for abuse of process. These are, first, where the court concludes that the accused can no longer receive a fair hearing; and, second, where it would otherwise be unfair to try the accused or, put another way, where a stay is necessary to protect the integrity of the criminal justice system. The first limb focuses on the trial process and where the court concludes that the accused would not receive a fair hearing it will stay the proceedings; no balancing exercise is required. The second limb concerns the integrity of the criminal justice system and applies where the Court considers that the accused should not be standing trial at all, irrespective of the potential fairness of the trial itself.
>
> ... [T]here is a strong public interest in the prosecution of crime and in ensuring that those charged with serious criminal offences are tried. Ordering a stay of proceedings, which in criminal law is effectively a permanent remedy, is thus a remedy of last resort.

His Lordship observed (at [21]) that 'cases in which it may be unfair to try the accused (the second category of case) will include, but are not confined to, those cases where there has been bad faith, unlawfulness or executive misconduct'. In such a case, 'the court is concerned not to create the perception that it is condoning malpractice by law enforcement agencies or to convey the impression that it will adopt the approach that the end justifies the means: the touchstone is the integrity of the criminal justice system' (at [23]).

In R v *Horseferry Road Magistrates' Court, ex parte Bennett* [1994] 1 AC 42, Lord Griffiths (at p.61H) said that if the courts have a power to interfere with the prosecution in such cases:

> ... it must be because the judiciary accept a responsibility for the maintenance of the rule of law that embraces a willingness to oversee executive action and to refuse to countenance behaviour that threatens either basic human rights or the rule of law ... I have no doubt that the judiciary should accept this responsibility in the field of criminal law.

There are thus two main categories of abuse of process:

● cases where the court concludes that the accused cannot receive a fair trial;
● cases where the court concludes that it would be unfair for the accused to be tried.

The former focuses on the trial process; the latter is applicable where the accused should not be standing trial at all (irrespective of the fairness of the actual trial).

In *DPP v Humphrys* [1977] AC 1, Lord Salmon (at p.46) commented that a judge does not have 'any power to refuse to allow a prosecution to proceed merely because he considers that, as a matter of policy, it ought not to have been brought. It is only if the prosecution amounts to an abuse of the process of the court and is oppressive and vexatious that the judge has the power to intervene'.

There is no definitive list of matters which are capable of amounting to abuse of process, but it is possible to derive some broad categories of abuse from the case law. For example:

● Lengthy delay which causes prejudice to the accused (see, for example, *A-G's Ref (No. 1 of 1990)* [1992] QB 630, where it was held that the defendant has to show on the balance of probabilities that, owing to the delay, he will suffer serious prejudice to the extent that no fair trial can be held);
● Failure to honour an undertaking given to the accused (see, for example, *R v Abu Hamza* [2006] EWCA Crim 2918; [2007] QB 659, where Lord Phillips CJ (at [54]), said that 'it is not likely to constitute an abuse of process to proceed with a prosecution unless (i) there has been an unequivocal representation by those with the conduct of the investigation or prosecution of a case that the defendant will not be prosecuted and (ii) that the defendant has acted on that representation to his detriment. Even then, if facts come to light which were not known when the representation was made, these may justify proceeding with the prosecution despite the representation');
● Failing to secure evidence or destroying evidence (for example, *R (Ebrahim) v Feltham Magistrates' Court* [2001] 1 All ER 831; the defendant has to show, on the balance of probabilities, that because of the fact that evidence is missing, he will suffer serious prejudice to the extent that a fair trial cannot be held);
● Tactical manipulation or misuse of procedures in order to deprive the accused of some protection provided by the law, or taking unfair advantage of a technicality (for example, *R (Wardle) v Leeds Crown Court* [2001] UKHL 12; [2002] 1 AC 754, where a murder charge was replaced with a manslaughter charge in order to get around the expiry of the custody time-limit);
● Entrapment (in *R v Looseley; Attorney General's Reference (No 3 of 2000)* [2001] UKHL 53; [2001] 1 WLR 2060 it was held that the question was whether a person has been persuaded or pressurised by a law enforcement officer into committing a crime which he would not otherwise have committed. Although entrapment usually relates to the actions of law enforcement officers, in *R v TL* [2018] EWCA Crim 1821, Lord Burnett CJ accepted (at ([32]) that 'it is not inconceivable that, given sufficiently gross misconduct by a private citizen, it would be an abuse of the court's process (and a breach of Art.6 [of the ECHR]) for the state to seek to rely on the product of that misconduct [i.e. the evidence obtained thereby]');
● Abuse of executive power (for example, *R v Horseferry Road Magistrates' Court, ex parte Bennett* [1994] 1 AC 42, where the accused had been brought back forcibly to the UK in disregard of extradition procedures that were available).

For a critique of the decisions in *Warren* and *Mitchell*, see Patrick O'Connor, '*Abuse of process' after Warren and Mitchell* [2012] Crim LR 672–686.

For a more detailed analysis of the case law on abuse of process and the principles which underpin in, see Peter Hungerford-Welch, '*Abuse of process: does it really protect the suspect's rights?*' [2017] Crim LR 3–17.

Chapter 2

Bail

Chapter Contents

In this chapter, we look at the court power to adjourn cases, and at the principles which govern whether the defendant should be held in custody or granted bail prior to the trial.

2.1 Adjournments

Adjournments are often necessary to enable the prosecution or the defence to prepare their case for trial. The granting of an adjournment is a matter for the court's discretion, but the rules of natural justice require that both sides should be allowed to prepare and present their cases properly (*R v Thames Magistrates' Court ex p Polemis* [1974] 1 WLR 1371).

In *R v Kingston-upon-Thames Justices ex p Martin* [1994] Imm AR 172, it was said that the following factors should be taken into account in deciding whether or not to grant an adjournment:

- the importance of the proceedings;
- the likely adverse consequences for the person seeking the adjournment;
- the risk of prejudice if the application is not granted;
- the convenience of the court;
- the interests of justice in ensuring that cases are dealt with efficiently; and
- the extent to which the applicant has been responsible for the circumstances which have led to the application for an adjournment.

In *R v Hereford Magistrates' Court ex p Rowlands* [1998] QB 110, at p.127, Lord Bingham of Cornhill CJ said:

> It is not possible or desirable to identify hard and fast rules as to when adjournments should or should not be granted. The guiding principle must be that justices should fully examine the circumstances leading to applications for delay, the reasons for those applications and the consequences both to the prosecution and the defence. Ultimately, they must decide what is fair in the light of all those circumstances.
>
> [...]
>
> Applications for adjournments must be subjected to rigorous scrutiny. Any defendant who is guilty of deliberately seeking to postpone a trial without good reason has no cause for complaint if his application for an adjournment is refused ... In deciding whether to grant an adjournment, justices will bear in mind that they have a responsibility for ensuring, so far as possible, that summary justice is speedy justice.

Further guidance was given by Jack J in *DPP v Picton* [2006] EWHC 1108 (Admin); (2006) 170 JP 567, at [9]:

> (a) A decision whether to adjourn is a decision within the discretion of the trial court. An appellate court will interfere only if very clear grounds for doing so are shown.
>
> (b) Magistrates should pay great attention to the need for expedition in the prosecution of criminal proceedings; delays are scandalous; they bring the law into disrepute; summary justice should be speedy justice; an application for an adjournment should be rigorously scrutinised.
>
> (c) Where an adjournment is sought by the prosecution, magistrates must consider both the interest of the defendant in getting the matter dealt with, and the interest of the public that criminal charges should be adjudicated upon, and the guilty convicted as well as the innocent acquitted. With a more serious charge the public interest that there be a trial will carry greater weight.

(d) Where an adjournment is sought by the accused, the magistrates must consider whether, if it is not granted, he will be able fully to present his defence and, if he will not be able to do so, the degree to which his ability to do so is compromised.

(e) In considering the competing interests of the parties the magistrates should examine the likely consequences of the proposed adjournment, in particular its likely length, and the need to decide the facts while recollections are fresh.

(f) The reason that the adjournment is required should be examined and, if it arises through the fault of the party asking for the adjournment, that is a factor against granting the adjournment, carrying weight in accordance with the gravity of the fault. If that party was not at fault, that may favour an adjournment. Likewise if the party opposing the adjournment has been at fault, that will favour an adjournment.

(g) The magistrates should take appropriate account of the history of the case, and whether there have been earlier adjournments and at whose request and why.

(h) Lastly, of course, the factors to be considered cannot be comprehensively stated but depend upon the particular circumstances of each case, and they will often overlap. The court's duty is to do justice between the parties in the circumstances as they have arisen.

In *DPP v Petrie* [2015] EWHC 48 (Admin); (2015) 179 JP 251, Gross LJ (at [19]) observed that 'efficiency, expedition, the discouraging of delay and the avoidance of unnecessary hearings are adjuncts of dealing with cases justly and it may be said, in the summary jurisdiction, summarily. Adjournments ... run contrary to these important objectives'. His Lordship went on to say (at [20]):

Although there are of course instances where the interests of justice require the grant of an adjournment, this should be a course of last rather than first resort – and after other alternatives have been considered ... It is essential that parties to proceedings in the magistrates' court should proceed on the basis of a need to get matters right first time; any suggestion of a culture readily permitting an opportunity to correct failures of preparation should be firmly dispelled.

His Lordship added (at [21]) that appellate courts should be "slow to interfere" with case management decisions which have endeavoured to give effect to this approach, and that the grant or refusal of an adjournment 'is a paradigm example of a discretionary case management decision where an appeal ought only to succeed on well-recognised but limited grounds (for example, error of principle, error of law or where the decision can properly be characterised as plainly wrong)'.

In *R v Bolton Magistrates' Court ex p Merna* (1991) 155 JP 612, the Divisional Court considered the position where the accused is absent, and seeks an adjournment on medical grounds. Bingham LJ (at p.622) said that if the court suspects the grounds to be spurious or believes them to be inadequate, it should ordinarily express its doubts, giving the defendant an opportunity to seek to resolve them. The court may call for better evidence, require further inquiries to be made or adopt any other expedient that is fair to both parties. His Lordship added that a claim of illness with apparently responsible professional support should not be rejected without the court satisfying itself that it is proper to reject it and that no unfairness would result.

Criminal Practice Direction III, para.14B.2, says that a defendant who will be unable for medical reasons to attend court must (prior to the hearing) obtain a certificate from his/her general practitioner or another appropriate medical practitioner such as the doctor with care of the defendant at a hospital. Without a medical certificate, or if an unsatisfactory certificate is provided, the court is likely to consider that the defendant has failed to surrender to bail (para.14B.3).

However, the fact that a medical certificate has been received from the accused is not conclusive. Criminal Practice Direction I para.5C.3 notes that a court is 'not absolutely bound by a medical certificate. The medical practitioner providing the certificate may be required by the court to give evidence. Alternatively the court may exercise its discretion to disregard a certificate which it finds unsatisfactory'. In R v *Ealing Magistrates' Court ex p Burgess* (2001) 165 JP 82, the Divisional Court said that justices have a discretion to reject an accused's medical certificate, refuse an adjournment and proceed to hear the case in his absence. That discretion has to be exercised with proper regard to the principle that a defendant has a right to a fair trial and a fair opportunity to be present. However, the principle only extended to a *fair* opportunity to be present and not an unlimited one.

Paragraph 5C.4 goes on to say that circumstances where the court may find a medical certificate to be unsatisfactory include:

(a) Where the certificate indicates that the defendant is unfit to attend work (rather than to attend court);
(b) Where the nature of the defendant's ailment (e.g. a broken arm) does not appear to be capable of preventing his attendance at court;
(c) Where the defendant is certified as suffering from stress/anxiety/depression and there is no indication of the defendant recovering within a realistic timescale.

The first of these is of great practical importance, as there is a significant difference between being 'unfit for work' and 'unfit to attend court'.

Paragraph 5C.5 sets out what it describes as the 'minimum standards' for a medical certificate:

(a) The date on which the medical practitioner examined the defendant;
(b) The exact nature of the defendants ailments;
(c) If it is not self-evident, why the ailment prevents the defendant attending court;
(d) An indication as to when the defendant is likely to be able to attend court, or a date when the current certificate expires.

Where an application for an adjournment is refused, a further application for an adjournment can be granted only if there has been a material change of circumstances (R *(Watson)* v *Dartford Magistrates' Court* [2005] EWHC 905; R *(F)* v *Knowsley Youth Court* [2006] EWHC 695).

Reasons for granting, or refusing, an adjournment should be given, but they do not have to be elaborate, so long as the basis for the decision is clear (*Essen* v *DPP* [2005] EWHC 1077).

2.2 Remands: procedure in court

Where a defendant is before the court because he has been arrested and charged, an adjournment is called a 'remand'. The remand may be in custody or on bail. This decision is governed by the Bail Act 1976.

Rule 14.5 of the Criminal Procedure Rules applies whenever the court can grant or withhold bail. Under r.14.5(2), the prosecutor must, as soon as practicable, provide the defendant and the court with all the information in the prosecutor's possession which is material to the question of bail. Rule 14.5(3) requires a prosecutor who opposes the grant of bail to specify each statutory ground for withholding bail on which the prosecutor relies, and each consideration that the prosecutor thinks relevant. Under r.14.5(4), a prosecutor who wants the court to impose a condition on any grant of bail must specify each proposed condition, and explain what purpose would be served by such a condition.

It is usually the prosecutor who makes the formal application for the adjournment (although there is no reason why it could not be the defence, if the prosecution are ready to proceed but the defence are not). The Crown Prosecution Service (CPS) representative is asked by the court if there are any objections to bail and, if so, to summarise them. The objections are based on a form in the CPS file which has been filled in by the police. A list of the defendant's previous convictions (if any) will also be provided to the court.

There is no requirement for formal evidence of the matters which give rise to the objections to bail to be given (R v Mansfield Justices ex p Sharkey [1985] QB 613). The objections to bail are simply given by the CPS representative in court; a police officer will not usually be called to give evidence in support of the objections.

The defendant may then make an application for bail. The defence will try to show either that the prosecution objections are ill-founded, or that the objections can be met by the imposition of appropriate conditions. The prosecution will not normally reply to the defence bail application. However, in R v Isleworth Crown Court ex p Commissioner of Customs & Excise [1990] Crim LR 859, it was said that the prosecution have a right to reply to the defence submissions if this is necessary to correct alleged mis-statements of fact in what the defence have said.

The court then comes to a decision. If bail is refused, the court must say why. The reason(s) must be based on the grounds for withholding bail set out in the Bail Act 1976 and must be recorded in a certificate which is handed to the defendant.

Paragraphs 9 and 10 of sch.1 to the Justices Clerks Rules 2015 empower a justice's legal adviser to adjourn a case with the consent of both parties, so long as the question of either a remand in custody or on bail does not also arise, or the accused is to be remanded on bail either on the same terms as before or on terms to which both parties agree. However, in R (Bourne) v Scarborough Magistrates' Court [2017] EWHC 2828 (Admin); [2018] 4 WLR 29, the justices' legal adviser had been nominated by the court to manage this case. The Divisional Court held that the legal adviser therefore had power, by virtue of r.3.5(2)(f) of the Criminal Procedure Rules, to adjourn the trial on the prosecution's application even though that application was opposed by the defence. It is submitted, with respect, that this decision is questionable, and that the fact that r.3.5 allows the court to 'nominate a … justices' legal adviser to manage the case' should not necessarily be taken to permit the court to delegate judicial powers to the legal adviser.

2.2.1 Period of remand in custody prior to conviction

The maximum period of a remand in custody prior to conviction is 'eight clear days' unless s.128A of the Magistrates' Courts Act 1980 applies (s.128(6) of the Magistrates' Courts Act 1980). The term 'eight clear days' means that if a hearing takes place on Monday, the next hearing must take place no later than the following Wednesday.

Section 128A(2) provides that a magistrates' court may remand the accused in custody for a period exceeding eight clear days if it has previously remanded him in custody for the same offence, and he is now before the court, but only if, after affording the parties an opportunity to make representations, it has set a date on which it expects that it will be possible for the next stage in the proceedings, other than a hearing relating to a further remand in custody or on bail, to take place. In such a case, the accused may be remanded in custody for a period ending not later than that date, or for a period of 28 clear days, whichever is the less.

Thus, s.128A allows a remand in custody for up to 28 days but does not apply to the first remand hearing, as the defendant must have previously been remanded in custody for the same offence. Furthermore, for s.128A to apply, the next hearing must be 'effective', in the sense that (for example) the mode of trial hearing or summary trial will take place. Both the prosecution and the defendant must be allowed to make representations before a remand in excess of eight days is ordered, but the defendant's consent is not required. It should be noted that s.128A(3) provides that 'nothing in this section affects the right of the accused to apply for bail during the period of the remand'.

By way of context, the annual report on the prison population in the Offender Management statistics for the year to 30 June 2018 showed a total prison population of 82,773 (85,863 for the year to 30 June 2017), of whom 9,285 (9,638 the previous year) were on remand (i.e. they were not serving a custodial sentence). Of those remand prisoners, 6,307 were awaiting trial and 2,978 had been convicted but were awaiting sentence (in the previous year, 6,601 and 3,037 respectively). It is salutary to note that 7.6% of the prison population (7.7% the previous year) were unconvicted defendants.

2.2.2 Remands in the absence of the defendant

The provisions of s.128A of the 1980 Act should be contrasted with remands in the absence of the defendant which are possible, provided that the defendant:

- has the assistance of a legal representative to represent him in the proceedings in that court' (s.128 (1B)); and
- consents to not being present at future remand hearings (s.128(1C)).

The defendant must be brought before the court on at least every fourth application for his remand (s.128(1A)(ii)). Thus, there can be a maximum of three remands in the absence of the defendant, and so the defendant has to appear in court at least once a month.

It is open to the defendant to withdraw his consent to being remanded in his absence (s.128 (3A)(d)). It follows that the defendant can still apply for bail during the 28-day period by giving notice to the court that he wishes to do so.

2.2.2.1 Use of live links

Section 57B of the Crime and Disorder Act 1998 applies to preliminary hearings in a magistrates' court or the Crown Court. The court may give a 'live link' direction requiring the accused, if he is being held in custody, to attend the hearing through a live link from the place at which he is being held (subs.(3)). The court cannot give or rescind such a direction unless the parties to the proceedings have been given the opportunity to make representations (subs.(5)). Where the court is a magistrates' court and it decides not to give a live link direction where it has power to do so, it must give reasons for not doing so (subs.(6)). Section 57A(3) defines a 'live link' as 'an arrangement by which a person (when not in the place where the hearing is being held) is able to see and hear, and to be seen and heard by, the court during a hearing'.

2.2.3 Remand after conviction

Following summary conviction, there may be a remand in custody of up to three weeks (four weeks if the offender is on bail) to enable the preparation of a pre-sentence report (s.10(3) of the Magistrates' Courts Act 1980).

2.3 The Bail Act 1976

Section 4(1) of the Bail Act 1976 provides that 'a person to whom this section applies shall be granted bail except as provided in Schedule 1 to this Act'. This is sometimes said to create a 'right to bail'. It would, however, be more accurate to describe s.4 as creating a (rebuttable) presumption in favour of bail.

Section 4(2) says that s.4 applies where the accused appears before a magistrates' court or the Crown Court in connection with proceedings for an offence, or when he applies to a court for bail or for a variation of the conditions of bail in connection with those proceedings. Under s.4(4), s.4 also applies to a person who has been convicted of an offence and whose case is adjourned for the purpose of enabling inquiries or a report to be made to assist the court in dealing with him for the offence.

In summary, therefore, the presumption in favour of bail applies at all stages prior to conviction, and also after conviction, but only where the case is adjourned for a pre-sentence report.

Where s.4 does not apply (for example, when the defendant appeals against conviction and/ or sentence, or where the defendant is committed for sentence following summary conviction of an either-way offence), the court nevertheless has a *discretion* to grant bail.

2.3.1 Imprisonable offences

If the defendant is charged with (or has been convicted of) an offence which is punishable with imprisonment (but which is not a summary offence), the presumption in favour of bail may be rebutted if the court finds that one or more of the grounds for withholding bail set out in Part 1 of Sch.1 to the Bail Act applies. This is the provision which applies to indictable (including either-way) offences.

2.3.1.1 Grounds for withholding bail

Under para.2(1), the defendant need not be granted bail if the court is satisfied that there are substantial grounds for believing that the defendant, if released on bail, would:

(a) fail to surrender to custody; or
(b) commit an offence while on bail; or
(c) interfere with witnesses or otherwise obstruct the course of justice, whether in relation to himself or any other person.

The importance of there being 'substantial grounds to believe' that one or more of these consequences would result from the defendant's release on bail (whether or not subject to any conditions) should be emphasised. This sets a high threshold for withholding bail.

Paragraph 2ZA(1) applies to cases of domestic violence. It provides that the defendant need not be granted bail if the court is satisfied that there are substantial grounds for believing that the defendant, if released on bail, would commit an offence while on bail by engaging in conduct that would, or would be likely to, cause:

(a) physical or mental injury to an associated person; or
(b) an associated person (as defined by s.62 of the Family Law Act 1996) to fear physical or mental injury.

Under para.2A, the defendant need not be granted bail if:

(a) the offence is an indictable offence or an offence triable either way; and
(b) it appears to the court that the defendant was on bail in criminal proceedings on the date of the offence.

Under para.3, the defendant 'need not be granted bail if the court is satisfied that the defendant should be kept in custody for his own protection or, if he is a child or young person, for his own welfare'.

Under para.4, the defendant need not be granted bail if he is serving a custodial sentence imposed on an earlier occasion.

Under para.5, the defendant need not be granted bail where the court is satisfied that it has not been practicable to obtain sufficient information for the purpose of taking the bail decisions required by the Act 'because of want of time since the institution of the proceedings against him'.

Under para.6, the defendant need not be granted bail if, having previously been released on bail in the proceedings, he has been arrested under s.7 of the Act.

Under para.7, where the case is adjourned for inquiries or a report, the defendant 'need not be granted bail if it appears to the court that it would be impracticable to complete the inquiries or make the report without keeping the defendant in custody'.

By virtue of para.1A, certain paragraphs in Part 1 do not apply where the defendant has attained the age of 18, has not been convicted of an offence in the proceedings, and 'it appears to the court that there is no real prospect that he will be sentenced to a custodial sentence in the proceedings'. The paragraphs which do not apply in these circumstances are:

- para.2 (refusal of bail where defendant may fail to surrender to custody, commit offences on bail or interfere with witnesses);
- para.2A (refusal of bail where defendant appears to have committed indictable or either way offence while on bail); and
- para.6 (refusal of bail where defendant has been arrested under s.7).

Paragraph 1A is intended to reduce the risk of a defendant being remanded in custody but then, after conviction, receiving a non-custodial sentence. However, there remains the risk that, even if a custodial sentence is passed, the defendant may have been remanded in custody for a period in excess of that sentence (especially having regard to the fact that prisoners are released from custody half-way through a custodial sentence). Moreover, the significant reduction in the ability of the court to withhold bail in cases that are likely to be non-custodial means that it is more difficult to ensure that defendants attend court in such cases.

2.3.1.2 Factors to be considered

Paragraph 9 requires the court to have regard to:

(a) The 'nature and seriousness of the offence', and the 'probable method of dealing with the defendant for it'. This draws attention to the gravity of the alleged offence: the more serious the offence, the more likely it is that a custodial sentence will be imposed, giving an incentive to abscond. It should noted, however, that in *Hurnam v State of Mauritius* [2005] UKPC 49; [2006] 1 WLR 857, the Privy Council said that the seriousness of an offence cannot be treated as a conclusive reason for refusing bail to an unconvicted suspect: the right to personal liberty is an important constitutional right and a suspect should remain at large unless it is necessary to refuse bail in order to serve one of the ends for which detention before trial is permissible. Lord Bingham of Cornhill, at [15], said:

> The seriousness of the offence and the severity of the penalty likely to be imposed on conviction may well ... provide grounds for refusing bail, but they do not do so of themselves, without more: they are factors relevant to the judgment whether, in all the circumstances, it is necessary to deprive the applicant of his liberty.

(b) The 'character and antecedents', and the 'associations and community ties' of the defendant:

    (i) 'character and antecedents' refers principally to previous convictions: these may make a custodial sentence more likely (especially if the defendant, if convicted of the present offence, will be in breach of a suspended sentence of imprisonment);

    (ii) the word 'associations' is generally taken to refer to undesirable friends with criminal records;

    (iii) examining the defendant's 'community ties' involves looking at how easy it would be for the defendant to abscond and how much he has to lose by absconding. For example, how long has the defendant lived at his present address? Is he single or married? Does he have dependent children? Is he in employment? How long has he had his present job? Does he have a mortgage or a protected tenancy?

(c) The defendant's 'record as respects the fulfilment of his obligations under previous grants of bail in criminal proceedings'. In other words, has the defendant absconded or committed offences while on bail in the past? Absconding or offending whilst on bail in earlier proceedings may be regarded as evidence of a risk that the defendant may do so again.

(d) Except in the case of a defendant whose case is adjourned for a pre-sentence report, the 'strength of the evidence of his having committed the offence'. The strength of the prosecution case is relevant in that, if the defendant has a good chance of acquittal, it can be argued that there is no point in absconding; conversely, if the prosecution case is strong, so that conviction is likely, the defendant may abscond rather than 'face the music', especially if a custodial sentence is likely.

(e) If the court is satisfied that there are substantial grounds for believing that the defendant, if released on bail (whether subject to conditions or not), would commit an offence while on bail, 'the risk that the defendant may do so by engaging in conduct that would, or would be likely to, cause physical or mental injury to any person other than the defendant'.

The court also has to have regard to 'any others matters which appear to be relevant' (making it clear that the list of factors set out above is not exhaustive). In particular, it should also be noted that s.4(9) of the Bail Act stipulates that, in taking any decisions under schedule 1, the considerations to which the court is to have regard 'include, so far as relevant, any misuse of controlled drugs by the defendant'.

2.3.1.3 The bail decision

Where the statute says that the defendant 'need not be granted bail', this effectively reverses the presumption in favour of bail. It then becomes necessary for the court to be persuaded that there is no significant risk that the defendant would fail to surrender to custody, or commit an offence etc. (R (*Wiggins*) v *Harrow Crown Court* [2005] EWHC 882 (Admin), per Collins J at [24]).

The approach to be taken was summarised by Collins J in R (*Thompson*) v *Central Criminal Court* [2005] EWHC 2345 (Admin), at [10]:

> [T]here must be a grant of bail unless there are good reasons to refuse. The approach, therefore, really is not should bail be granted, but should custody be imposed, that is: is it necessary for the defendant to be in custody? ... Only if persuaded that it is necessary, should a remand in custody take place. It will be necessary if the court decides that whatever conditions can reasonably be imposed in relation to bail, there are nonetheless substantial grounds for believing that the defendant would either fail to surrender to custody, commit an offence, interfere with witnesses or otherwise obstruct justice.

Where the presumption in favour of bail under s.4 applies, it must be clear that the court has applied the statutory test. In R(F) v Southampton Crown Court [2009] EWHC 2206 (Admin), the judge refused to grant bail because he was 'not sure' the accused would 'turn up or stay out of trouble'. Collins J (at [8]) said that it was 'not a question of him not being sure that the defendant would turn up or stay out of trouble'; the judge was 'only entitled to refuse bail if there were substantial grounds for believing that he would breach, he would fail to turn up or would commit further offences'.

In R (R) v Snaresbrook Crown Court [2011] EWHC 3569 (Admin), the Crown Court judge withheld bail on the basis that a custodial sentence was inevitable. Holman J (at [31]) said that:

> even the inevitability of a custodial sentence is not itself an exception to the right to bail, unless it justifies a court being satisfied that there are substantial grounds for believing that the defendant would fail to surrender to custody.

A similar case is R (Shehzad) v Newcastle Crown Court [2012] EWHC 1453 (Admin). The Crown Court judge refused bail because the defendant had 'every reason to fail to surrender, there is the possibility of further offences and there is a risk of interference with witnesses'. Foskett J (at [10] and [11]) said that the judge was 'very unlikely to have misapplied the usual approach to decisions of this nature'. However, it was 'right that the defendant should have his case assessed by the correct statutory formulation'; the refusal of bail was therefore quashed.

2.3.1.4 Children and young persons

Paragraph 9AA applies where the defendant is under the age of 18, and it appears to the court that he was on bail in criminal proceedings on the date of the present offence. When deciding (under para.2(1)) whether there are substantial grounds for believing that the defendant, if released on bail, would commit an offence while on bail, the court must 'give particular weight' to the fact that the defendant was on bail in criminal proceedings on the date of the offence.

Paragraph 9AB applies where the defendant is under the age of 18, and it appears to the court that, having been released on bail in the proceedings for the present offence, he failed to surrender to custody. When deciding (under para.2(1)) whether there are substantial grounds for believing that the defendant, if released on bail, would fail to surrender to custody, the court must give particular weight to:

(a) where the defendant did not have reasonable cause for his failure to surrender to custody, the fact that he failed to surrender to custody; or

(b) where he did have reasonable cause for his failure to surrender to custody, the fact that he failed to surrender to custody at the appointed place as soon as reasonably practicable after the appointed time.

2.3.1.5 Murder, manslaughter and rape

Paragraph 6ZA of Part 1 of Sch.1 to the Bail Act 1976 applies only to murder cases, and provides that if the defendant is charged with murder, he must not be granted bail unless the court is of the opinion that there is no significant risk of his committing, while on bail, an offence that would, or would be likely to, cause physical or mental injury to any other person. It should also be noted that s.115 of the Coroners and Justice Act 2009 restricts the granting of bail in murder cases. It provides that a person charged with murder may only be granted bail by a Crown Court judge, and so a person charged with murder must be committed to the Crown Court for the question of bail to be decided.

Section 25 of the Criminal Justice and Public Order Act 1994 applies where the defendant is charged with murder, attempted murder, manslaughter, rape or attempted rape and has been convicted of one of these offences in the past. In a case to which s.25 applies, bail may only be granted if there are 'exceptional circumstances' which justify the grant of bail. In R (O) v *Harrow Crown Court* [2006] UKHL 42; [2007] 1 AC 249, it was held that s.25 should be regarded as imposing an evidential burden on the defendant to point to or produce material which supports the existence of exceptional circumstances (not a full legal burden to establish such circumstances on the balance of probabilities). The House of Lords went on to hold that s.25 operates to disapply the ordinary requirement, under reg.6(6) of the Prosecution of Offences (Custody Time Limits) Regulations 1987, namely that bail should be granted automatically to anyone whose custody time limit has expired.

2.3.2 Summary offences

Paragraph 1(2) of Part 1 of Sch.1 to the Bail Act 1976 provides that where the imprisonable offence is a summary offence, or an offence to which s.22 of the Magistrates' Courts Act 1980 applies (criminal damage where the value involved is £5,000 or less), Part 1 of the schedule does not apply. Instead, Part 1A of the schedule applies in such cases.

Under para.2, the defendant need not be granted bail if it appears to the court that, having been previously granted bail in criminal proceedings, he has failed to surrender to custody in accordance with his obligations under the grant of bail, and the court believes, in view of that failure, that the defendant, if released on bail, would fail to surrender to custody.

Under para.3, the defendant need not be granted bail if it appears to the court that he was on bail in criminal proceedings on the date of the present offence, and the court is satisfied that there are substantial grounds for believing that the defendant, if released on bail, would commit an offence while on bail.

Paragraph 4 relates to domestic violence. It provides that the defendant need not be granted bail if the court is satisfied that there are substantial grounds for believing that, if released on bail, he would commit an offence while on bail by engaging in conduct that would, or would be likely to, cause physical or mental injury to an 'associated person' or to cause an 'associated person' to fear physical or mental injury. An 'associated person' is someone associated with the defendant within the meaning of s.62 of the Family Law Act 1996.

Under para.5, the defendant need not be granted bail if the court is satisfied that he should be kept in custody for his own protection (or, if he is a child or young person, for his own welfare).

Under para.6, the defendant need not be granted bail if he is serving a custodial sentence in respect of another offence.

Under para.7, the defendant need not be granted bail if, having been released on bail in the proceedings for the present offence, he has been arrested under s.7 of the Act, and the court is satisfied that there are substantial grounds for believing that the defendant, if released on bail, would fail to surrender to custody, commit an offence while on bail or interfere with witnesses or otherwise obstruct the course of justice (whether in relation to himself or any other person).

Under para.8, the defendant need not be granted bail where the court is satisfied that it has not been practicable to obtain sufficient information for the purpose of taking the decisions required by the Act for want of time since the institution of the proceedings against him.

Paragraph 1A provides that certain paragraphs in Part 1A do not apply where the defendant has attained the age of 18, he has not been convicted of an offence in the proceedings, and it appears to the court that there is no real prospect that he will be sentenced to a custodial sentence in the proceedings. The paragraphs which are disapplied in such cases are:

- para.2 (refusal of bail for failure to surrender to custody);
- para.3 (refusal of bail where defendant would commit further offences on bail); and
- para.7 (refusal of bail in certain circumstances when arrested under s.7).

2.3.3 Non-imprisonable offences

Bail may be withheld even if the offence with which the defendant is charged does not carry a sentence of imprisonment. Part 2 of Schedule 1 to the Bail Act applies where the offence, or every offence, of which the defendant is accused or convicted is one which is not punishable with imprisonment.

Under para.2, the defendant need not be granted bail if either he is under the age of 18, or he has been convicted of an offence in the proceedings of an offence, and it appears to the court that, having been previously granted bail in criminal proceedings, he has failed to surrender to custody in accordance with his obligations under the grant of bail, and the court believes, in view of that failure, he would (if released on bail) fail to surrender to custody.

Under para.3, the defendant need not be granted bail if the court is satisfied that the defendant should be kept in custody for his own protection (or, if he is a child or young person, for his own welfare).

Under para.4, the defendant need not be granted bail if he is serving a custodial sentence in respect of another offence.

Under para.5, the defendant need not be granted bail if either he is under the age of 18, or he has been convicted of an offence in the proceedings, and having been released on bail in the proceedings he has been arrested under s.7 of the Act, and the court is satisfied that there are substantial grounds for believing that the defendant, if released on bail, would fail to surrender to custody, commit an offence on bail or interfere with witnesses or otherwise obstruct the course of justice (whether in relation to himself or any other person).

Under para.6, the defendant need not be granted bail if, having been released on bail in the proceedings, he has been arrested under s.7, and the court is satisfied that there are substantial grounds for believing that he would, if released on bail, commit an offence while on bail by engaging in conduct that would, or would be likely to, cause physical or mental injury to an associated person (within the meaning of s.62 of the Family Law Act 1996), or to cause an associated person to fear physical or mental injury (i.e. domestic violence).

2.4 Conditional bail

If the court grants unconditional bail, the defendant's only duty is to attend court on the date of the next hearing (s.3(1) of the Bail Act). It is, however, open to the court to attach conditions to the grant of bail. Section 3(6) of the Act provides that the defendant may be required to comply with such requirements as appear to the court to be necessary:

- to secure that he surrenders to custody;
- to secure that he does not commit an offence while on bail;
- to secure that he does not interfere with witnesses or otherwise obstruct the course of justice whether in relation to himself or any other person;
- for his own protection or, if a child or young person, for his own welfare or in his own interests;
- to secure that he makes himself available for the purpose of enabling inquiries or a report to be made to assist the court in dealing with him for the offence;
- to secure that, before the time appointed for him to surrender to custody, he attends an interview with a lawyer.

Section 3 also makes provision for specific conditions: subs.(4) says that the defendant may be required, before release on bail, to provide a surety or sureties to secure his surrender to custody, and subs.(5) says that he may be required, before release on bail, to give security for his surrender to custody (the security may be given by him or by someone else on his behalf).

Section 3(6ZAA) adds that the requirements which may be imposed under subs.(6) include electronic monitoring requirements.

It should be noted that para.8 of Part 1 of Sch.1 to the Bail Act also makes provision for conditional bail.

2.4.1 Examples of commonly imposed conditions

While certain types of condition are mentioned in s.3, it does not provide a comprehensive list of conditions that may be attached to the grant of bail. The court can impose *any* condition it thinks appropriate, provided that the condition is necessary. Commonly imposed conditions include:

- surety (where one or more persons, other than the defendant, promise to pay a specified sum to the court if the defendant absconds: see below for further details);
- security (where the defendant deposits money or one or more valuable items with the court: if the defendant absconds the court can order the forfeiture of some or all of the security);
- residence (that is, living and sleeping at a specified address);
- residence in a bail hostel (the defendant may also be required to comply with the rules of the hostel (s.3(6ZA));
- reporting to a specified police station (on specified days and at specified times);
- curfew (requiring the defendant to stay indoors during specified hours at night);
- not to enter a particular building or to go to a specified place or to go within a specified distance of a certain address;
- not to contact, directly or indirectly, the alleged victim or any named prosecution witnesses;
- surrender of defendant's passport to the police.

2.4.1.1 Sureties

A surety makes a formal promise to pay a fixed sum of money (known as the 'recognisance') if the defendant fails to surrender to custody. In deciding whether to grant bail subject to a surety, the court has to consider the suitability of the proposed surety. Section 8(2) of the Bail Act provides that regard may be had (among other things) to:

- the surety's financial resources (could the surety pay the sum which he is promising to pay?);
- the surety's character and any previous convictions (is the surety a trustworthy person?); and
- the surety's 'proximity (whether in point of kinship, place of residence or otherwise) to the person for whom he is to be surety' (is the proposed surety a friend, relative or employer? How far away does he live from the defendant? The most important consideration under this heading is the relationship of the proposed surety to the defendant: will the surety have the ability to control the defendant so as to ensure that he attends court when he should? Put another way, would the fact the surety stands to lose money if the defendant absconds operate on the mind of the defendant so as to deter him from absconding?).

If the proposed surety is in court, he gives evidence of these matters and confirms that he understands the obligations he will be undertaking.

The financial circumstances of the proposed surety are crucial. In R v Birmingham Crown Court ex p Ali (1999) 163 JP 145, Kennedy LJ (at p. 147) said that:

> it is irresponsible (and possibly a matter for consideration by a professional disciplinary
> body) for a qualified lawyer ... to tender anyone as a surety unless he or she has reasonable

grounds for believing that the surety will, if necessary, be able to meet his or her financial undertaking.

In fixing the amount of the surety, the court has regard to the seriousness of the offence, the degree of risk that the defendant will abscond, and to the means of the proposed surety. It is quite common to have two or more sureties. If the court will only grant bail subject to a recognisance of a certain amount and that amount is beyond the means of the proposed surety, then another person will have to be found. It should be noted that the defendant cannot stand as a surety for himself (s.3(2) of the Bail Act 1976).

If the defence are aware that someone has offered to act as a surety but that person is not in court, and the magistrates are satisfied that the person is a satisfactory surety, the court may grant bail subject to that named surety entering into the recognisance (that is, signing the formal document which sets out the agreement to act as surety) in front of a justice of the peace or a justices' clerk, or at a police station in front of an officer of the rank of Inspector or above (s.8 (4)). The defendant remains in custody until this has been done.

If there is no one whom the defence can offer as a surety at the time of the hearing, the magistrates may grant bail subject to a surety who is acceptable to the police entering into a recognisance (for the amount fixed by the court) at a magistrates' court or a police station (s.8 (3)). Again, the defendant stays in custody until a satisfactory surety has entered into a recognisance. If the potential surety is rejected by the magistrates' court clerk or police Inspector (as the case may be) because that person is not satisfied of the surety's suitability, the potential surety may apply to the magistrates' court to take his recognisance (s.8(5)).

In *S v Winchester Crown Court* [2013] EWHC 1050 (Admin), Kenneth Parker J ruled that surety should be provided only to secure surrender to custody and not to secure performance of any other condition (see [24] and [38]).

2.4.1.2 When may conditions be imposed?

In *R v Mansfield Justices ex p Sharkey* [1985] QB 613, Lord Lane CJ said (at p.625) that, whereas there have to be substantial grounds for believing that the defendant will abscond, commit further offences, etc., for bail to be withheld altogether, the test for the imposition of conditions is a lower one. To impose conditions on the grant of bail, it is enough if the justices 'perceive a real and not a fanciful risk' of the defendant absconding, committing further offences, etc. In R (CPS) v Chorley Justices [2002] EWHC 2162; (2002) 166 JP 764, the court noted that the only prerequisite for imposing conditions on bail under s.3(6) is that, in the circumstances of the particular case, imposition of the condition is 'necessary' to achieve the aims specified in the section.

In *R v Bournemouth Magistrates ex p Cross* (1989) 89 Cr App R 90, it was held that conditions may be imposed when bail is granted to someone who is charged with a non-imprisonable offence.

2.4.2 Breaking conditions of bail

If the defendant is granted conditional bail but then breaches a condition of that bail, he is liable to be arrested under s.7(3) of the Bail Act 1976, which provides that a person who has been released on bail in criminal proceedings and who is under a duty to surrender into the custody of a court may be arrested without warrant by a police officer:

- if the officer has reasonable grounds for believing that he is not likely to surrender to custody;
- if the constable has reasonable grounds for believing that he likely to break any of the conditions of his bail, or for suspecting that he has broken any of those conditions; or

• in a case where the person was released on bail with one or more sureties, if a surety notifies the police in writing that the person is unlikely to surrender to custody and that for that reason the surety wishes to be relieved of his obligations as a surety.

Under s.7(4), a person arrested under subs.(3) must be 'brought as soon as practicable and in any event within 24 hours after his arrest before a justice of the peace'. For these purposes Christmas Day, Good Friday and any Sunday are disregarded (s.7(7)).

In R v Governor of Glen Parva Young Offender Institution ex p G [1998] QB 877, the defendant was arrested for breach of bail conditions; he was taken to the cells of a magistrates' court within 24 hours of arrest but was not brought before a magistrate until two hours after the expiry of the 24-hour time limit. The Divisional Court held that the detention after 24 hours was unlawful: s.7(4) requires the defendant to be brought before a Justice of the Peace (not merely brought within the court precincts) within 24 hours of arrest.

The importance of dealing with the accused within 24 hours was again emphasised in R (Culley) v Crown Court sitting at Dorchester [2007] EWHC 109 (Admin); (2007) 171 JP 373, where it was held that the magistrate is required to complete the decision-making process within the 24-hour period. If the magistrate fails to do so, the continued custody of the accused becomes unlawful from the moment the 24-hour period has expired.

In R v Liverpool Justices ex p DPP [1993] QB 233, it was held that where the police arrest someone who is in breach of a bail condition, or who the police believe is about to abscond, a single lay magistrate has the power to remand the defendant in custody or to grant bail subject to further conditions.

Section 7(5) of the Bail Act provides that a magistrate before whom a person is brought under subs.(4) may, if of the opinion that he is not likely to surrender to custody, or has broken (or is likely to break) any condition of his bail, remand him in custody or grant him bail subject to the same or to different conditions, but if not of that opinion must grant him bail subject to the same conditions (if any) as were originally imposed. In other words, the court has to decide whether the accused is indeed likely to fail to surrender to custody or has broken (or is likely to breach) any condition of his bail. If so, the defendant's bail may be withdrawn, so that he will be held in custody pending trial, or else bail may be granted again but subject to more stringent conditions.

However, it must be borne in mind that, under s.7(5A), where the defendant has attained the age of 18 and has not been convicted of an offence in the proceedings, the magistrate cannot remand the defendant in custody under s.7(5) if it appears that 'there is no real prospect that the person will be sentenced to a custodial sentence in the proceedings'. This is a significant restriction on the power to revoke bail where the defendant breaches bail conditions.

In R (DPP) v Havering Magistrates' Court [2001] 1 WLR 805, the Divisional Court considered s.7 in the context of Art.5 and Art.6 of the European Convention on Human Rights. The court said that Art.6 has no direct relevance where magistrates are exercising their judgment whether or not to commit a person to custody following breach of bail conditions, since s.7 does not create any criminal offence. However, the court went on to hold that Art.5 is directly relevant; however, the procedures applicable under domestic law are entirely compatible with the requirements of Art.5. The court went on to give guidance on proceedings under s.7. Latham LJ, at [38], said:

> Proceedings under s.7(5) are by their nature emergency proceedings to determine whether or not a person, who was not considered to present the risks which would have justified remanding in custody in the first instance, nonetheless does now present one or other of those risks ... [I]n exercising [the power under s.7(5),] the justice would not be entitled to order detention by reason simply of the finding of a breach; that in itself is not a justification for the refusal of bail ... The fact of a breach of a condition may be some evidence, even powerful evidence, of a relevant risk arising. But it is no more than one of the factors which a justice must consider in exercising his discretion under s.7(5).

His Lordship added (at [40] and [41]):

> [T]he material upon which a justice is entitled ... to come to his opinion is not restricted to admissible evidence in the strict sense ... What undoubtedly is necessary is that the justice, when forming his opinion, takes proper account of the quality of the material upon which he is asked to adjudicate. This material is likely to range from mere assertion at the one end of the spectrum which is unlikely to have any probative effect, to documentary proof at the other end of the spectrum. The procedural task of the justice is to ensure that the defendant has a full and fair opportunity to comment on and answer that material. If that material includes evidence from a witness who gives oral testimony clearly the defendant must be given an opportunity to cross-examine. Likewise, if he wishes to give oral evidence he should be entitled to. The ultimate obligation of the justice is to evaluate that material in the light of the serious potential consequences to the defendant ... and the particular nature of the material ... taking into account, if hearsay is relied upon by either side, the fact that it is hearsay and has not been the subject of cross-examination, and form an honest and rational opinion. If his opinion is that the defendant has broken a condition of his bail, he must then go on to consider whether or not, in view of that opinion, and in all the circumstances of the case, he should commit the defendant in custody or grant bail on the same or other conditions.

This echoes the comments in *R v Liverpool City Justices ex p DPP* [1993] QB 233 (per Roch, J, at p.241), that s.7(5) of the 1976 Act requires the magistrate to conduct an 'informal inquiry' into the reasons for the defendant's arrest; the subsection provides a 'simple and expeditious' method of dealing with a person arrested under s.7, and so the procedure is 'informal' (ibid., p.242). In *R (Thomas) v Greenwich Magistrates' Court* [2009] EWHC 1180 (Admin); (2009) 173 JP 345, Hickinbottom J reiterated (at [12]) that a magistrate who is considering whether the defendant has broken any condition of bail is 'entitled to rely upon written hearsay material, so long as the material is properly evaluated.

In *R (Vickers) v West London Magistrates' Court* [2003] EWHC 1809; (2003) 167 JP 473, it was held that s.7(5) requires a two-stage approach. Gage J ([16]) describes the two stages thus:

> First a decision must be made as to whether or not there has been a breach of a condition. If there has been no breach of a condition then the bailed person is entitled to be admitted to bail on precisely the same conditions – in other words, bail continues. If the justices are of the opinion that there has been a breach of the condition, then they must go on to consider whether or not the bailed person can be admitted again to bail or must be remanded in custody – that is the second stage.

At [17] and [18], his Lordship went on to say that the first stage 'does not involve the justices in an inquiry as to whether the arrested person had a reasonable excuse for being in breach'. However, at the second stage, the question why the defendant breached his bail condition will be relevant and so, at that stage, the justices will have to consider whether he had a reasonable excuse for the breach.

In *R (Ellison) v Teeside Magistrates' Court* [2001] EWHC 12 (Admin); (2001) 165 JP 355, the defendant was arrested for breaking bail conditions imposed by the Crown Court. He was taken before a magistrates' court (under s.7). The magistrates remanded him in custody to appear at the Crown Court to deal with the question of bail. It was held by the Divisional Court that, where a defendant is brought before a magistrates' court for breaching a condition of his bail, the magistrates must deal with the matter. They have no power to commit the defendant to the Crown Court to be dealt with for the breach.

It should be emphasised that s.7 does not create a separate offence: it merely confers a power of arrest (R (Gangar) v Leicester Crown Court [2008] EWCA Crim 2987). Nonetheless, the defendant might commit an offence through the conduct that also amounts to the breach of the bail condition (R v Ashley [2003] EWCA Crim 2571; [2004] 1 WLR 2057).

2.4.3 Application for variation of conditions

Under s.3(8) of the Bail Act 1976, where bail is granted subject to conditions, the defendant or the prosecution may apply to vary those conditions; if unconditional bail was granted, the prosecution may apply to the court for conditions to be added.

2.5 Options open to defendant where bail refused

Section 5(3) of the Bail Act 1976 provides that where a court withholds bail, or grants conditional bail, or varies conditions of bail, in a case where the presumption in favour of bail applies under s.4, then the court must give reasons for withholding bail or for imposing or varying the conditions. A record of the decision, including the reasons for it, must be given to the defendant (s.5(4)). In R (R) v Snaresbrook Crown Court [2011] EWHC 3569 (Admin), Holman J said (at [21]) that, where bail is withheld, such reasons had to identify the ground(s) upon which the court was satisfied that bail should be refused and identify the case-specific reasons for being so satisfied.

Thus, the defendant receives a document setting out which statutory ground(s) for withholding bail were held to be applicable, and what factors were taken into account in deciding that those grounds were made out.

Furthermore, s.5(6A) says that if a magistrates' court refuses bail after hearing a fully-argued bail application, and either it has not previously heard a fully-argued application in those proceedings or it has previously heard full argument but is satisfied that there has been a change in circumstances or that new considerations have been placed before it, then the court must provide the defendant with a certificate that this is the case. If the magistrates allow a defendant to make a bail application because there has been a material change of circumstances but do not grant bail, they must state in the certificate what change of circumstances persuaded them to hear the application (s.5(6B)).

Once the defendant has a certificate that full argument has been heard, he may apply for bail to the Crown Court in order to challenge the refusal of bail by the magistrates.

2.5.1 Repeated bail applications

Paragraph 1 of Part IIA of Schedule 1 to the Bail Act 1976 says that if the court decides not to grant the defendant bail, it is the court's duty to consider, at each subsequent hearing at which the presumption in favour of bail (under s.4) applies, whether the defendant ought to be granted bail. However, this does not mean that a bail application can be made at each hearing. Paragraphs (2) and (3) go on to say that:

(2) At the first hearing after that at which the court decided not to grant the defendant bail he may support an application for bail with any argument as to fact or law that he desires (whether or not he has advanced that argument previously).

(3) At subsequent hearings the court need not hear arguments as to fact or law which it has heard previously.

Thus, at the first hearing after that the hearing at which bail was refused, the defendant can make a bail application whether or not it is based on arguments that were advanced on the first occasion. This means that the defendant may make bail applications on his first and second appearances before the court and may advance precisely the same arguments in each application if he so wishes. Or, if no application is made on the first appearance, the defendant may make an application on his second appearance. Thereafter, new arguments relevant to bail are required if a further bail application is to be made. So, in subsequent remands, the court should only consider whether the circumstances have changed since the last fully-argued bail application was heard (for example, a possible surety comes forward or the defendant is offered employment). If there is new information to put before the court, then a fully-argued bail application may be made.

This provision is based on R v Nottingham Justices ex p Davies [1981] 1 QB 38, in which the Divisional Court said the defendant should be allowed two fully-argued applications. This was because the first application is often under-prepared due to lack of time, and so fairness demands that a second application be heard. Thereafter, however, the court would simply be hearing arguments that had been heard before; hence, the restriction that a third application for bail can be made only if there is some fresh material for the court to consider.

The test to be applied is whether there are 'new considerations', which is not necessarily the same as asking whether there has been a 'change of circumstances'. In R (B) v Brent Youth Court [2010] EWHC 1893 (Admin), there had been two bail applications to the magistrates and one at the Crown Court; the defence sought to make a further application to the magistrates on the basis, inter alia, of a new set of possible conditions. The magistrates ruled that the possibility of new conditions did not amount to a change of circumstances because the revised conditions could have been put before the court on a previous occasion; accordingly, they refused to hear the application. This refusal was quashed by the High Court. Wilkie J (at [9]) said:

> [T]he court is obliged to entertain two bail applications regardless of whether the arguments put forward in the second are arguments which have been advanced previously. But if those arguments are sought to be put forward a third time the court is not obliged to entertain them, though it may do so. But this only applies to the extent that arguments put forward as to fact or law are arguments which the court has heard previously.

His Lordship went on to say this is almost invariably referred to as the 'change of circumstance' condition but that this phrase 'does not accurately reflect the statutory provisions. His Lordship said (at [16]):

> The mere fact that the [condition] could have possibly been put forward before but had not been is not an argument for concluding that there was no statutory obligation to consider it ... [T]he question is a little wider than 'Has there been a change?'; it is 'Are there any new considerations which were not before the court when the accused was last remanded in custody?'.

In R v Dover and East Kent Justices ex p Dean [1992] Crim LR 33, the defendant did not make a bail application on his first appearance at court and he consented to being remanded in his absence (under s.128 of the Magistrates' Courts Act 1980) for the next three weeks. On the occasion of his next appearance before the court (a month after his first appearance), the defendant sought to make a bail application. The magistrates would not let him do so, but the Divisional Court held that remands in the defendant's absence did not count as hearings for the purpose of determining whether a bail application could be made. The defendant's second appearance before the court was to be regarded as the second hearing (even though the case had been listed in the intervening weeks) and so he had a right to make a bail application.

In R v *Calder Justices ex p Kennedy* (1992) 156 JP 716, it was held that, if the magistrates remand the defendant in custody on the basis that there is insufficient information to make a decision on bail, this hearing does not count for these purposes. So, a full bail application may be made on the occasion of the defendant's next appearance and, if that application is unsuccessful, a second fully argued bail application can be made on his subsequent appearance before the court.

2.5.2 Application to the Crown Court

An application for bail may be made to the Crown Court if the defendant has a certificate (under s.5(6A) of the Bail Act 1976) from the magistrates' court that a fully-argued bail application was made there. The defendant's application to the Crown Court should explain why the Crown Court should not withhold bail (or, as the case may be, why it should vary the condition(s) under appeal; what further information or legal argument, if any, has become available since the magistrates' court's decision; and propose the terms of any suggested condition of bail.

The application may be heard in public or in private (r.14.2(2) of the Criminal Procedure Rules); however, such applications are often heard in private. In R (*Malik*) v *Central Criminal Court* [2006] EWHC 1539 (Admin); [2006] 4 All ER 1141, Gray J (at [40]) said that the court must start from the 'fundamental presumption in favour of open justice'. The court must therefore consider whether it is necessary, in the interests of justice, to depart from the ordinary rule of open justice. The judgment makes it clear that this is not an exercise of discretion (which implies a judicial choice between two or more equally proper courses), but of judgement as to whether a departure from the norm is justified (at [30]).

The application will be heard by a circuit judge or recorder. The hearing follows the same procedure as a bail application in the magistrates' court, with the prosecution summarising the objections to bail and the defence responding to those objections.

2.5.2.1 Appeal against conditions of bail

Section 16(1) of the Criminal Justice Act 2003 also enables the defendant to appeal to the Crown Court against the imposition of certain bail conditions, namely:

- residing away from a particular place or area;
- residing at a particular place other than a bail hostel;
- providing one or more sureties, or the giving of security;
- remaining indoors between certain hours (i.e. a curfew);
- electronic monitoring; or
- refraining from making contact with another person.

This right of appeal can be exercised only if the defendant has previously made an application to the magistrates (under s.3(8)(a) of the Bail Act) for the conditions to be varied (s.16(5)) or where the prosecution have previously made an application under s.3(8)(b) or s.5B(1) of the Bail Act (s.16(6)). On an appeal under s.16, the Crown Court may vary the conditions of bail (s.16(7)). Once the Crown Court has disposed of the appeal, no further appeal can be brought unless a further application under s.3(8)(a) has been made to the magistrates (s.16(8)).

2.5.3 Jurisdiction of High Court

Section 29(3) of the Senior Courts Act 1981 excludes judicial review of decisions of the Crown Court in 'matters relating to trial on indictment'. However, in R (M) v *Isleworth Crown Court* [2005] EWHC 363, Maurice Kay LJ said (at [11]), that the High Court has jurisdiction to review a bail decision by the Crown Court, but that this is a jurisdiction which should be exercised 'very sparingly indeed'. The exceptional nature of this jurisdiction was emphasised in R (*Galliano*) v *Crown Court at Manchester* [2005] EWHC 1125 (Admin), where Collins J (at [11]) said that the defendant will succeed only if he can persuade the court that the decision of the Crown Court judge 'fell outside the bounds of what could be regarded as reasonable'; the High Court 'will be reluctant to entertain claims for judicial review of a failure to grant bail and will only do so if satisfied that the decision of the Crown Court judge was an irrational one'.

Section 29(3) prevents a judicial review challenge to a decision by a trial judge during a Crown Court trial to revoke bail of a defendant (R (*Uddin*) v *Leeds Crown Court* [2013] EWHC 2752 (Admin); [2014] 1 WLR 1742).

2.6 Prosecution challenges to decision to grant bail

Under s.5(2A) of the Bail Act, where a court grants bail to a person to whom s.4 applies after hearing representations from the prosecutor in favour of withholding bail, the court must give reasons for granting bail.

2.6.1 Application for reconsideration of bail

Section 5B(1) of the Bail Act 1976 provides that where a magistrates' court has granted bail (or the defendant was granted police bail), the prosecution may apply to the magistrates' court for that decision to be reconsidered, asking the court to:

(a) vary the conditions of bail; or
(b) impose conditions in respect of bail which has been granted unconditionally; or
(c) withhold bail.

This provision applies only where the defendant is accused of an indictable (including triable either-way) offence (s.5B(2)).

An application under s.5B is not, strictly speaking, an appeal, since it is not challenging the correctness of the original decision. Section 5B(3) provides:

> No application for the reconsideration of a decision under this section shall be made unless it is based on information which was not available to the court or constable when the decision was taken.

Thus, an application under s.5B is possible only if it is based on new information (in the sense of information which was not available when the original decision regarding bail was taken). The basis of the application is therefore not to impugn the original decision to grant bail but to draw to the court's attention a relevant change in circumstances.

2.6.2 Appeal to the Crown Court

The Bail (Amendment) Act 1993 allows the prosecution to appeal, in certain circumstances, against decisions by magistrates to grant bail.

Section 1(1) of the Bail (Amendment) Act 1993 provides that, where a magistrates' court grants bail to a person who is charged with, or convicted of, an offence punishable by imprisonment, the prosecution may appeal to the Crown Court against the granting of bail.

Section 1(1B) provides that where a Crown Court judge grants bail to a person who is charged with, or convicted of, an offence punishable by imprisonment, the prosecution may appeal to the High Court against the granting of bail. However, under s.1(1C), such an appeal cannot be made where the judge has granted bail in the context of a prosecution appeal under s.1(1).

Under s.1(2) of the 1993 Act, the prosecution right of appeal applies only where the prosecution is conducted by or on behalf of the Director of Public Prosecutions (this includes CPS prosecutions). Furthermore, for the Act to apply, the prosecution must have opposed the grant of bail before it was granted (s.1(3)).

If the prosecution wish to exercise the right of appeal, oral notice of appeal must be given to the court 'at the conclusion of the proceedings in which bail has been granted and before the release from custody of the person concerned' (s.1(4)) and written notice of appeal must be served on the court and on the defendant within two hours of the conclusion of the bail hearing (s.1(5)).

Where oral notice of appeal has been given, the court must remand the accused in custody until the appeal is determined (s.1(6)). The defendant is then held in custody pending the hearing of the appeal, which must take place within 48 hours from the date on which oral notice of appeal is given (excluding weekends and public holidays): s.1(8). If, having given oral notice of appeal, the prosecution fails to serve a written notice of appeal within the two-hour period specified in s.1(5) of the Act, the appeal is deemed to have been disposed of (s.1(7)) and the defendant must be released. The appeal takes the form of a rehearing, and the judge may remand the defendant in custody or may grant bail subject to such conditions (if any) as he thinks fit (s.1(9)).

The courts have accorded some latitude to prosecutors when interpreting the apparently strict time limits in the Act. For example, in R v Isleworth Crown Court ex p Clarke [1998] 1 Cr App R 257, the Divisional Court held that the requirement that the prosecutor must give oral notice of appeal against the decision to grant bail 'at the conclusion of the proceedings' was satisfied in a case where such notice was given to the magistrates' court clerk some five minutes after the court had risen. Similarly, in R (Jeffrey) v Warwick Crown Court [2002] EWHC 2469, the written notice of appeal was served on the court three minutes late. The Divisional Court held that Parliament did not intend that the time limit for serving the notice of appeal should defeat an appeal if the prosecution had given itself ample time to serve the notice on the defendant within the two-hour period, had used due diligence to serve the notice within that period, and the failure to do so was not the fault of the prosecution, but was due to circumstances outside its control. Furthermore, the delay of three minutes had not caused the accused any prejudice (since he knew at the conclusion of the proceedings before the magistrates that the prosecution was exercising its right of appeal, and he knew that he was being detained in custody as a result of the oral application for him to be remanded in custody until the appeal was disposed of).

The same approach was taken in (Cardin) v Birmingham Crown Court [2017] EWHC 2101 (Admin); [2018] 1 Cr App R 3, where the prosecutor gave oral notice of an intention to appeal the granting of bail at 12.54 p.m. Written notice of the prosecution's intention to appeal the granting of bail was given to the court officer at the magistrates' court at 1.56 p.m. However, the remand warrant incorrectly stated that the written notice of appeal had been served on the defendant at 12.54 p.m. The written notice was not served on the defendant because he had (in error) already been sent to the prison where he was to be held pending the disposal of the prosecution appeal against the grant of bail. Attempts by the court to secure service of the notice on the defendant at the prison were unsuccessful. The Bail (Amendment) Act 1993, s.1(5), stipulates that written notice of appeal must be served on the magistrates' court and on the defendant 'within two hours of the conclusion of the bail proceedings; subs.(7) goes on to state that, where the prosecution fails, within that period of two hours, to serve one or both of those notices, 'the appeal shall be deemed to have been disposed of'. Andrews J ruled (at [46]) that:

> [I]t cannot have been Parliament's intention that the Crown should lose the opportunity to reverse a decision that was wrong in principle, with the result that a defendant who might abscond or commit further offences or interfere with prosecution witnesses was released on bail, if the reason why the notice of appeal was not served in time (or indeed at all) was outside the prosecution's control.

She added (at [47]):

> The word 'fails' in this context carries with it an implication of fault, and would not generally be used to describe the situation in which a person is unable to do something. One dictionary definition of 'fails' is 'to neglect to do something', and in our judgment that is the sense, rather than the wider sense of 'being unsuccessful in achieving one's goals' in which the word should be understood in this specific context.

In R v Middlesex Guildhall Crown Court ex p Okoli [2001] 1 Cr App R 1, the Divisional Court had to consider the effect of the 48-hour time limit contained in s.1(8). On 7 June 2000, the defendant was granted bail by a magistrates' court. The prosecution sought to appeal under the 1993 Act. The appeal was listed for 3 p.m. on 9 June. The defendant argued that, because this was more than 48 hours after the notice of appeal had been given, the Crown Court had no jurisdiction to hear the appeal. It was held that where an oral notice of appeal against a decision to grant bail has been given, the appeal hearing must commence within two working days of the date − not the time − on which notice of appeal was given. The Crown Court therefore had jurisdiction to hear the appeal.

The need to have a written notice following the oral notice of appeal is to enable the question whether or not to appeal to be considered by a Senior Crown Prosecutor.

Guidance issued to Crown Prosecutors by the CPS (available on their website) says that. in considering whether an appeal is appropriate, 'the key factor to consider is the level of risk posed to a victim, group of victims or the public at large'.

2.7 Failure to surrender to custody

Section 2(2) of the Bail Act 1976 defines 'surrender to custody' to mean the accused 'surrendering himself into the custody of the court … at the time and place for the time being appointed for him to do so'. In other words, the defendant 'surrenders' to custody by attending the correct court, on the correct date and at the correct time, and by complying with that court's procedure for surrender, for example, reporting to a particular office or a particular person (DPP v Richards [1988] QB 701). Thus, a defendant surrenders to custody when he puts himself at the direction of the court or an officer of the court (R v Central Criminal Court ex p Guney [1996] AC 616).

In R v Evans [2011] EWCA Crim 2842; [2012] 1 WLR 1192, Hughes LJ (at [36]) said that, in the Crown Court, surrender is 'accomplished when the defendant presents himself to the custody officers by entering the dock or where a hearing before the judge commences at which he is formally identified as present'. His Lordship observed (at [32]) that, though arrival at the court building does not amount to surrender, once a defendant arrives at the Crown Court he is not entirely at liberty to come and go as he wishes; he may be required at any moment to do so and in consequence he would be very unwise to wander away.

Moreover, having surrendered to the custody of the court, the defendant must remain within the precincts of the court unless and until the court grants him bail again. Section 7(2) of the Bail Act provides that if a person who has been released on bail absents himself from the court at any time after he has surrendered into the custody of the court and before the court is ready to begin or to resume the hearing of the proceedings, the court may (unless he is absent in accordance with leave given to him by the court) issue a warrant for his arrest.

In R v Evans, Hughes LJ (at [9]–[11]) noted that the Bail Act distinguishes between two situations: first, where a defendant is on bail but fails without reasonable excuse to surrender to custody (an offence under s.6(1)); second, where a defendant has surrendered to bail but then absents himself from the court before the hearing either begins or resumes, as the case may be (not a Bail Act offence, though the court may issue a warrant for the defendant's arrest under s.7(2)).

2.7.1 Adjournment

If the defendant clearly has a good reason for not attending court, the court should simply adjourn the case in the absence of the defendant, with the defendant being remanded on bail as before (s.129(3) of the Magistrates' Courts Act 1980). This is sometimes known as 'enlarging bail'.

2.7.2 Police powers

Under s.7(3)(a) of the Bail Act, the police have the power to arrest without warrant a person who is on bail if there are reasonable grounds for believing that he 'is not likely to surrender to custody'. After arrest, the defendant will be brought before the court.

2.7.3 Proceeding in the absence of the defendant

In some instances, it may be possible to continue with the case even though the defendant is not present in the courtroom. This is dealt with in Chapters 5 and 10 (which examine trial in the magistrates' court and in the Crown Court respectively).

2.7.4 Bench warrants

Under s.7(1), if the defendant has been released on bail, the court can issue a warrant for his arrest if he fails to surrender to custody at the time appointed for him to do so. Such a warrant is sometimes known as a 'bench warrant'.

If a defendant fails to attend court but there is a suggestion that he has a good reason for not doing so (but there is insufficient information to be sure of this), the court may issue a bench warrant 'backed for bail' (permitted by s.117 of the Magistrates' Courts Act 1980 and s.81(4) of the Senior Courts Act 1981 for magistrates' courts and the Crown Court respectively). In other words, the warrant is endorsed with a direction to the police to release the defendant once he has been arrested and informed of the next date he must attend court. This serves to warn the defendant that failure to attend court may lead to his arrest. Such warrants are, however, sometimes viewed as consuming a disproportionate amount of police time and effort in return for little or no advantage. A possible alternative to the issue of a warrant backed for bail where the accused fails to attend is to send him a warning letter, directing him to attend on the date of the next hearing and warning him of the consequences of non-attendance, namely that if he fails to attend the next hearing, it is likely that the court will proceed in his absence or issue a bench warrant that is not backed for bail.

2.7.4.1 Failure to attend to answer requisition or summons

If the defendant was supposed to attend court to answer a requisition or summons (that is, he was not originally arrested and charged), a bench warrant can be issued under s.1(6) of the

Magistrates' Courts Act 1980 provided that the offence charged is an indictable offence (that is, one that may or must be tried in the Crown Court). A warrant may be issued by a single magistrate.

2.7.4.2 After arrest under a bench warrant

After arrest pursuant to a bench warrant not backed for bail, the defendant will be taken before the court which granted the warrant, and the question whether or not he should be released on bail (perhaps with more stringent conditions) or kept in custody will be decided by the court.

2.7.5 Loss of presumption in favour of bail

As a result of absconding, the defendant's chances of being granted bail in the same, and any later, proceedings are reduced.

Under para.6 of Part 1 of Sch.1 to the Bail Act 1976, the defendant need not be granted bail in the proceedings if, having previously been released on bail, he has been arrested in pursuance of s.7 (though it should be noted that, because of para.1A, bail cannot be withheld under para.6 if there is no real prospect that the defendant will be sentenced to a custodial sentence in the proceedings).

By virtue of para.9(c) of Part 1 of Sch.1, when deciding whether it is satisfied there are substantial grounds for believing that the defendant will fail to surrender to custody, the court may have regard to the defendant's record as respects the fulfilment of his obligations under previous grants of bail.

2.7.6 Forfeiture of recognisance

If the defendant was granted bail subject to one or more sureties, and the defendant then fails to surrender to custody when he should, there is a presumption that the full sum promised by each surety will be forfeited, unless it is fair and just that a lesser sum (or none at all) should be forfeited. The principles to be applied were summarised by McCullough J in R v Uxbridge Justices ex p Heward-Mills [1983] 1 WLR 56 (at p.62):

> (1) When a defendant for whose attendance a person has stood surety fails to appear, the full recognisance should be forfeited, unless it appears fair and just that a lesser sum should be forfeited or none at all.
> (2) The burden of satisfying the court that the full sum should not be forfeited rests on the surety and is a heavy one. It is for him to lay before the court the evidence of want of culpability and of means on which he relies.

Another helpful summary was provided by Gibbs J in Choudhry v Birmingham Crown Court [2007] EWHC 2764 (Admin); (2008) 172 JP 33 (at [15]):

> (a) The purpose of a recognizance is to bring the defendant to court for trial.
> (b) The forfeiture of recognizance is not a penalty imposed on the surety for misconduct.
> (c) It is for the surety to establish to the satisfaction of the court that there are grounds upon which the court may remit from forfeiture part or, wholly exceptionally, the whole recognizance.
> (d) The absence of culpability on the part of the surety is not of itself a reason to set aside or reduce the obligation entered into.
> (e) Absence of culpability is a factor to be considered. The court may, in the exercise of a wide discretion, decide it would be fair and just to [forfeit] some or all of the recognizance.

His Lordship added (at [43]) that the court *may*, in the exercise of its discretion, remit the whole or the substantial part of the amount of the recognisance in an exceptional case, but that 'there is no principle of law which *requires* it to do so'.

It follows that relevant factors include:

- The surety's means: has there been a change in financial circumstances since he agreed to act as surety which would make it unfair to order him to forfeit the sum promised?
- Culpability: did the surety take all reasonable steps to secure the defendant's attendance at court, again making it unfair to penalise the surety?

The position is summarised thus in Criminal Practice Direction 19F (para.19F.5):

The court has discretion to forfeit the whole sum, part only of the sum, or to remit the sum. The starting point is that the surety is forfeited in full. It would be unfortunate if this valuable method of allowing a defendant to remain at liberty were undermined. Courts would have less confidence in the efficacy of sureties. It is also important to note that a defendant who absconds without in any way forewarning his sureties does not thereby release them from any or all of their responsibilities. Even if a surety does his best, he remains liable for the full amount, except at the discretion of the court. However, all factors should be taken into account and the following are noted for guidance only:

(i)   The presence or absence of culpability is a factor, but is not in itself a reason to reduce or set aside the obligations entered into by the surety.

(ii) The means of a surety, and in particular changed means, are relevant.

(iii) The court should forfeit no more than is necessary, in public policy, to maintain the integrity and confidence of the system of taking sureties.

2.7.7 The offence of absconding

Section 6(1) of the Bail Act 1976 states that a person who has been released on bail and who fails, without reasonable cause, to surrender to custody, is guilty of an offence.

Under s.6(2), if it is not reasonably practicable for the defendant to surrender to custody at the appointed time, he must do so as soon thereafter as it is reasonably practicable, or else is guilty of an offence.

Section 6 does not require that the defendant be formally charged with an offence (*Schiavo v Anderton* [1987] QB 20) but, once the court has decided to proceed under s.6, there is then a hearing to determine whether or not the defendant is guilty of absconding.

Failure to answer bail which was granted by a court (that is, rather than by the police) will be dealt with by the court at which the proceedings in respect of which bail was granted are to be heard. In other words, if the defendant is to be tried for the substantive offence in the magistrates' court, the Bail Act 1976 offence will be dealt with in that court; if the defendant is to be tried in the Crown Court, the Bail Act offence will be dealt with in that court (by a judge sitting alone, not by a jury). Current practice is to deal with the Bail Act offence immediately, not to postpone consideration of it until the conclusion of the substantive proceedings.

An offence is committed under s.6 only if the defendant has no reasonable cause for the failure to surrender. The burden of proof rests on the accused to prove (on the balance of probabilities) that he had reasonable cause for his failure to surrender to custody (s.6(3)).

In R v *Watson* (1990–91) 12 Cr App R(S) 227, the Court of Appeal emphasised that, when the court is dealing with an allegation of absconding, the defendant must be given an opportunity to explain the failure to surrender to custody, or (if he admits the offence) to put forward any mitigation. Furthermore, where the defendant denies the offence, he should be given the chance to adduce evidence that he had good cause for the failure to surrender.

In R v Scott [2007] EWCA Crim 2757; (2008) 172 JP 149, Toulson LJ (at [14]) said that, 'the mere fact that a defendant is only slightly late cannot afford him a defence'. His Lordship explained this approach (at [16]) by saying that even if a delay is small, 'it can still cause inconvenience and waste of time. If a culture of lateness is tolerated the results can be cumulative and bad for the administration of justice'.

It must be emphasised that if reasonable cause exists at the time the defendant should have surrendered, then he should surrender as soon as reasonably practicable thereafter.

2.7.7.1 The penalty for absconding

The Sentencing Council Guideline for Breach Offences includes a Guideline for the offence under s.6 of the Bail Act 1976. According to that Guideline, failure to surrender which represents a 'deliberate attempt to evade or delay justice' is the most serious category of culpability; the lowest category of culpability is where the reason for the failure to surrender is just short of amounting to reasonable cause. Failure to attend a Crown Court hearing resulting in substantial delay and/or interference with the administration of justice is the most serious category of harm; failure to attend a magistrates' court hearing with that result is the middle category of harm; cases where the non-attendance does not result in substantial delay and/or interference with the administration of justice are in the lowest category of harm. The aggravating features identified in the Guideline include a history of breaches of court orders or police bail, and distress caused to victims and/or witnesses. The mitigating factors specifically identified are: genuine misunderstanding of bail or its requirements, prompt voluntary surrender, and the accused being sole or primary carer for a dependent relative.

Criminal Practice Direction III para.14C.9 says that the offence under s.6 'stands apart from the proceedings in respect of which bail was granted. The seriousness of the offence can be reflected by an appropriate and generally separate penalty being imposed for the Bail Act offence'. Paragraph 14C.10 goes on to state that, where the appropriate penalty is a custodial sentence, consecutive sentences should be imposed unless there are circumstances that make this inappropriate. Indeed, in R v White; R v McKinnon [2002] EWCA Crim 2952; [2003] 2 Cr App R(S) 29, the Court of Appeal had said that a custodial sentence imposed for failure to surrender to custody under s.6 should normally be ordered to be served consecutively to any sentence of imprisonment imposed for the substantive offence for which the defendant was before the court. The court also made it clear that there is no principle of law that the sentence for failing to surrender to custody should be proportionate to the sentence for the substantive offence of which the defendant stands convicted. Moreover, the court pointed out that in R v Neve (1986) 8 Cr App R(S) 270, the Court of Appeal had upheld the imposition of a sentence of six months' imprisonment for failing to surrender to custody even though the defendant had been acquitted of the substantive offence.

In R v Leigh [2012] EWCA Crim 621, the Court of Appeal said that failures to surrender to custody 'are to be taken seriously and a custodial sentence, consecutive to any other sentences imposed, should be the starting point. Bail offences not only reflect a disregard for an order of the court but they also can make a serious contribution to delay, cost and inefficiency in the court system' (per Treacy J, at [8]).

2.8 Custody time limits

Section 22 of the Prosecution of Offences Act 1985 provides for 'custody time limits'. The custody time limits themselves are set out in the Prosecution of Offences (Custody Time Limits) Regulations 1987 (SI 1987/299):

- For either-way offences, the maximum period of custody between the accused's first appearance and the start of summary trial or the time when the court decides to send the accused to the Crown Court for trial is 70 days (reg.4(2)) unless, before the expiry of 56 days following the day of the accused's first appearance, the court decides to proceed to summary trial, in which case the maximum period of custody between the accused's first appearance and the start of the summary trial is 56 days (reg.4(3)).
- For indictable-only offences, the maximum period of custody between the accused's first appearance and the time when the court decides to send the accused to the Crown Court for trial is 70 days (reg.4(4)).
- For summary offences, the maximum period of custody beginning with the date of the accused's first appearance and ending with the date of the start of the summary trial is 56 days (reg.4(4A)).
- Where a case is sent for trial in the Crown Court, the maximum period of custody between the time when the accused is sent for trial and the start of the trial is 112 days (reg.5(3)).

These provisions apply to proceedings in the youth court even though the usual distinction between summary and indictable offences does not apply there (R v Stratford Youth Court ex p S [1998] 1 WLR 1758).

Under reg.8 of the Prosecution of Offences (Custody Time Limits) Regulations 1987, where the custody time limit has expired:

- the defendant has an absolute right to bail;
- the court cannot require sureties, or the giving of security, as a condition of granting bail (but it can impose other conditions, such as conditions of residence, reporting to a police station, etc.); and
- following the grant of bail, the defendant may not be arrested without warrant (under s.7 of the Bail Act 1976) on the ground that a police officer believes he is unlikely to surrender to custody or that that he has broken, or is likely to break, a condition of bail.

If the defendant is granted bail because the custody time limit has expired, his right to bail continues only until he enters a plea. Thereafter, the court can withhold bail if any of the reasons for doing so under the Bail Act 1976 apply (R v Croydon Crown Court ex p Lewis (1994) 158 JP 886).

2.8.1 Extending the time limit

Section 22(3) of the Prosecution of Offences 1985 Act provides that the appropriate court may:

> at any time before the expiry of a time limit imposed by the regulations, extend, or further extend, that limit; but the court shall not do so unless it is satisfied –
>
> (a) that the need for the extension is due to –
> 　(i) the illness or absence of the accused, a necessary witness, a judge or a magistrate;
> 　(ii) a postponement which is occasioned by the ordering by the court of separate trials in the case of two or more accused or two or more offences; or
> 　(iii) some other good and sufficient cause; and
> (b) that the prosecution has acted with all due diligence and expedition.

The 'appropriate court' to do so is the Crown Court if the defendant has been sent for trial to the Crown Court; otherwise the application should be made to the magistrates' court (subs.(11)).

The application to extend the time limit must be made prior to the expiry of the limit; once the limit has expired, there is no power to extend it (R v *Sheffield Justices ex p Turner* [1991] 2 QB 472).

The court can decide whether or not to extend time on the basis of submissions; there is no need for evidence to be called if the court thinks that this would be unnecessary (R v *Norwich Crown Court ex p Parker and Ward* (1992) 96 Cr App R 68).

Guidance on extensions of custody time limits was given by the Court of Appeal in R v *Manchester Crown Court ex p McDonald* [1999] 1 WLR 841. Lord Bingham of Cornhill CJ said (at p.846) that, 'it is for the prosecution to satisfy the court on the balance of probabilities that both the statutory conditions in s.22(3) are met'. At p.847, his Lordship considered the condition in s.22(3)(b), that the prosecution should have acted with all due expedition:

> The condition looks to the conduct of the prosecuting authority (police, solicitors, counsel). To satisfy the court that this condition is met the prosecution need not show that every stage of preparation of the case has been accomplished as quickly and efficiently as humanly possible ... What the court must require is such diligence and expedition as would be shown by a competent prosecutor conscious of his duty to bring the case to trial as quickly as reasonably and fairly possible. In considering whether that standard is met, the court will of course have regard to the nature and complexity of the case, the extent of preparation necessary, the conduct (whether co-operative or obstructive) of the defence, the extent to which the prosecutor is dependent on the co-operation of others outside his control and other matters directly and genuinely bearing on the preparation of the case for trial.

His Lordship then addressed s.22(3)(a), which requires good and sufficient cause for extending the maximum period of custody:

> The seriousness of the offence with which the defendant is charged cannot of itself be good and sufficient cause within the section ... Nor can the need to protect the public ... Nor ... can it be a good cause that the extension is only for a short period ...

His Lordship went on to note that the unavailability of a suitable judge or a suitable courtroom within the maximum period specified in the regulations may amount to good and sufficient cause for granting an extension of the custody time limit but only 'in special cases and on appropriate facts'. However, in R (*McAuley*) v *Coventry Crown Court* [2012] EWHC 680 (Admin); [2012] 1 WLR 2766, Sir John Thomas P said (at [35]):

> Although other considerations may apply to cases which are not routine, lack of money provided by Parliament in circumstances where the custody time limits are unchanged, will rarely, if ever, provide any justification for the extension of a CTL.

In *O'Dowd v UK* [2010] ECHR 1324, the European Court of Human Rights ruled (at [73]) that the 'due diligence' required by s.22(3) of the 1985 Act cannot be equated to the 'special diligence' required by Art.5(3). The Court went on to explain that:

> Unlike the approach of the domestic courts to compliance with the 1985 Act, in assessing compliance with Art.5(3), this Court will examine the proceedings as a whole and assess any particular periods of inactivity or delay by the authorities within the context of the overall period of pre-trial detention, with particular regard to any recognition by the authorities of the length of time already spent in detention and the need to take additional steps to bring about a more speedy trial.

However, the Court found that, in the present case, there had been no breach of Art.5(3). This was largely because the accused had contributed substantially to the overall length of his pre-trial detention (for example, dismissing his legal advisers shortly before hearings, which resulted in the hearings being postponed).

2.9 Bail and the European Convention on Human Rights

Article 5 of the European Convention on Human Rights ('ECHR') provides that 'everyone has the right to liberty' and states that no one should be deprived of their liberty save in the six sets of circumstances specified in Art.5(1)(a) to (f):

(a) the lawful detention of a person after conviction by a competent court;

(b) the lawful arrest or detention of a person for non-compliance with the lawful order of a court or in order to secure the fulfilment of any obligation prescribed by law;

(c) the lawful arrest or detention of a person effected for the purpose of bringing him before the competent legal authority on reasonable suspicion of having committed an offence or when it is reasonably considered necessary to prevent his committing an offence or fleeing after having done so;

(d) the detention of a minor by lawful order for the purpose of educational supervision or his lawful detention for the purpose of bringing him before the competent legal authority;

(e) the lawful detention of persons for the prevention of the spreading of infectious diseases, of persons of unsound mind, alcoholics or drug addicts or vagrants;

(f) the lawful arrest or detention of a person to prevent his effecting an unauthorised entry into the country or of a person against whom action is being taken with a view to deportation or extradition.

The list of exceptions is exhaustive, and has been described in Strasbourg as ensuring that no one is deprived of liberty in an 'arbitrary fashion' (*Engel v Netherlands* (1979–80) 1 EHRR 647, at [58])).

The Law Commission (Law Com No. 269, June 2001) considered the impact of the Human Rights Act 1988 on the law governing bail decisions and noted that, although reasonable suspicion that the detained person has committed an offence can be sufficient to justify pre-trial detention for a short time, the national authorities must thereafter show additional grounds for detention (para.6.8). They summarised (at para.2.29) the five additional grounds recognised under the ECHR as follows, namely where the purpose of detention is to avoid a real risk that, were the accused to be released:

- he would fail to attend trial;
- he would interfere with evidence or witnesses, or otherwise obstruct the course of justice;
- he would commit an offence while on bail;
- he would be at risk of harm against which he would be inadequately protected; or
- a disturbance to public order would result.

The Law Commission concluded that there are no provisions in the Bail Act 1976 which are incompatible with Convention rights. However, the Commission did produce a guide to assist decision-makers to apply the Act in a way that is compatible with the ECHR. Paragraph 2 emphasises that an accused should be refused bail only where detention is necessary for a purpose which Strasbourg jurisprudence has recognised as legitimate, in the sense that detention may be compatible with the accused's right to release under Art.5(3). Thus, a domestic court exercising its powers in a way which is compatible with the Convention rights should refuse bail only where it can be justified under both the ECHR, as interpreted in Strasbourg jurisprudence, and domestic legislation. Paragraph 3 points out that detention will be necessary only if the risk relied upon as the ground for withholding bail could not be adequately addressed by the imposition of appropriate bail conditions. It follows that conditional bail should be used in preference to detention where one or more bail conditions could adequately address the risk that would otherwise justify detention. Paragraph 4 emphasises that the court refusing bail should give reasons for finding that detention is necessary. Those reasons should be closely related to the individual circumstances pertaining to the accused, and be capable of supporting the conclusion of the court.

In R (Fergus) v Southampton Crown Court [2008] EWHC 3273 (Admin), Silber J (at [19]) referred to R (Thompson) v Central Criminal Court [2005] EWHC 2345 (Admin), in which Collins J (at [10]) had said:

> The approach under the Bail Act is entirely consistent with the approach which the European Court has regarded as proper under Art.5, namely there must be a grant of bail unless there are good reasons to refuse. The approach therefore really is not should there be bail granted but should custody be opposed, that is, is it necessary for the defendant to be in custody. That is the approach that the court should take. Only if persuaded that it is necessary should a remand in custody take place. It would be necessary if the court decides that whatever conditions can be reasonably imposed in relation to bail there are nevertheless substantial grounds for believing that the defendant will either fail to surrender to custody, commit an offence, interfere with witnesses or otherwise obstruct justice.

Silber J concluded (at [21]) that certain consequences flowed from this:

> First, it is not reasonable for a court to withdraw bail unless it is necessary to do so especially as any decision to withdraw bail engages rights under Article 5. Second, any such reason justifying the decision to withdraw bail must be stated by the decision maker explaining why bail should be withdrawn and that reason must relate to the facts. Such a reason must be more than merely reciting that one of the statutory grounds has been made out. The underlying facts have to be put forward.

2.9.1 Strasbourg case law

Under Art.5, a person charged with an offence must be released pending trial unless there are 'relevant and sufficient' reasons to justify continued detention (Wemhoff v Germany (1979–80) 1 EHRR 55, at [12]). The case law of the European Court of Human Rights ('ECtHR') shows that this is interpreted in a way that is consistent with the Bail Act 1976. The grounds accepted by the European Court of Human Rights for withholding bail include:

● The risk that the accused will fail to appear at the trial. This requires 'a whole set of circumstances . . . which give reason to suppose that the consequences and hazards of flight will seem to him to be a lesser evil than continued imprisonment' (Stogmuller v Austria (1979–80) 1 EHRR 155, at [15]). The court can take account of 'the character of the person involved, his morals, his home, his occupation, his assets, his family ties, and all kinds of links with the country in which he is being prosecuted' (Neumeister v Austria (1979–80) 1 EHRR 91, at [10]). The likely sentence is relevant but cannot of itself justify the refusal of bail (Letellier v France (1992) 14 EHRR 83, at [43]).

- The risk that the accused will interfere with the course of justice (e.g., interfering with witnesses, warning other suspects, destroying relevant evidence). There must be an identifiable risk and there must be plausible evidence in support (cf. *Clooth v Belgium* (1992) 14 EHRR 717).
- Preventing the commission of further offences. There must be good reason to believe that the accused will commit offences while on bail (cf. *Toth v Austria* (1992) 14 EHRR 551).
- The preservation of public order. Bail may be withheld where the nature of the alleged crime and the likely public reaction to it are such that the release of the accused may give rise to public disorder (*Letellier v France*, at [51]).

It should be noted that the 'equality of arms' principle applies to bail applications (*Woukam Moudefo v France* (1991) 13 EHRR 549). This includes:

- the right to disclosure of prosecution evidence for purposes of making a bail application: *Lamy v Belgium* (1989) 11 EHRR 529, at [29] (the decision of the Divisional Court, *R v DPP, ex parte Lee* [1999] 2 Cr App R 304 is broadly consistent with this approach);
- the requirement that the court should give reasons for the refusal of bail (*Tomasi v France* (1993) 15 EHRR 1, at [84]) and should permit renewed applications for bail at reasonable intervals (*Bezicheri v Italy* (1990) 12 EHRR 210, at [21]).

In *O'Dowd v UK* [2010] ECHR 1324, the ECtHR observed (at [68]) that:

Continued detention can be justified in a given case only if there are specific indications of a genuine requirement of public interest which, notwithstanding the presumption of innocence, outweighs the rule of respect for individual liberty laid down in Article 5 of the Convention.

It follows, said the Court (at [69]), that it falls to the 'national judicial authorities to ensure that, in a given case, the pre-trial detention of an accused person does not exceed a reasonable time'. The Court went on to say (at [70]) that the 'persistence of reasonable suspicion that the person arrested has committed an offence is a condition *sine qua non* for the lawfulness of the continued detention, but after a certain lapse of time it no longer suffices'. At that point, there must not only be 'sufficient' grounds to justify the deprivation of liberty, but the 'national authorities' (that is, the prosecution) must display 'special diligence' in the conduct of the proceedings. In assessing whether the 'special diligence' requirement has been met, regard must be had 'to periods of unjustified delay, to the overall complexity of the proceedings and to any steps taken by the authorities to speed up proceedings to ensure that the overall length of detention remains "reasonable"'.

Chapter 3

Classification of Offences and Allocation of Either-Way Offences

In this chapter, we examine how the decision is made as to which court (a magistrates' court or the Crown Court) the offence should be tried in, if that offence is one which can be tried in either court. Allocation (or 'mode of trial' as it is sometimes known) can be determined in any magistrates' court; it does not matter where in England and Wales the offence was allegedly committed (s.2 of the Magistrates' Courts Act 1980).

3.1 Classification of offences

According to Sch.1 to the Interpretation Act 1978, there are three types of criminal offence:

(a) 'summary' offences (offences which are triable only in a magistrates' court);
(b) 'indictable' offences, which are either:
   (i) triable only on indictment (triable only in the Crown Court); or
   (ii) triable either way (triable either in the magistrates' court or the Crown Court).

To determine which category a particular offence falls into one should look at:
- Schedule 1 to the Magistrates' Courts Act 1980, which lists a number of offences that are triable either way; and
- the statute which creates the offence: if the penalty refers both to summary conviction and to conviction on indictment, the offence is triable either way; if it refers only to conviction on indictment, the offence can be tried only in the Crown Court; if it refers only to summary conviction, the offence can be tried only in the magistrates' court.

If an offence is listed in Sch.1 to the Magistrates' Courts Act 1980 Act or its penalty is expressed in a way which refers to both summary trial and trial on indictment, it is triable either way.

3.1.1 Procedural consequences of classification

If the offence is a summary offence and the defendant pleads guilty, sentence will be passed by the magistrates' court. If the defendant pleads not guilty, the trial will take place in the magistrates' court (and sentence will be passed there if the defendant is convicted). See Figure.3.1.

If the offence is triable either way, a 'plea before venue' hearing takes place. If the defendant pleads guilty, sentence may be passed either by the magistrates' court or by the Crown Court, depending on the seriousness of the offence; if the defendant indicates an intention to plead not guilty, an allocation hearing then takes place to determine where the trial will take place (see below). See Figure.3.2.

If the offence is triable only on indictment, the case will be sent to the Crown Court, where a Plea and Trial Preparation Hearing ('PTPH') will take place. See Figure.3.3.

3.2 Either-way offences: the 'plea before venue' hearing

The allocation or 'mode of trial' procedure begins with the court seeking to find out the defendant's intended plea, a procedure known to practitioners as 'plea before venue'. This process is set out in ss.17A and 17B of the Magistrates' Courts Act 1980.

Section 17A applies where a defendant who has attained the age of 18 is charged with an offence that is triable either way (s.17A(1)). The s.17A procedure has to be carried out in the presence of the defendant (s.17A(2)). It begins with the charge being written down (if this has not already been done) and being read to the defendant (s.17A(3)). The court then explains to the defendant that he may indicate whether he intends to plead guilty or not guilty; the defendant must also be warned that an indication of an intention to plead guilty will be regarded as an actual plea of guilty and that the magistrates then have the power to commit for sentence to the Crown Court if they take the view that their sentencing powers are inadequate (s.17A(4)).

The defendant is then asked whether he intends to plead guilty or not guilty (s.17A(5)).

3.2.1 Indication of guilty plea

If the defendant indicates an intention to plead guilty, the magistrates must proceed as if the case were a summary trial at which the defendant had pleaded guilty (s.17A(6)). In other words, the indication of an intention to plead guilty is to be regarded as a plea of guilty, and so the court proceeds to the sentencing stage. If the case is a serious one, in the sense that it calls for a sentence beyond the powers of the magistrates, the defendant will be committed for sentence to the Crown Court.

In *Westminster City Council v Owadally* [2017] EWHC 1092 (Admin); [2017] 1 WLR 4350, at the plea before venue hearing, guilty pleas were indicated on behalf of the accused by their counsel. The Divisional Court held (at [45]) that, as in the Crown Court, an accused in a magistrates' court must enter a guilty plea personally. The requirements of s.17A of the Magistrates' Courts Act 1980 are to be treated as going to the jurisdiction of the court. It follows that, if a guilty plea is not entered by the accused personally, that plea (and any proceedings subsequent to that plea, such as committal for sentence) is to be regarded as a nullity.

3.2.2 Indication of not guilty plea

If the defendant indicates an intention to plead not guilty, the court goes through the allocation procedure set out in ss.18–21 of the Magistrates' Courts Act 1980 (s.17A(7)). Where the defendant declines to give an indication of intended plea, the court must assume that the defendant intends to plead not guilty and so must go through the allocation procedure (s.17A(8)).

3.2.3 'Mixed' pleas

Where the defendant indicates an intention to plead guilty to one or more either-way offences but is also sent to the Crown Court for trial in respect of a related either-way offence to which he intends to plead not guilty, or in respect of a related offence which is triable only on indictment, the magistrates may commit the defendant to the Crown Court for sentence (under s.4 of the Powers of Criminal Courts (Sentencing) Act 2000) in respect of the offence(s) to which he had indicated a guilty plea (even if their sentencing powers would be adequate to deal with the offence(s)).

3.2.4 Proceedings in absence of defendant

Section 17B of the Magistrates' Courts Act 1980 applies where:

- the accused is represented by a legal representative;
- the court considers that by reason of the accused's disorderly conduct before the court it is not practicable for proceedings under s.17A to be conducted in his presence; and
- the court considers that it should proceed in the absence of the accused (s.17B(1)).

In such a case, the legal representative gives the indication of intended plea (s.17B(2), (3)).

3.3 Procedure for determining allocation

The procedure to be followed where a defendant who has attained the age of 18 indicates an intention to plead not guilty (or gives no indication of intended plea) in respect of one or more either-way offences, is set out in ss.18–21 of the Magistrates' Courts Act 1980.

Under s.18(5), this procedure may take place before a single lay justice. However, if the accused is given the option of summary trial and accepts that option, a single justice cannot try the case (and so, where the preliminary hearing takes place before a single justice and the accused pleads not guilty, the case will have to be adjourned for hearing before a full bench (or a District Judge)). Similarly, although a single lay justice may take a guilty plea, sentence must be imposed by a full bench (or a District Judge).

3.3.1 The mode of trial hearing

Under s.19(1), the court has to decide whether the offence appears to be more suitable for summary trial or for trial on indictment. Before making that decision, the court must give the prosecution an opportunity to inform the court of any previous convictions recorded against the accused, and must give the prosecution and the accused an opportunity to make representations as to whether summary trial or trial on indictment would be more suitable (s.19(2)).

When deciding which mode of trial is more appropriate, the court must consider:

- whether the sentence which a magistrates' court would have power to impose for the offence would be adequate;
- any representations made by the parties;
- the allocation guidelines issued by the Sentencing Council under s.122 of the Coroners and Justice Act 2009.

Where the accused is charged with two or more offences, and it appears to the court that those offences could be joined in the same indictment or that they arise out of the same or connected circumstances, the maximum aggregate sentence which a magistrates' court would have power to impose for all of the offences taken together is the sentence taken into account for this purpose (s.19(4)).

If the defendant wishes to be tried at the Crown Court, no defence representations will be made since, even if the magistrates decide that the case is suitable for summary trial, the defendant can nevertheless choose trial on indictment. If, on the other hand, the prosecution seek trial on indictment but the defendant wishes to be tried summarily, the defendant will first have to persuade the magistrates to accept jurisdiction (that is, to rule that the case is suitable for summary trial).

The Sentencing Council Guideline on Allocation states that:

In general, either way offences should be tried summarily unless:

- the outcome would clearly be a sentence in excess of the court's powers for the offence (s) concerned after taking into account personal mitigation and any potential reduction for a guilty plea; or
- for reasons of unusual legal, procedural or factual complexity, the case should be tried in the Crown Court. This exception may apply in cases where a very substantial fine is

the likely sentence. Other circumstances where this exception will apply are likely to be rare and case specific ...

The Guideline goes on to emphasise the presumption in favour of summary trial, pointing out that a defendant who is convicted of an either-way offence in a magistrates' court may nonetheless be sentenced for that offence in the Crown Court, because the magistrates' court is able (by virtue of s.3 of the Powers of Criminal Courts (Sentencing) Act 2000) to commit the defendant to the Crown Court for sentence following summary conviction:

> In cases with no factual or legal complications the court should bear in mind its power to commit for sentence after a trial and may retain jurisdiction notwithstanding that the likely sentence might exceed its powers.

The Allocation Guideline also emphasises the need to give the parties an opportunity to make representation as to which mode of trial would be most appropriate:

> All parties should be asked by the court to make representations as to whether the case is suitable for summary trial. The court should refer to definitive guidelines (if any) to assess the likely sentence for the offence in the light of the facts alleged by the prosecution case, taking into account all aspects of the case including those advanced by the defence, including any personal mitigation to which the defence wish to refer.

Rule 9.2(6) of the Criminal Procedure Rules provides that, where the court is dealing with two or more defendants who are charged jointly with an offence that can be tried in the Crown Court, the court must explain that, if it sends one of them to the Crown Court for trial, then it must also send to the Crown Court any other defendant who is charged with the same offence (or with an offence which is related to that offence) and who does not wish to plead guilty to each offence with which he is charged, even if the court has by then decided to allocate that other defendant for magistrates' court trial. This means that where one defendant is sent for trial (e.g. because he elects Crown Court trial), any co-accused must also be sent to the Crown Court for trial even if the offence(s) would otherwise be suitable for summary trial. This is sometimes referred to by practitioners as 'one up, all up'.

3.3.1.1 Presence of accused

The defendant must be present at the allocation hearing unless either of the following two exceptions applies:

- Under s.18(3) of the Magistrates' Courts Act, the court may proceed in the absence of the accused if the court considers that, by reason of his disorderly conduct before the court, it is not practicable for the proceedings to be conducted in his presence;
- Under s.23(1) of the Magistrates' Courts Act, if (a) the accused is represented by a legal representative who, in his absence, signifies to the court the accused's consent to the proceedings for determining allocation being conducted in his absence, and (b) the court is satisfied that there is good reason for proceeding in the absence of the accused, then the court may proceed in the absence of the accused, in which case the legal representative can speak on behalf of the absent defendant. It must be emphasised that this provision applies only where there is a good reason for the absence of the accused, such as illness; it does not apply if the accused simply fails to attend court.

3.3.1.2 Procedure where court decides in favour of summary trial

If the court decides that the offence appears to be more suitable for summary trial, the procedure set out in s.20 is followed. The court informs the accused that it appears to the court more suitable for summary trial to take place for the offence, and that he can either consent to summary trial or, if he wishes, elect trial on indictment. He must also be warned that, if he is tried summarily and convicted, he may be committed to the Crown Court for sentence if the magistrates' sentencing powers are inadequate (s.20(2)).

The accused may then request an indication of sentence, namely whether a custodial or non-custodial sentence would be more likely if he were to plead guilty at that stage (s.20(3)). If the accused requests an indication of sentence, the court is not obliged to give one (s.20(4)). If the accused does request, and the court gives, an indication of sentence, the court then asks the accused whether he wishes, on the basis of the indication, to reconsider the indication of plea which he gave at the plea before venue hearing (s.20(5)). If the accused indicates that he does wish to reconsider the indication given at the plea before venue hearing, the court repeats the plea before venue procedure (s.20(6)). If the accused then indicates that he would plead guilty, this is treated as a plea of guilty, and so the court will then proceed to the sentencing stage (s.20(7)).

If the court does not give an indication of sentence (either because the accused does not request one or because the court declines to give one) or an indication is given but the accused does not change his plea to guilty, the court asks the accused whether he consents to be tried summarily or wishes to be tried on indictment. If he consents to summary trial, the case proceeds to summary trial (if necessary, after an adjournment); if he does not consent to summary trial, the case is sent to the Crown Court for trial under s.51 of the Crime and Disorder Act 1998 (s.20(8), (9)).

Where a sentence indication is given and the defendant changes his plea to guilty, a custodial sentence may be imposed for the offence only if such a sentence was indicated (s.20A(1)). However, where an indication of sentence is given and the defendant does not choose to plead guilty on the basis of it, the sentence indication is not binding on the magistrates who later try the case summarily, or on the Crown Court if the defendant elects trial on indictment (s.20A(3)).

3.3.1.3 Procedure where court decides in favour of trial on indictment

If the court decides that the offence appears to be more suitable for trial on indictment, the court informs the accused of this decision, and the case is sent to the Crown Court for trial under s.51 of the Crime and Disorder Act 1998 (s.21).

3.3.1.4 Restriction on summary trial for either-way offences

The key point to emphasise about the allocation procedure is that summary trial of an either-way offence is possible only if both the magistrates and the defendant agree to it. If either the magistrates or the defendant want the case to be tried in the Crown Court, the case will have to be sent to the Crown Court for trial.

3.3.1.5 The accused's decision

If the magistrates do not offer the defendant the chance of summary trial, the defendant has no choice in the matter: the trial has to take place in the Crown Court. If the magistrates do accept jurisdiction, should the defendant agree to summary trial?

The main advantages of summary trial are said to be as follows:

- The trial procedure is less formal. This means that the trial is less daunting, a fact which may be particularly relevant if the defendant is going to be unrepresented at trial, as will be the case if the defendant is not granted publicly-funded representation and yet cannot afford legal representation.
- Summary trial takes a shorter time than a trial in the Crown Court. This means that summary trial

is cheaper (again particularly relevant if the defendant is not publicly funded but has chosen to pay for representation).

- It is sometimes said that an advantage of summary trial is that there is a limit on the sentence which the magistrates' court can pass (six months' imprisonment for one either-way offence, 12 months for two or more). However, this advantage is nullified by the power of the magistrates to commit an offender for sentence (under s.3 of the Powers of Criminal Courts (Sentencing) Act 2000) if, having convicted him, they decide that their sentencing powers are inadequate to deal with him for the offence(s) in question.

The main advantages of trial on indictment are said to be as follows:

- In the magistrates' court, the justices are triers of law and fact whereas, in the Crown Court, the judge is the trier of law and the jurors are the triers of fact. Two advantages of Crown Court trial flow from this fact:
  - Where the admissibility of a piece of evidence is challenged in the Crown Court, the challenge is made in the absence of the jury and, if the judge rules the evidence inadmissible, the jury hear nothing of this evidence. By contrast, in the magistrates' court, the justices themselves have to rule on any question concerning the admissibility of evidence. If they decide that a particular piece of evidence is inadmissible, they must then put it from their minds. It is difficult to be sure that the justices are able to ignore, for example, evidence that the defendant made a confession even where they have ruled that the confession is inadmissible. However, under s.8A of the Magistrates' Courts Act 1980, a bench is empowered to give a pre-trial ruling on the admissibility of evidence and that ruling will bind the bench that eventually tries the case. This, to a large extent, negates the advantage of Crown Court trial where there is an issue over the admissibility of evidence, at least in cases where the admissibility point becomes apparent well before the start of the trial.
  - If there is a point of law to be decided, it is easier to deal with that point in the Crown Court, presided over by a professional judge, than in the magistrates' court, where the justices (who have only elementary legal training) depend on the court legal adviser for advice on questions of law (unless the trial takes place before a legally qualified District Judge). Legal errors are also easier to detect in the Crown Court, as the judge has to set out the relevant law in the summing up to the jury.
- Another advantage of trial on indictment is said to be that the prosecution have to disclose copies of the statements made by the witnesses they will be calling at the Crown Court. This is because the witness statements of the people the prosecution propose to call as witnesses have to be served on the defence as an integral part of the process through which the case is transferred to the Crown Court. However, this advantage is largely negated by the fact that, in the case of summary trial, the prosecutor should provide to the defence all evidence upon which the Crown proposes to rely, and such provision should allow the accused and their legal advisers sufficient time properly to consider the evidence before it is called. The effect of this is to place a defendant who is being tried in the magistrates' court in the same position as a defendant who is being tried in the Crown Court as regards obtaining copies of the statements of the people to be called as prosecution witnesses.
- Perhaps the most significant advantage of Crown Court trial is that the acquittal rate is higher in the Crown Court than in the magistrates' courts. However, the gap is much smaller than is often realised, as is shown by the statistics that follow:
  - According to the casework statistics that accompany the CPS Annual Report for 2017–18, of defendants in the magistrates' court who pleaded not guilty, 62% were convicted (60% in 2016–17 and 58% in 2015–16) whereas in the Crown Court 54% of those pleading not guilty were convicted (52% in both 2016–17 and in 2015–16). It is also noteworthy that in 2017–18 only 4% of either-way offences tried in the Crown Court (2% in 2016–17 and 3% in 2015–16) were tried in that court because the defendant had elected trial (the rest were so tried because

the magistrates declined jurisdiction). It is clear from these figures that the proportion of acquittals in CPS cases in the Crown Court is higher than the acquittal rate in the magistrates' court (suggesting that defendants are, as is commonly supposed, more likely to be acquitted in the Crown Court). However, a number of points can be made about this conclusion:

- the gap between the acquittal rates of the two courts is not perhaps as high as some people might expect;
- national figures may well mask significant local variations (tough juries/lenient magistrates);
- it may well be that a number of cases which resulted in acquittal in the Crown Court would also have resulted in acquittal had they been tried in the magistrates' court; and
- considerably more either-way cases are tried in the Crown Court because the magistrates declined jurisdiction than are sent there because the defendant elected trial on indictment.

● Another factor which might be relevant to the defendant's choice as regards mode of trial is the length of time to wait for a summary trial or a trial on indictment to take place. This depends very much on local conditions, as waiting lists vary considerably.

3.4 Failure to follow correct procedure in determining mode of trial

In R v Kent Justices, ex p Machin [1952] 2 QB 355, it was held that, because the jurisdiction of magistrates' courts to try either-way offences derives solely from statute, any failure to comply with the statutory procedure laid down for determining mode of trial renders any summary trial which follows that defective procedure *ultra vires* and therefore a nullity. In R v Ashton [2006] EWCA Crim 794; [2007] 1 WLR 181 (where it was held that, in the absence of a clear indication that Parliament intended jurisdiction automatically to be removed following a procedural failure, the decision of the court should be based on an assessment of the interests of justice, with particular focus on whether there was a real possibility that the prosecution or the defendant may suffer prejudice: if that risk is present, the court should then decide whether it is just to permit the proceedings to continue) the court said that a number of authorities, including *Machin*, would have to be reconsidered (see [67]–[69]). However, in R (Rahmdezfouli) v Wood Green Crown Court [2013] EWHC 2998 (Admin); [2014] 1 WLR 1793, Mackay J (at [16]) said that where a magistrates' court failed to follow the requirements of the statutory allocation procedure, the court was acting without jurisdiction (and so the allocation proceedings, and any subsequent proceedings based on that allocation decision, would be a nullity).

3.5 Challenging a decision to accept jurisdiction

It is difficult for the prosecution to mount a challenge against a decision in favour of summary trial, since it is essentially a matter within the magistrates' discretion. An application to quash a decision to accept jurisdiction will succeed only if the magistrates' decision was so obviously wrong that no reasonable magistrate could have arrived at it (R v McLean ex p Metropolitan Police Commissioner [1975] Crim LR 289). Nevertheless, in an appropriately clear-cut case, the Divisional Court will grant judicial review. In R v Northampton Magistrates' Court ex p Commissioners of Customs and Excise [1994] Crim LR 598, for example, the accused was charged with a VAT fraud which, on the prosecution case, had caused a loss of £193,000. The magistrates decided to try him summarily and the prosecution sought judicial review. The Divisional Court said that the correct approach was to ask whether the acceptance of jurisdiction was 'truly astonishing'. Here they must have concluded that it was, as they allowed the application and remitted the matter with a direction to the magistrates to reject jurisdiction.

3.6 Changing the decision as to mode of trial

Under s.25(2) of the Magistrates' Courts Act 1980, where a magistrates' court has accepted jurisdiction and the defendant has consented to summary trial, the prosecution may apply to the court for the offence to be tried on indictment instead. This application must be made before the summary trial begins (s.25(2A)). The court may grant the application only if it is satisfied that the sentence which a magistrates' court would have power to impose for the offence(s) would be inadequate (s.25(2B)). Where the magistrates accede to the prosecution application, the case is sent to the Crown Court for trial (s.25(2D)).

3.6.1 Withdrawal of consent to summary trial

The magistrates also have a discretion to allow the defendant to withdraw consent to summary trial. The test to be applied in deciding whether to exercise this discretion in the defendant's favour was set out in R v Birmingham Justices ex p Hodgson [1985] QB 1131, and R v Highbury Corner Magistrates ex p Weekes [1985] QB 1147: did the defendant understand the 'nature and significance' of the choice that had to be made at the allocation hearing? In deciding this question, the magistrates should have regard to factors such as:

● whether the defendant knew that he had a possible defence to the charge;
● whether the defendant had access to legal advice before making the decision as to mode of trial;
● the defendant's age and apparent intelligence;
● whether the defendant has previous convictions (and so is likely to know something about criminal procedure).

It should be noted that the burden of proof lies with the defendant to show that he did not understand the nature and significance of the choice (R v Forest Magistrates ex p Spicer (1989) 153 JP 81).

Mode of trial also has to be reconsidered where the defendant successfully applies to change his plea. In R v Bow Street Magistrates ex p Welcombe (1992) 156 JP 609, it was held that if the defendant is allowed to change his plea from guilty to not guilty, he must also be given the opportunity to elect trial on indictment if he so wishes. Moreover, if the defendant entered a guilty plea and later seeks to change his plea from guilty to not guilty, the magistrates should (if they allow him to do so) also reconsider mode of trial and send him for trial if they take the view that their sentencing powers are inadequate.

3.7 Criminal damage: special provisions

Section 22 of the Magistrates' Courts Act 1980 sets out a special procedure to be applied in cases of criminal damage (excluding arson) where the value involved does not exceed the 'relevant sum' (currently £5,000).

Under s.22(2), if the amount involved does not exceed £5,000, the court must 'proceed as if the offence were triable only summarily' (and so the question of allocation does not arise). Therefore, where the value involved is £5,000 or less, the case must be tried summarily.

Under s.33 of the Magistrates' Courts Act 1980, the maximum sentence in such a case is three months' imprisonment or a fine of up to £2,500; furthermore, there can be no committal for sentence to the Crown Court under s.3 of the Powers of Criminal Courts (Sentencing) Act 2000.

If 'it appears to the court clear that, for the offence charged, the value involved exceeds the relevant sum', the court will proceed to determine mode of trial in the usual way (s.22(3)). Thus, where the value is more than £5,000, the usual allocation procedure applies. If the defendant consents to summary trial and is convicted, the usual penalties apply and committal for sentence under s.3 of the 2000 Act is possible.

Under s.22(4)–(6), if there is doubt as to whether the value involved is more or less than £5,000, the magistrates must offer the defendant the chance of summary trial. If he consents to summary trial, the trial will take place in the magistrates' court and, if he is convicted, the court will not be able to impose more than three months' imprisonment or a fine up to £2,500, and there is no power to commit for sentence under s.3 of the Powers of Criminal Courts (Sentencing) Act 2000.

It follows that the first step in a case involving criminal damage is to ascertain the 'value involved'. This is defined (in Sch.2) as the cost of repair or, if the article is damaged beyond repair, replacement. The value may be ascertained on the basis of representations by the prosecution and defence. There is no obligation on the magistrates to hear evidence as to the value, though they have a discretion to do so (R v Canterbury Justices ex p Klisiak [1982] QB 398).

Section 22(11) provides that where the accused is charged with two or more offences to which the section applies and which 'constitute or form part of a series of two or more offences of the same or a similar character', the court should take the value involved as being the aggregate of the values involved in each offence for the purpose of determining whether the special procedure applies.

Under s.22(8), where the defendant is convicted by a magistrates' court of an offence to which s.22 applies, he cannot appeal to the Crown Court against the conviction on the ground that the magistrates' decision as to the value involved was mistaken.

It must be emphasised that these special provisions apply only to criminal damage (and to offences under s.12A of the Theft Act 1968 – aggravated vehicle-taking – but only where the only aggravating feature alleged is criminal damage).

Section 17D(1) of the Magistrates' Courts Act 1980, provides that where the accused, at the plea before venue hearing, indicates a guilty plea to an offence to which s.22 applies (and so is deemed to have pleaded guilty to it), the court must consider whether, having regard to any representations made by the accused or by the prosecutor, the value involved exceeds £5,000. If it appears clear to the court that the value involved does not exceed £5,000, or it is unclear whether the value involved exceeds £5,000, the court's sentencing powers are subject to the limits set out in s.33 of the Act, and there is no power to commit for sentence.

3.8 Low-value shoplifting

Section 22A(1) of the Magistrates' Courts Act 1980 provides that 'low-value' shoplifting (defined as shoplifting where the value of the stolen goods does not exceed £200) is triable only summarily. However, s.22A(2) goes on to provide that, where a defendant who has attained the age of 18 is charged with low-value shoplifting, the court must, before the summary trial of the offence begins, give the defendant the opportunity of electing Crown Court trial for the offence; if he elects to be so tried, the magistrates' court must send him to the Crown Court for trial. Unlike the special procedure for criminal damage (under s.22), in the case of low-value shoplifting the accused retains the right to elect Crown Court trial. Rule 9.7(4)(c) of the Criminal Procedure Rules makes it clear that, where the offence is low-value shoplifting, the magistrates' court must offer the accused the opportunity to require trial in the Crown Court.

In R v Maxwell [2017] EWCA Crim 1233; [2018] 1 Cr App R 5, the court noted that, if the accused is charged (at the same time) with two or more offences of low-value shoplifting, the value is aggregated; if the total value exceeds £200, the offences are treated as ordinary either-way offences (Magistrates' Courts Act 1980, s.22A(4)(b)). However, low-value shoplifting charges cannot be aggregated with shoplifting offences to which s.22A does not apply (and so it is only the 'low-value' offences that can be aggregated). In this case, the three low-value offences came nowhere near £200 in total and so were (unless the accused elected Crown Court trial) triable only summarily.

3.9 Adjusting the charge to dictate mode of trial

It is possible for the prosecution to drop an existing charge and replace it with a new charge. Sometimes the effect of replacing one charge with another will be to replace an offence which is triable either way with one which is triable only summarily, thus depriving the accused of the possibility of Crown Court trial. In *DPP v Hammerton* [2009] EWHC 921 (Admin); [2010] QB 79, Davis J (at [30]) said that, 'where a lesser charge is to be substituted ... it must be proper and appropriate to the facts of the case'.

It is also possible for a charge which is triable either way to be replaced by an offence which is triable only on indictment. However, in *R v Brooks* [1985] Crim LR 385, the Court of Appeal warned that it would generally be unjust and wrong for the prosecution to do this if the magistrates have already accepted jurisdiction in respect of the either-way offence, since the prosecution would be frustrating that decision by changing the charge.

The Code for Crown Prosecutors says that prosecutors should select charges which:

- reflect the seriousness and extent of the offending supported by the evidence;
- give the court adequate powers to sentence and impose appropriate post-conviction orders; and
- enable the case to be presented in a clear and simple way.

The prosecutor should also bear in mind the need for the court to be able to make a confiscation order under the Proceeds of Crime Act 2002.

The Code also makes it clear that prosecutors should not change the charge simply because of the decision made by the court or the defendant about where the case will be heard (and so should not, for example, replace an either-way offence with a summary offence in order to frustrate the defendant's choice to be tried in the Crown Court).

3.10 Procedural consequences of the classification of the offence

The flow charts which follow illustrate the procedural differences which result from the classification of an offence as summary, either-way or indictable-only.

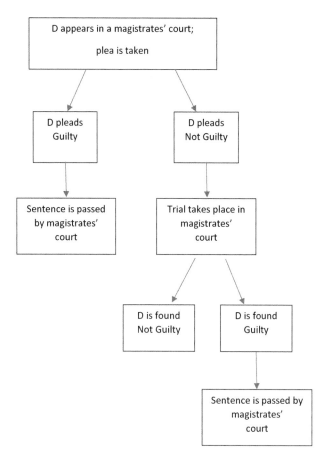

Figure 3.1 Summary offences

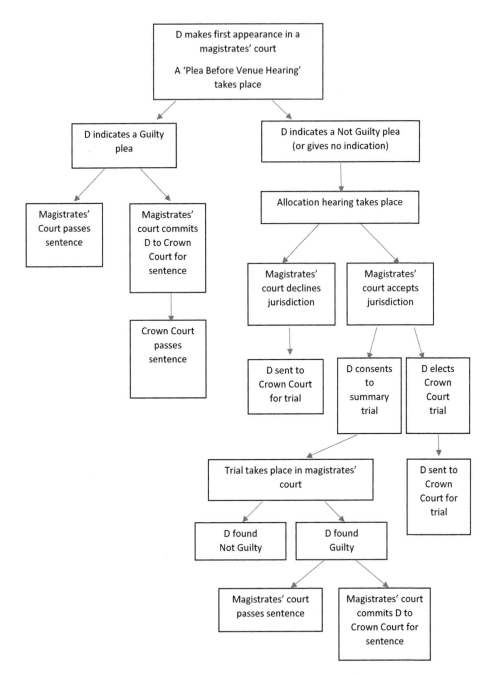

Figure 3.2 Either-way offences

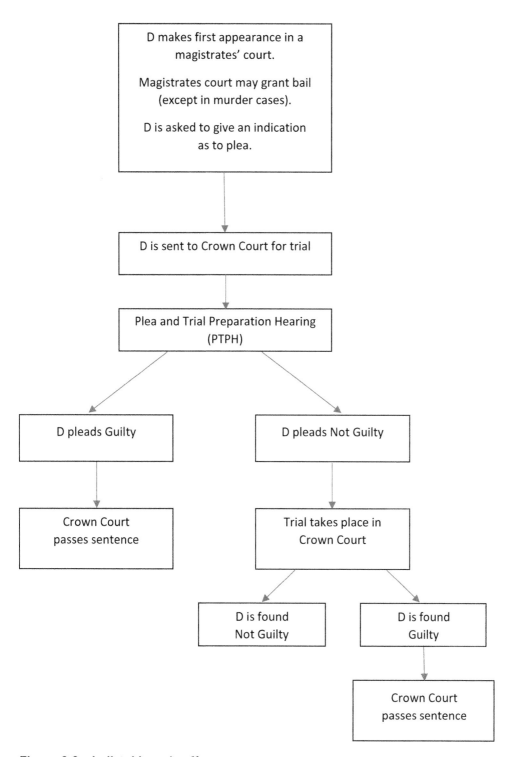

Figure 3.3 Indictable-only offences

Chapter 4

Disclosure

Chapter Contents

In this chapter, we consider various aspects of the rules relating to disclosure, including the duty of the prosecution to disclose the evidence on which it intends to rely prior to the trial, the duty of the prosecution to disclose relevant 'unused' material to the defence, and the duty of the defence to disclose their case to the prosecution.

Criminal Practice Direction IV para.15A.1 emphasises that all parties must be familiar with, and must comply with their obligations under, the *Judicial Protocol on the Disclosure of Unused Material in Criminal Cases* and the *Attorney-General's Guidelines on Disclosure*.

4.1 Initial details of the prosecution case

Rule 8.2 of the Criminal Procedure Rules requires the prosecutor to serve initial details of the prosecution case on the court (and on the defendant, if the defendant so requests) as soon as practicable and, in any event, no later than the beginning of the day of the first hearing. If the defendant does not request those details, the prosecutor must make them available to the defendant at, or before, the beginning of the day of the first hearing.

Rule 8.3 defines what has to be supplied by way of 'initial details of the prosecution case'. Where, immediately before the first hearing in the magistrates' court, the defendant is in police custody for the offence charged, initial details comprise:

- a summary of the circumstances of the offence, and
- the defendant's criminal record, if any.

If, on the other hand, the defendant is not in custody, the initial details that are supplied must *also* include:

- any account given by the defendant in interview;
- any written witness statement or exhibit that the prosecutor then has available and considers material to plea, or to the allocation of the case for trial, or to sentence;
- any available statement of the effect of the offence on a victim, a victim's family or others.

Criminal Practice Direction I, para.3A.4, states that the information supplied pursuant to CrimPR 8.3 must be sufficient to allow the accused and the court, at the first hearing, to take an informed view on plea and (where applicable) venue for trial. Paragraph 3A.12 makes the point that, if the accused is on bail and the prosecutor does not anticipate a guilty plea at the first hearing in a magistrates' court, the initial details of the prosecution case that are provided for that first hearing must be sufficient to assist the court to identify the real issues and to give appropriate directions for an effective trial (regardless of whether the trial is to be heard in the magistrates' court or the Crown Court). Moreover, by virtue of para.3A.13, as well as the material required by r.8.3, the information required by the Preparation for Effective Trial form must be available to be submitted at the first hearing, and the parties must complete that form.

In an attempt to encourage compliance with these obligations, r.8.4 states that, where the prosecutor wants to introduce information contained in a document listed in r.8.3 but has not served that document on the defendant, or otherwise made that information available to the defendant, then the court 'must not allow the prosecutor to introduce that information unless the court first allows the defendant sufficient time to consider it'.

Part 8 contains no specific sanction if the prosecution fail to supply the required initial details. However, it would be open to the magistrates' court to make a direction (under r.3.5) requiring the prosecution to comply. It should be noted that r.3.5(6)(a) provides that, if a party fails to comply with a direction given by the court, the court may (for example) adjourn the hearing. Failure on the part of the prosecution to comply with Part 8 is likely to result in an adjournment (and possibly a costs sanction under r.3.5(6)(b)). However, the court cannot dismiss the charges brought by the prosecution because of non-compliance (*King v Kucharz* (1989) 153 JP 336 and R (*AP, MD and JS*) v *Leeds Youth Court* [2001] EWHC 215 (Admin); (2001) 165 JP 684, decided under an earlier version of the Rules).

4.2 Disclosure of prosecution evidence

Where the offence is to be tried in the Crown Court, the evidence upon which the prosecution intend to rely at trial has to be served (in the form of witness statements) on the defence as part of the process (under s.51 of the Crime and Disorder Act 1998) whereby the case is transferred to the Crown Court.

Where the offence is to be tried in a magistrates' court, good practice requires that the prosecutor should provide to the defence all the evidence upon which the Crown proposes to rely. Such provision should allow the accused and their legal advisers sufficient time properly to consider the evidence before it is called.

The effect of this is to put a defendant who is being tried in the magistrates' court in the same position as one who is being tried in the Crown Court as regards obtaining copies of the statements of the people to be called as prosecution witnesses.

4.3 Prosecution disclosure of 'unused' material

Under s.1 of the Criminal Procedure and Investigations Act 1996 ('CPIA 1996'), the statutory disclosure provisions apply to all trials in the magistrates' court or youth court where the defendant pleads not guilty and to all cases being tried in the Crown Court.

4.3.1 The duty of the investigator

A system of disclosure of unused material held by the prosecution will be only as good as the investigation which was conducted by the police, since the prosecution cannot disclose material that has not been found during the investigation. Furthermore, the system depends on relevant information that is discovered during the investigation being retained and its existence accurately recorded. It is essential that the police draw up accurate schedules of the material in their possession, and that those schedules contain sufficient detail when describing that material to enable the prosecutor to make an informed judgment as to whether the material should be disclosed (and for the defence to challenge non-disclosure). The investigating officer is therefore required to retain material obtained in a criminal investigation which may be relevant to that investigation. Paragraph 17 of the *Attorney General's Guidelines on Disclosure* says:

> A fair investigation involves the pursuit of material following all reasonable lines of enquiry, whether they point towards or away from the suspect. What is 'reasonable' will depend on the context of the case. A fair investigation does not mean an endless investigation: investigators and disclosure officers must give thought to defining, and thereby limiting, the scope of their investigations, seeking the guidance of the prosecutor where appropriate.

4.3.2 The duty of disclosure

Section 3(1) of the CPIA 1996 provides that the prosecutor must:

(a) disclose to the accused any prosecution material which has not previously been disclosed to the accused and which might reasonably be considered capable of undermining the case for the prosecution against the accused or of assisting the case for the accused; or

(b) give to the accused a written statement that there is no material of a description mentioned in paragraph (a).

'Prosecution material' is defined by s.3(2) as material which 'is in the prosecutor's possession, and came into his possession in connection with the case for the prosecution against the accused', or which 'he has inspected in connection with the case for the prosecution against the accused'.

4.3.2.1 The scope of the prosecution disclosure obligations under s.3

The disclosure requirements contained in s.3 cover a wide range of material. Paragraph 6 of the *Attorney-General's Guidelines on Disclosure* says that:

In deciding whether material satisfies the disclosure test, consideration should be given among other things to:

(a) the use that might be made of it in cross-examination;

(b) its capacity to support submissions that could lead to:
  (i) the exclusion of evidence; or
  (ii) a stay of proceedings, where the material is required to allow a proper application to be made; or
  (iii) a court or tribunal finding that any public authority had acted incompatibly with the accused's rights under the ECHR; or

(c) its capacity to suggest an explanation or partial explanation of the accused's actions; or

(d) the capacity of the material to have a bearing on scientific or medical evidence in the case.

Paragraph 7 goes on to say that:

It should also be borne in mind that while items of material viewed in isolation may not be reasonably considered to be capable of undermining the prosecution case or assisting the accused, several items together can have that effect.

On the basis of this guidance, a useful rule-of-thumb test is that material ought to be disclosed if it would give the defence a useful basis for cross-examination or if it would support defence arguments that prosecution evidence is inadmissible or that the proceedings should be stayed. In R v *Makin* [2004] EWCA Crim 1607, Hooper LJ (at [30]) expressed it thus:

[T]here is an obligation to disclose material if it assists the defence by allowing the defendant to put forward a tenable case in the best possible light or if the material could assist the defence to make further enquiries and those enquiries might assist in showing the defendant's innocence or avoid a miscarriage of justice.

In R v *Mills* [1998] AC 382, the House of Lords held that the prosecution should provide the defence with a copy of the witness statement containing relevant material even if the prosecution take the view that the witness is not a credible witness.

Information which must be disclosed under s.3 includes anything that casts doubt on the reliability of a prosecution witness by undermining their credibility. So, for example, the prosecution should disclose any relevant previous convictions of their witnesses. In *Her Majesty's Advocate v Murtagh* [2009] UKPC 36; [2011] 1 AC 731 (a Scottish case, but based on disclosure rules that are very similar to those in England and Wales), Lord Hope of Craighead (at [29]) said that only previous convictions that are 'material' ought to be disclosed to the defence. His Lordship said (at [30]) that:

> Materiality in this context must depend on whether the information could have any possible bearing on the witnesses' credibility or character ... Previous convictions which would be relevant to a legitimate attack on their character or to their credibility would plainly be relevant to the accused's defence.

At [32], his Lordship said that:

> [A] conviction for an offence many years ago which was, on any view, of a trivial nature only and was not repeated would fall well outside the threshold of what was relevant. Other cases where care will need to be taken are where the conviction that might not be material was for an offence of a sensitive nature, disclosure of which could seriously affect the witness's relationship with others such as his neighbours, employer or members of his family.

The prosecution should disclose the fact that a prosecution witness has sought a reward payable on the defendant's conviction (as in *R v Rasheed* (1994) 158 JP 914).

In *R v Guney* [1998] 2 Cr App R 242, the Court of Appeal held that the defence are entitled to be informed of any convictions or disciplinary findings recorded against a police officer involved in the present case, and of any decisions by trial judges where a trial was stopped, or Court of Appeal judgments where a conviction was quashed, because of misconduct or lack of veracity of police officers who are also involved in the present case.

In *R v R* [2015] EWCA Crim 1941; [2016] 1 WLR 1872, the Court of Appeal gave detailed guidance on disclosure in cases where there is a large volume of material. The Court set out a number of key principles to govern disclosure in such cases:

- The prosecution is and must be in the driving seat at the stage of initial disclosure;
- the prosecution must then encourage dialogue and prompt engagement with the defence;
- the law is prescriptive of the result, not the method;
- the process of disclosure should be subject to robust case management by the judge, utilising the full range of case management powers;
- flexibility is critical.

Material which potentially harms the defence case does not have to be disclosed. In *R v Brown* [1998] AC 367, the prosecution had failed to disclose to the defence information which reflected on the credibility of two defence witnesses. It was held by the House of Lords that the Crown is not under a duty to disclose to the defence material which is relevant only to the credibility of defence witnesses.

In *R v DPP ex p Lee* [1999] 1 WLR 1950, the Divisional Court noted that the CPIA 1996 does not specifically address disclosure during the period between arrest and the case being sent to the Crown Court. The court said that the prosecutor must always be alive to the need to make advance disclosure of material that should be disclosed at an earlier stage. Examples given by Kennedy LJ, at p.1962, include:

- Previous convictions of a complainant or deceased if that information could reasonably be expected to assist the defence when applying for bail;

- Material which might enable a defendant to make an early application to stay the proceedings as an abuse of process;
- Material which might enable a defendant to submit that he should only be sent for trial on a lesser charge, or perhaps that he should not be sent for trial at all;
- Material which will enable the defendant and his legal advisers to make preparations for trial, which may be significantly less effective if disclosure is delayed (e.g. names of eye-witnesses who the prosecution do not intend to use).

Section 3(6) enables the prosecutor to withhold material if 'the court, on an application by the prosecutor, concludes it is not in the public interest to disclose it and orders accordingly'. The question of 'public interest immunity' is considered in detail later in this chapter. However, the key point to emphasise is that if material should be disclosed under s.3, the prosecution may withhold that material from the defence only if permitted to do so by the court.

4.3.2.2 Continuing duty of disclosure

Section 7A of the 1996 Act creates a duty to keep the question of disclosure under review as the case progresses:

(1) This section applies at all times –
   (a) after the prosecutor has complied with s.3 or purported to comply with it; and
   (b) before the accused is acquitted or convicted or the prosecutor decides not to proceed with the case concerned.
(2) The prosecutor must keep under review the question whether at any given time (and, in particular, following the giving of a defence statement) there is prosecution material which –
   (a) might reasonably be considered capable of undermining the case for the prosecution against the accused or of assisting the case for the accused; and
   (b) has not been disclosed to the accused.
(3) If at any time there is any such material as is mentioned in subs.(2) the prosecutor must disclose it to the accused.

4.4 Disclosure by the defence

Where the case is to be tried in the Crown Court, the defence are required, by s.5 of the CPIA 1996, to serve a 'defence statement'. Where the case is to be tried in a magistrates' court or youth court, service of a defence statement is voluntary (s.6 of the Act).

In the Crown Court, the defence statement must be served within 28 days of the date when the prosecution comply (or purport to comply) with the duty of disclosure under s.3 of the CPIA 1996; in the magistrates' court, if the accused chooses to serve a defence statement, this must be done within 14 days of that date (reg.2 of the Criminal Procedure and Investigations Act 1996 (Defence Disclosure Time Limits) Regulations 2011 (SI 2011/209).

Section 5(5) requires the defendant to give a defence statement to both the court and the prosecution. This content of 'defence statement' is prescribed by s.6A(1) as follows:

(1) [A] defence statement is a written statement –
   (a) setting out the nature of the accused's defence, including any particular defences on which he intends to rely;
   (b) indicating the matters of fact on which he takes issue with the prosecution;

(c) setting out, in the case of each such matter, why he takes issue with the prosecution; (ca) setting out particulars of the matters of fact on which he intends to rely for the purposes of his defence; and

(d) indicating any point of law (including any point as to the admissibility of evidence or an abuse of process) which he wishes to take, and any authority on which he intends to rely for that purpose.

4.4.1 Alibis

Section 6A(2) makes specific provision for cases where the defendant relies on an alibi:

A defence statement that discloses an alibi must give particulars of it, including –

(a) the name, address and date of birth of any witness the accused believes is able to give evidence in support of the alibi, or as many of those details as are known to the accused when the statement is given;

(b) any information in the accused's possession which might be of material assistance in identifying or finding any such witness in whose case any of the details mentioned in paragraph (a) are not known to the accused when the statement is given.

Evidence in support of an alibi is defined, by s.6A(3), as:

evidence tending to show that by reason of the presence of the accused at a particular place or in a particular area at a particular time he was not, or was unlikely to have been, at the place where the offence is alleged to have been committed at the time of its alleged commission.

Evidence amounts to alibi evidence only if it is evidence that the defendant was somewhere other than the place where the offence was allegedly committed at the relevant time; evidence that simply shows that the defendant was not present at the commission of the offence is not alibi evidence (R v Johnson [1995] 2 Cr App R 1).

The particulars of an alibi should set out where the defendant claims to have been at the relevant time even if the only evidence in support of that alibi is to come from the defendant himself (cf. R v Jackson [1973] Crim LR 356). Moreover, in Joseph Hill Solicitors (Wasted Costs Order [2013] EWCA Crim 775; [2014] 1 WLR 786, Openshaw J (at [34]) said:

The statutory obligation to give the name and address of an alibi witness is triggered by the defendant's belief that the witness is able to give evidence in support of the alibi. It is not necessary that the alibi witness can give such evidence let alone that he or she is also willing to do so. Nor is the defendant's belief in the witness's ability to give evidence dependent on the witness giving a proof of evidence.

It should be noted that the defence of alibi applies only to offences that are linked to a particular time and place. In R v Hassan [1970] 1 QB 423, for example, the defendant was charged with living off immoral earnings and claimed in his defence that he was out of the country at the time he was alleged to have been so doing. This defence was held not to amount to an alibi because the allegation was not specific to a particular place. The court said that the definition of an alibi contemplated the commission of an offence at a particular place; the present offence was not anchored to any particular location.

An alibi is concerned with the defendant's whereabouts at the time when the offence is alleged to have been committed. Evidence as to his whereabouts on another occasion does not amount to alibi evidence (R v Lewis [1969] 2 QB 1). However, in R v Fields and Adams [1991] Crim LR 38, the defendant was allegedly seen twice by a prosecution witness, once during the robbery with which he was charged and once three hours before the robbery. The defendant had no alibi for the time of the robbery itself but said that three hours before the robbery he was 25 miles away and so could not have been the person seen by the witness. This was held to amount to an alibi even though it did not relate to the time of the offence itself. This decision of the Court of Appeal may be justified on the basis that the two sightings were very close together in time and that they were inextricably linked, given the evidence of the witness; also, that the person seen three hours before the robbery was at the scene in order to prepare for the robbery and so his presence there could (loosely) be said to be part of the robbery itself.

4.4.2 Drafting defence statements

Defence statements are normally drafted by the accused's solicitor, since counsel may not be involved during the early stages of the case. However, counsel will sometimes be instructed to draft a defence statement. In any event, it is important that the client understands the importance of the accuracy and adequacy of the defence statement, and has had the opportunity of carefully considering and approve the statement before it is sent to the prosecution and the court.

Even though it is desirable that the defendant should sign the defence statement (R v Wheeler (2000) 164 JP 565), the court has no power to impose a requirement that a defence statement be signed personally by the defendant (R (Sullivan) v Maidstone Crown Court [2002] EWHC 967; [2002] 1 WLR 2747).

Section 6E(1) of the 1996 Act provides that where a solicitor purports to give a defence statement on behalf of the accused, the statement shall, unless the contrary is proved, be deemed to be given with the authority of the accused.

Section 6E(4) of the CPIA increases the importance of the defence statement by empowering the judge to direct that a copy of the defence statement (edited, if necessary, to remove any inadmissible evidence) be shown to the jury. Under subs.(5), such a direction may be given of the judge's own motion or on the application of any party; however, the direction may be made only if the judge is of the opinion that seeing a copy of the defence statement would help the jury to understand the case or to resolve any issue in the case.

In R v Rochford [2010] EWCA Crim 1928; [2011] 1 WLR 534, the Court of Appeal considered the advice which should be given to an accused about the duty to provide a defence statement. Hughes LJ (at [22]) said:

Can the lawyer properly advise a defendant not to file a defence statement? The answer to that is 'No'. The obligation to file a defence statement is a statutory obligation on the defendant. It is not open to a lawyer to advise his client to disobey the client's statutory obligation. It is as simple as that.

His Lordship continued, at [24]–[25]:

What is the duty of the lawyer if the defendant has no positive case to advance at trial but declines to plead guilty? ... The defence statement must say that the defendant does not admit the offence ... and calls for the Crown to prove it. But it must also say that he advances no positive case because if he is going to advance a positive case that must appear in the defence statement and notice of it must be given ... Accordingly, in all those circumstances the lawyer's duty is first of all never to advise either the absence of a defence statement or the omission from it of something which section 6A requires to be there because of the way the trial is going to be conducted ... The lawyer's duty is to explain the statutory obligation that he has and to explain the consequences which follow from disobedience of it.

4.4.3 Disclosure of expert evidence

Under r.19.3(3) of the Criminal Procedure Rules, a party who wants to introduce expert evidence must serve a report by the expert which complies with r.19.4 (which sets out the rules governing such reports) on the court and on each other party. This obligation applies equally to the defence and the prosecution.

4.4.4 Notification of intention to call defence witnesses

Section 6C(1) of the CPIA 1996 provides:

The accused must give to the court and the prosecutor a notice indicating whether he intends to call any persons (other than himself) as witnesses at his trial and, if so –

(a) giving the name, address and date of birth of each such proposed witness, or as many of those details as are known to the accused when the notice is given;

(b) providing any information in the accused's possession which might be of material assistance in identifying or finding any such proposed witness in whose case any of the details mentioned in paragraph (a) are not known to the accused when the notice is given.

Under s.6C(4), the accused has to serve an amended notice if he decides to call someone who is not identified on the notice that has been served.

The notice under s.6C is mandatory whether the case is being tried in the Crown Court or the magistrates' court. In Crown Court cases, it has to be served within 28 days of the date when the prosecution comply (or purport to comply) with s.3; in magistrates' court cases, it must be served within 14 days of that date (reg.2 of the Criminal Procedure and Investigations Act 1996 (Defence Disclosure Time Limits) Regulations 2011 (SI 2011/209).

The proposal that the defence should have to reveal details of their witnesses to the prosecution was a cause of some concern. It is likely that, at least in serious cases, the police will want to interview some or all of the witnesses who are named, and there is a risk that the witnesses may thereby be put off from testifying. In an attempt to allay these fears, s.21A(1) of the 1996 Act requires the Secretary of State to publish a Code of Practice which gives guidance to police officers (and other people who are responsible for investigating offences) in respect of arranging and conducting interviews of defence witnesses.

Safeguards in the Code include requirements that the witness must be asked whether he consents to being interviewed, that he must be informed that he is not obliged to attend the interview, and that he is entitled to be accompanied by a solicitor (para.3.1). It should be noted, however, that public funding for the attendance of a solicitor is unlikely to be forthcoming.

Paragraph 4.1 of the Code requires the investigator to inform the accused (or his legal representative, if he has one) if an interview has been requested and whether the witness has agreed to be interviewed. Under para.6, if the witness has consented to the presence of the accused's solicitor, the solicitor must be notified that the interview is taking place and be invited to observe.

A witness who consents to being interviewed must be asked whether he consents to a solicitor attending the interview on behalf of the accused (para.3.2), and the witness can, at any time, withdraw consent to the presence of the accused's solicitor (para.8.1). The accused's solicitor may attend only as an observer (para.8.2), and so is not entitled to intervene if, for example, the police put inappropriate questions to the witness.

Under para.3.2 of the Code, a witness who consents to being interviewed must also be asked whether he consents to a copy of the record of the interview being sent to the accused.

It follows from this that, if the witness withholds consent, the defendant's solicitor cannot attend the interview and the defendant will not receive a record of the interview.

For a critique of these provisions, see Peter Hungerford-Welch, *Prosecution interviews of defence witnesses* [2010] Crim LR 690–701.

4.4.6 Summary trial: voluntary disclosure by defence

Where the defendant is to be tried in the magistrates' court (or, if a juvenile, the youth court), s.6 of the CPIA 1996 makes provision for voluntary disclosure by the defence.

Section 6(2) provides that, if the defendant gives a defence statement to the prosecutor, it must also be given to the court.

The incentive for the defence to make disclosure even though it is not compulsory is that, if they do so, this will assist the prosecution to identify any material which has not been disclosed thus far and which might assist the defence. In effect, it triggers a review under s.7A.

4.4.7 Sanctions for failure to comply with defence disclosure obligations

The sanction for non-compliance with the defence disclosure obligations is set out in s.11 of the CPIA 1996. Section 11 applies where the defendant:

- fails to give a defence statement where one is required under s.5 (Crown Court cases); or
- provides a defence statement but does so late; or
- sets out inconsistent defences in the defence statement; or
- at the trial, puts forward a defence which was not mentioned in his defence statement or is different from any defence set out in that statement; or
- at the trial, relies on a matter which was not mentioned in his defence statement but which should have been so mentioned; or
- at the trial, adduces evidence in support of an alibi without having given particulars of the alibi in the defence statement; or
- at the trial, calls an alibi witness without having given appropriate notice of the alibi, or details of that particular witness, in the defence statement; or
- gives a witness notice (under s.6C) but does so late; or
- at the trial, calls a witness who was not included, or not adequately identified, in a witness notice.

Where s.11 applies:

- the court or any other party may make such comment as appears appropriate;
- the court or jury may draw such inferences as appear proper in deciding whether the accused is guilty of the offence concerned.

Where the accused puts forward a defence which is different from any defence set out in his defence statement, the court must have regard to the extent of the differences in the defences, and whether there is any justification for it. Where the accused calls a witness whom he has failed to include, or to identify adequately, in a witness notice, the court must have regard to whether there is any justification for the failure.

Crucially, a defendant cannot be convicted of an offence solely on an inference drawn under s.11.

The list of sanctions in s.11 is exhaustive. For example, a defendant does not lose his entitlement to disclosure under the CPIA 1996 merely because defence statement is served out of time (*Murphy v DPP* [2006] EWHC 1753 (Admin)).

In *R (Tinnion) v Reading Crown Court* [2009] EWHC 2930 (Admin); (2010) 174 JP 36, the defendant was being tried in the Crown Court (by way of an appeal from the youth court). The judge refused to allow the defendant to call two alibi witnesses because no notice had been given to the Crown of the intention to call those two witnesses as alibi witnesses (and they had not been named by the defendant when he was interviewed by the police). Given that the trial was an appeal from a summary trial, the provision of a defence statement would have been voluntary (under s.6 of the 1996 Act). However, David Clarke J ([8]) said that:

> Even if the Recorder had been right to hold that the claimant was under a requirement to provide a defence statement, either in the Youth Court or in the Crown Court on appeal, with details of his alibi witnesses, it does not follow that the failure to comply with this requirement rendered the evidence inadmissible. The sanction against a defendant who fails to give such notice is not that a witness cannot be called, but that adverse comment can be made and cross-examination can be conducted, and that the court or jury may draw such inference as is proper from the failure to give such notice.

It followed that the Crown Court had no power to prevent the witnesses being called, and so the Divisional Court directed the appeal be reheard before a different judge and justices.

In *R v Rochford* [2010] EWCA Crim 1928; [2011] 1 WLR 534, the Crown Court judge regarded failure to provide a defence statement that satisfied the requirements of s.6A as being contempt of court. The Court of Appeal disagreed. Hughes LJ ([18]) said:

> The sanction for non-compliance is explicit in the statute in s.11. It is not open to the court to add an additional extra-statutory sanction of punishment for contempt of court.

It is clear from this case law that the only sanctions for non-compliance are those set out in s.11.

4.4.8 Defence application for disclosure

Section 8(1) and (2) of the CPIA 1996 provide that, where the accused has given a defence statement under s.5 or 6 and has, at any time, reasonable cause to believe that there is prosecution material which should have been disclosed to him but which has not been disclosed, he may apply to the court for an order requiring the prosecution to disclose it to him. It is, however, open to the prosecutor to argue that disclosure is not in the public interest, in which case the court may authorise the withholding of the material from the defence (s.8(5)).

4.4.9 Third-party disclosure

Sometimes material that may support the defence case is in the hands of a third party. For example, the accused might be charged with a sexual offence involving a child, and the child's school, or the relevant social services department, might have records of false allegations made by the child who is the alleged victim of the offence (as in *R v Brushett* [2001] Crim LR 471).

If material remains in the hands of the third party, then the accused is obviously entitled to request it. If the third party is not prepared to hand it over, then the accused can seek a witness summons (using the procedure laid down by s.2 of the Criminal Procedure (Attendance of Witnesses) Act 1965 in Crown Court cases, or s.97 of the Magistrates' Courts Act 1980 in magistrates' court cases). The accused would have to be able to show that the third party is likely to be able to give or produce material evidence in the case, and that it is in the interests of justice to issue a summons.

4.5 Public interest immunity

Sections 3(6) (initial duty of disclosure) and 7A(8) (continuing duty of disclosure) of the CPIA 1996 enable the prosecutor to withhold material that would normally have to be disclosed if the court, on an application by the prosecutor, concludes that it is not in the public interest to disclose it and orders accordingly. For these purposes, the relevant court is the court in which the defendant is to be tried (so the magistrates' court has no jurisdiction in respect of disclosure once the defendant has been sent to the Crown Court for trial: R v CPS ex p Warby (1994) 158 JP 190). Public interest immunity ('PII') is similarly relevant under s.8(5), being a defence to an application for disclosure.

A common example of a case where PII is raised is where the prosecution wish to protect the identity of an informant whom the prosecutor does not intend to call as a witness at the trial (as in R v Turner [1995] 1 WLR 264). A similar example is where the police wish to keep secret the location of an observation post from which they were watching the movements of the accused (as in R v Johnson [1988] 1 WLR 1377).

The essence of the PII provisions in the CPIA 1996 is that, if material should otherwise be disclosed because it undermines the prosecution case or assists the defence case, that material must be disclosed to the defence *unless* the court gives permission for it to be withheld from the defence.

4.5.1 Principles underpinning public interest immunity

In Jasper v UK (2000) 30 EHRR 441, the European Court of Human Rights said (at [51]) that Art.6 (1) of the European Convention on Human Rights requires that 'the prosecution authorities should disclose to the defence all material evidence in their possession for or against the accused'. However, the Court went on to note (at [52]) that it is not only the interests of the accused that have to be taken into account. It follows that:

> the entitlement to disclosure of relevant evidence is not an absolute right. In any criminal proceedings there may be competing interests, such as national security or the need to protect witnesses at risk of reprisals or keep secret police methods of investigation of crime, which must be weighed against the rights of the accused ... In some cases it may be necessary to withhold certain evidence from the defence so as to preserve the fundamental rights of another individual or to safeguard an important public interest. However, only such measures restricting the rights of the defence which are strictly necessary are permissible under Article 6§1 ... Moreover, in order to ensure that the accused receives a fair trial, any difficulties caused to the defence by a limitation on its rights must be sufficiently counter-balanced by the procedures followed by the judicial authorities ....

The leading case on the principles to be applied where public interest immunity is claimed were set out by the House of Lords in R v H [2004] UKHL 3; [2004] 2 AC 134. Lord Bingham of Cornhill said (at [18]) that 'derogation from the golden rule of full disclosure may be justified but such derogation must always be the minimum derogation necessary to protect the public interest in question and must never imperil the overall fairness of the trial'.

His Lordship emphasised (at [35]) that material only has to be disclosed to the defence if it is relevant:

> If material does not weaken the prosecution case or strengthen that of the defendant, there is no requirement to disclose it ... Neutral material or material damaging to the defendant need not be disclosed and should not be brought to the attention of the court. Only in truly borderline cases should the prosecution seek a judicial ruling on the disclosability of material in its hands.

Lord Bingham went on to give detailed guidance on how the courts should approach PII hearings (at [36]):

- Is the material such as may weaken the prosecution case or strengthen the defence case?
  - No: disclosure should not be ordered.
  - Yes: full disclosure should (subject to PII) be ordered.
- Is there a real risk of serious prejudice to an important public interest if full disclosure of the material is ordered?
  - No: full disclosure should be ordered.
  - Yes: can the defendant's interest be protected without disclosure, or can disclosure be ordered to such an extent or in such a way which will give adequate protection to the public interest in question and also afford adequate protection to the interests of the defence? For example, through summaries of evidence or the provision of documents in edited or anonymised form. The court should order such disclosure as will represent the 'minimum derogation from the golden rule of full disclosure'.
  - If limited disclosure may render the trial process unfair to the defendant, fuller disclosure should be ordered 'even if this leads or may lead the prosecution to discontinue the proceedings so as to avoid having to make disclosure'.

Even if the judge rules in favour of non-disclosure or limited disclosure, the position may change during the course of the trial, so the court has to keep the question of disclosure under review during the trial.

4.5.2 Procedure for determining public interest immunity claims

The procedure where the prosecution seek permission to withhold material from the defence on the basis of PII is set out in r.15.3 of the Criminal Procedure Rules. This procedure is based largely on the procedure set out, prior to the 1996 Act, in R v Ward [1993] 1 WLR 619 and R v Davis [1993] 1 WLR 613 at 617–18. The Court of Appeal identified three classes of case, which Lord Bingham of Cornhill, in R v H [2004] UKHL 3; [2004] 2 AC 134, summarised (at [20]) thus:

- Cases where the prosecution give notice to the defence that they are applying for a ruling, and indicate to the defence at least the category of the material to which the application relates, and the defence then have the opportunity to make representations to the court. This category comprises 'most of the cases in which a PII issue arises'.
- Cases where disclosure even of the category of material would be tantamount to revealing whatever it is that the prosecution are seeking not to disclose: the prosecution should still notify the defence of the application, but need not specify the category of material; in such a case, the

application will take place in the absence of the accused and his representatives, although it would be open to the defence to make representations (usually in writing) to the judge.

● Cases where the public interest would be injured even by disclosure that an application is being made: in such cases, the application to the court is made without notice to the defence. These cases are 'highly exceptional'; if the court considers that the case should be treated as falling within the second or the first class, it will so order.

If the public interest in non-disclosure is then outweighed by the need to order disclosure in the interests of securing fairness to the defendant, the prosecution will have to decide whether to disclose the material in question or to offer no further evidence in the case.

4.5.2.1 Use of 'special counsel' in PII applications

In R v H the House of Lords also considered the potential role for 'special independent counsel', appointed by the Attorney General, in PII hearings. Such a 'special advocate' was described by Lord Bingham (at [21]) as being someone who is appointed 'to protect the interests of a party against whom an adverse order may be made and who cannot (either personally or through his legal representative), for security reasons, be fully informed of all the material relied on against him', and who 'may not disclose to the subject of the proceedings the secret material disclosed to him, and is not in the ordinary sense professionally responsible to that party, but who, subject to those constraints, is charged to represent that party's interests'. However, his Lordship said ([22]):

> Such an appointment will always be exceptional, never automatic ... It should not be ordered unless and until the trial judge is satisfied that no other course will adequately meet the overriding requirement of fairness to the defendant.

4.6 Shortcomings in the disclosure regime

In July 2018, the Parliamentary Justice Committee published the report of its findings following an enquiry into failures in the system of disclosure. The report noted that it had been widely acknowledged for some time that there are persistent problems with the practice of disclosure (at [22]). A number of earlier reports had highlighted problems with the disclosure regime, including:

2011: *Review of Disclosure in Criminal Proceedings*, Lord Justice Gross, September 2011
2012: *Further review of disclosure in criminal proceedings: sanctions for disclosure failure*, Lord Justice Gross and Lord Justice Treacy, November 2012
2014: *Magistrates' Court Disclosure Review*, Lord Justice Gross, May 2014
2015: *Review of Efficiency in Criminal Proceedings*, Sir Brian Leveson President of the Queen's Bench Division, January 2015
2017: *Making it fair a Joint Inspection of Disclosure of Unused Material in Volume Crown Court Cases*, The Criminal Justice Joint Inspectorate, HM Inspectorate of Constabulary, Fire and Rescue Services, and HM Crown Prosecution Service Inspectorate, July 2017.

Subsequently, in November 2018, the Attorney General's *Review of the efficiency and effectiveness of disclosure in the criminal justice system* was published.

All of these reports, together with enquiries into failings in particular cases, highlighted serious shortcomings in the disclosure regime. It is possible to discern a number of underlying themes from these reports.

First and foremost, it is essential that disclosure be seen as an integral part of the criminal process, not something to be added on at the end as an afterthought: it is fundamental to the fairness of that process.

It is therefore important that police officers investigating alleged offences keep an open mind and do not dismiss as irrelevant evidence that points away from the person they suspect to be guilty of the offence. It is in some ways counter-intuitive to be looking for evidence that points away from the suspect when trying to build a case against that suspect, but that is what fairness demands. Investigating officers need to be aware of the risk of 'confirmation bias' (the tendency to accept information that confirms the correctness of one's opinions whilst ignoring, or rejecting, information that casts doubt on those opinions).

A particular challenge is created by the sheer volume of material that can be collected during an investigation. This is not a feature confined to major financial and economic crime investigations. Downloading material from mobile phones (for example in cases of alleged sexual offences or assaults) generates a very significant amount of material. It can take a very long time indeed to sift through this material to see whether there is any of relevance in it. In such cases, the investigating officers are required by para. 3.5 of the CPIA Code of Practice to 'pursue all reasonable lines of inquiry, whether these point towards or away from the suspect'; what is a reasonable line of inquiry is necessarily a decision that is 'fact specific in each and every case' (see R v E [2018] EWCA Crim 2426, at [23]).

It is also very important that the schedule of unused material that is supplied to the CPS by the police describes the material accurately (otherwise, the Crown Prosecutor is unable to assess correctly whether that material ought to be disclosed to the defence).

Resourcing is, of course, key. In an under-funded system, the burden on the police, the CPS and defence lawyers makes it very difficult for disclosure to be approached as thoroughly as it should be. This leads to a very serious risk of miscarriages of justice taking place.

For a discussion of some of these issues, see Tom Smith, The 'near miss' of Liam Allan: critical problems in police disclosure, investigation culture and the resourcing of criminal justice [2018] Crim LR 711–731 and Ian Dennis, Prosecution disclosure: are the problems insoluble? [2018] Crim LR 829–842.

Chapter 5

Summary Trial

In this chapter we look at summary trial in magistrates' courts.

5.1 Territorial jurisdiction

Section 2(1) of the Magistrates' Courts Act 1980 provides that a magistrates' court 'has jurisdiction to try any summary offence'. Under s.2(3), a magistrates' court 'has jurisdiction to try summarily any offence which is triable either way' (assuming the allocation hearing results in a decision in favour of summary trial).

5.2 Time limits

There are no time limits applicable to indictable (including either-way) offences. However, proceedings in respect of a summary offence must be started within six months of the commission of the offence, unless the statute creating the offence provides otherwise (s.127 of the Magistrates' Courts Act 1980). Where a statute creates a continuing summary offence, a prosecution can be brought at any time until six months have elapsed from the date when the offence ceased to be committed (*British Telecommunications plc v Nottinghamshire CC* [1999] Crim LR 217).

In *Atkinson v DPP* [2004] EWHC 1457; [2005] 1 WLR 96, it was held that where there is uncertainty as to whether proceedings have been commenced in time, the question should be determined according to the criminal burden and standard of proof, and so the magistrates should decline to hear the matter unless satisfied so that they are sure that the proceedings were started in time.

5.3 The contents of the charge

Rule 7.3(1) of the Criminal Procedure Rules provides that the charge must contain:

(a) a statement of the offence that –
    (i) describes the offence in ordinary language; and
    (ii) identifies any legislation that creates it; and
(b) such particulars of the conduct constituting the commission of the offence as to make clear what the prosecutor alleges against the defendant.

A single charge should allege just one offence, but r.7.3(2) says that:

More than one incident of the commission of the offence may be included in the allegation if those incidents taken together amount to a course of conduct having regard to the time, place or purpose of commission.

A charge which alleges more than one offence but which does not fall within the proviso created by r.7.3(2) will be 'duplicitous' and ought to be amended. A charge would be duplicitous if, for example, the defendant to be were charged with receiving stolen goods and another form of handling stolen goods in the same charge. However, because of r.7.3(2), a series of acts may amount to a single offence if those acts constitute a course of conduct; for example, stealing a number of items from a supermarket would be charged as a single allegation of theft, since it may fairly be described as comprising one single activity (*Heaton v Costello* (1984) 148 JP 688). In *DPP v McCabe* (1993) 157 JP 443, a single charge alleging theft of 76 library books over a period of a year was held not to be duplicitous. Similarly, in *Barton v DPP* [2001] EWHC Admin 223; (2001)

165 JP 779, the defendant was accused of taking sums of money, on 94 occasions, totalling of £1,338. The Divisional Court held that it was a 'continuous offence', so the charge was not duplicitous. The court noted that this was not a case where the accused had put forward a specific answer to some of the alleged takings and not to others, requiring the specific answers to be considered separately.

5.4 Case management

As we saw in Chapter 1, active case management is seen as fundamental to achieving the overriding objective.

5.4.1 Active case management

There is a Preparation for Effective Trial form for use in the magistrates' courts. Completion of this form assists with case management, and it requires the issues in the case to be identified, together with the witnesses who will testify in respect of those issues. This in turns helps with the construction of a timetable for the trial. During the trial, the court must ensure that the evidence, questions, and submissions are strictly directed to the relevant disputed issues.

In *Drinkwater v Solihull Magistrates' Court* [2012] EWHC 765 (Admin); (2012) 176 JP 401, Sir John Thomas P emphasised the importance of active case management in magistrates' courts:

> [50] In setting the timetable, the court should scrutinise the reasons why it is said a witness is necessary and the time examination and cross-examination would take. It is also important in setting a timetable to have regard to the nature of the issues and the fact that the trial is a summary trial; any estimate of more than a day in the Magistrates' Courts should be scrutinised with the utmost rigour. Parties must realise that a summary trial requires a proportionate approach. If a timetable for the trial is not set, it is difficult to have any real confidence that the estimate is accurate.
>
> [51] At the commencement of the trial, the Magistrates' Court should check with the parties that the timetable and the estimates remain valid. If there is any variation which lengthens the estimate, the court should make every effort to see if the trial can still be accommodated that day by sitting late or otherwise.
>
> [52] Once the trial has started, the court must actively manage the trial, keeping an eye on progress in relation to the timetable ...
>
> [54] The consequences of the failure of setting a timetable and actively managing a case in the Magistrates' Courts can be much more serious in a particular case than in the Crown Court. In the Crown Court if a trial does not conclude within the estimate, the case will continue on the following day ... In the Magistrates' Court, it is often not possible for a case to continue the following day ... particularly given the commitments of the Magistrates and other business that has been scheduled for succeeding days ... A delay in the middle of a case for a period of two to three weeks is plainly inimical to the principles of speedy and summary justice. It is ... essential that the closest attention is paid to timetabling, that the case is actively managed and concluded within the estimate.

In R (Firth) v Epping Justices [2011] EWHC 388 (Admin); [2011] 1 WLR 1818, it was held that the magistrates were entitled to treat an assertion of self-defence in the case management form as an admission by the defence that the accused was present at the scene of the offence. However, this decision must be seen in the light of R v Newell [2012] EWCA Crim 650; (2012) 176 JP 273, where Sir John Thomas P (at [35]), said that:

The Trial Preparation Form ... should be completed at the first hearing. It provides for the making of admissions or the acknowledgement that matters are not in issue. Where admissions are made in that way they will be admissible at the trial. Where statements are made on the form which are not made under the section relating to admissions, such statements should be made without the risk that they would be used at trial as statements of the defendant admissible in evidence against the defendant, provided the advocate follows the letter and the spirit of the Criminal Procedure Rules.

In *Valiati v DPP* [2018] EWHC 2908 (Admin), the Divisional Court again considered the admissibility of admissions made in Preparation for Effective Trial forms in magistrates' courts, holding that, if the defence fail to comply with the obligation to identify the issues in the case, such admissions could (if the prosecution make the appropriate application) be admissible as hearsay evidence, subject to the power to exclude evidence under s.78 of the Police and Criminal Evidence Act 1984. Sir Brian Leveson P reiterated (at [15]-[16]) that requiring a defendant to identify the issues (so that any trial can be conducted efficiently and expeditiously) 'does not offend the twin principles that the prosecution must prove its case and that a defendant is not obliged to inculpate himself'.

Criminal Practice Direction VI, para.24B.4, summarises the position thus:

The identification of issues at the case management stage will have been made without the risk that they would be used at trial as statements of the defendant admissible in evidence against the defendant, provided the advocate follows the letter and the spirit of the Criminal Procedure Rules. The court may take the view that a party is not acting in the spirit of the Criminal Procedure Rules in seeking to ambush the other party or raising late and technical legal arguments that were not previously raised as issues. No party that seeks to ambush the other at trial should derive an advantage from such a course of action. The court may also take the view that a defendant is not acting in the spirit of the Criminal Procedure Rules if he or she refuses to identify the issues and puts the prosecutor to proof at the case management stage. In both such circumstances the court may limit the proceedings on the day of trial in accordance with CrimPR 3.11(d). In addition any significant divergence from the issues identified at case management at this late stage may well result in the exercise of the court's powers under CrimPR 3.5(6), the powers to impose sanctions.

This is consistent with the approach required under the Criminal Procedure Rules, namely that the issues in the case should be identified prior to the start of the trial, so that the trial can focus exclusively on the matters that are in dispute.

5.4.2 Power to make pre-trial rulings

Section 8A(4) of the Magistrates' Courts Act 1980 empowers magistrates to make binding rulings on:

(a) any question as to the admissibility of evidence;
(b) any other question of law relating to the case.

These provisions apply to summary offences, and either-way offences that are to be tried summarily, where the accused has pleaded not guilty; the power is exercisable at any stage up to the start of the trial once the accused has entered a not guilty plea (s.8A(1)). A ruling may be made following an application by a party to the case, or of the court's own motion (s.8A(6)). Under s.8A(3), a pre-trial ruling may only be given if it is in the interests of justice to do so and if the court has given the parties an opportunity to be heard. When the accused is unrepresented but wishes to be represented, the court must ask if he wishes to apply for legal aid and, if so, must enable him to apply for it (s.8A(5)).

A pre-trial ruling made by a magistrates' court remains binding until the case against the accused or, if there is more than one, against each of them, is disposed of (s.8B(1)). The case is disposed of when the accused is convicted or acquitted, or is sent to the Crown Court for trial (s.8B(2) and (6)).

The magistrates' court may discharge or vary a pre-trial ruling on application by a party to the case or of its own motion, so long as the court has given the parties an opportunity to be heard and it is in the interests of justice to discharge or vary the ruling (s.8B(3) and (4)). An application for the discharge or variation of an order may be made only if there has been a material change of circumstances since the ruling was made or, if a previous application has been made, since the application (or last application) was made (subs.(5)).

There is no separate right of appeal against a pre-trial ruling (if the accused is ultimately convicted, he can appeal to the Crown Court in the usual way; in the case of an acquittal, the prosecution could ask the magistrates to state a case to the Divisional Court).

The power to vary pre-trial rulings was considered in R (CPS) v *Gloucester Justices* [2008] EWHC 1488 (Admin); (2008) 172 JP 506. MacKay J, construing s.8B, said (at [10] and [12]):

> It appears ... on a strict reading of this section, that where the court acts of its own motion to vary a previous ruling, the grounds for discharge or variation are simply the interests of justice, and where an application is made by a party, there is an additional requirement for proof of material change of circumstances ...
>
> I for my part find it difficult, indeed impossible, to accept that it can be in the interests of justice for the same court to feel free, in effect, to annul or discharge its own earlier ruling without there being some compelling reason, such as changed circumstances or fresh evidence, so to do. I would not regard it as being in the interests of justice for one bench to set aside a previous bench's ruling previously because on the same material it thought it would reach a different conclusion.

5.4.3 'Special measures' directions

An application can be made under s.19 of the Youth Justice and Criminal Evidence Act 1999 for 'special measures' to assist witnesses to testify. These measures are also applicable in the Crown Court, and are dealt with in Chapter 10, when we look at Crown Court trial.

5.4.4 Preparation for Trial Hearings

Rule 3.27(1)(a) requires the magistrates' court to conduct a Preparation for Trial Hearing unless the defendant is sent to the Crown Court for trial or a trial is not expected to place. Rule 3.27(1)(b) enables the magistrates' court to conduct a further pre-trial case management hearing (and if necessary more than one such hearing) only where:

(i)   the court anticipates a guilty plea,
(ii) it is necessary to conduct such a hearing in order to give directions for an effective trial, or
(iii) such a hearing is required to set ground rules for the conduct of the questioning of a witness or defendant.

At a preparation for trial hearing the court must give directions for an effective trial (r.3.27(2)).

Rule 3.27(3) states that, at the preparation for trial hearing, the court must (if the defendant is present:

(a) satisfy itself that there has been explained to the defendant, in terms the defendant can understand (with help, if necessary), that the defendant will receive credit for a guilty plea;

(b) take the defendant's plea or if no plea can be taken then find out whether the defendant is likely to plead guilty or not guilty; and

(c) unless the defendant pleads guilty, satisfy itself that there has been explained to the defendant, in terms the defendant can understand (with help, if necessary), that at the trial—

   (i) the defendant will have the right to give evidence after the court has heard the prosecution case,

   (ii) if the defendant does not attend, the trial is likely to take place in the defendant's absence, and

   (iii) where the defendant is released on bail, failure to attend court when required is an offence for which the defendant may be arrested and punished and bail may be withdrawn.

5.5 Securing the attendance of witnesses

Section 97(1) of the Magistrates' Courts Act 1980 empowers a magistrate (or a clerk) to issue a witness summons if satisfied that a person is 'likely to be able to give material evidence' (or produce any document or other item of evidence that is likely to be material evidence) at a summary trial and that it is in the interests of justice to issue a witness summons to secure the attendance of the witness.

'Material evidence' means evidence of some value to the party seeking the order. In *R v Peterborough Magistrates' Court ex p Willis* (1987) 151 JP 785, it was held that a witness summons should not be issued to enable someone to find out whether the witness can give any material evidence, as there has to be material before the court on which it may be satisfied that the witness will be able to give material evidence. Similarly, before the magistrate (or clerk) can issue a summons requiring the production of documents or other items of evidence under s.97, he must be satisfied that the person is likely to be able to produce the requested documents, and that the documents contain material evidence (that is, evidence which is both relevant and admissible). It is for the party who seeks the production of the documents to adduce evidence which satisfies the magistrate that there is a real possibility that the documents are material.

Documents which are requested merely for the purpose of possible cross-examination are not material (see *R v Reading Justices ex p Berkshire County Council* [1996] 1 Cr App R 239). Moreover, the applicant must be able to show that the item to be produced would be admissible evidence and not, for example, subject to legal professional privilege (*R v Derby Magistrates' Court ex p B* [1996] AC 487).

Where it has been established by evidence given on oath that the witness is likely to be able to give material evidence, and it is probable that a summons would not procure the attendance of the witness, the magistrate (but not a clerk) may, instead of issuing a summons, issue a warrant for the arrest of the witness (s.97(2)).

Under s.97(2B), the magistrate may refuse to issue a witness summons if not satisfied that an application for the summons has been made as soon as reasonably practicable after the accused pleaded not guilty.

Section 97(3) deals with the situation where the witness fails to attend, despite the issue of a witness summons. If the court is satisfied by evidence given on oath that the witness is likely to be able to give material evidence (or produce any document likely to be material evidence), and it is proved that he has been served with the summons in the manner prescribed by Part 4 of the

Criminal Procedure Rules (the procedure for service of a witness summons is the same as that for service of any summons or requisition), and it appears to the court that there is no 'just excuse' for the failure to attend, the court may issue a warrant for his arrest. Under s.97(4), a witness who attends before the court but refuses without just excuse to give evidence can be imprisoned for up to one month or until he gives evidence (if sooner), and/or he may be fined.

5.6 Defects in the charge or information

Section 123 of the Magistrates' Courts Act 1980 provides that:

(1)   No objection shall be allowed to any information ... or to any summons or warrant to procure the presence of the defendant, for any defect in it in substance or in form, or for any variance between it and the evidence adduced on behalf of the prosecutor or complainant at the hearing of the information or complaint.

(2)   If it appears to a magistrates' court that any variance between a summons or warrant and the evidence adduced on behalf of the prosecutor or complainant is such that the defendant has been misled by the variance, the court shall, on the application of the defendant, adjourn the hearing.

The effect of s.123 is that all but the gravest of errors can either be ignored or else cured by amendment. It appears from the case law that there are three categories of defect for this purpose.

5.6.1 Minor defects

First, there are minor defects which do not require amendment. This would include a minor misspelling or other inconsequential error that has misled no one. In R v Sandwell Justices ex p West Midlands Passenger Transport Executive [1979] RTR 17, for example, the charge alleged a defective rear nearside tyre, when in fact it was a rear offside tyre which was defective; a conviction based on this unamended charge was upheld.

5.6.2 Defects requiring amendment

Second, there are defects which require amendment (which is possible under s.123) but which are not so grave as to be incurable. If the defendant has been misled by the error, the court should remedy this by granting an adjournment to enable the defence to prepare their case in the light of the amendment.

An example of a remediable defect is where the charge alleges an offence under a section of an Act which has been repealed and re-enacted in identical terms in a later statute (Meek v Powell [1952] 1 KB 164).

Similarly, in Wright v Nicholson [1970] 1 WLR 142, it was held that a charge can be amended to show a different date for the alleged commission of the offence, provided that an adjournment is granted if the defence need more time to prepare their case in the light of the amendment. This was so even though the defendant had an alibi for the date originally alleged.

In the case of summary offences, an important question is whether or not the six-month time limit for commencing a prosecution (see s.127 of the Magistrates' Courts Act 1980) has expired; if it has not, then there is nothing to stop the prosecution simply starting the proceedings again, and this is a strong factor in favour of allowing an amendment to the existing charge. However, the fact that the time limit has expired is not necessarily fatal to an application to amend the existing charge. In R v Scunthorpe Justices ex p McPhee and Gallagher (1998) 162 JP 635, the defendant was charged with robbery; the prosecution sought to amend the charge to allege theft and common assault (a summary offence) instead. Dyson J said the charge can be amended under s.123 even if the amendment takes place more than six months after the commission of the alleged offence. This is so even if the amendment involves alleging a different offence, provided that (a) the new offence alleges the 'same misdoing' as the original offence (in other words, 'the new offence should arise out of the same (or substantially the same) facts as gave rise to the original offence'); and (b) the amendment can be made in the interests of justice. In considering whether it is in the interests of justice for the amendment to be made, the court should pay particular regard to the interests of the accused. If the amendment would result in the defendant facing a 'significantly more serious charge', it is likely to be against the interests of justice to allow such an amendment; similarly, the need for an adjournment would militate against the court granting leave for the amendment of the charge.

The same approach had been taken in R v Newcastle-upon-Tyne Justices ex p John Bryce (Contractors) Ltd [1976] 1 WLR 517, where the prosecution were allowed to amend a charge which alleged 'use' rather than 'permitting use' of a vehicle, even though the effect was to charge a different summary offence and even though a new charge could not have been brought because more than six months had elapsed from the date of the alleged offence. It was said that the defence were not prejudiced by this amendment as the true nature of the offence was clear from the statement of facts on the original summons.

Another example is DPP v Short [2001] EWHC 885 (Admin); (2002) 166 JP 474, where the charge alleged that the defendant 'used' a vehicle with excess alcohol (rather than 'drove') under s.5 of the Road Traffic Act 1988. At the end of the evidence, the prosecution invited the justices to exercise their power under s.123 to amend the information to substitute 'drove' for 'used', thus bringing the charge into line with the wording of s.5. The magistrates refused to allow the information to be amended. It was held by the Divisional Court that s.123 confers a wide discretion on justices to amend a charge, and that discretion should ordinarily be exercised in favour of amendment unless so amending would result in injustice to a defendant (per Owen J, at [22]). In the present case, no injustice would have been caused to the defendant by the proposed amendment, since he was fully aware of the case against him. Accordingly, the justices had erred in refusing the prosecution amendment.

The very wide ambit of s.123 is shown by James v DPP [2004] EWHC 1663 (Admin); (2004) 168 JP 596. The defendant was charged with supplying a Class B drug. At the close of her case, it was submitted that the evidence, although demonstrating an attempt to supply the drug, did not demonstrate an actual supply. The prosecution, relying on s.123 of the 1980 Act, applied to amend the information to allege an offence of attempting to supply a Class B drug (contrary to the Criminal Attempts Act 1981). Issues arose as to whether the justices were right to allow the amendment after the close of the defendant's case and whether they were right not to hold fresh allocation proceedings after allowing the amendment. The Divisional Court held that there is no fetter on the justices relying on the very wide wording of s.123 to substitute a different offence, even where that offence arises under a different Act of Parliament, provided that no injustice is caused to the defendant in so doing. In the present case, the defendant had suffered no prejudice. The court went on to hold that, where there is no injustice to the defendant, there is no requirement on the magistrates to undertake the allocation procedure upon the amendment of the charge, even where one offence is substituted for another.

However, in Shaw v DPP [2007] EWHC 207 (Admin); (2007) 171 JP 254, the justices allowed an information to be amended to allege a different offence. The new offence carried imprisonment, whereas the original one did not. Significantly, the amendment had permitted the introduction of a new charge outside the six-month time limit imposed in respect of summary offences by s.127 of the 1980 Act. It was held that the substitution of a new offence with a significantly heavier penalty, especially one where the defendant faces the possibility of a custodial sentence, should have led the justices to reach the conclusion that it was not in the interests of justice to allow such an amendment.

Where the effect of the amendment would be to replace one offence with a different one, a key question is how similar those offences are. In *Williams v DPP* [2009] EWHC 2354 (Admin), the accused was suspected of drink-driving. At the police station, he failed to give an adequate breath sample and was asked for a blood or urine sample. He refused to give a blood sample, on the basis that he was afraid of needles, and failed to provide a urine sample. However, he was charged with failure to provide a breath specimen. On the day of the trial (some nine months later), the magistrates acceded to an application by the CPS to amend the charge to allege failure to provide a urine sample. The Divisional Court ruled that this amendment would have been permissible but for the fact that the magistrates also allowed a further adjournment of four months.

In *Dougall v CPS* [2018] EWHC 1367 (Admin); [2018] 2 Cr App R 24, the Divisional Court held that an amendment which seeks to replace an indictable-only or either-way offence with a summary offence can be permitted (even if arising out of the 'same misdoing') only if the proceedings for the original offence were commenced within six months of the alleged commission of that offence. Holroyde LJ (at [22]) said that the words of s.127

> stipulate that a magistrates' court may not try an information alleging a summary offence unless the information on which the prosecution is founded was laid within the statutory time limit. That is so, whether the information initially charges the summary offence or initially charges an indictable offence but is later amended to charge a summary offence. If no information is laid within the period of six months, but an indictable offence is later charged and then subsequently amended to charge a summary offence, that amendment does not avoid the consequence of the statutory time limit.

5.6.3 Irremediable defects

Third, there are fundamental errors which cannot be corrected by amendment (despite the wide wording of s.123 of the 1980 Act). This includes a charge which names the wrong person (for example, *Marco (Croydon) Ltd v Metropolitan Police* [1984] RTR 24; *R v Greater Manchester Justices ex p Aldi GmbH & Co KG* (1995) 159 JP 717). The only remedy for the prosecution in such a case is to start fresh proceedings (which, in the case of a summary offence, is only possible if less than six months have elapsed since the alleged commission of the offence).

In *R (J Sainsbury plc) v Plymouth Magistrates Court* [2006] EWHC 1749; (2006) 170 JP 690, a charge was brought under food safety legislation naming the defendant as 'J Sainsbury plc (trading as Sainsburys Supermarket Ltd)'. It was argued that the charge did not name the proper defendant, since the relevant store was operated by Sainsbury's Supermarkets Ltd. The prosecution applied under s.123 to substitute Sainsbury's Supermarkets Ltd as defendant. The District Judge allowed the amendment notwithstanding that the time limit for bringing a prosecution had since expired. The Divisional Court ruled that the proper defendant had not been before the court and so the effect of the decision was improperly to prefer a charge against it out of time.

Where the accused is misnamed but nonetheless appears before the court, this may have the effect of waiving the error and rendering amendment permissible (see *Allan v Wiseman* [1975] RTR 217, where the wrong surname was used but the right person was nonetheless before the court).

In *Platinum Crown Investments Ltd v North East Essex Magistrates' Court* [2017] EWHC 2761 (Admin); [2018] 4 WLR 11, the informations and summonses referred to Platinum Crown Ltd. That company was defunct. The defendant should have been identified as Platinum Crown Investments Ltd. The question was whether the name of the company could be amended under the s.123, even though the six-month time limit applicable under s.127 had expired. Treacy LJ considered *R. (Essence Bars Ltd) v Wimbledon Magistrates' Court* [2016] EWCA Civ 63; [2016] 1 WLR 3265, and (at 35]) said that this decision 'shows that a degree of factual inquiry is necessary before the court can distinguish between a mistake as to identity (which cannot be corrected out of time) and a mis-statement of name (which may be corrected out of time)'. His Lordship went on to say that, 'the local authority always intended to prosecute PCIL' and 'both PCIL and its director [who also faced charges] were aware of that fact prior to the laying of information. On the first court appearance when [the director] attended and entered not guilty pleas it is clear that he must have intended to enter pleas on behalf of PCIL' ([37]). It followed that this involved 'a mistake or mis-statement of name in circumstances where there could be no reasonable doubt as to the identity of the defendant entertained by the court or indeed by the defendant itself' ([38]). Accordingly, the magistrates were entitled to permit amendment of the name of the company, notwithstanding the expiry of the statutory time limit ([39]). It is submitted that this decision may suggest some relaxation of the strictness of the approach taken in earlier case law where the defendant was mis-named.

5.7 Trying more than one offence or more than one defendant

Where several defendants are charged with the same offence, they will be tried together.

Where an accused faces more than one charge, or there are several defendants charged with separate (but linked) offences, a joint trial is possible.

More than one charge may be tried at the same time if the magistrates are satisfied that there is a sufficient link between the offences. This is a matter for the discretion of the justices, who should ask themselves whether the interests of justice are best served by a joint trial or separate trials, balancing convenience for the prosecution against the risk of any prejudice to the defendant. As Lord Roskill put it in *Chief Constable of Norfolk v Clayton* [1983] 2 AC 473 at p.492: 'The justices should always ask themselves whether it would be fair and just to the defendant or defendants to allow a joint trial.'

5.8 Attendance of the parties

5.8.1 Non-attendance by the prosecution

Section 15(1) of the Magistrates' Courts Act 1980 provides that if the prosecutor fails to attend the trial, the court may dismiss the case or, if evidence has been received on a previous occasion, proceed in the absence of the prosecutor. If, instead of dismissing the case or proceeding in the absence of the prosecutor, the court adjourns the trial, it can only remand the accused in custody if he was already in custody or cannot be remanded on bail by reason of his failure to find sureties (s.15(2)).

In DPP v Shuttleworth [2002] EWHC 621 (Admin); (2002) 166 JP 417, it was held that s.15 does not apply where the prosecution are represented at the hearing but the prosecutor is unable to proceed because he does not have the relevant file.

Where a magistrates' court dismisses a case under s.15 without consideration of the merits of the case because of the non-attendance of the prosecutor, there is no rule of law which prevents the court from dealing with an identical charge subsequently laid against the same defendant; the question to be decided is whether the new charge amounts to an abuse of process, and so the court must consider what prejudice would be caused to the defendant by the new charge (*Holmes v Campbell* (1998) 162 JP 655, where it was also held that, because the accused was not at risk of conviction when the case was dismissed because of the absence of the prosecutor, it was not open to him to invoke the rule against 'double jeopardy' by claiming *autrefois acquit*).

In DPP v Jarman [2013] EWHC 4391 (Admin); (2014) 178 JP 89, the prosecutor failed to attend and the magistrates dismissed the case for want of prosecution under s.15 of the Magistrates' Courts Act 1980. Fresh proceedings were then instituted. It was held that a dismissal by a magistrates' court of a charge owing to the absence of prosecution counsel was not akin to an acquittal, as the defendant had not been in peril of conviction, and a stay of proceedings barring further prosecution for similar offences was therefore lifted. Griffith Williams J (at [30]) reiterated that the scope of *autrefois acquit* 'is narrowly confined to those cases where the accused is put in peril of conviction for the same offence as that with which he is then charged'. This requires that 'the court must be in a position to conduct a hearing and so it follows that there must be a prosecutor to prosecute and a defendant to defend unless, of course, the defendant has wilfully absented himself or herself and so the trial proceeds in his or her absence' (at [31]). In the present case, the accused 'was in no way in peril because, while the court was competent to try him and there was a valid charge upon which he was to be tried, the dismissal was not on the merits; there was no prosecutor and the magistrates had heard no evidence' ([32]). His Lordship added (at [36]):

> While the overriding objective [in Part 1 of the Criminal Procedure Rules] includes ... the requirement to deal with cases efficiently and expeditiously, the ... power to dismiss proceedings pursuant to s.15 of the Act must not ... be used, save in the most exceptional cases, to, in effect, punish the prosecution for its inefficiency.

It should be noted that, in R v *Watford Justices ex p DPP* [1990] RTR 374, it was held that the justices cannot dismiss a charge on the ground that the case is too trivial to justify the continuance of the proceedings. If the prosecution wish to adduce evidence, the magistrates must hear that evidence unless the prosecution amounts to an abuse of process.

5.8.2 Non-attendance by the defendant

Section 122(1) of the Magistrates' Courts Act 1980 provides that a party to any proceedings before a magistrates' court may be represented by a legal representative. Under subs.(2), an absent party who is so represented is to be deemed present. However, subs.(3) makes it clear that this does not apply where the accused is under a duty to attend court. Therefore, where the defendant was originally arrested and charged, he must attend court personally or else he is in breach of his bail, entitling the court to issue a bench warrant for his arrest under s.7 of the Bail Act 1976.

It follows that where proceedings were commenced by written charge and requisition (or by information and summons), rather than by arrest and charge, the defendant is deemed to be present if his legal representative is in court (and the legal representative may enter a plea on behalf of the defendant if the latter is not in court). However, where the proceedings were started with the accused being arrested and charged by the police, the accused (if not in custody) will be at liberty because he has been granted bail (either by the police or by a magistrates' court) and so is under a duty to attend court; s.122 cannot excuse his non-attendance.

Section 13 of the Magistrates' Courts Act 1980 provides that where the accused fails to attend court and the magistrates decide not to proceed in his absence but to adjourn instead, they may issue a warrant for his arrest. However, s.13(2) stipulates that, where a summons or requisition was issued, a warrant may only be issued if the conditions set out in subs.(2A) or (2B) are satisfied:

- it is proved the summons or requisition was served on the accused within what appears to the court to be a reasonable time before the trial; or
- the present adjournment is a second or subsequent adjournment of the trial, the accused was present on the last occasion when the trial was adjourned, and on that occasion the court determined the time for the hearing at which the adjournment is now being made (i.e. it has to be proved that the defendant knew of the date of the present hearing).

A warrant may be issued under s.13 only if the offence with which the defendant is charged is punishable with imprisonment, or the court, having convicted him of the offence, proposes to impose a disqualification on him (s.13(3) (adults); s.13(3A) (juveniles)).

5.8.2.1 Trial in absence of the defendant

Section 11(1) of the Magistrates' Courts Act 1980 provides that where the accused fails to attend at the time and place appointed for trial:

(a)   if the accused is under 18 years of age, the court may proceed in his absence; and

(b)   if the accused has attained the age of 18 years, the court shall proceed in his absence, unless it appears to the court to be contrary to the interests of justice to do so" (emphasis added).

It should be noted, however, that if the offence charged is triable either way, the trial can only take place in the absence of the defendant if, on an earlier occasion, he consented to summary trial.

Under s.11(2), where the proceedings were started by means of a written charge and requisition, or information and summons, the court cannot try the case in the absence of the defendant unless either it is proved to the satisfaction of the court that the requisition or summons was served on the accused within a reasonable time before the trial, or that the accused has appeared on a previous occasion to answer to the charge.

Section 11(2A) says that the court must not proceed in the absence of the accused 'if it considers that there is an acceptable reason for his failure to appear'. However, subs.(6) makes it clear that the court is not required to enquire into the reasons for the accused's failure to appear before deciding whether to proceed in his absence.

The procedure to be followed where the defendant is absent is set out in r.24.12(3):

Where the defendant is absent—

(a)   the general rule is that the court must proceed as if the defendant—
   (i)   were present, and
   (ii)   had pleaded not guilty (unless a plea already has been taken)
and the court must give reasons if it does not do so; but
(b)   the general rule does not apply if the defendant is under 18;
(c)   the general rule is subject to the court being satisfied that—
   (i)   any summons or requisition was served on the defendant a reasonable time before the hearing, or
   (ii)   in a case in which the hearing has been adjourned, the defendant had reasonable notice of where and when it would resume.

In *Killick v West London Magistrates' Court* [2012] EWHC 3864 (Admin), Sharp J summarised the relevant principles thus, at [17]:

(1)   The overriding principle is that the court should not proceed to hear a case in the defendant's absence without satisfying itself that the claim for an adjournment may properly be rejected and that no unfairness will thereby be done ...

(2)   The discretion to commence a trial in the absence of a defendant should be exercised with the utmost care and caution. Where a defendant to a criminal charge wishes to resist it and is shown by medical evidence to be unfit to attend court to do so, either as a result of involuntary illness or incapacity, it would be very rarely, if indeed ever, right for the court to exercise its

discretion in favour of commencing the trial, or to proceed to hear the case in his absence, at any rate unless the defendant is represented and asks that the trial should begin ...

(3) If a court asked for an adjournment on medical grounds, suspects the grounds to be spurious or believes them to be inadequate, the court should ordinarily express its doubts and thereby give the defendant an opportunity to resolve those doubts ...

(4) A court considering an application to adjourn will need carefully to distinguish between genuine reasons for the defendant not being present and those reasons which are spuriously advanced or designed to frustrate the process. However, if the court comes to the conclusion that either of the latter is the case, it should say so. It cannot simply be inferred that a court has come to that conclusion unless that is clearly stated by the magistrates ...

(5) If a conclusion is open to the court reasonably on the material before it either to the effect that an excuse given is spurious or there is a truly compelling and exceptional reason for proceeding notwithstanding a good excuse for non-attendance, the court has the power to do so. This however will be an exceptional case ....

5.8.2.2 Setting aside conviction where the defendant did not know of proceedings

Under r.4.4 of the Criminal Procedure Rules, a summons or requisition may be served by posting it to an address where it is reasonably believed that the defendant will receive it, or by leaving it at such an address. There is therefore a risk that the summons or requisition will not, in fact, come to the attention of the defendant, and that the defendant will be tried and convicted in his absence under s.11 of the Magistrates' Courts Act 1980. The potential injustice of this is mitigated by s.14 of the 1980 Act, which provides that in these circumstances the conviction may be set aside.

Under s.14(1), the accused may, at any time during or after the trial, make a statutory declaration (that is, a written statement under oath) averring that he did not know of the summons/requisition, or the subsequent proceedings, until after the court had begun to try the case. The declaration must also state the date on which the defendant first became aware of the proceedings. The declaration must be served on the magistrates' court within 21 days of the date when the accused became aware of the proceedings. The effect of the service of the declaration is to render void the summons or requisition, and all subsequent proceedings. However, the original information or written charge remains unaffected, and so a fresh summons or requisition can be served.

Under s.14(3), a magistrate may allow a declaration to take effect even if it was served after the 21-day time limit, if it was not reasonable to expect the defendant to effect service of the declaration within that time (for example, where the accused is out of the country at the relevant time).

The problem of a defendant not knowing about proceedings never arises where proceedings are commenced by arrest and charge, since the charge sheet tells the defendant the date of his first court appearance.

5.8.3 Pleading guilty by post

Section 12 of the Magistrates' Courts Act 1980 provides that the defendant may be offered the opportunity of pleading guilty by post. However, this applies only to summary offences.

The defendant is sent a special form, which includes a statement of the facts alleged against him. On the form, the defendant can indicate a plea of guilty and can also draw to the court's attention any mitigating circumstances that may persuade the court to impose a more lenient sentence. At court, neither the prosecution nor the defence are represented. In open court, the court legal adviser reads out the statement of facts which was sent to the defendant and whatever the defendant has written on the form or in an accompanying letter. The court then proceeds to pass sentence. However, a sentence of imprisonment or disqualification from driving cannot be imposed in the absence of the defendant. If the court is minded to impose such a sentence, the defendant will be summoned to attend on a later occasion (see s.11(3) and (4) of the Magistrates' Courts Act 1980).

Section 12A of the Magistrates' Courts Act 1980 makes provision for the application of s.12 where the defendant appears in court. If the accused has indicated that he wishes to plead guilty by post but nevertheless appears before the court, the court may (if the accused consents) proceed as if the defendant were absent. Similarly, if the accused has not indicated that he wishes to plead guilty by post but, when he attends court, indicates that he wishes to plead guilty, the court may (if the accused consents) proceed as if he were absent and had indicated an intention to plead guilty by post. Where the court proceeds as if the defendant were absent, the prosecution summary of the facts of the case must not go beyond the statement served on the defendant when he was given the option of pleading guilty by post. However, if the accused is, in fact, present in court, he must be given the opportunity to make an oral submission with a view to mitigation of sentence.

5.8.4 The 'single justice' procedure

Section 16A of the Magistrates' Courts Act 1980 enables a single justice to try certain cases 'on the papers'. This procedure is limited to cases where a person who has attained the age of 18 is charged with a summary offence that does not carry imprisonment; it does not apply where the defendant serves a written notice indicating a desire either to plead not guilty or not to be tried under s.16A.

Where s.16A applies, the court (which may be composed of a single justice) hears no oral evidence but considers only the documents served on the court by the prosecution and the accused. The court is not required to conduct any part of the proceedings in open court, and tries the charge in the absence of the parties; if a party appears, the court must proceed as if the party were absent.

Under s.16B, if the court decides, before the accused is convicted of the offence, that it is not appropriate to proceed under s.16A, the trial will (if it has begun) be adjourned, and a summons will be issued requiring the accused to appear before a magistrates' court for the trial.

Similarly, under s.16C(1), if the court decides, after the accused has been convicted of the offence, that it is not appropriate to proceed under s.16A, the court must adjourn the case and issue a summons requiring the accused to appear before a magistrates' court to be dealt with. Under s.16C(2), if a magistrates' court which has been proceeding under s.16A, having convicted the accused, proposes to impose disqualification from driving, the court must give the accused the opportunity to make representations about the proposed disqualification; if the accused indicates a wish to make such representations, the court may not continue to proceed under s.16A (and so must adjourn and issue a summons requiring the attendance of the offender).

Where a case has been adjourned under s.16B or s.16C, the court which hears the case when it resumes will be composed in the usual way (namely, at least two lay justices, as required by s.121(1) of the Magistrates' Courts Act 1980 or a District Judge (Magistrates' Courts)).

Where the case is being dealt with under s.16A, the powers of the court as regards sentence are limited by s.121(5A) of the Magistrates' Courts Act 1980: the court may (for example) discharge the offender (conditionally or absolutely) or impose a fine, and may make a number of ancillary orders (such as compensation and disqualification from driving), but cannot impose a community order or a custodial sentence.

5.9 Withdrawal of charge/offering no evidence

If the defendant has not yet entered a plea, the prosecution can (with the agreement of the justices) withdraw the charge (R v Redbridge Justices ex p Sainty [1981] RTR 13). The prosecution may make such an application if, for example, one of their witnesses is not available but the court will not grant an adjournment because it takes the view that the prosecution should be in a position to proceed. Withdrawal of a charge in this way does not constitute an acquittal, so fresh proceedings may be brought unless it would amount to an abuse of process (R v Grays Justices ex p Low [1990] 1 QB 54). If the defendant has entered a plea of not guilty, it is too late to withdraw the charge and so the prosecution, if they are not ready to proceed on the date fixed for trial, must:

- seek an adjournment; or
- proceed with the trial as best they can;
- or offer no evidence.

The other situations where the prosecution may offer no evidence are where:

- the defendant has pleaded guilty to one offence and the prosecution do not wish to proceed with another (closely related) charge; or
- new evidence exonerating the defendant has come to light; or
- the CPS have reviewed the evidence and decided that there is insufficient prospect of securing a conviction to merit continuing the proceedings.

If the prosecution offer no evidence, an acquittal is recorded. As a result, fresh proceedings may be brought if (but only if) the defendant was never in jeopardy of conviction (R v Dabhade [1993] QB 329). For example, in Holmes v Campbell (1998) 162 JP 655, a magistrates' court dismissed the case against the defendants when the prosecutor failed to appear at the hearing. The prosecutor subsequently brought fresh proceedings (making the same allegations) but the magistrates' court declined to try the case on the ground that it would be an abuse of process. The Divisional Court held that, by virtue of s.15 of the 1980 Act, the defendants could not have been convicted at a hearing where the prosecutor was absent. They had therefore not been in jeopardy of conviction at that hearing and so the doctrine of autrefois acquit did not prevent the bringing of the fresh charge.

5.10 Summary trial procedure

A magistrates' court conducting a summary trial will consist either of three lay justices or a District Judge; there will also be a clerk/court legal adviser to assist the court.

5.10.1 Outline of a summary trial

Section 9 of the Magistrates' Courts Act 1980 provides as follows:

(1) On the summary trial of an information [or charge], the court shall, if the accused appears, state to him the substance of the information [or charge] and ask him whether he pleads guilty or not guilty.

(2) The court, after hearing the evidence and the parties, shall convict the accused or dismiss the information [or charge].

(3) If the accused pleads guilty, the court may convict him without hearing evidence.

A more detailed outline of a summary trial may be found in Part 24 of the Criminal Procedure Rules.

Rule 24.2(2) sets out what happens at the start of the trial:

Unless already done, the justices' legal adviser or the court must –

(a) read the allegation of the offence to the defendant;
(b) explain, in terms the defendant can understand (with help, if necessary) –
  (i) the allegation; and
  (ii) what the procedure at the hearing will be;
(c) ask whether the defendant has been advised about the potential effect on sentence of a guilty plea;
(d) ask whether the defendant pleads guilty or not guilty; and
(e) take the defendant's plea.

Moreover, r.24.15(2) requires the court legal adviser, before the hearing begins and by reference to what has been provided in the case management documents (in particular, the preparation for trial form), to draw the court's attention to:

(i) what the prosecutor alleges,
(ii) what the parties say is agreed,
(iii) what the parties say is in dispute, and
(iv) what the parties say about how each expects to present the case, especially where that may affect its duration and timetabling.

Rule 24.3(3) then sets out what happens where the accused pleads not guilty (or declines to enter a plea, in which case a not guilty plea will be entered on his behalf):

In the following sequence—
(a) the prosecutor may summarise the prosecution case, concisely identifying the relevant law, outlining the facts and indicating the matters likely to be in dispute;
(b) to help the members of the court to understand the case and resolve any issue in it, the court may invite the defendant concisely to identify what is in issue;
(c) the prosecutor must introduce the evidence on which the prosecution case relies;
(d) at the conclusion of the prosecution case, on the defendant's application or on its own initiative, the court:
  (i) may acquit on the ground that the prosecution evidence is insufficient for any reasonable court properly to convict, but
  (ii) must not do so unless the prosecutor has had an opportunity to make representations;
(e) the justices' legal adviser or the court must explain, in terms the defendant can understand (with help, if necessary):
  (i) the right to give evidence, and
  (ii) the potential effect of not doing so at all, or of refusing to answer a question while doing so;
(f) the defendant may introduce evidence;
(g) a party may introduce further evidence if it is then admissible (for example, because it is in rebuttal of evidence already introduced);
(h) the prosecutor may make final representations in support of the prosecution case, where:
  (i) the defendant is represented by a legal representative, or
  (ii) whether represented or not, the defendant has introduced evidence other than his or her own; and
  (iii) the defendant may make final representations in support of the defence case.

Thus, the main stages of a summary trial are as follows:

(1) The prosecutor may make an opening speech, introducing the prosecution case to the magistrates.

(2) The defendant may be asked to clarify what the issues are (i.e. which aspects of the prosecution case are disputed). Criminal Practice Direction VI, para.24B.2, notes that the purpose of this is to provide the court with 'focus as to what it is likely to be called upon to decide', so that the justices will be 'alert to those issues from the outset and can evaluate the prosecution evidence that they hear accordingly'. Paragraph 24B.3 goes on to note that the parties 'should keep in mind that, in most cases, the members of the court already will be aware of what has been declared to be issue' (through the preparation for trial form and the legal adviser's summary at the start of the trial). Therefore, if a party 'has nothing of substance to add to that, then he or she should say so. The requirement to be concise will be enforced and the exchange with the court properly may be confined to enquiry and confirmation that the court's understanding of those allegations and issues is correct'.

(3) The prosecution evidence is then called.

(4) At the close of the prosecution case, the defence may make a submission of no case to answer. Unless the magistrates are minded to rule that there is a case to answer, they must give the prosecution a chance to respond to the defence submission before making their decision. The magistrates may indicate that they are minded to dismiss the case at this stage without the defence inviting them to do so, but the prosecution must be given the opportunity to make representations first. Submissions of no case to answer are considered in more detail below.

(5) The court (usually through the justices' legal adviser) must inform the defendant that he has the right to give evidence and must warn the defendant of the risk of adverse inferences being drawn (under s.35 of the Criminal Justice and Public Order Act 1994) if he does not testify (or refuses to answer questions while testifying).

(6) The defendant may then testify and call any supporting witnesses.

(7) Either party may call further evidence, for example evidence in rebuttal. Since the defence will have just called their evidence, it is likely to be the prosecution who seek to make use of this provision. In any event, the calling of rebuttal evidence should be regarded as an exceptional course of action.

(8) The prosecution may make a closing speech (unless the defendant is unrepresented *and* called no witnesses other than his own testimony).

(9) The defence may make a closing speech (thus, the defence will always have the last word before the magistrates decide their verdict).

Under r.24.3(4)(a), where a party wants to introduce evidence or make representations after their opportunity to do so under r.24.3(3), the court may refuse to receive any such evidence or representations. Rule 24.3(4)(b) preserves the principle of finality by providing that the court must not receive any such evidence or representations after it has announced its verdict.

5.10.2 Witnesses

Rule 24.4(2)(a) says that a witness who is waiting to give evidence must wait outside the courtroom unless that witness is a party or an expert witness. Under r.24.4(3), before giving evidence, a witness must either take an oath or affirm (that is, promise, rather swear, to tell the truth). Rule 24.4(4) goes on to stipulate that:

In the following sequence –
(a) the party who calls a witness must ask questions in examination-in-chief;
(b) every other party may ask questions in cross-examination;
(c) the party who called the witness may ask questions in re-examination.

5.10.2.1 Reading witness statements

Under s.9(2) of the Criminal Justice Act 1967, a written statement may be read aloud to the court as evidence (instead of the maker of the statement giving oral evidence) if:

- the statement is signed by its maker;
- the statement contains a declaration by the maker that it is true to the best of his knowledge and belief, and that he makes it knowing that he is liable to prosecution if he has wilfully stated in it anything which he knows to be false or does not believe to be true;
- a copy of the statement has been served on all the other parties to the proceedings; and
- none of the parties on whom the statement is served objects within seven days of service to the statement being used as evidence.

The last two requirements do not apply if the parties agree immediately before or during the hearing that the statement may be used as evidence rather than the witness giving 'live' testimony (see the proviso to s.9(2)). Where the conditions in subs.(2) are satisfied, the statement is admissible as evidence to the same extent as oral evidence to the like effect by that person (s.9(1)).

Rule 24.5(2) of the Criminal Procedure Rules stipulates that if the court admits such evidence:

(a) the court must read the statement; and
(b) unless the court otherwise directs, if any member of the public, including any reporter, is present, each relevant part of the statement must be read or summarised aloud.

It is usually the statements of prosecution witnesses which are read out in this way, with the consent of the defence, on the basis that the defence concedes that the evidence of that witness is uncontroversial and so the defence do not wish to cross-examine that witness. However, there is no reason why the evidence of a defence witness cannot be given in this way (if the prosecution agree).

5.10.2.2 Witnesses the prosecution must call

Where the prosecutor serves a bundle of witness statements on the defence prior to summary trial, the prosecution must call as witnesses all the people whose statements have been served, unless any of the exceptions which relate to Crown Court trials (set out in R v Russell-Jones [1995] 1 Cr App R 538 at 544–5, per Kennedy LJ) are applicable (R v Haringey Justices ex p DPP [1996] QB 351 at 357, per Stuart-Smith LJ). These exceptions are considered later in the context of trial on indictment.

5.10.3 Admissions

Rule 24.6 applies where a party introduces in evidence a fact admitted by another party, or parties jointly admit a fact (for example, under s.10 of the Criminal Justice Act 1967). Unless the court otherwise directs, a written record must be made of the admission.

5.10.4 Objecting to prosecution evidence in a summary trial

Objections to prosecution evidence are made under s.76 or s.78 of the Police and Criminal Evidence Act 1984.

The procedure to be followed where the defence object to prosecution evidence is made more challenging because of the fact that the magistrates are the judges of both fact and law. There is a danger that the magistrates will learn the nature of the evidence in the course of the arguments about its admissibility; should they then rule the evidence inadmissible, they may have difficulty in ignoring it when reaching a verdict. This problem is mitigated to some extent by the availability of pre-trial rulings (under s.8A of the Magistrates' Courts Act 1980), but these will not avail where issues of admissibility are raised for the first time during the course of the trial itself.

The stage of the trial at which the magistrates rule upon a question of admissibility of evidence is a matter for their discretion (per Lord Lane CJ in *F v Chief Constable of Kent* [1982] Crim LR 682, followed in *R v Epping and Ongar Justices ex p Manby* [1986] Crim LR 555 and *A v DPP* (2000) 164 JP 317).

5.10.4.1 Section 76 of PACE

If the defence invoke s.76 and allege that a confession has been obtained by oppression or in circumstances where anything said by the defendant is likely to be unreliable, the magistrates have to hold a *voir dire* or 'trial within a trial' (*R v Liverpool Juvenile Court ex p R* [1988] QB 1). The terms in which s.76 is drafted stipulate that the court must not admit the confession into evidence unless satisfied that it was not obtained by oppression or by words or conduct likely to render it unreliable. It follows that magistrates (just like the Crown Court) are obliged to hear evidence on the admissibility of the confession. The prosecution will generally have to call the police officers who were present when the defendant confessed and they can be cross-examined by the defence; the defendant may then give evidence (and be cross-examined by the prosecution). At this stage, it is only the admissibility of the confession, not its truth, which is in issue.

If the magistrates decide that the confession is inadmissible, the trial will continue (assuming there is other evidence against the accused), but no further mention may be made of the confession. If the confession is ruled admissible, the trial will resume with the police officer giving evidence of what the defendant said (unless this has already been done in the *voir dire*, in which case the evidence does not have to be repeated as the magistrates have already heard it).

5.10.4.2 Section 78 of PACE

Where the defence argue that a confession should be excluded under s.76 of PACE, the court is obliged to hear evidence about the obtaining of the confession (as the prosecution have to prove that the confession was not obtained in a manner forbidden by s.76); where, however, the admissibility of prosecution evidence falls to be considered under the general exclusionary power in s.78, the court has a discretion to hear evidence on the issue of admissibility but is not obliged to do so (and so may rule on the matter following submissions on behalf of the parties). In the latter type of case, it remains a matter for the justices' discretion when they determine the question of admissibility (*Vel v Chief Constable of North Wales* (1987) 151 JP 510 and *Halawa v Federation Against Copyright Theft* [1995] 1 Cr App R 21). In *Vel*, it was held that magistrates may deal with an application to exclude evidence under s.78 when it arises or may leave the decision until the end of the hearing. The court declined to lay down any general rule, other than that the object should always be to secure a trial which is fair and just to both sides. In *Halawa*, Gibson LJ said (at p.34) that, in most cases, it is generally better for the magistrates to hear all the prosecution evidence (including the disputed evidence) before considering an application to exclude evidence under s.78. This does, of course, leave the justices with the very difficult (some might say impossible) task of putting from their minds prejudicial evidence that they have heard but then decide is inadmissible.

5.10.5 Submission of no case to answer

By virtue of r.24.3(3)(d)(i), the magistrates may, after the close of the prosecution case, 'acquit on the ground that the prosecution evidence is insufficient for any reasonable court properly to convict'. Where the justices are minded to dismiss a case prior to the start of the defence case (whether following a submission of no case to answer by the defence or of their own motion), the prosecution should be given the opportunity to address the court to show why the case should not be dismissed (R v Barking and Dagenham Justices ex p DPP (1995) 159 JP 373; r.24.3(3)(d)(ii)). This means that the prosecution have the right to reply to the defence submission that there is no case to answer unless, having heard the defence submission, the magistrates decide to rule against the defence and they indicate this fact to the prosecutor. If the submission is successful, the defendant is acquitted. If it is unsuccessful, the trial continues.

An important question that arises in the context of submissions of no case to answer in the magistrates' court is the extent to which the justices may have regard to the credibility of prosecution witnesses when considering such a submission. In the Crown Court, the judge has to be careful not to trespass on the territory of the jury. The test to be applied by the judge when ruling on a submission of no case to answer is set out in R v Galbraith [1981] 1 WLR 1039: is the prosecution evidence so tenuous that, even taken at its highest, a jury properly directed could not properly convict on it? The requirement that the Crown Court judge should 'take the prosecution evidence at its highest' is intended to leave questions of credibility to the jury. Thus, submissions of no case to answer based on the credibility of the prosecution evidence should only succeed in the Crown Court where the prosecution evidence is clearly incredible. In R v Barking and Dagenham Justices ex p DPP, the Divisional Court said that questions of credibility should, except in the clearest of cases, not normally be taken into account by justices considering a submission of no case to answer in the magistrates' court.

Nonetheless, some justices may well take the pragmatic view that it would be inappropriate for them to go through the motions of hearing defence evidence if they have already formed the view that the prosecution evidence is so unconvincing that they will not convict on it in any event. However, the general principle remains that, so long as the necessary minimum amount of prosecution evidence has been adduced so as to raise a case on which a reasonable tribunal could convict, the justices should allow the trial to run its course rather than acquitting on a submission of no case to answer.

There is no legal obligation on magistrates to give reasons for rejecting a submission of no case to answer (Moran v DPP [2002] EWHC 89; (2002) 166 JP 467).

5.10.5.1 Reopening the prosecution case

A successful submission of no case to answer results in the acquittal of the defendant. However, in some cases, the deficiency in the prosecution case, which is highlighted by the defence submission of no case to answer, may be cured by allowing the prosecution to re-open their case, rather than upholding the submission of no case to answer and acquitting the accused.

In Khatibi v DPP [2004] EWHC 83; (2004) 168 JP 361, Nelson J said (at [17]):

> There is a general discretion to admit evidence after the close of the prosecution ... [This] discretion must be exercised with great caution and the strictly adversarial nature of the English criminal process, whereby the cases for the prosecution and the defence are presented consecutively in their entirety, should be borne in mind and the normal order of events not departed from substantially unless justice really demands.

If the defect in the prosecution case is one that could be cured simply and speedily by allowing them to re-open their case and recall a witness, it may well be that the interests of justice require that the prosecution be given the chance to remedy the defect. It is difficult to see how the defendant would be prejudiced by this decision. However, if the re-opening of the prosecution case would require an adjournment, and thus cause delay in the disposal of the case, the balance of the interests of justice might require that the submission should be upheld and the defendant acquitted.

In *Tuck v Vehicle Inspectorate* [2004] EWHC 728 (Admin), the Divisional Court considered a case in which magistrates had permitted the prosecution to repair omissions in their evidence after they had closed their case, following a submission of no case to answer. MacKay J summarised the applicable principles as follows (at [15]):

> The general rule remains that the prosecution must finish its case once and for all … and the test to be applied is narrower than consideration of whether the additional evidence would be of value to the tribunal … The discretion will only be exercised 'on the rarest of occasions' … The discretion must be exercised carefully having regard to the need to be fair to the defendant … and giving consideration to the question of whether any prejudice to the defendant will be caused.

In *R (DPP) v Chorley Magistrates' Court* [2006] EWHC 1795, Thomas LJ (at [27]), gave a warning that the defence must raise issues as early as possible in the case:

> The duty of the court is to see that justice is done. That does not involve allowing people to escape on technical points or by attempting, as happened here, an ambush. It involves the courts in looking at the real justice of the case and seeing whether the rules have been complied with by 'cards being put on the table' at the outset and the issues being clearly identified.

This point was reiterated in *R (CPS) v Norwich Magistrates' Court* [2011] EWHC 82 (Admin), where the prosecution opened the case (a charge of assault) by stating that identification was not in dispute (the section of the case management form completed by the defence having raised the issue of self-defence). At the close of the prosecution case, the defence made a submission of no case based on the lack of adequate identification. The prosecution sought to call additional evidence, but the magistrates refused to allow this. The Divisional Court said that the decision of the magistrates was wrong. Richards LJ said (at [22]):

> [I]f the defence was going to take a positive point on identification, it was incumbent on it to flag the point at an early stage, not to wait until the close of the prosecution case before raising it for the first time in a submission of no case. It should have been expressed during the case management process and included in terms in the trial information form … It was not appropriate … simply to sit tight and to raise it at the end of the prosecution case by way of a submission of no case.

5.10.6 The defendant's evidence

If a submission of no case to answer is not made (or is unsuccessful), the defence then have the opportunity to present evidence to the court. If the defendant is going to call other witnesses as well as giving evidence himself, the defendant should give evidence first unless the court otherwise directs (see s.79 of PACE).

If the defendant decides not to give evidence, he runs the risk that the magistrates will be entitled to draw adverse inferences from his silence under s.35 of the Criminal Justice and Public Order Act (CJPOA) 1994. The magistrates should warn the defendant of the possible consequences of not testifying (this warning is required by s.35(2) of the Act). However, in *Radford v Kent County Council* (1998) 162 JP 697, the magistrates failed to warn the defendant that adverse inferences could be drawn if he failed to testify. In their stated case, the justices said that 'we drew no inferences whatsoever from the failure of the appellant to give evidence, but simply were aware that the evidence for the prosecution was not rebutted by evidence from or on behalf of the appellant'. The Divisional Court held that, in the circumstances, although the warning of the consequences of not testifying is very important, the failure to give the warning in the present case did not render the appellant's conviction unsafe.

The adverse inference provisions in s.34 of the CJPOA 1994 also apply to summary trials where the accused has failed to mention when questioned matters on which he subsequently relies his defence. In T v DPP [2007] EWHC 1793 (Admin); (2007) 171 JP 605, the Court summarised the approach to be taken in a case where a magistrates' court is considering whether to draw adverse inferences in such a case. The justices should ask themselves three questions (per Hughes LJ [26]):

(1) Has the defendant relied in his defence on a fact which he could reasonably have been expected to mention in his interview, but did not? If so, what is it?
(2) What is his explanation for not having mentioned it?
(3) If that explanation is not a reasonable one, is the proper inference to be drawn that he is guilty?

5.10.7 Reopening the prosecution case after defence evidence has been called

Rule 24.3(3)(g) of the Criminal Procedure Rules provides that, after the defence evidence has been presented, 'a party may introduce further evidence if it is then admissible (for example, because it is in rebuttal of evidence already introduced)'. As the defence will have just presented their evidence, it is likely that it will normally be the prosecution who seek to invoke this provision.

In *Khatibi v DPP* [2004] EWHC 83; (2004) 168 JP 361, Nelson J said (at [18]) that there is 'a general discretion to permit the calling of evidence at a stage later than the closing of the prosecution case but prior to the moment the justices retire', and said that 'before exercising that discretion the court will look carefully at the interests of justice overall and in particular the risk of any prejudice whatsoever to the Defendant'.

For example, in *James v South Glamorgan County Council* [1994] 99 Cr App R 321, the main prosecution witness had not arrived but the trial proceeded nonetheless; after the prosecution case had been closed and while the defendant was giving evidence, the witness arrived. It was accepted by the magistrates that the witness had a good reason for being late and the prosecution were allowed to call him as a witness. It was held by the Divisional Court that, since the evidence had not been available at the proper time and there was no unfairness to the defendant (there was no suggestion that the defendant's case would have been differently conducted had the witness' evidence been given timeously), the decision of the magistrates was correct.

In *R (Lawson) v Stafford Magistrates' Court* [2007] EWHC 2490 (Admin), the defendant was charged with driving in excess of the speed limit. During his closing submissions, defence counsel raised for the first time the issues that the prosecution had to satisfy the court that the signs indicating the limit complied with the relevant regulations and that the speed-measuring device should be tested. The Divisional Court said that the accused had sought to ambush the prosecution and the magistrates were entitled to adjourn the case to receive further evidence. Aikens J (at [39]) said that:

> [T]he courts' power to allow a case to be re-opened is a power which must be exercised rarely and having regard to the need to be fair to the defendant. A court must bear in mind the question of whether any prejudice to the defendant will be caused by a case being re-opened. However those points do not detract from the legal proposition that justices are entitled to hear evidence after the case has been closed where special circumstances exist.

5.10.7.1 Hearing further evidence after the justices have retired to consider their verdict

It is only in the rarest of cases that further evidence may be adduced once the justices have retired to consider their verdict. In *Webb v Leadbetter* [1966] 1 WLR 245, one of two prosecution witnesses failed to arrive. The justices had retired to consider their decision when they were informed that the second prosecution witness had arrived. They returned to court and allowed the prosecution to call him. The Divisional Court held that, although justices have a discretion to allow further evidence to be called in particular circumstances, the manner of the exercise of that discretion depends on the stage of the case. In the absence of 'special circumstances' (per Lord Parker CJ) or even 'very special circumstances' (per Sachs J), they should not allow evidence to be called after they have retired. In the instant case, such circumstances were absent and so the further evidence had been wrongly admitted.

In *Malcolm v DPP* [2007] EWHC 363 (Admin); [2007] 1 WLR 1230, the Divisional Court took a broad of view of what would amount to 'special circumstances' enabling the case to be re-opened even after the justices had retired to consider their verdict. The accused had been charged with driving with excess alcohol. In her final speech, defence counsel submitted that there had been no warning, as required by the relevant legislation, that a failure to provide a specimen might render the accused liable to prosecution and that, accordingly, there was no admissible evidence of the analysis of alcohol in her breath. The magistrates retired to consider the submissions. They returned to court and gave their conclusions that the case would have to be dismissed because of the lack of admissible evidence of the proportion of alcohol in the appellant's breath. Before they formally dismissed the case, however, counsel for the prosecution requested leave to recall the officer in charge of the breath test procedure to establish that the required warning had been given. Stanley Burnton J said ([31]) that 'it is the duty of the defence to make the real issues clear at the latest before the prosecution closes its case'; the failure to do so amounted to special circumstances entitling the magistrates to allow the case to be reopened.

5.10.8 Change of plea

The magistrates can allow a defendant to change his plea from not guilty to guilty at any time before a verdict is returned.

The magistrates also have a discretion to allow a defendant to change his plea from guilty to not guilty at any stage before sentence is passed (*S (An Infant) v Recorder of Manchester* [1971] AC 481). Lord Upjohn, at p.507, observed that 'this discretionary power is one which should only be exercised in clear cases and very sparingly'. The question for the magistrates is whether the original plea was unequivocal and entered with a proper understanding of what the charge entailed. If the offence is triable either way and the defendant is allowed to change his plea to one of not guilty, he should also be allowed to reconsider his consent to summary trial (*R v Bow Street Magistrates ex p Welcombe* (1992) 156 JP 609).

In *Revitt v DPP* [2006] EWHC 2266 (Admin); [2006] 1 WLR 3172, the court observed that the onus lies on a party seeking to vacate a guilty plea to demonstrate that justice requires that this should be permitted. If, after an unequivocal plea of guilty, it becomes apparent that the defendant did not appreciate the elements of the offence to which he was pleading guilty, it is likely to be appropriate to permit him to withdraw his plea; similarly, where the facts relied upon by the prosecution do not add up to the offence charged, justice will normally demand that the defendant be permitted to withdraw his plea.

The procedure for seeking to change a plea from guilty to not guilty is set out in r.24.10 of the Criminal Procedure Rules, which provides as follows:

(2) The defendant must apply to [withdraw a guilty plea] –

    (a) as soon as practicable after becoming aware of the reasons for doing so; and

    (b) before sentence.

(3) Unless the court otherwise directs, the application must be in writing ...

(4) The application must –

    (a) explain why it would be unjust not to allow the defendant to withdraw the guilty plea;

    (b) identify –

        (a) any witness that the defendant wants to call; and

        (b) any other proposed evidence; and

    (c) say whether the defendant waives legal professional privilege, giving any relevant name and date.

5.10.9 Seeing the magistrates in private

It is open to the justices to hear representations from the parties in private, but they should do so only in exceptional cases. Steps must be taken to ensure that all parties are aware of the private hearing and are represented at it. The clerk must take a contemporaneous note of the hearing (see *R v Nottingham Justices ex p Furnell* (1995) 160 JP 201).

5.10.10 The magistrates' decision

Usually, there are three lay magistrates. Their decision to acquit or to convict is by simple majority. The decision is announced in open court by the chairman. He does not state whether it is unanimous or by a majority. The chairman does not have a second or casting vote. If only two lay justices hear a case but cannot agree on a verdict, they have no option but to adjourn the case for retrial in front of a bench with three justices (*R v Redbridge Justices ex p Ram* [1992] QB 384).

Under r.24.3(5), if the court convicts the defendant, it *must* give 'sufficient reasons to explain its decision'. In *McKerry v Teesdale & Wear Valley Justices* (2000) 164 JP 355, Lord Bingham CJ said (at [23]) that justices 'are not obliged to state reasons in the form of a judgment or to give reasons in any elaborate form'. In *R (McGowan) v Brent Justices* [2001] EWHC Admin 814; (2002) 166 JP 29, Tuckey LJ said (at [18]) that 'the essence of the exercise ... is to inform the defendant why he has been found guilty. That can usually be done in a few simple sentences'.

Under r.24.3(6)(a), if the court acquits the defendant, it *may* (but is not required to) give an explanation of its decision.

In reaching their decision on a question of fact, it is open to magistrates to use their personal local knowledge, but they should inform the prosecution and the defence that they are doing so, so that those representing the parties have the opportunity of commenting upon the knowledge which the justices claim to have (*Bowman v DPP* [1991] RTR 263; *Norbrook Laboratories (GB) Ltd v Health and Safety Executive* [1998] EHLR 207).

Care must be taken by the magistrates when they are formulating the reasons for their decision. For example, in *JS (a Child) v DPP* [2017] EWHC 1162 (Admin); [2017] 4 WLR 102, the accused was charged with the offence of tampering with a motor vehicle. The magistrates convicted him, saying that the accused 'did not say anything to persuade us that he did not tamper with the moped' and they were therefore 'sure' that he was guilty. The conviction was quashed. The words used by the magistrates created the impression that they had convicted the accused because he had not proved his innocence (thus reversing the burden of proof).

5.10.10.1 Alternative verdicts

Whereas a jury can sometimes convict the defendant of a lesser offence even though that offence is not on the indictment (for example, theft instead of robbery) under s.3 of the Criminal Law Act 1967, the magistrates have no such power (*Lawrence v Same* [1968] 2 QB 93). Section 3 of the 1967 applies only to trials on indictment, and there is no equivalent general power for magistrates' courts.

However, there are certain statutory exceptions to this, such as the power to convict of careless driving instead of dangerous driving (see s.24 of the Road Traffic Offenders Act 1988) and the power to convict of taking a vehicle without the owner's consent instead of aggravated vehicle taking (see s.24A(5) of the Theft Act 1968). A magistrates' court can convict of a lesser offence only if there is a specific statutory power relating to that offence which empowers them to do so.

Otherwise, if the prosecution wish the justices to consider alternative offences, those offences must be charged separately. The charges can then be tried together. If the defendant faces only one charge to begin with, but the prosecution want the court to have the power to convict the defendant of a different offence, the defendant has to be 'further charged' with the other offence. This course of action will be appropriate if, for example, the defendant is willing to plead guilty to an offence which is less serious than that originally charged and the prosecution are willing to accept that plea and drop the more serious charge.

If the accused is charged with alternative offences and pleads not guilty to both, the magistrates should not convict him of both offences. In R (*Dyer*) v *Watford Magistrates' Court* [2013] EWHC 547 (Admin); (2013) 177 JP 265, the accused was charged with an offence under s.4 of the Public Order Act 1986, and also with the racially aggravated version of the offence under s.31 (1)(a) of the Crime and Disorder Act 1998. Before trial, he offered to plead guilty to the s.4 offence, but that offer was rejected by the prosecution. Following trial, he was convicted of both offences. The Divisional Court declined to follow its earlier decisions in DPP v *Gane* (1991) 155 JP 846 and R (*CPS*) v *Blaydon Youth Court* (2004) 168 JP 638 (where it had been held that it was open to the magistrates' court to convict the accused of both offences in similar circumstances), and quashed the conviction on the lesser charge. The Court held that it was 'unfair and disproportionate' for an accused to be convicted twice for a single wrong, since a person's criminal record should record what he had done, no more and no less (per Laws LJ, at [11]). In such a case, the magistrates should adjourn the lesser charge at the end of the trial but before conviction so that, if an appeal succeeded against conviction on the greater charge, a conviction on the lesser offence might thereafter properly be recorded against the accused (at [12]); in other words, the court gives no verdict on the lesser alternative and adjourns that lesser charge *sine die* (that is, without fixing a date) under s.10 of the Magistrates' Courts Act 1980, so that the lesser charge can be brought back, if appropriate, if the accused appeals successfully against the conviction for the more serious offence (per Hickinbottom J, at [14]).

Dyer was followed in *Henderson v CPS* [2016] EWHC 464 (Admin); [2016] 1 WLR 1990, where Simon LJ (at [40]) reiterated that:

> In order to avoid the objectionable course of convicting for both the underlying offence and the aggravated offence, the sensible course is to adjourn the trial of the underlying offence sine die; and we do not consider that any practical difficulty involved in dealing with the files in such cases is an insurmountable objection to this course.

The Court of Appeal expressed agreement with this approach in R v *Nelson* [2016] EWCA Crim 1517; [2017] 1 WLR 491, so long as the two charges can properly be regarded as 'genuine' or 'true' alternatives, in that they 'overlap in terms of their ingredients'.

5.11 Procedure where the defendant is convicted

Rule 24.11 sets out the procedure where the defendant is convicted (either because he pleads guilty or is found guilty):

(2)   The court –

(a)   may exercise its power to require –

(i)   a statement of the defendant's assets and other financial circumstances,

(ii)   a pre-sentence report ...

(3)   The prosecutor must –

(a)   summarise the prosecution case, if the sentencing court has not heard evidence;

(b)   identify any offence to be taken into consideration in sentencing;

(c)   provide information relevant to sentence, including any statement of the effect of the offence on the victim, the victim's family or others; and

(d)   where it is likely to assist the court, identify any other matter relevant to sentence, including –

(i)   the legislation applicable,

(ii)   any sentencing guidelines, or guideline cases,

(iii)   aggravating and mitigating features affecting the defendant's culpability and the harm which the offence caused, was intended to cause or might fore-seeably have caused, and

(iv)   the effect of such of the information listed in paragraph (2)(a) as the court may need to take into account.

(4)   The defendant must provide details of financial circumstances ...

(7)   Before the court passes sentence –

(a)   the court must –

(i)   give the defendant an opportunity to make representations and introduce evidence relevant to sentence ...

(b)   the justices' legal adviser or the court must elicit any further information relevant to sentence that the court may require ...

(9)   When the court has taken into account all the evidence, information and any report available, the court must –

(a)   as a general rule, pass sentence there and then;

(b)   when passing sentence, explain the reasons for deciding on that sentence, unless neither the defendant nor any member of the public is present ....

Where the defendant pleads guilty, or is being sentenced after an adjournment following his conviction at trial, the prosecutor will summarise the facts of the offence and will draw the court's attention to any previous convictions recorded against the defendant. Once the prosecution have summarised the facts, the magistrates may decide to adjourn for a pre-sentence report. If not, the defence will make a plea in mitigation in order to try to persuade the court to impose a more lenient sentence. Having heard the plea in mitigation, the magistrates may pass sentence or may then decide to adjourn for a pre-sentence report. The adjournment cannot be for more than four weeks if the defendant is on bail, or three weeks if he is in custody (s.10(3) of the Magistrates' Courts Act 1980). If there has been an adjournment for a pre-sentence report, it is unlikely that the same magistrates will be sitting on the next occasion, so the prosecution will have to summarise the facts of the offence and the defence will have to do a full plea in mitigation. Sentence is then passed.

If the defendant pleads guilty but argues that the facts of the case are not as serious as the prosecution suggest, r.24.11(5) applies. This provides:

Where the defendant pleads guilty but wants to be sentenced on a different basis to that disclosed by the prosecution case –

(a) the defendant must set out that basis in writing, identifying what is in dispute;

(b) the court may invite the parties to make representations about whether the dispute is material to sentence; and

(c) if the court decides that it is a material dispute, the court must –

    (i) invite such further representations or evidence as it may require; and

    (ii) decide the dispute.

Thus, where there is a significant difference between the prosecution version of the facts and the version to be put forward by the defence (for example, in the case of an offence of dishonesty, there is a dispute over the value involved in the offence), the court should either accept the defence version or else hear evidence on the question and then come to a decision on which version to believe (*R v Newton* (1983) 77 Cr App R 13). Although r.24.11(5)(c) appears to suggest that, where the difference in versions put forward by the parties is significant (in that it would make a difference to the sentence passed), the court has a choice of hearing further representations or evidence, it is submitted that magistrates should follow the procedure laid down by *R v Newton* (1982) 77 Cr App R 13, and (if they are unwilling simply to accept the defence version of events) hear evidence (that is, hold a *Newton* hearing) and then make findings of fact and sentence accordingly. In any event, it is unlikely that there are many cases in which the magistrates will be able to resolve the dispute without hearing evidence on the matter.

5.12 The role of the court clerk/justices' legal adviser

The functions of the clerk/justices' legal adviser are set out in s.28 of the Courts Act 2003, which provides that:

(4) The functions of a justices' clerk include giving advice to any or all of the justices of the peace to whom he is clerk about matters of law (including procedure and practice) on questions arising in connection with the discharge of their functions, including questions arising when the clerk is not personally attending on them.

(5) The powers of a justices' clerk include, at any time when he thinks he should do so, bringing to the attention of any or all of the justices of the peace to whom he is clerk any point of law (including procedure and practice) that is or may be involved in any question so arising.

The role is described in greater detail in r.24.15 of the Criminal Procedure Rules:

(1) A justices' legal adviser must attend the court and carry out the duties listed in this rule, as applicable, unless the court –

    (a) includes a District Judge (Magistrates' Courts); and

    (b) otherwise directs.

(2) A justices' legal adviser must –

    (a) before the hearing begins ... draw the court's attention to –

        (i) what the prosecutor alleges;

        (ii) what the parties say is agreed;

        (iii) what the parties say is in dispute; and

        (iv) what the parties say about how each expects to present the case, especially where that may affect its duration and timetabling;

    (b) whenever necessary, give the court legal advice and –

(i) if necessary, attend the members of the court outside the courtroom to give such advice; but

(ii) inform the parties (if present) of any such advice given outside the courtroom; and

(c) assist the court, where appropriate, in the formulation of its reasons and the recording of those reasons.

(3) A justices' legal adviser must –

(a) assist an unrepresented defendant;

(b) assist the court by –

(i) making a note of the substance of any oral evidence or representations, to help the court recall that information;

(ii) if the court rules inadmissible part of a written statement introduced in evidence, marking that statement in such a way as to make that clear;

(iii) ensuring that an adequate record is kept of the court's decisions and the reasons for them; and

(iv) making any announcement, other than of the verdict or sentence.

Additionally, r.24.4(6) says that the justices' legal adviser (or the court) may ask a witness questions and, in particular, where the defendant is not represented, may ask any question that is 'necessary in the defendant's interests'.

Criminal Practice Direction VI, para.24A.5, adds further detail:

It shall be the responsibility of the justices' clerk or legal adviser to provide the justices with any advice they require to perform their functions justly, whether or not the advice has been requested, on:

(a) questions of law;

(b) questions of mixed law and fact;

(c) matters of practice and procedure;

(d) the process to be followed at sentence and the matters to be taken into account, together with the range of penalties and ancillary orders available, in accordance with the relevant sentencing guidelines;

(e) any relevant decisions of the superior courts or other guidelines;

(f) the appropriate decision-making structure to be applied in any given case; and

(g) other issues relevant to the matter before the court.

The justices' legal adviser also has responsibility for assisting the court, where appropriate, 'as to the formulation of reasons and the recording of those reasons' (para.24A.6), and a duty to assist an unrepresented defendant, in particular when the court making a decision on allocation, bail, at trial and on sentence (para.24A.7).

Immediately prior to the commencement of a trial, the legal adviser must summarise for the court the agreed and disputed issues, together with the way in which the parties propose to present their cases. If this is done by way of pre-court briefing, it should be confirmed in court or agreed with the parties (para.24A.11).

During the trial, the court legal adviser 'may ask questions of witnesses and the parties, in order to clarify the evidence and any issues in the case. A legal adviser has a duty to ensure that every case is conducted justly' (para.24A.13).

A key aspect of the role is giving advice to the justices. It is important that the parties have an opportunity to comment on any advice given by the court legal adviser. Paragraph 24A.15 says:

At any time, justices are entitled to receive advice to assist them in discharging their responsibilities. If they are in any doubt as to the evidence which has been given, they should seek the aid of their legal adviser, referring to his notes as appropriate. This should ordinarily be done in open court. Where the justices request their adviser to join them in the retiring room, this request should be made in the presence of the parties in court. Any legal advice given to the justices other than in open court should be clearly stated to be provisional; and the adviser should subsequently repeat the substance of the advice in open court and give the parties the opportunity to make any representations they wish on that provisional advice. The legal adviser should then state in open court whether the provisional advice is confirmed or, if it is varied, the nature of the variation.

Accordingly, when a point of law arises during the course of proceedings, any advice given by the clerk to the magistrates should be given publicly in open court, so that the parties can make submissions to the bench on that advice. The clerk should not leave the court room with the justices when they retire to consider their verdict. If the magistrates require assistance from the clerk, he should join them only when asked to do so and should return to the court room once the advice has been given, so as to avoid giving the impression that he is participating improperly in the decision-making process.

Paragraph 24A.12 also makes it clear that:

A justices' clerk or legal adviser must not play any part in making findings of fact, but may assist the bench by reminding them of the evidence, using any notes of the proceedings for this purpose, and clarifying the issues which are agreed and those which are to be determined.

It follows that the clerk should not say whether or not he believes a particular witness. For example, in R v Stafford Justices ex p Ross [1962] 1 WLR 456, the conviction was quashed because, while the accused was giving evidence in his own defence, the clerk handed the bench a note which, in effect, suggested that the defendant's evidence ought not to be believed.

The adviser also has a duty to assist unrepresented parties, whether defendants or not, to present their case, but:

must do so without appearing to become an advocate for the party concerned. The legal adviser should also ensure that members of the court are aware of obligations under the Victims' Code (para.24A.16).

5.13 Committal for sentence

Even if a defendant is tried and convicted by a magistrates' court, he may still in certain circumstances be sentenced by the Crown Court.

5.13.1 Section 3 of the Powers of Criminal Courts (Sentencing) Act 2000

Section 3 of the Powers of Criminal Courts (Sentencing) Act 2000 applies where a defendant is convicted in a magistrates' court of an either-way offence. The effect of a committal under s.3 is that the defendant will be sentenced by the Crown Court, whose sentencing powers are greater than those of the magistrates' court. Section 3(2) provides that:

If the court is of the opinion that the offence or the combination of the offence and one or more offences associated with it was so serious that the Crown Court should, in the court's opinion, have the power to deal with the offender in any way it could deal with him if he had been convicted on indictment, the court may commit the offender in custody or on bail to the Crown Court for sentence in accordance with s.5(1) below.

Where the defendant is sentenced by the Crown Court following a s.3 committal, the maximum sentence which the Crown Court can impose is the same as if the defendant had just been convicted on indictment (s.5 of the Powers of Criminal Courts (Sentencing) Act 2000).

Where the defendant is committed for sentence, the committal may be on bail or in custody (s.3(1)) of the Powers of Criminal Courts (Sentencing) Act 2000). There is no presumption in favour of bail, as s.4 of the Bail Act 1976 does not apply. In R v Rafferty [1999] 1 Cr App R 235, Thomas J said (at p.237) that:

[I]n most cases where a plea of guilty is made at the plea before venue, it will not be usual to alter the position as regards bail or custody. In the usual case, when a person who has been on bail pleads guilty at the plea before venue, the usual practice should be to continue bail, even if it is anticipated that a custodial sentence will be imposed by the Crown Court, unless there are good reasons for remanding the defendant in custody. If the defendant is in custody, then after entering a plea of guilty at the plea before venue, it would be unusual, if the reasons for remanding him in custody remained unchanged, to alter the position.

Guidance on the relationship between committal for sentence and the 'plea before venue' procedure was given in R v Warley Magistrates' Court ex p DPP [1999] 1 WLR 216:

- Where a defendant indicates a guilty plea under the 'plea before venue' procedure, the magistrates must take account of the discount to be granted for that guilty plea when deciding whether or not their sentencing powers are adequate to deal with the defendant.
- Where it is clear that the case is beyond the sentencing powers of the magistrates, they should be prepared to commit the defendant to the Crown Court for sentence without first seeking a pre-sentence report or hearing a full plea in mitigation (although they should warn the defence that they have this in mind, so that the defence can make brief representations to oppose that course of action; if the magistrates are persuaded to change their minds, the prosecutor should be given a chance to reply). In other cases, the hearing should proceed as usual.
- Where there is a difference between the prosecution and defence versions of the facts of the offence:
  - if the magistrates think that their sentencing powers will be adequate however the dispute is resolved, they should adopt the procedure laid down in R v Newton (1983) 77 Cr App R 13 (either accepting the defence version or else hearing evidence and making findings of fact);
  - if they think that their sentencing powers will not be adequate however the dispute is resolved, they should simply commit for sentence, leaving the Crown Court to follow the Newton procedure;
  - if the decision whether or not to commit turns, or may turn, on which version is found to be correct, the magistrates should follow the Newton procedure; if the offender is then committed for sentence, the Crown Court should adopt the findings of fact made by the magistrates at the Newton hearing unless the defendant can point to some significant development, such as the discovery of important new evidence in his favour.

5.13.1.1 Challenging a decision to commit for sentence

If a defendant is aggrieved at a decision to commit him for sentence to the Crown Court, there is little that can be done about it. The Crown Court Crown Court cannot reject a committal for sentence unless it is 'bad on its face'. In *Sheffield Crown Court ex p DPP* (1994) 15 Cr App R (S) 768, the Crown Court declined to pass sentence following a committal for sentence and purported to remit the case back to the magistrates' court. Kennedy LJ (at p.771) said that:

> the Crown Court had no power to go behind the order of the magistrates' court which committed these matters to the Crown Court for sentence. That order was, on the face of it, a valid order. If it was to be challenged, it could only be properly challenged in this court. The position can be different where the order is obviously bad on the face of it, for example, where a case has been purportedly committed for trial when the offence is one which can only be tried summarily . . ..

A challenge by way of judicial review would succeed only if the committal were perverse (in the sense that no reasonable bench of magistrates could have decided to commit the defendant for sentence).

However, the defendant may derive some comfort from two points: firstly, it is by no means inevitable that the Crown Court will in fact impose a sentence which is more severe than the sentence which the magistrates' court could have imposed (it should be noted that s.5 of the 2000 Act says that, following a committal for sentence (e.g. under s.3), the Crown Court 'may deal with the offender in any way in which it could deal with him if he had just been convicted of the offence on indictment before the court', and so the Crown Court is not obliged to impose a sentence greater than the sentence the magistrates' court could have imposed); secondly, the Court of Appeal has jurisdiction (under s.10 of the Criminal Appeal Act 1968) to entertain an appeal against the sentence that the Crown Court imposes if it is excessive.

One basis which has been accepted for challenging the decision to commit for sentence under s.3 of the Criminal Courts (Sentencing) Act 2000 Act is where the defendant had a legitimate expectation that he would be sentenced in the magistrates' court (*R v Horseferry Road Magistrates' Court ex p Rugless* [2000] 1 Cr App R(S) 484). Indeed, in *R (Rees) v Feltham Justices* [2001] 2 Cr App R(S) 1, Rose LJ ([12]) said that, 'if justices have in mind that one of the options which is open to them is to commit for sentence, they should specifically say so'.

However, the expectation has to be a legitimate one (*R (White) v Barking Magistrates' Court* [2004] EWHC 417 (Admin)). In *R (Harrington) v Bromley Magistrates Court* [2007] EWHC 2896 (Admin), Mitting J (at [12]) said that he could not conceive of circumstances in which a properly given indication could be gone back on by a subsequent decision without that decision being held to be irrational or unlawful. Whenever the challenge arises, whether it is to the original or subsequent decision, it is the rationality and lawfulness of the first decision which ultimately determines the issue.

The Divisional Court will interfere with a decision by the magistrates' court to retain jurisdiction, rather than commit for sentence, only if that decision is 'truly astonishing' (*R v Warley Magistrates' Court ex p DPP* [1999] 1 WLR 216, p 225, per Kennedy LJ; *R (DPP) v Devizes Magistrates' Court* [2006] EWHC 1072 (Admin) at [25], per Maurice Kay LJ).

5.13.1.2 Procedure in the Crown Court

The Crown Court, when hearing a committal pursuant to s.3, comprises a circuit judge or recorder (s.74 of the Senior Courts Act 1981).

The hearing takes the same form as the sentencing procedure in the magistrates' court, and so the prosecution summarise the facts of the case and give details of the defendant's previous convictions (if any), followed by a defence plea in mitigation.

If there is a dispute between the prosecution and the defence regarding the facts of the offence, and a *Newton* hearing took place at the magistrates' court, the Crown Court should adopt the outcome. If the divergence between prosecution and defence versions becomes apparent for the first time at the Crown Court (or if no *Newton* hearing was held at the magistrates' court), the Crown Court should hold a *Newton* hearing to determine the issue (see *Munroe v DPP* (1988) 152 JP 657). A Crown Court judge has jurisdiction to allow a fresh *Newton* hearing to take place (even though one took place in the magistrates' court before the defendant was committed for sentence) if satisfied that it is in the interests of fairness and justice to do so. However, the judge should not ordinarily allow a defendant to re-open findings of fact determined by a magistrates' court unless the defendant can point to some significant development or matter, such as important further evidence discovered since the magistrates' court reached its conclusion on the facts (per Forbes J in R (*Gillan*) v DPP [2007] EWHC 380; [2007] 1 WLR 2214, at [29]).

5.13.2 Committal for breach of Crown Court order

Where a magistrates' court has convicted a defendant of any offence committed during the currency of a suspended sentence or a community order or conditional discharge imposed by the Crown Court, the magistrates can commit the defendant to be dealt with by the Crown Court for the breach of the Crown Court order (which may mean the Crown Court re-sentencing the defendant for the offence originally dealt with by the Crown Court). The relevant provisions are: s.13(5) of the Powers of Criminal Courts (Sentencing) Act 2000 (breach of Crown Court conditional discharge); sch.12, paras.8(6) and 11(2), of the Criminal Justice Act 2003 ('the 2003 Act') (breach of a requirement under a Crown Court suspended sentence and power to commit an offender convicted of an offence committed during the operational period of a Crown Court suspended sentence); sch.8, para.9(6) of the 2003 Act (power to commit an offender who is in breach of a Crown Court community order).

Where the offender is committed for sentence under these provisions, the Crown Court comprises a judge sitting alone.

5.13.3 Section 4 of the Powers of Criminal Courts (Sentencing) Act 2000

Section 4 of the Powers of Criminal Courts (Sentencing) Act 2000 provides that where the defendant has indicated that he will plead guilty to an either-way offence (and so is deemed to have pleaded guilty to it under the 'plea before venue procedure') and he is also sent for trial for one or more related offences, the magistrates may commit him to the Crown Court for sentence in respect of the either-way offence to which he has pleaded guilty. For the purposes of these provisions, one offence is related to another if the charges for them could (if both were to be tried in the Crown Court) be joined in the same indictment (s.4(7)), so the two charges must be founded on the same facts or must be a series (or part of a series) of offences of the same or similar character.

Section 4(4) provides that, where the justices have committed a defendant for sentence pursuant to s.4(2), the Crown Court can exceed the sentencing powers of the magistrates' court in respect of the either-way offence to which the defendant indicated a plea of guilty only if either:

- the magistrates, when they committed for sentence under s.4, stated that they considered their sentencing powers were inadequate to deal with the defendant for that offence (and so they also had power to commit him for sentence under s.3); or
- he is also convicted by the Crown Court of one or more of the related offences.

The relationship between s.3 and s.4 of the Powers of Criminal Courts (Sentencing) Act 2000 may seem rather confusing. The purpose of s.4 is to ensure that, if the defendant is to be tried in the Crown Court for an offence which is related to an offence to which he has indicated a guilty plea at the 'plea before venue' hearing, then the magistrates can commit him to the Crown Court for sentence for that latter offence even if their sentencing powers are adequate to deal with that offence (and so a committal under s.3 would be not be possible).

If the magistrates take the view that their sentencing powers are adequate to deal with the offence in respect of which the defendant has indicated a guilty plea, then only s.4 allows them to commit him to the Crown Court for sentence for that offence. On the other hand, if the magistrates take the view that their sentencing powers are not adequate to deal with that offence, they have two options: they can either commit him for sentence for that offence under s.3, or they can commit him for sentence under s.4 but indicate that they took the view that their sentencing powers were inadequate and so could have invoked s.3. Obviously, the best practice would be to use s.3 where the magistrates' sentencing powers are not adequate and to use s.4 where their powers are adequate. In any event, when committing a defendant for sentence in these circumstances, the court should state whether it is doing so under s.3 or s.4. If the magistrates commit under s.4 but do not consider that their sentencing powers are adequate to deal with the offence, they should state (under s.4(4)) that they also had the power to commit the defendant for sentence under s.3, so as to avoid inadvertently fettering the powers of the Crown Court when dealing with the offence if the defendant is not convicted of the offence(s) being tried in the Crown Court.

5.13.4 Dangerous offenders: s.3A of the Powers of Criminal Courts (Sentencing) Act 2000

Section 3A of the 2000 Act applies where, following the summary trial of a specified offence which is triable either way (that is, one to which the 'dangerous offender' provisions in the Criminal Justice Act 2003 apply), a person aged 18 or over is convicted of the offence. By virtue of s.3A(2), if it appears to the court that the criteria for the imposition of a sentence under s.226A of the Criminal Justice Act 2003 would be met, the court must commit the offender to the Crown Court for sentence.

Where the magistrates' sentencing powers for the offence in question are inadequate, the option of committing under s.3 remains available (s.3A(5)).

Any other offences that the magistrates would otherwise be dealing with may be committed to the Crown Court for sentence under s.6 (s.3A(3)).

5.13.5 Section 6 of the Powers of Criminal Courts (Sentencing) Act 2000

Section 6 of the Powers of Criminal Courts (Sentencing) Act 2000 gives a power to commit for sentence which may be used to supplement a committal under any of the following provisions:

- ss.3 to 4A of the 2000 Act;
- s.13(5) of the 2000 Act (conviction places defendant in breach of a Crown Court conditional discharge);
- sch.12, para.11(2), of the Criminal Justice Act 2003 (committal to Crown Court where offender convicted during operational period of suspended sentence).

These committal powers may conveniently be referred to as 'primary powers'.

Under s.6(2) of the 2000 Act, when a magistrates' court exercises a primary committal power in respect of an indictable (including either-way) offence, it may also commit the offender to the Crown Court to be dealt with in respect of any other offence of which he stands convicted (whether summary or indictable) that the magistrates' court has jurisdiction to deal with. Thus, to take the example of a magistrates' court which has decided to commit an offender (under s.3) for an either-way offence, a committal under s.6 may (for example) relate to:

- another, less serious, either-way offence of which the magistrates have convicted the offender on the same occasion; or
- a summary offence of which they have convicted the offender on the same occasion.

Committal under s.3 for the secondary offence would not be appropriate in the first of these situations because the offence is not sufficiently serious, so the magistrates' powers of sentencing for it are adequate. In the second situation, a s.3 committal would be not be possible because that section does not apply to summary offences.

Another use of s.6 is where a conviction in the magistrates' court puts the offender in breach of a suspended sentence passed by the Crown Court and the magistrates consider that, although the breach should be committed to the Crown Court under sch.12, para.11(2)(a) of the Criminal Justice Act 2003, the offence giving rise to the breach is not in itself serious enough to warrant committal under s.3. The court should then commit the offender under para.11(2)(a), for possible activation of the suspended sentence, and under s.6, for sentence for the present offence.

Section 7(1) of the 2000 Act provides that, following a committal under s.6, the Crown Court may deal with the offender in any way the magistrates' court might have done had it not committed the offender to the Crown Court under s.6. The Crown Court's powers on a committal under s.6 are thus identical to the powers of the magistrates' court. This is because the purpose of a s.6 committal is to enable one court to deal with an offender for all matters outstanding against him, not to increase the sentence that may be imposed.

Two examples may help to illustrate the scope of s.6 of the 2000 Act:

- The defendant is charged with theft (triable either way) and common assault (a summary offence) and the magistrates convict him of both charges. The magistrates decide that their sentencing powers are inadequate to deal with the theft and so they commit the defendant to the Crown Court in respect of that offence under s.3 of the 2000 Act. This section does not apply to summary offences and so cannot be used to enable the magistrates to commit the defendant to the Crown Court for the common assault. However, s.6 enables the magistrates to commit the defendant to the Crown Court for the common assault, and so the Crown Court can sentence him for both offences.
- The defendant is charged with theft. The theft in question is a very minor offence and so the magistrates cannot invoke s.3 of the 2000 Act (since their sentencing powers are plainly adequate to deal with the theft). However, the defendant committed the theft while he was subject to a conditional discharge imposed by the Crown Court. If the magistrates want the Crown Court to deal with the defendant for the theft as well as dealing with him for the breach of the conditional discharge, they can commit him to the Crown Court to be dealt with for the breach of the conditional discharge and, under s.6, in respect of the theft.

Section 7(2) of the 2000 Act provides that the limitation on sentencing powers contained in s.7(1) does not apply where a magistrates' court commits a person under s.6 to be dealt with by the Crown Court in respect of a suspended sentence; instead, the powers in paras.8 and 9 of sch.12 to the Criminal Justice Act 2003 apply. In R v Bateman [2012] EWCA Crim 2158; [2013] 1 WLR 1710, Moore-Bick LJ said (at [20]) that s.7(2) is referring to a suspended sentence previously imposed by a magistrates' court. This provision enables the Crown Court to exercise the powers under the 2003 Act which could otherwise have been exercised by the magistrates themselves, and ensures that, on committal to the Crown Court under s.6, a person is not exposed to a more severe penalty than could have been imposed on him by the magistrates.

Where the offender is in breach of a suspended sentence imposed by the Crown Court, and the breach is because of the commission of an either-way offence, the magistrates' court should consider carefully whether its sentencing powers are adequate in respect of the offence which constituted the breach. If the magistrates consider that the gravity of the offence which constitutes the breach, together with any associated matters, is such as to justify committal under s.3 (on the basis that their sentencing powers are inadequate), then the offence(s) should be committed pursuant to s.3, rather than s.6, so that the Crown Court's powers are those contained in s.5, not those contained in s.7 (per Moore-Bick LJ in *Bateman*, at [31]).

5.13.6 Errors in the committal process

Sometimes the basis of a committal for sentence is mis-described by the magistrates' court. In R v *Ayhan* [2011] EWCA Crim 3184; [2012] 1 WLR 1775, Lord Judge CJ said (at [22]):

> [P]rovided the power of the magistrates' court to commit for sentence was properly exercised in respect of one or more either way offences in accordance with s.3 of the 2000 Act, a mistake in recording the statutory basis for a committal of summary only offences does not invalidate the committal. The principle is that thereafter the Crown Court must abide by the sentencing powers available to the magistrates' court in relation to the summary only offences. If that principle is not followed, then the sentences must be reduced to sentences which fall within the jurisdiction of the magistrates.

This approach was followed in R v *Luff* [2013] EWCA Crim 1958, where Bean J (at [23]) said:

> The appellant's committal for sentence on the breach charge should have been under s.4. The justices had that power and should have been advised to use it. They could not have committed under s.6 because they had no such jurisdiction. The reference to s.6 was therefore a mistake, and the committal should be treated as having been under s.4.

Chapter 6

Young Defendants and Youth Court Trials

In this chapter we look at the trial of young defendants (those under the age of 18) in the youth court and those exceptional situations where a young defendant must or may be tried in an adult court.

6.1 The aims of the youth justice system

Section s.37(1) of the Crime and Disorder Act 1998 provides that it 'shall be the principal aim of the youth justice system to prevent offending by children and young persons'. However, s.44(1) of the Children and Young Persons Act 1933 provides that every court 'in dealing with a child or young person who is brought before it, either as an offender or otherwise, shall have regard to the welfare of the child or young person'.

6.1.1 Terminology

The 'youth court' has jurisdiction to deal with young defendants, namely those aged 10–17 years (inclusive); 10–13-year-olds are called 'children' and 14–17-year-olds are called 'young persons'.

6.1.2 Age of criminal responsibility

There is an irrebuttable presumption that a person who is under the age of 10 cannot be guilty of a criminal offence (s.50 of the Children and Young Persons Act 1933). In T v United Kingdom (2000) 30 EHRR 121, the European Court of Human Rights rejected the argument that this age was too low. The Court noted (at [48]) that the age of criminal responsibility varies widely across Europe, from 7 to 18, and went on to say (at [72]):

> The Court does not consider that there is at this stage any clear common standard amongst the member States of the Council of Europe as to the minimum age of criminal responsibility. Even if England and Wales is among the few European jurisdictions to retain a low age of criminal responsibility, the age of ten cannot be said to be so young as to differ disproportionately from the age-limit followed by other European States. The Court concludes that the attribution of criminal responsibility to the applicant does not in itself give rise to a breach of Art.3 of the Convention.

There used to be a rebuttable presumption that a child aged between 10 and 14 was incapable of committing an offence. This presumption, sometimes called *doli incapax*, was that children under the age of 14 did not know the difference between right and wrong (and therefore were incapable of committing a crime) unless the prosecution were able to prove that they did have this understanding. Hence, a child aged under 14 could be convicted of a criminal offence only if the presumption of *doli incapax* was first rebutted. To rebut the presumption, the prosecution had to adduce evidence to prove that the child knew that what he was doing was seriously wrong, rather than simply naughty. This presumption was, however, abolished by s.34 of the Crime and Disorder Act 1998. In R v JTB [2009] UKHL 20; [2009] 1 AC 1310, the House of Lords confirmed that, by enacting s.34, Parliament intended to abolish both the presumption and the defence of *doli incapax*, so it is not open to a defendant to raise *doli incapax* as a defence.

For a brief discussion of the age of criminal responsibility, see Penelope Brown, 'Reviewing the age of criminal responsibility' [2018] Crim LR 904-909.

6.1.3 Youth offending teams

Pursuant to s.39 of the Crime and Disorder Act 1998, each local authority has to establish a youth offending team ('YOT'). Each YOT includes a probation officer, a person with experience of social work in relation to children, a social worker, a police officer and a person with experience in education. The functions of the YOT are to co-ordinate the provision of youth justice services for all those in the authority's area who need them, and to carry out such functions as are assigned to it in the local authority's 'youth justice plan'.

6.2 Youth courts

By virtue of s.45(2) of the Children and Young Persons Act 1933, a lay justice or district judge has to be authorised to sit in a youth court before he/she can do so. Magistrates (including district judges) have to receive special training before being authorised to sit in the youth court.

A key point to underline about the jurisdiction of the youth court is that the distinction between indictable, triable either way and summary offences does not apply to young defendants. Thus, a bench of justices in the youth court may try an offence which, in the case of an adult defendant, would be triable only in the Crown Court. Furthermore, a child/young person has no right to elect Crown Court trial in any case where an adult defendant would have such a right (although the justices in the youth court may decline jurisdiction in respect of certain indictable offences – see below).

A useful resource is the *Youth Court Bench Book* (Judicial College, August 2017).

6.2.1 Attendance of parent or guardian

Section 34A(1) of the Children and Young Persons Act 1933 provides that if the child/young person is under 16, the court must (or, if the child/young person is 16 or 17, the court may) require a parent or guardian 'to attend at the court during all the stages of the proceedings, unless and to the extent that the court is satisfied that it would be unreasonable to require such attendance, having regard to the circumstances of the case'. A child or young person who is in local authority care will be accompanied by a local authority social worker or foster parent (see s.34A(2)).

The Sentencing Council Guideline on children and young persons (at para.3.2) says that, although this requirement can cause a delay, 'it is important it is adhered to. If a court does find exception to proceed in the absence of a responsible adult then extra care must be taken to ensure the outcomes are clearly communicated to and understood by the child or young person'.

6.2.2 Reporting restrictions in the youth court

Under s.49(1) of the Children and Young Persons Act 1933, no matter relating to any child or young person concerned in youth court proceedings (or appeals from youth court proceedings) may, while he is under the age of 18, be included in any publication if it is likely to lead members of the public to identify him as someone concerned in the proceedings. For these purposes, a person is 'concerned in the proceedings' if he is the accused or a witness (subs.(4)). The protected information includes the person's name and address, the identity of any school or other educational establishment he attends, and the identity of any place of work; the restriction also applies to any 'still or moving picture of him' (subs.3A)).

For these purposes, 'publication' is defined very widely, and includes 'any speech, writing, relevant programme or other communication in whatever form, which is addressed to the public at large or any section of the public (subs.(3)).

It should be noted that the restrictions imposed by s.49 apply only while the person in question remains under the age of 18. This is seen by some as a disadvantage because of the risk that media reporting of the offending once the person becomes an adult may have an adverse effect on their rehabilitation.

Breach of the restrictions imposed by s.49 is a summary offence, punishable with a fine of any amount (subs.(9)).

The court may lift the ban on publicity to the extent it considers necessary either to avoid injustice to the child or young person (s.49(5)(a)) or, in the case of one who is unlawfully at large, where it is necessary to do so for the purpose of apprehending him (s.49(5)(b)). However, s.49(5)(b) applies only to a child or young person who is charged with, or convicted of, a violent or sexual offence or an offence punishable in the case of an adult with imprisonment for 14 years or more; moreover, the power conferred by s.49(5)(b) may be exercised only upon the application of the DPP (this includes Crown Prosecutors) (s.49(7)). An order under s.49(5)(a) might be appropriate where, for example, the defence wish to make an appeal for potential witnesses to come forward.

The court may also lift the ban on publicity where a child or young person has been convicted of an offence, if it is satisfied that it is in the public interest to do so (s.49(4A)). Before doing so, it must afford an opportunity to the parties to make representations (s.49(4B)).

In *McKerry v Teesdale Justices* (2000) 164 JP 355, Lord Bingham CJ stressed (at [25]) that the power to dispense with anonymity must be exercised with 'very great care, caution and circumspection', and added:

> It would be wholly wrong for any court to dispense with a child/young person's prima facie right to anonymity as an additional punishment. It is also very difficult to see any place for 'naming and shaming'. The court must be satisfied that the statutory criterion that it is in the public interest to dispense with the reporting restriction is satisfied. This will very rarely be the case, and justices making an order under s.49(4A) must be clear in their minds why it is in the public interest to dispense with the restrictions.

6.2.3 Detention where bail is withheld

Section 91 of the Legal Aid, Sentencing and Punishment of Offenders Act 2012 applies where a person under 18 is charged with, or convicted of, one or more offences. It provides that, if the child/young person is not released on bail, the court must remand him to local authority accommodation, in accordance with s.92, or to youth detention accommodation, in accordance with s.102.

6.2.3.1 Remands to local authority accommodation

This is a remand to accommodation provided by or on behalf of the local authority designated by the court (s.92(1)).

Section 93 enables the court, when remanding to local authority accommodation, to impose any conditions that could be imposed under s.3(6) of the Bail Act 1976. Under s.93(3), a court remanding a child/young person to local authority accommodation may also impose requirements on the designated authority to secure compliance with the conditions imposed on the child/young person; the court can also stipulate that the child/young person must not be placed with a named person.

6.2.3.2 Remands to youth detention accommodation

Remand to 'youth detention accommodation' means remand to a secure children's home, a secure training centre, a young offender institution, or detention accommodation for detention and training orders (s.102). Remand to youth detention accommodation is possible only where either of two sets of conditions (set out in ss.98 and 99) is satisfied (s.91(4)).

The first set of conditions (in s.98) is as follows:

- *age condition*: the child/young person must have attained the age of twelve;
- *offence condition*: one or more of the offences must be:
  - a violent or sexual offence (specified in sch.15 to the Criminal Justice Act 2003); or
  - an offence punishable with at least 14 years' imprisonment;
- *necessity condition*: the court must be of the opinion, after considering all the options for the remand of the child/young person, that only a remand to youth detention accommodation would be adequate to:
  - protect the public from death or serious personal injury (whether physical or psychological) occasioned by further offences committed by the child/young person; or
  - to prevent the child/young person committing imprisonable offences;
- *representation condition*:
  - the child/young person is legally represented at court; or
  - representation has been withdrawn because of the child/young person's conduct or because it appeared that the child/young person's financial resources were such that he was not eligible for such representation; or
  - representation was refused because it appeared that the child/young person's financial resources rendered him ineligible for such representation; or
  - the child/young person has refused to apply for representation.

The second set of conditions (in s.99) is as follows:

- *age condition*: the child/young person must have attained the age of twelve;
- *sentencing condition*: there must be a real prospect that the child/young person will be sentenced to a custodial sentence;
- *offence condition*: one or more of the offences is imprisonable;
- *history condition*:
  - the child/young person has a recent history of absconding while subject to a custodial remand and one or more of the present offences is alleged (or found) to have been committed while he was remanded to local authority accommodation or youth detention accommodation; or
  - the offence(s) amount, or would (assuming the child/young person is convicted) amount, to a recent history of committing imprisonable offences while on bail or subject to a custodial remand;
- *necessity condition* (as under s.98);
- *representation condition* (as under s.98).

6.2.4 Differences between the youth court and the adult magistrates' court

The main difference between the youth court and the ordinary (adult) magistrates' court is that there is less formality in the youth court than in an adult magistrates' court. For example:

- there is no dock;
- the accused and any witnesses under the age of 18 are addressed by their first names;
- the oath taken by witnesses is to promise (not swear) to tell the truth;
- the terminology differs slightly, for example, a 'finding of guilt' (not a 'conviction') and an 'order made upon a finding of guilt' (not a 'sentence'). Note, however, that the child/young person pleads 'guilty' or 'not guilty'.

6.2.4.1 Exclusion of the public

The public are excluded from the courtroom by virtue of s.47(2) of the Children and Young Persons Act 1933, the effect of which is summarised by r.24.2(1)(c) of the Criminal Procedure Rules:

> [U]nless the court otherwise directs, only the following may attend a hearing in a youth court –
> (i) the parties and their legal representatives;
> (ii) a defendant's parents, guardian or other supporting adult;
> (iii) a witness;
> (iv) anyone else directly concerned in the case; and
> (v) a representative of a news-gathering or reporting organisation.

The youth court can (under s.47(2)(d)) specially authorise other people (such as law students) to be present.

Note that if a child/young person is appearing as an accused, or as a witness, in the adult magistrates' court or the Crown Court, the public have the right to be present unless the court takes the exceptional step of sitting in private.

6.2.5 Summary trial procedure

Where the child/young person pleads not guilty, the trial procedure is the same as that in the adult magistrates' court (and so the sequence of events set out in r.24.3 of the Criminal Procedure Rules takes place).

Under r.24.11(7)(a), if the child/young person pleads guilty or is found guilty, the court must, before passing sentence, give the defendant, and his parents, guardian or other supporting adult, if present, an opportunity to make representations.

6.3 Court of first appearance

The young defendant's first court appearance in respect of an offence will be in the youth court unless the case is one of the exceptional ones where the first appearance is in the adult magistrates' court. Those exceptional cases are where:

● the child/young person is jointly charged with an adult; or
● the child/young person is charged with aiding and abetting an adult to commit an offence (or vice versa); or
● the child/young person is charged with an offence which arises out of circumstances which are the same as (or connected with) those which resulted in the charge faced by an adult accused.

These exceptions exist because no one who is 18 or older at the time of their first court appearance will appear in the youth court, yet defendants who are jointly charged (or charged with closely connected offences) should appear together in court. The result is that a child/young person in such a case appears alongside the adult in an adult magistrates' court.

6.4 Place of trial

A child/young person may be tried in the youth court for an offence which is triable only on indictment in the case of an adult offender, and a child/young person never has a right to elect trial on indictment.

However, there are circumstances in which a child/young person may be tried in the Crown Court or in an adult magistrates' court. The law in this area is rather complicated, as it is to be found in a combination of statutory sources:

- s.46 of the Children and Young Persons Act 1933;
- s.18 of the Children and Young Persons Act 1963;
- s.24 of the Magistrates' Courts Act 1980;
- s.29 of the Magistrates' Courts Act 1980;
- s.51A of the Crime and Disorder Act 1998.

The key points may, however, be summarised quite briefly. There are five circumstances in which the trial of a child/young person may take place in the Crown Court. These are where the child/young person is charged with:

- homicide (i.e. murder or manslaughter);
- an offence to which a mandatory minimum sentence applies:
  - a firearms offence where there is a mandatory minimum sentence under s.51A of the Firearms Act 1968;
  - s.29(3) of Violent Crime Reduction Act 2006 (minimum sentences in certain cases of using someone to mind a weapon);
- an offence to which s.91 of the Powers of Criminal Courts (Sentencing) Act 2000 applies (i.e. an offence which carries at least 14 years' imprisonment in the case of an adult or one that is specified in s.91 itself);
- a 'specified' offence as defined by s.224 of the Criminal Justice Act 2003 (and so falling within the ambit of the 'dangerous offender' provisions of that Act); or
- an offence where there is an adult co-accused.

There is only one situation where the trial of a child/young person may take place in an adult magistrates' court, namely where the child/young person is charged alongside an adult.

6.5 Crown Court trial of child/young persons

Firstly, we examine the situations where a child/young person either must or else may be tried in the Crown Court. See also Figure 6.1.

6.5.1 Murder and manslaughter

Where a child/young person is charged with homicide (that is, murder or manslaughter), the trial must take place in the Crown Court (s.51A(2) of Crime and Disorder Act 1998).

6.5.2 Section 91 of the Powers of Criminal Courts (Sentencing) Act 2000

Another situation where a child/young person may be tried in the Crown Court is where s.91 of the Powers of Criminal Courts (Sentencing) Act 2000 applies to the offence. Section 91 empowers the Crown Court to order that a child/young person be detained for a period not exceeding the

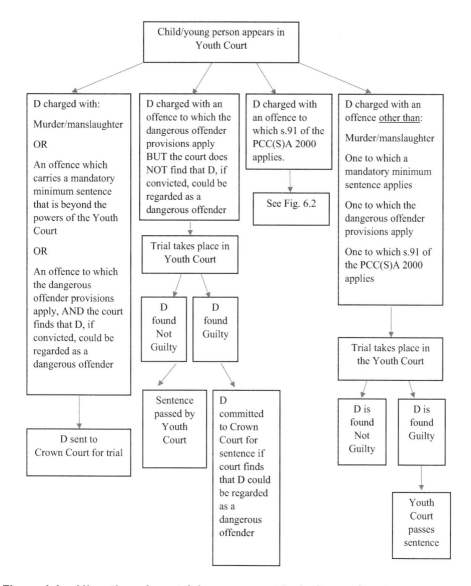

Figure 6.1 Allocation where trial may or must be in Crown Court

maximum sentence of imprisonment which may be imposed on an adult offender for the offence in question. Under s.91(1), this power applies only where a child/young person who has attained the age of 10 is charged with:

- an offence which carries at least 14 years' imprisonment in the case of an adult offender;
- certain offences under the Sexual Offences Act 2003, including s.3 of that Act (sexual assault);
- a firearms offence to which the mandatory minimum sentence provisions in s.51A of the Firearms Act 1968 apply; or
- an offence under s.28 of the Violent Crime Reduction Act 2006 (using someone to mind a weapon) to which the minimum sentence provisions in s.29(3) of that Act apply.

The offences to which s.91 applies are sometimes referred to as 'grave' crimes.

The power to send a child/young person for trial in the Crown Court if charged with one or more of these offences is contained in s.51A(3)(b) of the Crime and Disorder Act 1998, which empowers the magistrates to send the child/young person to the Crown Court for trial if:

- s.91 of the 2000 Act applies to the offence; *and*
- the court "considers that if he is found guilty of the offence it ought to be possible to sentence him" to detention under s.91.

These provisions are necessary because of the relatively limited ambit of the custodial sentence that would normally be applicable in the case of an offender under the age of 18, namely the detention and training order ('DTO'). The DTO is limited to a total of 24 months (12 months' custody followed by 12 months' supervision); where the offender has not attained the age of 15, a DTO can be made only if he is a 'persistent offender'; and the DTO is not available at all where the offender is under 12. Section 91 of the Powers of Criminal Courts (Sentencing) Act 2000 enables the Crown Court to pass a longer term of detention than would otherwise be possible (given the 24-month limit on the duration of the DTO), and it enables the Crown Court to impose a term of detention where otherwise no detention would be possible (in the case of an offender under the age of 12, or an offender under the age of 15 who is not a persistent offender).

It should be noted that the Crown Court is not obliged to pass a sentence of detention under s.91 of the 2000 Act. The court retains the power to deal with the offender in any way that the youth court could have done. If the Crown Court decides not to sentence the child/young person under s.91, it is undesirable for the Crown Court to remit the case to the youth court for sentence (under s.8 of the 2000 Act), since the youth court will already have expressed the view that the case is too serious for its powers (see R v *Allen and Lambert* (1999) 163 JP 841).

See also Figure 6.2.

6.5.2.1 The decision to send for trial in a s.91 case

A young defendant should be sent for Crown Court trial under these provisions only if the case is sufficiently serious to justify a sentence of detention under s.91 of the 2000 Act. In R (D) v *Manchester City Youth Court* [2001] EWHC 860 (Admin); [2002] 1 Cr App R(S) 135, Gage J said (at [22]) that:

> a magistrates' court should not decline jurisdiction unless the offence and the circum-stances surrounding it and the offender are such as to make it more than a vague or theoretical possibility that a sentence of detention [under s.91] may be passed.

There is nothing in the statute to prevent the Crown Court using its powers under s.91 to impose a sentence of less than two years' detention. However, in R (W) v *Thetford Youth Court* [2002] EWHC 1252; [2003] 1 Cr App R(S) 67, Gage J said (at [29]–[30]):

> [W]here an offence or offences are likely to attract a sentence of less than two years' custody the appropriate sentence will be a detention and training order. In the case of an offender under 15, who is not a persistent offender or a child under 12, the most likely sentence will be a noncustodial sentence. It follows that in most cases the appropriate place of trial will be the youth court ... [C]ases involving offenders under 15 for whom a detention and training order is not available will only rarely attract a period of detention under s.91; the more rarely if the offender is under 12.

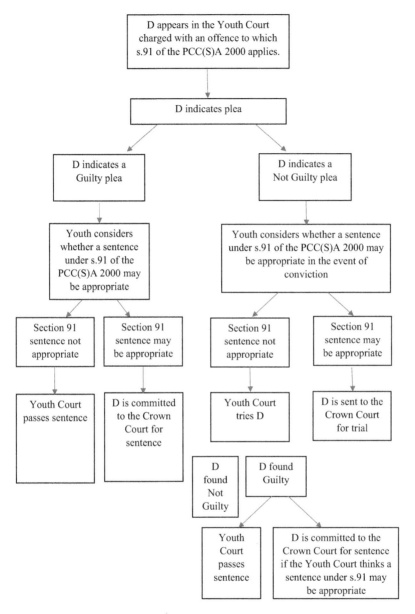

Figure 6.2   Allocation where s. 91 of the PCC(S)A 2000 applies

Similarly, in R (B) v Norfolk Youth Court [2013] EWHC 1459 (Admin), Cox J (at [50]) said that, 'a trial in the Crown Court should be reserved for those most serious and ... exceptional cases, which truly merit the description "grave crimes"', adding that, to fall within that definition, an offence would have to be 'so serious that it necessitated the exceptional course of declining jurisdiction for such crimes. The exceptional power to detain for grave crimes should not be used to water down the general principle that a child ... should stand trial in the Youth Court, which is, for him, the appropriate place of trial'.

Leveson J summarised the relevant principles in R (H) v *Southampton Youth Court* [2004] EWHC 2912 (Admin); [2005] 2 Cr App R (S) 30, at [33]–[35]:

(1) The general policy of the legislature is that those who are under 18 years of age and in particular children of under 15 years of age should, wherever possible, be tried in the youth court. It is that court which is best designed to meet their specific needs. A trial in the Crown Court with the inevitably greater formality and greatly increased number of people involved (including a jury and the public) should be reserved for the most serious cases.

(2) It is a further policy of the legislature that, generally speaking, first-time offenders aged 12 to 14 and all offenders under 12 should not be detained in custody and decisions as to jurisdiction should have regard to the fact that the exceptional power to detain for grave offences should not be used to water down the general principle. Those under 15 will rarely attract a period of detention and, even more rarely, those who are under 12.

(3) In each case the court should ask itself whether there is a real prospect, having regard to his or her age, that this defendant whose case they are considering might require a sentence of, or in excess of, two years or, alternatively, whether although the sentence might be less than two years, there is some unusual feature of the case which justifies declining jurisdiction, bearing in mind that the absence of a power to impose a detention and training order because the defendant is under 15 is not an unusual feature.

Another helpful summary may be found in R (CPS) v *Redbridge Youth Court* [2005] EWHC 1390; (2005) 169 JP 393, at [11]:

- Although it is not necessary, in order to invoke the provisions under s.91, that the crime be one of exceptional gravity, the power to make an order for detention is a 'long-stop reserved for very serious offences'.
- The Youth Court should start with a strong presumption against sending a young defendant to the Crown Court unless it is satisfied that this is clearly required, notwithstanding the fact that the forum for trial will not be so appropriate for trial as the Youth Court. The general policy of the legislature is that those who are under 18 years of age and, in particular, children under 15 years of age, should, wherever possible, be tried in the Youth Court. A trial in the Crown Court should be reserved for the most serious cases.
- Accordingly, a magistrates' court should not decline jurisdiction unless the offence and the circumstances surrounding it and the offender are such as to make it more than a vague or theoretical possibility that a sentence of detention for a long period may be passed under s.91.
- Given that the maximum period for which a magistrates' court may impose a detention and training order is 24 months, s.91 is primarily applicable to cases of such gravity that the court is or may be considering a sentence of at least two years.

An important consideration is the power to commit to the Crown Court for sentence in s.91 cases under s.3B of the Powers of Criminal Courts (Sentencing) Act 2000 (see Chapter 15). When originally enacted, this power applied only where the child/young person had been convicted following trial in the Crown Court. However, s.3B was subsequently amended so that it also permits committal for sentence in s.91 cases where the child/young person pleads guilty in the youth court. Prior to this amendment, if the youth court accepted jurisdiction to try a s.91 case, that removed the possibility of a committal for sentence under s.3B and with it the possibility of an order for long-term detention under s.91. The amendment has the effect that, even if the trial of the s.91 offence takes place in the youth court, a sentence under s.91 may nonetheless be passed by the Crown Court. In R (DPP) v South Tyneside Youth Court [2015] EWHC 1455 (Admin); [2015] 2 Cr App R (S) 59, the court considered the effect of this amendment of s.3B. Sir Brian Leveson P (at [31]) observed that, because s.3B (as amended) 'means that the youth court is not making a once and for all decision at the point of allocation, the "real prospect" assessment requires a different emphasis'. His Lordship continued:

> [T]here will, of course, be cases in which the alleged offending is so grave that a sentence of or [in] excess of two years will be a 'real prospect' irrespective of particular considerations in relation either to the offence or the offender's role in it: such cases are, however, likely to be rare. As the time of allocation and determination of venue, the court will doubtless take the views of the prosecution and defence into account; these views could include representations as [to] the value of privacy of the proceedings or, alternatively, the desire for a jury trial. Subject to such submissions, however, in most cases whether there is such a 'real prospect' will generally be apparent only when the court has determined the full circumstances of the offence and has a far greater understanding of the position of the offender. Since the youth court now has the option of committing a defendant for sentence after conviction if the court considers that the Crown Court should have the power to impose a sentence of detention pursuant to s.91(3) of the 2000 Act, it will generally be at that point when the assessment can and should be made. In that way, the observations in Southampton Youth Court (at [33]) that Crown Court trial for a youth 'should be reserved for the most serious cases' remain entirely apposite.

The Sentencing Council Guideline on Sentencing Children and Young People (para.2.10) adds that it should be borne in mind that there is a power to commit grave crimes for sentence:

> Before deciding whether to send the case to the Crown Court or retain jurisdiction in the youth court, the court should hear submissions from the prosecution and defence. As there is now a power to commit grave crimes for sentence, the court should no longer take the prosecution case at its highest when deciding whether to retain jurisdiction. In most cases it is likely to be impossible to decide whether there is a real prospect that a sentence in excess of two years' detention will be imposed without knowing more about the facts of the case and the circumstances of the child or young person. In those circumstances the youth court should retain jurisdiction and commit for sentence if it is of the view, having heard more about the facts and the circumstances of the child or young person, that its powers of sentence are insufficient.
>
> . . .
>
> Children and young people should only be sent for trial or committed for sentence to the Crown Court when charged with or found guilty of an offence of such gravity that a custodial sentence substantially exceeding two years is a realistic possibility. For children aged 10 or 11, and children/young people aged 12–14 who are not persistent offenders, the court should take into account the normal prohibition on imposing custodial sentences.

In R (W & others) v Brent Youth Court [2006] EWHC 95; (2006) 170 JP 198, Smith LJ (at [9]) pointed out that where several defendants are charged together and all are under 18, the court must consider the position of each defendant separately 'even if this results in one defendant being tried in the Youth Court and others in the Crown Court'. It follows that one child/young person cannot be sent to the Crown Court for trial merely because a child/young person co-accused is being sent there (R (W and M) v Oldham Youth Court [2010] EWHC 661 (Admin)).

The decision to send a child/young person for trial under s.51A of the Crime and Disorder Act is based on representations made by the prosecution and the defence. No evidence is called (R v South Hackney Child/young person Court ex p RB and CB (1983) 77 Cr App R 294).

In reaching its decision, the court is entitled to know about any previous findings of guilt recorded against the child/young person (R (Tullet) v Medway Magistrates' Court [2003] EWHC 2279 (Admin); (2003) 167 JP 541).

Where a youth court intends to decline jurisdiction to hear a case and send a young defendant for trial at the Crown Court, the magistrates should give reasons for this decision (R (C) v Balham Youth Court [2003] EWHC 1332 (Admin); [2004] 1 Cr App R (S) 22 (per Scott Baker LJ, at [14]).

6.5.2.2 Related offences

Section 51A(4) of the Crime and Disorder Act 1998 empowers the magistrates, if they send a child/young person for trial for an offence to which s.91 of the 2000 Act applies, to send him for trial for any indictable or summary offence with which he is also charged and which appears to the court to be related to the s.91 offence (if the offence is a summary one it must be punishable with imprisonment or involve disqualification from driving).

6.5.2.3 Challenging refusal to send for trial in a s.91 case

If the child/young person is charged with an offence which falls within the ambit of s.91 of the Powers of Criminal Courts (Sentencing) Act 2000 but the magistrates decide to try the case summarily, the prosecution may seek judicial review to quash that decision if it is unreasonable (R v Inner London Youth Court ex p DPP (1997) 161 JP 178).

6.5.2.4 Challenging the decision to send for trial in a s.91 case

Similarly, the appropriate procedure for challenging a decision to send a child/young person to the Crown Court for trial is to seek judicial review in the High Court (R v AH [2002] EWCA Crim 2938; (2003) 167 JP 30).

In R (W) v Thetford Youth Court [2002] EWHC 1252; [2003] 1 Cr App R(S)67, Sedley LJ (at [40]) said that the question is 'not whether the youth court's judgment has crossed the bounds of rationality but whether in our judgment it is wrong'.

6.5.3 Joint charge with adult to be tried in the Crown Court

The next situation where a child/young person may be tried in the Crown Court is where the child/young person is charged alongside an adult. In that case, their first court appearance will be in an adult magistrates' court.

Section 51(7) of the Crime and Disorder Act 1998 provides that, where the magistrates' court sends an adult for trial under s.51, and a child/young person appears before the court on the same or a subsequent occasion charged jointly with the adult with the offence for which the adult is sent for trial (or is charged with an indictable offence which appears to the court to be related to that offence), the court 'shall, if it considers it necessary in the interests of justice to do so, send the child or young person forthwith to the Crown Court for trial for the indictable offence'.

By virtue of s.51(8), where the court sends a child/young person for trial under s. 51(7), it may also send him to the Crown Court for trial for any indictable or summary offence with which he is charged and which is related to the offence for which he is sent for trial (if it is a summary offence, it must be punishable with imprisonment or involve obligatory or discretionary disqualification from driving).

In deciding whether or not it is 'necessary in the interests of justice' to send the child/young person to the Crown Court under s.51(7), the court has to balance what may well be conflicting interests. On the one hand, it is desirable that there should be a joint trial, to avoid the cost and inconvenience of having two trials (for example, prosecution witnesses having to give their evidence twice), to avoid the risk of inconsistent verdicts, and to avoid the risk of disparity in the sentences which are passed in the event of conviction. On the other hand, a young defendant may well find appearing in the Crown Court an unduly traumatic experience.

Generally speaking, the younger the child/young person and the less serious the charge, the more reluctant the justices should be to send the child/young person to the Crown Court. Also relevant is the likely plea of the young defendant and the degree of his involvement in the offence. If the young defendant is likely to plead guilty and it is accepted by the prosecution that he played only a minor role in the offence, it is likely to be more appropriate to deal with him separately.

In R(CPS) v South East Surrey Youth Court [2005] EWHC 2929 (Admin); [2006] 1 WLR 2543, Rose LJ (at [17]) said that:

> when a youth under 18 is jointly charged with an adult, an exercise of judgment will be called for by the youth court when assessing the competing presumptions in favour of (a) joint trial of those jointly charged and (b) the trial of youths in the youth court. Factors relevant to that judgment will include the age and maturity of the youth, the comparative culpability in relation to the offence and the previous convictions of the two and whether the trial can be severed without either injustice or undue inconvenience to witnesses.

The Sentencing Council Guideline on Sentencing Children and Young Persons emphasises (at para.2.11) that the proper venue for the trial of any child or young person is normally the youth court. Subject to statutory restrictions, that remains the case where they are charged jointly with an adult. If the adult is sent for trial to the Crown Court, 'the court should conclude that the child or young person must be tried separately in the youth court unless it is in the interests of justice for the child or young person and the adult to be tried jointly'. The Guideline then goes on to give (para.2.12) *examples* of factors that should be considered when deciding whether to send the child or young person to the Crown Court (rather than having a trial in the youth court). These include:

- whether separate trials will cause injustice to witnesses or to the case as a whole (consideration should be given to the provisions of ss.27 and 28 of the Youth Justice and Criminal Evidence Act 1999);
- the age of the child or young person; the younger the child or young person, the greater the desirability that the child or young person be tried in the youth court;
- the age gap between the child or young person and the adult; a substantial gap in age militates in favour of the child or young person being tried in the youth court;
- the lack of maturity of the child or young person;
- the relative culpability of the child or young person compared with the adult and whether the alleged role played by the child or young person was minor; and/or
- the lack of previous findings of guilt on the part of the child or young person.

The Guideline also notes (at para.2.13) that the court should bear in mind that the youth court now has a general power to commit for sentence following conviction pursuant to s.3B of the Powers of Criminal Courts (Sentencing) Act 2000 (see below). In appropriate cases (where the offence in question is one to which s.91 of the 2000 applies), 'this will permit the same court to sentence adults and youths who have been tried separately'.

In R (W and R) v Leeds Crown Court [2011] EWHC 2326; [2012] 1 WLR 2786, the Divisional Court ruled that where the magistrates' court decides that it is necessary in the interests of justice for the child/young person to be tried in the Crown Court, the Crown Court has no power to remit the child/young person to the youth court for trial even if, for example, the adult pleads guilty in the Crown Court and so the child/young person will be tried alone in the Crown Court.

See Figure 6.3.

6.5.4 Plea before venue

Sections 24A–24D of the Magistrates' Courts Act 1980 apply a procedure similar to that contained in ss.17A–17C (the 'plea before venue' hearing) to cases involving a defendant who is under the age of 18 where the court has to decide whether to send him to the Crown Court for trial, either because he is charged with an offence to which s.91 of the Powers of Criminal Courts (Sentencing) Act 2000 applies, or because he is charged alongside an adult co-accused.

In such cases, the child/young person is asked to indicate how he intends to plead to the offence(s). If he indicates an intention to plead guilty, he will be regarded as having entered a plea of guilty (subs.(7)); if he indicates that he intends to plead not guilty (or gives no indication), the court proceeds to determine where the child/young person will be tried:

- In the case of offences to which s.91 of the 2000 Act applies, the youth court will send the child/young person to the Crown Court for trial if the court considers that, if he is found guilty of the offence, it 'ought to be possible to sentence him' under s.91;
- If the child/young person is charged alongside an adult, the court will send the young defendant to the Crown Court for trial if it considers it 'necessary in the interests of justice' to do so.

Section 24B of the Magistrates' Courts Act 1980 enables the 'plea before venue' procedure to take place in the absence of the child/young person where he is represented by a legal representative, the court considers that by reason of the accused's disorderly conduct before the court it is not practicable for proceedings under s.24A to be conducted in his presence, and the court considers that it should proceed in the absence of the accused. In such a case, the legal representative speaks on behalf of the accused.

6.5.4.1 Committal for sentence following plea before venue

Section 3B of the Powers of Criminal Courts (Sentencing) Act 2000 enables the youth court to commit a child/young person (in custody or bail on bail) to the Crown Court to be sentenced where:

- the child/young person is charged with an offence to which s.91 applies;
- the child/young person indicates a guilty plea at the 'plea before venue' hearing; and
- the court is of the opinion that the offence(s) are such that 'the Crown Court should ... have power to deal with the offender' under s.91.

Section 3B applies whether the young defendant pleads guilty or is found guilty of an offence to which s.91 applies.

Section 3B(3) provides that where a child/young person is committed for sentence under s.3B, s 6 of the 2000 Act (which enables a magistrates' court to commit the offender to the Crown Court to be dealt with in respect of other offences for which the court would otherwise be passing sentence) is applicable.

Under s.5A(1) of the 2000 Act, where an offender is committed for sentence under s.3B, the Crown Court may deal with the offender in any way in which it could deal with him if he had just been convicted of the offence on indictment before the court (this includes detention under s.91).

Section 4A of the Powers of Criminal Courts (Sentencing) Act 2000 applies where a child/young person is charged with an offence falling within the ambit of s.91 of the 2000 Act and, at the 'plea before venue' hearing, indicates an intention to plead guilty to that offence. Under s.4A(2), if the court sends the child/young person to the Crown Court for trial for one or more offences that are related to the s.91 offence, it may commit him (in custody or on bail) to the Crown Court to be dealt with in respect of the s.91 offence to which he has indicated a guilty plea. Under s.4A(4), if the magistrates commit the s.91 offence to the Crown Court for sentence but do not state that, in their opinion, the case is one where it ought to be possible to impose detention under s.91, the Crown Court cannot impose detention under s.91 for that offence (and so is limited to the sentences that could be imposed by the youth court) unless the child/young person is convicted by the Crown Court of one or more of the related offences which were sent for trial. This provision thus mirrors s.4 of the 2000 Act, which is applicable to adult offenders.

6.5.5 Dangerous offenders

Section 51A(3)(d) of the Crime and Disorder Act 1998 provides that the court must send the child/young person to the Crown Court for trial if he is charged with a specified offence (within the meaning of s.224 of the Criminal Justice Act 2003 – that is, one listed in sch.15 to that Act) and it appears to the court that, if he is found guilty of the offence, the criteria for the imposition of an extended sentence under s.226B of the 2003 Act would be met.

Section 3C of the Powers of Criminal Courts (Sentencing) Act 2000 enables committal for sentence of dangerous young offenders. Where a child/young person is convicted of a 'specified offence' (as defined by s.224 of the 2003 Act), and it appears to the court that the criteria for the imposition of an extended sentence under s.226B of the 2003 Act would be met, the court must commit the offender (in custody or on bail) to the Crown Court for sentence (s.3C(2)).

Following committal under s.3C, the Crown Court can deal with the offender in any way in which it could deal with him if he had just been convicted of the offence on indictment before the court (s.5A(1)).

The offender can also be committed (under s.6 of the 2000 Act) to be sentenced for other offences that the magistrates would otherwise be dealing with (s.3C(3)).

It should be noted that s.3C applies both where a child/young person indicates an intention to plead guilty and also where a child/young person is convicted following summary trial.

The Sentencing Council guideline on Sentencing Children and Young Persons makes the point (at para.2.4) that a sentence under the dangerous offender provisions can be imposed only if:

- the child or young person is found guilty of a specified violent or sexual offence; and
- the court is of the opinion that there is a significant risk to the public of serious harm caused by the child or young person committing further specified offences; and
- a custodial term of at least four years would be imposed for the offence.

Paragraph 2.5 states that a 'significant risk' is 'more than a mere possibility of occurrence' and that, in making this assessment, it will be essential to obtain a pre-sentence report. Paragraph 2.6 adds that children and young people 'may change and develop within a shorter time than adults and this factor, along with their level of maturity, may be highly relevant when assessing probable future conduct and whether it may cause a significant risk of serious harm'. Paragraph 2.7 makes the important point that trial in the youth court, followed by committal for sentence to the Crown Court (if appropriate) will generally be the most appropriate course of action:

> In anything but the most serious cases it may be impossible for the court to form a view as to whether the child or young person would meet the criteria of the dangerous offender provisions without greater knowledge of the circumstances of the offence and the child or young person. In those circumstances jurisdiction for the case should be retained in the youth court. If, following a guilty plea or a finding of guilt, the dangerousness criteria appear to be met then the child or young person should be committed for sentence.

6.5.6 Special arrangements where a child/young person is tried in an adult court

In *V v UK* (2000) 30 EHRR 121, the European Court of Human Rights scrutinised the procedure adopted for the murder trial of two child/young persons in the Crown Court. The trial took place in the full glare of national and international publicity. The Court held that the right of the two accused to a fair trial under Art.6(1) of the ECHR had been violated. The Court stated that it is essential that a young child charged with a serious offence attracting high levels of media interest should be tried in such a way as to reduce as far as possible any feelings of intimidation. It considered that the formality and ritual of the Crown Court must at times have seemed incomprehensible and intimidating for a child aged 11. Moreover, there was evidence that certain of the modifications to the courtroom, in particular the raised dock (which was designed to enable the accused to see what was going on) had the adverse effect of increasing their sense of discomfort during the trial, since they felt exposed to the scrutiny of the press and public. Further, there was evidence that the post-traumatic stress disorder suffered by the accused, combined with the lack of any therapeutic work since the offence, had limited their ability to instruct lawyers or testify in their own defence. The Court found that they were unable to follow the trial or take decisions in their own best interests. They were therefore unable to participate effectively in the criminal proceedings against them and were, in consequence, denied a fair hearing in breach of Art.6(1).

It should be emphasised that the Court did not find that trial of child/young persons in the Crown Court is necessarily unfair, only that appropriate adaptations to the procedure have to be made to accommodate the needs of the young defendant.

In *SC v UK* (2005) 40 EHRR 10, the European Court of Human Rights (at [28]) said:

> The right of an accused to effective participation in his or her criminal trial generally includes ... not only the right to be present, but also to hear and follow the proceedings. In the case of a child, it is essential that he be dealt with in a manner which takes full account of his age, level of maturity and intellectual and emotional capacities, and that steps are taken to promote his ability to understand and participate in the proceedings, including conducting the hearing in such a way as to reduce as far as possible his feelings of intimidation and inhibition.

The Court went on (at [29]) to add that:

> The defendant should be able to follow what is said by the prosecution witnesses and, if represented, to explain to his own lawyers his version of events, point out any statements with which he disagrees and make them aware of any facts which should be put forward in his defence.

The Court concluded (at [35]):

> [W]hen the decision is taken to deal with a child, such as the applicant, who risks not being able to participate effectively because of his young age and limited intellectual capacity, by way of criminal proceedings rather than some other form of disposal directed primarily at determining the child's best interests and those of the community, it is essential that he be tried in a specialist tribunal which is able to give full consideration to and make proper allowance for the handicaps under which he labours, and adapt its procedure accordingly.

Criminal Practice Direction I 3G contains a number of measures aimed at ensuring that court procedures are adapted to take account of the needs of young (and other vulnerable) defendants and witnesses. For example, it may be appropriate to arrange that a vulnerable defendant should visit, out of court hours and before the case is heard, the courtroom in which that hearing is to take for the purpose of familiarisation (para.3G.2). Where an intermediary is being used to help the defendant to communicate at court, the intermediary should accompany the defendant on this pre-trial visit (para.3G.3). [It should be noted that, at the time of writing, s.33BA of the Youth Justice and Criminal Evidence Act 1999, which makes provision for the questioning of a defendant to be carried out through an intermediary, has not been brought into force. However, the court may nonetheless permit the use of an intermediary if the fairness of the trial so demands: R (C) v *Sevenoaks Youth Court* [2009] EWHC 3088 (Admin); (2010) 174 JP 224)]. If the defendant is to use a live link, a practice session may be appropriate (para.3G.4). The proceedings should, if practicable, be held in a courtroom in which all the participants are on the same, or almost the same, level (para.3G.7). The defendant should normally be free to sit with members of his family or others in a like relationship, and with some other suitable supporting adult such as a social worker, and in a place which permits easy, informal communication with his legal representatives (para.3G.8). The court must ensure that the defendant understands what is happening and what has been said by those on the bench, the advocates and witnesses (para.3G.9). The trial should be conducted according to a timetable which takes full account of the defendant's ability to concentrate: 'frequent and regular breaks will often be appropriate' (para.3G.10). In the Crown Court (or where the child/young person is being tried in an adult magistrates' court), the court should be prepared to restrict attendance by members of the public in the courtroom to a small number, 'perhaps limited to those with an immediate and direct interest in the outcome' (para.3G.13).

In R (TP) v *West London Youth Court* [2005] EWHC 2583 (Admin), [2006] 1 WLR 1219, Scott Baker LJ (at [26]) summarised the key steps that are needed:

(i) keeping the [defendant]'s level of cognitive functioning in mind;

(ii) using concise and simple language;

(iii) having regular breaks;

(iv) taking additional time to explain court proceedings;

(v) being proactive in ensuring the [defendant] has access to support;

(vi) explaining and ensuring the [defendant] understands the ingredients of the charge;

(vii) explaining the possible outcomes and sentences;

(viii) ensuring that cross-examination is carefully controlled so that questions are short and clear and frustration is minimized.

Criminal Practice Direction I, para.3G.1, makes the point that, if a vulnerable defendant, especially one who is young, is to be tried jointly with one who is not, the court should consider whether the vulnerable defendant should be tried on his own, but should only so order if satisfied that a fair trial cannot be achieved by use of appropriate special measures or other support for the defendant. If a vulnerable defendant is tried jointly with one who is not, the court should consider whether any of the special arrangements set out in the practice direction should apply to the joint trial.

6.5.6.1 Accused testifying via live link

Section 33A of the Youth Justice and Criminal Evidence Act 1999 allows the court (whether the Crown Court or a magistrates' court), on application by the accused, to direct that any evidence given by him should be given via a 'live link'. Section 33B defines 'live link' very broadly; it encompasses any technology that enables the accused to see and hear a person in the courtroom, and to be seen and heard by the persons listed in subs.(2), namely the judge or justices (or both) and the jury (if there is one); where there are two or more accused in the proceedings, each of the other accused; the legal representatives acting in the proceedings, and any interpreter or other person appointed by the court to assist the accused.

Under s.33A(2), before giving a live link direction, the court must be satisfied that it would be in the interests of justice to do so, and (where the accused is under 18) that:

(a) his ability to participate effectively in the proceedings as a witness giving oral evidence in court is compromised by his level of intellectual ability or social functioning; and

(b) use of a live link would enable him to participate more effectively in the proceedings as a witness (whether by improving the quality of his evidence or otherwise).

6.5.7 Sentencing young defendants after Crown Court trial alongside an adult

If a child/young person is convicted at the Crown Court following joint trial with an adult, the Crown Court should remit the child/young person to the youth court for sentence unless it is 'undesirable' to do so (s.8(2) of the Powers of Criminal Courts (Sentencing) Act 2000). In R v Lewis (1984) 79 Cr App R 94, however, Lord Lane CJ said (p.99) that remittal to the youth court would generally be undesirable because:

- the Crown Court judge (having presided over the trial) will be better informed as to the facts of the case;
- there would otherwise be a risk of unacceptable disparity in the sentences if co-accused are to be sentenced in different courts on different occasions;
- there would be unnecessary duplication of proceedings (causing unnecessary delay and fruitless expense).

The Sentencing Council Guideline on Sentencing Children and Young Persons (para.2.15) says that, in considering whether remittal is undesirable, the court 'should balance the need for expertise in the sentencing of children and young people with the benefits of the sentence being imposed by the court which determined guilt'. Paragraph 2.16 makes the point that referral orders (see Chapter 15) are generally not available in the Crown Court but may be the most appropriate sentence.

6.6 Summary trial of child/young persons in adult magistrates' court

A child/young person can be tried in an adult magistrates' court only if the case is one that involves an adult co-accused.

6.6.1 Adult being tried in Crown Court

If the child/young person is jointly charged with an adult, and the justices decide that it is not necessary in the interests of justice to send the child/young person to the Crown Court for trial, even though the adult co-accused is to be tried by the Crown Court (either because the offence is triable only on indictment or, if it is an either-way offence, because the adult elects Crown Court trial), the charge will be put to the child/young person in the adult magistrates' court and a plea taken from him.

If the child/young person pleads not guilty, the adult magistrates' court may try him (under s.29(2) of the Magistrates' Courts Act 1980). However, in the absence of a good reason to the contrary (for example, the prosecution wish to offer no evidence), he should normally be remitted to the youth court for trial (again under s.29(2)).

If the child/young person pleads guilty (or is found guilty following trial in the adult magistrates' court), the magistrates will consider whether their sentencing powers in respect of the child/young person are adequate. Those powers, which are contained in s.8(7) and (8) of the 2000 Act, are to make any one or more of the following orders:

- a referral order (where the conditions for making such an order are satisfied);
- an absolute or conditional discharge;

- a fine;
- an order requiring the young defendant's parents to enter into a recognisance to exercise proper control over him.

In addition, the court may make ancillary orders such as compensation or costs.

If none of these powers is appropriate, the adult magistrates' court will remit the offender to the youth court to be dealt with (s.8(6)).

See Figure 6.3, below.

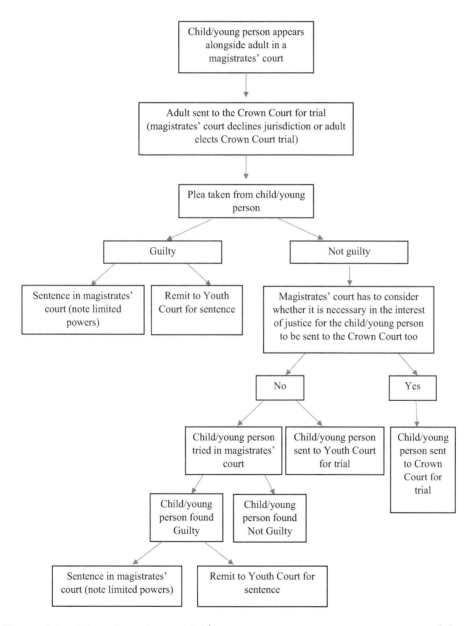

Figure 6.3 Allocation where child/young person charged alongside adult (1)

6.6.2 Adult being tried in the magistrates' court

Where the child/young person is charged with an adult who is to be tried summarily (either because it is a summary offence or, if it is an either-way offence, because the adult consents to summary trial), the place of trial for the child/young person may differ depending on the plea entered by the adult and on whether the charge is a joint charge or merely a related charge:

(a) *Joint charge*: if the adult and the child/young person are jointly charged, and the adult pleads not guilty to the joint charge, the magistrates' court will ask the child/young person to enter a plea. If the child/young person also pleads not guilty, the adult court must try him (s.46(1) (a) of the Children and Young Persons Act 1933). If he pleads guilty or is found guilty, the magistrates will remit him to the youth court for sentence if none of the sentences which the adult court can impose (see above) is inappropriate.

(b) *Aiding and abetting; connected offences*: if the child/young person is charged with aiding and abetting the adult, or the adult is charged with aiding and abetting the child/young person, and they both plead not guilty, the adult magistrates' court has a *discretion* to try them both (s.46(1)(b) of the Children And Young Persons Act 1933; s.18(a) of the Children And Young Persons Act 1963). Similarly, if the adult and child/young person are charged with offences which arise out of the same or connected circumstances and both plead not guilty, the adult magistrates' court may *either* try the child/young person or remit him to the youth court for trial (s.18(b) of the Children and Young Persons Act 1963). If the adult pleads guilty and the child/young person not guilty, the magistrates are likely to remit the young defendant to the youth court for trial. If the adult magistrates' court tries the child/young person and convicts him, he will be remitted to the youth court for sentence if the magistrates' sentencing powers (see above) are inappropriate.

(c) *The adult pleads guilty to the joint charge*: if the child/young person pleads not guilty, the adult magistrates' court may try him under s.29(2) of the Magistrates' Courts Act 1980 or else remit him to the youth court for trial. Although the magistrates could theoretically try the child/young person (even though the adult has pleaded guilty, so that there will be no trial of the adult), it is much more likely that they will remit him to the youth court for trial. If the child/young person pleads guilty (or the adult court does try him and he is found guilty), the adult court will remit him to the youth court for sentence if none of the sentences which the adult court can impose is appropriate.

See Figures 6.4 and 6.5, below.

6.6.3 Determining the age of the defendant

In R (M) v *Hammersmith Magistrates' Court* [2017] EWHC 1359 (Admin), the accused said that he was 16. At his first appearance, the court expressed doubts about his age, based only on a visual assessment, and deemed him to be 18. Irwin LJ (at [14]) said that where there is a real issue about the age of a defendant, criminal courts should adjourn proceedings so as to conduct the 'age inquiry' permitted by s.99(1) of the Children and Young Persons Act 1933. He added (at [16]) that

> In cases where there is a real doubt as to the claimed age, the proper course is to make directions for an age assessment to be conducted. The relevant local authority, through the medium of the youth offending team or service, will usually be the appropriate avenue to pursue.

If an adult magistrates' court starts to deal with a defendant believing him to be 18 or over and it then transpires that he is a child/young person, the court can either continue to hear the

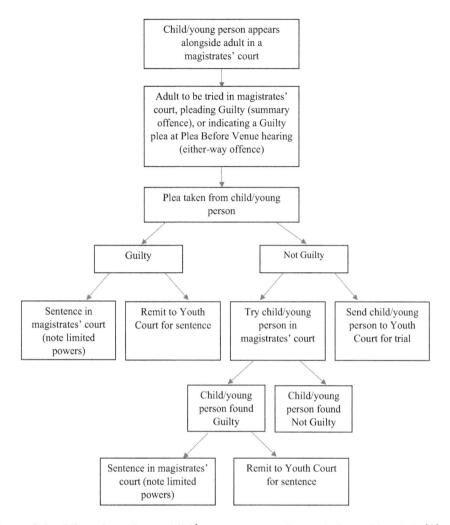

Figure 6.4 Allocation where child/young person charged alongside adult (2)

case or remit it to the youth court, whichever seems most appropriate in the circumstances (s.46 (1)(c) of the Children and Young Persons Act 1933).

6.7 Reporting restrictions in the adult courts

Section 45 of the Youth Justice and Criminal Evidence Act 1999 (which replaced s.39 of the Children and Young Persons Act in criminal proceedings) applies to criminal proceedings in any court in England and Wales except for youth court proceedings (to which s.49 of the Children and Young Persons Act 1933 applies).

Under s.45(3), the court may direct that no matter relating to any person concerned in the proceedings shall, while he is under the age of 18, be included in any publication if it is likely to lead members of the public to identify him as a person concerned in the proceedings. For these purposes, a person is 'concerned in the proceedings' if he is the accused or a witness (subs.(7)).

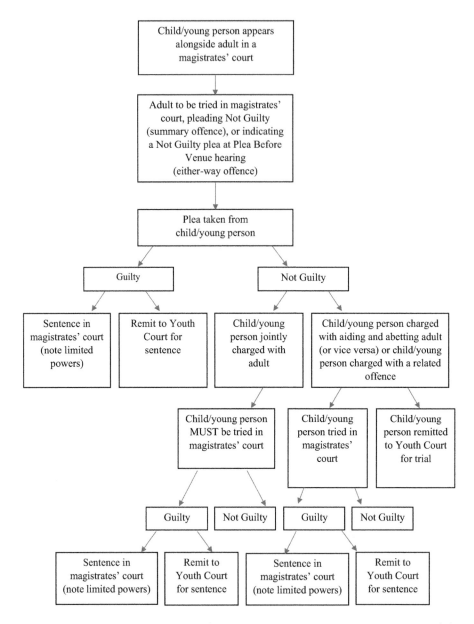

Figure 6.5 Allocation where child/young person charged alongside adult (3)

The protected information includes the person's name and address, the identity of any school or other educational establishment he attends, and the identity of any place of work; the restriction also applies to any 'still or moving picture of him' (subs.(8)).

The court may (at the time the direction is given under subs.(3) or subsequently) make an 'excepting direction', which dispenses, to any extent specified, with the restrictions imposed by a direction under subs.(3), if it is satisfied either that it is 'necessary in the interests of justice' to do so (subs.(4)) or that the effect of the restrictions imposed under subs.(3) 'is to impose a substantial and unreasonable restriction on the reporting of the proceedings', and that 'it is in the public interest to remove or relax that restriction' (subs.(5)). An 'excepting direction' cannot be given under subs.(5) solely on the basis that the proceedings have been determined in any way or have been abandoned.

When deciding whether to make a direction under s.45(3), or an 'excepting direction', the court must have regard to the welfare of the person in question (subs.(6)).

In R v Central Criminal Court ex p S (1999) 163 JP 776, the Divisional Court held that there has to be a good reason for making an order preventing identification of a child/young person who appears before an adult court. In considering the range of factors that may be considered by a court when determining whether or not to make such a direction, some useful guidance comes from the judgment of Simon Brown LJ in R v Winchester Crown Court ex p B [1999] 1 WLR 788, at p.790:

(i) In deciding whether to impose or thereafter to lift reporting restrictions, the court will consider whether there are good reasons for naming the defendant.

(ii) In reaching that decision, the court will give considerable weight to the age of the offender and to the potential damage to any young person of public identification as a criminal before the offender has the benefit or burden of adulthood.

(iii) [T]he court must 'have regard to the welfare of the child or young person'.

(iv) The prospect of being named in court with the accompanying disgrace is a powerful deterrent and the naming of a defendant in the context of his punishment serves as a deterrent to others. These deterrents are proper objectives for the court to seek.

(v) There is a strong public interest in open justice and in the public knowing as much as possible about what has happened in court, including the identity of those who have committed crime.

(vi) The weight to be attributed to the different factors may shift at different stages of the proceedings and, in particular, after the defendant has been found, or pleads, guilty and is sentenced. It may then be appropriate to place greater weight on the interest of the public in knowing the identity of those who have committed crimes, particularly serious and detestable crimes.

(vii) The fact that an appeal has been made may be a material consideration.

In R (Y) v Aylesbury Crown Court [2012] EWHC 1140 (Admin), Hooper LJ (at [46]–[48]) said:

The court must ... balance the welfare of the child or young person which is likely to favour a restriction on publication with the public interest and the requirements of Article 10 which are likely to favour no restriction on publication. Prior to conviction the welfare of the child or young person is likely to take precedence over the public interest. After conviction, the age of the defendant and the seriousness of the crime of which he or she has been convicted will be particularly relevant.

What the court should do is to identify the factors that would favour restriction on publication and the factors that would favour no restriction. The court may also decide ... to permit the publication of some details but not all.

If having conducted the balancing exercise between the welfare of the child or young person, on the one hand, and the public interest and the requirements of Article 10 on the other, the factors favouring a restriction on publication and the factors favouring publication are very evenly balanced, then it seems to us ... that a court should make an order restricting publication.

In R v Cornick [2014] EWHC 3623 (QB), Coulson J (at [10]) noted that 'in the vast majority of cases, a defendant in a criminal case can be expected to be named, unless there is an absolute necessity for anonymity'. His Lordship went on to say (at [12]) that 'the onus is on the party seeking an order [for anonymity] to establish, either by way of Art.2 or by way of Art.8 [of the ECHR], that the rights of the press and public under Art.10 should be trumped by the welfare of the child'. His Lordship said there had to be 'a good reason for making an order [for anonymity]'. His Lordship added (at [14]) that it is only the child whose interests can be considered in the balancing exercise: save for any indirect impact on the child, the effect of his identification on his family is not a relevant consideration.

In R v Markham [2017] EWCA Crim 739; [2017] 2 Cr App R (S) 30, the Court of Appeal considered an appeal against the lifting of reporting restrictions in a case involving what the trial judge described as a 'terrible and unnatural crime', namely, the murder by the offenders of the mother and sister of one of them. They were both aged 15. Sir Brian Leveson noted (at [83]) that 'when a juvenile is tried on indictment in the Crown Court ... there is a strong presumption that justice takes place in open, and the press may report the proceedings'. His Lordship said that the facts of the case (and the judge's sentencing remarks) could not be properly understood without identifying the offenders; that no material was before the court to justify the conclusion that lifting anonymity would cause harm to either offender; that there was no evidence before the court that reporting their identities would adversely affect the future rehabilitation of the offenders (and, thus, be contrary to their welfare); that the anonymity granted by s.45 lasts only until 18 years of age and that both offenders faced a very considerable term of detention that would stretch long into their adult lives (see [88] and [89]). In the circumstances, the court held that the lifting of reporting restrictions pursued a legitimate aim and was a reasonable and proportionate measure, properly balancing the welfare of the appellants (and other factors identified Art.8 of the ECHR) against the Art.10 rights of the press and the interests of the public (see [90]).

6.8 Relevant date for determining age

Section 29(1) of the Children and Young Persons Act 1963 provides that:

> Where proceedings in respect of a young person are begun for an offence and he attains the age of eighteen before the conclusion of the proceedings, the court may continue to deal with the case and make any order which it could have made if he had not attained that age.

Thus, the youth court has jurisdiction if the accused is under the age of 18 when the proceedings are begun. For these purposes, proceedings are begun when the accused makes his first court appearance in connection with the offence, not the date when he is charged with the offence (R v Uxbridge Youth Court ex p H (1998) 162 JP 327).

What happens if a 17-year-old has his 18th birthday during the course of proceedings in the youth court? The House of Lords held in R v Islington North Child/young person Court ex p Daley [1983] 1 AC 347 at 364, per Lord Diplock, that:

> the only appropriate date at which to determine whether an accused person has attained an age which entitles him to elect to be tried by jury for offences which ... are triable either way is the date of his appearance before the court on the occasion when the court makes its decision as to the mode of trial.

Given that Crown Court trial of a child/young person is possible only in certain cases, there will often not be an occasion on which mode of trial (or 'allocation') for a child/young person is determined. It is submitted that Lord Diplock must be taken as having meant that the right of a person who attains the relevant age during the currency of proceedings against him to be tried on indictment for an indictable offence depends either upon his age when mode of trial/allocation is determined, or – if there is no express determination of mode of trial – upon his age when the court is ready for the charge to be put. If he is under that age on the relevant date, he has no right to elect trial on indictment, even if the matter is forthwith adjourned for trial at a later date and he attains the age of 18 before any evidence is heard. The corollary is that, where the offence charged is triable only on indictment in the case of an adult, an erstwhile child/young person must go to the Crown Court for trial if he attains the age of 18 before a plea is taken (*Vale of Glamorgan Child/young person Justices, ex p Beattie* (1986) 82 Cr App R 1).

Cases where the defendant attains the age of 18 between conviction and sentence are dealt with by s.9 of the Powers of Criminal Courts (Sentencing) Act 2000. Under s.9(1), the youth court is empowered, in such a case, to remit the defendant to the adult magistrates' court to be sentenced. The adult magistrates' court may then 'deal with the case in any way in which it would have power to deal with it if all proceedings relating to the offence which took place before the youth court had taken place before [the adult court]' (s.9(2)(b)). There is no right of appeal against the order of remission (s.9(4)).

6.9 International instruments on youth justice

There are a number of international instruments of relevance to youth justice, the effect of which has been incorporated into domestic legislation and practice. These include:

- United Nations Standard Minimum Rules for the Administration of Juvenile Justice (the 'Beijing Rules'), November 1985
- Convention on the Rights of the Child (1990)
- Recommendation No. R(87)20 of the Committee of Ministers to Member States on Social Reactions to Juvenile Delinquency
- Recommendation Rec (2003)20 of the Committee of Ministers to member states

6.10 Reforming the youth justice system

Youth court advocacy can be very challenging indeed, dealing with vulnerable defendants and vulnerable witnesses. Magistrates receive additional training to equip them to hear youth court cases, and Crown Prosecutors who do youth court work also receive additional training. However, so far as the defence are concerned, youth court work is poorly remunerated and tends to be given to comparatively junior practitioners. There have been several calls for reform of the youth justice system.

For example, *Rules of Engagement – Changing the heart of youth justice: A policy report by the Youth Justice Working Group* (Centre for Social Justice, January 2012) recommended that, 'All defence lawyers appearing in youth and Crown Court proceedings should complete specialist youth training before they are allowed to practice'; that 'Crown Court judges should be "ticketed" to deal with youth cases'; that 'training for youth sentencers (lay magistrates and district judges) [should] be developed … to include comprehensive understanding of the distinct vulnerabilities of children and young people'. The training that was recommended for youth proceedings practitioners included:

- The distinct needs of children in trouble with the law (such as mental health needs, communication and learning needs, welfare issues and child development);
- effective participation to enable defendants to participate fully and fairly in courtroom proceedings (including how to manage learning and communication difficulties, mental health problems and vulnerability, and fitness to plead);
- the role of the family and importance of parental engagement.

The *Independent Parliamentarians' Inquiry into the Operation and Effectiveness of the Youth Court, Chaired by Lord Carlile of Berriew CBE QC* (June 2014) recommended that:

- Section 33BA of the Youth Justice and Criminal Evidence Act 1999 should be brought into force and also extended, through new legislation, to enable young defendants to have an intermediary to provide communication support throughout their case and not just for the giving of evidence.

● At substantive hearings, all children should be accompanied by the most appropriate adult supporter in their lives (for example, their Youth Offending Team case worker or a teacher) and that this should become a statutory requirement.

● There should be a requirement for all legal practitioners representing children at the police station and practising in youth proceedings to be accredited to do so.

● There should be a clear presumption in law that all child defendants are dealt with in the youth court. Any residue of cases to be heard in the Crown Court should be exceptional only, determined on a case-by-case basis where the circumstances are of exceptional gravity and it is clearly necessary and in the interests of justice for a trial to occur in the Crown Court.

The *Youth Proceedings Advocacy Review: Final Report* (Bar Standards Board et al, November 2015) recommended that:

● Legal practice in the Youth Court and Crown Court youth cases should be recognised as a specialism, through the introduction of mandatory training and a licensing system for youth justice advocates.

● Parity in funding for legal representation for serious youth court cases and for Crown Court cases of equivalent seriousness.

● Promotion of use of 'plain English' in the criminal courts.

● Systematic screening of young defendants to identify the likely presence of a mental health problems, learning disability or other need prior to their appearance at court.

● Mandatory training for all advocates who practise in youth proceedings, to include:
  ○ child development;
  ○ the nature and manifestations of behavioural, emotional and social difficulties and speech, language and communication needs among children and young people;
  ○ communication skills and dealing with vulnerability;
  ○ available adaptations to the court process to meet the needs of young court users, including working with intermediaries;
  ○ methods of engaging children and young people (including through role play-based training).

Charlie Taylor, in his *Review of the Youth Justice System in England and Wales* (Ministry of Justice, December 2016) reiterated the call for mandatory training for all lawyers appearing in the youth court. Additionally, he recommended:

● A presumption that all cases involving children should be heard in the youth court, with suitably qualified judges being brought in to oversee the most complex or serious cases in suitably modified proceedings [this would require a review of the relevant sentencing legislation too, as the maximum sentence that can be imposed by the youth court – even if presided over by a Circuit Judge – is currently a 24-month Detention and Training Order; only the Crown Court has the power to impose a sentence of long-term detention under s.91 of the Powers of Criminal Courts (Sentencing) Act 2000];

● Automatic reporting restrictions where young defendants appear in the Crown Court [and presumably the adult magistrates' court too] and lifelong reporting restrictions for young defendants [reporting restrictions currently cease to apply when the person attains the age of 18].

In November 2017, the Bar Standards Board published *Youth Proceedings Competences*. These include:

Dealing with vulnerability

2.1 Have knowledge and understanding of the additional vulnerabilities faced by young people in the criminal justice system.

2.2 Be able to recognise and identify where a young person might be vulnerable and ensure effective safeguarding measures are in place.

2.3 Be able to adapt the delivery of their service to meet the needs of vulnerable young people.

2.4 Ensure that the young person understands the circumstances of what is happening before, during and after the proceedings, including the consequences of a criminal conviction and any sentence and/or order imposed.

Awareness of background and needs

3.1 Take all reasonable steps to be alert to any developmental, communication and/or mental health needs of a young person.

3.2 Take all reasonable steps to be alert to any cultural, educational and/or social issues which may affect a young person.

3.3 Take all reasonable steps to be aware of the background (personal circumstances) of a young person, including the involvement of other agencies in the case.

3.4 Be ready to amend their approach based on those issues.

Communication and engagement

4.1 Speak in a clear and concise manner, using plain English when communicating with young people or in proceedings where young people are present.

4.2 Recognise that young people might find it difficult to engage with them and/or other professionals within the youth justice system.

4.3 Demonstrate emotional intelligence to communicate effectively with those who may not share their own style of spoken language or background – such as racial, gender, religious or any other background. In particular:

4.3.1 Exercise good communication skills. Have the ability to understand and build trust with young people and help them to understand procedure(s).

4.3.2 Be able to recognise and communicate effectively with young people with additional vulnerabilities. Where direct communication proves difficult for young people, to be able to give advice about the services available to make communication easier.

A point to underline is that the potential complexity of dealing with cases involving children and young people, who are often vulnerable and not skilled in communicating, must not be underestimated. Adequate training is essential for lawyers involved in such cases.

Chapter 7

Appeals from Magistrates' Courts and Youth Courts

In this chapter we look at:

- The power of a magistrates' court to correct errors
- Appeal to the Crown Court
- Appeal to the High Court by way of case stated
- Appeal to the High Court by way of judicial review

7.1 Setting aside conviction or sentence

Where an obvious error has been made, it is not always necessary to lodge an appeal, as the error can be corrected by the magistrates' court itself, under s.142 of the Magistrates' Courts Act 1980. This provides:

(1) A magistrates' court may vary or rescind a sentence or other order imposed or made by it when dealing with an offender if it appears to the court to be in the interests of justice to do so; and it is hereby declared that this power extends to replacing a sentence or order which for any reason appears to be invalid by another which the court has power to impose or make.

[...]

(2) Where a person is convicted by a magistrates' court and it subsequently appears to the court that it would be in the interests of justice that the case should be heard again by different justices, the court may so direct.

In *Zykin v CPS* [2009] EWHC 1469 (Admin); (2009) 173 JP 361, Bean J said (at [16]) that s.142 'does not confer a wide and general power on a magistrates' court to reopen a previous decision on the grounds that it is in the interests of justice to do so'; rather, it is 'a power to be used in a relatively limited situation, namely one which is akin to mistake or the slip rule'.

There is no time limit within which applications for the setting aside of a conviction or sentence under s.142 must be made. However, where a defendant applies under s.142(2) for the trial to be reheard, delay in making the application is a relevant consideration for the magistrates in deciding whether or not to grant that application (*R v Ealing Magistrates' Court ex p Sahota* (1998) 162 JP 73).

7.1.1 Setting aside a conviction

Section 142(2) enables a defendant who was convicted in the magistrates' court to ask the magistrates to set the conviction aside. This application can be considered by the same magistrates who convicted the defendant or by a different bench. If the conviction is set aside, the case is usually reheard by different magistrates from those who convicted the defendant.

An application under s.142(2) may be appropriate if, for example, the magistrates made an error of law or there was some defect in the procedure which led to the conviction. In *R v Croydon Youth Court ex p DPP* [1997] 2 Cr App R 411 (at p. 416), McCowan LJ said that the purpose of s.142(2) is most accurately described as a 'power to rectify mistakes', and that it is generally and correctly regarded as a 'slip rule' (that is, enabling the court to correct minor errors).

Section 142(2) can be invoked where a defendant is convicted in his absence. For example, in *R (Morsby) v Tower Bridge Magistrates' Court* [2007] EWHC 2766 (Admin); (2008) 172 JP 155, the defendant had been remanded in custody and so failed to attend his trial for another offence, of which he was convicted in his absence. He applied under s.142 to rescind his conviction and reopen the trial, but the magistrates' court refused. The Divisional Court held that the interests of justice clearly required the setting aside of the defendant's conviction and a retrial in his presence.

However, in R v Newport Magistrates' Court ex p Carey (1996) 160 JP 613, the Divisional Court held that magistrates have a broad discretion in deciding whether or not to reopen a case under s.142. They are entitled to have regard to the fact that the defendant failed to attend the original hearing through his own fault and that witnesses would be inconvenienced if a retrial were to be ordered. Henry LJ also pointed out that the magistrates, by refusing to reopen the case, were not 'finally shutting out the defendant from the judgment seat' because he still had his unfettered right of appeal to the Crown Court.

Section 142 is not generally available where the defendant pleaded guilty. In R (Williamson) v City of Westminster Magistrates' Court [2012] EWHC 1444 (Admin); [2012] 2 Cr App R 24, the defendant pleaded guilty in the magistrates' court but subsequently said that he did so on the basis of incompetent advice from his solicitor. Burnett J (at [36]) said:

> We accept that there may be circumstances in which s. 142(2) could be used to allow an unequivocal guilty plea to be set aside. Examples which spring to mind include cases in which a guilty plea had been entered to an offence unknown to the law … That would fall comfortably within the language of mistake. They may include cases where a jurisdictional bar was not appreciated by the defendant relating, for example, to a time limit or the identity of a prosecutor. There may be cases in which the proceedings were, in truth, a nullity.

It is clear that s.142 cannot be invoked simply to re-argue points that have been ventilated before the magistrates' court, in the hope that a different bench will take a different view. For s.142 to apply, it must be clear that the magistrates have made a mistake, either of law or of fact, when reaching their decision. The mistake must be an obvious one; if it is debatable whether or not a mistake has been made, the proper course for the defendant is to appeal against conviction.

7.1.2 Varying or rescinding a sentence

Section 142(1) empowers a magistrates' court to vary or rescind a sentence if it is in the interests of justice to do so. Again, this power may be exercised by a different bench from that which passed the original sentence. The main use of this power is to remedy the situation where an unlawful sentence is inadvertently passed on an offender.

The magistrates can reopen the case under s.142 regardless of whether the defendant pleaded guilty or was found guilty. However, s.142 cannot operate where the defendant was acquitted (see Coles v East Penwith Justices (1998) 162 JP 687, where the prosecution had withdrawn the charges and the Divisional Court held that there was no power under s.142(1) to rescind the defendant's costs order which had been made).

In R (Holme) v Liverpool Justices [2004] EWHC 3131 (Admin); (2005) 169 JP 306, the defendant pleaded guilty to dangerous driving; a pedestrian had sustained serious injuries. A community sentence was imposed. The CPS applied to re-open the case under s.142 on the basis the original counsel for the prosecution had not addressed the extent of the pedestrian's injuries and that the difference between the sentence imposed and the custodial sentence that would probably have been imposed had the court known all the facts offended the principles of justice. On appeal to the Divisional Court, Collins J (at [30]) said that:

> the power under s.142 is to be used in a relatively limited situation, namely one which is akin to mistake or, as the court says, the slip rule. But … if a court has been misled into imposing a particular sentence, and it is discovered that it has been so misled, then the sentence may properly be said to have been imposed because of a mistake; the mistake being the failure of the court to appreciate a relevant fact. That may well give power to the court to exercise the jurisdiction conferred by s.142, but it does not indicate that that power should necessarily be used.

His Lordship went on (at [33]) to say that the sort of case which is appropriate for use of the power under s.142 is one 'where the mistake is quickly identified and it is accepted on all sides that a mistake had been made'.

At [42]–[43], his Lordship said that it is:

> possible to envisage circumstances where the failure of the court to be aware of such material factors could properly mean that there could be resort to s.142 [but] it would only be in very rare circumstances that it would be appropriate to resort to s.142 to consider an increase in sentence, particularly if that increase ... brought the possibility of custody as opposed to another form of disposal.

The facts of the instant case, said the Court, did not come anywhere near justifying such a use of s.142.

7.2 Appeals to the Crown Court

The most common form of appeal from the magistrates' court and youth court is to the Crown Court. This is governed by s.108 of the Magistrates' Courts Act 1980. Under s.108(1):

> A person convicted by a magistrates' court may appeal to the Crown Court –
> (a)   if he pleaded guilty, against his sentence;
> (b)   if he did not, against the conviction or sentence.

Thus, a defendant who pleaded guilty cannot appeal against conviction (unless the plea was equivocal, considered later in this chapter) but can appeal against the sentence imposed. If the defendant pleaded not guilty but was convicted by the magistrates, he can appeal against conviction and/or sentence.

7.2.1 Procedure for appeal to the Crown Court

The procedure for appeal to the Crown Court is set out in Part 34 of the Criminal Procedure Rules. Notice of appeal must be given to the magistrates' court, to the prosecutor and to any co-defendant (r.34.2(1)). This notice must be given within 21 days of the passing of the sentence (r.34.2(2)). The 21-day period for giving notice of appeal runs from the date when sentence is passed even if the appeal is against conviction only.

The notice of appeal must be in writing and must 'summarise the issues' (r.34.3(1)(b)). In an appeal against conviction, r.34.3(1)(c) requires the notice, to the best of the appellant's ability, to:

(i)   identify the witnesses who gave oral evidence in the magistrates' court,
(ii)   identify the witnesses who gave written evidence in the magistrates' court,
(iii) identify the prosecution witnesses whom the appellant will want to question if they are called to give oral evidence in the Crown Court,
(iv)   identify the likely defence witnesses,
(v)   give notice of any special arrangements or other measures that the appellant thinks are needed for witnesses,
(vi)   explain whether the issues in the Crown Court differ from the issues in the magistrates' court, and if so how, and
(vii) say how long the trial lasted in the magistrates' court and how long the appeal is likely to last in the Crown Court.

In the case of an appeal against sentence, r.34.3(1)(d) requires the notice to:

(i) identify any circumstances, report or other information of which the appellant wants the court to take account, and

(ii) explain the significance of those circumstances or that information to what is in issue.

The notice should also say whether the appellant has asked the magistrates' court to reconsider the case (r.34.3(1)(f)). This is a reference to the power to set aside a conviction or sentence under s.142 of the Magistrates' Courts Act 1980 (see above).

The respondent then has 21 days in which to serve a respondent's notice (r.34.2(5)). This notice has to give very similar information to that contained in the appellant's notice: the witnesses whose evidence was adduced in the magistrates' court; the prosecution witnesses whom the respondent intends to call to give oral evidence in the Crown Court; any special arrangements that are likely to be needed for witnesses; whether the issues in the Crown Court differ from the issues in the magistrates' court, and if so how; and how long the trial lasted in the magistrates' court and how long the appeal is likely to last in the Crown Court (r.34.3(2)).

Criminal Practice Direction IX, para.34A.1, notes that the requirement to supply information needed for the effective case management of the appeal applies to both the appellant and respondent, but it is possible for the appellant, but not the respondent, to be relieved of that obligation, either in whole or in part.

It should be noted that permission to appeal to the Crown Court is not required.

The 21-day period for giving notice of appeal can be extended (even after it has expired) under the court's general power to extend time limits under r.34.10. Where an appeal notice is served after the expiry of the 21-day period, the notice must include an application for an extension of the time limit and must give reasons (r.34.2(3)).

Criminal Practice Direction IX, para.34B.3 says that, on an appeal against conviction, the reasons given by the magistrates for their decision should not be included with the documents that are sent to the Crown Court. This is because the appeal hearing is not a review of the magistrates' court's decision but a re-hearing. Similarly, para.34B.4 states that, on an appeal solely against sentence, the magistrates' court's reasons and factual finding leading to the finding of guilt should be included, but any reasons for the sentence imposed should be omitted (because the Crown Court will be conducting a fresh sentencing exercise).

7.2.2 Bail pending appeal

Where the defendant is given a custodial sentence, bail pending appeal may be granted by the magistrates who passed sentence (s.113 of the Magistrates' Courts Act 1980). However, there is no presumption in favour of bail, as s.4 of the Bail Act 1976 does not apply.

If the magistrates do not grant bail, the Crown Court may do so (under s.81(1)(b) of the Senior Courts Act 1981). The strongest argument that can usually be advanced in support of bail pending the hearing of the appeal is that a short sentence may have been served before the appeal is heard.

7.2.3 The hearing of the appeal in the Crown Court

The appeal is heard by a judge (a circuit judge or a recorder) and at least two (but not more than four) lay justices (s.74(1) of the Senior Courts Act 1981).

Section 73(3) of the Senior Courts Act 1981 stipulates that where a Crown Court judge sits with Justices of the Peace:

- he shall preside;
- the decision of the Crown Court may be a majority decision; and
- if the members of the court are equally divided, the Crown Court judge has a second and casting vote.

Rule 34.11 provides that, before or after the actual appeal hearing, the Crown Court may comprise a judge sitting alone (without lay justices) and, when so constituted, may exercise case management powers and state a case for the opinion of the High Court, or refuse to do so. Thus, where there has been an application to the Crown Court to state a case (see below), it is permissible for the judge to approve the formal statement of case, or to refuse to state a case, without recalling the magistrates who also heard the appeal.

7.2.3.1 Appeals against conviction

To enable effective case management of appeals, r.34.7 enables the Crown Court to conduct a 'preparation for appeal hearing' if it is necessary to do so in order to give directions for the effective determination of the appeal, or to set ground rules for the conduct of the questioning of a witness or appellant. It should be noted that the Crown Court may comprise only a judge (without lay justices) when exercising case management powers (r.34.11(3)).

An appeal against conviction takes the form of a complete rehearing, and so the procedure is the same as the trial in the magistrates' court or youth court (s.79(3) of the Senior Courts Act 1981).

Because an appeal against conviction is a rehearing, the parties are not limited to evidence which was called at the original trial. This has the important consequence that either party can call witnesses who were not called in the magistrates' court trial, or refrain from calling witnesses who did give evidence in the magistrates' court. However, the Crown Court cannot amend the charge on which the appellant was convicted (*Garfield v Maddocks* [1974] QB 7; *R v Swansea Crown Court ex p Stacey* [1990] RTR 183).

7.2.3.2 Appeals against sentence

An appeal against sentence similarly mirrors the sentencing procedure in the magistrates' court or youth court, with the prosecution summarising the facts and the defence making a plea in mitigation.

The Crown Court carries out a complete rehearing of the issues and forms an independent view as to the correct sentence. In *R v Swindon Crown Court ex p Murray* (1998) 162 JP 36, the Divisional Court held that, when dealing with an appeal against sentence, the Crown Court should not ask itself whether the sentence was within the discretion of the magistrates (the test which would be appropriate in judicial review) but should consider whether, in the light of all the matters which the Crown Court had heard, the sentence passed by the magistrates was the correct one. If it was not the correct sentence, the Crown Court should replace it with the sentence that the court holds to be the right one.

7.2.4 Decision

The decision of the Crown Court is a majority decision. This means that the lay justices can outvote the Crown Court judge. The lay justices must, however, accept any decisions on questions of law made by the judge.

In *R v Orpin* [1975] QB 283, p.287, Lord Widgery CJ said that:

in matters of law the lay justices must take a ruling from the presiding judge in precisely the same way as the jury is required to take his ruling when the jury considers its verdict ... [It should be] clearly understood: first, that decisions are the product of all members of the court but, secondly, that any question of law is a question upon which the lay members of the court must defer to the views of the qualified presiding judge.

In R v Newby (1984) 6 Cr App R (S) 148, the Court of Appeal emphasised the importance of the judge consulting with the lay justices.

7.2.4.1 Reasons for the decision

Where the Crown Court dismisses an appeal against conviction, the judge must give reasons (and judicial review can be sought to compel the judge to do so if necessary). The reasons need not be elaborate, but the judge must say enough to demonstrate that the court has identified the main contentious issues in the case and how it has resolved each of them; the appellant is entitled to know the basis upon which the prosecution case had been accepted by the court (R v Harrow Crown Court ex p Dave [1994] 1 WLR 98, per Pill J at p.107). In R v Snaresbrook Crown Court ex p Input Management Ltd (1999) 163 JP 533, the Divisional Court said that the reasons given by the court should enable the defendant to see the nature of the criminality found to exist by the court and to consider properly whether there are grounds for a further appeal to the Divisional Court by way of case stated. However, in R v Kingston Crown Court ex p Bell (2000) 164 JP 633, Jackson J said (at [34]):

> In the ordinary way, when the Crown Court hears an appeal from the magistrates' court, the Crown Court is under a duty to give reasons for its decision and a failure to give reasons will vitiate the Crown Court's decision. However, this is not a universal rule: for example, the reasons may be obvious, or the case may be simple or the subject matter of the appeal may be unimportant. In cases of that nature, a failure to give reasons would not be fatal.

Nonetheless, it is submitted that the invariable practice of the Crown Court should be to give reasons where it dismisses an appeal. In R (Alabi) v Crown Court at Ipswich [2014] EWHC 895 (Admin), Rafferty LJ (at [12]) cited with approval the words of Hickinbottom J in R (Aitchison) v Sheffield Crown Court [2012] EWHC 2844 (Admin), at [18]:

> [I]t is insufficient merely to declare or announce that the appeal is dismissed, because that does not amount to any substantive reasoning at all ... In its reasons, the Crown Court must show that it has adopted a proper approach and has not misdirected itself: it must at least identify the main issues in the appeal, and indicate how it has determined those issues.

Rafferty LJ went on to say that there is 'no particular magic' to the language used to state the reasons.

7.2.5 Equivocal pleas

Section 108(1)(a) of the Magistrates Courts' Act 1980 limits the right of appeal in the case of a defendant who pleaded guilty to an appeal against sentence. It follows that a defendant who pleads guilty in the magistrates' court cannot usually challenge that conviction by appealing to the Crown Court. However, if the plea of guilty was 'equivocal', the defendant can appeal against conviction despite having pleaded guilty. There are two types of equivocal plea:

● The plea which is equivocal in court (that is, it becomes equivocal because of something said prior to the passing of sentence). This will be the case if either:

   ○ when the charge is put, the defendant says 'Guilty but ...' (in other words, at the time of entering the guilty plea, the defendant says something which raises a defence, such as 'guilty of theft but I thought the property was mine'); or o   when the charge is put, the defendant says only 'Guilty', but this straightforward plea is followed by a plea in mitigation which raises a defence and so is inconsistent with the guilty plea (for example, R v Durham Quarter Sessions ex p Virgo [1952] 2 QB 1, where an unrepresented defendant pleaded guilty to stealing a motorbike. Before sentence was passed, he made a statement to the effect that his taking of the motorbike was a mistake as he thought it belonged to a friend of his who had told him to take it home. It was held that the justices should have entered a plea of not guilty in view of the defendant's statement, and the case was remitted to the magistrates' court with a direction to hear the case on the basis of a plea of not guilty); and

● The plea which is made equivocal not because of anything the defendant says in court but because the defendant pleaded guilty as a direct result of threats from a third party; then, at some time after the passing of sentence, the defendant alleges that he only pleaded guilty as a result of duress and now maintains that he is innocent (for example, R v Huntingdon Crown Court ex p Jordan [1981] QB 857, where the defendant, in the course of an appeal to the Crown Court, said that she had been threatened by her husband that he would physically ill-treat her if she did not plead guilty: it was held that the Crown Court should investigate the matter where it is alleged that there has been an equivocal plea in that sense and, if satisfied that there was an equivocal plea, send the matter back to the justices to enable them to re-hear the case on the basis of a not guilty plea).

In the case of the first type of equivocal plea, the problem should, of course, be dealt with at the original hearing. The charge should be put again by the magistrates' court once the relevant law has been explained to the defendant. If the plea remains equivocal, a 'not guilty' plea should be entered by the court on the defendant's behalf. If this does not occur, or if the plea is equivocal because of duress, the defendant should apply to the Crown Court to declare the plea equivocal. In this type of appeal, the only inquiry undertaken by the Crown Court is whether or not the plea was equivocal. If the Crown Court decides that the plea was indeed equivocal, it will remit the case to the magistrates' court for trial. If not, the conviction based on the guilty plea will be upheld.

Provided the Crown Court conducts a proper inquiry into what happened in the magistrates' court (the justices' legal adviser or the chairman of the bench which convicted the defendant may have to supply a statement to assist the Crown Court in that inquiry), a direction from the Crown Court regarding remission for trial is binding on the magistrates' court (R v Plymouth Justices ex p Hart [1986] QB 950).

There are no other grounds for going behind a plea of guilty and so no other cases where a defendant can appeal to the Crown Court after pleading guilty (R v Marylebone Justices ex p Westminster London Borough Council [1971] 1 WLR 567). It is therefore not sufficient for the defendant merely to show that he regrets pleading guilty and that he has an arguable defence.

7.2.6 Powers of the Crown Court

The powers of the Crown Court when disposing of an appeal under s.108 of the Magistrates' Courts Act 1980 are set out in s.48(2) of the Senior Courts Act 1981. This provides that, following an appeal from the magistrates' court, the Crown Court:

(a)   may confirm, reverse or vary any part of the decision appealed against, including a determination not to impose a separate penalty in respect of an offence; or

(b)   may remit the matter with its opinion thereon to the authority whose decision is appealed against; or

(c)   may make such other order in the matter as the court thinks just, and by such order exercise any power which the said authority might have exercised.

This means that, on an appeal against conviction, the Crown Court may:

- dismiss the appeal (and so uphold the conviction); or
- allow the appeal (and quash the conviction, placing the defendant in the position he would have been in had the magistrates acquitted him); or
- remit the case to the magistrates' court (as would be the case where the Crown Court holds a plea of guilty to be equivocal).

The Crown Court can also vary the sentence imposed by the magistrates' court. Section 48(4) of the 1981 Act says that:

> if the appeal is against a conviction or a sentence, the preceding provisions of this section shall be construed as including power to award any punishment, whether more or less severe than that awarded by the magistrates' court whose decision is appealed against, if that is a punishment which that magistrates' court might have awarded.

The Crown Court may thus vary the sentence imposed by the magistrates, and this includes the power to increase the sentence, but not beyond the maximum sentence which the magistrates' court could have passed.

Section 48(5) provides that s.48 'applies whether or not the appeal is against the whole of the decision' and, as we have seen, s.48(2) refers to varying 'any part' of the decision under appeal. The effect of these provisions is that, if the defendant appeals against only part of the decision of the magistrates' court, every aspect of the magistrates' decision can be reconsidered by the Crown Court. For example:

- even if the defendant appeals only against conviction, the Crown Court can still vary the sentence;
- if the defendant was convicted of two offences and appeals against only one conviction, the Crown Court could allow the appeal (and quash the conviction that is being appealed) but also vary the sentence for the other offence;
- if the defendant was convicted by the magistrates of one offence but acquitted of another and he now appeals against the conviction, the Crown Court could convict the defendant of the offence of which the magistrates' court acquitted him.

It should be emphasised that, if the Crown Court does vary the sentence, it cannot impose a sentence greater than the sentence that the magistrates could have imposed.

7.2.7 Further appeal from the Crown Court

The decision of the Crown Court on an appeal from a magistrates' court or youth court can only be challenged by means of an appeal to the Divisional Court by way of case stated or judicial review. There is no further appeal to the Court of Appeal.

7.3 Appeal to the High Court by way of case stated

Appeal to the Divisional Court (part of the High Court of Justice) is made possible by s.111(1) of the Magistrates' Courts Act 1980, which provides as follows:

> Any person who was a party to any proceeding before a magistrates' court or is aggrieved by the conviction, order, determination or other proceeding of the court may question the

proceeding on the ground that it is wrong in law or is in excess of jurisdiction by applying to the justices composing the court to state a case for the opinion of the High Court on the question of law or jurisdiction involved.

The right to appeal by way of case stated is only available where there has been a 'final determination' of the case in the magistrates' court (*Streames v Copping* [1985] QB 920 and *Loade v DPP* [1990] 1 QB 1052). It follows that s.111 does not apply to interlocutory decisions, such as a decision to commit the defendant to the Crown Court to be sentenced. The case law is fairly clear that there must have been a final determination before an appeal by way of case stated may be brought, but in *Essen v DPP* [2005] EWHC 1077 (Admin), Sedley LJ said (at [34]) observed that:

> It may be … this … could usefully be revisited. If neither judicial review nor appeal by a case stated is available against an interlocutory decision which would arguably have been dispositive of a case at an early and much less costly stage, a fixed rule that any challenge must abide a final outcome is capable of working injustice.

Nonetheless, the principle has been applied consistently. It can arise in particular where there is an issue about the jurisdiction of the magistrates' court to try the case. Whether appeal by way of case stated is available to challenge their decision depends on whether they accepted or rejected jurisdiction. In *Downes v Royal Society for the Prevention of Cruelty to Animals* [2017] EWHC 3622 (Admin); [2018] 2 Cr App R 3, Julian Knowles J (at [23]) said:

> (a) where a jurisdictional point is taken before the magistrates' court, then if the court declines jurisdiction that decision can be challenged either by judicial review or by way of case stated …; (b) where such a point is taken and a court accepts that it has jurisdiction [the] only remedy is for the aggrieved party to seek judicial review, and the magistrates in such an event should not adjourn unless there are particularly good reasons to do so. It will very usually be better to carry on and complete the case, allowing for all matters to be raised on appeal at the conclusion of the case in the normal way; (c) in all other cases there is no power to state a case in relation to an interlocutory ruling. A magistrate should proceed to determine the case finally and then to state a case if appropriate to do so …

Unlike the appeal to the Crown Court, appeal to the High Court by way of case stated is available to the prosecution as well as the defence. However, under s.111(1) of the Magistrates' Courts Act 1980, it is available only where the decision of the magistrates' court or youth court is:

- wrong in law; or
- in excess of jurisdiction.

This procedure is best suited to cases where it is suggested that the magistrates got the law wrong when coming to their decision – for example, that they misconstrued a statutory provision.

Where the defence wants to bring a challenge that is essentially about the correctness of the findings of fact by the magistrates, the better course is to appeal to the Crown Court, rather than to the High Court by way of case stated. In *Oladimeji v DPP* [2006] EWHC 1199 (Admin), Keene LJ said (at [4]):

> If there is no evidence for a finding of fact, that will give rise to an error of law. But the weight to be attached to particular pieces of evidence is a matter for the justices. Only if no reasonable Bench could have reached the finding in question will that finding produce an error of law or amount to an ultra vires act. If a defendant believes that the justices have arrived at a finding for which there was evidence but at which he contends they should not

have arrived (for example, because it was against the weight of the evidence), his remedy lies in an appeal to the Crown Court, not in an appeal by case stated to this court.

It follows that questions which go to the court's findings of fact are not appropriate for appeal by way of case stated (see, for example, R (Skelton) v Winchester Crown Court [2017] EWHC 3118 (Admin), at [34]). An appeal on a finding of fact can be regarded as an appeal on a point of law if, and only if, the finding is unreasonable (in the sense that no fact-finder, properly directed, could make that finding on the basis of the evidence that was heard). As Ward LJ expressed it (in the context of a social security appeal, which had to be on a point of law) in Braintree District Council v Thompson [2005] EWCA Civ 178 (at [19])

> It will be an error of law to find a fact if there is no evidence to support that finding … Findings of fact which are challenged as erroneous for being against the weight of the evidence do not involve any error of law. It only becomes an error of law if the finding of fact is perverse in the sense that no reasonable Tribunal could have reached that conclusion. An example of such perversity would be where the fact-finding body proceeded upon a blatant misunderstanding or in total ignorance of an established and relevant fact. It must be established that the Tribunal acted upon a wholly incorrect basis of fact but that only arises where the fact is plain and incontrovertible and where there is no room for difference of view about it.

7.3.1 Procedure for appealing by way of case stated

Section 111(2) requires that an application under s.111 must be made 'within 21 days after the day on which the decision of the magistrates' court was given'. Subsection (3) defines the date of decision, where the defendant has been convicted by a magistrates' court, as 'the day on which the court sentences or otherwise deals with the offender'.

The appellant begins the appeal by making an application to the magistrates to state a case. In accordance with s.111, this application must be made within 21 days of sentence and must identify the question of law or jurisdiction at issue.

This 21-day period cannot be extended (see Michael v Gowland [1977] 1 WLR 296). In Woolls v North Somerset Council [2016] EWHC 1410 (Admin), Jeremy Baker J declined to hold that the initial 21-day limit could not be extended. His Lordship (at [6]) invoked the Civil Procedure Rules, which provide that application may be made to the High Court to vary the time limit for filing an appeal notice. However, the Divisional Court reached the opposite conclusion in Mishra v Colchester Magistrates' Court [2017] EWHC 2869 (Admin); [2018] 1 WLR 1351. Sharp LJ said that there is 'no doubt that Parliament has decided in primary and secondary legislation that there should be a strict time limit of 21 days to state a case from the magistrates' courts' (at [33]). The provisions of the Civil Procedure Rules are part of the suite of rules governing the procedure for an appeal brought under s.28A of the Senior Courts Act 1981; they have no application to the right of a party to apply to the magistrates' court to state a case under s.111(2) of the Magistrates' Courts Act 1980. In other words, the Civil Procedures are relevant only once the case has reached the High Court. Accordingly, the contention that the 21-day time limit in s.111(2) of the 1980 Act can be extended by resort to the Civil Procedure Rules, which govern a different procedure, 'must be rejected' (at [34]). It follows that the approach suggested in Woolls should therefore not be followed, and that the initial 21-day period cannot be extended.

7.3.2 Refusal to state a case

By virtue of s.111(5), the justices may refuse to state a case if they are of opinion that the application is 'frivolous'. If the magistrates refuse to state a case on this basis, the applicant may seek a certificate confirming their refusal to state a case. Under subs.(6), where justices refuse to state a case, the applicant may seek judicial review of the refusal and the High Court may make an order requiring the justices to state a case.

The test of whether a request to state a case is 'frivolous' is whether the application raises an 'arguable' point of law (R v City of London Justices ex p Ocansey (1995), QBD, 17 February, unreported).

In R v Mildenhall Magistrates' Court ex p Forest Heath District Council (1997) 161 JP 401, Lord Bingham CJ said that the word 'frivolous' in this context means that the justices consider the application to be 'futile, misconceived, hopeless, or academic'. His Lordship went on to say that such a conclusion will be reached only rarely; it is not enough that the justices consider that their original decision was correct. Furthermore, where justices do refuse to state a case, they should give brief reasons explaining why they have done so.

Where the magistrates refuse to state a case and the appellant seeks judicial review of that refusal, the usual remedy (if the Divisional Court holds that the refusal to state a case was wrong) is for the Divisional Court to quash the refusal to state a case, so the magistrates have to state a case. However, it is open to the Divisional Court, when considering the application for judicial review of the refusal to state a case, to regard the written evidence used in the judicial review proceedings as the case stated and to treat the application for judicial review as if it were an appeal by way of case stated. In this way, the Divisional Court can, for example, quash a conviction without waiting for the case to go back to the magistrates to state a case (R v Crown Court at Blackfriars ex p Sunworld Ltd [2000] 1 WLR 2102, per Simon Brown LJ (at pp.2106–7).

Another reason for refusing to state a case is contained in s.114 of the Magistrates' Courts Act 1980, which empowers the magistrates to require the appellant to enter into a recognisance (that is, promise to pay a specified sum of money if the condition is not complied with) to pursue the appeal without delay and to pay any costs awarded against him by the High Court. If this power is invoked, a case will not be stated until the appellant has entered into a recognisance.

7.3.3 The statement of case

The procedure for an appeal by way of case stated is governed by Part 35 of the Criminal Procedure Rules. The application is made to the magistrates' court. Rule 35.2(2) requires that the application must:

- specify the decision in issue;
- specify the proposed question or questions of law or jurisdiction on which the opinion of the High Court will be asked;
- indicate the proposed grounds of appeal.

Under r.35.3(3), unless the court otherwise directs, not more than 21 days after the court's decision to state a case, the court officer must serve a draft case on each party.

Rule 35.3(4) provides that the draft case must:

- (a) specify the decision in issue;
- (b) specify the question(s) of law or jurisdiction on which the opinion of the High Court will be asked;
- (c) include a succinct summary of –
  - (i)   the nature and history of the proceedings;
  - (ii) the court's relevant findings of fact; and
  - (iii) the relevant contentions of the parties;
- (d) if a question is whether there was sufficient evidence on which the court reasonably could reach a finding of fact –

    (i)   specify that finding; and

    (ii) include a summary of the evidence on which the court reached that finding.

Rule 35.3(5) clarifies that, except to the extent that para.(4)(d) requires, 'the draft case must not include an account of the evidence received by the court'.

The reasons for the decision that are set out in the stated case must be those that were in the minds of the magistrates when they reached that decision. However, in *Marshall v CPS* [2015] EWHC 2333 (Admin); (2016) 180 JP 33, Kenneth Parker J (at [27]) said that 'the justices, within fair and reasonable limits, may amplify their reasons for the decision that they reached'.

The parties then have 21 days from service of the draft case to make representations on the content of the draft case (r.35.3(6)). The court must state the case not more than 21 days after the time for service of representations has expired (r.35.3(7)). The stated case is served on each party (r.35.3(9)).

The appellant should lodge the stated case at the Administrative Court Office within 10 days of receiving it from the magistrates' court (Civil Procedure Rules Practice Direction 52, para.18.4) and must serve the appellant's notice and accompanying documents on all respondents within four days after they are filed or lodged at the appeal court (para.18.6).

7.3.3.1 Further guidance on the content of the stated case

In *Vehicle Inspectorate v George Jenkins Transport Ltd* [2003] EWHC 2879 (Admin) (at [36]-[38], per Kennedy LJ), it was said that a stated case should set out:

- the facts as found or accepted for the purposes of the magistrates' ruling;
- in summary form, the submissions made on each side;
- the conclusions of the magistrates' court on the matters in issue; and
- the question(s) for the consideration of the Divisional Court.

In *Oladimeji v DPP* [2006] EWHC 1199 (Admin), Keene LJ said (at [4]) that the court needs:

clear findings of fact, and a clear identification of the questions of law which are said to arise. The justices should decline to pose questions for this court unless those questions are ones of law.

It should be borne in mind that when magistrates are asked to state a case, it is not open to them to put forward reasons their decision should not be challenged where those reasons were not part of their original decision (*Kent County Council v Curtis* (1998) EGCS 100). Furthermore, the justices should not change, or put a gloss on, the reasons which they gave in court for convicting or acquitting the defendant (*Evans v DPP* [2001] EWHC 369 (Admin), per Bell J, at [10])).

7.3.4 Bail pending appeal

If the defendant was given a custodial sentence, the magistrates may grant bail pending appeal under s.113 of the Magistrates' Courts Act 1980. If the magistrates refuse, the defendant can apply to a High Court judge under s.22 of the Criminal Justice Act 1967.

7.3.5 The hearing

The appeal is heard by a Divisional Court (that is, two or more High Court judges in open court). The hearing of the appeal takes the form of legal argument based on the facts stated in the case; no evidence is called, and so there are no witnesses.

A corollary of this is that a party is not entitled to take a new point, the decision of which might be affected by evidence which could have been, but was not, adduced before the magistrates. Similarly, where a defendant has been convicted by the magistrates and appeals to the Divisional Court, it is not possible to raise the issue that certain prosecution evidence should have been excluded if the defence had not asked the magistrates to exclude the evidence; such matters cannot be raised for the first time in the Divisional Court (see *Braham v DPP* (1995) 159 JP 527).

7.3.6 Powers of the Divisional Court

The powers of the Divisional Court on an appeal by way of case stated are contained in s.28A(3) of the Senior Courts Act 1981, which provides that the High Court may:

(a)   reverse, affirm or amend the determination in respect of which the case has been stated; or

(b)   remit the matter to the magistrates' court, or the Crown Court, with the opinion of the High Court, and may make such other order in relation to the matter (including as to costs) as it thinks fit.

It follows that:

- where the defendant was convicted by the magistrates' court the Divisional Court may replace the conviction with an acquittal;
- where the defendant was acquitted after a full trial (that is, not after a successful submission of no case to answer at the close of the prosecution case), the Divisional Court may remit the case back to the magistrates' court with a direction to convict and proceed to sentence (or, if it is plain what sentence should be passed, the Divisional Court may itself convict the appellant and then proceed to sentence him);
- where the defendant was acquitted otherwise than after a full trial (for example, following a successful submission of no case to answer), the Divisional Court may remit the case to the magistrates' court with a direction to continue with the trial or to start the trial afresh in front of a fresh bench.

In *Griffith v Jenkins* [1992] 2 AC 76, the House of Lords confirmed that the Divisional Court has the power to remit a case for a rehearing before the same or a different bench of magistrates. Thus, it does not matter if the original court cannot be reconstituted for some reason (for example, one of the justices has retired or died). However, a rehearing of the case will be ordered only if a fair trial is still possible given the lapse of time since the alleged offence.

7.3.7 Effect on the right of appeal to the Crown Court

The making of an application to the magistrates to state a case removes the defendant's right to appeal to the Crown Court (s.111(4) of the Magistrates' Courts Act 1980). Tactically, therefore, it may be wise to appeal to the Crown Court first and, if that appeal is unsuccessful, to appeal against the decision of the Crown Court to the Divisional Court if there is a point of law on which to base that appeal.

7.4 Judicial review

Like appeal by way of case stated, judicial review is available to the prosecution as well as the defence. However, an acquittal will not be quashed unless the trial was a nullity and so the defendant was not in danger of a valid conviction (for example, the purported summary trial of an indictable-only offence, or where the magistrates acquit without hearing any prosecution evidence, as in R v Dorking Justices ex p Harrington [1984] AC 743).

Unlike appeal by way of case stated, for judicial review to be available, there does not have to have been a final determination of the case. Nonetheless, any application for judicial review should usually be made at the conclusion of the proceedings in the magistrates' court. In R (Hoar-Stevens) v Richmond-upon-Thames Magistrates [2003] EWHC 2660 (Admin), Kennedy LJ (at [18]) said:

> [T]he course of a criminal trial in the Magistrates' Court should not be punctuated by applications for an adjournment to test a ruling in this court, especially when in reality if the case proceeds the ruling may turn out to be of little or no importance ... [E]ven when ... there is an important substantive point which arises during a trial this court should not and indeed cannot intervene. The proper course is to proceed to the end of the trial in the lower court and then to test the matter, almost certainly by way of case stated.

However, there are exceptions. In R (Watson) v Dartford Magistrates' Court [2005] EWHC 905 (Admin), the court entertained a challenge to an interlocutory decision on an application for an adjournment. Mitting J said (at [7]) that:

> in some cases, the prosecution would no doubt say at the conclusion of a trial resulting in a conviction that it was too late for the claimant to complain about an adjournment that should not have been granted before. In a case such as this, where the issue is straightforward and the principle clear, I do not see that there is any fetter on this court intervening.

Where the defendant pleaded guilty and wishes to challenge his conviction on the basis of a complaint about the conduct of the prosecution, the question is whether the prosecutor has acted in a way that has misled the defendant, whether deliberately or not (R v Burton-on-Trent Justices ex p Woolley (1995) 159 JP 165, followed in R v Dolgellau Justices ex p Cartledge [1996] RTR 207).

7.4.1 Grounds for seeking judicial review

The traditional statement of the ambit of judicial review comes from the speech of Lord Diplock in Council of Civil Service Unions v Minister for the Civil Service [1985] AC 374, at p.410:

> [O]ne can conveniently classify under three heads the grounds upon which administrative action is subject to control by judicial review. The first ground I would call 'illegality', the second 'irrationality' and the third 'procedural impropriety'.

Case law on the ambit of judicial review suggests that the following are the main grounds:

- Error of law on the face of the record (that is, an error disclosed in the court records). This could include, for example, convicting a defendant of an offence created by a statute that was not in force at the relevant time).
- Excess of jurisdiction (that is, the decision was ultra vires). This would include, for example, a magistrates' court trying an either-way offence without the defendant having first consented to summary trial.
- Breach of the rules of natural justice (for example, bias or failing to allow both sides to put their case).

Breach of natural justice has been widely construed. It includes, for example:

- the unreasonable refusal of an adjournment to enable a defendant to prepare his case (*R v Thames Magistrates' Court ex p Polemis* [1974] 1 WLR 1371);
- refusing an adjournment where a defence witness could not attend on the day of the trial without first considering the effect on the defence of having to go ahead without that witness (*R v Bracknell Justices ex p Hughes* (1990) 154 JP 98);
- failure by the prosecution to notify the defence of the existence of witnesses who could support the defence case (*R v Leyland Justices ex p Hawthorn* [1979] QB 283);
- failure by the prosecution to inform the defence that a key prosecution witness had a previous conviction for wasting police time, arising out of a false allegation of theft (*R v Knightsbridge Crown Court ex p Goonatilleke* [1986] QB 1, where the accused was charged with shoplifting);
- ordering a defendant to pay costs without considering his means to pay them (*R v Newham Justices ex p Samuels* [1991] COD 412).

7.4.1.1 Availability of appeal to the Crown Court

In *R v Peterborough Justices ex p Dowler* [1997] QB 911, it was held that it is unnecessary to grant judicial review of a conviction by magistrates where the procedural unfairness complained of could be rectified by a fair hearing (by way of appeal) before the Crown Court, appealing to that court being 'clearly more effective and more convenient as well as being more expeditious' (per Henry LJ, p.923). However, in *R v Hereford Magistrates' Court ex p Rowlands* [1998] QB 110, Lord Bingham CJ (at p.125) said that *Dowler* should not be treated as authority that a party complaining of procedural unfairness in a magistrates' court should invariably exercise his right of appeal to the Crown Court rather than seek judicial review; the existence of a right of appeal to the Crown Court, particularly if unexercised, should not ordinarily weigh against judicial review, in a proper case.

Nonetheless, given the length of time that it takes to obtain judicial review, and the cost that is involved, a defendant will almost always be best advised to appeal against conviction to the Crown Court rather than seek to have the conviction overturned through judicial review.

7.4.2 Procedure

Judicial review is governed by Part 54 of the Civil Procedure Rules (CPR) and the Practice Direction 54A which supplements Part 54.

Rule 54.5(1) states that the claim form must be filed promptly and, in any event, 'not later than 3 months after the grounds to make the claim first arose'.

The first stage is to seek permission to pursue a claim for judicial review (s.31(3) of the Senior Courts Act 1981). The procedure is as follows.

The first step in a claim for judicial review is to file a claim form. Paragraph 5.6 of the Practice Direction says that the claim form must include or be accompanied by a detailed statement of the claimant's grounds for bringing the claim for judicial review and a statement of the facts relied upon. Paragraph 5.7 goes on to say that the claim form must also be accompanied by any written evidence in support of the claim, a copy of any order that the claimant seeks to have quashed, an approved copy of the lower court's reasons for reaching the decision under challenge, copies of any documents on which the claimant proposes to rely, copies of any relevant statutory material, and a list of essential documents for reading in advance by the court.

Where the claim is for judicial review of a decision of a magistrates' court or the Crown Court, the prosecution must always be named as an interested party (para.5.2).

The defendant must file an acknowledgement of service not more than 21 days after the service of the claim form; the acknowledgment of service must be served on the claimant and on any other person named in the claim form, not later than seven days after it is filed (r.54.8(2)). The acknowledgement of service must (if the person filing it intends to contest the claim) set out a summary of the grounds for contesting the claim (r.54.8(4)).

Paragraph 8.4 of the Practice Direction says that the court will generally consider the question of permission without a hearing. Where there is a hearing, neither the defendant nor any other interested party need attend the hearing unless the court directs otherwise (para.8.5). Where the defendant or any interested party does attend a hearing, the court will not generally make an order for costs against the claimant (para.8.6).

The test applied in deciding the question of permission is whether the application discloses an arguable case. Rule 54.12 provides that if the court, without a hearing, refuses permission to proceed or gives permission that is subject to conditions or on certain grounds only, the court will serve its reasons for making the order along with the order itself. Under r.54.12(3), the claimant may not appeal but may request the decision to be reconsidered at a hearing. Neither the defendant nor anyone else served with the claim form may apply to set aside an order giving the claimant permission to proceed (r.54.13).

Under r.54.14, once the claimant has been given permission to proceed, the defendant (and anyone else served with the claim form who wishes to contest the claim) must, within 35 days after service of the order giving permission, serve detailed grounds for contesting the claim, and any written evidence.

Where all the parties agree, the court may decide the claim for judicial review without a hearing (r.54.18). Otherwise, the claimant must file and serve a skeleton argument not less than 21 working days before the date of the hearing of the judicial review claim (para.15.1 of the Practice Direction). The defendant (and any other party wishing to make representations at the hearing) must file and serve a skeleton argument not less than 14 working days before the date of the hearing (para.15.2). The skeleton arguments must contain a list of issues, a list of the legal points to be taken (together with any relevant authorities), a chronology of events, a list of essential documents for advance reading by the court, and a list of persons referred to (para.15.3).

In a criminal case, a judicial review hearing takes place before a Divisional Court (that is, two or more High Court judges sitting in an open court). It usually takes the form of legal argument based on the written evidence, though it is possible for oral evidence to be called if necessary.

7.4.3 Bail

Where the defendant was given a custodial sentence by the magistrates and is applying to the Divisional Court to quash the conviction, the magistrates do not have the power to grant bail pending the hearing of the application for judicial review. An application for bail may, however, be made to the High Court under s.37(1)(d) of the Criminal Justice Act 1948.

7.4.4 Remedies

The main judicial review remedies (listed in s.31(1)(a) of the Senior Courts Act 1981) are:

- quashing order (formerly called 'certiorari'), which has the effect of quashing the original decision (where a conviction is quashed, the defendant stands acquitted of the offence);
- mandatory order (formerly called 'mandamus'), which requires the lower court to do something, for example, to go through the allocation procedure again;
- prohibiting order (formerly called 'prohibition'), which prevents the lower court from doing

something that it should not do, for example, trying the defendant in circumstances that amount to an abuse of process.

Sometimes more than one order is made – for example, there might be a quashing order to quash the decision of the court below, and a mandatory order compelling the lower court to reconsider the matter.

Section 31(5) of the Senior Courts Act 1981 provides that, if the High Court quashes the decision to which the application relates, it may also:

(a) remit the matter to the court, tribunal or authority which made the decision, with a direction to reconsider the matter and reach a decision in accordance with the findings of the High Court; or

(b) substitute its own decision for the decision in question.

However, it may only do the latter if the decision in question was made by a court or tribunal, the decision is quashed on the ground that there has been an error of law and, without the error, there would have been only one decision which the court or tribunal could have reached.

The granting of a judicial review remedy is always discretionary. Even if the applicant is able to succeed on the merits, the High Court may decide that it is inappropriate to grant a remedy. In *Santos v Stratford Magistrates' Court* [2012] EWHC 752 (Admin), for example, the court declined to grant relief, mainly because the applicant had failed to raise the issue relied on at the time of the trial and that issue was 'in reality, pure technicality' (per Treacy J [17]).

Delay is one reason for withholding relief. In R v *Neath and Port Talbot Justices ex p DPP* [2000] 1 WLR 1376, Simon Brown LJ (at p.1381) said that the circumstances to be taken into account when the court is exercising its discretion in criminal proceedings whether to grant relief in a judicial review application (or indeed an appeal by way of case stated) where there has been delay include:

(a) the seriousness of the criminal charges, (b) the nature of the evidence in the case and in particular the extent to which its quality may be affected by the delay, (c) the extent, if any, to which the defendant has brought about or contributed to the justice's error, (d) the extent, if any, to which the defendant has brought about or contributed to the delay in the hearing of the challenge, and (e) how far the complainant would feel justifiably aggrieved by the proceedings being halted and the defendant would feel justifiably aggrieved by their being continued.

7.5 Appeals against sentence

Although it would theoretically be possible to appeal by way of case stated (or to seek judicial review) if the magistrates impose a sentence which is beyond their powers, it is quicker and easier simply to appeal to the Crown Court against sentence.

Even where the appeal is on the basis that the sentence is wrong in law (or outside jurisdiction) because it is so severe that no reasonable bench could impose such a sentence, the proper appeal is to the Crown Court rather than to the Divisional Court. In *Tucker v DPP* (1992) 13 Cr App R(S) 495, Woolf LJ said (at p.498):

If a person who is convicted by the magistrates wishes to challenge the sentence which is imposed, in all but the most exceptional case, the appropriate course for them to adopt is to go before the Crown Court where there will be a rehearing.

In R v Gloucester Crown Court ex p McGeary [1999] 2 Cr App R(S) 263, Lord Bingham CJ said (at p.268) that, 'before any challenge can succeed, the departure of the sentencing court from normal standards or levels or practice of sentencing must be so great as to constitute an excess of jurisdiction or an error of law'.

7.6 Case stated or judicial review

The grounds on which judicial review can be sought and an appeal by way of case stated made are virtually the same: an error of law or jurisdiction.

In R v Oldbury Justices ex p Smith (1994) 159 JP 316, it was said that where appeal by way of case stated is available, it is preferable to challenge a decision of a magistrates' court by means of appeal by way of case stated rather than judicial review. This is because judicial review is to be regarded as a remedy of last resort and because on an appeal by way of case stated the Divisional Court is presented with all the findings of fact made by the magistrates.

It has to be borne in mind that appeal by way of case stated is available only when there has been a final determination of the proceedings in the lower court.

Judicial review is particularly appropriate where the appeal raises jurisdictional issues (R v North Essex Justices ex p Lloyd [2001] 2 Cr App R(S) 15, per Lord Woolf CJ (at [11])).

In R (P) v Liverpool City Magistrates [2006] EWHC 887 (Admin), Collins J (at [7]–[8]) said that judicial review is appropriate 'where it is alleged that there has been unfairness in the way that the justices conducted the case'; however, 'where it is alleged that justices have misdirected themselves or got the law wrong in their approach to a decision, case stated is the appropriate way of dealing with it'. In B v Carlisle Crown Court [2009] EWHC 3540 (Admin), Langstaff J (at [18]) said that: 'In those cases where there is said to be a material irregularity in the procedure adopted in the court hearing the appeal, judicial review may well be an appropriate route'.

In R (Kracher) v Leicester Magistrates' Court [2013] EWHC 4627 (Admin), Hickinbottom J (at [18]) emphasised the importance of challenges to magistrates' court convictions being by way of appeal by way of case stated, rather than judicial review, 'in those cases where the challenge is other than one of some procedural failure by the court below'.

It follows that, provided there has been a final determination, if it is alleged that the magistrates have (for example) misconstrued a statutory provision, appeal by way of case stated is preferable as it enables the question(s) at issue to be set out more clearly. On the other hand, judicial review is more appropriate where it is alleged that there has been procedural unfairness.

7.7 Further appeals

If the initial appeal is unsuccessful, a further appeal may be possible.

7.7.1 From the Crown Court

Where the Crown Court is sitting in an appellate capacity from the magistrates' court, the appellant may appeal against the decision of the Crown Court to the Divisional Court by way of case stated, or seek judicial review, but only where the Crown Court has made an error of law or jurisdiction (ss.28(1) and 29(3) of the Senior Courts Act 1981).

It should be noted that, when stating a case for the opinion of the High Court, or refusing to do so, the Crown Court may comprise only a judge, and so the lay justices who sat with the judge to hear the appeal from the magistrates' court do not have to be involved (r.34.11(3) of the Criminal Procedure Rules).

7.7.2 Appeal from the Divisional Court

Appeal from the Divisional Court lies direct to the Supreme Court, bypassing the Court of Appeal (s.1(1)(a) of the Administration of Justice Act 1960). The Divisional Court must certify that there is a point of law of general public importance involved and either the Divisional Court or the Supreme Court must give leave to appeal (s.1(2)).

7.8 Proposals for reform of the system of appeals from magistrates' courts

Sir Brian Leveson, in his *Review of Efficiency in Criminal Proceedings* (January 2015) makes the point, at para.324, that 'the less serious the alleged offence, the greater the possible rights of appeal', and that is it has been suggested that this is 'disproportionate' and 'no longer justifiable'. The principal criticism of the system is the fact that, even though magistrates' court deal with less serious crime, is that the avenues for appeal are very generous. In particular:

- Appeal to the Crown Court takes the form of a new trial;
- There is no requirement for leave to appeal;
- Additionally, there are two different routes by which an appeal can be made to the High Court.

By contrast, the Crown Court is generally concerned with more serious criminal cases, but:

- There is only one avenue of appeal (to the Court of Appeal (Criminal Division));
- Leave to appeal is required;
- It does not consist of any form of rehearing (instead the appellant has to show that the conviction was unsafe or the sentence wrong in principle or manifestly excessive).

The Review suggests that it would be more proportionate to have a single avenue of appeal from decisions of magistrates' courts, with a requirement of leave to appeal and the appeal taking the form of a review of the decision of the magistrates' court rather than a re-hearing.

This proposal mirrored recommendations made earlier by Lord Justice Auld in his report of the *Review of the Criminal Courts of England and Wales* (2001), Chapter 12.

This proposal for a more streamlined process has much to commend it. However, only a small proportion of magistrates' court decision are appealed to the Crown Court (possibly because of the power of the Crown Court to increase sentence if there is an appeal against conviction and/or sentence), and very few cases indeed are appealed to the High Court, either by way of case stated or judicial review. Moreover, appeal to the High Court is the only avenue by which the prosecution can challenge decisions of magistrates' courts. It should also be borne in mind that decisions of the Crown Court tend not to be reported, whereas those of the High Court are; appeals from magistrates' courts have generated a very useful body of case law on criminal procedure and evidence, as well as substantive criminal law.

Chapter 8

Sending Cases to the Crown Court for Trial

Chapter Contents

In this chapter, we examine the process for transferring a case from the magistrates' court to the Crown Court.

8.1 Introduction

We have already seen that criminal cases begin in the magistrates' court (the requisition or summons requiring the defendant to attend the magistrates' court, or else the defendant being arrested and charged, and then either bailed to appear at the magistrates' court or kept in custody and brought before the magistrates' court). If the offence is triable only in the Crown Court, it must be transferred to that court. If it is triable either way, it will be transferred to the Crown Court for trial if the accused indicates a not guilty plea at the 'plea before venue' hearing and the allocation hearing that follows results in a decision in favour of Crown Court trial (either because the magistrates decline jurisdiction or because the accused elects Crown Court trial). The transfer to the Crown Court takes place through s.51 of the Crime and Disorder Act 1998.

8.2 Section 51 of the Crime and Disorder Act 1998

Section 51 applies where an adult appears before a magistrates' court:

- charged with an indictable-only offence; or
- charged with an either-way offence where the allocation hearing resulted in a decision in favour of trial on indictment (i.e. the accused indicated a 'not guilty' plea at the plea before venue hearing and either the magistrates declined jurisdiction or else the accused was offered summary trial but chose Crown Court trial instead); or
- where notice has been given to the court under s.51B (serious or complex fraud cases) or s.51C (certain cases involving children).

In such cases, 'the court shall send him forthwith to the Crown Court for trial for the offence' (s.51(1), (2)).

The magistrates' court specifies in a notice the offence(s) for which the defendant is being sent for trial, and the location of the Crown Court where the trial is to take place (s.51D(1)).

Under r.9.7(5) of the Criminal Procedure Rules, if the court is dealing with an offence that is triable only on indictment and sends the defendant to the Crown Court for trial, it must ask whether the defendant intends to plead guilty in the Crown Court and, if the answer is 'yes', make arrangements for the Crown Court to take the defendant's plea as soon as possible; if the defendant does not answer, or the answer is 'no', the court should make arrangements for a case management hearing in the Crown Court. Criminal Practice Direction I, para.3A.9, says that if the defendant has indicated an intention to plead guilty in a matter which is to be sent to the Crown Court, the magistrates' court should request the preparation of a pre-sentence report for the Crown Court's use if the magistrates' court considers that:

(a) there is a realistic alternative to a custodial sentence; or
(b) the defendant may satisfy the criteria for classification as a dangerous offender; or
(c) there is some other appropriate reason for doing so.

The court must also set a date for a Plea and Trial Preparation Hearing, to enable the defendant to enter the guilty plea as soon as possible.

In any case sent to the Crown Court for trial, other than one in which the defendant indicates an intention to plead guilty, the magistrates' court must set a date for a Plea and Trial Preparation Hearing, which should usually be held within 28 days of sending (para.3A.11).

The functions of a magistrates' court under s.51 may be discharged by a single justice (s.51(13)).

8.2.1 Linked offences

Section 51(3) deals with linked offences. It provides that where an adult is sent for trial under s.51, the court must also send the accused to the Crown Court for trial for any either-way or summary offence with which he is also charged, so long as that offence is related to the main offence (and in the case of a summary offence is also punishable with imprisonment or involves obligatory or discretionary disqualification from driving: s. 51(11)). For these purposes, an either-way offence is related to an indictable offence if the charge for the either-way offence could be joined in the same indictment as the charge for the indictable offence, and a summary offence is related to an indictable offence if it arises out of circumstances which are the same as or connected with those giving rise to the indictable offence (s.51E(c) and (d)).

One of the consequences of the provisions contained in s.51(3) is that, if the accused is charged with an indictable-only offence, there will not be any question as to the mode of trial in respect of any related either-way offences with which he is charged and to which he pleads not guilty (since any related either-way offences will be sent for trial automatically alongside the indictable-only offence). If a summary offence is sent to the Crown Court under s.51(3), it will be dealt with in accordance with the para.6 of sch.3 to the Act (see below).

Under s.51(4), if an adult has already been sent to the Crown Court for trial under s.51(1) and then subsequently appears before a magistrates' court charged with an either-way or summary offence that appears to the court to be related to the offence sent for trial under s.51(1), the court may send him forthwith to the Crown Court for trial for the either-way or summary offence (provided that, if the offence is a summary one, it is punishable with imprisonment or disqualification from driving). This is a discretionary power, so there will be a plea before venue and allocation hearing in respect of any either-way offence to which s.51(4) applies.

8.2.2 Co-accused

Section 51(5) of the CDA 1998 applies where the court sends an adult for trial (under s.51(1) or 51(3)), and another adult appears before the court, either on the same or a subsequent occasion, charged jointly with the first adult with an either-way offence, and that offence appears to the court to be related to an offence for which the first adult was sent for trial under s.51(1) or (3). The court must (where it is the same occasion), or may (where it is a subsequent occasion), send the other adult forthwith to the Crown Court for trial for the either-way offence.

Where the court sends an adult for trial under s.51(5), it must (by virtue of s. 51(6)) at the same time send him to the Crown Court for trial for any either-way or summary offence with which he is charged and which appears to the court to be related to the offence for which he is sent for trial (provided that, if it is a summary offence, it is punishable with imprisonment or disqualification from driving).

Section 51(7) applies where the court sends an adult to the Crown Court for trial under s.51 (1), (3) or (5), and a child or young person (that is, a person under the age of 18) appears before the court (on the same or a subsequent occasion) charged jointly with the adult with an indictable offence for which the adult is sent for trial under s.51(1), (3) or (5), or charged with an indictable offence that appears to the court to be related to that offence. The court 'shall, if it considers it necessary in the interests of justice to do so', send the juvenile forthwith to the Crown Court for trial for the indictable offence.

Under s.51(8), where the court sends a juvenile for trial under s.51(7), it may at the same time send him to the Crown Court for trial for any indictable or summary offence with which he is charged and which appears to the court to be related to the offence for which he is sent for trial (again, if the offence is a summary one, it must be punishable with imprisonment or disqualification from driving).

8.2.3 Reporting restrictions

Section 52A of the Crime and Disorder Act 1998 sets out reporting restrictions intended to prevent prejudicial pre-trial reportage of cases. Under s.52A(1), the restrictions apply to any allocation or sending proceedings, and cover both written reports and broadcast programmes. Section 52A(6) provides that it is unlawful to publish, or include in a broadcast programme, any matters except those specified in subs.(7). In other words, s.52A(7) sets out the only matters that can be reported, namely:

- the identity of the court and the name of the justice or justices;
- the name, age, home address and occupation of the accused;
- in the case of an accused charged with an offence in respect of which notice has been given to the court under s.51B (serious or complex fraud cases), any relevant business information;
- the offence or offences, or a summary of them, with which the accused is or are charged;
- the names of counsel and solicitors engaged in the proceedings;
- details of any adjournments;
- the arrangements as to bail;
- whether legal aid was granted.

Under s.52A(2), the magistrates have the power to lift these reporting restrictions. Where the accused (or any of the accused) objects to the lifting of the restrictions, the court may lift the restrictions only if it is satisfied, after hearing representations from (each of) the accused, that it is in the interests of justice to do so (s.52A(3) and (4)).

It is submitted that if there is only one defendant, and he asks for the restrictions to be lifted, the court should make an order lifting the restrictions. In R v Leeds Justices, ex parte Sykes [1983] 1 WLR 132, it was held (construing earlier legislation) that, in the event of disagreement between the defendants, the burden was on the one(s) who wanted reporting to show that it was in the interests of justice for the normal restrictions to be lifted. Griffiths LJ said (at pp.134–5) that 'the interests of justice incorporate as a paramount consideration that the defendants should have a fair trial' and that, because Parliament has laid down a general rule against reporting, 'a powerful case' has to made out to lift the reporting restrictions. His Lordship suggested (at p.137) that an application for restrictions to be lifted on the ground that publicity might induce potential witnesses for the defendant making the application to come forward would 'merit really serious consideration by the justices'.

The court must give all the co-accused a chance to make representations. Failure to do so is a serious breach of procedure and is likely to result in the quashing of the order lifting the reporting restrictions (R v Wirral District Magistrates' Court, ex parte Meikle (1990) 154 JP 1035).

Under s.52B, breach of the reporting restrictions set out in s.52A is a summary offence. Proceedings under s.52B can only be brought by, or with the consent of, the Attorney General (s.52B(3)).

In Sykes, Griffiths LJ (at p.136) said that: 'If the reporting restrictions are to be lifted, then they are to be lifted ... in their entirety. They cannot be lifted piecemeal'. Thus, if the restrictions are lifted, then all of the restrictions have to be lifted; the justices cannot pick and choose which of the restrictions are lifted and which remain. However, if the justices wish to lift the reporting restrictions but nonetheless wish to prevent the full reporting of all the details of the case, they can lift the restrictions but then make an order under s.4(2) of the Contempt of Court Act 1981. This allows the court to order postponement of the contemporaneous reporting of some or all of any legal proceedings where such action is necessary to prevent a 'substantial risk of prejudice to the administration of justice'. Thus, if the s.52A restrictions have been lifted, the court can effectively define what may be reported by making an order under the Contempt of Court Act 1981.

In R v *Sarker* [2018] EWCA Crim 1341, Lord Burnett CJ (at [22]) gave guidance on what the application for an order under s.4(2) should address:

> [T]he explanation for why the order is necessary needs to address, clearly (and ordinarily in writing): (i) how contemporaneous fair and accurate reports of the trial will cause a substantial risk of prejudice? and (ii) why a postponement order would avoid the identified risk of prejudice?.

His Lordship went on to stress the importance of open justice, saying (at [29]):

> When dealing with applications for reporting restrictions, the default position is the general principle that all proceedings in courts and tribunals are conducted in public. This is the principle of open justice. Media reports of legal proceedings are an extension of the concept of open justice.

Turning to the proper approach to a s.4(2) postponement order application, his Lordship referred to the guidance given R v *Sherwood ex p Telegraph Group plc* [2001] EWCA Crim 1075; [2001] 1 WLR 1983 (at [22], per Longmore LJ), summarising it as follows (at [30]):

> (i) The first question is whether reporting would give rise to a substantial risk of prejudice to the administration of justice in the relevant proceedings ... If not, that will be the end of the matter.
>
> (ii) If such a risk is perceived to exist, then the second question arises: would a s.4(2) order eliminate it? If not, there could be no necessity to impose such a ban. On the other hand, even if the judge is satisfied that an order would achieve the objective, he or she would still have to consider whether the risk could satisfactorily be overcome by some less restrictive means. If so, it could not be said to be 'necessary' to take the more drastic approach ...
>
> (iii) If the judge is satisfied that there is indeed no other way of eliminating the perceived risk of prejudice; it still does not necessarily follow that an order has to be made. The judge may still have to ask whether the degree of risk contemplated should be regarded as tolerable in the sense of being 'the lesser of two evils'. It is at this stage that value judgments may have to be made as to the priority between the competing public interests; fair trial and freedom of expression/open justice.

The word 'substantial' in this context means 'not insubstantial' or 'not minimal' (at [31]). The exceptional nature of reporting restrictions is emphasised when his Lordship makes the point that, in most cases, 'no possible prejudice to the immediate trial could arise from the publication of contemporaneous reports of the trial itself (at least so much of the proceedings that take place in front of the jury)', given that: (i) the jury will have heard the evidence or submissions that are the subject of the report; (ii) the jury will have been directed by the judge to try the case on the evidence presented during the trial, not to carry out any research themselves, to ignore any media reports that they may see of the case they are trying; moreover, the court must proceed on the basis that juries are committed to the right of the accused to receive a fair trial and that they will abide by the directions given by the judge, and also that media reports of the trial will be 'responsible, fair and accurate' (see [32]).

It could be argued that that the willingness of the jury to comply with the directions from the judge is overstated, but Lord Burnett does make reference to the Law Commission's 2014 Report, *Contempt of Court (2): Court Reporting* (Law Com No.344). Paragraph 2.30(3) says that 'what research is available suggests that jurors find the trial process absorbing, and significantly prioritise what they hear during the trial over what they might have heard from the media outside of the trial'. The Report cites New Zealand Law Commission Report No 69, *Juries in Criminal Trials* (2001) and M Chesterman, J Chan and S Hampton, *Managing Prejudicial Publicity: An Empirical Study of Criminal Jury Trial in New South Wales* (2001).

As regards cases of sequential or connected trials, his Lordship observed that, where a s.4(2) order is made in the first trial to protect the second trial or re-trial, 'the judge must still consider carefully the nature of the prejudice that is relied upon to justify the order'. If the subsequent trial will take place some months after the first, the court should bear in mind the 'fade factor', namely the effect of the lapse of time between publication and trial (see [34]).

Turning to the question whether an order is 'necessary', Lord Burnett said that, if any order is thought to be required, the key question is 'whether a less restrictive order might avoid the risk of prejudice that has been identified'. By way of example, his Lordship noted that it may be sufficient to limit the order to the postponement of the identification of certain persons involved in the first trial or to particular aspects of the evidence in the first trial. It follows that 'consideration must be given to whether an order stopping short of a total postponement of reporting of the proceedings can be fashioned' (at [35]).

Finally, Lord Burnett said that it was not strictly accurate to say that the court ultimately had a 'discretion' whether to make an order under s.4(2); rather the court was required 'to make a value judgment about the competing rights and interests' (at [36]).

As Lord Burnett points out (at [29]), referring to the words of Lord Steyn in Re S [2005] AC 593 (at [18]):

Attending court in person is not practical for any but a handful of people, and live-streaming and broadcasting of court proceedings remain restricted. The only way that citizens can be informed about what takes place in most of our courts is through media reports. In that way the media serve both as the eyes and ears of the wider public and also as a watchdog.

His Lordship also agreed (at [26]) with comments in previous case law to the effect that, 'in the modern era of communications, it is truer than ever that "stale news is no news".'

Where the court is minded to make an order under the Contempt of Court Act 1981, it should listen to any representations made on behalf of the press (R v Clerkenwell Magistrates ex p The Telegraph plc [1993] QB 462).

8.2.4 Procedure after the case has been sent to the Crown Court

Under reg.2 of the Crime and Disorder Act 1998 (Service of Prosecution Evidence) Regulations 2005 (SI 2005/902), where a person is sent for trial under s.51, copies of the documents containing the evidence on which the charge(s) are based must, within 70 days (50 days if the accused is in custody) from the date on which the accused was sent for trial, be served on the accused and on the Crown Court.

The prosecution may apply for an extension of this time limit, under reg.3. In *Fehily v Governor of Wandsworth Prison* [2002] EWHC 1295; [2003] 1 Cr App R 10, it was held that the Crown Court has jurisdiction to extend time for service of the documents on an application by the prosecution even if the application is made after the expiry of the time limit.

The draft indictment must be served on the Crown Court within 28 days of the defendant being served with copies of the documents containing the evidence on which the charge(s) are based (see r.10.4(2) of the Criminal Procedure Rules).

8.2.4.1 Applications for dismissal of charge

Para.2(1) of sch.3 enables a person who has been sent for trial under s.51 to apply to the Crown Court for the charge(s) to be dismissed. Such an application may be made, orally or in writing, at any time after he has been served with copies of the documents containing the evidence on which the charge(s) are based but before he is arraigned (that is, before he is asked to enter a plea). An oral application is permitted only if the accused has given written notice of intention to make such an application (para.2(3)).

Paragraph 2(2) provides that the judge must dismiss the charge (and quash any count in the indictment relating to it) if it appears that 'the evidence against the applicant would not be sufficient for him to be properly convicted'. Moreover, by virtue of para.2(6), where a charge has been dismissed in this way, no further proceedings may be brought on that charge except by means of the preferment of a voluntary bill of indictment.

In R (Snelgrove) v Crown Court at Woolwich [2004] EWHC 2172 (Admin); [2005] 1 WLR 3223 (followed in R (O) v Central Criminal Court [2006] EWHC 256 (Admin)), it was held that a judge's decision to refuse to dismiss a case under para.2 is a matter relating to trial on indictment (an integral part of the trial process and an issue between the Crown and the defendant arising out of issues formulated by the charge), and therefore not susceptible to judicial review (as a result of s.29(3) of the Senior Courts Act 1981).

8.2.4.2 Power of the Crown Court to deal with summary offence

Indictable-only or either-way offences appear on the indictment and are tried in the Crown Court. However, any summary offences that are sent to the Crown Court under s.51 do not appear on the indictment.

Paragraph 6 of Sch.3 to the 1998 Act sets out the procedure to be followed where a summary offence is included in the offences sent for trial under s.51 (adults) or s.51A (young defendants). Paragraph 6(2) says that, if the defendant is convicted on the indictment, the Crown Court must first consider whether the summary offence is related to the indictable offence for which he was sent for trial (or any of the indictable offences, if he was sent for trial for more than one). For these purposes, an offence is related to another offence if it 'arises out of circumstances which are the same as or connected with those giving rise to the other offence' (para.6(12)). If the court considers that the summary offence is indeed so related, the defendant is asked to enter a plea to the summary offence (para.6(3)). If he pleads guilty, the Crown Court passes sentence in respect of the summary offence, but may deal with him only in a manner in which a magistrates' court could have dealt with him (para.6(4)). If he pleads not guilty, 'the powers of the Crown Court shall cease in respect of the summary offence' (para.6(5)), unless the prosecution inform the court that they would not desire to submit evidence in respect of the summary offence, in which case 'the court shall dismiss it' (para.6 (6)); if the prosecution wish to proceed with the charge, they have to do so in the magistrates' court.

Although para.6 does not address the possibility, it is possible for the Crown Court judge, exercising the jurisdiction conferred by s.66 of the Courts Act 2003, to try the summary offence, sitting as a District Judge (Magistrates' Courts).

8.2.4.3 Procedure where main offence sent for trial is not on the indictment

Paragraph 7 of Sch.3 deals with the situation where the defendant is sent for trial in respect of an indictable-only offence (with any related either-way offences therefore being sent to the Crown Court for trial without an allocation hearing taking place) but the indictment that is then drafted includes only one or more either-way offences (for example, where the defendant was sent for trial for robbery but the indictment charges theft instead).

In such a case, the court will ask the accused whether (if the offence in question were to proceed to trial) he would plead guilty or not guilty (para.7(5)). If the accused indicates that he would plead guilty, the court proceeds as if he has pleaded guilty (para.7(6)). If he indicates that he would plead not guilty (or does not give an indication of intended plea), the court decides whether the offence is more suitable for summary trial or for trial on indictment (para.7(7)). Before deciding this question, the court must give the prosecution an opportunity to inform the court of any previous convictions recorded against the accused, and must give the prosecution and the accused an opportunity to make representations as to which mode of trial would be more suitable (para.9(2)). The decision will be taken having regard to whether the sentence which a magistrates' court would have power to impose for the offence would be adequate, to any representations made by the parties, and to the allocation guidelines issued by the Sentencing Council (para.9(3)).

If the Crown Court considers that the offence is more suitable for summary trial, the court asks the defendant whether he wishes to be tried summarily or on indictment. If he indicates that he wishes to be tried summarily, he will be remitted for trial to the magistrates' court (para.10 (3)). If the Crown Court considers that an offence is more suitable for trial on indictment, the court will inform the accused of this fact (para.11).

In R v Haye [2002] EWCA Crim 2476, the defendant was charged with robbery. He was sent for trial at the Crown Court. The prosecution then dropped the charge of robbery and replaced it with a charge of theft. The defendant pleaded not guilty to theft. When the matter came on for trial, the defendant was rearraigned on the theft charge and entered a guilty plea. However, he subsequently appealed against conviction on the ground that the procedure set out in para. 7 had not been followed prior to the arraignment on the theft charge; in particular, he complained that proper consideration had not been given to the question whether he should be tried summarily or whether the Crown Court should continue to deal with the case. He argued that the proceedings which followed the plea of guilty were, therefore, a nullity. The Court of Appeal agreed, holding that any failure to comply with the statutory procedure in relation to the right of a defendant to make representations and/or to exercise choice as to mode of trial would render any subsequent hearing in respect of that offence *ultra vires*.

However, in R v Thwaites [2006] EWCA Crim 3235, the defendant was sent for trial to the Crown Court charged with conspiracy to handle stolen goods. Subsequently, he was arraigned and tried on an indictment containing counts of burglary. The judge failed to conduct the mode of trial procedure required by para.7. The Court of Appeal dismissed the appeal, holding that there was no unfairness or prejudice to the defendant, who had received a fair trial.

Similarly, in R v Gul [2012] EWCA Crim 1761; [2013] 1 WLR 1136, the defendant was sent for trial in respect of an indictable-only offence. However, the indictment, when drafted, contained only either-way offences. The defendant was not afforded the opportunity to make representations about the mode of trial. Lord Judge CJ said (at [20] and [21]) that the case had been properly submitted to the Crown Court under s.51 of the 1998 Act, the offences arose from precisely the same facts and were based on the same evidence as the single indictable-only charge upon which the defendant had been sent to the Crown Court, the defendant had been asked to enter a plea to each of the counts in the indictment, and he had pleaded guilty to each count. Once the defendant had pleaded guilty to the offences, the case was bound to remain in the Crown Court. On this basis the Court of Appeal rejected the argument that para.7 had not been complied with. Lord Judge CJ went on say (at [23]) that the

> entitlement of the defendant is to make submissions in support of summary trial if he wishes to do so, but the defendant does not enjoy an unfettered entitlement to summary trial ... If however the defendant wishes to be tried summarily and the court has failed to give him the opportunity to ask for it, there is nothing in the procedure which prevents an application by him to that effect.

It followed that the proceedings were not nullified by the flaw in the process in the Crown Court.

8.3 Notices of transfer

8.3.1 Serious or complex fraud cases

Section 51B(1) of the 1998 Act applies where the prosecution is brought by the Director of Public Prosecutions, the Director of the Serious Fraud Office, or a Secretary of State (s.51B(9)), and the prosecutor is of the opinion that the evidence of the offence charged:

(a) is sufficient for the person charged to be put on trial for the offence; and

(b) reveals a case of fraud of such seriousness or complexity that it is appropriate that the management of the case should without delay be taken over by the Crown Court.

The prosecuting authority serves a notice on the magistrates' court specifying the proposed place of trial (subs.(3)). The effect of such a notice is that the functions of the magistrates' court cease in respect of the case (subs.(6)) and the Crown Court has jurisdiction to try the case on the basis of the notice.

8.3.2 Child witness cases

Section 51C of the Crime and Disorder Act 1998 applies where the Director of Public Prosecutions (DPP; in practice, this includes any Crown Prosecutor) is of the opinion that:

(a) the evidence of the offence would be sufficient for the person charged to be put on trial for the offence;

(b) a child would be called as a witness at the trial; and

(c) for the purpose of avoiding any prejudice to the welfare of the child, the case should be taken over and proceeded with without delay by the Crown Court.

Under subs.(3), s.51C applies only to certain offences, including those which involve 'an assault on, or injury or a threat of injury to, a person' and offences under the Protection of Children Act 1978 and the Sexual Offences Act 2003. As with s.51B, the effect of such a notice is that the functions of the magistrates' court cease in respect of the case and the Crown Court has jurisdiction to try the case on the basis of the notice.

Where the defendant is under 18 and the offence is one that falls within the ambit of s.91 of the Powers of Criminal Courts (Sentencing) Act 2000, there should be no transfer to the Crown Court for trial unless the prosecution could conclude that a magistrates' court would be likely to find that the case falls within the requirements of seriousness that would enable them to send the case to the Crown Court for trial (R v T and K [2001] 1 Cr App R 32 at [37]).

8.3.3 Submissions of no case to answer

Section 51 of the 1998 Act applies when notice is given to the court under s.51B or 51C in respect of an offence, and so para.2 of Sch.3 applies in such cases, enabling an application for dismissal of the charge(s) to be made.

8.3.4 Linked offences

In R v Wrench [1996] 1 Cr App R 340, it was held that, if one of the offences of which the defendant is accused is one to which the transfer provisions apply, then the procedure can also be used in respect of any other offences provided that they can validly be joined on the same indictment.

8.4 Voluntary bills of indictment

Another way of securing the Crown Court trial of a defendant is for the prosecution to seek a 'voluntary bill of indictment'. Essentially, this is an order by a High Court judge requiring the defendant to stand trial for the offence(s) specified in the order.

The obtaining of a voluntary bill of indictment is made possible by s.2(2)(b) of the Administration of Justice (Miscellaneous Provisions) Act 1933 and the procedure for doing so, as set out in r.10.9 of the Criminal Procedure Rules, now applies 'where a prosecutor wants a High Court judge's permission to serve a draft indictment' (in other words, seeks a 'voluntary bill of indictment'). The prosecutor has to serve a written application on the court and (unless the judge otherwise directs) on the proposed defendant; if the prosecutor asks for a hearing, the application must explain why a hearing is needed (r.10.9(2)).

The application must attach (i) the proposed indictment; (ii) copies of the documents containing the evidence on which the prosecutor relies, including any written witness statements and documentary exhibits; (iii) a copy of any indictment on which the defendant already has been arraigned; and (iv) if not contained in such an indictment, a list of any offence(s) for which the defendant already has been sent for trial (r.10.9(3)(a)). The application must also include (i) 'a concise statement of the circumstances in which, and the reasons why, the application is made', and (ii) a concise summary of the evidence contained in the documents which accompany the application, relating that evidence to each count in the proposed indictment (r.10.9(3)(b)). Unless the application is made on behalf of the DPP or the Director of the SFO, the application must also contain a statement that, to the best of the prosecutor's knowledge, information and belief, (i) the evidence on which the prosecutor relies will be available at the trial, and (ii) the allegations contained in the application are substantially true (r.10.9(3)(c)).

Under r.10.9(4), a proposed defendant served with an application who wants to make representations to the judge must serve written representations on the court and on the prosecutor, as soon as practicable. If the proposed defendant asks for a hearing, he must explain why a hearing is needed.

Rule 10.9(5) provides that the judge may determine the application without a hearing, or at a hearing (in public or in private), and may do so with or without receiving the oral evidence of any proposed witness.

Voluntary bills of indictment are comparatively rare. Criminal Practice Direction II para.10B.4 says:

> The preferment of a voluntary bill is an exceptional procedure. Consent should only be granted where good reason to depart from the normal procedure is clearly shown and only where the interests of justice, rather than considerations of administrative convenience, require it.

Paragraph 10B.6 goes on to say:

> The judge may invite oral submissions from either party, or accede to a request for an opportunity to make oral submissions, if the judge considers it necessary or desirable to receive oral submissions in order to make a sound and fair decision on the application. Any such oral submissions should be made on notice to the other party and in open court unless the judge otherwise directs.

One possible use of the 'voluntary bill' procedure is where one defendant has already been sent for trial and another suspect is arrested shortly before the trial of the first defendant, and it is desirable that there be a joint trial. If it is undesirable to seek an adjournment of the first defendant's trial, the voluntary bill procedure is a speedy way of getting the second suspect to the Crown Court so that there can be a joint trial.

However, the most important use for voluntary bills of indictment is where a charge has been dismissed (under para.2 of Sch.3 to the Crime and Disorder Act 1998). In *Serious Fraud Office v Evans* [2014] EWHC 3803 (QB); [2015] 1 WLR 3526, the prosecution sought a voluntary bill of indictment following such a dismissal. Fulford LJ said (at [85]) that:

> Granting a voluntary bill of indictment is an exceptional course, and it will only be issued following a successful application to dismiss if (i) the court has made a basic and substantive error of law that is clear or obvious; or (ii) new evidence has become available that the prosecution could not put before the court at the time of the dismissal hearing which (along with any existing evidence) provides the prosecution with a sustainable factual basis for the charge; or (iii) there was a serious procedural irregularity ... [T]his is not an exhaustive list because there will be other exceptional situations when it may be appropriate to grant a voluntary bill, for instance if the charges against the accused were dismissed on the basis of a technicality, particularly if it was one that the prosecution reasonably failed to anticipate.

His Lordship noted that, in R v Muse [2007] EWHC 2924, Openshaw J had held that it was wrong in principle for the prosecution to be able to get round a decision that it did not like by inviting another judge to take a different view of the same material that had been before the judge who had dismissed the charge(s). However, his Lordship had also suggested that there was no inflexible rule that a voluntary bill of indictment could never be granted to correct a mistaken decision of the prosecution or to reflect a change of mind by the prosecuting authority, albeit the power to do so should be used sparingly, in truly exceptional cases.

In *Evans*, Fulford LJ (at [86]) also said:

> In my view whether or not a voluntary bill is granted under this heading will depend on the nature and the extent of the prosecution's changed position, the reasons that have led to the new approach and the implications for the proceedings as a whole. Therefore, the court will need to consider carefully the prosecution's suggested justification against the background of the relevant procedural history. Furthermore, it is to be emphasised although the accused will always be prejudiced by the prosecution's application to revive dismissed criminal proceedings, his position will necessarily require careful consideration.

It follows from this that the judge must give careful consideration to the reason for the change of mind on the part of the prosecution and to any injustice to the defendant if the proceedings are to be reinstated.

If the judge directs that a voluntary bill of indictment be preferred (that is, orders the defendant to stand trial in the Crown Court), that decision cannot be challenged by way of judicial review (R v Manchester Crown Court ex p Williams (1990) 154 JP 589).

Similarly, the judge who presides over the trial in the Crown Court cannot quash the indictment if he disagrees with the decision of the High Court judge (R v Rothfield (1937) 26 Cr App R 103 at 105, per Humphreys J). Moreover, the Court of Appeal will not inquire into the exercise of the discretion of a judge to direct the preferment of a voluntary bill, so long as it is clear that he had jurisdiction to entertain the application (Rothfield, p.106).

Even though the decision of a High Court judge to issue a voluntary bill of indictment is not subject to judicial review, the decision of a prosecutor to seek a voluntary bill is susceptible to review, but only on very limited grounds, such as bad faith or alleged personal malice on the part of the prosecutor (R v Inland Revenue Commissioners ex p Dhesi (1995) The Independent, 14 August).

Chapter 9

Indictments

9.1 Terminology

The 'indictment' is the document that sets out the charges which the defendant faces at the Crown Court. Each offence charged is known as a 'count'. Where there is more than one count, they must be numbered consecutively.

9.2 Drafting the indictment

Section 2(1) of the Administration of Justice (Miscellaneous Provisions) Act 1933 provides:

> Subject to the provisions of this section, a bill of indictment charging any person with an indictable offence may be preferred by any person before a court in which the person charged may lawfully be indicted for that offence and it shall thereupon become an indictment and be proceeded with accordingly.

A 'bill of indictment' simply means a draft indictment. It is 'preferred' when it is served on the Crown Court.

By virtue of s.2(6ZA), any objections to an indictment based on an alleged failure to observe the procedural rules governing indictments may not be taken after the start of the trial (that is, when the jury has been sworn). The right to object to the form of the indictment is therefore lost once the trial has commenced: see R v Johnson [2018] EWCA Crim 2485, at [49]. Moreover, if a trial proceeds on the basis of a defective form of indictment, the primary consideration in any appeal against conviction based on that defect 'will be the fairness of the trial and the safety of the conviction, not the technical validity of the indictment' (at [54], per Sir Brian Leveson P).

The indictment will usually be drafted by a Crown Prosecutor.

9.3 Time limit

Under r.10.4(1) of the Criminal Procedure Rules, unless the draft indictment is generated electronically when the defendant is sent for trial, the prosecutor must serve a draft indictment on the Crown Court not more than 28 days after service on the defendant and on the Crown Court officer of copies of the documents containing the evidence on which the charge(s) are based.

Under r.10.2(5), a draft indictment (historically known as a 'bill of indictment') is 'preferred' (i.e. served on the Crown Court), thereby becoming the indictment either:

- where (under r.10.3), the draft indictment is generated electronically on sending for trial), immediately before the first count (or the only count, if there is only one) is put to the defendant for plea;
- otherwise, when the prosecutor (under r.10.4) serves the draft indictment on the Crown Court after the sending for trial (where the draft is served on the Crown Court by uploading the indictment onto the Digital Case System ('DCS'), it is 'preferred' once it is entered electronically onto the DCS: R v PW [2016] EWCA Crim 745; [2017] 4 WLR 79).

Once the draft indictment has become an indictment, it can be amended only with leave from the court (under s.5(1) of the Indictments Act 1915).

9.4 Form of indictment

Section 3(1) of the Indictments Act 1915 provides that:

Every indictment shall contain, and shall be sufficient if it contains, a statement of the specific offence or offences with which the accused person is charged, together with such particulars as may be necessary for giving reasonable information as to the nature of the charge.

Rule 10.2(1) of the Criminal Procedure Rules provides that an indictment must be in writing and must contain at least one paragraph, called a 'count'. Each count must contain:

(a) a statement of the offence charged that –
   (i) describes the offence in ordinary language; and
   (ii) identifies any legislation that creates it; and
(b) such particulars of the conduct constituting the commission of the offence as to make clear what the prosecutor alleges against the defendant.

The 'statement of offence' is a brief description of the offence; if the offence is a statutory one, the relevant section of the statute will be given. The 'particulars of offence' summarise what is alleged against the defendant. The particulars should set out who is charged, the date of the alleged offence, the act allegedly done, an allegation of *mens rea* (that is, the mental element of the crime), and the identity of the alleged victim. In R v *Clarke* [2015] EWCA Crim 350; [2015] 2 Cr App R 6, Lord Thomas CJ (at [18]) said that the 'sole question is whether the particulars make clear what the prosecutor alleges against the defendant'.

An indictment therefore looks like this:

No 20/01321

INDICTMENT
THE CROWN COURT AT CROYDON
THE QUEEN V VICTOR JAMES WARD

VICTOR JAMES WARD is charged as follows:
COUNT 1
Statement of Offence

Burglary, contrary to s 9(1)(b) of the Theft Act 1968.
Particulars of Offence

VICTOR JAMES WARD, on 2 September 2020, having entered as a trespasser a building known as 17 Maidwell Avenue, Croydon, stole therein a television set and a DVD recorder, the property of John Green.

COUNT 2
Statement of Offence

Unlawful wounding, contrary to section 20 of the Offences Against the Person Act 1861.
Particulars of Offence

VICTOR JAMES WARD, on 2 September 2020, unlawfully and maliciously wounded John Green.

Where the date of the commission of the offence is not known for certain, it is usual to say either 'on or about [date]' or 'on a date unknown between [day before the earliest date when the offence could have been committed] and [day after the latest date when the offence could have been committed]'. If the date is incorrectly stated, it is not fatal to the prosecution case since the indictment can be amended, though the defendant may well be entitled to an adjournment if necessary to prepare his defence on the basis of the new date.

Where there is more than one defendant, the order in which the names of defendants are placed on an indictment is the responsibility of the prosecutor, who has a discretion as to that order (R v Cairns [2002] EWCA Crim 2838; [2003] 1 WLR 796).

Each count in an indictment is a separate entity. In R v O'Neill [2003] EWCA Crim 411, the defendant was charged in an indictment which included a count that was defective, in that it was based on a statutory provision which had not been in force at the relevant time. The Court of Appeal confirmed that even if one count charges an offence not known to the law, any other counts in the same indictment can stand and need not be quashed.

Rule 10.2(7) states that, unless the Crown Court otherwise directs, the court officer must endorse any paper copy of the indictment made for the court with a note to identify it as a copy of the indictment, together with the date on which the draft indictment became the indictment, and serve a copy on all parties.

9.5 The rule against duplicity

The general rule is that a count should allege only one offence. However, r.10.2(2) of the Criminal Procedure Rules states that:

> More than one incident of the commission of the offence may be included in a count if those incidents taken together amount to a course of conduct having regard to the time, place or purpose of commission.

Criminal Practice Direction II, para.10A.11, notes that, for r.10.2(2) to apply, each incident 'must be of the same offence'. Circumstances in which such a count may be appropriate include cases where the victim on each occasion was the same, or where there was no identifiable individual victim; where the alleged incidents involve a 'marked degree of repetition in the method employed or in their location, or both'; or where the alleged incidents took place over a clearly defined period (generally no more than about a year). In any event, the defence must be the same for every alleged incident: where what is in issue differs between different incidents, a single 'multiple incidents' count will not be appropriate.

The specimen indictment shown above has as its first count an allegation of burglary involving the theft of two items. Where the acts form part of 'the same transaction or criminal enterprise', they may properly be said to amount to a single offence (DPP v Merriman [1973] AC 584). This means, for example, that if a defendant steals a number of items from the same person at more or less the same time, it will be regarded as a single act of theft (R v Wilson (1979) 69 Cr App R 83). In that case, the defendant was charged with stealing eight records and a bottle of aftershave from Boots (count 1) and stealing three jumpers, a pair of shorts, two pairs of trousers, four dimmer switches and a cassette tape from Debenhams (count 2). It was argued on behalf of the defendant that both counts were bad for duplicity, as the stolen items came from different departments of the stores in question. The argument was rejected on the basis that each count alleged acts forming a single activity, and so neither count was duplicitous. Thus, where a series of acts in effect amounts to a single course of conduct, those acts can validly be regarded as amounting to a single offence. For example, in DPP v McCabe (1993) 157 JP 443, it was held by the Divisional Court that an allegation that the defendant stole 76 library books between two specified dates was a single offence and so a single charge alleging this theft was not bad for duplicity. Similarly, in Barton v DPP (2001) 165 JP 779, a single charge alleged theft of a total of £1,338.23. The prosecution case was that, on 94 separate occasions, the accused had taken small amounts of cash from the till. The accused gave no specific explanation for the individual takings and put forward the same defence for all. The charge was held not to be duplicitous. Indeed, to bring 94 separate charges would rightly have been regarded as oppressive. *Barton* was approved by the Court of Appeal in R v *Tovey* [2005] 2 Cr App R (S) 606 and R v *Lunn* [2017] EWCA Crim 34; [2017] 4 WLR 214 (cases concerning indictments).

Where there are several victims, it is usual to have a separate count for each victim, as in R v *Mansfield* [1977] 1 WLR 1102, where the defendant was charged with seven different counts of murder arising from a single act of arson. This is so, even though only one act was involved.

However, a count which alleged that the defendant stole £200 from A one day and £200 from B the next would be duplicitous because there are two separate acts of theft.

If a section of a statute creates one offence that may be committed in a number of ways, the alternatives may be charged in a single count (although it might sometimes be better to charge them in separate counts if this would make the task of the jury easier). If, however, the section creates more than one offence, each offence that the prosecution wish the jury to consider must be put in a separate count.

An example of where this might arise is to be found in respect of handling stolen goods contrary to s.22 of the Theft Act 1968. Handling effectively comprises two different offences. The first is that of dishonestly receiving stolen goods; the second comprises all the other ways of handling (these ways are all different ways of committing a single offence). The various ways of committing the second form of handling can, and usually will, be charged in a single count. However, a count that charged receiving and the other forms of handling together would be regarded as defective.

Thus, there are two basic handling counts – either:

- AB on [date] dishonestly received stolen goods, namely [description of goods], knowing or believing the same to be stolen goods; or
- AB on [date] dishonestly undertook or assisted in the retention, removal, disposal or realisation of stolen goods, namely [description of goods], by or for the benefit of another, or dishonestly arranged to do so, knowing or believing the same to be stolen goods.

If a count alleges more than one offence and the defence raise an objection to this, the prosecution will usually seek leave to amend the indictment under s.5(1) of the Indictments Act 1915 to split the 'duplicitous' count into two separate counts. Even if a count includes allegations that do not amount to a single course of conduct (as permitted by r.10.2(2)), this does not necessarily mean that a conviction would be quashed. In R v *Levantiz* [1999] 1 Cr App R 465, several discrete acts of supplying a controlled drug were alleged in a single count in the indictment. The Court of Appeal held that, where a count in an indictment is duplicitous (that is, charges more than one offence), that count is not void and the conviction is not necessarily unsafe. It follows that an appeal against conviction on that count can be dismissed if the Court of Appeal decides that the conviction is safe despite the irregularity in the indictment. In R v *Marchese* [2008] EWCA Crim 389; [2009] 1 WLR 992, Lord Phillips CJ (at [48]) said that it is necessary to consider whether the form of the indictment resulted in the risk of injustice to the accused.

9.6 Co-defendants

Where there is alleged to have been more than one participant in the offence, all the parties to that offence may be joined in a single count (*DPP v Merriman* [1973] AC 584). The jury will be directed that they must consider each defendant separately, so where there are two defendants, they may acquit both defendants, convict both defendants or convict one and acquit the other.

Secondary parties (that is, those who aid, abet, counsel or procure the commission of the offence) are usually charged as principal offenders (s.8 of the Accessories and Abettors Act 1861).

Thus, in a burglary case where one person enters the premises and another person stays outside as a look-out, both will usually be charged with burglary, and the particulars will allege that both entered the premises and stole. Similarly, the getaway driver in a robbery will usually be charged in the same count as the defendants who actually carry out the robbery. The fact that a defendant is really alleged to have been a secondary party is thus not apparent from the indictment itself, but is made clear to the jury in the course of the prosecution opening speech.

Nonetheless, there will be cases where the prosecution choose to draft a count that specifically alleges aiding and abetting.

9.7 Joinder of counts

A single indictment may (and often will) allege several different offences (each set out in a different 'count'). Rule 3.21(4) provides that:

> Where the same indictment charges more than one offence, the court may exercise its power to order separate trials of those offences if of the opinion that—
> (a) the defendant otherwise may be prejudiced or embarrassed in his or her defence (for example, where the offences to be tried together are neither founded on the same facts nor form or are part of a series of offences of the same or a similar character); or
> (b) for any other reason it is desirable that the defendant should be tried separately for any one or more of those offences.

Criminal Practice Direction II, para.10A.3, notes that the rule has been abolished which formerly required an indictment containing more than one count to include only offences founded on the same facts, or offences which constituted all or part of a series of the same or a similar character. However, if an indictment charges more than one offence, and one or more of those offences does not meet those criteria, then the court may decide to exercise its power to order separate trials under s.5(3) of the Indictments Act 1915. Paragraph 10A.3 goes on to say that it is for the court to decide which allegations, against whom, should be tried at the same time, having regard to the prosecutor's proposals, the parties' representations, the court's powers to order separate trials, and the overriding objective. The Practice Direction adds that it is generally undesirable for a large number of counts to be tried at the same time, and the prosecutor may be required to identify a selection of counts on which the trial should proceed, leaving a decision to be taken later whether to try any of the remainder.

It is submitted that, where counts are not founded on the same facts and do not form (part of) a series of offences of the same or a similar character, it is likely that the court will order separate trials. It is therefore necessary to consider how those phases have been construed (in case law decided at a time when there was a strict rule against having an indictment which contained counts that did not satisfy that test for 'joinder').

9.7.1 Same facts

Two offences may be said to be founded on the same facts if either:

- They arise from a single incident or are part of the same 'transaction'. For example, in the specimen indictment shown above, the defendant wounds the householder in the course of committing the burglary. The same principles would apply where someone steals a car in order to use it as a getaway vehicle in a robbery: the taking of the car and the robbery would be charged in a single indictment. Similarly, someone who causes criminal damage in order to commit a burglary may be charged with both offences in a single indictment (the criminal damage being charged pursuant to s.40 of the Criminal Justice Act 1988 if the value of the damage is less than £5,000); or

- The later offence would not have been committed but for the commission of an earlier offence. For example, in R v Barrell and Wilson (1979) 69 Cr App R 250, a defendant was charged with affray and assault (both arising out of a single incident) and with attempting to pervert the course of justice, as the defendant had tried to bribe witnesses to the affray and assault not to give evidence against him. The defence objected to the joinder of the latter charge. However, the Court of Appeal held that, because the attempt at bribery would not have taken place but for the charges arising out of the affray, the charges all had a "common factual origin" (per Shaw LJ, at p.253). It was held, therefore, that all these charges could appear in a single indictment.

9.7.1.1 Contradictory counts

In R v Bellman [1989] AC 836, the House of Lords held that counts can be joined in an indictment even if they are mutually contradictory. The defendant in that case was charged with conspiracy to evade the prohibition on the importation of controlled drugs and with obtaining property by deception. If the defendant had intended to import the drugs, he was guilty of the first offence; if he took the money from the buyers but did not intend to import the drugs to give to them, he was guilty of the second offence. The House of Lords ruled that these inconsistent allegations could properly appear in a single indictment.

9.7.2 Same or similar character

In Ludlow v Metropolitan Police Commissioner [1971] AC 29, the House of Lords had to consider whether two offences formed, or were part of, a series of offences of the same or a similar character. The defendant faced two allegations, one of attempted theft on 20 August 1968 (the theft allegedly taking place at a public house in Acton) and one of robbery on 5 September 1968 (the allegation arising out of an altercation with a barman in a public house in Acton). The House of Lords held that these two allegations could be made in the same indictment. In coming to this conclusion, the following points were made:

- two offences are capable of amounting to a 'series';
- 'both the law and the facts ... should be taken into account in deciding whether offences are similar or dissimilar in character ... For this purpose there has to be some nexus between the offences' (per Lord Pearson, at p.39);
- the evidence in respect of one count need not be admissible evidence in respect of the other count(s).

In R v Marsh (1986) 83 Cr App R 165, Mustill LJ (at p.171) said that:

[T]hose faced with the question of joinder should approach the matter by seeking to ascertain whether or not the counts have similar or dissimilar legal characteristics, whether or not they have similar or dissimilar factual characteristics, and whether or not in all the circumstances such features of similarity as are found enable the offences to be properly described as a series.

Similarly, in R v McGlinchey (1984) 78 Cr App R 282, French J (p.285) said:

[T]he offences should exhibit such similar features that they can conveniently be tried together in the general interests of justice, including those of the defendants, the Crown, the witnesses and the public.

9.7.3 Joinder of defendants

The provisions of r.3.21(4) apply whether the counts are against the same defendant or different defendants. Two or more defendants may be joined in the same indictment even if no count applies to both/all of them, provided that the counts are sufficiently linked for joint trial to be appropriate. For example, in R v *Assim* [1966] 2 QB 249, there were two defendants, a receptionist and a doorman at a night club. The receptionist was charged with wounding one person, and the doorman was charged with assault occasioning actual bodily harm against a different person. Even though there was no joint count in the indictment, it was held to be appropriate for the two defendants to be tried together, as there was sufficient link in both time and place: both victims had tried to leave without paying; D1 allegedly attacked one victim with a knife; the other victim intervened and was attacked by D2. Thus, there was a sufficiently close connection between the incidents for a joint trial to take place Sachs J (at p.260) said:

> Where ... the matters which constitute the individual offences of the several offenders are upon the available evidence so related, whether in time or by other factors, that the interests of justice are best served by their being tried together, then they can properly be the subject of counts in one indictment and can, subject always to the discretion of the court, be tried together.

9.7.4 Joinder of summary offences under s.40 of the Criminal Justice Act 1988

Section 40 of the Criminal Justice Act 1988 applies if the defendant is sent for trial in respect of an indictable (that is, indictable-only or triable either way) offence and the witness statements served on the accused when the case is sent for trial also disclose any one or more of the following summary offences:

- common assault;
- taking a conveyance without the owner's consent (s.12 of the Theft Act 1968);
- driving a motor vehicle while disqualified;
- criminal damage where the value involved is £5,000 or less;
- assaulting a prison custody officer or a secure training centre custody officer.

The summary offence(s) may then be included on the indictment if (under s.40(1)) they are:

- founded on the same facts or evidence as a count charging an indictable offence; or
- part of a series of offences of the same or similar character as an indictable offence which is also charged.

Examples of the operation of s.40 would include cases where:

- a getaway driver at a robbery who has taken the car without the owner's consent can be indicted for robbery and for taking the vehicle without consent (even though the latter is a summary offence);
- a burglar who commits criminal damage in order to effect entry to the premises can be indicted for burglary and criminal damage even if the value of the criminal damage is less than £5,000 (and therefore triable summarily under s.22 of the Magistrates' Courts Act 1980).

It is the prosecution (not the magistrates) who decide whether or not the linked summary offence(s) should appear on the indictment so that the Crown Court can try the summary offence (s) as well as the indictable offence.

Where s.40 applies, the summary offence(s) appear on the indictment and are tried as if indictable. However, if the defendant is convicted of a s.40 summary offence, the Crown Court cannot impose more than the maximum sentence which the magistrates' court could have imposed for that offence.

Under s.40(4), the Secretary of State is empowered to specify additional summary offences to come within the ambit of s.40 (provided that any such offence is punishable with imprisonment or involves obligatory or discretionary disqualification from driving).

In R v Lewis [2013] EWCA Crim 2596; [2014] 1 Cr App R 25, the defendant was sent to the Crown Court for trial on a charge of attempted theft. Two charges of common assault, which were founded on the same facts as the attempted theft, were joined in the indictment pursuant to s.40. The prosecution subsequently offered no evidence on the attempted theft (and so the defendant stood acquitted of that offence). The defendant was then tried for the two summary offences, and found guilty by the jury. On appeal, McCombe LJ, at [15], said that s.40:

> is relevant to the stage at which an indictment is drawn up. Once the indictment is preferred, it remains the indictment before the court. The loss of one charge by reason of an acquittal, either by a jury verdict at the conclusion of the trial, or on earlier judicial direction, or on the entry of a formal verdict on the offering of no evidence on that charge at whatever stage, does not remove the count from the indictment. It remains in the indictment on which the defendant is charged and tried.

It followed that the Crown Court retained jurisdiction to try the summary offences, even though the either-way offence was no longer before the court. Lewis was followed in R v Taylor [2014] EWCA Crim 2411.

9.8 Discretion to order separate trials

Where an indictment alleges that a defendant committed more than one offence or alleges that more than one defendant was involved in the offence(s), the judge may order that separate trials take place. The power to order separate trials of offences on an indictment is sometimes known as 'severing the indictment'. It applies both to a defendant who seeks separate trials for a number of offences and to co-defendants who seek separate trials.

9.8.1 Separate counts

Section 5(3) of the Indictments Act 1915 provides:

> Where, before trial, or at any stage of a trial, the court is of opinion that a person accused may be prejudiced or embarrassed in his defence by reason of being charged with more than one offence in the same indictment, or that for any other reason it is desirable to direct that the person should be tried separately for any one or more offences charged in an indictment, the court may order a separate trial of any count or counts of such indictment.

The defendant has to show that he will not receive a fair trial if all the counts are dealt with together. In Ludlow v Metropolitan Police Commissioner [1971] AC 29, it was held that, if the counts arise from the same facts or form part of a series of offences of the same or a similar character, those counts should usually be tried together and the defendant must show a 'special feature', which means that separate trials are required in the interests of justice (per Lord Pearson, at p.41). In other words, the burden rests on the defendant to show that exceptional circumstances merit separate trials. This case was decided at a time when there was a strict rule that an indictment could contain only counts that were founded on the same facts or which form [part of] a series of offences of the same or a similar character. Even though r.3.21(4) now leaves the matter much more within the discretion of the court, it is submitted that a 'special feature' will still need to be shown where there is an application for separate trials.

Arguments in favour of separate trials which may succeed in appropriate cases include the following:

- the jury may find it difficult to disentangle the evidence, with the risk that they will rely on evidence that does not relate to a particular count when considering that count;
- one count is of a nature likely to arouse hostility in the minds of the jurors, and so they may not approach the other counts with open minds;
- the evidence on one count is strong but on the other is weak, and there is a risk that the jury will assume the defendant is guilty of the second count merely because they find him guilty of the first;
- the evidence in respect of each count is weak, but the jury may convict on the basis that there is 'no smoke without fire', taking an overview of the allegations rather than (as they should) considering each count individually;
- the number of counts and/or defendants is such that the jury will be overwhelmed by the sheer weight of evidence, and the interests of justice are therefore better served by having a number of shorter trials (see, for example, R v Novac (1976) 65 Cr App R 107, where Bridge LJ (at p.119) said that if multiplicity of defendants and charges threatens undue length and complexity of trial, then a heavy responsibility must rest on the prosecution to consider whether joinder is essential in the interests of justice or whether the case can reasonably be subdivided).

It has to be borne in mind that the effect of all these risks, except the last, can be minimised, if not removed altogether, by appropriately worded directions from the judge on how the jury should approach the task of analysing the evidence. A defendant seeking separate trials would therefore have to show why such a direction would not provide sufficient protection in his case.

9.8.2 Co-defendants

Where two or more defendants are charged in a single count, the judge has a discretion to order separate trials. Again, it has to be shown that a fair trial cannot be achieved without severance. Judges are reluctant to order separate trials of defendants charged with the same offence; if there are two separate trials, the cost of the proceedings will be doubled, the witnesses will have to testify twice, and there is a risk of inconsistent verdicts. It is for this reason that separate trials will be ordered only if there are exceptional circumstances that require this course of action.

In R v Grondkowski and Malinowski [1946] KB 369, the Court of Appeal upheld the refusal to order separate trials even though the defendants were blaming each other (the so-called 'cut-throat defence', a defence that often results in both defendants being convicted). Similarly, in R v Lake (1976) 64 Cr App R 172, the trial judge's refusal to order separate trials was upheld by the Court of Appeal even though there was some evidence in the case that was admissible against one defendant but inadmissible against (and highly prejudicial to) the other. The Court of Appeal agreed with the trial judge that the danger of prejudice could be removed by an appropriate direction to the jury. Likewise, in R v Eriemo [1995] 2 Cr App R 206, it was held that a judge was justified in refusing an application to sever an indictment where one defendant intends to argue that he was acting under the duress of another defendant.

The usual response to the argument that the jury will hear evidence that is inadmissible against one defendant, or that they might give undue weight to the evidence of one defendant if he gives evidence that implicates his co-accused, is that the jury will be directed by the judge to consider the case of each defendant separately and to ignore any evidence that has been ruled inadmissible against a particular defendant when they consider the case against that defendant (and that they should bear in mind that one defendant might be serving his own interests by giving evidence against a co-accused). In R v Miah [2011] EWCA Crim 945, the Court of Appeal proceeded on the basis that it is only in 'very exceptional' cases that a judge should exercise his judgment in favour of ordering separate trials. Aikens LJ (at [59]) said:

> [T]he fact that a co-defendant is running a 'cut-throat' defence is common and is very seldom a successful ground, standing alone, for severance. Nor is the fact that one co-defendant has implicated another in the offences charged in the course of a police interview, which is denied by that second co-defendant and which is not admissible as evidence against him. Further, there is always the possibility that a co-defendant who has made an exculpatory statement in interview but at the same time has implicated co-defendants will decide not to give evidence at the trial and rely on just his police interview. Those factors are commonplace.

9.9 Deciding the contents of the indictment

In most cases, the counts on the indictment are the same as the charges in respect of which the defendant was sent for trial. However, s.2(2) of the Administration of Justice (Miscellaneous Provisions) Act 1933 states that where a defendant has been sent for trial at the Crown Court, the draft indictment against the person charged may include, either in substitution for or in addition to counts charging the offence(s) for which the defendant was sent for trial, any counts founded on the evidence served on the accused when the case was sent for trial, provided that the various counts may lawfully be joined in the same indictment.

Section 2(2) effectively confers two powers:

- the power to indict an offender for offences in addition to those for which he has been sent for trial by the magistrates; and
- the power to replace the offences for which he has been sent for trial with different offences.

9.9.1 Substituting offences

An example of the power in s.2 of the Administration of Justice (Miscellaneous Provisions) Act 1933 to substitute a different offence would be a case where the magistrates send the defendant for trial on a charge of burglary (entering premises as a trespasser and then stealing). The prosecution, after the case has been sent to the Crown Court, decide that the evidence on the issue of trespass is very weak, but that they can prove that the defendant stole what he is alleged to have stolen during the course of the 'burglary'. The prosecution could indict the defendant for theft instead of burglary.

Similarly, if the magistrates send the defendant for trial on a charge of theft but the prosecution subsequently decide that there is sufficient evidence to prove that the theft was committed in the course of a burglary, the prosecution could indict the defendant for burglary instead of theft.

9.9.2 Adding additional offences

Section 2(2) of the Administration of Justice (Miscellaneous Provisions) Act 1933 also enables the prosecution to indict the defendant for charges that are additional to those in respect of which he was sent for trial. However, it includes a proviso that the additional counts must be ones which 'may lawfully be joined in the same indictment'. In construing this proviso, it has to be borne in mind that the rules governing joinder of counts in indictments have been relaxed, and there is no longer an absolute rule that, to be in the same indictment, counts have to founded on the same facts or form [part of] a series of offences of the same or a similar character. However, when exercising the power conferred by s.2(2), a prosecutor should add only counts which the court is likely to be permitted to try together. Indeed, r.10.2(4) states that an indictment may contain:

(a) any count charging substantially the same offence as one for which the defendant was sent for trial;

...

(c) any other count charging an offence that the Crown Court can try and which is based on the prosecution evidence that has been served.

An example of use of s.2(2) would be where the defendant is sent for trial on a single charge of robbery. The prosecution witness statements relied upon by the prosecution also disclose the fact that the defendant was in possession of a firearm when carrying out the robbery. The prosecution could add a firearms offence to the indictment. Even though the defendant has not been sent for trial in respect of the firearms charge, it is a charge that is sufficiently closely related to the charge in respect of which the defendant has been sent for trial to justify being tried at the same time as the robbery.

An example of where it would not be appropriate for the prosecution to add a count to the indictment would be where the defendant is sent for trial on a charge of burglary. The prosecution witness statements also reveal evidence that would support a completely unrelated drugs charge. However, the defendant has not been sent for trial in respect of that charge. The prosecution should not add the drugs charge to the indictment which contains the burglary charge. The two charges are wholly unrelated, and it is (it is submitted) inevitable that the court would order separate trials. Adding the drugs count would clearly not be within the spirit of s.2(2).

9.9.3 More than one indictment

In *Lombardi*, Lord Lane CJ said (at p.77) that where the magistrates have sent a defendant to the Crown Court on more than one charge, the prosecution are at liberty to prefer a number of separate indictments if they feel that it is appropriate to do so. If, for example, a defendant is sent for trial on two charges that could legitimately be joined on the same indictment, but which the prosecution feel ought to be tried separately, two separate indictments could be drafted, since the defendant has been sent for trial in respect of both offences.

However, what the prosecution cannot do is to prefer one indictment containing the charge (s) in respect of which the defendant was sent for trial, and a second indictment containing only charges in respect of which the defendant has not been sent for trial. Take, for example, a case where the defendant is sent to the Crown Court for trial on a charge of burglary, but the prosecution witness statements also reveal evidence of a wholly unrelated drugs offence. The prosecution can prefer an indictment for burglary because the defendant has been sent for trial in respect of that charge. They cannot add the unrelated drugs offence to that indictment (because a joint trial would not appropriate), and they cannot prefer a separate indictment in respect of the drugs offence, because the defendant has not been sent for trial in respect of that offence and that offence is not being substituted for an offence in respect of which the defendant was sent for trial.

9.9.4 Adding an additional defendant

If defendants are not sent for trial at the same time, it is nevertheless open to the prosecution to join those defendants in the same indictment, assuming a joint trial is appropriate (see *R v Groom* [1977] QB 6).

If the indictment is already in existence, the prosecution can apply (under s.5(1) of the Indictments Act 1915) to amend the indictment to add an additional defendant.

9.9.5 Alternative counts

In many cases, the prosecution will include alternative counts on the indictment. For instance, an allegation of wounding with intent (s.18 of the Offences Against the Person Act 1861) may be accompanied by a separate count alleging unlawful wounding (s.20 of the same Act). This would be appropriate where the prosecution are not sure that they can prove that the accused had the requisite intent to commit the s.18 offence. There is nothing on the indictment to show that these are alternatives (the word 'or' does not appear) but counsel for the prosecution, during the opening speech, will inform the jury that the prosecution seek a conviction on one or other of the two counts but not both.

9.10 Amending the indictment

Section 5(1) of the Indictments Act 1915 provides:

> Where, before trial, or at any stages of a trial, it appears to the court that the indictment is defective, the court shall make such order for the amendment of the indictment as the court thinks necessary to meet the circumstances of the case, unless, having regard to the merits of the case, the required amendments cannot be made without injustice.
>
> This provision thus allows an indictment to be amended at any stage, provided that the amendment can be made without causing injustice.

In R v Pople [1951] 1 KB 53, it was held that it is not necessary that an indictment, in order to be 'defective' within the meaning of s.5(1), should be one that is bad on its face (for example, one that charges an offence unknown to the law). On the contrary, said the court, any alteration in matters of description may be made in order to meet the evidence in the case, so long as the amendment causes no injustice to the accused. In that case, the indictment alleged the obtaining of sums of money by false pretences; the trial judge allowed the indictment to be amended by replacing the sums in question with the words 'a valuable security, to wit, a cheque'. The Court of Appeal upheld this amendment, ruling that the defence were not prejudiced, since the substance of the allegation was unaltered.

The amendment may take the form of inserting a new count in the indictment, whether in addition to or instead of the original count (R v Johal [1973] QB 475).

In R v Thompson [2011] EWCA Crim 102; [2012] 1 WLR 571, the issue was whether an indictment can be amended to add counts in respect of matters which have arisen after the date when the accused was sent to the Crown Court for trial. Thomas LJ concluded (at [29]) that, although there is the power to amend the indictment to add matters subsequent to the sending for trial, the circumstances in which that might be done are likely to be 'rare'. His Lordship added (at [32]) that the real issue 'is whether there is any prejudice or injustice to a defendant or to the fair and proper conduct of an orderly trial if this is done'.

Applications to amend the indictment may be made at the Plea and Trial Preparation Hearing (PTPH). If an amendment is made just before the start of the trial, and the amendment changes the nature of the prosecution case, the defence should be allowed an adjournment to enable them to review their case in the light of the new allegations. If a jury has already been empanelled, it may be necessary for the judge to discharge that jury and order a retrial.

It is permissible (subject to the possible need for an adjournment) for the indictment to be amended during the course of the trial (although if the amendment is a fundamental one, so that the defence would need a long adjournment, it may be appropriate for the judge to discharge the jury and order a retrial instead). In R v *Foster* [2007] EWCA Crim 2869; [2008] 1 WLR 1615, Sir Igor Judge P said (at [65]):

> [I]t is now common practice to permit amendments to the indictment at any stage of the trial, whether by amending or adding or substituting new counts, provided that these steps may be taken without unfairness to the accused. Whether unfairness results will usually depend on the purpose of the amendment, the stage of the trial at which the amendment is sought, the degree, if any, to which the defendant is required by the amendment to meet a new prosecution case and whether he would be disadvantaged in the presentation of his defence.

Such an amendment may even be permitted after the jury have retired to consider their verdict. In R v *Collison* (1980) 71 Cr App R 249, for example, the defendant was charged with a single count of wounding with intent. The jury were unable to reach either a unanimous or a majority verdict on this count, but wanted to convict the defendant of the lesser offence of unlawful wounding. Since they could not agree on an acquittal of the offence on the indictment, they could not simply return a verdict of guilty to the lesser offence under s.6(3) of the Criminal Law Act 1967, since that provision only applies where the jury first acquits of the offence on the indictment. The judge therefore allowed the prosecution to add a further count, alleging the lesser offence, to the indictment. The Court of Appeal upheld this course of action, as no injustice was caused to the defendant by the addition of the new count. Given their power to acquit of wounding with intent but convict instead of unlawful wounding, the lesser offence was, effectively, already before the jury.

The important question in deciding whether or not to allow an amendment once the trial has started is whether the defence case would have been conducted differently had the amendment taken place at the outset. In R v *Thomas* [1983] Crim LR 619, for example, the Court of Appeal quashed a conviction where a count of receiving stolen property was added to an indictment which hitherto alleged only theft. This amendment took place after the close of the prosecution case and the defence would have cross-examined the prosecution witnesses differently if both allegations had been made at the outset.

9.11 Quashing the indictment

It is open to the defence to make an application to 'quash' the indictment. Such an application would normally be made at the PTPH. There are three grounds for quashing an indictment:

(a) the indictment (or a count on the indictment) is bad on its face, in that it alleges an offence which is not known to the law, or a single count alleges more than one offence (and so is 'duplicitous');

(b) the indictment (or one of its counts) has been preferred without authority, in that there has been no valid sending of the case from the magistrates' court to the Crown Court, and no voluntary bill of indictment;

(c) the indictment contains a count in respect of which the defendant was not sent for trial (and there was no voluntary bill of indictment in respect of that count) and the prosecution witness statements do not disclose a case to answer on that count.

The distinction between (b) and (c) is that in the case of (b), there was no valid sending of the case to the Crown Court; in the case of (c), there was a valid sending to the Crown Court, but the person drafting the indictment added a new offence in addition to the offence(s) in respect of which the defendant was originally sent for trial.

The only instance in which the trial judge is entitled to look at the prosecution witness statements to see if they disclose a case to answer is in case (c), in respect of the 'new' count (R v Jones (1974) 59 Cr App R 120). It follows that if the offence is one in respect of which the defendant was sent for trial, the judge cannot be asked to quash the indictment on the basis that there is insufficient evidence in respect of that offence (R v London Quarter Sessions ex p Downes [1954] 1 QB 1).

Motions to quash are of little practical importance since these grounds are very limited and, in any event, most errors can be cured by the prosecution seeking to amend the defective indictment under s.5(1) of the Indictments Act 1915.

Furthermore, if the indictment is quashed, the defendant is not regarded as having been acquitted and so can be prosecuted again. However, if the whole indictment is quashed, the defendant can only be indicted for the same offence again if he is sent for trial a second time for that offence by a magistrates' court or if a voluntary bill of indictment is obtained from a High Court judge (R v Thompson [1975] 1 WLR 1425).

In R v FB [2010] EWCA Crim 1857; [2011] 1 WLR 844, it was held that a Crown Court judge has no power to quash an indictment simply because he does not believe that the proceedings should have been brought.

9.12 Historical note: the previous rules on joinder

It used to be the case that, if an indictment contained counts that were not founded on the same facts or else [part of] a series of offences of the same or a similar character, then the indictment was regarded as defective. The court would either have to delete one or more counts so as to leave only those which were sufficiently connected, or else 'stay' the existing (defective) indictment and allow the prosecution to create two or more new indictments (see R v Newland [1988] QB 402 and R v Follett [1989] QB 338). A subsequent amendment to the Criminal Procedure Rules enabled the court simply to make an order for separate trials in such a case (effectively overruling Newland, where the Court of Appeal had ruled that there was no power to order separate trials in such circumstances). The current version of the rules clarifies that the court always has a discretion to order separate trials.

Chapter 10

Crown Court Trial

In this chapter, we look at trial on indictment in the Crown Court.

10.1 Pre-trial hearings

Section 39 of the Criminal Procedure and Investigations Act 1996 makes provision for pre-trial hearings in cases to be tried in the Crown Court. These hearings take place before the jury is empanelled. Under s.40(1), a judge may make at a pre-trial hearing a ruling as to:

(a) any question as to the admissibility of evidence;
(b) any other question of law relating to the case concerned.

Under s.40(2), a ruling may be made either following an application by a party to the case, or of the judge's own motion.

Section 40(3) states that a ruling made under s.40 is binding from the time it is made until the case against the accused is disposed of (that is, when the accused is acquitted or convicted, or the prosecutor decides not to proceed with the case).

However, s.40(4) empowers the judge to discharge or vary a ruling made under s.40 (following an application by a party to the case, or of the judge's own motion) if it appears to him that it is in the interests of justice to do so. Under subs.(5), an application for a ruling to be discharged or varied cannot be made unless there has been a material change of circumstances since the ruling was made.

10.1.1 Plea and Trial Preparation Hearing ('PTPH')

If the defendant is charged with an either-way offence, a guilty plea is entered through indicating a guilty plea at the 'plea before venue hearing' in the magistrates' court. If the sentencing powers of the magistrates' court are insufficient, the defendant will be committed to the Crown Court for sentence. However, if the offence is triable only on indictment, there is no opportunity to enter a formal plea in the magistrates' court. However, at the time of sending the case to the Crown Court for trial under s.51 of the Crime and Disorder Act 1998, the magistrates' court is required by r.9.7 (5) to ask the defendant about intended plea, and so a defendant who intends to plead guilty has an opportunity to indicate that intention then (in which case a hearing for the guilty plea to be entered in the Crown Court will be arranged to take place as soon as possible). In any other case, Criminal Practice Direction I, para.3A.11 states that a PTPH must be held within 28 days of the case being sent to the Crown Court.

However, r.3.24(5) of the Criminal Procedure Rules provides that where a magistrates' court sends the defendant for trial, the Crown Court must take the defendant's plea not less than two weeks after the date on which the sending takes place (unless the parties otherwise agree) and not more than 16 weeks after that date, unless the court otherwise directs.

Paragraph 3A.16 goes on to say that an indictment should be lodged at least seven days in advance of the PTPH. Additional case management hearings are discouraged (para.3A.21). Any case progression hearings should take place without courtroom hearings, using electronic communications (para.3A.24).

Rule 3.13(1) provides that the Crown Court must conduct a plea and trial preparation hearing, and may conduct one or more further pre-trial case management hearings only where the court anticipates a guilty plea, or it is necessary to conduct such a hearing in order to give directions for an effective trial, or such a hearing is required to set ground rules for the conduct of the questioning of a witness or defendant.

Rules 3.13(2) goes on to provide that, at the plea and trial preparation hearing the court must:

(a) satisfy itself that there has been explained to the defendant, in terms the defendant can understand (with help, if necessary), that the defendant will receive credit for a guilty plea;

(b) take the defendant's plea or if no plea can be taken then find out whether the defendant is likely to plead guilty or not guilty;

(c) unless the defendant pleads guilty, satisfy itself that there has been explained to the defendant, in terms the defendant can understand (with help, if necessary), that at the trial—

(i) the defendant will have the right to give evidence after the court has heard the prosecution case,

(ii) if the defendant does not attend, the trial may take place in the defendant's absence,

(iii) if the trial takes place in the defendant's absence, the judge may inform the jury of the reason for that absence, and

(iv) where the defendant is released on bail, failure to attend court when required is an offence for which the defendant may be arrested and punished and bail may be withdrawn; and

(d) give directions for an effective trial.

The PTPH includes the completion, by all parties, of an advocates' questionnaire. In R v Newell [2012] EWCA Crim 650; [2012] 1 WLR 3142, the Court of Appeal ruled that it will only be in exceptional cases that the prosecution will be able to rely on admissions made by the accused in case management forms. Sir John Thomas P said (at [36]):

[P]rovided the case is conducted in accordance with the letter and spirit of the Criminal Procedure Rules ... information or a statement written on a [PTPH] form should in the exercise of the court's discretion under s.78 [of PACE] not be admitted in evidence as a statement that can be used against the defendant.

10.1.1.1 Arraignment

At the PTPH, the defendant is asked to enter a plea to the offence(s) on the indictment (this is sometimes known as 'arraigning' the defendant). The indictment is read out by the clerk of the court and after each count the defendant says 'guilty' or 'not guilty'. Each count must be 'put' to the defendant separately, and a separate plea must be entered on each count. The plea must be entered by the defendant personally (not through his advocate), at least if the plea is one of guilty (R v Ellis (1973) 57 Cr App R 571; R v Williams [1978] QB 373).

If the defendant pleads guilty to some counts but not guilty to others, sentence will be postponed until the trial on the counts to which the defendant has pleaded not guilty has been completed, assuming that the prosecution wish to proceed with the trial of the offences to which the defendant pleaded not guilty.

10.1.1.2 Seeking an indication as to sentence

It is possible to seek an indication as to likely sentence from the judge. The process for doing so is laid down in R v Goodyear [2005] EWCA Crim 888; [2005] 1 WLR 2532. Lord Woolf CJ gave detailed guidance, including the following (at [54]–[77]):

- Any advance indication of sentence to be given by the judge should normally be confined to the maximum sentence if a plea of guilty were to be tendered at the stage at which the indication is sought.
- The judge should not give an advance indication of sentence unless one has been sought by the defendant.
- The judge retains an unfettered discretion to refuse to give an advance indication of sentence.
- Alternatively, the judge may reserve his position until such time as he feels able to give an indication (for example, when a pre-sentence report is available).
- Once an indication has been given, it is binding on the judge who has given it and on any other judge who becomes responsible for the case.
- If, after a reasonable opportunity to consider his position in the light of the indication, the defendant does not plead guilty, the indication will cease to have effect.
- The defendant's advocate should not seek an indication without written authority, signed by the defendant, confirming that he wishes to seek an indication.
- The advocate must ensure that the defendant fully appreciates that: (a) he should not plead guilty unless he is guilty; (b) any sentence indication given by the judge remains subject to the entitlement of the Attorney General (where it arises) to refer an unduly lenient sentence to the Court of Appeal; (c) any indication given by the judge reflects the situation at the time when it is given, and that if a guilty plea is not tendered in the light of that indication, the indication ceases to have effect.
- An indication should not be sought while there is any uncertainty between the prosecution and the defence about an acceptable plea to the indictment, or any factual basis relating to the plea. Any agreed basis should be reduced into writing before an indication is sought. Where there is a dispute about a particular fact which counsel for the defendant believes to be effectively immaterial to the sentencing decision, the difference should be recorded, so that the judge can make up his own mind.
- The judge should not be asked to indicate levels of sentence which he may have in mind depending on possible different pleas.
- The hearing should normally take place in open court, with both sides represented and in the defendant's presence.
- Any reference to a request for a sentence indication will be inadmissible in any subsequent trial (if the defendant maintains his not guilty plea).

These principles are summarised in Criminal Practice Direction Sentencing C (paras C.1–C.8).

10.1.1.3 Pleading guilty to an alternative offence

The indictment may contain alternative counts. For example, there might be one count alleging possession of controlled drugs with intent to supply and another alleging only possession. If the defendant pleads not guilty to the more serious offence but guilty to the lesser offence, it is up to the prosecution to decide whether to proceed with a trial of the count to which the defendant pleads not guilty. If a trial does follow and the defendant is acquitted of the more serious offence, he will then be sentenced for the lesser offence to which he pleaded guilty. If he is convicted of the more serious offence, the lesser offence will be ignored for sentencing purposes.

Normally, the prosecution will indicate to the defence beforehand whether a plea of guilty to the lesser offence will be acceptable. Where the plea to the lesser offence is acceptable, the lesser offence is put to the defendant first and (assuming he pleads guilty to it, as anticipated) the second offence will not be put to the defendant, or else it will be put and the prosecution will either offer no evidence (which amounts to an acquittal) or ask it to be left on the file (which does not amount to an acquittal as the court can give permission for the prosecution to proceed with a count that has been left on file).

If there is no alternative count on the indictment, the defendant may, by virtue of s.6(1)(b) of the Criminal Law Act 1967, plead not guilty to the count on the indictment but offer a plea of guilty to a lesser offence of which the jury would be able to convict him under s.6(3) of the Act (see below). If this plea is accepted, the defendant stands acquitted of the offence charged but convicted of the lesser offence, for which he will then be sentenced.

If the plea of guilty to the lesser offence is not accepted by the prosecution, the trial will proceed on the basis of a 'not guilty' plea to the offence on the indictment. The defendant's plea of guilty to the lesser offence is impliedly withdrawn; if the jury acquit the defendant of the offence on the indictment, and do not convict of the lesser offence under s.6(3), the defendant cannot then be sentenced for the lesser offence (R v Hazeltine [1967] 2 QB 857; R v Yeardley [2000] 1 QB 374).

If the prosecutor asks the judge to approve the acceptance of a plea to a lesser offence, the prosecutor must abide by the decision of the judge; if the prosecutor does not seek approval from the judge, it is open to the judge to express dissent with the course of action proposed and to ask the prosecutor to reconsider (Criminal Practice Direction Sentencing B, paras B.2 and B.3).

10.1.1.4 Offering no evidence; leaving counts on the file

Section 17 of the Criminal Justice Act 1967 provides that where the defendant pleads not guilty and the prosecutor proposes to offer no evidence against him, the court may order that a verdict of not guilty is to be recorded (and this has the same effect as if the defendant had been acquitted by the jury). This may be appropriate, for example, where a key prosecution witness refuses to testify, or where evidence exonerating the defendant comes to light, or where the defendant pleads guilty to one offence and the prosecution do not wish to proceed with another. Although s.17 says that the court 'may' enter a finding of not guilty where the prosecution offer no evidence, in practice a judge would not force the prosecution to present its case.

Alternatively, the prosecution may ask for one or more counts to be 'left on the file, marked not to be proceeded with without leave of the Crown Court or the Court of Appeal'. This may be appropriate where the defendant pleads guilty to some counts but not guilty to others, since leaving a count on the file does not amount to an acquittal. Thus, if the conviction is for some reason overturned on appeal, the prosecution can proceed with the other counts if the Crown Court or Court of Appeal gives permission. This could happen, for example, if the trial judge gives a preliminary ruling on the law adverse to the accused, so the accused pleads guilty but then challenges the judge's ruling by means of an appeal against conviction; the prosecution could then seek leave to proceed with the other counts.

Thus, the main difference between offering no evidence and leaving counts on the file is that the former results in an acquittal, whereas the latter leave open the possibility (with the leave of the court) of the case against the defendant being revived.

10.1.1.5 Different pleas from different defendants

If more than one defendant is charged in the same indictment, it may well be that one defendant will plead guilty and another will plead not guilty.

Where this occurs, counsel for the prosecution should only tell the jury that tries the defendant who pleads not guilty that '[name of defendant who pleads guilty], of whom you may hear mention in the course of this case, is not before you and is none of your concern'.

Usually, sentencing of the defendant who pleads guilty will be adjourned until after the trial of the defendant who pleads not guilty. There is less risk of disparity between the sentences if the judge sentences the defendants together, and the judge is in a better position to sentence as he will have heard the evidence about the gravity of the offence and the respective roles played by the defendants during the course of the trial (R v Payne (1950) 34 Cr App R 43).

However, where the defendant who pleads guilty also agrees to be a witness for the prosecution against the defendant who pleads not guilty (sometimes known as 'turns Queen's evidence'), it is open to the court to sentence him there and then, so that there should be no suspicion of his evidence being affected by the fact that he hopes to get a lighter sentence because of the evidence which he gives (*Payne*). However, in R v *Weekes* (1980) 2 Cr App R (S) 377, it was said to be better that all are sentenced at the same time by the same court whenever that is possible, and so sentence should normally be postponed until after the trial of the defendant who pleads not guilty. Ultimately, however, the decision whether or not to postpone sentence on a defendant who pleads guilty and indicates that he is willing to give evidence against a co-defendant until the end of the trial is a matter for the discretion of the trial judge (R v *Clement* (1991) *The Times*, 12 December).

10.1.2 Preparatory hearings

Section 29(1) of the of the Criminal Procedure and Investigations Act 1996 empowers a Crown Court judge to order that a 'preparatory hearing' be held, but only where 'an indictment reveals a case of such complexity, a case of such seriousness or a case whose trial is likely to be of such length, that substantial benefits are likely to accrue from [such] a hearing'.

Section 29(2) sets out the purposes of the preparatory hearing. They include:

- identifying issues which are likely to be material to the determinations and findings which are likely to be required during the trial;
- if there is to be a jury, assisting their comprehension of those issues and expediting the proceedings before them;
- assisting the judge's management of the trial;
- considering questions as to the severance or joinder of charges.

Section 31(3) sets out the powers which the judge may exercise at the preparatory hearing. He may make a ruling as to:

(a) any question as to the admissibility of evidence;
(b) any other question of law relating to the case;
(c) any question as to the severance or joinder of charges.

Section 35(1) of the CPIA provides that an appeal may be made to the Court of Appeal against any ruling under s.31(3), but only with the leave of the judge or of the Court of Appeal. This is what makes a preparatory hearing significantly different to a PTPH, as appeals cannot be brought against decisions made at a PTPH.

In R v I [2009] EWCA Crim 1793; [2010] 1 Cr App R 10, the Court of Appeal made it clear that preparatory hearings should rarely take place. Hughes LJ (at [21]) said:

> Virtually the only reason for directing such a hearing nowadays is if the judge is going to have to give a ruling which ought to be the subject of an interlocutory appeal. Such rulings are few and far between and do not extend to most rulings of law. An interlocutory appeal can be a most beneficial process in a few, very limited, circumstances.

In R v *Quillan* [2015] EWCA Crim 538; [2015] 1 WLR 4673, the Court of Appeal (at [7]–[8]) said:

> One of the purposes of making an order for a preparatory hearing is to assist the judge's management of the trial. Deciding issues such as those which arise on this appeal in

advance of the trial ... allows the trial to proceed uninterrupted, if that is the result of the determination of the legal issue. If there is an appeal, it allows this court to determine issues without the pressure of time created by the need to ensure that the jury which has spent weeks dealing with the case is not further inconvenienced. Even more importantly, if the decision is that the judge was right to stop the case, then no trial is required at all and enormous public expenditure is saved.

Criminal proceedings are burdensome for all involved, particularly witnesses, jurors and other members of the public who become embroiled in them. In addition such prosecutions are a very considerable burden on public finances; a misconceived prosecution is therefore a very serious matter. If counts in the indictment are misconceived in law it is essential that this is determined at the earliest stage ....

The Court referred to the dictum of Hughes LJ in R v I, quoted above, and went on to say (at [10]–[11]):

Whilst that is almost invariably the position, there may be special circumstances where a trial will be very long and very costly and where a ruling on a point of law in relation to the legal basis on which a count in the indictment is founded may determine whether or not a trial is required at all. In such a case such a point of law should be determined well before any trial starts. That is not the same thing as saying that it must be resolved in a preparatory hearing. There is a power in any case under s.40 of the 1996 Act to hold a pre-trial hearing and to decide any question of law relating to the case concerned. This procedure does not involve any of the technicalities which have caused some difficulty in relation to preparatory hearings and there is no interlocutory right of appeal (except where the prosecution treats any ruling as a terminating ruling).

A further benefit of the preparatory hearing procedure is that the prosecution is not required to undertake that a defendant is entitled to be acquitted if an appeal it brings against a ruling in a preparatory hearing fails. Cases of real complexity are crucially affected by the charges the prosecution chooses to prefer and the way in which it formulates its case. ... It is obviously of benefit for such issues to be determined in advance of the trial so that, if it can be fairly done, the prosecution has an opportunity to reflect on any adverse ruling and to consider whether an amendment to the indictment should be sought.

10.2 Securing the attendance of witnesses

Section 2 of the Criminal Procedure (Attendance of Witnesses) Act 1965 enables the Crown Court to issue a witness summons requiring the attendance at the Crown Court of a person who is likely to be able to give material evidence (or produce any document or thing likely to be material evidence). This power may be exercised only if it is in the interests of justice to issue a summons.

Under subs.(4), an application for a witness summons must be made as soon as reasonably practicable after the defendant has been sent to the Crown Court for trial.

Section 4(2) provides that, if a witness fails to attend in compliance with the summons, the court may (if it is satisfied that there are reasonable grounds for believing that he has failed to attend without just excuse) issue a warrant for his arrest. Someone arrested under such a warrant will be taken before the Crown Court and may be remanded in custody or on bail until the time his evidence is required (s.4(3)).

The power to remand a witness in custody, pursuant to s.4(3), does not expire when the witness starts to give evidence; rather it continues until the witness is released from further attendance at court. The correct test is whether there is a real possibility that either side might recall the witness (R (TH) v Crown Court at Wood Green [2006] EWHC 2683 (Admin); [2007] 1 WLR 1670, per Wilkie J, at [29]).

Failure to comply with a witness summons also amounts to contempt of court (s.3(1)), punishable with up to three months' imprisonment.

Section 4(1) of the Act enables pre-emptive action if a witness summons has been obtained and there are grounds to believe that the person will not attend court. It provides that, if a Crown Court judge is satisfied by evidence on oath that a witness in respect of whom a witness summons is in force is unlikely to comply with it, he may issue a warrant to arrest the witness and bring him before the court.

10.3 Presence of defendant

In the Crown Court, the defendant must be present in order to enter a plea to the counts on the indictment. If, after entering a plea, the defendant absconds (or misbehaves and disrupts the proceedings), the trial judge has a discretion to continue the trial in the defendant's absence. However, r.25.2(1)(b) of the Criminal Procedure Rules provides that the court must not proceed if the defendant is absent, unless the court is satisfied both that the defendant has waived the right to attend, and that the trial will be fair despite the defendant's absence.

Guidance on the exercise of the discretion to proceed in the absence of the defendant was given by the House of Lords in R v Jones [2002] UKHL 5; [2003] 1 AC 1. Lord Bingham said (at [13]) that:

> the discretion to commence a trial in the absence of a defendant should be exercised with the utmost care and caution. If the absence of the defendant is attributable to involuntary illness or incapacity it would very rarely, if ever, be right to exercise the discretion in favour of commencing the trial, at any rate unless the defendant is represented and asks that the trial should begin.

Criminal Practice Direction III, para.14E.3, says that proceeding in the absence of a defendant is a step that ought normally to be taken 'only if it is unavoidable' and that the court must exercise its discretion as to whether a trial should take place or continue in the defendant's absence with 'the utmost care and caution'. Circumstances to be taken into account before proceeding include:

(i) the conduct of the defendant;

(ii) the disadvantage to the defendant;

(iii) the public interest, taking account of the inconvenience and hardship to witnesses, and especially to any complainant, of a delay; if the witnesses have attended court and are ready to give evidence, that will weigh in favour of continuing with the trial;

(iv) the effect of any delay;

(v) whether the attendance of the defendant could be secured at a later hearing; and

(vi) the likely outcome if the defendant is found guilty.

Where a defendant is taken ill during the course of the trial and cannot attend court, the usual practice is for the trial to continue in his absence if he consents; if he does not consent to the trial continuing in his absence, and the illness is likely to last more than a few days, the jury will be discharged and a new trial will begin when the defendant is well enough to attend court.

In R v Welland [2018] EWCA Crim 2036, the defendant suffered several seizures during the trial. The judge rejected an application to discharge the jury and so the trial continued, with the defendant observing the proceedings through a video link. The defendant did not give evidence (because of concerns that he would be taken ill if he did so). Leggatt LJ (at [18] said that the right of a defendant who wishes to do so to give evidence in his own defence is an important element of the right to a fair trial, and so a defendant who wishes to testify 'must be given a full and fair opportunity to do so'. It followed that a 'decision to proceed in circumstances where such a defendant is understood not to be in a fit state to give evidence should be taken, if at all, only after the most full and careful consideration'. In the present case, there had not been proper consideration of whether any steps could be taken (such as medication) which might have enabled the defendant to give evidence. The court concluded (at [21]) that: 'To insist that the trial must proceed without exploring that possibility and without establishing through medical evidence that there was no realistic means of enabling [the defendant] to give evidence was unfair'. If there is sufficient basis for concluding that there are no measures which could reasonably be taken to enable the defendant to testify but that the trial should nevertheless proceed, the direction to the jury must spell out the consequences of the fact that the defendant had been unable to give evidence; in particular, the point should be made that the jury has not been able to hear at first hand the defendant's account of events, including where that account conflicted with that of other witnesses, and to assess its credibility (see [22]).

Where a trial has started in the presence of a defendant, it may continue in his absence if he misbehaves in court. However, in such a case the judge ought to allow the defendant a 'cooling off' period and an opportunity thereafter to apologise and undertake to behave properly (see R v Hussain [2018] EWCA Crim 1785).

In many cases, the decision on whether or not to try a defendant in his or her absence has to be taken because the defendant has failed to surrender to custody. To discourage defendants from absconding, in R v O'Hare [2006] EWCA Crim 471, Thomas LJ (at [35]) recommended that it should be made clear to each defendant when bail is granted that, 'if he fails to attend a trial, the consequences may well be that the trial will proceed in his absence and without legal representation'. A defendant who then fails to attend could be regarded as having waived his right to be present.

Paragraph 14E.3 of the Practice Direction also says that, even if the defendant is voluntarily absent, 'it is still generally desirable that he or she is represented'. In R v Kepple [2007] EWCA Crim 1339, the Court of Appeal said that where the defendant is being tried in his absence but counsel continues to act, he should conduct the case as though his client were still present in court but had decided not to give evidence, on the basis of any instructions he had received. He is free to use any material contained in his brief and may cross-examine prosecution witnesses and call defence witnesses. Counsel is entitled to ask questions of prosecution witnesses based on his instructions, but without indicating what the defendant's evidence might have been and in the knowledge that he will not be able to call evidence to contradict the answers given. He is entitled to conduct cross-examination on this basis in the hope of either showing that his absent client's instructions are accepted by the witnesses or casting doubt upon the coherence or accuracy of their accounts.

10.3.1 Bail

If the defendant is remanded in custody prior to his trial, he will remain in custody during the trial itself (unless the trial judge grants bail, which is very unlikely).

In R v Central Criminal Court ex p Guney [1996] AC 616, the House of Lords held that when a defendant who is on bail and who has not previously surrendered to the custody of the court is arraigned (that is, called upon to plead guilty or not guilty), he surrenders to the custody of the court at that moment. The result is that the Crown Court judge then has to decide whether or not to grant him bail; unless the judge grants bail, the defendant will remain in custody pending and during the trial. In R v *Evans* [2011] EWCA Crim 2842; [2012] 1 WLR 1192, Hughes LJ (at [20]) said that practical effect of *Guney* is that:

> once arraignment has taken place, however informal its particular circumstances may be, the court must review the question of bail and if a surety is involved direct a fresh taking of a reconnaissance … [W]henever else it may happen surrender is deemed to have taken place on arraignment.

His Lordship also pointed out (at [33]) that bail (and any surety) lapses on the first appearance in the Crown Court. It follows that, at the conclusion of the first hearing in the Crown Court, bail should always be considered. The question of bail will therefore have to be considered at the PTPH.

In any event, if the defendant is on bail before the trial, his bail effectively expires at the start of the trial. It is therefore a matter for the discretion of the trial judge whether or not bail is granted to the defendant for lunchtime and/or overnight adjournments. Criminal Practice Direction III, para.14G.2 says that it 'may be a proper exercise of this discretion to refuse bail during the short adjournment if the accused cannot otherwise be segregated from witnesses and jurors'. However, a defendant who is on bail prior to the trial should not be refused bail during the trial 'unless, in the opinion of the court, there are positive reasons to justify this refusal'; such reasons might include '(a) that a point has been reached where there is a real danger that the accused will abscond, either because the case is going badly for him, or for any other reason, or (b) that there is a real danger that he may interfere with witnesses, jurors or co-defendants' (para.19G.3). If the defendant is convicted, the grant of bail prior to sentence 'should be decided in the light of the gravity of the offence, any friction between co-defendants and the likely sentence to be passed' (para.19G.4).

10.4 The jury

In this section we focus on the jury who are at the centre of a Crown Court trial.

10.4.1 Who can serve on a jury?

Jurors are drawn from the electoral register. Anyone on the register and aged between 18 and 75 can be summoned for jury service (s.1 of the Juries Act 1974). The principle underpinning the operation of the Juries Act 1974 is that the jury should be a cross-section of society, drawn at random.

Schedule 1 to the Act disqualifies two categories of people:

- those who are liable to be detained under the Mental Health Act 1983, or who lack capacity, within the meaning of the Mental Capacity Act 2005, to serve as a jurors; and
- those who have certain previous convictions:
  - a term of imprisonment for five years or more disqualifies the person for life;
  - a sentence of less than five years, a suspended sentence or a community order disqualifies the person for ten years.

In R v *Abdroikov* [2007] UKHL 37, [2007] 1 WLR 2679, three appeals were heard together. In two cases, the trial jury included among its members a serving police officer, and in the third case it included a solicitor employed by the Crown Prosecution Service. The House held that the question to be asked was whether, on the particular facts of each case, a fair-minded and informed observer would conclude that there was a real possibility that the jurors in question were biased, having regard to the fact that Parliament had declared that in England and Wales such persons were eligible to sit on juries, envisaging that any objection to their sitting would be the subject of judicial decision. They went on to hold (by a 3:2 majority) that the convictions should be quashed in the case where one of the jurors was an employee of the CPS (that fact was enough to create a suspicion of bias in a case where the prosecution was brought by the CPS) and the case where one of the jurors was a serving police officer who worked in the same area as police witnesses in the case; however, the conviction should not be quashed in the other case, where the police officer who was on the jury did not work in the same area as the police witnesses.

In R v Khan [2008] EWCA Crim 531; [2008] 3 All ER 502, the appeals were each based on the ground that a member of the jury had, by reason of their occupation, an appearance of bias. The relevant jurors were a serving police officer, an employee of the CPS (in a case being prosecuted by the Department of Trade and Industry), and two prison officers. Lord Phillips CJ said (at [10]):

> Where an impartial juror is shown to have had reason to favour a particular witness, this will not necessarily result in the quashing of a conviction. It will only do so if this has rendered the trial unfair, or given it an appearance of unfairness. To decide this it is necessary to consider two questions: (i) Would the fair-minded observer consider that partiality of the juror to the witness may have caused the jury to accept the evidence of that witness? If so (ii) Would the fair-minded observer consider that this may have affected the outcome of the trial? If the answer to both questions is in the affirmative, then the trial will not have the appearance of fairness. If the answer to the first or the second question is in the negative, then the partiality of the juror to the witness will not have affected the safety of the verdict and there will be no reason to consider the trial unfair.

The case of Khan subsequently went to the European Court of Human Rights, reported as Hanif and Khan v UK (2012) 55 EHRR 16. The Court said that a jury 'must be impartial from an objective as well as a subjective point of view' ([138]). The 'personal impartiality of a judge or a jury member must be presumed until there is proof to the contrary' ([139]). In considering whether there was impartiality from an objective point of view, the Court 'must examine whether in the circumstances there were sufficient guarantees to exclude any objectively justified or legitimate doubts as to the impartiality of the jury' ([140]). Moreover,

> it does not necessarily follow from the fact that a member of a tribunal has some personal knowledge of one of the witnesses in a case that he will be prejudiced in favour of that person's testimony. In each individual case it must be decided whether the familiarity in question is of such a nature and degree as to indicate a lack of impartiality on the part of the tribunal ([141]).

In the case under consideration, there was nothing to suggest that there had been actual partiality on the part of the police officer, so the question was whether there were 'sufficient guarantees to exclude any objectively justified doubts as to his impartiality' ([142]). The Court regarded it as important that the defence case 'depended to a significant extent upon his challenge to the evidence of the police officers' ([146]). The Court said (at [148]) that:

> leaving aside the question whether the presence of a police officer or a juror could ever be compatible with Art.6, where there is an important conflict regarding police evidence in the case and a police officer who is personally acquainted with the police officer witness giving the relevant evidence is a member of the jury, jury directions and judicial warnings are

insufficient to guard against the risk that the juror may, albeit subconsciously, favour the evidence of the police.

In the present case, the juror in question had known one of the officers in the case for ten years and, although not from the same station, had worked with him on three occasions. The other witnesses who supported that officer's account of events were also police officers. On this basis, the Court found (at [149]) that there had been a violation of Art.6.1 of the Convention, since the trial had not taken place before an impartial tribunal.

In *Armstrong v UK* [2014] ECHR 1368, there were two police officers (one retired, one still serving) on the jury. The European Court of Human Rights rejected the claim that the trial had therefore been unfair. Firstly, the officers had alerted the court to the fact that they were police officers (one retired and one still serving) and enquiries were made to establish whether there was a real risk of bias. Secondly, 'the defence had every opportunity to object to the continued presence of the men on the jury but chose not to do so' (see [41] and [42]). Thirdly, this was 'not a case where a police officer who was personally acquainted with a police officer witness giving relevant evidence was a member of the jury' (see [43]). Finally, the defence case 'did not depend to any significant extent – if at all – upon a challenge to the evidence of the police officer witnesses' (at [44]).

Criminal Practice Direction VI, para.26C.7, states that where a potential juror is a police officer, the judge will have to assess whether he may serve as a juror. Regard should be had to:

> whether evidence from the police is in dispute in the case and the extent to which that dispute involves allegations made against the police; whether the potential juror knows or has worked with the officers involved in the case; whether the potential juror has served or continues to serve in the same police units within the force as those dealing with the investigation of the case or is likely to have a shared local service background with police witnesses in a trial.

Paragraph 26C.9 adds that employees of prosecuting authorities must not serve on a trial prosecuted by the prosecuting authority by which they are employed, but they can serve on a trial prosecuted by another prosecuting authority. Similarly, a serving police officer can serve where there is no particular link between the court and the station where the police officer serves.

For a critique of the presence of police officers and prosecutors on juries, see Peter Hungerford-Welch, *'Police Officers as Jurors'* [2012] Crim LR 320–342.

For a research-based appraisal of the fairness of the system of jury trial, see Cheryl Thomas, *Are juries fair?* (Ministry of Justice, 2010).

10.4.2 Excusal and deferral

Section 9(2) of the Juries Act 1974 provides that a person who has been summoned for jury service may seek excusal if they can show a 'good reason' for this.

Section 9A(1) enables a person summoned for jury service to seek deferral of that service if there is good reason (and so if, for example, the dates specified in the summons clash with the person's holiday arrangements or business commitments, attendance can be deferred to a later date); s.9B enables a person to be excused from jury service because he/she is not capable of acting effectively as a juror because of a physical disability.

Excusal is generally reserved for cases where it would be unreasonable to require the person to serve at any time within the next 12 months.

10.4.3 Empanelling a jury

The term 'jury panel' is used to describe the body of people who have been summoned for jury service at a particular Crown Court.

Because of concerns about misconduct on the part of jurors, in particular carrying out their own research into the cases they are trying, r.26.3 of the Criminal Procedure Rules requires the court officer to arrange for each juror to receive general information about jury service and about a juror's responsibilities. In particular, the juror must receive written notice of the prohibitions against research by a juror into the case; disclosure by a juror of any such research to another juror during the trial; conduct by a juror which suggests that that juror intends to try the case otherwise than on the evidence; and disclosure by a juror of the deliberations of the jury. The written notice must contain a warning that the penalty for breach of those prohibitions is imprisonment and/or a fine. This is because s.20A of the Juries Act 1974 makes it an offence for a member of a jury 'to research the case during the trial period' (subs.(1)). For this purpose, research means intentionally seeking information, when the juror 'knows or ought reasonably to know that the information is or may be relevant to the case' (subs.(2)). Seeking information includes searching on the internet, visiting or inspecting a place or object, conducting an experiment, or asking another person to seek the information (subs. (3)).

Rule 25.6(4) of the Criminal Procedure Rules states that:

The court must select the jury by drawing at random each juror's name from among those so summoned, and

(a) announcing each name so drawn; or

(b) announcing an identifying number assigned by the court officer to that person, where the court is satisfied that that is necessary.

The ability to identify a juror by using a number, rather than their name, is relevant in cases where there is a fear of possible jury intimidation.

Where a defendant has pleaded not guilty to an indictment, at least 12 members of the jury panel are brought into the court room; they are then known as the 'jury in waiting'. The clerk of the court calls out the names (or numbers) of 12 of them, chosen at random.

Each of the jurors (one after the other) takes the juror's oath, reading the words from a card and holding in his right hand the appropriate Holy Book (New Testament for Christians, Old Testament for Jews, Koran for Muslims). Jurors who do not wish to swear an oath are permitted to make an affirmation instead. Under r.25.6(9), the oath or affirmation taken by each juror is as follows: 'I swear by Almighty God [or I do solemnly, sincerely and truly declare and affirm] that I will faithfully try the defendant and give a true verdict according to the evidence'.

Once all 12 have taken the oath (or affirmed), the clerk reads out the indictment and then says: 'To this indictment the defendant has pleaded not guilty. It is your charge, having heard the evidence, to say whether he be guilty or not'.

If the defendant has pleaded guilty to some of the counts on the indictment, but not guilty to the others, the jury will not be told about the guilty pleas.

10.4.3.1 Starting with more than 12 jurors

Rule 25.6(6) provides that the jury selected must comprise no fewer than 12 jurors and that it may, where the court expects the trial to last for more than four weeks, comprise as many as 14 jurors to begin with. Under r.25.6(7), where the court selects a jury comprising more than 12 jurors, the court must explain to them that:

(a) the purpose of selecting more than 12 jurors to begin with is to fill any vacancy or vacancies caused by the discharge of any of the first 12 before the prosecution evidence begins;

(b) any such vacancy or vacancies will be filled by the extra jurors in order of their selection from the panel;

(c) the court will discharge any extra juror or jurors remaining by no later than the beginning of the prosecution evidence; and

(d) any juror who is discharged for that reason then will be available to be selected for service on another jury, during the period for which that juror has been summoned.

Rule 25.7(2) stipulates that, no later than the beginning of the prosecution evidence, if the jury then comprises more than 12 jurors, the court must discharge any in excess of 12 in reverse order of their selection from the panel.

The provision for having more than 12 jurors at the start of the trial is intended to prevent a trial from collapsing at its early stages because one or more of the jurors have to be discharged (for example, where it becomes apparent during the prosecution opening that one of the jurors is acquainted with a party to the case).

10.4.4 Challenges to jurors

It is possible for would-be jurors to be prevented from sitting on the jury which is to try the defendant.

10.4.4.1 Standing a juror by

The prosecution have a right to challenge a juror without giving reasons; this is known as 'standing the juror by'. To exercise this right, prosecuting counsel simply says 'stand by' just before the juror takes his oath. It is then explained to the juror that he cannot sit on this jury, but will go back to the jury panel and may be called on to try another case.

Under r.25.8(3), a prosecutor who exercises the prosecution right without giving reasons to prevent the court selecting an individual juror must announce the exercise of that right before the juror completes the oath or affirmation.

Guidance issued by the Attorney General, *Jury vetting: right of stand by guidelines* (2012), makes it clear that the right of stand-by should be exercised only in exceptional circumstances.

The judge also has the power to stand a juror by. This power is hardly ever exercised. In R v Ford [1989] QB 868, the Court of Appeal held that a judge must not use this power to try to ensure a racially balanced jury.

Criminal Practice Direction VI, para.26D.2, states that the judge's discretion to discharge a particular juror who ought not to be serving 'but this discretion can only be exercised to prevent an individual juror who is not competent from serving. It does not include a discretion to discharge a jury drawn from particular sections of the community or otherwise to influence the overall composition of the jury'.

10.4.4.2 Challenging for cause

It is open to the prosecution to challenge a juror for cause rather than stand the juror by. However, challenging for cause is the only way in which the defence can challenge a juror.

Rule 25.8(2) provides that a party who objects to the selection of an individual juror must tell the court of the objection after the juror's name or number is announced but before the juror completes the oath or affirmation, and must explain the objection.

To challenge for cause, the advocate says 'challenge' just before the would-be juror takes the oath. The reason for the challenge is then explained to the judge. In a straightforward case, the judge will hear submissions from counsel and, if he agrees with the challenge, will ask the would-be juror to leave the jury box. Otherwise, jurors who have already been sworn in and the rest of the 'jury in waiting' will be asked to leave the courtroom and evidence will be called to substantiate the challenge.

Where it is suspected that the would-be juror might be biased, the question is whether the fair-minded and informed observer, having considered the facts, would conclude that there was a real possibility that the he or she was biased (cf. Porter v Magill [2002] 2 AC 357, per Lord Hope, at [103]).

The challenger must provide prima facie evidence in support of the challenge before being allowed to question the juror (R v Chandler (No 2) [1964] 2 QB 322, per Lord Parker CJ, at p.338).

Questioning of potential jurors will rarely be permitted. In R v Andrews [1999] Crim LR 156, the Court of Appeal said that questioning of jurors (whether done orally or by means of a questionnaire) is of doubtful efficacy and may even be counter-productive (by reminding the jurors of the adverse publicity); it should therefore be done only in the most exceptional circumstances.

10.4.5 Discharge of individual jurors during the trial

Under s.16 of the Juries Act 1974, up to three jurors may be discharged during the course of the trial in case of illness or other reason (for example, bereavement). What constitutes a valid reason is a matter for the trial judge. If more than three jurors can no longer serve, the trial has to be abandoned; a fresh trial will usually take place later.

10.4.6 Discharge of the entire jury

The entire jury may be discharged if, for example:

- The jury hears evidence which is inadmissible and prejudicial to the defendant and the judge decides that a direction to ignore this evidence would not be sufficient. Where something prejudicial to the defendant has inadvertently been admitted in evidence, it is not necessarily the case that the jury should be discharged; whether or not the jury should be discharged is a matter for the discretion of the trial judge (R v Weaver [1968] 1 QB 353). In R v Docherty [1999] 1 Cr App R 274, Roch LJ (at p.280) said that 'the question is whether there is a real danger of injustice occurring because the jury, having heard the prejudicial matter, may be biased'; similarly, in R v Lawson [2005] EWCA Crim 84; [2007] 1 Cr App R 20, Auld LJ (at [65]) said that the 'test is always the same, whether to continue with the trial would or could, by reason of the admission of the unfairly prejudicial material, result in an unsafe conviction'.
- The jury cannot agree on a verdict (see below);
- An individual juror has to be discharged and there is a risk that he may have contaminated the rest of the jury – for example, he happens to know that the defendant has previous convictions which have not been ruled admissible or is facing further trials for other offences (R v Hutton [1990] Crim LR 875).

Where the jury is discharged from giving a verdict, the defendant can be retried, as he is not regarded as having been acquitted.

10.4.6.1 Jury irregularities

Criminal Practice Direction VI, para.6M.2, says that a jury irregularity

> is anything that may prevent one or more jurors from remaining faithful to their oath or affirmation to 'faithfully try the defendant and give a true verdict according to the evidence.' Jury irregularities take many forms. Some are clear-cut such as a juror conducting research about the case or an attempt to suborn or intimidate a juror. Others are less clear-cut – for example, when there is potential bias or friction between jurors.

Paragraph 26M.6 stipulates that a jury irregularity 'should be drawn to the attention of the judge in the absence of the jury as soon as it becomes known'. Paragraph 26M.7 summarises the steps that should be taken thereafter:

Step 1: Consider isolating juror(s)
Step 2: Consult with advocates [in open court, in the presence of the defendant]
Step 3: Consider appropriate provisional measures (which may include surrender/seizure of electronic communications devices and taking defendant into custody)
Step 4: Seek to establish basic facts of jury irregularity
Step 5: Further consult with advocates
Step 6: Decide what to do in relation to conduct of trial
Step 7: Consider ancillary matters (contempt in face of court and/or commission of criminal offence)

As regards the conduct of the trial, there are three possibilities (para.26M.26):

- Take no action and continue with the trial;
- discharge the juror(s) concerned and continue with the trial; or
- discharge the whole jury.

If members of the jury misbehave during the course of the trial, the jury should be discharged if there is a 'real danger' of prejudice to the accused (R v Sawyer (1980) 71 Cr App R 283).

Where a juror has specialised knowledge of something relevant to the case against the defendant, and has communicated that knowledge to the rest of the jury, the judge is obliged to discharge the jury if this comes to light at a stage of the trial such that the defendant has had no opportunity to challenge what amounts to new evidence or to put forward his own explanation (R v Fricker (1999) The Times, 13 July).

10.5 Special measures

The court can adopt a range of measures to help witnesses who might otherwise find it difficult to testify.

10.5.1 Special measures directions

Section 19 of the Youth Justice and Criminal Evidence Act 1999 makes provision for various 'special measures' which the court can direct in respect of certain witnesses (other than the defendant).

By virtue of s.16(1), a witness in criminal proceedings is eligible for assistance if

- under the age of 18 at the time of the hearing; or
- the court considers that the quality of evidence given by the witness is likely to be diminished because the witness
  - suffers from mental disorder within the meaning of the Mental Health Act 1983; or
  - otherwise has a significant impairment of intelligence and social functioning;
  - has a physical disability or is suffering from a physical disorder.

Under s.17(1), a witness is also eligible for assistance:

if the court is satisfied that the quality of evidence given by the witness is likely to be diminished by reason of fear or distress on the part of the witness in connection with testifying in the proceedings.

The special measures under the Act include:

- screening the witness from the accused (s.23);
- giving evidence by live link (s.24);
- giving evidence in private, in a sexual offence case, or where there is a fear that the witness may be intimidated (s.25);
- removal of wigs and gowns (s.26);
- video recording of evidence-in-chief (s.27);
- video recording of cross-examination and re-examination where the evidence-in-chief of the witness has been video recorded (s.28);
- use of an intermediary, to communicate questions to the witness and their answers to the questioner (s.29);
- provision of aids to communication (s.30).

These special measures apply to witnesses other than the accused.

Section 51 of the Criminal Justice Act 2003 provides that a witness (other than the defendant) may, if the court so directs, give evidence through a live link in a trial in the magistrates' court or Crown Court. Section 56(2) defines a 'live link' as a live television link or other arrangement by which a witness, who is not in the building where the proceedings are being held, is able to see and hear, and be seen and heard by, the defendant(s), the justices or the judge and jury, and the legal representatives acting in the proceedings. Under s.51(4), a direction may not be given unless the court is satisfied that it is 'in the interests of the efficient or effective administration of justice for the person concerned to give evidence in the proceedings through a live link'.

Section 137(1) of the Criminal Justice Act 2003 empowers the court to allow a video recording of an interview with a witness (other than the defendant) to be admitted as evidence-in-chief of the witness (that is, to replace live evidence-in-chief of that witness) provided that:

- the offence is triable only on indictment, or a prescribed either-way offence;
- the witness's recollection of the events in question is likely to have been significantly better when he gave the recorded account than it will be when he gives oral evidence in the proceedings, and
- it is in the interests of justice for the recording to be admitted as evidence.

Additionally, s.86 of the Coroners and Justice Act 2009 empowers the court to make a 'witness anonymity order', that is an order 'requiring such specified measures to be taken in relation to a witness in criminal proceedings as the court considers appropriate to ensure that the identity of the witness is not disclosed in or in connection with the proceedings'. Under s.88 (3)–(5), three conditions have to be met:

Condition A is that the proposed order is necessary—

(a) in order to protect the safety of the witness or another person or to prevent any serious damage to property, or

(b) in order to prevent real harm to the public interest (whether affecting the carrying on of any activities in the public interest or the safety of a person involved in carrying on such activities, or otherwise).

Condition B is that, having regard to all the circumstances, the effect of the proposed order would be consistent with the defendant receiving a fair trial.

Condition C is that the importance of the witness's testimony is such that in the interests of justice the witness ought to testify and—

(a) the witness would not testify if the proposed order were not made, or

(b) there would be real harm to the public interest if the witness were to testify without the proposed order being made.

In R v Lubemba [2014] EWCA Crim 2064 the Court of Appeal considered the methods which may be employed to facilitate vulnerable witnesses giving evidence. Hallett LJ quoted extensively from the judgement of the Court of Appeal R v Barker [2010] EWCA Crim 4 (whose approach was adopted in R v Wills [2011] EWCA Crim 1938, [2012] 1 Cr App R 2). Her Ladyship went on (at [42]–[45]):

The court is required to take every reasonable step to encourage and facilitate the attendance of vulnerable witnesses and their participation in the trial process ... [I]t is best practice to hold hearings in advance of the trial to ensure the smooth running of the trial, to give any special measures directions and to set the ground rules for the treatment of a vulnerable witness. We would expect a ground rules hearing in every case involving a vulnerable witness, save in very exceptional circumstances. If there are any doubts on how to proceed, guidance should be sought from those who have the responsibility for looking after the witness and or an expert.

... The ground rules hearing should cover, amongst other matters, the general care of the witness, if, when and where the witness is to be shown their video interview, when, where and how the parties (and the judge if identified) intend to introduce themselves to the witness, the length of questioning and frequency of breaks and the nature of the questions to be asked. So as to avoid any unfortunate misunderstanding at trial, it would be an entirely reasonable step for a judge at the ground rules hearing to invite defence advocates to reduce their questions to writing in advance.

... The trial judge is responsible for controlling questioning and ensuring that vulnerable witnesses and defendants are enabled to give the best evidence they can. The judge has a duty to intervene, therefore, if an advocate's questioning is confusing or inappropriate.

... It is now generally accepted that if justice is to be done to the vulnerable witness and also to the accused, a radical departure from the traditional style of advocacy will be necessary. Advocates must adapt to the witness, not the other way round. They cannot insist upon any supposed right 'to put one's case' or previous inconsistent statements to a vulnerable witness. If there is a right to 'put one's case' (about which we have our doubts) it must be modified for young or vulnerable witnesses. It is perfectly possible to ensure the jury are made aware of the defence case and of significant inconsistencies without intimidation or distressing a witness ...

Rule 3.13(1)(c)(iii) of the Criminal Procedure Rules provides that the Crown Court may hold a pre-trial case management hearing where 'such a hearing is required to set ground rules for the conduct of the questioning of a witness or defendant'. Rule 3.9(7) makes more detailed provision for 'ground rules' hearings, at which the court can give directions for the appropriate treatment and questioning of vulnerable witnesses and defendants:

> Where directions for appropriate treatment and questioning are required, the court must—
> (a) invite representations by the parties and by any intermediary; and
> (b) set ground rules for the conduct of the questioning, which rules may include—
> > (i) a direction relieving a party of any duty to put that party's case to a witness or a defendant in its entirety,
> > (ii) directions about the manner of questioning,
> > (iii) directions about the duration of questioning,
> > (iv) if necessary, directions about the questions that may or may not be asked,
> > (v) where there is more than one defendant, the allocation among them of the topics about which a witness may be asked, and
> > (vi) directions about the use of models, plans, body maps or similar aids to help communicate a question or an answer.

10.5.2 Special measure for defendants

Section 33A(2) of the Youth Justice and Criminal Evidence Act 1999 allows the court (whether the Crown Court or a magistrates' court), on application by the accused, to direct that any evidence given by him should be given via a 'live link'. Before giving a live link direction, the court must be satisfied that it would be in the interests of justice to do so, and:

- if the accused is under the age of 18, that his ability to participate effectively as a witness giving oral evidence is compromised by his 'level of intellectual ability or social functioning', and that use of a live link would enable him to participate more effectively as a witness, whether by improving the quality of his evidence or otherwise (s.33A(4)); or
- if the accused is aged 18 or over, that he is unable to participate effectively in the proceedings effectively as a witness giving oral evidence because he has a mental disorder (within the meaning of the Mental Health Act 1983) or a 'significant impairment of intelligence and social function', and that use of a live link would enable him to participate more effectively as a witness, whether by improving the quality of his evidence or otherwise (s.33A(5)).

Section 33BA of the 1999 Act (not in force at the time of writing) makes provision for the court to give a direction that provides for any examination of the accused to be conducted through an interpreter or intermediary in the same circumstances where a live link direction could be made.

It should also be noted that the court has the power to adopt special measures for an accused independently of the 1999 Act where such steps are necessary to ensure a fair trial (see R (C) v Sevenoaks Youth Court [2009] EWHC 3088 (Admin); [2010] 1 All ER 735). Criminal Practice Direction I, para.3F.12, states that there is no presumption that a defendant will be assisted in this way and so, even where an intermediary would improve the trial process, the appointment of an intermediary to assist the defendant is not mandatory. The court will rarely exercise its inherent powers to direct the appointment of an intermediary but, where a defendant is vulnerable or for some other reason experiences communication or hearing difficulties, such that they need more help to follow the proceedings than their legal representatives are readily able to provide, then the court should 'consider sympathetically any application for the defendant to be accompanied throughout the trial by a support worker or other appropriate companion who can provide that assistance'.

It is regrettable that there is no statutory requirement in force for an intermediary to assist a defendant who has communication difficulties. However, s.33BA of the Youth Justice and Criminal Evidence Act 1999 s.33BA, which makes provision for any examination (i.e. questioning) of the accused to be conducted through an intermediary (to communicate (a) to the accused, questions put to the accused, and (b) to any person asking such questions, the answers given by the accused in reply to them), has not been brought into force. Moreover, its scope quite limited because of its application only to the questioning of the defendant. Some judges may feel that there is a legislative steer that Parliament's view is that intermediaries should have at best a limited role supporting defendants. However, it is submitted that judges and magistrates should give careful consideration to the use of an appropriately qualified intermediary where a defendant has difficulties communicating or understanding the proceedings, not just for the questioning of the defendant but throughout the trial, where that is necessary in order to safeguard the fairness of the trial.

10.6 The trial

In this section, we examine the stages of a Crown Court trial.

10.6.1 An outline of trial

Rule 25.9(2) of the Criminal Procedure Rules sets out the procedure to be followed where the defendant pleads not guilty. It provides that, in the following sequence:

(a) where there is a jury, the court must:
  (i) inform the jurors of each offence charged in the indictment to which the defendant pleads not guilty, and
  (ii) explain to the jurors that it is their duty, after hearing the evidence, to decide whether the defendant is guilty or not guilty of each offence;
(b) the prosecutor may summarise the prosecution case;
(c) where there is a jury, to help the jurors to understand the case and resolve any issue in it the court may:
  (i) invite the defendant concisely to identify what is in issue, if necessary in terms approved by the court,
  (ii) if the defendant declines to do so, direct that the jurors be given a copy of any defence statement served under rule 15.4 (Defence disclosure), edited if necessary to exclude any reference to inappropriate matters or to matters evidence of which would not be admissible;
(d) the prosecutor must introduce the evidence on which the prosecution case relies;
(e) ... at the end of the prosecution evidence, on the defendant's application or on its own initiative, the court:
  (i) may direct the jury (if there is one) to acquit on the ground that the prosecution evidence is insufficient for any reasonable court properly to convict, but
  (ii) must not do so unless the prosecutor has had an opportunity to make representations;
(f) ... at the end of the prosecution evidence, the court must ask whether the defendant intends to give evidence in person and, if the answer is 'no', then the court must satisfy

itself that there has been explained to the defendant, in terms the defendant can understand (with help, if necessary):

    (i)   the right to give evidence in person, and

    (ii) that if the defendant does not give evidence in person, or refuses to answer a question while giving evidence, the court may draw such inferences as seem proper;

(g) the defendant may summarise the defence case, if he or she intends to call at least one witness other than him or herself to give evidence in person about the facts of the case;

(h) in this order (or in a different order, if the court so directs) the defendant may:

    (i)   give evidence in person,

    (ii) call another witness, or witnesses, to give evidence in person, and introduce any other evidence;

(i) a party may introduce further evidence if it is then admissible (for example, because it is in rebuttal of evidence already introduced);

(j) the prosecutor may make final representations, where

    (i)   the defendant has a legal representative,

    (ii) the defendant has called at least one witness, other than the defendant him or herself, to give evidence in person about the facts of the case, or

    (iii) the court so permits; and

(k) the defendant may make final representations.

Under r.25.9(5), where there is more than one defendant, this procedure applies to each of them in the order in which their names appear in the indictment, or in an order directed by the court.

10.6.1 Witnesses waiting to testify

Rule 25.11(2) of the Criminal Procedure Rules requires that, unless the court otherwise directs, a witness waiting to give evidence must not wait inside the courtroom, unless that witness is either a party or an expert witness.

10.6.2 The start of the trial: preliminary directions to the jury

At the start of the trial the judge should give some general instructions to the jury. According to Criminal Practice Direction VI, para.26G.3, guidance should always be given on:

    (i)   The need to try the case only on the evidence and remain faithful to their oath or affirmation;

    (ii) The prohibition on internet searches for matters related to the trial, issues arising or the parties;

    (iii) The importance of not discussing any aspect of the case with anyone outside their own number or allowing anyone to talk to them about it, whether directly, by telephone, through internet facilities such as Facebook or Twitter or in any other way;

    (iv) The importance of taking no account of any media reports about the case;

    (v) The collective responsibility of the jury ...;

    (vi) The need to bring any concerns, including concerns about the conduct of other jurors, to the attention of the judge at the time, and not to wait until the case is concluded ...

10.6.3 Prosecution opening speech

Once the jury has been empanelled, the prosecution present their case. Counsel for the prosecution begins by making an opening speech, summarising the case against the accused.

Criminal Practice Direction VI, para.25A.1, says that the prosecution opening speech should 'set out for the jury the principal issues in the trial, and the evidence which is to be introduced in support of the prosecution case', and that the purpose is 'to help the jury understand what the case concerns, not necessarily to present a detailed account of all the prosecution evidence due to be introduced'.

In R v *Lashley* [2005] EWCA Crim 2016, Judge LJ (at [13]) said that the

> presumption should be that an opening address by counsel for the Crown should not address the law, save in cases of real complication and difficulty where counsel believes and the trial judge agrees that the jury may be assisted by a brief and well-focused submission.

10.6.4 Defence confirmation of the issues

After the prosecution speech, the defence may (where appropriate) be called upon to clarify the issues in the case. Criminal Practice Direction VI, para.25A.2, states that the purpose is to 'provide the jury with focus as to the issues that they are likely to be called upon to decide, so that jurors will be alert to those issues from the outset and can evaluate the prosecution evidence that they hear accordingly'. This may be unnecessary if, for example, the case is 'such that the issues are apparent', or the prosecutor 'has given a fair, accurate and comprehensive account of the issues in opening, rendering repetition superfluous' (para.26A.4).

Paragraph 25A.3 goes on to say that, at this point, the judge may give appropriate directions about the law (for example, as to what features of the prosecution evidence they should look out for in a case in which what is in issue is the identification of the defendant by an eye-witness). 'Giving such directions at the outset is another means by which the jury can be helped to focus on the significant features of the evidence, in the interests of a fair and effective trial.'

10.6.5 Prosecution evidence

The prosecution evidence may take a variety of forms.

10.6.5.1 Formal admissions

If the defendant pleads not guilty, the prosecution are put to proof of their entire case, and so must adduce evidence on all the elements of the alleged offence(s). The only exception to this rule is where the defence make a 'formal admission' so that something that would otherwise be an issue is no longer an issue.

Under s.10 of the Criminal Justice Act 1967, the prosecution or the defence (in practice, it is usually the defence) may admit any fact that would otherwise be an issue; this admission is conclusive evidence of the fact admitted. If, for example, the defendant is charged with causing death by dangerous driving, he might admit that he was driving the car at the time of the accident. Under r.25.13, a written record must be made of the admission.

10.6.5.2 Prosecution witnesses

Rule 25.11(4) sets out the process for eliciting evidence from the witness. It provides that, in the following sequence:

> (a) the party who calls a witness may ask questions in examination-in-chief;
> (b) if the witness gives evidence for the prosecution—

(i) the defendant, if there is only one, may ask questions in cross-examination, or

(ii) subject to the court's directions, each defendant, if there is more than one, may ask such questions, in the order their names appear in the indictment or as directed by the court;

...

(d) the party who called the witness may ask questions in re-examination arising out of any cross-examination.

The prosecution witnesses whose written statements the defence do not allow to be read to the court each give evidence in turn. Evidence is usually given under oath, the witness saying, 'I swear by almighty God that the evidence I shall give shall be the truth, the whole truth, and nothing but the truth'. A witness who does not wish to take the oath may affirm instead, promising to tell the truth.

Each witness is examined-in-chief by the prosecution, then cross-examined by the defence, and (if necessary) re-examined by the prosecution.

In R v Butt [2005] EWCA Crim 805, Dyson LJ (at [10]) said that, although defence counsel has a duty to present the defence fearlessly, there is also an obligation to avoid repetition and prolixity, and to discriminate between relevant and irrelevant matters. The judge is therefore entitled to impose a time limit on cross-examination.

Section 139(1) of the Criminal Justice Act 2003 provides that a person giving oral evidence in criminal proceedings may, at any stage in the course of doing so, 'refresh his memory of it from a document made or verified by him at an earlier time' provided that:

(a) he states in his oral evidence that the document records his recollection of the matter at that earlier time; and

(b) his recollection of the matter is likely to have been significantly better at that time than it is at the time of his oral evidence.

This is invariably done to enable police officers to refer to their notebooks while giving evidence, but any witness who satisfies the criteria in s.139 may refresh their memory in accordance with its provisions.

10.6.5.3 Reading witness statements with the consent of the defence

Section 9(1) of the Criminal Justice Act 1967 provides that a written statement is admissible in evidence as if it were oral testimony provided that the requirements set out in subs.(2) are satisfied, namely:

- the statement is signed by the maker;
- the statement contains a declaration by that person to the effect that it is true to the best of his knowledge and belief and that he made the statement knowing that, if it is tendered in evidence, he will be liable to prosecution if he wilfully stated in it anything which he knew to be false or did not believe to be true;
- a copy of the statement has been served on each of the other parties to the proceedings; and
- none of the other parties objects to the statement being tendered in evidence.

This very useful provision will be invoked, for example, where the defence in a theft case is not that the property was not stolen but that the defendant was not the thief; the evidence of the loser of the property, saying that the property is his and that he gave no one permission to take it, will not therefore be disputed by the defence and so the written statement of the loser will be read out to the court.

Under r.25.12, where the court permits a party to introduce in evidence the written statement of a witness, each relevant part of the statement must be read or summarised aloud, unless the court otherwise directs.

The judge should direct the jury that a statement read out under this provision has the same evidential value as 'live' testimony.

10.6.5.4 Reading witness statements without the consent of the defence

Section 116 of the Criminal Justice Act 2003 makes provision for the reading of witness statements, without the consent of the defence, in cases where the witness is unavailable. Under s.116(2) this applies where the witness:

- is dead;
- is 'unfit to be a witness because of his bodily or mental condition';
- is outside the United Kingdom and it is not reasonably practicable to secure his attendance;
- cannot be found although such steps as it is reasonably practicable to take to find him have been taken;
- is not testifying because of 'fear', and the court gives leave for the statement to be given in evidence:
  - under s.116(3), fear 'is to be widely construed and (for example) includes fear of the death or injury of another person or of financial loss';
  - under s.116(4), leave can be given on basis of fear only if the court considers that the statement ought to be admitted in the interests of justice, having regard to any risk that its admission or exclusion will result in unfairness to any party to the proceedings (and in particular to how difficult it will be to challenge the statement if the witness does not give oral evidence) and to the fact that a special measures direction might be available under s.19 of the Youth Justice and Criminal Evidence Act 1999.

Where it is asserted that the witness is not testifying through fear, that fear must be proved by admissible evidence (*Neill v North Antrim Magistrates' Court* [1992] 1 WLR 1220; *R v Belmarsh Magistrates' Court ex p Gilligan* [1998] 1 Cr App R 14).

Where a statement is read to the jury without the consent of the defence, the jury should be warned that the evidence needs to be viewed in light of the fact that the defence have not had the opportunity to cross-examine the witness. It is not sufficient simply to draw the jury's attention to the fact that evidence has been given by way of a witness statement. The jury should be warned to use particular care when considering the witness statement, since the maker of the statement was not in court to be cross-examined as to its contents. Where the witness statement is vital to the prosecution case, failure to give such a direction will render any subsequent conviction unsafe (*R v Curry* (1998) *The Times*, 23 March).

The Crown Court Compendium (Part 14-1) says that a jury should be directed that hearsay evidence may suffer from the following limitations when compared with evidence given on oath by a witness at trial.

(a) There has usually been no opportunity to see the demeanour of the person who made the statement.

(b) The statement admitted as hearsay was not made on oath.

(c) There has been no opportunity to see the witness's account tested under cross-examination, for example as to accuracy, truthfulness, ambiguity or misperception, and how the witness would have responded to this process. In some cases the credibility of the absent witness and/or their consistency will have been challenged under s.124 of the Act. In such cases the jury needs to be reminded of those challenges and of any discrepancies or weaknesses revealed.

10.6.5.5 Real evidence

Real evidence means tangible evidence such as the murder weapon or the stolen goods. An item of real evidence has to be 'produced' (that is, formally identified and its relevance established) by a witness. Once this has been done, the advocate says to the judge 'may this be exhibit [number]?' and (assuming the judge agrees) the item then becomes an exhibit in the case. Exhibits are numbered sequentially.

10.6.5.6 Witnesses whom the prosecution must call

The prosecution must call all the witnesses whose statements were served on the defence when the case was sent to the Crown Court. However, there are some exceptions (R v Russell-Jones [1995] 1 Cr App R 538, per Kennedy LJ, at pp.544–5), namely where:

- the defence consent to the written statement of the witness being read to the court; or
- the prosecution take the view that the witness is no longer credible; or
- the witness would so fundamentally contradict the prosecution case that it would be better for that witness to be called by the defence.

If one witness duplicates the evidence of another, the prosecution may simply 'tender' that witness for cross-examination; in other words, call the witness, establish his identity and relevance to the case, and then invite the defence to cross-examine. This is often done with police witnesses, where the evidence of one officer largely replicates that of another.

10.6.5.7 Expert evidence

Rule r.19.2(1)(a) of the Criminal Procedure Rules states that an expert must help the court to achieve the overriding objective by giving opinion which is (i) objective and unbiased, and (ii) within the expert's area or areas of expertise. Rule 19.2(2) makes it clear that the expert's duty to the court overrides any obligation to the person from whom the expert receives instructions or by whom the expert is paid. Rule 19.2(3) goes on to say that the expert must define his/her area(s) of expertise and must, when giving evidence in person, to draw the court's attention to any question to which the answer would be outside the expert's area(s) of expertise.

In R v Harris [2005] EWCA Crim 1980, Gage LJ (at [271]) said this:

> It may be helpful for judges, practitioners and experts to be reminded of the obligations of an expert witness summarised by Cresswell J in the Ikerian Reefer [1993] 2 Lloyds Rep 68 at p.81. Cresswell J pointed out amongst other factors the following, which we summarise as follows:
>
> (1) Expert evidence presented to the court should be and be seen to be the independent product of the expert uninfluenced as to form or content by the exigencies of litigation.
>
> (2) An expert witness should provide independent assistance to the court by way of objective unbiased opinion in relation to matters within his expertise. An expert witness in the High Court should never assume the role of advocate.
>
> (3) An expert witness should state the facts or assumptions on which his opinion is based. He should not omit to consider material facts which detract from his concluded opinions.
>
> (4) An expert should make it clear when a particular question or issue falls outside his expertise.
>
> (5) If an expert's opinion is not properly researched because he considers that insufficient data are available then this must be stated with an indication that the opinion is no more than a provisional one.

(6) If after exchange of reports, an expert witness changes his view on material matters, such change of view should be communicated to the other side without delay and when appropriate to the court.

The content of the expert report is governed by r.19.4.

10.6.6 Challenging the admissibility of prosecution evidence

In this section we consider how the admissibility of prosecution evidence may be challenged. Two key provisions require examination: s.76 and s.78 of the Police and Criminal Evidence Act 1984.

10.6.6.1 Confessions: s.76 of PACE

Section 76(2) of PACE provides:

> If, in any proceedings where the prosecution proposes to give in evidence a confession made by an accused person, it is represented to the court that the confession was or may have been obtained –
> (a) by oppression of the person who made it; or
> (b) in consequence of anything said or done which was likely, in the circumstances existing at the time, to render unreliable any confession which might be made by him in consequence thereof,
>
> the court shall not allow the confession to be given in evidence against him except in so far as the prosecution proves to the court beyond reasonable doubt that the confession (notwithstanding that it may be true) was not obtained as aforesaid.

Subsection (8) defines 'oppression' as including 'torture, inhuman or degrading treatment, and the use or threat of violence (whether or not amounting to torture)'.

A number of important points should be noted about s.76:

- Section 76 applies only to confessions;
- the defendant merely has to 'represent' that the confession was obtained in the manner forbidden by s.76; in other words, the defendant bears only an 'evidential' burden to raise the issue;
- if the defendant does raise the issue that the confession was obtained in the manner forbidden by s.76, the prosecution then have to prove beyond reasonable doubt that the confession was not so obtained;
  - this is a 'legal' burden of proof and so it has to be discharged through calling evidence.

Where s.76 is invoked during the course of a trial, a *voir dire* ('trial within a trial') takes place.

Unless the witness is in the middle of giving (or has already given) evidence in the course of the trial, a witness giving evidence on a *voir dire* takes a special form of oath: 'I swear by almighty God that I will answer truthfully all such questions as the court may ask.'

Each prosecution witness called in the *voir dire* may be cross-examined by the defence. When the relevant prosecution witnesses have given evidence, the defence may then call evidence (including the evidence of the defendant himself); each defence witness may be cross-examined by the prosecution.

It should be noted that the questioning must be confined to the obtaining of the question. For these purposes, it is irrelevant whether the confession is true or not.

After the evidence has been called, both advocates may address the judge and the judge then rules on the admissibility of the confession. Where the judge is satisfied beyond reasonable doubt that the confession was not obtained improperly, and so rules that the confession is admissible, the jury should not be told of the ruling (the trial should simply continue with the prosecution calling evidence of the confession); if the judge indicates that he has ruled against the accused, this might lead the jury to think that the judge does not believe the accused.

10.6.6.2 Unfairness: s.78 of PACE

Section 78(1) of PACE provides:

> In any proceedings the court may refuse to allow evidence on which the prosecution proposes to rely to be given if it appears to the court that, having regard to all the circumstances, including the circumstances in which the evidence was obtained, the admission of the evidence would have such an adverse effect on the fairness of the proceedings that the court ought not to admit it.

Key points to note are:

- Section 78 (unlike s.76) applies to any prosecution evidence, not just confessions;
- Where the defence object to prosecution evidence on the ground that its admission would be unfair, this objection is made in the absence of the jury but need not involve the judge hearing evidence. In other words, a *voir dire* need not take place if the judge is able to decide the question of admissibility under s.78 just by hearing legal argument from the advocates and without hearing evidence. This will be the case, for example, where the breach of provisions of the Codes of Practice made under PACE are apparent from the custody record and/or the witness statements of the prosecution witnesses and the judge merely has to decide the effect of those breaches.

Section 78 is sometimes described as conferring an exclusionary discretion. This is, however, not entirely accurate. If the judge decides that it would be unfair to allow the evidence in question to be adduced, that evidence must be ruled inadmissible. In other words, this is an exercise of judgment rather than discretion.

10.7 Submission of no case to answer

After the close of the prosecution case, the defence may make a submission that there is no case to answer. This submission is made in the absence of the jury, who might otherwise be prejudiced against the defendant if the submission fails (R v Smith (1987) 85 Cr App R 197; Crosdale v R [1995] 1 WLR 864).

Under r.25.9(2)(e)(i), this submission is made on the ground that 'the prosecution evidence is insufficient for any reasonable court properly to convict'. In R v Galbraith [1981] 1 WLR 1039, it was held (per Lord Lane CJ, at p.1042):

> (1) If there is no evidence that the crime alleged has been committed by the defendant, there is no difficulty. The judge will of course stop the case. (2) The difficulty arises where there is some evidence but it is of a tenuous character, for example because of inherent weakness or vagueness or because it is inconsistent with other evidence. (a) Where the judge comes to the conclusion that the prosecution evidence, taken at its highest, is such that a jury properly directed could not properly convict upon it, it is his duty, upon a submission being made, to stop the case. (b) Where however the prosecution evidence is such that its strength or weakness depends on the view to be taken of a witness's reliability, or other matters which are generally speaking within the province of the jury and where on one possible view of the facts there is evidence upon which a jury could properly come to the conclusion that the defendant is guilty, then the judge should allow the matter to be tried by the jury.

Two key principles flow from *Galbraith*:

- If the judge comes to the conclusion that the prosecution evidence, taken at its highest, is such that a jury, properly directed, could not properly convict upon it, the judge must rule that there is no case to answer; and
- If the strength or weakness of the prosecution evidence depends on the view to be taken of a witness's reliability, and on one possible view there is evidence on which a jury could properly convict, the judge should allow the matter to be tried by the jury.

Thus, a judge should only accept a submission of no case to answer in a clear case; otherwise the judge is trespassing on the function of the jury.

The phrase 'taken at its highest' is generally taken to require the judge to assume that the prosecution witnesses are telling the truth. However, in R v *Shippey* [1988] Crim LR 767, for example, Turner J found no case to answer in a rape trial because of 'really significant inherent inconsistencies' in the complainant's uncorroborated evidence, which his Lordship found 'frankly incredible'. It had been conceded by the defence that there was undoubtedly some evidence that went to support the prosecution case. However, the judge agreed that taking the prosecution case at its highest did not mean 'picking out the plums and leaving the duff behind'. Rather, the judge held that he must assess the evidence as a whole. It would, he said, not be right to interpret *Galbraith* as saying that if there are parts of the evidence which support the charge, then no matter what the state of the rest of the evidence, that is enough to leave the matter to the jury.

It is clear from this that the case must not be withdrawn from the jury simply because the judge doubts whether the principal prosecution witnesses are telling the truth, since that would be to usurp the function of the jury. However, the judge is entitled to rule that there is no case to answer if he takes the view that no reasonable jury could find that the prosecution witnesses are telling the truth. If that is so, there would, of course, be no point in leaving the case to them, since they would inevitably acquit.

It follows that the judge can have regard to:

- the sheer improbability of what a witness says;
- internal inconsistencies in the testimony of a particular witness; and
- inconsistencies between one prosecution witness and another.

In R v *Pryer* [2004] EWCA Crim 1163, Hooper LJ said (at [27]) that *Shippey* is a decision on the facts, not a decision on the law. However, as Keene LJ said in R v *Broadhead* [2006] EWCA Crim 1705 (at [17]):

> The judge's task in considering such a submission at the end of the prosecution's case is to assess the prosecution's evidence as a whole. He has to take into account the weaknesses of the evidence as well as such strengths as there are.

The essential point is that the testimony of a 'good' witness will not usually be nullified merely because other witnesses are poor or incredible; similarly, a jury might sometimes have reason to believe one part of a witness's testimony without necessarily believing another part of it. In R v *Goring* [2011] EWCA Crim 2, Leveson LJ (at [37]) pointed out that the fact that a witness called by the Crown gives evidence in some respects inconsistent with the inferential case being advanced by the Crown cannot, by itself, be determinative of a submission of no case to answer, although it is a factor to be taken into account.

In R v *Vaid* [2015] EWCA Crim 298, Gross LJ (at [20]) noted that when considering (pursuant to *Galbraith*) whether the prosecution evidence, taken at its highest, is such that a jury properly directed could properly convict on it, 'the question is whether a reasonable jury could, on one possible view of the evidence, reject all realistic possibilities consistent with innocence, not whether all reasonable juries would do so'.

In R v *Darnley* [2012] EWCA Crim 1148, Elias LJ (at [21]) said:

> [T]he focus should be on the traditional question, namely whether there was evidence on which a jury, properly directed, could infer guilt. It is an easier test, not least because it focuses on what a reasonable jury could do rather than what it could not do. Reasonable juries may differ because the assessment of the facts is not simply a logical exercise and different views may reasonably be taken about the weight to be given to potentially relevant evidence. The judge must be alive to that when considering a half-time application. Of course, if the judge is satisfied that even on the view of the facts most favourable to the prosecution no reasonable jury could convict, then the case should be stopped.

In R v *Sardar* [2016] EWCA Crim 1616; [2017] 1 WLR 917, Sir Brian Leveson P (at [17]) cited with approval the decision of the Supreme Court of South Australia, in *Questions of Law Reserved on Acquittal* (No 2 of 1993) (1993) 61 SASR 1, where King CJ had said:

> [I]t is not the function of the judge in considering a submission of no case to choose between inferences which are reasonably open to the jury. He must decide upon the basis that the jury will draw such of the inferences which are reasonably open, as are most favourable to the prosecution. . . . Neither is it any part of his function to decide whether any possible hypotheses consistent with innocence are reasonably open on the evidence. . . . He is concerned only with whether a reasonable jury could reach a conclusion of guilty beyond reasonable doubt and therefore exclude any competing hypothesis as not reasonably open on the evidence.
>
> I would re-state the principles, in summary form, as follows. If there is direct evidence which is capable of proving the charge, there is a case to answer no matter how weak or tenuous the judge might consider such evidence to be. If the case depends upon circumstantial evidence, and that evidence, if accepted, is capable of producing in a reasonable mind a conclusion of guilt beyond reasonable doubt and thus is capable of causing a reasonable mind to exclude any competing hypotheses as unreasonable, there is a case to answer. There is no case to answer only if the evidence is not capable in law of supporting a conviction. In a circumstantial case, that implies that even if all the evidence for the prosecution was accepted and all inferences most favourable to the prosecution which are reasonably open were drawn, a reasonable mind could not reach a conclusion of guilty beyond reasonable doubt, or to put it another way, could not exclude all hypotheses consistent with innocence, as not reasonably open on the evidence.

The rationale for the submission of no case to answer is based on the desirability of removing the need for the defence to present its case where the prosecution case appears doomed to failure. This spares the accused the stress of testifying (and the risk of incriminating himself during the course of the defence case), and reduces the time spent on the case (and therefore the cost). However, it is submitted that it is only appropriate to stop a case at 'half time' if the prosecution case is clearly doomed. If the judge is uncertain whether or not there is a case to answer, the presumption should be that the case will continue and the jury be given the opportunity to decide on guilt or innocence.

It should be noted that where identification is an issue, special rules apply. In R v *Turnbull* [1977] QB 224, Lord Widgery CJ (at p.229–30) said:

> When, in the judgment of the trial judge, the quality of the identifying evidence is poor, as for example when it depends solely on a fleeting glance or on a longer observation made in difficult conditions, the situation is very different. The judge should then withdraw the case

from the jury and direct an acquittal unless there is other evidence which goes to support the correctness of the identification.

If the submission of no case to answer succeeds in respect of all the counts being tried, the judge directs the jury to acquit the defendant on all those counts. If the submission fails on all counts, the trial proceeds and the jury know nothing about the making of the submission. If the submission succeeds on some, but not all, of the counts in the indictment, the trial of those counts in respect of which the judge has found there to be a case to answer continues; the jury are told that they are to consider only the counts that are left, and a formal acquittal on those counts where the submission succeeded will be directed when the jury give their verdict on the remaining counts.

The Court of Appeal has cautioned against the tactical use of submissions of no case to answer. If defence counsel notices a procedural error on the part of the prosecution, he should take the point at the outset, and not wait until the close of the prosecution case. In R v *Gleeson* [2003] EWCA Crim 3357; [2004] 1 Cr App R 29, Auld LJ (at [35]) said:

> For defence advocates to seek to take advantage of such errors by deliberately delaying identification of an issue of fact or law in the case until the last possible moment is ... no longer acceptable.

The importance of the defence raising issues at an early stage, and not leaving it until the close of the prosecution case, was reiterated in R v *Penner* [2010] EWCA Crim 1155, per Thomas LJ (at [16]–[19]).

In R v *Powell* [2006] EWCA Crim 685, Moore-Bick LJ (at [19]) said that where a submission of no case to answer is made but rejected, the judge should give brief reasons for deciding that there is sufficient evidence to go before a jury.

10.7.1 Acquittal by judge of his own motion

The judge can order an acquittal of his own motion (in other words, without the need for a submission of no case to answer). However, in *Attorney General's Reference (No 2 of 2000)* [2001] 1 Cr App R 36, the Court of Appeal held that where a prosecution has been properly brought (that is, it is not an 'abuse of process'), a trial judge has no power to prevent the prosecution from calling evidence, or to direct the jury to acquit, simply on the basis that he thinks a conviction is unlikely.

In R v *Brown* [2001] EWCA Crim 961; [2002] 1 Cr App R 5, the Court of Appeal held that a Crown Court judge is entitled to rule, even at the end of the defence case, that there is no case to go before the jury if there is no evidence on a count or if no reasonable jury could convict on the evidence available. A judge is under a duty to keep under review the question whether a properly directed jury could convict at the close of evidence before leaving the matter to the jury. However, the judge's power to rule that there is no case to go before the jury should be exercised 'very sparingly' and 'only if the judge really is satisfied that no reasonable jury, properly directed, could on the evidence safely convict' (per Longmore J, at [12]).

10.8 The defence case

If there is no submission of no case to answer, or a submission is made and the judge finds a case to answer in respect of some or all of the counts, evidence may then be adduced on behalf of the defendant.

Counsel for the defence may begin the defence case by making an opening speech if he proposes to call one or more witnesses (other than the defendant) as to the facts. If the only witness as to the facts is the defendant (that is, only the defendant gives evidence or there is evidence only from the defendant and one or more character witnesses) there will be no defence opening speech. This is apparent from r.25.9(2)(g), and also from s.2 of the Criminal Evidence Act 1898, which provides:

> Where the only witness to the facts of the case called by the defence is the person charged, he shall be called as a witness immediately after the close of the evidence for the prosecution.

10.8.1 Defence evidence

Where there is more than one defence witness, including the defendant, the defendant must give evidence first unless the court otherwise directs (s.79 of PACE). Each defence witness (including the defendant himself, if he chooses to give evidence) is liable to be cross-examined by the prosecution and may then be re-examined by defence counsel, if necessary. Rule 25.11(4)(c) states that if a witness gives evidence for a defendant:

> (i) subject to the court's directions, each other defendant, if there is more than one, may ask questions in cross-examination, in the order their names appear in the indictment or as directed by the court, and
>
> (ii) the prosecutor may ask such questions.

The defendant is not obliged to testify. However, s.35 of the Criminal Justice and Public Order Act 1994 enables the jury 'to draw such inferences as appear proper from his failure to give evidence or his refusal, without good cause, to answer any question'. Section 35 requires that the defendant be warned that adverse inferences may be drawn from his silence unless he (or his advocate) has informed the court that he will give evidence.

In R v Bevan (1994) 98 Cr App R 354, the Court of Appeal said that if the defendant chooses not to give evidence in his own defence, counsel should make sure that this decision is recorded (usually, this will be done by an endorsement on the brief). Watkins LJ said (at p.358) that:

> it should be the invariable practice of counsel to have that decision recorded and to cause the defendant to sign the record, giving a clear indication that (1) he has by his own will decided not to give evidence and (2) that he has so decided bearing in mind the advice, if any, given to him by his counsel.

10.9 Closing speeches

Once all the defence evidence has been called, both counsel may generally make a closing speech. The prosecution make the first speech (although prosecuting counsel may decide not to make a speech if the trial has been a very short one).

Rule 25.9(2)(j) states that the prosecutor may make final representations if the defendant has a legal representative, or the defendant has called at least one witness (apart from his own testimony) about the facts of the case, or the court so permits. The latter proviso is important as it gives a degree of flexibility.

However, r.25.9 does encapsulate the effect of earlier case law, where it was held that, if the accused is unrepresented and either calls no evidence at all or else was himself the only witness as to the facts, then the prosecution have no right to make a closing speech (R v Mondon (1968) 52 Cr App R 695); R v Paul [2013] EWCA Crim 978; [2013] 2 Cr App R 26). In R v Cojan [2014] EWCA Crim 2512; [2015] 2 Cr App R 20, the court referred to Paul. Hallett LJ noted (at [12]) that the court in that case had considered that, despite any breach of a rule or 'convention' about the prosecution advocate not being entitled to make a closing speech, the verdicts were nonetheless safe on the basis that the strength of the evidence against the defendant. Her Ladyship went on to say (at [12]):

> [W]e share the doubts of the court in Paul as to whether there is still any rule that prosecuting counsel may not make a closing speech where the accused is unrepresented ... In any event, we are not prepared to contemplate a rule, the effect of which would be to enable an accused deliberately to dispense with the services of his representatives so as to prevent prosecuting counsel making a closing speech in an appropriate case.

Hallett LJ went on to say (at [13]) that the court preferred:

> to approach the matter as an issue of balance and fairness. It is the overriding duty of any trial judge to ensure that an accused has a fair trial. As part of that duty it would be incumbent upon a trial judge, faced with an unrepresented accused, to assess all the circumstances of the case and decide whether or not it would be fair to allow prosecuting counsel to make a speech.

Where the prosecutor does make a closing speech, s.1(b) of the Criminal Procedure (Right of Reply) Act 1964 requires that such a speech must 'be after the close of the evidence for the defence and before the closing speech (if any) by or on behalf of the accused'.

Thus, the prosecutor has the first closing speech and the defence advocate has the last word before the judge's summing up.

10.10 Variation in procedure where there is more than one defendant

The procedure adopted where there is more than one defendant depends on whether or not the defendants are separately represented.

10.10.1 Defendants separately represented

Where two or more defendants are charged in the same indictment and are separately represented, their cases are presented in the order in which their names appear on the indictment:

| Regina | v | D1 |
| | | D2 |

Each prosecution witness is cross-examined first on behalf of D1, then on behalf of D2. The defence case is then presented as follows:

- Opening speech on behalf of D1.
- D1 called as a witness (if he chooses to give evidence):
  - examination-in-chief by his own counsel;
  - cross-examination on behalf of D2;

- ○ cross-examination by prosecution;
- ○ re-examination by his own counsel (if necessary).
- Any witnesses called on behalf of D1 give evidence; the order of questioning is the same as above.
- Opening speech on behalf of D2.
- D2 called as a witness (if he chooses to give evidence):
  - ○ examination-in-chief by his own counsel;
  - ○ cross-examination on behalf of D1;
  - ○ cross-examination by prosecution;
  - ○ re-examination by his own counsel (if necessary).
- Any witnesses called on behalf of D2 give evidence; the order of questioning is the same as above.
- Prosecution closing speech.
- Closing speech on behalf of D1.
- Closing speech on behalf of D2.

10.10.2 Defendants jointly represented

If the defendants are jointly represented, they are regarded as presenting a joint defence. Consequently, the defence case will be presented as follows:

- a single opening speech on behalf of all the defendants;
- D1 gives evidence if he wishes to do so;
- D2 gives evidence if he wishes to do so;
- any other defence witnesses give evidence;
- prosecution closing speech;
- closing speech on behalf of all defendants.

10.11 The judge's directions to the jury

After the prosecution and defence counsel have made their closing speeches, the judge sums the case up to the jury. The judge must do this in all cases, however simple the case may seem. Although traditionally the judge produces the summing up without reference to counsel, in *R v Taylor* [2003] EWCA Crim 2447, Latham LJ (at [16]) said that where complex directions are to be given to the jury, counsel in the case should be permitted to consider and comment upon the draft directions before the judge addresses the jury.

Traditionally, the directions to the jury were given at the end of the trial, in the judge's summing up. However, the Criminal Procedure Rules and Criminal Practice Directions have introduced greater flexibility. Rule 25.14(2) requires the court to 'give the jury directions about the relevant law at any time at which to do so will assist jurors to evaluate the evidence'. Such directions may be given at any stage of the trial, not just in the summing up. Criminal Practice Direction VI, para.26K.10, gives some examples of where an 'early direction' might be appropriate before:

- identification evidence in a case where identification is in issue;
- expert evidence;
- evidence of bad character;
- hearsay evidence.

The purpose of such an 'early direction' is to help the jury evaluate the evidence as they hear it.

10.11.1 The summing up to the jury

Useful guidance on the summing up may be found in the *Crown Court Compendium, Part I: Jury and Trial Management and Summing Up* (Judicial College, June 2018)

Rule 25.14(3) goes on to set out the contents of the judge's summing up to the jury and subsequent stages of the trial. It provides that the court must:

- summarise for the jury, to such extent as is necessary, the evidence relevant to the issues they must decide;
- give the jury such questions, if any, as the court invites jurors to answer in coming to a verdict;
- direct the jury to retire to consider its verdict;
- if necessary, recall the jury to answer jurors' questions;
- if appropriate, recall the jury to give directions for a verdict by a majority; and
- recall the jury when it informs the court that it has reached a verdict.

Under r.25.14(4), the court may give the jury directions, questions or other assistance in writing.

Some matters should be dealt with in every summing up; others only have to be dealt with if they are relevant in the particular case.

The summary of the evidence referred to in r.25.14 requires a 'summary of the nature of the evidence relating to each issue', and a 'balanced account of the points raised by the parties' (Criminal Practice Direction VI, para.26K.21).

The reference in r.25.14 to questions that may be put to the jury relates to what is sometimes known as a 'route to verdict'; it poses a series of questions the answers to which will lead the jury to their verdict. Criminal Practice Direction VI, para.26K.12, says that, unless the case is so straightforward that it would be superfluous to do so, the judge should provide a written route to verdict, which may be presented (on paper or digitally) in the form of 'text, bullet points, a flowchart or other graphic'. Sir Brian Leveson in his *Review of Efficiency in Criminal Proceedings* (2015) had (at paras 307–8) recommended as follows:

> The Judge should devise and put to the jury a series of written factual questions, the answers to which logically lead to an appropriate verdict in the case. Each question should be tailored to the law as the Judge understands it to be and to the issues and evidence in the case.
>
> These questions – the 'route to verdict' – should be clear enough that the defendant (and the public) may understand the basis for the verdict that has been reached.

The *Crown Court Compendium*, at 1–7, says:

> The provision of written materials to jurors has two main benefits. First, and most importantly, there is now clear evidence that juror understanding and recollection of the legal directions during deliberations increases significantly if they are given written directions alongside the oral directions. Secondly, the provision of written materials is likely to reduce the scope for any meritorious appeal in the event of any conviction.

The Compendium goes on to say this about routes to verdict:

> When a jury is faced with more than one issue in a case, judicial experience suggests that jurors can be assisted by having a written sequential list of questions, or what is often referred to as a 'Route to Verdict'. Such a document can help focus jury deliberations and

provide them with a logical route to verdict/s. In more complicated cases some judges have a practice of providing a chart showing the jury the permissible combinations of verdicts.

Annex 1 of the *Compendium* gives the following example of a route to verdict:

It is agreed that V sustained a wound and that this was caused when a pint glass held by D broke against the side of V's face.

Questions for Verdicts

Question 1
Are you sure that D struck V deliberately?
- If your answer is 'No' your verdict will be one of Not Guilty on Count 1 and Count 2.
- If your answer is 'Yes', go on to Question 2.

Question 2
Are you sure that when D struck V he was not acting in lawful self-defence?
- If your answer is 'No' your verdict will be one of Not Guilty on Count 1 and Count 2
- If your answer is 'Yes', go on to Question 3.

Question 3
Are you sure that when D struck V, D intended to cause a really serious injury?
- If your answer is 'No' your verdict will be Not Guilty on Count 1 and you must go on to consider Question 4.
- If your answer is 'Yes' your verdict will be Guilty on Count 1 and you will not consider Count 2.

Question 4
Are you sure that when D struck V, D realised he might cause him some injury?
- If your answer is 'No' your verdict will be one of Not Guilty on Count 2.
- If your answer is 'Yes' your verdict will be one of Guilty to Count 2.

In R v Kay [2017] EWCA Crim 2214, where the Court of Appeal noted (see [34]) 'with some concern that the jury was not assisted by written directions as to the elements of the offence that had to be proved, or a route to verdict', adding that 'written directions or a route to verdict would have been of great assistance' (see [34]). Shortly afterwards, in R v Atta-Dankwa [2018] EWCA Crim 320; [2018] 2 Cr App R 16, Holroyde LJ said (at [31]):

... one should never be too quick to assume that a case is so straightforward that a route to verdict would be superfluous. Experience shows that problems can arise even in cases which seem straightforward ... Moreover, quite apart from the assistance which the end product will provide to the jury, the mental discipline of drafting a route to verdict in itself assists the court to identify the essential ingredients of the offences charged and the issues on which the jury must focus.

His Lordship acknowledged the pressure of work on judges and recorders sitting in the Crown Court, and accepted that 'some cases are so straightforward that no written materials for the jury are necessary'. However, 'such cases are in a minority' (at [32]).

It should also be noted that the summing up does not have to be given in a single block, as there is now provision for a 'split' summing up. Criminal Practice Direction VI, para.26K.16, says that:

Where the judge decides it will assist the jury when listening to the closing speeches, a split summing up should be provided. For example, the provision of appropriate directions prior to the closing speeches may avoid repetitious explanations of the law by the advocates.

Paragraph 26K.17 says that, by way of illustration, such directions may include:

- Functions of the judge and jury;
- Burden and standard of proof;
- Separate consideration of counts;
- Separate consideration of defendants;
- Elements of offence(s);
- Defence(s);
- Route to verdict;
- Circumstantial evidence; and
- Inferences from silence.

10.11.1 Respective functions of judge and jury

In a trial on indictment, matters of law are for the judge, whereas matters of fact are for the jury. This means that the jury must accept what the judge says about the law, whether they agree or not. The judge should be careful not to express an opinion on the facts and should make it clear to the jury that if he does express an opinion on the facts, the jury are free to come to a different conclusion. The direction approved in R v Jackson [1992] Crim LR 214 was:

> It is my job to tell you what the law is and how to apply it to the issues of fact that you have to decide and to remind you of the important evidence on these issues. As to the law, you must accept what I tell you. As to the facts, you alone are the judges. It is for you to decide what evidence you accept and what evidence you reject or of which you are unsure. If I appear to have a view of the evidence or of the facts with which you do not agree, reject my view. If I mention or emphasise evidence that you regard as unimportant, disregard that evidence. If I do not mention what you regard as important, follow your own view and take that evidence into account.

See Part 4 of the *Crown Court Compendium*.

10.11.2 Burden and standard of proof

Every summing up must contain a direction to the jury as to the burden and standard of proof, and as to the ingredients of the offence or the offences which the jury are called upon to consider (R v Miah [2018] EWCA Crim 563, at [33])).

See Part 5 of the *Crown Court Compendium*.

10.11.2.1 Burden of proof

The jury should be told that it is for the prosecution to prove that the defendant is guilty; he does not have to prove his innocence.

10.11.2.2 Standard of proof

The jury should be told that they can convict the defendant if they are 'sure' of his guilt. If they are not sure, they must find the defendant not guilty. Directing the jury that they must be 'sure' of the defendant's guilt is regarded as preferable to the well-known phrase 'beyond reasonable doubt'. The words suggested in the Compendium are as follows:

The prosecution must prove that D is guilty. D does not have to prove anything to you. D does not have to prove that he/she is innocent. The prosecution will only succeed in proving that D is guilty if you have been made sure of D's guilt. If, after considering all of the evidence, you are sure that D is guilty, your verdict must be 'Guilty'. If you are not sure that D is guilty, your verdict must be 'Not Guilty'.

10.11.2.3 Exceptional cases where the burden is on the defendant

Exceptionally, the defendant may bear a burden of proof. For example, if the defendant is charged with possession of an offensive weapon, it is open to him to show that he had lawful authority or reasonable excuse. In such a case, it must be made clear to the jury that the defendant can satisfy this burden of proof on the balance of probabilities (that is, showing that it is more likely than not that he had lawful authority or reasonable excuse).

There is only a burden of proof on the defendant if statute so provides; otherwise it is for the prosecution to disprove any defence. Thus, for example, if the defendant raises the defence of self-defence, it is for the prosecution to prove beyond reasonable doubt that he was not so acting.

10.11.3 Explanation of the law involved and how it relates to the facts

Even in a straightforward case, directions on the ingredients of the offence are an essential part of the summing up (R v McVey). Thus, the judge must explain what the prosecution have to prove and must remind the jury of the evidence they have heard.

The judge should remind the jury of the main features of the prosecution and defence evidence, even if the case is a straightforward one (R v Gregory [1993] Crim LR 623).

In R v Lawrence [1982] AC 510, Lord Hailsham of St Marylebone LC (p.519) said that the summing up must:

include a succinct but accurate summary of the issues of fact as to which a decision is required, a correct but concise summary of the evidence and arguments on both sides, and a correct statement of the inferences which the jury are entitled to draw from their particular conclusions about the primary facts.

With the help of the summing up, the jury should thus be able to relate the evidence which they have heard to the legal principles which they have to apply.

In R v Bowerman [2000] 2 Cr App R 189, Henry LJ (at pp.192–3) said:

it is generally of assistance to the jury if the judge summarises those factual issues which are not disputed, and, where there is a significant dispute as to material facts, identifies succinctly those pieces of evidence which are in conflict. By so doing, the judge can focus the jury's attention on those factual issues which they must resolve. It is never appropriate, however, for a summing-up to be a mere rehearsal of the evidence.

The summing up must be properly balanced. In R v Marchant [2018] EWCA Crim 2606 (at [15]), Leggatt LJ said:

[T]he essential tasks for the judge are, first, to explain the law which the jury needs to apply and, second, to review the essential features of the evidence. In reviewing the evidence, the judge should seek to focus the jury's attention on the issues of fact which they need or may think it important to decide and to remind them of the main evidence bearing on those issues. The judge must also identify the defence case. The judge is perfectly entitled to comment on the evidence by pointing out matters which may tend to support or undermine either party's case on an issue. Nor is there any requirement that a summing up should be balanced in the sense that a judge should seek to compensate for a weak case or downplay a strong one. What is vital is, first, that the judge should not trespass on the role of the jury by telling them what conclusions they should draw on matters which are for them to determine and, second, that the judge's review of the evidence should be objective and impartial and not skewed unfairly in favour of the prosecution (or the defence).

10.11.4 Such warnings as are appropriate
A number of matters have to be addressed in the summing up if they are relevant.

10.11.4.1 Co-defendants or more than one count
Where there is more than one count and/or more than one defendant, the judge must direct the jury to consider each count and each defendant separately.

In R v Jones and Jenkins [2003] EWCA Crim 1966; [2004] 1 Cr App R 5, Auld LJ (at [47]), agreed with counsel that where there are co-defendants, and each defendant says that he is not responsible for the alleged crime, the jury should be directed as follows:

> First, the jury should consider the case for and against each defendant separately. Second, the jury should decide the case on all the evidence, including the evidence of each defendant's co-defendant. Third, when considering the evidence of co-defendants, the jury should bear in mind that he or she may have an interest to serve or, as it is often put, an axe to grind. Fourth, the jury should assess the evidence of co-defendants in the same way as that of the evidence of any other witness in the case.

10.11.4.2 Identification evidence
If the case rests on identification evidence, the judge must warn the jury that such evidence is notoriously unreliable and that they should examine very closely the circumstances in which the identification took place when assessing the weight of that evidence. The judge should give a detailed direction on the factors which strengthen or weaken the identification evidence (R v Turnbull [1977] QB 224). The effect of Turnbull is summarised in Part 15 of the Crown Court Compendium:

> The jury must be warned that:
> (1)   there is a need for caution to avoid the risk of injustice;
> (2)   a witness who is honest and convinced in his own mind may be wrong;
> (3)   a witness who is convincing may be wrong;
> (4)   more than one witness may be wrong ...;
> (5)   a witness who is able to recognise the defendant, even when the witness knows the defendant very well, may be wrong.
>
> The jury should be directed to put caution into practice by carefully examining the surrounding circumstances of the evidence of identification, in particular:
> (1)   the time during which the witness had the person he says was D under observation; in particular the time during which the witness could see the person's face;
> (2)   the distance between the witness and the person observed;
> (3)   the state of the light;
> (4)   whether there was any interference with the observation (such as either a physical obstruction or other things going on at the same time);

(5) whether the witness had ever seen D before and if so how many times and in what circumstances (i.e. whether the witness had any reason to be able to recognise D);

(6) the length of time between the original observation of the person said to be D (usually at the time of the incident) and the identification by the witness of D the police (often at an identification procedure);

(7) whether there is any significant difference between the description the witness gave to the police and the appearance of D.

Moreover, any weaknesses in the identification evidence must be drawn to the attention of the jury; any evidence 'which is capable and, if applicable, evidence which is not capable of supporting and/or is capable of undermining the identification must be identified'.

10.11.4.3 Adverse inferences for silence

Given the fact that a jury may draw adverse inferences from the failure of a defendant to answer police questions (under s.34 of the Criminal Justice and Public Order Act 1994) or to testify in court (s.35), they have to be given some guidance on how to approach this aspect of the case.

In R v Cowan [1996] QB 373, the Court of Appeal considered what should be said in the summing up if the case is one where adverse inferences might be drawn under s.35 from the defendant's failure to testify. Lord Taylor CJ (at p.381) said that the essential elements of the direction are as follows:

(1) The judge will have told the jury that the burden of proof remains upon the prosecution throughout and what the required standard is. (2) It is necessary for the judge to make clear to the jury that the defendant is entitled to remain silent. That is his right and his choice. The right of silence remains. (3) An inference from failure to give evidence cannot on its own prove guilt ... (4) Therefore, the jury must be satisfied that the prosecution have established a case to answer before drawing any inferences from silence ... (5) If, despite any evidence relied upon to explain his silence or in the absence of any such evidence, the jury conclude the silence can only sensibly be attributed to the defendant's having no answer or none that would stand up to cross-examination, they may draw an adverse inference.

In R v Argent [1997] 2 Cr App R 27, Lord Bingham CJ (at p.33) considered the requirement that the accused must have failed to mention a fact which, in the circumstances existing at the time, he could reasonably have been expected to mention when so questioned, before adverse inferences can be drawn under s.34:

The time referred to is the time of questioning, and account must be taken of all the relevant circumstances existing at that time ... [M]atters such as time of day, the defendant's age, experience, mental capacity, state of health, sobriety, tiredness, knowledge, personality and legal advice are all part of the relevant circumstances; and those are only examples of things which may be relevant. When reference is made to 'the accused' attention is directed not to some hypothetical, reasonable accused of ordinary phlegm and fortitude but to the actual accused with such qualities, apprehensions, knowledge and advice as he is shown to have had at the time.

A defendant may seek to explain silence on the basis of legal advice. The European Court of Human Rights in Beckles v United Kingdom (2003) 36 EHRR 13 ruled (at [64]) that the jury in that case should have been directed that, 'if it was satisfied that the [defendant's] silence at the police interview could not sensibly be attributed to his having no answer or none that would stand up to police questioning, it should not draw an adverse inference'. When the case returned to the Court of Appeal (R v Beckles [2004] EWCA Crim 2766; [2005] 1 WLR 2829), Lord Woolf CJ said (at [46]):

[I]n a case where a solicitor's advice is relied upon by the defendant, the ultimate question for the jury remains under s.34 whether the facts relied on at the trial were facts which the defendant could reasonably have been expected to mention at interview. If they were not, that is the end of the matter. If the jury consider that the defendant genuinely relied on the advice, that is not necessarily the end of the matter. It may still not have been reasonable for him to rely on the advice, or the advice may not have been the true explanation for his silence.

Similarly, in R v Hoare [2004] EWCA Crim 784; [2005] 1 WLR 1804, Auld LJ said (at [46]):

[H]owever sound the advice in law or as a matter of tactics, a defendant is not entitled to hide behind it if, at the time, the true reason for not mentioning the facts was that he had no or no satisfactory explanation consistent with his innocence to offer.

See Part 17 of the *Crown Court Compendium*.

10.11.4.4 Alibi evidence

Where the defendant puts forward an alibi, the judge must direct the jury that the burden of proof rests on the prosecution to disprove it (not on the defendant to prove it) beyond reasonable doubt. The jury should also be directed that even if they conclude that the alibi was false, that does not by itself entitle them to convict the defendant; an alibi is sometimes invented to bolster a genuine defence.

A failure to give such a direction does not automatically render a conviction unsafe; the Court of Appeal will consider whether the jury might have come to a different conclusion had the direction been given (R v Harron [1996] 2 Cr App R 457; R v Lesley [1996] 1 Cr App R 39).

See Part 18-2 of the *Crown Court Compendium*.

10.11.4.5 Lies by the defendant

Where there is evidence before the jury that the defendant has lied about something, and there is a risk of the jury thinking that, because the defendant has lied, he must therefore be guilty of the offence with which he is charged, they should be directed that proof of lying is not proof of guilt (in that an innocent defendant might lie). See R v Lucas [1981] QB 720, where Lord Lane CJ said (at p.724):

To be capable of amounting to corroboration the lie told out of court must first of all be deliberate. Secondly it must relate to a material issue. Thirdly the motive for the lie must be a realisation of guilt and a fear of the truth. The jury should in appropriate cases be reminded that people sometimes lie, for example, in an attempt to bolster up a just cause, or out of shame or out of a wish to conceal disgraceful behaviour from their family. Fourthly the statement must be clearly shown to be a lie ... by admission or by evidence from an independent witness.

Part 16-3 of the *Crown Court Compendium* summarises the effect of *Lucas* thus:

Before the jury may use an alleged or admitted lie against D they must be sure of all of the following:

(1) that it is either admitted or shown, by other evidence in the case, to be a deliberate untruth: i.e. it did not arise from confusion or mistake;

(2) that it relates to a significant issue; and

(3) that it was not told for a reason advanced by or on behalf of D, or some other reason arising from the evidence, which does not point to D's guilt.

The jury must be directed that unless they are sure of all of the above the [alleged] lie is not relevant and must be ignored.

If the jury are sure of all of the above they may use the lie as some support for the prosecution case, but it must be made clear that a lie can never by itself prove guilt.

10.11.4.6 Defendant's previous convictions

To understand the directions that have to be given where a defendant has previous convictions, it is necessary to understand something of the basis upon which previous convictions may be admissible. The detail of the relevant statutory provisions is beyond the scope of this work, but the main provisions are as follows:

Section 101(1) of the Criminal Justice Act 2003 provides that:

In criminal proceedings evidence of the defendant's bad character is admissible if, but only if—
(a) all parties to the proceedings agree to the evidence being admissible,
(b) the evidence is adduced by the defendant himself or is given in answer to a question asked by him in cross-examination and intended to elicit it,
(c) it is important explanatory evidence,
(d) it is relevant to an important matter in issue between the defendant and the prosecution,
(e) it has substantial probative value in relation to an important matter in issue between the defendant and a co-defendant,
(f) it is evidence to correct a false impression given by the defendant, or
(g) the defendant has made an attack on another person's character.

Sections 102–106 offer interpretative assistance on some of these 'gateways' to the admissibility of the defendant's previous convictions:

Important explanatory evidence (s.102): evidence is important explanatory evidence if:

(a) without it, the court or jury would find it impossible or difficult properly to understand other evidence in the case, and
(b) its value for understanding the case as a whole is substantial.

Important matter in issue between the defendant and the prosecution (s.103(1)): the matters in issue between the defendant and the prosecution include:

(a) the question whether the defendant has a propensity to commit offences of the kind with which he is charged, except where his having such a propensity makes it no more likely that he is guilty of the offence;
(b) the question whether the defendant has a propensity to be untruthful, except where it is not suggested that the defendant's case is untruthful in any respect.

The phrase 'important matter' means 'a matter of substantial importance in the context of the case as a whole' (s.112(1)).

In R v *Hanson* [2005] EWCA Crim 824; [2005] 1 WLR 3169, Rose LJ (at [7]) noted that where propensity to commit the offence is relied upon there are three questions to be considered:

(i) Does the history of conviction(s) establish a propensity to commit offences of the kind charged?
(ii) Does that propensity make it more likely that the defendant committed the offence charged?

(iii) Is it unjust to rely on the conviction(s) of the same description or category; and, in any event, will the proceedings be unfair if they are admitted?

Matter in issue between the defendant and a co-defendant (s.104):

(1) Evidence which is relevant to the question whether the defendant has a propensity to be untruthful is admissible on that basis under s.101(1)(e) only if the nature or conduct of his defence is such as to undermine the co-defendant's defence.

(2) Only evidence—
  (a) which is to be (or has been) adduced by the co-defendant, or
  (b) which a witness is to be invited to give (or has given) in cross-examination by the co-defendant, is admissible under s.101(1)(e).

Evidence to correct a false impression (s.105(1)):

(a) the defendant gives a false impression if he is responsible for the making of an express or implied assertion which is apt to give the court or jury a false or misleading impression about the defendant;

(b) evidence to correct such an impression is evidence which has probative value in correcting it.

For these purposes, the assertion may be made by the defendant, by a witness called by the defendant, or by any witness in cross-examination in response to a question asked by the defendant that is intended (or likely) to elicit it (s.105(2)).

Attack on another person's character (s.106(1)): a defendant makes an attack on another person's character if:

(a) he adduces evidence attacking the other person's character,

(b) he ... asks questions in cross-examination that are intended to elicit such evidence, or are likely to do so, or

(c) evidence is given of an imputation about the other person made by the defendant—

on being questioned under caution ....

For these purposes, 'evidence attacking the other person's character' means evidence to the effect that the other person has committed an offence or has behaved, or is disposed to behave, in a reprehensible way (s.106(2)).

A careful direction is needed where the jury have been made aware that the defendant has previous convictions. In *R v Hanson* [2005] EWCA Crim 824; [2005] 1 WLR 3169, Rose LJ (at [18]) said that:

[T]he judge in summing up should warn the jury clearly against placing undue reliance on previous convictions. Evidence of bad character cannot be used simply to bolster a weak case, or to prejudice the minds of a jury against a defendant. In particular, the jury should be directed: that they should not conclude that the defendant is guilty or untruthful merely because he has these convictions; that, although the convictions may show a propensity, this does not mean that he has committed this offence or been untruthful in this case; that whether they in fact show a propensity is for them to decide; that they must take into account what the defendant has said about his previous convictions; and that, although they are entitled, if they find propensity as shown, to take this into account when determining guilt, propensity is only one relevant factor and they must assess its significance in the light of all the other evidence in the case.

See Part 12 of the Crown Court Compendium.

10.11.4.7 The defendant's good character

Where the defendant has no previous convictions, the jury should be directed that this is relevant both to his credibility as a witness and to the likelihood of his having committed the offence. If the defendant does not testify, then his previous good character goes to the credibility of any denial that he made to the police when interviewed as well as being relevant to the likelihood of his having committed the offence alleged (R v Vye [1993] 1 WLR 471). In R v Hunter [2015] EWCA Crim 631; [2015] 1 WLR 5367, the Court of Appeal reviewed extensively the case law on *Vye* directions. Hallett LJ (at [68]) said that:

(a) The general rule is that a direction as to the relevance of good character to a defendant's credibility is to be given where a defendant has a good character and has testified or made pre-trial statements.

(b) The general rule is that a direction as to the relevance of a good character to the likelihood of a defendant's having committed the offence charged is to be given where a defendant has a good character whether or not he has testified or made pre-trial answers or statements.

(c) Where defendant A, of good character, is tried jointly with B who does not have a good character, (a) and (b) still apply.

(d) There are exceptions to the general rule for example where a defendant has no previous convictions but has admitted other reprehensible conduct and the judge considers it would be an insult to common sense to give directions in accordance with Vye. The judge then has a residual discretion to decline to give a good character direction.

(e) A jury must not be misled. . . .

See Part 11 of the Crown Court Compendium.

10.11.4.8 Accomplices

Where an accomplice testifies as a prosecution witness against a defendant, there is no duty to warn the jury about the dangers of convicting on the basis of that evidence (s.32 of the Criminal Justice and Public Order Act 1994). However, the trial judge has a discretion to warn the jury in regard to a particular witness. In R v Makanjuola [1995] 1 WLR 1348 (at pp.1351–2), Lord Taylor CJ summarised the law as follows:

It is a matter for the judge's discretion what, if any warning, he considers appropriate in respect of such a witness as indeed in respect of any other witness in whatever type of case. Whether he chooses to give a warning and in what terms will depend on the circumstances of the case, the issues raised and the content and quality of the witness's evidence.

In some cases, it may be appropriate for the judge to warn the jury to exercise caution before acting upon the unsupported evidence of a witness . . . There will need to be an evidential basis for suggesting that the evidence of the witness may be unreliable . . .

Where some warning is required, it will be for the judge to decide the strength and terms of the warning.

See Part 10-2 of the Crown Court Compendium.

10.11.4.9 Expert evidence

In a case involving expert evidence, it is important that the judge should make clear to the jury that they are not bound by the expert's opinion, and that the issue is for them to decide (R v Stockwell

(1993) 97 Cr App R 260, per Lord Taylor CJ, at p.266). Part 10-3 of the *Crown Court Compendium* says that, in every case where expert evidence has been heard, the jury should be directed as follows:

(a) Expert witnesses regularly give evidence and opinions in criminal trials to assist juries on matters of a specialist kind which are not of common knowledge.

(b) However, as with any other witness, it is the jury's task to weigh up the evidence of the expert(s), which includes any evidence of opinion, and to decide which they accept and which they do not. The jury should take into account [as appropriate] the qualifications/ practical experience/methodology/source material/quality of analysis/objectivity of the experts, and the impression they made when giving evidence.

(c) The jury's verdicts must be based on the evidence as a whole, of which the expert evidence and opinion forms only a part.

10.11.4.10 Alternative counts

If the indictment contains alternative counts where one is more serious than the other, the judge will tell the jury to consider the more serious count first. If they convict on that count, they should not go on to consider the other count; if they acquit on the more serious count, they should proceed to consider the less serious charge. Thus, the jury could convict the defendant on one of the two counts, but not both; or they could acquit the defendant of both.

See Part 6-3 of the *Crown Court Compendium*.

10.11.4.11 Concluding directions

Criminal Practice Direction VI, para.26K.22, says that certain directions must be given to the jury at the conclusion of the summing up. It says that,

At the conclusion of the summing up, the judge should provide final directions to the jury on the need:
● For unanimity (in respect of each count and defendant, where relevant);
● To dismiss any thoughts of majority verdicts until further direction; and
● To select a juror to chair their discussions and speak on their behalf to the court.

So far as majority verdicts are concerns, Criminal Practice Direction VI, para 26Q.1, suggests this form of words:

As you may know, the law permits me, in certain circumstances, to accept a verdict which is not the verdict of you all. Those circumstances have not as yet arisen, so that when you retire I must ask you to reach a verdict upon which each one of you is agreed. Should, however, the time come when it is possible for me to accept a majority verdict, I will give you a further direction.

10.12 Retirement of the jury

After the conclusion of the summing up, the jury are delivered into the custody of the jury bailiff, who takes an oath to take them to a private place to consider their verdict and to prevent anyone from communicating with them. The jury then go to the jury room to consider their verdict.

During lunchtime and overnight adjournments during the trial, the jury are allowed to go their separate ways. Part 21-2 of the *Crown Court Compendium* refers to the decision of the Court of Appeal in R v Oliver [1995] 2 Cr App R 514 at 520, and summarises that decision thus:

It is not necessary to use any precise form of words provided that the jury are directed that:

(1) when they leave the court room and until they return to the courtroom {specify e.g. this afternoon/tomorrow morning} they must not talk about the case to anyone;

(2) this includes talking to one another because, if any of them were to do so, they would not be deliberating as a jury but having separate discussions in which not all the jury would be involved;

(3) they must decide the case on the evidence and the arguments that they have seen and heard in court and not on anything that they may see or hear outside the court room. For this reason no juror must look for or receive any further information about the case, whether by talking to someone or by making their own investigations e.g. on the internet.

10.13 No further evidence after retirement

Once the jury has retired, the general rule is that no further evidence can be called (R v Owen [1952] 2 QB 362). In that case, the jury came out of retirement to ask whether the premises where a sexual assault was alleged to have taken place would have been occupied or not at the relevant time. The Court of Appeal held that no further evidence (whether from a witness who has already been called or from a fresh witness) can be called after the jury has retired to consider its verdict. However, in R v Hallam [2007] EWCA Crim 1495, Toulson LJ said (at [22]) that there is no longer an absolute rule to the effect that evidence cannot be admitted after the retirement of the jury; rather, 'the question is what justice requires'. The same view was expressed by Gage LJ in R v Khan [2008] EWCA Crim 1112 (at [39]), where his Lordship said that although, historically, the authorities state that there is an absolute principle that no further evidence should be given after the judge's summing-up has been concluded and the jury has retired, this principle has, in recent years, been subject to some relaxation.

10.14 Questions from the jury after retirement

If the jury wish to communicate with the judge (for example, they need further directions on the law or to be reminded of some of the evidence), they do so by means of a note sent to the judge via the jury bailiff. A judge who receives such a note should follow the procedure set out in R v Gorman [1987] 1 WLR 545 (per Lord Lane CJ, at pp.550–1):

First of all, if the communication raises something unconnected with the trial, for example a request that some message be sent to a relative of one of the jurors, it can simply be dealt with without any reference to counsel and without bringing the jury back to court ...

Secondly, in almost every other case a judge should state in open court the nature and content of the communication which he has received from the jury and, if he considers it helpful so to do, seek the assistance of counsel. This assistance will normally be sought before the jury is asked to return to court, and then, when the jury returns, the judge will deal with their communication.

Exceptionally if ... the communication from the jury contains information which the jury need not, and indeed should not, have imparted, such as details of voting figures ... then, so far as possible the communication should be dealt with in the normal way, save that the judge should not disclose the detailed information which the jury ought not to have revealed.

10.15 Returning a verdict

Rule 25.14(5) says that when the court directs the jury to deliver its verdict(s), the court must ask the foreman chosen by the jury, in respect of each count: (a) whether the jury has reached a verdict on which all the jurors agree; (b) if so, whether that verdict is guilty or not guilty.

So, when the jury come back into court in a case where a majority verdict direction has not been given (see below), the clerk asks them: 'Have you reached a verdict upon which you are all agreed?' If the answer is 'yes', the foreman will be asked to announce the verdict on each count of the indictment.

Where the defendant is charged with a number of offences and the jury indicate that they have agreed verdicts on some, but not all, of the offences, r.25.14(3) applies. It provides that the court should,

(f)   in a case in which the jury is required to return two or more verdicts—
  (i)   recall the jury (unless already recalled) when it informs the court that it has reached a verdict or verdicts, and
  (ii) ask the jury whether its members all agree on every verdict required;
(g)   if the answer to that question is 'yes', direct the delivery of each of those verdicts there and then; and
(h)   if the answer to that question is 'no'—
  (i)   direct the delivery there and then of any unanimous verdict that has been reached, or
  (ii) postpone the taking of any such verdict while the jury considers each other verdict required.

It follows that where the case is one in which more than one jury verdict is required, the judge should take the verdicts on those counts upon which the jury are agreed before they continue considering the other counts (R v F [1994] Crim LR 377).

If the indictment contains counts which are in the alternative, the usual practice is for the clerk to ask for a verdict on the more serious allegation first. If the verdict on that count is 'not guilty', the clerk will go on to ask for the verdict on the other count. If, on the other hand, the verdict on the more serious count is 'guilty', the jury should be discharged from giving a verdict on the less serious charge.

10.16 Majority verdicts

Section 17 of the Juries Act 1974 Act makes provision for majority verdicts. Bearing in mind that one or more jurors may be discharged during the course of the trial, the permissible majorities (under s.17(1)) are:

Up to three jurors may be discharged, leaving a nine-person jury. If that occurs, their verdict has to be unanimous.

12 jurors:	11–1 or 10–2;
11 jurors:	10–1;
10 jurors:	9–1.

The court will not accept a majority verdict until the jury have been told that such a verdict is acceptable. Until then, the jury must try to reach a unanimous verdict.

Whereas a unanimous verdict can be accepted at any time after the jury have retired to consider their verdict, s.17(4) states that the court cannot accept a majority verdict:

> unless it appears to the court that the jury have had such period of time for deliberation as the court thinks reasonable having regard to the nature and complexity of the case; and the Crown Court shall in any event not accept such a verdict unless it appears to the court that the jury have had at least two hours for deliberation.

The jury is usually given an additional 10 minutes to settle down in the jury room and elect a foreman, so a majority verdict direction will not be given until at least two hours 10 minutes have elapsed since the jury retired to consider its verdict. This is the minimum time they must be given; the more complex the case, the longer they will be given before a majority verdict direction is given.

The majority verdict direction asks the jury to try once again to reach a verdict upon which all the jurors are agreed, but informs them that the time has now come when the court can accept a majority verdict. They should be asked to retire once more and told they should continue to endeavour to reach a unanimous verdict but that, if they cannot, the judge will accept a majority verdict (see Criminal Practice Direction VI, para.26Q.3).

Rule 25.14(5)(c) states that, where the jury has deliberated for at least two hours and if the court decides to invite a majority verdict, the court must ask the foreman chosen by the jury, in respect of each count:

(i) whether at least 10 (of 11 or 12 jurors), or 9 (of 10 jurors), agreed on a verdict,
(ii) if so, is that verdict guilty or not guilty, and
(iii) if (and only if) such a verdict is guilty, how many jurors agreed to that verdict and
(iv) how many disagreed.

Accordingly, Criminal Practice Direction VI, para.26Q.4, requires that, after a majority verdict direction has been given, when the jurors return to court they will be asked: 'Have at least ten (or nine as the case may be) of you agreed on your verdict?'. If the answer is 'Yes', they will be asked for their verdict. If the verdict is 'Not Guilty', that is the end of the matter (and so it will never be known whether the acquittal was unanimous or by majority). If (and only if) the verdict is 'Guilty', they will be asked whether the verdict is unanimous or by majority, and if so, how many agreed to the verdict and how many dissented.

This is to ensure compliance with s.17(3), which states that the court cannot accept a majority verdict of guilty unless the foreman of the jury states in open court 'the number of jurors who respectively agreed to and dissented from the verdict'. If this is not done, the verdict is a nullity (R v Pigg [1983] 1 WLR 6).

See Part 21-4 of the Crown Court Compendium.

10.17 Jury still unable to reach a verdict

The judge must not exert undue pressure on the jury to reach a verdict (R v McKenna [1960] 1 QB 411). However, the judge can inquire whether there is a reasonable prospect of a verdict's being reached, and may tell the jury that if there is no reasonable prospect of their reaching a verdict they will be discharged but that, if there is, then they can have as much time as they need (R v Modeste [1983] Crim LR 746).

10.17.1 The **Watson** direction

In R v *Watson* [1988] QB 690, the Court of Appeal said that a judge must not point out to the jury that if they do not reach a verdict there will have to be a retrial which will cause inconvenience and expense. However, Lord Lane CJ said (at p.700) that the jury could be directed:

> Each of you has taken an oath to return a true verdict according to the evidence. No one must be false to that oath, but you have a duty not only as individuals but collectively. That is the strength of the jury system. Each of you takes into the jury box with you your individual experience and wisdom. Your task is to pool that experience and wisdom. You do that by giving your views and listening to the views of the others. There must necessarily be discussion, argument and give and take within the scope of your oath. That is the way in which agreement is reached. If, unhappily, [10 of] you cannot reach agreement you must say so.

Further guidance on *Watson* directions was given in R v *Arthur* [2013] EWCA Crim 1852, where Pitchford LJ (at [43]–[44]) said:

> [O]nce the jury is in retirement it is of the first importance that no individual juror should feel under any compulsion or pressure to conform with the views of the majority if to do so would compromise their conscience and, therefore, their oath. Furthermore, the jury as a whole, despite the heavy cost and inconvenience of a re-trial, should not feel under any pressure to return a verdict if, conscientiously, they are not unanimous or cannot reach the required majority ... It is undesirable to give a Watson direction before or at the time of the majority verdict direction because its effect may be to undo the benefit of the majority verdict direction for which Parliament has provided. Exceptional circumstances may arise that will require the trial judge to deal with the exigencies of the moment but, in general, there is no occasion to make exhortations to the jury to arrive at a verdict. This is why the Watson direction is rarely given by trial judges and, when it is, only as a last resort following a prolonged retirement after the majority verdict direction has been given.
>
> [I]f complaint is made about the trial judge's words of explanation, encouragement or exhortation the question for [the Court of Appeal] is whether the words used were appropriate in the circumstances or carried with them the risk that jurors would feel undue pressure to reach a verdict. If the effect of the judge's direction to the jury is to create a significant risk that the jury or individual jurors may have felt under pressure to compromise their oaths, the verdict is likely to be unsafe. No juror should feel required to compromise their oath in order to fall in with the majority and no jury should feel under pressure to reach a verdict if to do so would require any one of them to compromise their oath. The danger is that all jurors, particularly the minority, will feel pressure to return a verdict unanimously or by an acceptable majority at the expense of conscientious consideration of the evidence. The closer the jury is to unanimity or to an acceptable majority the greater is the pressure to which the minority may feel exposed.

In R v M [2014] EWCA Crim 2590, the Court of Appeal considered R v *Arthur*, Bean LJ (at [20]) summarised the effect thus:

> [T]here are cumulative tests which must be satisfied before a Watson direction can be given: (i) it requires exceptional circumstances, which is why it is rarely given; and even then (ii) it can only be given as a last resort where prolonged retirement following the giving of a majority direction.

Watson directions were considered again in R v *Logo* [2015] 2 Cr App R 17. Saunders J said (at [20]) that the key principles were that (i) 'such a direction should only be given after the majority direction has been given and after some time has elapsed or a further direction is sought from the judge by the jury'; (ii) there will 'usually be no need' for such a direction; (iii) the judge should follow the wording set out in *Watson*. His Lordship added (at [25]) that, given the difficulties that this direction can cause, 'trial judges may wish to think long and hard before exercising their discretion to do so and ... they will also be well advised to seek the submissions of counsel to assist them reach a considered decision'.

See Part 21-5 of the *Crown Court Compendium*.

10.17.2 Discharge of jury

If there is no possibility of the jury's reaching a verdict within what the judge regards as a reasonable time, the jury will be discharged. This does not count as an acquittal, so the accused can be retried. In R v *Byrne* [2002] EWCA Crim 632; [2002] 2 Cr App R 21, Aikens J (at [14]) said that:

> There is a convention that if a jury disagrees on the first trial and then a second jury also disagrees, the prosecution will then formally offer no evidence ... However, this is no more than a convention. There is no rule of law that forbids a prosecutor from seeking a second retrial after a jury has disagreed.

Nonetheless, a third trial will be very rare. In R v *Bell* [2010] EWCA Crim 3; [2010] 1 Cr App R 27, Lord Judge CJ said (at [46]):

> [T]he jurisdiction which permits a second re-trial after two jury disagreements ... must be exercised with extreme caution ... [A] second re-trial should be confined to the very small number of cases in which the jury is being invited to address a crime of extreme gravity which has undoubtedly occurred ... and in which the evidence that the defendant committed the crime ... on any fair minded objective judgment remains very powerful.

In R v *Burton* [2015] EWCA Crim 1307; [2016] 1 Cr App R 7, the Court of Appeal reiterated that 'the prosecution will not seek a third trial in the absence of special factors that would justify such a course' (per Treacy LJ at [24]). His Lordship went on to observe (at [36]):

> [T]he number of cases in which a third trial is permitted should be strictly limited in order to maintain public confidence in the criminal justice system and provide a degree of finality for a defendant. It is for that reason that the court must proceed with extreme caution. If a crime is truly one of extreme gravity and the evidence is cogent despite the problems experienced by previous juries then it may well be an affront to justice and more likely to undermine public confidence not to pursue the aims of convicting the guilty and deterring the most serious crimes.

10.18 Verdict of guilty to an alternative offence

Under s.6(3) of the Criminal Law Act 1967, where 'the allegations in the indictment amount to or include (expressly or by implication) an allegation of another offence' which may be tried on indictment, the jury may acquit on the offence charged and convict on the included offence.

10.18.1 Express inclusion

An offence is expressly included in the indictment if words can be deleted from the existing count so as to leave words alleging another offence (R v Lillis [1972] 2 QB 236).

Suppose, for example, that it is alleged that the defendant 'entered 4 Gray's Inn Place as a trespasser and stole therein a computer'. If the words 'entered 4 Gray's Inn Place as a trespasser and' and 'therein' are deleted, that leaves an allegation that the defendant 'stole a computer'. Therefore, theft is expressly included in the allegation of burglary.

Thus, if a jury decides that they are not satisfied so that they are sure that the defendant entered as a trespasser but are sure that he stole the goods alleged in the indictment, they can acquit of burglary but convict of theft.

10.18.2 Implied inclusion

The meaning of implied inclusion was considered by the House of Lords in *Metropolitan Police Commissioner v Wilson* [1984] AC 242. Where the commission of the offence alleged in the indictment will, in the normal course of events (that is, in the great majority of cases), involve the commission of another offence, that other offence is impliedly included in the offence charged in the indictment.

In *Wilson*, for example, it was held that inflicting grievous bodily harm (s.20 of the Offences Against the Person Act 1861) usually involves assault occasioning actual bodily harm (s.47 of the same Act), so the jury can acquit of grievous bodily harm but convict of actual bodily harm. It may well be possible to inflict grievous bodily harm without assaulting the victim (for example, by deliberately creating a panic in a crowded building intending that people are seriously hurt in the rush to escape) but, in the normal course of events, grievous bodily harm will involve assault occasioning actual bodily harm.

The same applies to an allegation of wounding under s.20 of the Offences Against the Person Act 1861, so s.47 is an alternative offence to that charge too (R v Savage [1992] 1 AC 699). A charge of causing grievous bodily harm with intent (s.18) includes a charge of inflicting grievous bodily harm (s.20) (R v Mandair [1995] 1 AC 208). Likewise, sexual assault is an alternative to rape (R v Hodgson [1973] QB 565) and theft is an alternative to robbery.

There are also a number of statutory provisions which set out possible alternative offences, including:

- s.6(2) of the Criminal Law Act 1967: the jury may acquit of murder but convict of (inter alia) manslaughter or causing grievous bodily harm with intent;
- s.6(4) of the same Act: the jury may acquit of the offence charged but convict of attempt to commit that offence;
- s.12(4) of the Theft Act 1968: on a count of theft of a motor vehicle, the jury may acquit of theft but convict the defendant of taking the vehicle without the owner's consent (even though the latter is a summary offence);
- s.24 of the Road Traffic Offenders Act 1988: for example, on a count alleging dangerous driving or causing death or serious injury by dangerous driving, the jury may convict the defendant instead of careless driving (again, even though the latter is a summary offence).

Section 6(3A) provides that summary offences to which s.40 of the Criminal Justice Act 1988 applies (common assault etc.) come within the ambit of subs.(3), and that this is so even if a count charging that summary offence is not included in the indictment. For example, if the accused is charged with assault occasioning actual bodily harm (s.47 of the Offences Against the Person Act 1861) but the jury find that no actual bodily harm was caused, they may acquit of that charge but convict of common assault (to which s.40 of the 1988 Act applies) even though that charge does not appear on the indictment.

Convicting of an alternative offence is possible only if the jury first agree to acquit on the offence on the indictment. If the jury cannot agree on an acquittal on the offence charged, the only way they can convict of another offence is if that offence is added to the indictment as a new count. See, for example, R v Collison (1980) 71 Cr App R 249, where a count was added to the indictment after the jury had been considering their verdict for some while for this very reason.

10.18.3 Directing the jury on alternative offences

The jury can return a verdict of guilty to an alternative offence only if permitted to do by the judge. In Metropolitan Police Commissioner v Wilson [1984] AC 242, Lord Roskill said (at p.261) that the trial judge:

> must always ensure, before deciding to leave the possibility of conviction of another offence to the jury under s.6(3), that that course will involve no risk of injustice to the defendant and that he has had the opportunity of fully meeting that alternative in the course of his defence.

If the possibility of an alternative offence is only canvassed at the end of the trial, the key question is whether the defence would have cross-examined prosecution witnesses differently or would have adduced different defence evidence had the alternative offence been mentioned at the start of the trial.

The question of when the jury should be directed about the possibility of convicting of an alternative offence has been considered in a large number of cases, including R v Fairbanks [1986] 1 WLR 1202, R v Maxwell [1990] 1 WLR 401, and R v Coutts [2006] UKHL 39; [2006] 1 WLR 2154. The real tension in such cases arises from the possibility that the jury will decide that the defendant is not guilty of the offence on the indictment, but is guilty of 'something'. This in turn raises the risk that either the jury will convict him of the more serious offence to ensure he does not escape punishment altogether (which would clearly be unfair on the defendant), or else acquit him even though they have decided that there are sure that he is guilty of some criminality (thus leaving criminality unpunished).

In R v Foster [2007] EWCA Crim 2869; [2008] 1 WLR 1615, Sir Igor Judge P (at [60]–[61]) made the following points:

> [U]nderlining the duty of the trial judge to leave alternative verdicts to the jury, is the risk that faced with the stark choice between convicting a defendant whose behaviour was on any view utterly deplorable, and acquitting him altogether, the jury may unconsciously but wrongly allow its decision to be influenced by considerations extraneous to the evidence and convict of the more serious charges rather than acquit altogether. In such circumstances to omit directions about a possible lesser alternative verdict may therefore work to the defendant's disadvantage ...
>
> Accordingly, not every alternative verdict must be left to the jury. In addition to any specific issues of fairness, there is what we shall describe as a proportionality consideration. The judge is not in error if he decides that a lesser alternative verdict should not be left to the jury if that verdict can properly be described in its legal and factual context as trivial, or insubstantial, or where any possible compromise verdict would not reflect the real issues in the case ... However when the defence to a specific charge amounts to the admission or assertion of a lesser offence, the primary obligation of the judge is to ensure that the defence is left to the jury. If it is not, on elementary principles, the summing up will be seriously defective and the conviction will almost inevitably be unsafe. The judgment whether a 'lesser alternative verdict'

should be left to the jury involves an examination of all the evidence, disputed and undisputed, and the issues of law and fact to which it has given rise. Within that case specific framework the judge must examine whether the absence of a direction about a lesser alternative verdict or verdicts would oblige the jury to make an unrealistic choice between the serious charge and complete acquittal which would unfairly disadvantage the defendant.

In R v *Caven* [2011] EWCA Crim 3239, Aikens LJ helpfully summarised (at [12]) the relevant law:

(1) [B]efore any requirement to leave an alternative verdict to the jury arises, that alternative verdict must be 'obviously' raised on the evidence ...

(2) [T]he alternative is one which really arises on the issues as presented at the trial.

(3) There is no duty to put an alternative verdict if such a verdict would be remote from the real point of the case.

(4) However, each case must depend on its particular facts.

(5) The evidence, disputed and undisputed, and the issues of law and fact to which it gives rise, must be examined ... A judge will not be in error if he decides that a lesser alternative verdict should not be left to the jury if that verdict can properly be described in its legal and factual context as trivial, or insubstantial, or where any possible compromise verdict would not reflect the real issue in the case ...

(6) Where the defence to a specific charge amounts to the admission or assertion of a lesser offence, the primary obligation of the judge is to ensure that that defence is left to the jury. If it is not, then the summing-up will be seriously defective and the conviction unsafe.

(7) A judge may have to reconsider a decision not to leave an alternative verdict to the jury in the light of any question which the jury may see fit to ask ...

(8) At all stages the judge has to ask the question: will the absence of a lesser alternative verdict oblige the jury to make an unrealistic choice between the serious charge and a complete acquittal in a way which would unfairly disadvantage the defendant ....

In R v *Hodson* [2009] EWCA Crim 1590, Keene LJ expressed it thus (at [10]):

There is no automatic requirement on a judge to leave an alternative verdict if such a verdict would not properly reflect the facts of the case, when judged realistically, or would not do justice to the gravity of the case ... [W]hether it is necessary to leave such a verdict, even when legally available as an alternative, will depend on the facts of the individual case. But if it is a realistically available verdict on the evidence, as an interpretation properly open to the jury, without trivialising the offending conduct, then it should be left.

It follows that, for the judge to leave the alternative offence to the jury:

- it must be appropriate (for example, it would not be appropriate where the defence is one of alibi, since it would distract the jury from the main issue in the case, namely the whereabouts of the defendant at the time of the alleged offence);
- it must have been at least implicit in the defence questioning of prosecution witnesses and the defence evidence (otherwise, it will be unfair to the defence);
- if the alternative is trivial in comparison with the offence charged, it may be an unnecessary and undesirable complication.

A simpler course of action, instead of relying upon s.6(3), is to add a count to the indictment alleging the alternative offence, which the jury can then consider in the usual way, a practice commended by Lord Mackay LC in R v *Mandair* [1995] 1 AC 208 at p.216, and Sir Igor Judge P, in R v *Lahaye* [2005] EWCA Crim 2847; [2006] 1 Cr App R 11 at [21].

10.19 Change of plea

The defendant may change his plea from not guilty to guilty at any stage before the verdict is given. Counsel for the defendant simply asks for the indictment to be put again, and the defendant pleads guilty.

The judge has a discretion to allow the defendant to change his plea of guilty to one of not guilty at any stage before sentence has been passed (R v *Dodd* (1982) 74 Cr App R 50). Rule 25.5 requires an application to withdraw a guilty plea to be made in writing. Rule 25.5(3) requires that the application must:

    (a)   explain why it would be unjust for the guilty plea to remain unchanged;

    (b)   indicate what, if any, evidence the applicant wishes to call;

    (c)   identify any proposed witness; and

    (d)   indicate whether legal professional privilege is waived, specifying any material name and date.

Permission to withdraw a guilty plea is unlikely to be given unless the defendant did not realise that he had a defence when he pleaded guilty (R v *McNally* [1954] 1 WLR 933). In R v *Sheikh* [2004] EWCA Crim 492; [2004] 2 Cr App R 13, Mantell LJ (at [19]) said that the court has a discretion to allow the withdrawal of a guilty plea:

> where not to do so might work an injustice. Examples might be where a defendant has been misinformed about the nature of the charge or the availability of a defence or where he has been put under pressure to plead guilty in circumstances where he is not truly admitting guilt.

In *Sookram v R* [2011] UKPC 5, one of the defendants changed his plea to guilty during the course of the trial. The issue arose whether the trial of the remaining defendant should have continued. Lord Brown (at [19]) said that there are cases where, upon a co-accused changing his plea to guilty, justice requires the jury to be discharged and the other accused to be tried afresh by a new jury. However, that will be the case only where it is possible to point to a 'particular unfairness' which would result from that accused continuing to be tried by the same jury.

10.20 Procedure where defendant is convicted

Rule 25.16 of the Criminal Procedure Rules governs the procedure where the defendant either pleads guilty or is found guilty. Rule 25.16(2) provides that, where the defendant is an individual, the court may exercise its power:

    (i)   to require a pre-sentence report,

    (ii)   to request a medical report,

    (iii)   to require a statement of the defendant's financial circumstances.

If the defendant is a company, the court may require such information as it directs about the defendant's corporate structure and financial resources.

Rule 25.16(3) sets out the role of the prosecutor at the sentencing hearing:

The prosecutor must—

(a) summarise the prosecution case, if the sentencing court has not heard evidence;

(b) identify in writing any offence that the prosecutor proposes should be taken into consideration in sentencing;

(c) provide information relevant to sentence, including—
   (i) any previous conviction of the defendant, and the circumstances where relevant,
   (ii) any statement of the effect of the offence on the victim, the victim's family or others; and

(d) identify any other matter relevant to sentence, including—
   (i) the legislation applicable,
   (ii) any sentencing guidelines, or guideline cases,
   (iii) aggravating and mitigating features affecting the defendant's culpability and the harm which the offence caused, was intended to cause or might foreseeably have caused, and
   (iv) the effect of such of the information listed in para.(2) as the court may need to take into account.

Under r.25.16(6), before passing sentence, the court must give the defendant an opportunity to make representations and to introduce evidence relevant to sentence (and where the defendant is under 18, the court may give the defendant's parents, guardian or other supporting adult, if present, such an opportunity as well).

Rule 25.16(7)(a) provides that, when the court has taken into account all the evidence, information and any report available, the court must, as a general rule, pass sentence at the earliest opportunity. When passing sentence, r.25.16(7)(b) requires the court to:

(i) explain the reasons,

(ii) explain to the defendant its effect, the consequences of failing to comply with any order or pay any fine, and any power that the court has to vary or review the sentence, unless the defendant is absent or the defendant's ill-health or disorderly conduct makes such an explanation impracticable, and

(iii) give any such explanation in terms the defendant, if present, can understand (with help, if necessary) . . .

10.21 Variation of sentence

Section 155 of the Powers of Criminal Courts (Sentencing) Act 2000 empowers the Crown Court to vary or rescind a sentence within 56 days of the date when the court imposed that sentence. Under subs.(4), only the judge who imposed the sentence can vary or rescind it.

This power is rarely invoked. It would be appropriate where, for example, an unlawful sentence has inadvertently been passed.

Section 155 can, in exceptional circumstances, be used to increase sentence. In R v *Hadley* (1995) 16 Cr App R(S) 358, for example, the judge thought that the maximum sentence for the offence of which the defendant had been convicted was lower than in fact it was. When he discovered his error, he increased the defendant's sentence. The Court of Appeal upheld this use of s.155.

In R v *Warren* [2017] EWCA Crim 226; [2017] 4 WLR 71 (at [22]), the Court of Appeal gave guidance on the operation of s.155:

(1) Where an error occurs in the factual basis of sentence it should be pointed out to the court as soon as possible and consideration should be given to correcting it at the earliest opportunity, preferably by revisiting sentence on the same day rather than a subsequent day.

(2) A judge should not use the slip rule simply because there is a change of mind about the nature or length of the sentence but the slip rule is available where the judge is persuaded that he had made a material error in the sentencing process whether of fact or law. It is relevant in considering whether he had made a material error that that error might be corrected by the Court of Appeal on the Attorney General's application.

(3) The sooner the slip rule is invoked in such a case the better. The passage of time from the first decision to its revision is a material consideration as to how the power should be exercised but there is a 56-day cut off in any event.

(4) A judge should not be unduly influenced by the prospect of a reference being made to change the sentence that he thought was right at the time by the mere threat of a review by the Attorney General. If the judge concludes that the sentence was not wrong in principle and was not unduly lenient, he should not change his mind simply because there is the possibility of a reference. The judge can then use the opportunity at the further sentencing hearing to give any further explanations for the original decision for the sentence.

(5) Sentencing and re-sentencing should take place in the presence of the appellant and administrative convenience should not be allowed to degrade that principle. But if for one reason or another the appellant cannot be brought to court in the 56 days there is a discretion to proceed in his absence so long as there is an advocate who can fully represent in the sense of who is properly instructed as to the relevant facts and is able to assist the court to make pertinent submissions on the facts and the law, as clearly this appellant's advocate was on the date of the re-sentence.

(6) [T]he appearance of justice and the impact of the change on a defendant where an error has not been induced by anything that he has said or done is a relevant consideration and in appropriate cases it can be reflected in a modest discount to the proposed revised sentence to reflect this fact ....

10.22 Fitness to plead

A defendant is unfit to plead if he suffers from a disability which prevents him from being able to understand the course of the proceedings and the evidence which is given. Such a defendant would not be able to give proper instructions to his lawyer. It is not enough for the accused to be mentally disturbed or to be suffering from amnesia so that he cannot remember the events in question (see R v *Podola* [1960] 1 QB 325). In R v *Erskine* [2009] EWCA Crim 1425; [2009] 2 Cr App R 29, Lord Judge CJ (at [88]) said that: 'Provided the defendant can understand the proceedings, he will be deemed fit to plead.'

The procedure to be followed in a case where fitness to plead is an issue is contained in the Criminal Procedure (Insanity) Act 1964.

If the issue of fitness is determined at the start of the trial, it is determined by the judge (s.4 (5)), and if the defendant is found fit to plead, a jury is empanelled to try the case in the usual way.

Under s.4(2), the court may, if it is of the opinion that it is 'expedient to do so and in the interests of the accused', postpone consideration of the question of fitness until any time up to the opening of the case for the defence. This enables a submission of no case to answer to be made and, if the submission is successful, the defendant is acquitted, and so the question of fitness does not need to be determined (s.4(3)).

To determine the issue of fitness to plead, the evidence of at least two doctors (at least one of whom must specialise in mental disorder) is required (s.4(6)).

Where the defendant is found by the judge unfit to plead, a jury has to consider whether he committed the act or omission charged against him. The procedure for this is governed by s.4A of the 1964 Act. If consideration of the question of fitness to plead was postponed, that issue is determined by the jury trying the case (otherwise, a jury is empanelled for the purpose of determining the issue). If the jury finds that he did not do the act alleged, then he must be acquitted (s.4A(4)).

Under s.5, where the defendant is found unfit to plead and it is also found that he committed the act alleged, the court is empowered to make a hospital order or supervision order (under the Mental Health Act 1983), or to grant an absolute discharge.

See also r.25.10 of the Criminal Procedure Rules for a summary of this procedure.

It is likely that medical evidence will be required in order to determine fitness to plead. Directions for commissioning medical reports, other than for sentencing purposes, are contained in r.3.28. In particular, the court must identify each issue in respect of which it requires expert medical opinion and specify the nature of the expertise likely to be required for giving such opinion; the court must also set (and enforce) a timetable for the production of the report.

10.23 *Autrefois convict* and *autrefois acquit*

The basic principle of *autrefois convict* and *autrefois acquit* (double jeopardy) is that a person should not be tried twice for the same offence. In other words, a person should not be tried for a crime in respect of which he has already been acquitted or convicted (*Connelly v DPP* [1964] AC 1254). From the speeches in *Connelly*, it is possible to identify three other principles:

- the defendant cannot be tried for a crime in respect of which he could have been convicted on an earlier occasion (and so cannot be convicted of an offence which was an alternative offence of which the jury could have convicted him under s.6(3) of the Criminal Law Act 1967). Thus, a defendant who has been tried for robbery cannot subsequently be tried for the theft which comprised that robbery;
- the defendant cannot be tried for a crime, proof of which would necessarily entail proof of another crime of which he has already been acquitted (that is, the offence of which he has been acquitted is a necessary step towards establishing the second offence). Thus, if the defendant is acquitted of theft, he cannot later be charged with robbery alleging that same theft; and
- the defendant cannot be tried for a crime which is, in effect, the same (or substantially the same) as one of which he has previously been acquitted or convicted, or of which he could have been convicted by way of a verdict of guilty to an alternative offence.

In *R v JFJ* [2013] EWCA Crim 569; [2013] 2 Cr App R 10, Sir John Thomas P (at [29]) observed that the *autrefois* doctrine is complemented by abuse of process:

In any case where the narrow application of the principle would result in unfairness or injustice to a defendant amounting to oppression, the remedy lies in the power of the court to stay the proceedings.

10.24 Trial on indictment without a jury

Trial on indictment almost invariable means trial before a judge and jury. However, there are circumstances where a Crown Court trial may take place in front of a judge sitting without a jury.

10.24.1 Jury tampering

Section 44 of the Criminal Justice Act 2003 enables an application to be made by the prosecution for a trial to be conducted without a jury where there is a danger of jury tampering. The judge may make such an order only if two conditions are satisfied:

- there must be 'evidence of a real and present danger that jury tampering would take place' (s.44 (4)); and
- 'notwithstanding any steps (including the provision of police protection) which might reasonably be taken to prevent jury tampering, the likelihood that it would take place would be so substantial as to make it necessary in the interests of justice for the trial to be conducted without a jury' (s.44(5)).

Section 46 of the 2003 Act makes provision for the discharge of a jury because of jury tampering. Under subs.(3), if the judge (after hearing representations from the parties) discharges the jury, he may make an order that the trial is to continue without a jury if he is satisfied that:

- jury tampering has taken place; and
- to continue the trial without a jury would be fair to the defendant(s).

However, under subs.(4), if the judge considers that it is necessary in the interests of justice for the trial to be terminated, he must terminate the trial.

In R v T [2009] EWCA Crim 1035; [2010] 1 WLR 630, Lord Judge CJ said (at [16]) that the judge has to be satisfied to the criminal standard (that is, beyond reasonable doubt) that the conditions in ss.44(4) and 44(5) are fulfilled. The exceptional nature of judge-only trials was emphasised in R v J [2010] EWCA Crim 1755; [2011] 1 Cr App R 5. Lord Judge CJ (at [8]) said ordering the trial of as a serious criminal offence without a jury

> remains and must remain the decision of last resort, only to be ordered when the court is sure (not that it entertains doubts, suspicions or reservations) that the statutory conditions are fulfilled. Save in extreme cases, where the necessary protective measures constitute an unreasonable intrusion into the lives of the jurors ... the confident expectation must be that the jury will perform its duties with its customary determination to do justice.

10.24.2 Trial by judge following trial by jury on sample counts

Section 17(1) of the Domestic Violence, Crime and Victims Act 2004 enables the prosecution to apply to a Crown Court judge for an order that some, but not all, of the counts included in the indictment should be tried without a jury. Under s.17(2), the judge may make such an order if the conditions set out in subss.(3)–(5) are satisfied, namely that:

- the number of counts included in the indictment is likely to mean that a trial by jury involving all of those counts would be impracticable;

- each count or group of counts to be tried with a jury can be regarded as a sample of counts which could be tried without a jury;
- it is in the interests of justice for the order to be made.

Section 17(6) requires the judge to have regard 'to any steps which might reasonably be taken to facilitate a trial by jury' but, under subs.(7), 'a step is not to be regarded as reasonable if it could lead to the possibility of a defendant in the trial receiving a lesser sentence than would be the case if that step were not taken'.

Under s.19(1), where an order is made under s.17(2) and the defendant is found guilty by a jury on a count that may be regarded as a sample of other counts to be tried in those proceedings, those other counts may then be tried without a jury (that is, by a judge alone).

Chapter 11

Appeals to the Court of Appeal

Chapter Contents

Appeal against conviction and/or sentence in the Crown Court lies to the Court of Appeal (Criminal Division). In this chapter, we look at the procedure for appealing against conviction and/or sentence following trial on indictment and at the criteria applied by the Court of Appeal when disposing of such appeals.

11.1 The Court of Appeal (Criminal Division)

The Court of Appeal (Criminal Division) comprises Lords Justices of Appeal, together with High Court judges whom the Lord Chief Justice has asked to assist with the work of the Court of Appeal (ss.2, 3 and 9 of the Senior Courts Act 1981).

The number of judges required for a sitting of the Court of Appeal is governed by s.55 of the 1981 Act:

- When determining an appeal against conviction, the Court of Appeal must comprise at least three judges; one or more of the judges must be a Lord Justice of Appeal. The decision is by majority (the presiding judge does not have a casting vote). Usually, only one judgment will be delivered.
- When determining an appeal against sentence, the Court of Appeal may consist of only two judges, but again one of them should be a Lord Justice of Appeal. Should an appeal be heard by a two-judge court (again, one would have to be a Lord Justice of Appeal) and the two judges disagree, the appeal will be reheard by a three-judge court.

We shall see later that some of the powers of the Court of Appeal may be exercised by a single judge (for example, the granting of leave to appeal). The single judge may be a Lord Justice of Appeal or else a High Court judge whom the Lord Chief Justice has asked to assist with the work of the Court of Appeal.

Certain circuit judges may also be approved by the Lord Chancellor to sit in the Court of Appeal (Criminal Division). A sitting of the court must not include more than one circuit judge (s.55(6)), and a circuit judge is not permitted to exercise the powers of the single judge (considering applications for leave to appeal and related matters).

The administrative work of the court is carried out by the office of the Registrar of Criminal Appeals.

There is very helpful information in the *Guide to commencing proceedings in the Court of Appeal Criminal Division* (2018).

11.2 Appeal against conviction

In this section we consider appeals against conviction, before going on to examine appeals against sentence.

11.2.1 The need for leave to appeal

Under s.1(2) of the Criminal Appeal Act 1968, an appeal against conviction may only be made if either:

- the Court of Appeal gives leave to appeal (s.1(2)(a)); or
- the trial judge (within 28 days of the date of conviction) certifies that the case is 'fit for appeal' (s.1(2)(b)).

In R v Inskip [2005] EWCA Crim 3372, it was emphasised that such certificates should be granted only in exceptional cases. The normal rule is that it should be left to the Court of Appeal to decide whether a case is suitable for the grant of leave to appeal (per Richards LJ, at [28]). A certificate would ordinarily be granted only 'if there was a very clear reason for doing so, such as an unresolved issue of law or where there were clear reasons for supposing that the appeal was likely to succeed' (R v Harries [2007] EWCA Crim 820, per Scott Baker LJ (at [4])). In R v Matthews [2014] EWCA Crim 2757, Lord Thomas CJ (at [2]–[3]) said:

> ... Crown Court Judges should certify cases only in exceptional circumstances ... [A] judge should not grant a certificate with regard to sentence merely in the light of the mitigation to which he has, in his opinion, given due weight. A judge should also bear in mind that applications may always be made to this court for leave to appeal and for bail, or, if bail is not granted, expedition of the hearing of the appeal. If a short sentence is imposed, every effort is made by the Court of Appeal to bring the case on very quickly. Difficulties arise for an appellant if he is granted bail and the court hearing the appeal concludes that there was no basis for the appeal.
>
> [I]t is essential that if a judge is to consider exercising the power to grant a certificate and to grant bail, he should set out his reasons for taking such a course. His reasons should explain why the exceptional procedure is being used.

In R v Atta-Dankwa [2018] EWCA Crim 320; [2018] 2 Cr App R 16, Holroyde LJ said (at [20]) that, even if the case is one where the criteria for a certificate by the trial judge appear to be met, it should still be borne in mind that:

> the Registrar of Criminal Appeals has the power to refer an application for leave to appeal directly to the full Court, which can be done very quickly, and that in an appropriate case, steps can be taken to ensure that an appeal is heard within a short period of time.

Indeed, Criminal Practice Direction III, para.14H.3 says that 'it is expected that certificates will only be granted in exceptional circumstances'.

11.2.2 Appeal against conviction where the defendant pleaded guilty

The Court of Appeal is very unwilling to give leave to appeal against conviction to a defendant who pleaded guilty in the Crown Court. In R v Forde [1923] 2 KB 400, Avory J said (at p.403):

> A plea of guilty having been recorded, this Court can only entertain an appeal against conviction if it appears (1) that the appellant did not appreciate the nature of the charge or did not intend to admit he was guilty of it, or (2) that upon the admitted facts he could not in law have been convicted of the offence charged.

In R v Eriemo [1995] 2 Cr App R 206, the Court of Appeal reaffirmed its reluctance to entertain appeals where the defendant pleaded guilty. In that case, the applicant (who had changed his plea to guilty following the trial judge's refusal to sever the indictment on the basis that the applicant was going to allege that he committed the offence under the duress of the co-defendant) was refused leave to appeal. It was said by Glidewell LJ (at p.210) that where a defendant pleads guilty, he is making an admission of the facts which form the basis of the offence with which he is charged and therefore loses his right to appeal against conviction.

In *R v Chalkley* [1998] QB 848, the Court of Appeal returned to the question whether a defendant who pleads guilty in the Crown Court can appeal against conviction to the Court of Appeal. The defendants had originally pleaded not guilty, but the judge ruled that certain evidence against them (covertly obtained tape-recordings of conversations) was admissible; the defendants then changed their pleas to guilty. It was held that the Court of Appeal may quash a conviction based on a guilty plea 'where the plea was mistaken or without intention to admit the truth of the offence charged' (per Auld LJ, at p.859). His Lordship went on to say (at p.864):

> [A] conviction would be unsafe where the effect of an incorrect ruling of law on admitted facts was to leave an accused with no legal escape from a verdict of guilty on those facts. But a conviction would not normally be unsafe where an accused is influenced to change his plea to guilty because he recognises that, as a result of a ruling to admit strong evidence against him, his case on the facts is hopeless. A change of plea to guilty in such circumstances would normally be regarded as an acknowledgement of the truth of the facts constituting the offence charged.

In *R v Asiedu* [2015] EWCA Crim 714; [2015] 2 Cr App R 8, Lord Hughes drew an important distinction (at [20]), saying that a guilty plea is not a bar to a subsequent appeal against conviction

> where the plea of guilty was compelled as a matter of law by an adverse ruling by the trial judge which left no arguable defence to be put before the jury. So, if the judge rules as a matter of law that on the defendant's own case, that is on agreed or assumed facts, the offence has been committed, there is no arguable defence which the defendant can put before the jury. In that situation he can plead guilty and challenge the adverse ruling by appeal to this court. If the ruling is adjudged to have been wrong, the conviction is likely to be quashed. Contrast the situation where an adverse ruling at the trial (for example as to the admissibility of evidence) renders the defence being advanced more difficult, perhaps dramatically so. There, the ruling does not leave the defendant no case to advance to the jury. He remains able, despite the evidence against him, to advance his defence and, if convicted, to challenge the judicial ruling as to admissibility by way of appeal. If he chooses to plead guilty, he will be admitting the facts which constitute the offence and it will be too late to mount an appeal to this court.

It follows that a conviction would be unsafe where, on the basis of the erroneous ruling, an acquittal would be legally impossible (for example, where the judge rejects the defendant's submission that admitted facts do not in law amount to the offence charged, and so there is no issue of fact for the jury to try). In such a case, an appeal will be entertained despite the guilty plea. Otherwise (for example, where the defendant pleads guilty following an erroneous ruling to admit strong evidence against the defendant), the guilty plea amounts to an admission of the truth of the allegations made against the defendant, and so no appeal will be entertained.

In *Asiedu*, Lord Hughes also referred (at [21]) to a second situation in which a plea of guilty will not prevent an appeal. This is 'where, even if on the admitted or assumed facts the defendant was guilty, there was a legal obstacle to his being tried for the offence'. That will be the case where, for example, the prosecution should have been stayed as an abuse of process. His Lordship said that such cases would be rare. However, such cases do occur. In *R v Early* [2002] EWCA Crim 1904; [2003] 1 Cr App R 288, for example, it was held that where the prosecution have failed to make proper pre-trial disclosure and prosecution witnesses have lied to the court on a *voir dire*, and the defendant enters a plea of guilty on the assumption that full disclosure has been made, the Court of Appeal will set aside that guilty plea however strong the prosecution case might appear to be. Rose LJ (at [10]) said that freely entered pleas of guilty will not be interfered with by the Court of Appeal unless the prosecution's misconduct is of a category which justifies this. It follows that a plea of guilty is binding unless the defendant was ignorant of evidence going to innocence or guilt; ignorance of material which goes merely to credibility of a prosecution witness does not justify re-opening a plea of guilty.

Defendants sometimes seek to argue that they pleaded guilty only because of defective legal advice. In R v Saik [2004] EWCA Crim 2936, Scott Baker LJ said (at [57]) that for an appeal against conviction to succeed on the basis that a guilty plea was tendered following erroneous legal advice, the facts must be so strong as to show that the plea of guilty was not a true acknowledgement of guilt. The advice, he said, must go to the heart of the plea, so that the plea would not be a free plea and what followed would be a nullity. This aspect of the decision is not affected by the successful appeal to the House of Lords [2006] UKHL 18; [2007] 1 AC 18. In R v McCarthy [2015] EWCA Crim 1185, Hallett LJ identified 'two essential principles which govern the present situation where a defendant pleads guilty and subsequently attempts to appeal against his conviction' (at [61]), namely (i) 'if a defendant has been deprived of a defence which [the court] believes would probably have succeeded' ([62]); and (ii) the defendant 'must be free to choose whether to plead guilty or not guilty' ([63]).

11.2.3 Procedure for obtaining leave to appeal

A notice of application for leave to appeal must be served on the Registrar of Criminal Appeals not more than 28 days after conviction (see r.39.2 of the Criminal Procedure Rules). By virtue of r.39.3(1), the notice of appeal must:

> (b) identify each ground of appeal on which the appellant relies ...;
> (c) identify the transcript that the appellant thinks the court will need, if the appellant wants to appeal against a conviction.

Rule 39.3(2) goes on to set out what the grounds of appeal must contain. They must:

> (a) include in no more than the first two pages a summary of the grounds that makes what then follows easy to understand;
> (b) in each ground of appeal identify the event or decision to which that ground relates;
> (c) in each ground of appeal summarise the facts relevant to that ground, but only to the extent necessary to make clear what is in issue;
> (d) concisely outline each argument in support of each ground;
> (e) number each ground consecutively, if there is more than one;
> (f) identify any relevant authority and—
>   (i) state the proposition of law that the authority demonstrates, and
>   (ii) identify the parts of the authority that support that proposition ....

The *Guide* (2018) (para.A3-1) says that the grounds 'must be settled with sufficient particularity to enable the Registrar, and subsequently the Court, to identify clearly the matters relied upon'. The *Guide* goes on (para.A3-6) to warn that:

> Advocates should not settle or sign grounds unless they consider that they are properly arguable. An advocate should not settle grounds they cannot support because they are 'instructed' to do so by a defendant.

11.2.3.1 Time limit

The notice of application for leave to appeal against conviction (or, in those rare cases where the trial judge certified the case fit for appeal, the notice of appeal) must be lodged within 28 days from the date of conviction (s.18(2) of the Criminal Appeal Act 1968).

In R v *Long* [1998] 2 Cr App R 326, the Court of Appeal emphasised that a notice of application for leave to appeal against conviction must be lodged within 28 days of conviction even if there is lapse of time between conviction and sentence. It is clear from the wording of s.18(2) that, for an appeal against conviction, time begins to run from the date of conviction (and not from the date of sentence).

The time for giving notice under s.18 may be extended, either before or after it expires, by the Court of Appeal (s.18(3)). In R v *Hawkins* [1997] 1 Cr App R 234 at p.239, Lord Bingham CJ noted that the Court of Appeal has 'traditionally been reluctant to do so save where the extension sought is relatively short and good reason is shown for the failure to apply in time'. In R v *Bestel* [2013] EWCA Crim 1305; [2014] 1 WLR 4579, Pitchford LJ (at [9]) said that an extension of time will generally be granted when 'the defendant provides a satisfactory explanation for missing the deadline by a narrow margin and there appears to be merit in the grounds of appeal', or 'where relevant and cogent fresh evidence admitted ... has emerged for the first time well after conviction. Nonetheless, evidence as to the circumstances in which the fresh evidence emerged will be required and prompt action thereafter will be expected'.

In R v *Cook* [2017] EWCA Crim 353, the Court of Appeal emphasised the importance of not waiting for sentence to be passed before lodging an application to appeal against conviction. Fulford LJ said (at [3]):

> It is said that the justification for the delay as regards the application for leave to appeal against conviction is to be found in a decision ... to delay the application for leave to appeal until after the applicant had been sentenced so as not to prejudice her at the sentencing hearing, because the judge might have discovered that there was an extant appeal. We indicate immediately that that explanation for the delay in filing grounds of appeal against conviction is entirely devoid of merit. A defendant will never be prejudiced at his or her sentencing hearing because he or she had filed an application for leave to appeal against conviction. The applicant's submission involves the starkly disrespectful suggestion that the judge may sentence the defendant less favourably because he or she was seeking to challenge the safety of the conviction. It is to be regretted that the applicant's representatives have chosen to advance such a fallacious argument ...

11.2.3.2 Transcript of evidence and summing up

The Registrar decides whether a transcript is necessary and, if so, how extensive it should be. Normally, the transcript is limited to the summing up and to any judgment given by the judge during the course of the trial. If counsel for the would-be appellant wants a more extensive transcript, reasons for this request must be given.

11.2.3.3 'Perfecting' the grounds of appeal

The original grounds of appeal will be based on notes taken by the advocate at the time of the trial. It may be that these notes are not entirely accurate (for example, some of the judge's comments may have been omitted or noted down incorrectly). The transcript of the summing up is sent to the appellant so that the grounds of appeal can be 'perfected'.

The original grounds of appeal should be amended so that they refer to specific passages of the transcript.

Once the grounds of appeal have been perfected, the papers are referred to a single judge of the Court of Appeal to decide the question of leave to appeal.

The *Guide* makes the point (para.A8-1) that:

> The purpose of perfection is (a) to save valuable judicial time by enabling the Court to identify at once the relevant parts of the transcript and (b) to give the advocate the opportunity to

reconsider the original grounds in the light of the transcript. Perfected grounds should consist of a fresh document which supersedes the original grounds of appeal and contains inter alia references by page number and letter (or paragraph number) to all relevant passages in the transcript.

11.2.3.4 Change of representative

It will not infrequently be the case that the lawyers who represent the defendant on appeal will not be the same as those who provided representation in the Crown Court. In such cases, the fresh representatives must comply with the duty of due diligence set out in R v McCook [2014] EWCA Crim 734; [2016] 2 Cr App R 30 (per Lord Thomas CJ, at [11]):

In any case where fresh solicitors or fresh counsel are instructed, it will henceforth be necessary for those solicitors or counsel to go to the solicitors and/or counsel who have previously acted to ensure that the facts are correct, unless there are in exceptional circumstances good and compelling reasons not to do so.

This is to ensure that the Court of Appeal is not inadvertently misled about what happened prior to the appeal.

11.2.3.5 Granting of leave to appeal: the single judge

The single judge considers the papers (without a hearing) and decides whether the appeal has a sufficient prospect of success to justify the granting of leave to appeal (s.31(2)(a) of the Criminal Appeal Act 1968).

In most cases, a single judge granting leave to appeal will give leave to appeal generally. However, the single judge may grant leave on some grounds and expressly refuse leave on others. Where leave to appeal has been refused on particular grounds, those grounds can only be argued before the court with its leave (R v Cox [1999] 2 Cr App R 6; R v Jackson [1999] 1 All ER 572).

If the single judge refuses leave to appeal, the appellant has 14 days in which to renew the application for leave (r.36.5(2)). If the appellant does renew the application, it will be heard by two or three Court of Appeal judges sitting in open court (s.31(3) of the Criminal Appeal Act 1968).

In the very rare cases where leave to appeal is not required because the trial judge certified that the case was fit for appeal, grounds of appeal still have to be drafted. The only difference in procedure is that the registrar will not refer the papers to a single judge; instead, the case will be listed for a full hearing by the Court of Appeal.

Under s.20 of the Criminal Appeal Act 1968, if the Registrar takes the view that a notice of appeal or an application for leave to appeal 'does not show any substantial ground of appeal', he can refer it to a sitting of the Court of Appeal for summary determination. The Court may, if they consider that the appeal or application for leave is 'frivolous or vexatious', determine it without adjourning it for a full hearing, dismissing the appeal or application for leave summarily.

It should be noted that, if the appellant wants to rely on a ground of appeal that is not identified by the appeal notice, an application under r.36.14(5) is required. Practice Direction IX, para.39C.4, refers to R v James [2018] EWCA Crim 285; [2018] 1 WLR 2749. In particular, the court will take into account the extent of the delay in advancing the fresh ground or grounds, the reasons for that delay, whether the facts or issues the subject of the fresh ground were known to the appellant's representatives when they advised on appeal, and the interests of justice and the overriding objective (see [38]).

11.2.3.6 Bail

The Crown Court only has jurisdiction to grant bail to someone who is appealing against conviction and/or sentence if the trial judge has certified that the case is fit for appeal (s.81(1)(f) of the Senior Court Act 1981). However, under s.19 of the Criminal Appeal Act 1968, the Court of Appeal may grant an appellant bail pending the determination of his appeal. An application for bail is made in writing and is considered by the single judge (under s.31(2)(e)) without a hearing, though the prosecution must be given an opportunity to make written representations (r.39.8).

Bail pending appeal will be granted only 'where it appears prima facie that the appeal is likely to be successful or where there is a risk that the sentence will have been served by the time the appeal is heard'; the question to be addressed is whether there are 'exceptional circumstances, which would drive the Court to the conclusion that justice can only be done by the granting of bail' (R v Watton (1979) 68 Cr App R 293, at p.297, per Lord Lane CJ).

11.2.3.7 Presence of the appellant

Where the appellant is not in custody, he may be present on any occasion when his appeal is being heard or where interlocutory applications in respect of his appeal are being made in open court. However, an appellant who is in custody may attend interlocutory applications in respect of his appeal and, if the appeal is on a ground of law alone, the hearing of the appeal itself, only with permission from the court (s.22 of the Criminal Appeal Act 1968). Where the appellant is in custody, the single judge may make an order permitting him to be present at the hearing of the appeal if he does not have a right to attend (s.31(2)(c)). No order is needed, as the appellant has the right to attend, if the appeal involves questions of fact.

11.2.4 The hearing of the appeal against conviction

Criminal Practice Direction IX, para.39F.1, provides that, in the case of an appeal against conviction, the advocates must serve a skeleton argument when the appeal notice does not sufficiently outline the grounds of the appeal, particularly in cases where a complex or novel point of law has been raised. In an appeal against sentence it may be helpful for an advocate to serve a skeleton argument when a complex issue is raised.

At the hearing, the appellant's case is presented first and the respondent (the prosecution) then has a right of reply. The appeal takes the form of argument based on the grounds of appeal, the transcript of the summing up and any other documentary evidence. Unless it is a case where the conviction is said to be unsafe because of fresh evidence, no oral evidence will be heard by the court.

11.3 Grounds of appeal against conviction

Section 2(1) of the Criminal Appeal Act 1968 provides that the Court of Appeal:

> (a) shall allow an appeal against conviction if they think that the conviction is unsafe; and
> (b) shall dismiss such an appeal in any other case.

There is no statutory definition of the word 'unsafe'. However, a conviction should be regarded as 'unsafe' if the members of the Court of Appeal feel that there is 'some lurking doubt in our minds which makes us wonder whether an injustice has been done' (R v Cooper [1969] 1 QB 267, at p.271, per Lord Widgery CJ). In Stafford v DPP [1974] AC 878, at p.912, Lord Kilbrandon expressed the question a judge of the Court of Appeal should pose: 'Have I a reasonable doubt, or perhaps even a lurking doubt, that this conviction may be unsafe ... ? If I have I must quash. If I have not, I have no power to do so.'

In R v Graham [1997] 1 Cr App R 302, at p. 308, Lord Bingham CJ said:

> If the Court is satisfied, despite any misdirection of law or any irregularity in the conduct of the trial or any fresh evidence, that the conviction is safe, the Court will dismiss the appeal.

But if, for whatever reason, the Court concludes that the appellant was wrongly convicted of the offence charged, or is left in doubt whether the appellant was rightly convicted of that offence or not, then it must of necessity consider the conviction unsafe. The Court is then subject to a binding duty to allow the appeal.

However, care must be taken in applying the 'lurking doubt' test. In R v Heron [2005] EWCA Crim 3245, Scott Baker LJ said (at [38]) that, 'if we are not persuaded for some specific reason that the conviction is unsafe, the appellant does not succeed on lurking doubt or any general feeling of unease about the conviction'.

Similarly, in R v Pope [2012] EWCA Crim 2241; [2013] 1 Cr App Rep 214, Lord Judge CJ (at [14]) said:

If ... there is a case to answer and, after proper directions, the jury has convicted, it is not open to the court to set aside the verdict on the basis of some collective, subjective judicial hunch that the conviction is or maybe unsafe. Where it arises for consideration at all, the application of the 'lurking doubt' concept requires reasoned analysis of the evidence or the trial process, or both, which leads to the inexorable conclusion that the conviction is unsafe. It can therefore only be in the most exceptional circumstances that a conviction will be quashed on this ground alone, and even more exceptional if the attention of the court is confined to a re-examination of the material before the jury.

It is possible to identify from the case law a number of matters that are capable of making a conviction unsafe.

11.3.1 Errors in the course of the trial

Examples of errors which may render a conviction unsafe include the following:

- A decision by the judge that certain evidence against the defendant was admissible. If the Court of Appeal decides that the evidence in question ought to have been excluded, the court will go on to consider what impact this mistake had on the trial – for example, how strong was the other (admissible) evidence against the accused. The ultimate question is whether the erroneous admission of the evidence rendered the conviction unsafe.
- The wrongful rejection by the judge of a submission that there is no case to answer. Where a defendant appeals against conviction on the ground that the trial judge wrongly rejected a submission of no case to answer at the end of the prosecution case, the Court of Appeal should ignore any evidence admitted after the submission of no case. In R v Smith [1999] 2 Cr App R 238, Mantell LJ (at p.242) said:

What if a submission is wrongly rejected but the defendant is cross-examined into admitting his guilt? Should the conviction be said to be unsafe? We think it should. The defendant was entitled to be acquitted after the evidence against him had been heard. To allow the trial to continue beyond the end of the prosecution case would be an abuse of process and fundamentally unfair. So even in the extreme case, the conviction should be regarded as unsafe ...

Therefore, if the defendant admits his guilt during cross-examination, the conviction will be set aside on the basis that the conviction is unsafe because the defendant should not have had to testify: if the submission of no case to answer had been upheld as it should have been, the defendant would not have been subject to cross-examination. This approach emphasises the need to achieve fairness for the defendant. On the other hand, it could be argued that it is contrary to one of the other elements of the overriding objective, namely 'acquitting the innocent and convicting the guilty'.

- Irregularities occurring during the course of the trial. This includes, for example, misconduct on the part of a juror (see below).

- Errors in the summing up. In R v Williams [2001] EWCA Crim 932, Dyson LJ (at [28]) said that, 'A legal misdirection or non-direction is not significant unless it is possible that, but for the error of law, the jury would have acquitted'. Because jurors do not give reasons for their verdict (simply announcing a finding that the defendant is 'guilty' or 'not guilty'), one can never be sure of the basis of their decision. The secrecy of the jury room (see below) means that the basis for the conviction or acquittal will only be known to the jurors themselves. The Court of Appeal therefore has to proceed on the basis that the jury both understood and applied the directions on the law that they received from the judge. In R v Taylor [2013] UKPC 8; [2013] 1 WLR 1144, Lord Hope (at [25]) said that the 'assumption must be that the jury understood and followed the direction that they were given ... [T]he law proceeds on the footing that the jury, acting in accordance with the instructions given to them by the trial judge, will render a true verdict in accordance with the evidence. To conclude otherwise would be to underrate the integrity of the system of trial by jury and the effect on the jury of the instructions by the trial judge'. That said, the only way in which the basis of the jury's decision can be made clearer is if the judge provides the jury with a written route to verdict (see Chapter 10). Whilst one cannot be sure what use a jury made of the written route to verdict, it does offer them a structure for their deliberations and (perhaps more importantly as regards appeals) does make it easier to detect errors of law in the directions given to the jury.

- The judge's conduct of the trial. In R v Inns [2018] EWCA Crim 1081, Singh LJ (at [33]–[38]) summarised the need for judicial neutrality, identifying six principles: (i) 'the tribunal of fact in a criminal trial in the Crown Court is the jury and no one else'; (ii) 'ours is an adversarial system, not an inquisitorial one. The role of the judge is therefore to act as a neutral umpire, to ensure a fair trial between the prosecution and the defence. The judge should not enter the arena so as to appear to be taking sides'; (iii) 'there is nothing wrong in principle with a trial judge asking questions of witnesses in order to assist the jury'; (iv) 'since ours is an adversarial system it is for the prosecution to prove its case and it will have the opportunity to cross-examine the defendant if he or she chooses to give evidence. It will often be unnecessary for the judge to ask any questions during the defendant's evidence-in-chief because it should be for the prosecution to cross-examine the defendant. It is certainly not the role of the judge to cross-examine the defendant'; (v) 'it is particularly important that the defendant should have the opportunity to give his or her account to the jury in the way that he or she would like that evidence to come out, elicited through questions from their own advocate'; (vi) 'this is not affected by the fact that the defence account may appear to be implausible or even fanciful. If it is truly incredible, the prosecution can reasonably be expected to expose its deficiencies in cross-examination and the jury will see through it. If anything, unwarranted interventions by a judge may simply prove to be counterproductive'.

Active case management is encouraged, but judges must take care not to go too far. For example, in R v Harirbafan [2008] EWCA Crim 1967, Toulson LJ (at [3]) noted that:

> Interruptions by a judge which are excessive or which demonstrate a lack or apparent lack of impartiality, by taking on the role of a prosecutor, may prejudice a fair trial and jeopardise the safety of a conviction in two particular ways, which may be cumulative. First, they may disrupt the process by which the defence advocate seeks to adduce evidence, whether by examination in-chief or cross-examination, in such a way that the defendant is prejudiced by the jury being deprived of the opportunity of hearing that evidence given and challenged in an orderly and coherent way. Secondly, such interruptions, if they are excessive and take on the substance of cross-

examination, may have the potential to poison the minds of the jury against the defendant, by causing the jury to perceive that the judge, who is supposedly an independent figure and likely to carry respect in the eyes of the jury, clearly thinks that the defendant is trying to fool the jury.

Similarly, in R v *Perren* [2009] EWCA Crim 348, Toulson LJ (at [34]–[35]) said that

there are good reasons why a judge should be particularly careful about refraining from intervening during a witness's evidence in-chief, except insofar as it is necessary to clarify, to keep the evidence moving on and, if necessary, to avoid prolixity or irrelevancies. The first is that it is for the prosecution to cross-examine, not for the judge. The second is that the right time for the prosecution to cross-examine is after a witness has given his evidence in-chief … A jury will inevitably form a view of each witness as the case goes along. As the witness is giving his or her evidence in-chief, so the jury will be absorbing that account and forming their own impression of the witness.

The [defendant's] story may have been highly improbable, but he was entitled to explain it to the jury without being subjected to sniper fire in the course of doing so. The potential for injustice is that if the jury, at the very time when they are listening to the witness giving his narrative account of events, do so to the accompaniment of questions from the Bench indicating to anybody with common sense that the judge does not believe a word of it, this may affect the mind of the jury as they listen to the account.

In R v *McClelland* [2015] EWCA Crim 1080, it was argued by the appellant that the judge had intervened excessively in the trial. Sir Brain Leveson P said (at [14]) that:

The judge is no longer required to allow the trial to take whatever course counsel seek to take it. His responsibilities include appropriate case management before, during and subsequent to all aspects of the trial. It is his responsibility to ensure that questions are direct and not prolix, that counsel pursue the trial with expedition, and that issues which he believes are relevant to the jury's consideration are appropriately examined. That is not to say that the judge could or should act as a second prosecutor (or a second defence counsel). When intervening to seek elaboration, it is appropriate to do so in an open and careful manner, not least because the impact of appearing partial may carry through into the jury's deliberations.

His Lordship added (at [16]) that 'excessive or inappropriate interventions of a judge are not sufficient to justify the quashing of a conviction. The decision for this court is whether the nature and the extent of the interventions have resulted in the appellant's trial becoming unfair'; where it is alleged that a judge has over-stepped the mark, it has to be decided whether he 'effectively acted as a second prosecutor and thereby deprived the appellant of a fair trial' (at [18]). It is only if that is the case that the conviction will be unsafe.

A similar approach was taken in R v *Aujla* [2015] EWCA Crim 853, where Hickinbottom J (at [26]) said:

Conduct of a judge will only lead to doubt with regard to a conviction if, looking at the matter as a whole, this court considers that, to let the conviction stand, risks an injustice being done or legitimately gives rise to a real perception that justice has not been done.

It follows that the ultimate question for the Court of Appeal is 'whether the judge's conduct, looked at in the context of the trial as a whole, was such as to lead us to doubt that to let the convictions stand would risk an injustice being done to the Appellant' (at [34]). As Leggatt LJ said in R v *Marchant* [2018] EWCA Crim 2606 (at [17]), the key question is whether there is 'a real risk that the jury was materially impeded from considering the prosecution and defence cases fairly and reaching a just verdict according to the evidence'.

In R v Naz [2017] EWCA Crim 482, [2018] 4 WLR 28 (at [32]), the Court of Appeal noted that,

> If the matters complained of rendered the trial unfair, then the strength of the case against the appellant is totally irrelevant. Every defendant, including a defendant faced with a strong prosecution case, is entitled to a fair trial. That is an absolute right irrespective of the strength of the evidence.

● Errors by defence counsel: in R v Ullah [2000] 1 Cr App R 351, it was held that a conviction will not be unsafe merely because defence counsel took a decision that another advocate might not have taken. Rose LJ (at p.358) said that the Court of Appeal will only have regard to 'significant' fault by trial counsel or solicitor: the question is whether the decision was one that no reasonable advocate could have reached. In R v Boal [1992] QB 591, where Simon Brown LJ said (at p.600) that an appeal on the ground of erroneous legal advice, resulting in a defence not being raised, will succeed only where the court 'believes the defence would quite probably have succeeded and concludes, therefore, that a clear injustice has been done'.

11.3.1.1 Safety of conviction and fairness of trial

An important question is the relationship between the 'safety' of the conviction (the test applicable under the Criminal Appeal Act 1968) and the 'fairness' of the trial (the test applicable under Art. 6 of the European Convention on Human Rights).

In R v Francom [2001] 1 Cr App R 17, Lord Woolf CJ said (at [43]) that the test of whether a conviction is 'unsafe' is not identical to the issue of 'unfairness'; the term 'unfair' is not limited to the safety of the conviction itself, but encompasses the entire prosecution process. However, his Lordship said (at [47]) that, in a case involving misdirection of the jury, the Court of Appeal should approach the issue of lack of safety in the same way that the European Court of Human Rights approaches lack of fairness. A misdirection might render a conviction unsafe and/or the trial unfair, but it does not necessarily do so.

However, in R v Togher [2001] 1 Cr App R 33, Lord Woolf CJ said (at [30]) that 'if a defendant has been denied a fair trial it will almost be inevitable that the conviction will be regarded as unsafe'.

Nevertheless, in R v Davies, Rowe and Johnson [2001] 1 Cr App R 8, the Court of Appeal said that, even if there has been a finding by the European Court of Human Rights that Art.6(1) of the Convention has been violated, that will not *necessarily* lead to the quashing of a conviction, since it is for the domestic court to examine the safety of the conviction in accordance with s.2 of the Criminal Appeal Act 1968. Mantell LJ said (at [56]) that a conviction can never be safe if there is doubt about the appellant's guilt. However, his Lordship said that the converse is not true: a conviction might be unsafe even where there is no doubt about guilt, but the trial process was vitiated by serious unfairness or significant legal misdirection. It follows that if a trial is found to be unfair, that could have an impact on the safety of the conviction even in the face of overwhelming evidence against the defendant. His Lordship went on to say that, usually, the court should ask itself: 'Assuming the wrong decision on law or the irregularity had not occurred and the trial had been free from legal error, would the only reasonable and proper verdict have been one of guilty?' At [65], his Lordship added that a finding of a breach of Art.6(1) would not lead 'inexorably' to the quashing of a conviction: the effect of any unfairness upon the safety of a conviction will vary according to its nature and degree.

The position was summarised by Mitting J in Dowsett v Criminal Cases Review Commission [2007] EWHC 1923 (Admin), at [16]: '[N]ot every breach of Article 6 will make a conviction unsafe. The nature of the breach and the facts of the case must in every case be analysed.'

In *R v A* (No 2) [2001] UKHL 25; [2002] 1 AC 45, Lord Steyn took a slightly different approach, saying (at [38]):

> It is well established that the guarantee of a fair trial under Art.6 is absolute: a conviction obtained in breach of it cannot stand … The only balancing permitted is in respect of what the concept of a fair trial entails: here account may be taken of the familiar triangulation of interests of the accused, the victim and society. In this context proportionality has a role to play.

Put another way, a breach of the right to a fair trial should result in the conviction being held to be unsafe, but not every error in the course of a trial is of sufficient gravity to result in unfairness. If there is doubt about guilt, then the conviction must be held to be unsafe. But if there is no doubt about guilt, it is not every case where an unfairness can be identified that will necessarily and inevitably lead to a quashing of the conviction. As Lord Bingham put it in *R v Randall* [2002] UKPC 19; [2002] 1 WLR 2237 (at [28]):

> [I]t is not every departure from good practice which renders a trial unfair … But the right of a criminal defendant to a fair trial is absolute. There will come a point when the departure from good practice is so gross, or so persistent, or so prejudicial, or so irremediable that an appellate court will have no choice but to condemn a trial as unfair and quash a conviction as unsafe, however strong the grounds for believing the defendant to be guilty. The right to a fair trial is one to be enjoyed by the guilty as well as the innocent, for a defendant is presumed to be innocent until proved to be otherwise in a fairly conducted trial.

The importance of the right to a fair trial was emphasised in *R v Myers* [2018] EWCA Crim 2191. The Court of Appeal (at [49]) cited with approval *R v Perren* [2009] EWCA Crim 348, where Toulon LJ had said (at [24]):

> [I]f the court is driven to the conclusion that the defendant has not had a fair trial, when the matter is looked at in the round, the natural conclusion will be that the verdict is unsafe because our system of criminal justice is dependent upon the fundamental principle of the provision of a fair trial. To allow an appeal in such circumstances, even though the evidence for the prosecution may have been exceedingly strong, is not to allow an appeal on a technicality, but to allow it upon a fundamental principle which underlines our criminal justice system.

11.3.1.2 Appeals relating to the jury

Under s.18 of the Juries Act 1974, a conviction may not be quashed on the ground that the provisions in the Act regarding the selection of the jury have not been complied with, or that a juror was not qualified to serve, or that a juror was unfit to serve.

In addition to the restriction contained in s.18, it is also a strict rule that the Court of Appeal will not investigate what went on in the jury room while the jury were considering their verdict. This is partly because of the effect of what is now s.20D of the Juries Act 1974, which makes it an offence, subject to a number of exceptions, for a person intentionally to 'disclose information about statements made, opinions expressed, arguments advanced or votes cast by members of a jury in the course of their deliberations in proceedings before a court, or to solicit or obtain such information'. This provision is subject to exceptions in s.20E–G which ensure that the offence does not prevent the proper investigation of alleged juror offences or irregularities.

There is, in any event, a long-standing common law rule that the Court of Appeal will not admit evidence of jury deliberations after a verdict has been delivered. For example, in R v Bean [1991] Crim LR 843, the defence wanted to adduce evidence from the jury bailiff that he had overheard an exchange which could be regarded as one juror being pressurised into voting in favour of conviction, but the Court of Appeal refused to entertain this evidence. Similarly, in R v Schofield [1993] Crim LR 217, the Court of Appeal refused to entertain evidence of a conversation between a juror and the jury bailiff in which it became apparent that the jury did not understand the legal definition of the charge.

In Gregory v UK (1998) 25 EHRR 577, after the jury had retired to consider its verdict, a note was passed from the jury to the judge. It read: 'Jury showing racial overtones. One member to be excused'. The trial judge warned the jury to try the case according to the evidence and to put aside any prejudice. The jury eventually, by a majority of 10 to 2, returned a verdict of guilty. The European Court of Human Rights (at [44]) acknowledged

> that the rule governing the secrecy of jury deliberations is a crucial and legitimate feature of English trial law which serves to reinforce the jury's role as the ultimate arbiter of fact and to guarantee open and frank deliberations among jurors on the evidence which they have heard.

In R v Connor; R v Mirza [2004] UKHL 2; [2004] 1 AC 1118, both appeals were based on a letter sent by a member of the jury after the trial was over. Lord Hope of Craighead took as his starting point three propositions (at [61]): (i) that confidentiality is essential to the proper functioning of the jury process; (ii) that there is merit in finality; and (iii) that jurors must be protected from harassment. At [107], Lord Hope summarised the exceptions to the jury secrecy rule:

- events that took place outside the jury room;
- irregularities which may have led to the jury being provided with information which they should not have had, or
- the possession by a juror of knowledge or characteristics which made it inappropriate for that person to serve on the jury.

Lord Rodger of Earlsferry (at [156]) noted that:

> Allegations of misconduct by jurors may surface at any stage of a trial before the jury has returned a verdict. In such cases there is no reason why the allegations should not be investigated. Judges must accordingly take appropriate steps to investigate and deal with any such matter that arises then ... If it turns out on investigation of an allegation that the jury as a whole is fatally compromised, the judge will discharge them. Where only one particular juror is fatally compromised, the judge will discharge that juror and the trial will proceed with the remaining jurors. In less serious cases the judge will deal with the matter by giving the jury appropriate directions.

The decision in Connor was considered by the House of Lords in R v Smith; R v Mercieca [2005] UKHL 12; [2005] 1 WLR 704. After the jury had been deliberating for some time, the judge received a letter from one of the jurors, stating that a certain group of jurors had been badgering, coercing and intimidating other jurors into changing their verdicts. The judge, after consulting with counsel, gave a further direction to the jury, telling them that there had to be discussion and give and take, and exhorting them not to be bullied or cajoled into giving a verdict with which they did not agree. It was held that the judge was not obliged to question the jurors about the contents of the letter, nor would it have been appropriate for him to do so; if he had gone into the allegations, he would inevitably have had to question them about the subject of their deliberations (namely, whether the defendants were guilty of any of the offences charged). Moreover, where the juror's communication alleges wilful misconduct on the part of certain jurors and deliberate disregard of the judge's directions on the law, the prospects of obtaining satisfactory answers to questioning would be rather limited. The judge in such a case is left with the choice of discharging the jury or giving them a further direction. If the jury have been behaving as alleged in the juror's letter, they require a strong, even stern, warning that they have to follow the judge's directions on the law, adhere to the evidence without speculation, and decide on the verdicts without pressure or bargaining. Without strong and detailed guidance and instruction it would be difficult to be satisfied that the discussion in the jury room was conducted in the proper manner.

In R v *Thompson* [2010] EWCA Crim 1623; [2011] 1 WLR 200, Lord Judge CJ (at [1]) said that, if jury irregularities

> become apparent during the course of the trial itself, they must be addressed and handled by the trial judge. Depending on the context he may give further directions to the jury, if necessary in severe and unequivocal language ... which he may or may not combine with discharging an individual juror or indeed, in the ultimate analysis, the entire jury.

However, where the irregularity comes to light after the verdict has been returned, the Court of Appeal 'is bound to apply the principle that the deliberations of the jury are confidential' ([2]). Lord Judge went on (at [4] and [5]) to address the two 'narrow exceptions' to the rule about the confidentiality of jury deliberations:

> The first arises if it emerges that there may have been a complete repudiation of the oath taken by the jurors to try the case according to the evidence ... If there are serious grounds for believing that such a repudiation may have taken place, this court will inquire into it, and may hear ... evidence, including the evidence of jurors themselves, in order to decide whether it has happened. If it has, the verdict will inevitably be unsafe, and any resulting conviction will be quashed.
>
> The second exception arises in cases where extraneous material has been introduced into the jury deliberations. The verdict must be reached, according to the jury oath, in accordance with the evidence ... [T]he introduction of extraneous material, that is non-evidential material, constitutes an irregularity ... Where the complaint is made that the jury has considered non-evidential material, the court is entitled to examine the evidence ... to ascertain the facts. If extraneous material has been introduced into the decision-making process, the conviction may be quashed.

Lord Judge went on (at [8]) to say:

> The directions given by trial judges should underline unequivocally the collective responsibility of jurors for their own conduct ... Jurors should readily understand that any irregularity, if unusually it should it occur must be brought to the attention of the trial judge immediately, since precisely because of confidentiality and collective responsibility for the verdict, it will be too late to do so after the end of the trial.

Lord Judge also addressed use of the internet by jurors. So far as appeals are concerned, his Lordship said (at [11]):

Just as it would in any other instance where it was satisfied that extraneous material had been introduced, the approach of this court is to make inquiries into the material. If, on examination, this material strikes at the fairness of the trial, because the jury has considered material adverse to the defendant with which he has had no or no proper opportunity to deal, the conviction is likely to be unsafe ... If the material does not affect the safety of the conviction, the appeal will fail.

His Lordship added (at [12]) that it was apparent that 'use of the internet is so common that some specific guidance must now be given to jurors'. On the guidance that should be given, Lord Judge said:

Jurors need to understand that although the internet is part of their daily lives, the case must not be researched there, or discussed there (for example, on social networking sites), any more than it can be researched with, or discussed among friends or family, and for the same reason ... Research of this kind may affect their decision, whether consciously or unconsciously, yet at the same time, neither side at trial will know what consideration might be entering into their deliberations and will therefore not be able to address arguments about it. This would represent a departure from the basic principle which requires that the defendant be tried on the evidence admitted and heard by them in court.

If a juror wishes to report concerns about the way the jury is approaching its task, those concerns should be raised as soon as possible. In R v Heward [2012] EWCA Crim 890, the judge received a note from one of the jurors, saying: 'To Judge, I believe that the members of the jury are being unfair, and supporting their own race. I wish this will stay confidential.' The jury returned with a verdict before the judge could take any action. Pitchford LJ (at [12]) said that the necessary course of action, before receiving any verdict from the jury, was to make some enquiry for the purpose of ensuring that the verdict which they wished to deliver was untainted by the bias apparently revealed by the note from the anonymous juror. As that had not been done, the court was 'left with the suspicion that the impartial observer would perceive the real risk of bias. If that was so, then the verdict cannot be safe' ([13]). It followed that the conviction had to be quashed.

However, if the juror delays in raising concerns, it is unlikely that evidence of those concerns will be accepted by the Court of Appeal. In R v Hinds [2018] EWCA Crim 833, a juror contacted defence counsel after the trial had concluded, saying that the jury had not approached their task with an open mind and had disregarded directions from the judge. Holroyde LJ (at [16]) noted the rationale for the rule about the secrecy of jury room, namely 'the need to protect jurors from any outside interference in or criticism of their collective decision-making', adding that this rule 'works in the same way whether the impugned verdict is one of guilty or not guilty'. Nonetheless, jurors 'can and should raise any allegations of misconduct by their colleagues during the trial and the Court of Appeal [is] entitled, in limited circumstances, to admit evidence of outside interference with jurors or of bribery of them'. It is for this reason that judges 'make it plain to jurors at the outset of a trial that they must raise any concerns with the judge before the trial ends, precisely because it may be too late for anything to be done after the trial has concluded'. His Lordship went on to note (at [17]) that the matters raised by the juror in the present case did not fall within the limited exception to the secrecy rule, namely those rare situations 'in which a jury completely repudiated their function of deliberating upon the evidence', for example by resorting to the tossing of a coin in order to determine the verdict (or as occurred in R v Young [1995] QB 324), consulting an ouija board in order to arrive at their verdict). The Court took the view that communications from the juror were to be regarded 'as coming into the category of an expression of dissent by a juror who disagreed with the majority', particularly given the fact that the juror did not raise any concerns during the evidence or whilst the jury were deliberating (see [30]).

Detailed guidance on the action to be taken where jury irregularities are suspected is set out in Criminal Practice Direction VI 26M (see Chapter 10).

11.3.1.3 Inconsistent verdicts

Where a defendant is convicted on one or more counts but acquitted on others, it is sometimes argued that the convictions are inconsistent with the acquittals. In R v Fanning [2016] EWCA Crim 550; [2016] 1 WLR 4175, the Court of Appeal held that, in cases in which an appeal was brought on the ground of inconsistent verdicts, there was a clear test in that the defendant had to satisfy the court that the two verdicts could not stand together, meaning thereby that no reasonable jury who had applied their mind properly to the facts of the case could have arrived at the conclusion being considered. The defendant had to satisfy the court that the verdicts were not merely inconsistent but were so inconsistent as to demand interference by an appropriate court. The test accorded with, and did not usurp, the constitutional position of the jury.

In R v Davey [2017] EWCA Crim 1062, the Court of Appeal confirmed that this is the definitive test.

In R v McDonald [2018] EWCA Crim 798, Gross LJ (at [24]) said that, before concluding that the verdicts are so inconsistent as to demand interference by an appellate court, 'it may be helpful to consider whether the jury simply followed the judge's direction to consider separate counts separately, or took a "merciful" or "ameliorative" view of the facts of one count'. In that case, the Court of Appeal rejected the argument that the jury's decision to convict the defendant of inflicting grievous bodily harm was inconsistent with their decision to acquit him of possession of the offensive weapon, namely a knife, used to inflict the grievous bodily harm. This conclusion may be justified on the basis that, if there was an error, it was the acquittal on the second count that was wrong, with the result that the safety of the appellant's conviction for the more serious offence was not imperilled.

11.3.2 Fresh evidence in the Court of Appeal

One reason for a conviction being unsafe may be that new evidence has come to light which casts doubt on the safety of the conviction. Another reason is that the trial judge wrongly declared certain evidence to be inadmissible. In either case, the Court of Appeal has a discretion to receive evidence which was not adduced at the trial. Section 23(1) of the Criminal Appeal Act 1968 empowers the Court of Appeal to receive fresh evidence.

The Court of Appeal decides whether or not to receive fresh evidence on the basis of written witness statements. If the Court of Appeal decides to receive the evidence, the witnesses have to attend court to give their evidence unless the court regards the written statements it has already seen as sufficient. Each witness is usually examined-in-chief on behalf of the appellant and cross-examined on behalf of the Crown.

Under s.23(2) of the 1968 Act, the Court of Appeal, when considering whether to receive any evidence, must have regard in particular to:

(a) whether the evidence appears to the Court to be capable of belief;
(b) whether it appears to the Court that the evidence may afford any ground for allowing the appeal;
(c) whether the evidence would have been admissible in the proceedings from which the appeal lies on an issue which is the subject of the appeal; and
(d) whether there is a reasonable explanation for the failure to adduce the evidence in those proceedings.

Thus, the criteria to which the court must have regard when deciding whether or not to receive fresh evidence are:

- the credibility of the new evidence;
- the relevance of the new evidence (i.e. whether would it have made a difference had it been adduced at trial);
- the admissibility of the evidence, applying the usual rules of evidence; and
- the reason for that evidence not being adduced at trial.

As far as s.23(2)(b) is concerned, in R v Gilfoyle [1996] 1 Cr App R 302, Beldam LJ (at p.320) said that the Court of Appeal

> has not only the power to receive admissible evidence which would afford a ground for allowing the appeal but has a wider discretion, if it thinks it necessary or expedient in the interests of justice, to order any witness to attend for examination and to be examined before the court whether or not he testified at the trial ... [T]he interests of justice are not simply confined to receiving evidence which would result in an appeal being allowed, particularly when the court is being asked to review as unsafe and unsatisfactory the verdict of a jury after an impeccable summing-up on the ground that it has a lurking doubt.

The court is therefore empowered to receive admissible evidence which reinforces or dispels a lurking doubt.

The fact that counsel for the defence took a tactical decision not to call a particular witness is not generally regarded as a reasonable explanation for the failure to adduce the evidence at trial for the purpose of s.23(2)(d). The relevant principles were summarised by Hooper LJ in R v Hampton [2004] EWCA Crim 2139 at [101]:

> The fundamental question in each case is whether the Court of Appeal thinks it is either necessary or expedient in the interests of justice to receive the evidence sought to be adduced. In answering that question the Court of Appeal must have regard to the four factors that are set out in s.23(2). They are not prerequisites that must be fulfilled before the Court of Appeal will receive the evidence that is sought to be adduced on appeal ... In relation to the fourth factor ... viz. whether there is a reasonable explanation of the failure to adduce the evidence at the trial, even if it is held that there is no reasonable explanation, that is not necessarily fatal to the application to adduce evidence on appeal. The Court of Appeal still has a duty to consider whether it is necessary or expedient in the interests of justice to receive the evidence ... In general a defendant is only entitled to one trial, so that it is his duty (as it is that of the prosecution) to put forward all his case and all the evidence that he wishes to be considered at that trial ... If the reason for a case not being argued or evidence not being adduced at the trial is that the defendant's legal advisers acted in such a way as to deprive the defendant of a fair trial, then that could amount to a reasonable explanation for the failure to adduce the evidence at the trial. However, if there was a deliberate, informed decision by a defendant and his advisers not to advance a defence or evidence known to be available and that decision is made for tactical reasons, then that will not amount to a reasonable explanation for the failure to adduce that evidence at trial ...

His Lordship concluded (at [103]):

> In any case, the Court of Appeal has always to ask the ultimate question: is it necessary or expedient in the interests of justice to receive the evidence that the appellant wishes to

adduce at the appeal? If an informed decision was made by the appellant and his advisers, for sound tactical reasons, not to call a witness at the trial, then even if the factors in s.23(2) (a), (b) and (c) are in the appellant's favour, the Court of Appeal is most likely to conclude that it is not expedient in the interests of justice to permit the evidence of that witness to be adduced on appeal.

In R v Singh [2017] EWCA Crim 466; [2018] 1 WLR 1425, Hallett LJ noted (at [45]) that:

> As is well-known by counsel and should be known by those who stand in the dock in the Crown Court, the time for calling evidence is at trial. It is not permissible to await conviction and then appeal on the basis of evidence that was available at trial but was 'not actively pursued'.

In R v Pendleton [2001] UKHL 66; [2002] 1 WLR 72, the House of Lords considered the test to be applied in deciding whether or not to allow an appeal against conviction where fresh evidence has been received under s.23 of the Criminal Appeal Act 1968. Lord Bingham (at [19]) said that:

> it will usually be wise for the Court of Appeal, in a case of any difficulty, to test their own provisional view by asking whether the evidence, if given at the trial, might reasonably have affected the decision of the trial jury to convict. If it might, the conviction must be thought to be unsafe.

Pendleton was considered by the Court of Appeal in R v Ahmed [2010] EWCA Crim 2899. Hughes LJ said (at [24]) said that the question which matters 'is whether the fresh material causes this court to doubt the safety of the verdict of guilty'. In R v George [2014] EWCA Crim 2507, [2015] 1 Cr App R 15, Sir Brian Leveson P (at [51]) reiterated that the essential question, where the Court of Appeal has to consider the impact of fresh evidence, is whether, in the light of that fresh evidence, the conviction is unsafe. His Lordship also referred to the test articulated by Lord Kerr in Lundy v The Queen [2013] UKPC 28 (at [150]):

> [T]he proper test to be applied by an appellate court in deciding whether a verdict is unsafe or a miscarriage of justice has occurred, where new evidence has been presented, is whether that evidence might reasonably have led to an acquittal.

In R v Garland [2016] EWCA Crim 1743; [2017] 4 WLR 117, the appeal was based on non-disclosure by the prosecution. The Court of Appeal noted that the statutory test requires the Court of Appeal to allow an appeal against conviction only if they think that the conviction is unsafe. The court went on to hold that the law as set out in Pendleton applies equally to non-disclosure. The court did not consider there was any material difference when determining the test to be applied. The ultimate question was whether the withheld material caused doubt about the safety of the conviction. Garland was followed in R v Embleton [2016] EWCA Crim 1968, where Macur LJ (at [37]), said that where a defendant appeals against conviction on the ground of non-disclosure by the prosecution:

> the first question for this court is whether the material withheld from the defence was material which ought to have been disclosed. If the answer is yes, the second question is whether, in the light of such non-disclosure, the appellate court considers that the conviction is unsafe.

For an analysis of the approach to the Court of Appeal in 'fresh evidence' cases, see Stephanie Roberts, *Fresh Evidence and Factual Innocence in the Criminal Division of the Court of Appeal* (2017) J Crim L 303–327.

11.4 Result of appeal against conviction

The Court of Appeal has a number of options open to it when disposing of an appeal against conviction.

11.4.1 Appeal dismissed

If the Court of Appeal decides that the appellant's conviction was safe, it will dismiss the appeal and the appellant's conviction will stand.

11.4.2 Successful appeal

If appeal is allowed, the conviction is quashed (s.2(2)); this means that, unless a retrial is ordered, the appellant is in the same position as if he had been acquitted at the Crown Court (s.2(3)).

However, in addition to quashing the conviction, the Court of Appeal has a number of options.

11.4.2.1 Ordering a retrial

Section 7(1) of the Criminal Appeal Act 1968 provides that the Court of Appeal may order a retrial where the court allows an appeal against conviction and it appears to the court that 'the interests of justice so require'.

Under s.7(2), a retrial may be ordered only in respect of:

- the offence of which the appellant was convicted at the original trial and in respect of which the appeal has been allowed;
- an offence of which the appellant could have been convicted at the original trial (i.e. by way of alternative verdict under s.6(3) of the Criminal Law Act 1967); or
- an offence which was charged in an alternative count at the original trial and on which no verdict was taken because of the appellant was convicted of the offence which was the subject of the appeal.

If the appeal is allowed after the Court of Appeal has heard fresh evidence, a retrial will usually be ordered so that a jury can hear all the evidence. If, however, the fresh evidence clearly establishes that the appellant is innocent of the charge, the Court of Appeal will simply quash the conviction. Moreover, no retrial will be ordered if the original trial took place so long ago that the memories of the witnesses would have faded, making a fair trial impossible (R v Saunders (1974) 58 Cr App R 248). Furthermore, if the appellant has already spent time in custody so that he has, in effect, already served whatever sentence would be appropriate were he to be found guilty on a retrial, no retrial will be ordered (R v Newland [1988] QB 402, at p.408).

It is permissible to introduce a new count to the indictment where there is a retrial, provided that this can be done without injustice to the defendant (R v Swaine [2001] Crim LR 166). In R v Feeley [2012] EWCA Crim 720; [2012] 2 Cr App R 13, Jackson LJ (at [28]) said that if

> the application to add further counts is a proper one, because further evidence has come to light since the original trial, then . . . the judge is not precluded . . . from allowing the amendment.

11.4.2.2 Substituting a conviction for an alternative offence

Section 3 of the Criminal Appeal Act 1968 provides that where the appellant has been convicted of an offence to which he did not plead guilty, and the jury could have found him guilty of another offence, and on the finding of the jury it appears to the Court of Appeal that the jury must have been satisfied of facts which proved him guilty of the other offence, then the court may, instead of allowing or dismissing the appeal, substitute for the verdict of the jury a verdict of guilty of the other offence.

Therefore, if:

- the jury could, on the indictment, have found the appellant guilty of some other offence (under s.6 of the Criminal Law Act 1967 or other statutory provisions dealing with specific offences); and
- the jury must have been satisfied of facts which proved him guilty of the other offence, the Court of Appeal may quash the conviction appealed against but replace it with a conviction for that other offence (R v Graham [1997] 1 Cr App R 302 (at pp.312–13), per Lord Bingham CJ).

If the Court of Appeal does quash the conviction appealed against but substitutes a conviction for a different offence, it must then go on to review the sentence imposed by the Crown Court. If the Court of Appeal alters the sentence, it must not impose a sentence that is more severe than the original sentence (see s.3(2)).

Section 3A of the 1968 Act applies where the appellant has been convicted of an offence to which he pleaded guilty; if he had not so pleaded, he could have pleaded guilty to, or been found guilty of, another offence; and it appears to the Court of Appeal that the plea of guilty indicates an admission by the appellant of facts that prove him guilty of the other offence. In that case, the Court of Appeal may, instead of allowing or dismissing the appeal, substitute for the appellant's plea of guilty a plea of guilty of the other offence. The operation of this provision is confined to cases where the guilty plea inevitably involves an admission to the alternative offence (R v Lawrence [2013] EWCA Crim 1054; [2014] 1 WLR 106, at [8]).

11.4.2.3 Unmeritorious appeals: directions for loss of time

Under s.29 of Criminal Appeal Act 1968, the time during which an appellant is in custody pending the determination of the appeal counts as part of the term of any custodial sentence imposed in respect of the offence which is the subject of the appeal, unless the Court of Appeal gives a direction (known as a 'direction for loss of time') to the contrary.

A direction for loss of time is relevant only if the appellant is serving a custodial sentence. The direction is that some or all of the sentence served by the appellant between the date of the commencement of the appeal proceedings and the date when the application for leave or (as the case may be) the renewed application for leave to appeal is dismissed does not count towards the service of the appellant's sentence.

Where the single judge gives leave to appeal (or the application is successfully renewed) but the Court of Appeal ultimately dismisses the appeal, a direction for loss of time cannot be made even though the appeal is ultimately unsuccessful (s.29(2)(a) of the Criminal Appeal Act 1968).

The *Guide* (para.A16-1) says that a direction for loss of time is appropriate where an application is 'wholly without merit'.

Criminal Practice Direction IX, para.39E.1 says:

> Where an application devoid of merit has been refused by the single judge he may indicate that the Full Court should consider making a direction for loss of time on renewal of the application. However, the Full Court may make such a direction whether or not such an indication has been given by the single judge.

Paragraph 39E.2 refers to R v Gray [2014] EWCA Crim 2372; [2015] 1 Cr App R (S) 27, where Hallett LJ (at [2]) said:

Unmeritorious renewal applications take up a wholly disproportionate amount of staff and judicial resources in preparation and hearing time. They also waste significant sums of public money, for example in obtaining transcripts, especially in applications for leave to appeal against conviction ... [A] clear picture of a pattern of unjustified renewals of applications for leave to appeal against conviction emerges ... The more time the Court of Appeal Office and the judges spend on unmeritorious cases, the longer the waiting times are likely to be.

Her Ladyship noted (at [3]) that the 'only means' the court has of 'discouraging unmeritorious applications which waste precious time and resources' is by using the power to make a direction for loss of time and to make an order for costs under the Prosecution of Offences Act 1985. She went on to say (at [7]) that the power to make a costs order 'is used infrequently' and the single judge's power to make an order for loss of time is exercised only very rarely, adding that:

Single judges today faced with what they consider to be a totally unmeritorious application generally prefer to initial a box on the form to indicate that if the application is renewed, the full court will consider the making of a loss-of-time order. However, the fact that the single judge has not initialled the box does not deprive the full court of the power to make a loss-of-time order ...

Finally, at [10], Hallett LJ said that:

The single judge should consider whether to initial the box, and if the application is renewed, the full court (be it a two- or three-judge court) should consider whether or not to make a loss-of-time order or costs order. If it decides to exercise the power, a statement to this effect would suffice:

'Despite being warned of the court's power to make a loss of time order, the applicant chose to pursue a totally unmeritorious application which has wasted the time of the court. Such applications hamper the court's ability to process meritorious applications in a timely fashion'.

The point about the warning from the single judge is an important one. Whilst the Court clearly has the power to make a direction for loss of time even if the single judge did not indicate that the case was an appropriate one for such a direction in the event of application for leave being renewed, it is submitted that the Court should be reluctant to do so unless there is a very cogent basis for doing so.

Paragraph 39E.3 goes on to refer to R v Hart [2006] EWCA Crim 3239; [2007] 1 Cr App R 31 (at [43]), where the court said:

We hope that both applicants and counsel will heed the fact that this court is prepared to exercise its power and will do so more frequently in the future than it has done so in the past. The mere fact that counsel has advised that there are grounds of appeal will not always be a sufficient answer to the question as to whether or not an application has indeed been brought which was totally without merit. It should not be thought that this court will not exercise its power on other occasions even if there is an advice from counsel supporting grounds of appeal.

Likewise, in R v Fortean [2009] EWCA Crim 437, Hughes LJ (at [17]) said that the power to make a direction for loss of time may be exercised 'in any meritless application which should never have been pursued after due warning', adding that the fact that counsel or solicitors have associated themselves with a renewal of an application for leave to appeal after the single judge has rejected it 'will be relevant, but it will not necessarily avoid such an order if there was no justification for continuing the case'.

The power to make a direction for loss of time, which effectively results in an increase in sentence because it means that part of the sentence has to be re-served as a consequence of bringing an unmeritorious appeal, may appear draconian. However, in *Monnell and Morris v UK* (1988) 10 EHRR 205, the European Court of Human Rights (at [46]) said that directions for loss of time are a legitimate 'component of the machinery existing under English law to ensure that criminal appeals are considered within a reasonable time and, in particular, to reduce the time spent in custody by those with meritorious grounds waiting for their appeal to be heard'. This reasoning was echoed in *R v Brind* [2008] EWCA Crim 934. Latham LJ said (at [1]) that:

> if the application is without merit then this court will consider ordering that time served should not count for the good reason that the renewal of such an application has a significant effect on the work of this court and adds to the potential backlog of cases to the detriment of those who have legitimate arguments to put before this court.

His Lordship added (at [2]) that, if the single judge expressed the view that the application is 'without merit . . . the would-be applicant must expect that this court will order that time served should not count' if the application for leave is renewed.

11.5 Appeal against sentence

Section 9(1) of the Criminal Appeal Act 1968 provides that a person who has been convicted of an offence on indictment may appeal to the Court of Appeal against the sentence passed on him for that offence. 'Sentence' includes an order to pay prosecution costs (R v *Hayden* [1975] 1 WLR 852) and a compensation order (R v *Vivian* [1979] 1 WLR 291).

Under s.10 of the Criminal Appeal Act 1968, an offender who has been committed to the Crown Court for sentence (for example, under s.3 of the Powers of Criminal Courts (Sentencing) Act 2000), may appeal to the Court of Appeal against any sentence passed for the offence by the Crown Court.

11.5.1 Leave to appeal

Section 11(1) and (1A) of the Criminal Appeal Act 1968 provide that leave is required in order to appeal against sentence unless (within 28 days of sentence being passed) the trial judge certifies the sentence fit for appeal. Certificates are hardly ever given and are strongly discouraged by the Court of Appeal (see, for example, R v *Grant* (1990–91) 12 Cr App R(S) 44, at p.443).

11.5.2 Procedure for appealing against sentence

The procedure for obtaining leave to appeal against sentence is virtually identical to that for obtaining leave to appeal against conviction. Within 28 days of the date on which sentence was passed (see s.18(2) of the 1968 Act), the appellant has to serve a notice of application for leave to appeal against sentence of the Registrar of Criminal Appeals. Grounds of appeal, based on the remarks made by the judge when passing sentence, have to be drafted. A single judge decides whether leave to appeal should be given.

11.5.3 Grounds of appeal against sentence

Unlike appeals against conviction, the Criminal Appeal Act 1968 does not specify grounds for appeal against sentence. However, case law suggests a number of grounds upon which a sentence may be challenged.

- Sentence is *wrong in law*. Where the judge imposes a sentence that he has no jurisdiction to impose, that sentence can be set aside by the Court of Appeal. This would apply, for example, if the judge imposed a sentence of three years' imprisonment for an offence that carries a maximum of two years' imprisonment.
- Sentence is *wrong in principle*. A sentence that is wrong in principle occurs where the Crown Court judge imposes the wrong form of sentence. For example, an appellant who receives a custodial sentence argues that the offence was not so serious that only a custodial sentence was appropriate and so the custody threshold had not been crossed. To succeed on this basis, the appellant must show that he was dealt with in a way that was outside the broad range of penalties appropriate to the case.
- Sentence is *manifestly excessive*. A sentence is manifestly excessive where the judge imposes the correct form of sentence but nevertheless imposes too severe a sentence. For example, the judge imposes a sentence of three years' imprisonment in a case where 18 months would be more appropriate. In R v Gumbs (1927) 19 Cr App R 74, Lord Hewart CJ (at p.75) said that the Court of Appeal 'never interferes with the discretion of the Court below merely on the ground that this Court might have passed a somewhat different sentence; for this Court to revise a sentence there must be some error in principle'. Similarly, in R v Gleeson [2001] EWCA Crim 2023; [2002] 1 Cr App R(S) 112, Rose LJ (at [16]) said that, save in 'wholly exceptional' cases, the Court of Appeal interferes if, but only if, the sentence passed was 'wrong in principle or manifestly excessive'.
- The judge adopted the *wrong approach to the sentencing process*. This occurs where the judge ignores relevant factors or takes account of irrelevant factors. In R v Skone (1967) 51 Cr App R 165 and R v Evans (1986) 8 Cr App R (S) 197, for example, the judge incorrectly penalised the defendant for casting imputations on the veracity of the prosecution witnesses.
- *Procedural errors*. An example of a procedural error is where the judge fails to hold a *Newton* hearing where the defendant pleads guilty but the defence and prosecution versions of events differ significantly.
- *Legitimate sense of grievance*. If a judge gives an indication that a custodial sentence will not be imposed, the Court of Appeal will interfere if a custodial sentence is subsequently imposed for that offence (R v Gillam (1980) 2 Cr App R(S) 267; R v Moss (1983) 5 Cr App R(S) 209).
- *Disparity*. Where two offenders are sentenced for an offence which they have committed jointly, any difference in sentence should result only from differing degrees of involvement in the offence or from personal circumstances. Even if a difference cannot be so justified, an appeal on the basis of disparity will only succeed in rare cases. If the heavier of the two sentences is the correct one, the Court of Appeal will not generally reduce it to bring it into line with the more lenient sentence; this would convert one right sentence and one wrong sentence into two wrong sentences. The main question is whether the appellant's sentence is excessive in itself (R v Tate [2006] EWCA Crim 2373). An appeal will succeed on the ground of disparity only if the appellant would otherwise be left with a justifiable and burning sense of grievance (R v Potter [1977] Crim LR 112; R v Dickinson [1977] Crim LR 303). As Lawton LJ put it in R v Fawcett (1983) 5 Cr App R(S) 158 (at p.161): 'would right-thinking members of the public, with full knowledge of all the relevant facts and circumstances, learning of this sentence consider that something had gone wrong with the administration of justice?'.

11.5.4 Effect of appeal against sentence

If the appeal is dismissed, the original sentence stands. If the Court of Appeal allows the appeal, it may quash the sentence and replace it with the appropriate sentence. Section 11(3) of the Criminal Appeal Act 1968 provides that, if the Court of Appeal considers that the appellant should be sentenced differently, it may quash any sentence which is the subject of the appeal, and replace it with such sentence as it thinks appropriate for the offence; however, when exercising this power, the court must ensure that, 'taking the case as a whole, the appellant is not more severely dealt with on appeal than he was dealt with by the court below'.

Thus, taking the case as a whole, the appellant should not be dealt with more severely by the Court of Appeal than he was dealt with by the Crown Court. Two examples may assist in interpreting the restrictions imposed by s.11(3):

- An appellant is sentenced to two years' imprisonment on count 1 and 12 months' imprisonment on count 2 and the judge ordered the terms to run consecutively, making a total of three years. The Court of Appeal could (for example) substitute sentences of 12 months on count 1 (a reduction) and two years on count 2 (an increase), to run consecutively; the original total of three years is not exceeded.
- An appellant is sentenced to two years on count 1 and three years on count 2, these terms to run consecutively (making a total of five years). The Court of Appeal could theoretically substitute sentences of five years on each count to run concurrently, as the total of five years is not exceeded.

Note that the Court of Appeal cannot replace a suspended sentence of imprisonment with a sentence of immediate custody, even if the term is the same as or less than the original term that was suspended (R v Peppard (1990–91) 12 Cr App R(S) 88), unless the term imposed means that the defendant is entitled to immediate release (R v Waters and Young [2008] EWCA Crim 2538).

11.6 Re-opening appeals

Once an appeal has been dismissed (assuming there is no further appeal to the Supreme Court), that is the end of the matter (subject to the power of the Criminal Cases Review Commission to refer a case back to the Court of Appeal, discussed below). However, in exceptional circumstances, the Court of Appeal will allow an appeal to be re-opened.

In R v Yasain [2015] EWCA Crim 1277; [2015] 3 WLR 1571, Lord Thomas CJ confirmed (at [19]) that the Court of Appeal (Criminal Division) has 'an implicit power to revise any order pronounced before it is recorded as an order of the court in the record of the relevant court'. However, even after the order has been entered on the (electronic) court record of the Crown Court, there are two situations where an appeal may be re-heard: (i) where the previous order was a nullity, and (ii) where 'a defect in the procedure may have led to some real injustice' (at [23]). His Lordship noted that the Court of Appeal (Civil Division) has power to re-open an appeal where it is necessary to do so in order to avoid real injustice (see Taylor v Lawrence [2002] EWCA Civ 90; [2003] QB 528, and r.52.30 of the Civil Procedure Rules). Lord Thomas went on to hold that the Court of Appeal (Criminal Division) had the same power.

In R v Hockey [2017] EWCA Crim 742; [2018] 1 WLR 343, Sir Brian Leveson P, said (at [14]) that the 'very limited jurisdiction identified by Yasain ... is absolutely not available in circumstances ... where it is alleged that the proper construction of the legislation was misunderstood and has been recognised as having been misunderstood in subsequent litigation'.

The exceptional nature of the power to re-open an appeal was emphasised again in R v *Gohil* [2018] EWCA Crim 140; [2018] 1 WLR 3697. Gross LJ (at [110]) said that the Court of Appeal (Criminal Division) will not re-open a final determination of any appeal unless:

(i) It is necessary to do so in order to avoid real injustice;
(ii) The circumstances are exceptional and make it appropriate to re-open the appeal; and
(iii) There is no alternative effective remedy.

Rule 36.15(3) of the Criminal Procedure Rules requires an application to re-open an appeal to explain:

(i) why it is necessary for the court to reopen that decision in order to avoid real injustice,
(ii) how the circumstances are exceptional and make it appropriate to reopen the decision notwithstanding the rights and interests of other participants and the importance of finality,
(iii) why there is no alternative effective remedy among any potentially available, and
(iv) any delay in making the application.

As Gross LJ said in *Gohil* (at [124]), recourse to the Criminal Cases Review Commission (see below) is the 'obvious route to follow or remedy to pursue, where fresh evidence or material (including by reason of non-disclosure) has come to light, following a concluded and unsuccessful appeal'; moreover, the CCRC has investigatory powers which the Court of Appeal does not have.

11.7 Appeals by the prosecution

The prosecution cannot appeal against an acquittal by a jury (though in limited circumstances they may seek a retrial if new evidence emerges). However, they can seek clarification of the law. Prosecution appeals are also possible where the trial is brought to an end by the judge, or where the sentence imposed is unduly lenient.

11.7.1 Attorney General's reference following acquittal

Where a defendant has been acquitted following trial on indictment and the Attorney General thinks that the trial judge misdirected the jury on a point of law, he may refer the case to the Court of Appeal under s.36 of the Criminal Justice Act 1972. The acquittal is not in jeopardy, as the Court of Appeal cannot reverse that acquittal, but the reference does enable the Court of Appeal to clarify the law for future cases.

11.7.2 Attorney General's reference: unduly lenient sentence

Sections 35 and 36 of the Criminal Justice Act 1988 enable the Attorney General to appeal against excessively lenient sentences imposed by the Crown Court. Three restrictions apply:

- this power applies only in respect of offences which are triable only on indictment, or which are triable either way and have been prescribed by statutory instrument;
- the Attorney General requires leave from a single judge of the Court of Appeal in order to bring such an appeal;

- the Court of Appeal may increase the sentence (but not beyond the maximum which the Crown Court could have imposed) only if it holds that the original sentence was 'unduly lenient'.

In *Attorney General's Reference* (No 4 of 1989) [1990] 1 WLR 41 (at p.46), Lord Lane CJ gave guidance on the use of s.36 references:

- a sentence is unduly lenient if it 'falls outside the range of sentences which the judge, applying his mind to all the relevant factors, could reasonably consider appropriate';
- even if the Court of Appeal does consider the original sentence to be unduly lenient, it does not have to increase that sentence. It may be that the sentence can be justified in the light of events since the trial, or that increasing the sentence would be unfair to the offender or detrimental to others for whose well-being the court should be concerned;
- if the Attorney General is given leave to refer a sentence to the Court of Appeal on the ground that it is unduly lenient, the court's powers are not confined to increasing the sentence. In theory, the sentence could be reduced.

In *Attorney-General's Reference* (No 31 of 2004) [2004] EWCA Crim 1934; [2005] 1 Cr App R (S) 76, the Court of Appeal reiterated that it will interfere with a sentence under s.36 only if it is shown that there was 'some error of principle in the judge's sentence, so that public confidence would be damaged if the sentence were not altered' (per Lord Woolf CJ, at [2]).

In *Attorney-General's Reference* Nos 4, 5, 6, 7 and 8 of 2014 (*R v Deacon*) [2014] EWCA Crim 651; [2014] 2 Cr App R (S) 51, the Court of Appeal considered a submission that the sentence substituted by the Court of Appeal should take account of the fact that the offender was being sentenced for the second time. Davis LJ (at [43]) said:

> We should add that some mention was made before us of what counsel described as 'double jeopardy'. Indeed, one counsel before us rather hopefully sought to invoke what was, he said, considered to be a notional deduction for double jeopardy of the order of 20% to 30% which had some currency some time ago. We do not think that such considerations of double jeopardy in cases of this particular kind, where significant custodial sentences, on any view, were imposed and had to be imposed should feature to any great extent in the appropriate sentence now to be imposed by this court.

11.7.3 Prosecution appeals terminating rulings

Section 58 of the Criminal Justice Act 2003 enables the prosecution to appeal against a 'terminating' ruling (such as upholding a submission of no case to answer). Following the ruling, the prosecution must either inform the court that they intend to appeal or request an adjournment to consider whether to appeal (s.58(4)(a)). Following such an adjournment, the prosecution must inform the court whether or not they in fact intend to appeal (s.58(4)(b)). By virtue of s.58(3), the judge's ruling has no effect while the prosecution are considering whether to appeal or are pursuing an appeal. Under s.58(8) and (9), the prosecution must agree that the defendant should be acquitted if the prosecution either fail to obtain leave to appeal or abandon the appeal.

Section 57 provides that an appeal under s.58 can be brought only with the leave of the trial judge or the Court of Appeal.

In *R v Quillan* [2015] EWCA Crim 538; [2015] 1 WLR 4673, Lord Thomas CJ noted (at [19]) that decisions of the Court of Appeal have established that, in an appeal under s.58, 'strict compliance with the requirements of that section by the prosecution is necessary before this court has jurisdiction to hear it'. In R v C [2017] EWCA Crim 2257, Sir Brian Leveson P (at [24]) emphasised that the key question is the order of events:

> What is critical is the sequencing of events and in particular that before the judge embarks on any consideration of the merits of an application for leave to appeal, the undertaking [required by subss.(8) and (9)] has been given so as to provide him with jurisdiction to consider whether to grant leave to appeal and this court jurisdiction to grant leave to appeal if he declines to do so.

He went on to clarify (at [25]) that 'undertaking must be given at the time when the court is being asked to embark upon the exercise of this jurisdiction'. There is no jurisdiction to embark on consideration of an application for leave to appeal under s.58 if the undertaking required by s.58(8) and (9) has not been given.

Under s.61(1), the Court of Appeal may confirm, reverse or vary the ruling that is under appeal. Under s.61(3) and (7), where the Court of Appeal confirms the ruling, it must order the acquittal of the defendant(s) for the offence(s) which are the subject of the appeal. If the Court of Appeal reverses or varies a ruling, it must (under s.61(4)) also order that the proceedings be resumed in the Crown Court, or that a fresh trial should take place, or that the defendant should be acquitted of the offence(s) that are subject to the appeal. By virtue of s.61(5), the trial must continue, or a fresh trial must take place, unless the court considers that the defendant 'could not receive a fair trial'.

Section 67 states that the Court of Appeal may not reverse a ruling unless satisfied:

(a)   that the ruling was wrong in law;
(b)   that the ruling involved an error of law or principle; or
(c)   that the ruling was a ruling that it was not reasonable for the judge to have made.

11.8 Appeals to the Supreme Court

Under s.33 of the Criminal Appeal Act 1968, either the prosecution or the defence can appeal to the Supreme Court against a decision of the Court of Appeal. This is subject to two conditions:

- the Court of Appeal must certify that a point of law of general public importance is involved; and
- leave to appeal must be given by the Court of Appeal or by the Supreme Court.

Given the ability of the prosecution to appeal, it should be noted that even if a conviction is quashed by the Court of Appeal, that conviction could be reinstated by the Supreme Court.

11.9 The role of the Divisional Court

Section 28(2) of the Senior Court Acts 1981 excludes from appeal by way of case stated any 'judgment or other decision of the Crown Court relating to trial on indictment'. Similarly, s.29(3) of the Act excludes from the scope of judicial review 'matters relating to trial on indictment'.

In DPP v Manchester Crown Court and Huckfield [1993] 1 WLR 1524, Lord Browne-Wilkinson suggested (at p.1530) that one 'pointer' to the true construction of s.29 would be:

> Is the decision sought to be reviewed one arising in the issue between the Crown and the defendant formulated by the indictment (including the costs of such issue)? If the answer is

'Yes', then to permit the decision to be challenged by judicial review may lead to delay in the trial: the matter is therefore probably excluded from review by the section. If the answer is 'No', the decision of the Crown Court is truly collateral to the indictment of the defendant and judicial review of that decision will not delay his trial therefore it may well not be excluded by the section.

A(F) v Crown Court at Kingston [2017] EWHC 2706 (Admin); [2018] 1 Cr App R 32 concerned an application for judicial review of the refusal of bail to a defendant who had been convicted in the Crown Court and had then been remanded in custody prior to being sentenced. The Divisional Court ruled that, because the decision to withhold bail was clearly related to trial indictment, it had no jurisdiction. Holroyde LJ (at [26]) said that 'there can in my judgment be no doubt that a decision refusing bail between the jury's verdict and sentence in the Crown Court is a matter relating to trial on indictment'; judicial review was therefore precluded by s.29(3) of the 1981 Act.

However, there may be cases where judicial review can be granted despite s.29(3). In *R (M) v Kingston Crown Court* [2014] EWHC 2702 (Admin); [2016] 1 WLR 1685, the court said (at [32]) that, where an order is made relating to a trial on indictment, it may be quashed (despite s.29(3)) 'in circumstances where the defect is so severe that it deprived the court below of jurisdiction to make it ... The question is whether there is a jurisdictional error of such gravity as to take the case out of the jurisdiction of the Crown Court'.

In *R (DPP) v Aylesbury Crown Court* [2017] EWHC 2987 (Admin); [2018] 1 Cr App R 22 (325), the Divisional Court was invited to consider an application for judicial review of a decision on a costs order in the context of proceedings on indictment. The court held that judicial review was possible, despite s.29(3), if 'there is a jurisdictional error of sufficient gravity to take the case out of the jurisdiction of the Crown Court' (per Sharp LJ, at [7]). It is submitted that the same principle could apply where the challenge relates to bail. If a judge has no jurisdiction to make the order he purported to make, it cannot not be categorised as a matter relating to a trial on indictment so as to fall within the exclusion in s.29(3) of the 1981 Act, and the order was thus amenable to judicial review. If a decision is so unreasonable that no reasonable judge could have reached that conclusion, there is a cogent argument that the purported decision falls outside the judge's jurisdiction. In essence, a 'decision' is not, in law, a 'decision' if it is reached without jurisdiction (compare *Anisminic Ltd. v Foreign Compensation Commission* [1969] 2 AC 147).

11.10 The Criminal Cases Review Commission

Section 8(1) of the Criminal Appeal Act 1995 created the Criminal Cases Review Commission ('CCRC'). Its function is to investigate possible miscarriages of justice.

Section 9(1) of the Criminal Appeal Act 1995 says that where a person has been convicted on indictment by the Crown Court, the Commission may, at any time, refer the conviction and/or the sentence to the Court of Appeal. Section 11(1) of the Act says that where a person has been convicted by a magistrates' court, the Commission may, at any time, refer the conviction and/or the sentence to the Crown Court. The power to refer a conviction to the Crown Court applies whether the defendant pleaded guilty or not guilty (s.11(2)).

Section 13(1)(a)–(c) sets out the three conditions which have to be satisfied before a reference can be made:

(a)   the Commission consider that there is a real possibility that the conviction or sentence would not be upheld were the reference to be made;

(b)   the Commission so consider –

(i) in the case of a conviction, because of an argument, or evidence, not raised in the proceedings which led to it or on any appeal or application for leave to appeal against it; or

(ii) in the case of a sentence, because of an argument on a point of law, or information, not so raised; and

(c) an appeal against the conviction or sentence has been determined or leave to appeal against it has been refused.

In R (Pearson) v Criminal Cases Review Commission [2000] 1 Cr App R 141, at p.149, Lord Bingham CJ said:

> The exercise of the power to refer ... depends on the judgment of the Commission, and it cannot be too strongly emphasised that this is a judgment entrusted to the Commission and to no one else ... The 'real possibility' test ... is imprecise but plainly denotes a contingency which, in the Commission's judgment, is more than an outside chance or a bare possibility, but which may be less than a probability or a likelihood or a racing certainty. The Commission must judge that there is at least a reasonable prospect of a conviction, if referred, not being upheld.

In R (Hunt) v Criminal Cases Review Commission [2001] QB 1108, at p.1112, Lord Woolf CJ said that the provision requiring a real possibility of the Court of Appeal intervening 'is worded in a manner which reserves a residual discretion to the Commission not to refer, albeit that the case is one where there is a real possibility the Court of Appeal would not uphold the conviction'. His Lordship went on to say, at p.1114, that 'it is important that this court restricts attempts to raise grounds for challenging the decision of the Commission unless a proper basis is established'. His Lordship added that the CCRC has to exercise the discretion which it has been given by Parliament carefully, and that it is important 'that the courts should not in inappropriate cases allow the Commission to be sucked into judicial review proceedings which are bound to distract it from fulfilling its statutory role'. The reluctance of the Divisional Court to interfere with the decisions of the CCRC was reiterated in R (Charles) v Criminal Cases Review Commission [2017] EWHC 1219 (Admin); [2017] 2 Cr App R 14, where Gross LJ (at [2]) reaffirmed the importance of the CCRC, saying that it is 'an integral part of the protection available in this jurisdiction against the risk and consequences of wrongful conviction'. His Lordship went on to say (at [47]) that the decision whether or not a case satisfies the threshold conditions and is to be referred to the Court of Appeal is for the CCRC and not the Divisional Court; it is not for the Divisional Court to usurp the CCRC's function. Moreover, it has to be borne in mind that, even if the threshold conditions are satisfied, the CCRC retains a discretion not to refer a case to the Court of Appeal.

11.10.1 Changes in the law as a ground of appeal

The fact that there has been a subsequent change of law after the defendant was convicted is rarely regarded as sufficient to justify re-opening an appeal. In R v Neuberg [2016] EWCA Crim 1927; [2017] 4 WLR 58, the Court of Appeal observed that it has been 'clearly established for some time that, where there is a change of law but the conviction was entirely proper under the law as it stood at the time of trial, leave to appeal out of time will only be granted where substantial injustice would otherwise be done' (per Lord Thomas CJ, at [47]). This principle applies in particular where the law has previously been misinterpreted. In R v Jogee [2016] UKSC 8; [2016] 2 WLR 681, where the Supreme Court corrected a long-standing misunderstanding about the nature of joint enterprise but, as regards convictions which took place prior to this decision, ruled (at [100]) that:

> [W]here a conviction has been arrived at by faithfully applying the law as it stood at the time, it can be set aside only by seeking exceptional leave to appeal to the Court of Appeal out of time. That court has power to grant such leave, and may do so if substantial injustice be demonstrated, but it will not do so simply because the law applied has now been declared to have been mistaken.

Accordingly, in R v Crilly [2018] EWCA Crim 168; [2018] 2 Cr App R 12, Hallett LJ (at [36]) summarised the relevant principles in 'change of law' cases thus:

> First, to qualify for the grant of exceptional leave the defendant must establish a 'substantial injustice' would be caused if it was denied. The fact that there has been a change in the law is not in itself sufficient where a person was properly convicted on the law as it stood at the time of trial, as here. Secondly, the threshold for demonstrating a substantial injustice is a high one. Thirdly, in determining whether that high threshold has been met the court will have regard to the strength of the case advanced, that a change in the law would in fact have made a difference.

11.11 Retrials for serious offences

Part 10 of the Criminal Justice Act 2003 creates a comparatively limited exception to the rule against 'double jeopardy'.

Under s.75, the power to order a retrial applies where a person has been acquitted of a 'qualifying offence' (i.e. an offence specified in the Act for this purpose; the list includes offences such as murder, rape, and arson).

Under s.77, the Court of Appeal may (despite the earlier acquittal) permit a retrial only if:

- there is 'new and compelling evidence against the acquitted person in relation to the qualifying offence' (s.78):
    - evidence is new if it was not adduced in the proceedings in which the person was acquitted;
    - evidence is compelling if it (a) is reliable; (b) is substantial, and (c) appears highly probative of the case against the acquitted person;

    and

- in all the circumstances it is in the interests of justice for the court to make the order (s.79), having regard to:
    - whether existing circumstances make a fair trial unlikely;
    - the length of time since the offence was allegedly committed;
    - whether it is likely that the new evidence would have been adduced in the earlier proceedings against the acquitted person but for a failure by an officer or by a prosecutor to act with due diligence or expedition;
    - whether, since those proceedings, any officer or prosecutor has failed to act with due diligence or expedition.

If the Court of Appeal is satisfied that the requirements of both s.78 and s.79 are met, the order for a retrial must be made; otherwise the application must be dismissed (s.77).

11.12 Court of Appeal statistics

The Court's Annual Report for 2016–17 (published August 2018) reveals some interesting information about the work of the Court.

- Appeals against conviction:
  - Percentage of cases where leave to appeal was refused by the single judge:

    - October 2014 – September 2015: 79%
    - October 2015 – September 2016: 75%
    - October 2016 – September 2017: 80%

  - Percentage of cases where appeal against conviction was allowed by the Court of Appeal:

    - October 2014 – September 2015: 40%
    - October 2015 – September 2016: 36%
    - October 2016 – September 2017: 36%

- Appeals against sentence:
  - Percentage of cases where leave to appeal was refused by the single judge:

    - October 2014 – September 2015: 70%
    - October 2015 – September 2016: 66%
    - October 2016 – September 2017: 68%

  - Percentage of cases where appeal against conviction was allowed by the Court of Appeal:

    - October 2014 – September 2015: 70%
    - October 2015 – September 2016: 71%
    - October 2016 – September 2017: 67%

Chapter 12

Legal Aid and Costs

Chapter Contents

In this chapter, we examine briefly some of the financial aspects of criminal litigation.

12.1 Advice and assistance for individuals in custody

Section 13 of the Legal Aid, Sentencing and Punishment of Offenders Act (LASPO) 2012 provides that:

> (1) Initial advice and initial assistance are to be available ... to an individual who is arrested and held in custody at a police station or other premises if the Director [of Legal Aid Casework] has determined that the individual qualifies for such advice and assistance ...
> (2) The Director must make a determination under this section having regard, in particular, to the interests of justice.

12.2 Legal aid in criminal proceedings

Section 14 of LASPO defines 'criminal proceedings' as including:

> (a) proceedings before a court for dealing with an individual accused of an offence;
> (b) proceedings before a court for dealing with an individual convicted of an offence, including proceedings in respect of a sentence or order.

By virtue of s.17(1) of LASPO, the decision whether an individual qualifies for legal aid depends on two criteria:

- a means test (s.21); and
- the interests of justice.

The Criminal Legal Aid (General) Regulations 2013 (SI 2013/9) make detailed provision for determinations in relation to whether an individual qualifies for criminal legal aid. In particular, para.29(1) provides that where legal aid is refused on the ground that the interests of justice do not require representation to be made available before the magistrates' court, an appeal lies to the magistrates' court, and para.30 makes provision for appeal to the Crown Court against refusal of legal aid in a Crown Court case.

Further details about the legal aid scheme are set out in a number of other statutory instruments.

12.2.1 The interests of justice test

Section 17(2) of LASPO sets out the basis of the 'interests of justice' test:

> In deciding what the interests of justice consist of for the purposes of such a determination, the following factors must be taken into account –
> (a) whether, if any matter arising in the proceedings is decided against the individual, the individual would be likely to lose his or her liberty or livelihood or to suffer serious damage to his or her reputation;
> (b) whether the determination of any matter arising in the proceedings may involve consideration of a substantial question of law;

(c) whether the individual may be unable to understand the proceedings or to state his or her own case;

(d) whether the proceedings may involve the tracing, interviewing or expert cross-examination of witnesses on behalf of the individual; and

(e) whether it is in the interests of another person that the individual be represented.

These factors are the same as those that were considered under earlier legislation and so earlier case law remains relevant.

When considering whether there is a risk of loss of liberty, there must be a real (not merely theoretical) risk of a custodial sentence being imposed. It is not enough that the offence carries a custodial sentence: the decision-maker must consider whether a custodial sentence might actually be imposed in this particular case R (*Sonn Macmillan Solicitors*) v *Gray's Magistrates' Court* [2006] EWHC 1103 (Admin).

In R v *Liverpool City Magistrates ex p McGhee* (1994) 158 JP 275, the Divisional Court rejected the contention that what would now be a community order with an unpaid work requirement could be regarded as a sentence which deprives the accused of liberty.

The factor which refers to 'expert cross-examination of witnesses' addresses the need to have an advocate cross-examination of witnesses, not cross-examination of expert witnesses (R v *Liverpool City Magistrates ex p McGhee*).

The provision of legal aid is a vital aspect of the right to a fair trial guaranteed by Art.6 of the European Convention on Human Rights. Article 6(3) includes the following rights:

(b) to have adequate time and facilities for the preparation of his defence;

(c) to defend himself in person or through legal assistance of his own choosing or, if he has not sufficient means to pay for legal assistance, to be given it free when the interests of justice so require.

12.2.2 The means test

The Criminal Legal Aid (Financial Resources) Regulations 2013 (SI 2013/471) make provision in relation to the circumstances in which an individual's financial resources are such that he/she is eligible for criminal legal aid. Part 2 makes provision in relation to the financial eligibility of an individual for advice and assistance provided under s.15 of LASPO (advice and assistance for criminal proceedings), and Part 3 makes provision in relation to the financial eligibility for representation provided under s.16 (representation in criminal proceedings).

The means test takes account of the applicant's income, family circumstances (e.g. number of children) and essential living costs (e.g. mortgage or rent). It should be noted that someone in receipt of 'qualifying benefits' (including income support, income-based jobseeker's allowance and universal credit) is automatically deemed to satisfy the means test.

12.2.3 Contribution orders

The Criminal Legal Aid (Contribution Orders) Regulations 2013 (SI 2013/483) make provision in relation to the liability of individuals who are in receipt of legal aid to make a payment in connection with the provision of such representation, based on an assessment of their financial resources. These orders apply only to Crown Court trials, and when the Crown Court is hearing appeals from magistrates' courts.

12.2.4 Recovery of Defence Costs Orders

The Criminal Legal Aid (Recovery of Defence Costs Orders) Regulations 2013 (SI 2013/511) provide that where an individual receives legal aid for representation in relation to criminal proceedings before any court other than the magistrates' court or the Crown Court (and so limited to proceedings in the Divisional Court, Court of Appeal and Supreme Court), the court hearing the proceedings must (unless an exception applies) make a determination at the conclusion of the proceedings requiring the individual to pay some or all of the cost of his/her representation.

12.3 Costs orders

The powers of the criminal courts to award costs are contained in ss.16–21 of the Prosecution of Offences Act 1985 and the Costs in Criminal Cases (General) Regulations 1986 (SI 1986/1335).

12.3.1 Defendant's costs orders

Section 16 empowers the court to make a defendant's costs order in any of the following circumstances:

- the prosecution decide not to proceed with a charge in the magistrates' court;
- the defendant is acquitted following summary trial;
- the prosecution at the Crown Court offer no evidence or ask that all counts remain on the file marked not to be proceeded with without leave;
- the defendant is acquitted following trial on indictment;
- the defendant successfully appeals against conviction and/or sentence.

However, by virtue of s.16A of the Act, individuals are able to recover their legal costs through a defendant's costs order made in respect of proceedings in a magistrates' court but not legal costs incurred in respect of Crown Court proceedings except where those costs related to an appeal against conviction and/or sentence from the magistrates' court or, in the case of a trial on indictment, the defendant was ineligible for legal aid owing to his means. For these purposes, legal costs are defined as 'fees, charges, disbursements and other amounts payable in respect of advocacy services or litigation services including, in particular, expert witness costs' (s.16A(10)).

Where available, a defendant's costs order should normally be made unless there are positive reasons for not doing so – for example, where the defendant's own conduct has brought suspicion on himself and has misled the prosecution into thinking that the case against him was stronger than it was (Practice Direction (Costs in Criminal Proceedings), para.2.1.1 (magistrates' courts) and para.2.2.1 (Crown Court)).

The amount of the costs order is governed by s.16(6) which provides that the amount is to be what the court considers 'reasonably sufficient' to compensate the defendant for 'any expenses properly incurred by him in the proceedings'. The order cannot include expenses that do not relate directly to the proceedings themselves, such as loss of earnings. However, where legal costs are recoverable, reg.4A of the Costs in Criminal Cases (General) Regulations 1986 (SI 1986/1335), says that the amount payable must be calculated in accordance with legal aid rates, whether or not that results in the fixing of an amount that the court considers reasonably sufficient or necessary to compensate the accused.

Section 21(4A)(a) of the Prosecution of Offences Act 1985 provides that where the defendant is legally aided then, for these purposes, his costs must be taken not to include the cost of representation paid for through legal aid (as these costs are being paid out of the public purse anyway).

12.3.2 Prosecution costs from central funds

An order that the prosecutor's costs be paid out of central funds may be made under s.17 of the Prosecution of Offences Act 1985. Section 17 applies only to private prosecutors, and so excludes the Crown Prosecution Service and any other public authority (for example, local authorities). Furthermore, this section applies only to the prosecution of indictable offences (whether indictable only or either way). Such an order can be made even though the defendant was acquitted. An order should be made save where there is good reason for not doing so, for example, where proceedings have been instituted or continued without good cause (Practice Direction (Costs in Criminal Proceedings), para.2.6.1).

The order under s.17(1) is an order for the payment out of central funds of such amount as the court considers 'reasonably sufficient' to compensate the prosecutor for any 'expenses properly incurred' in the proceedings. Section 17(2A) enables the court to award a lesser amount where the court 'considers that there are circumstances that make it inappropriate for the prosecution to recover the full amount'.

12.3.3 Defendant to pay prosecution costs

Section 18(1) of the Prosecution of Offences Act 1985 provides that where:

- a defendant is convicted of an offence by a magistrates' court;
- the Crown Court dismisses an appeal against such a conviction or against the sentence imposed by a magistrates' court; or
- a defendant is convicted of an offence by the Crown Court,

then the court may make 'such order as to the costs to be paid by the accused to the prosecutor as it considers just and reasonable'.

Section 18(2) allows the Court of Appeal to make a similar order where it dismisses an appeal or an application for leave to appeal.

Under s.18(5), where a defendant under the age of 18 is convicted of an offence by a magistrates' court (this term includes a youth court), the amount of any costs ordered to be paid by the accused under s.18 must not exceed the amount of any fine imposed on him.

An order will only be made under s.18 if the defendant has sufficient means to enable him to pay some or all of the prosecution costs (Practice Direction (Costs in Criminal Proceedings), para.3.4). In R v Northallerton Magistrates' Court ex p Dove [2000] 1 Cr App R(S) 136, Lord Bingham CJ (at p.142) set out the following principles:

(1) An order to pay costs to the prosecutor should never exceed the sum which, having regard to the defendant's means and any other financial order imposed upon him, the defendant is able to pay and which it is reasonable to order the defendant to pay.

(2) Such an order should never exceed the sum which the prosecutor has actually and reasonably incurred.

(3) The purpose of such an order is to compensate the prosecutor and not to punish the defendant. Where the defendant has by his conduct put the prosecutor to avoidable expense he may, subject to his means, be ordered to pay some or all of that sum to the

prosecutor. But he is not to be punished for exercising a constitutional right to defend himself ...

(4) While there is no requirement that any sum ordered by justices to be paid to a prosecutor by way of costs should stand in any arithmetical relationship to any fine imposed, the costs ordered to be paid should not in the ordinary way be grossly disproportionate to the fine ... If, when the costs sought by the prosecutor are added to the proposed fine, the total exceeds the sum which in the light of the defendant's means and all other relevant circumstances the defendant can reasonably be ordered to pay, it is preferable to achieve an acceptable total by reducing the sum of costs which the defendant is ordered to pay rather than by reducing the fine.

(5) It is for the defendant facing a financial penalty by way of fine or an order to pay costs to a prosecutor to disclose to magistrates such data relevant to his financial position as will enable justices to assess what he can reasonably afford to pay. In the absence of such disclosure justices may draw reasonable inferences as to the defendant's means from evidence they have heard and from all the circumstances of the case ...

(6) It is incumbent on any court which proposes to make any financial order against a defendant, whether by way of fine or costs, to give the defendant a fair opportunity to adduce any relevant financial information and make any appropriate submissions ...

Where costs are awarded against several defendants and one of them lacks the means to pay costs, the court should divide the total amount payable between the number of defendants (not just those who are able to pay) so that each defendant pays only his own share of the costs and does not subsidise the defendant who cannot pay (R v *Ronson* (1992) 13 Cr App R(S) 153, where there were four defendants of whom one could not afford to pay costs, and it was held by the Court of Appeal that the defendants who could afford to pay costs should each pay one-quarter of the total, not one-third). In R v *Harrison* (1993) 14 Cr App R(S) 419, however, the Court of Appeal upheld an order made against only one of the defendants; he was the principal offender (the other defendants had played relatively minor roles in the offences) and he had the means to pay the amount ordered.

Where a defendant is ordered to pay costs under s.18, the amount can include the cost of investigating the offence, as well as the costs of preparing and presenting the prosecution (R v *Associated Octel Co Ltd* [1997] 1 Cr App R (S) 435; *Balshaw v Crown Prosecution Service* [2009] EWCA Crim 470; [2009] 1 WLR 2301).

A judge in the Crown Court should not use a costs order as a means of penalising a defendant for electing Crown Court trial of an offence which could have been dealt with in the magistrates' court (R v *Hayden* [1975] 1 WLR 852). Nevertheless, it has been recognised by the Court of Appeal that trial on indictment is necessarily more expensive than summary trial and this will inevitably be reflected in the costs order (R v *Bushell* (1980) 2 Cr App R(S) 77; R v *Boyle* (1995) 16 Cr App R (S) 927).

A costs order is more likely to be made against a defendant where the prosecution case is manifestly strong and the defendant must have known all along that he was guilty (R v *Singh* (1982) 4 Cr App R(S) 38).

12.3.4 Wasted costs orders

There are three types of 'wasted costs' orders: against a party to the proceedings, against a legal representative, or against a third party.

12.3.4.1 Wasted costs orders against parties

Regulation 3 of the Costs in Criminal Cases (General) Regulations 1986 (SI 1986/1335) provides that where a magistrates' court, the Crown Court, or the Court of Appeal

> is satisfied that costs have been incurred in respect of the proceedings by one of the parties as a result of an unnecessary or improper act or omission by, or on behalf of, another party to the proceedings, the court may, after hearing the parties, order that all or part of the costs so incurred by that party shall be paid to him by the other party.

In R (*Commissioners of Customs & Excise*) v *Crown Court at Leicester* [2001] EWHC 33 (Admin), Lord Woolf CJ said (at [16]) that a structured approach should be followed:

(1) Has there been an unnecessary or improper act or omission?
(2) Have costs been incurred as a result of that unnecessary or improper act or omission?
(3) Should the court, as a matter of discretion, order all or part of the costs so incurred to be paid to the other party by the party in default?
(4) If so, what amount of costs should be paid?

In R v *Cornish* [2016] EWHC 779 (QB), Coulson J (at [16]) summarised the relevant principles thus:

(a) Simply because a prosecution fails, even if the defendant is found to have no case to answer, does not of itself overcome the threshold criteria of s.19 ...
(b) Improper conduct means an act or omission that would not have occurred if the party concerned had conducted his case properly ...
(c) The test is one of impropriety, not merely unreasonableness ... The conduct of the prosecution must be starkly improper such that no great investigation into the facts or decision-making process is necessary to establish it ...
(d) Where the case fails as a matter of law, the prosecutor may be more open to a claim that the decision to charge was improper, but even then, that does not necessarily follow because 'no one has a monopoly of legal wisdom, and many legal points are properly arguable' ...
(e) It is important that s.19 applications are not used to attack decisions to prosecute by way of a collateral challenge, and the courts must be ever vigilant to avoid any temptation to impose too high a burden or standard on a public prosecuting authority in respect of prosecution decisions ...
(f) In consequence of the foregoing principles, the granting of a s.19 application will be 'very rare' and will be 'restricted to those exceptional cases where the prosecution has made a clear and stark error as a result of which a defendant has incurred costs for which it is appropriate to compensate him' ....

In *Crowch v DPP* [2008] EWHC 948 (Admin), it was held that a wasted costs order cannot be made to compensate an unrepresented defendant for his own loss of time in preparing his case and attending court.

12.3.4.2 Wasted costs orders against representatives

Section 19A of the Prosecution of Offences Act 1985 empowers a magistrates' court, the Crown Court, or the Court of Appeal, to make a 'wasted costs order' against the representative acting for a party to criminal proceedings. The effect of the order is to disallow, or (as the case may be) order the legal or other representative concerned to meet, the whole or any part of the wasted costs.

Guidance was given by the Court of Appeal in *Re a Barrister (Wasted Costs Order) (No 1 of 1991)* [1993] QB 293, at p.301:

> A three-stage test or approach is recommended when a wasted costs order is contemplated. (i) Has there been an improper, unreasonable or negligent act or omission? (ii) As a result have any costs been incurred by a party? (iii) If the answers to (i) and (ii) are 'Yes,' should the court exercise its discretion to disallow or order the representative to meet the whole or any part of the relevant costs, and if so what specific sum is involved?

Further guidance was given in *Re P (a Barrister)* [2001] EWCA Crim 1728; [2002] 1 Cr App R 207 (per Kennedy LJ, at [44]):

> Because of the penal element a mere mistake is not sufficient to justify an order. There must be a more serious error ... If the allegation is one of serious misconduct or crime the standard of proof will be higher, but otherwise it will be the normal civil standard of proof.

It was held in *Re a Barrister (Wasted Costs Order) (No 9 of 1999)* (2000) *The Times*, 18 April, that such an order is appropriate only where the lawyer 'gave advice or committed an act or was responsible for an omission which no member of the profession, who was reasonably well informed and competent, would have given or done or omitted to do' (per Clarke LJ).

12.3.4.3 Wasted costs order against third parties

Section 19B(3) of the Prosecution of Offences Act 1985 enables costs to be awarded against a third party where there has been 'serious misconduct' by that third party, and the court considers it appropriate, having regard to that misconduct, to make a third-party costs order against him.

12.3.5 Appeals on costs

Neither party has a right of appeal to the Crown Court in respect of a costs order made by a magistrates' court; the prosecution have no right of appeal to the Crown Court, and s.108(3)(b) of the Magistrates' Courts Act 1980 specifically precludes a defence appeal to the Crown Court against a costs order. However, in *Hamilton-Johnson v RSPCA* (2000) 164 JP 345, it was held that, when the Crown Court dismisses an appeal against conviction or sentence, it has power to vary an order made by the magistrates' court requiring the defendant to pay the costs of the prosecutor in relation to the proceedings in the magistrates' court.

So far as costs orders made by the Crown Court are concerned, an order that the defendant pay part of the prosecution costs comes within the definition of a 'sentence' under s.50 of the Criminal Appeal Act 1968, so the defendant may appeal against the costs order under s.9 of the Act (*R v Heyden* [1975] 1 WLR 852).

Chapter 13

Sentencing Principles and Procedure

In this chapter, we examine some of the principles which underpin sentencing in England and Wales, and we then look at the process by which sentence is passed on someone who has pleaded guilty to, or been found guilty of, an offence.

13.1 The purposes of sentencing

Section 142(1) of the Criminal Justice Act 2003 states that any court dealing with an offender who has attained the age of 18 in respect of an offence must have regard to the following 'purposes of sentencing':

(a)   the punishment of offenders;
(b)   the reduction of crime (including its reduction by deterrence);
(c)   the reform and rehabilitation of offenders;
(d)   the protection of the public; and
(e)   the making of reparation by offenders to persons affected by their offences.

Section 142(2) states that subs.(1) does not apply to offenders under the age of 18 (they are dealt with by s.142A – see Chapter 15), or where there is a mandatory minimum sentence, or in relation to the making of hospital orders under the Mental Health Act 1983.

These statutory 'purposes' are not set out in order of priority and can in some circumstances conflict with one another (for example, a punitive sentence of imprisonment may remove the offender's ability to make reparation for the offence by paying compensation); the court has to decide which purpose(s) should take priority in the particular case it is dealing with.

13.2 Sentencing guidelines

Section 118 of the Coroners and Justice Act 2009 created the Sentencing Council for England and Wales. The membership is laid down by sch.15 of the Act: there are eight judicial members and six non-judicial members. The chair and deputy chair have to be drawn from the judicial members.

The Sentencing Council produces guidelines on general matters that are relevant to sentencing, and also guidelines on the approach to be taken in respect of specific offences.

Section 120(11) says that, when producing guidelines, the Sentencing Council must have regard to:

(a)   the sentences imposed by courts in England and Wales for offences;
(b)   the need to promote consistency in sentencing;
(c)   the impact of sentencing decisions on victims of offences;
(d)   the need to promote public confidence in the criminal justice system;
(e)   the cost of different sentences and their relative effectiveness in preventing reoffending;
(f)   the results of the monitoring carried out under s.128.

Section 121 sets out detailed requirements on the approach to be taken when producing sentencing guidelines. They should, if reasonably practicable given the nature of the offence, divide the offence into categories of seriousness, based on the offender's culpability, the harm caused, and any other particularly relevant factors.

The guidelines should state the range of sentences (the 'offence range') appropriate for a court to impose for the offence. If the guidelines divide the offence into categories of seriousness, they should also state the range of sentences appropriate for a court to impose for each category. The guidelines should also specify a starting point in the range for the offence or, if the guidelines divide the offence into categories of seriousness, a starting point for each category. The starting point is the sentence the Council considers to be appropriate in a case where the offender has pleaded not guilty, and before aggravating or mitigating factors are taken into account.

The guidelines should also list any relevant aggravating and mitigating factors that are likely to apply to the offence and the relevant mitigating factors personal to an offender. They should also include guidance on the weight to be given to an offender's previous convictions and to other aggravating and mitigating circumstances where these are of particular significance to the offence or the offender.

The offence-specific guidelines issued by the Sentencing Council adopt a standard format:

Step 1: Determining the offence category, which is done by reference to an *exhaustive* list of factors indicating greater and lesser harm and factors indicating higher and lower culpability. There are often (but not always) three categories (category 1: greater harm and higher culpability; category 2: greater harm and lower culpability, or lesser harm and higher culpability; and category 3: lesser harm and lower culpability).

Step 2: Starting point and category range: placing the offence in one of the categories determines both the starting point and the 'category range'. The court then determines where in the category range the offence falls. The guidelines suggest specific factors that increase seriousness, and those that reduce seriousness or reflect personal mitigation, but at this stage the court can take account of any factors that are relevant.

Step 3: Consider any other factors that indicate a reduction, such as assistance to the prosecution (see below).

Step 4: Reduction for guilty pleas (see below).

Step 5: Dangerousness (if the offence is one to which the 'dangerous offender' provisions of the Criminal Justice Act 2003 are applicable, the court has to consider whether such a sentence ought to be passed).

Step 6: Totality principle (where the offender is being sentenced for more than one offence, the court has to consider whether the total sentence is just and proportionate to the offending behaviour).

Step 7: Compensation and ancillary orders.

Step 8: Reasons (the court must formulate its reasons for the sentence passed).

Step 9: Consideration for remand time (credit for time spent on remand in custody).

For a discussion of this approach to the formulation of sentencing guidelines, see Julian V. Roberts & Anne Rafferty, *Sentencing guidelines in England and Wales: exploring the new format* [2011] Crim LR 681–689 and Mandeep K. Dhami, *Sentencing Guidelines in England and Wales: Missed Opportunities?* (2013) 76 Law and Contemporary Problems 289–307.

The Sentencing Council replaced the Sentencing Guidelines Council (SGC), which was established by the Criminal Justice Act 2003. The SGC guidelines (which are presented in a slightly different format) are being replaced by new Sentencing Council guidelines. However, unless and until they are superseded, guidelines issued by the SGC are deemed to be guidelines issued by the Sentencing Council (para.7 of the Coroners and Justice Act 2009 (Commencement No 4, Transitional and Saving Provisions) Order 2010 (SI 2010/816)).

Of particular relevance to magistrates' courts, the Magistrates' Court Sentencing Guidelines cover most of the offences that regularly come before a magistrates' court and also contain some very useful general explanatory material.

The existence of separate guidance for magistrates' courts means that the offence-specific guidelines are mainly relevant in the Crown Court.

Where there is no offence-specific guideline, the Crown Court has to rely on any relevant guideline judgements from the Court of Appeal.

13.2.1 Duty of court to follow guidelines

Section 125(1) says that every court:

(a) must, in sentencing an offender, follow any sentencing guidelines which are relevant to the offender's case; and

(b) must, in exercising any other function relating to the sentencing of offenders, follow any sentencing guidelines which are relevant to the exercise of the function, unless the court is satisfied that it would be contrary to the interests of justice to do so.

In R v Healey [2012] EWCA Crim 1005; [2013] 1 Cr App R (S) 33, the Court of Appeal emphasised the importance of following the Sentencing Council's guidelines. Hughes LJ said (at [5]) that a 'good deal of flexibility' is built into the guidelines. It is open to a judge to depart from the guidelines because the 'case has particular facts which warrant distinguishing it from the general level' of sentence, but not because the judge happens to take a different view about where the general level ought to be. His Lordship added (at [9]):

The format which is adopted by the Sentencing Council in producing its guidelines is to present the broad categories of offence frequently encountered pictorially in boxes … It may be that the pictorial boxes which are part of the presentation may lead a superficial reader to think that adjacent boxes are mutually exclusive, one or the other. They are not. There is an inevitable overlap between the scenarios that are described in adjacent boxes. In real life offending is found on a sliding scale of gravity with few hard lines. The guidelines set out to describe such sliding scales and graduations. We wholeheartedly endorse the approach of [counsel for one of the defendants] who asked us to find that a particular case was to be located on examination somewhere between two of the pictorial boxes.

In R v Dyer [2013] EWCA Crim 2114; [2014] 2 Cr App R (S) 11, Sir Brian Leveson P (at [13]) said that decisions of the Court of Appeal may help to interpret the guidance contained in Sentencing Council Guidelines, and provide illustrations of the circumstances in which they operate and when the interests of justice might justify departure from them: the Guidelines are intended to encapsulate the approach to the vast majority of cases that come before the court, but the interests of justice permit departure from the Guidelines in appropriate cases.

For a discussion of the duty of the court to follow sentencing guidelines and the circumstances in which the court can depart from those guidelines, see Julian V. Roberts, *Sentencing guidelines and judicial discretion: evolution of the duty of courts to comply in England and Wales* (2011) British Journal of Criminology 997–1013; Andrew Ashworth, *Departures from the sentencing guidelines* [2012] Crim LR 81–96 and Julian V. Roberts, *Points of departure: reflections on sentencing outside the definitive guidelines ranges* [2012] Crim LR 439–448.

On the role of judgment and discretion in sentencing, see Tom O'Malley, *Judgment and Calculation in the Selection of Sentence* (2017) 28 Criminal Law Forum 361–389 and Antje du Bois-Pedain, *In Defence of Substantial Sentencing Discretion* (2017) 28 Criminal Law Forum 391–435. See also Jose Pina-Sanchez et al, *Mind the step: A more insightful and robust analysis of the sentencing process in England and Wales under the new sentencing guidelines* (2018) Criminology and Criminal Justice 1–34.

In June 2018, the Sentencing Council published a draft General Guideline for sentencing offences for which there is no offence specific sentencing guideline. The final (definitive) version of this Guideline is not expected to be published before the autumn of 2019. The draft is therefore not in force at the time of writing, but it contains useful guidance that reflects the approach taken by the courts and so is referred to extensively in this chapter. Reference should be made to the final, definitive, version of this Guideline when it is published.

13.3 Determining the seriousness of the offence

Section 143(1) of the Criminal Justice Act 2003 Act provides:

> In considering the seriousness of any offence, the court must consider the offender's culpability in committing the offence and any harm which the offence caused, was intended to cause or might foreseeably have caused.

This means that the court is required to pass a sentence that is commensurate with the seriousness of the offence, with seriousness being determined by:

- the culpability of the offender, and
- the harm caused, intended or risked by the offending.

13.3.1 Culpability

The Sentencing Council's draft General Guideline (for sentencing offences for which there is no offence specific sentencing guideline) says that culpability 'is assessed with reference to the offender's role, level of intention and/or premeditation and the extent and sophistication of planning'.

The draft Guideline goes on to say that the relevance of particular factors will vary depending on the type of offending. However, some general points can be made:

- If a characteristic is inherent in the offence, the mere presence of that characteristic will not be determinative of the level of culpability.
- Deliberate or gratuitous violence or damage to property, over and above what is needed to carry out the offence, will normally indicate a higher level of culpability.
- For offences where there is no requirement for the offender to have any level of intention, the range of culpability may be inferred from the circumstances of the offence. Four levels of culpability, from highest to lowest, are identified:
  - deliberate – intentional act or omission;
  - reckless – acted or failed to act regardless of the foreseeable risk;
  - negligent – failed to take steps to guard against the act or omission;
  - low/no culpability – act or omission with none of the above features.
- For offences that require some level of culpability (e.g. intention, recklessness or knowledge) to be made out, the range of culpability will be narrower; relevant factors may include, from highest to lowest:
  - high level of planning/sophistication/leading role;
  - some planning/significant role;
  - little or no planning/minor role.

13.3.2 Harm

The Sentencing Council's draft General Guideline also makes a number of observations about harm.

The term 'victim' is used widely in the guideline. It can include 'one or more individuals, a community, the general public, the state, the environment and/or animal(s)'. In some cases, there may not be an identifiable victim.

The draft Guideline states that an assessment of harm should generally reflect the 'overall impact of the offence upon the victim(s) and may include direct harm (including physical injury, psychological harm and financial loss) and consequential harm'. When considering the value of property that has been lost or damaged, the court should take account of any 'sentimental value to the victim(s) and any disruption caused to a victim's life, activities or business'.

Sometimes the level of harm actually caused will be different from the level of harm intended. Where harm was intended but no harm was caused, or a lower level of harm resulted than was intended, the sentence will 'normally be assessed with reference to the level of harm intended'. Where, on the other hand, the harm actually caused is greater than that intended, the sentence will 'normally be assessed with reference to the level of harm suffered by the victim'.

Dealing with a risk of harm 'involves consideration of both the likelihood of harm occurring and the extent of it if it does'. Risk of harm is less serious than the same harm actually occurring. Where the offence has caused risk of harm but no (or less) harm has in fact been suffered, the 'normal approach is to move down to the next category of harm'. However, this may not be appropriate if either the likelihood or extent of potential harm is particularly high.

A Victim Personal Statement (see below) may assist the court in assessing harm, but the draft Guideline cautions that the absence of such a statement should not be taken to indicate the absence of harm.

13.4 Statutory aggravating factors

The 2003 Act sets out a number of factors that serve to increase the sentence imposed on an offender.

13.4.1 Previous convictions

Prior to the enactment of the Criminal Justice Act 2003, the existence of previous convictions was regarded as resulting in 'progressive loss of mitigation' (see, for example, R v Queen (1981) 3 Cr App R (S) 245). An offender with no previous convictions received 'credit' for that fact. The more previous convictions recorded against the offender, the more of that 'credit' was lost. According to this approach, the sentence for the present offence should not be increased because of the existence of previous convictions, as that would be tantamount to sentencing the offender again for offences which he has committed in the past and for which he has already been punished. However, in *Making Punishment Work: report of a review of the sentencing framework of England and Wales* (2001), John Halliday recommended that the severity of the sentence should increase when an offender has sufficiently recent and relevant previous convictions. In other words, the court should regard the existence of previous convictions as making the present offence itself more serious, and therefore deserving an increased sentence. The principle recommended by Halliday became enshrined in the Criminal Justice Act 2003.

Section 143(2) of the Act says:

In considering the seriousness of an offence ('the current offence') committed by an offender who has one or more previous convictions, the court must treat each previous conviction as an aggravating factor if (in the case of that conviction) the court considers that it can reasonably be so treated having regard, in particular, to –

(a) the nature of the offence to which the conviction relates and its relevance to the current offence; and

(b) the time that has elapsed since the conviction.

For a discussion of the so-called 'recidivist premium', see Julian V. Roberts, *Punishing persistence: explaining the enduring appeal of the recidivist sentencing premium* (2008) 48 British Journal of Criminology 468–481.

The Sentencing Council's draft General Guideline give guidance on the application of s.143 (2). The guidance notes that the 'primary significance of previous convictions is the extent to which they indicate trends in offending behaviour and possibly the offender's response to earlier sentences'. In assessing the relevance of the particular previous convictions, the Guideline suggests a number of considerations:

- Previous convictions are normally relevant to the current offence when they are of a similar type. However, previous convictions for a different type of offence may be relevant 'where they are an indication of persistent offending or escalation and/or a failure to comply with previous court orders'.
- Numerous and frequent previous convictions 'might indicate an underlying problem (for example, an addiction) that could be addressed more effectively in the community and so do not necessarily indicate that a custodial sentence is necessary'.
    - It follows from this that the fact that the defendant has a bad record does not necessarily mean that a custodial sentence is inevitable. It has often been recognised (for example, in R v Bowles [1996] 2 Cr App R(S) 248) that there are occasions when, in the case of persistent offenders, it is appropriate to impose a community order, rather than a custodial sentence, provided that there is sufficient reason to think that it might be possible to break the defendant's cycle of offending once and for all. To take such a course of action, the court should be satisfied that the offender is highly motivated to change his/her ways.
- If the offender received a non-custodial disposal for the previous offence, the court should not necessarily move to a custodial sentence for the current offence.
- In cases involving significant persistent offending, the community and custody thresholds (see below) may be crossed even though the current offence would otherwise warrant a lesser sentence.
- The aggravating effect of relevant previous convictions 'reduces with the passage of time; older convictions are less relevant to the offender's culpability for the current offence and less likely to be predictive of future offending'. Where the previous offence is particularly old it will normally have little relevance to sentencing for the current offence.
    - The court should therefore consider the time gap since the previous conviction and the reason for it. Where there has been a significant gap between previous and current convictions or a reduction in the frequency of offending, 'this may indicate that the offender has made attempts to desist from offending, in which case the aggravating effect of the previous offending will diminish'.
- Where the current offence is significantly less serious than the previous conviction (suggesting a decline in the gravity of offending), the previous conviction may carry less weight.
- When considering the totality of previous offending, a court should take a 'rounded view' of the previous crimes and not simply aggregate the individual offences.

It should also be noted that the fact that the offender has previously received non-custodial sentences, and yet has reoffended, may well be relevant under s.143(2). Reoffending could thus be taken as showing that non-custodial sentences do not prevent this offender from reoffending.

This argument is strongest where the offender has committed offences while being subject to a community order.

For an international perspective on the use of previous convictions, see Thomas Mahon, *Justifying the Use of Previous Convictions as an Aggravating Factor at Sentencing* [2012] Cork Online Law Review 85–97.

13.4.2 Offending while on bail

Section 143(3) says:

> In considering the seriousness of any offence committed while the offender was on bail, the court must treat the fact that it was committed in those circumstances as an aggravating factor.

The fact that the defendant was on bail at the time of the present offence must be regarded as an aggravating feature (resulting in an increase in sentence), whether or not he was subsequently convicted of that other offence. In R v *Thackwray* [2003] EWCA Crim 3362, the Court of Appeal confirmed that the fact that the defendant was subsequently acquitted of the offence for which he was on bail 'makes no difference' (per Lord Woolf CJ, at [7]).

13.4.3 Racial or religious aggravation

Section 145(2) says that, if the offence was 'racially or religiously aggravated', the court 'must treat that fact as an aggravating factor'.

The Sentencing Council's draft General Guideline says that an offence is racially or religiously aggravated for these purposes if:

- at the time of committing the offence, or immediately before or after doing so, the offender demonstrates towards the victim of the offence, hostility based on the victim's membership (or presumed membership) of a racial or religious group; or
- the offence is motivated (wholly or partly) by hostility towards members of a racial or religious group based on their membership of that group.

For these purposes, 'membership', in relation to a racial or religious group, 'includes association with members of that group'; and 'presumed' means 'presumed by the offender'; 'racial group' means 'a group of persons defined by reference to race, colour, nationality (including citizenship) or ethnic or national origins'; 'religious group' means 'a group of persons defined by reference to religious belief or lack of religious belief'.

In R v *Saunders* [2000] 1 Cr App R 458, the Court of Appeal said that where an offence involves racial aggravation, a term of up to two years' custody may be added to the sentence. Also, the presence of racial aggravation may make a custodial sentence appropriate for an offence which would otherwise have merited a non-custodial sentence (per Rose LJ, at p.462).

13.4.4 Disability, sexual orientation or transgender aggravation

Section 146(3) of the 2003 Act says that the court must treat as an aggravating factor the fact that the offence was committed in any of the following circumstances:

(a) that, at the time of committing the offence, or immediately before or after doing so, the offender demonstrated towards the victim of the offence hostility based on –

   (i)   the sexual orientation (or presumed sexual orientation) of the victim;

   (ii) a disability (or presumed disability) of the victim; or

   (iii) the victim being (or being presumed to be) transgender; or

(b) that the offence is motivated (wholly or partly) –

   (i)   by hostility towards persons who are of a particular sexual orientation;

   (ii) by hostility towards persons who have a disability or a particular disability; or

   (iii) by hostility towards persons who are transgender.

For these purposes, it does not matter whether the offender's hostility is also based, to any extent, on any other factor (s.146(4)). Disability means physical or mental impairment (subs.(5)).

13.4.5 Non-statutory aggravating factors

The Sentencing Council's draft General Guideline identifies a number of other aggravating factors, making it clear that the list is not exhaustive.

13.4.5.1 Commission of offence whilst under the influence of alcohol or drugs

The fact that an offender is voluntarily intoxicated at the time of the offence 'will tend to increase the seriousness of the offence provided that the intoxication has contributed to the offending'. In the case of a person who is addicted to drugs or alcohol, the intoxication 'may be considered not to be voluntary, but the court should have regard to the extent to which the offender has engaged with any assistance in dealing with the addiction in making that assessment'. An offender who has voluntarily consumed drugs and/or alcohol 'must accept the consequences of the behaviour that results, even if it is out of character'.

13.4.5.2 Offence committed as part of a group or gang

Where the offence was committed as part of a group or gang this will normally make it more serious because:

- the harm caused (both physical or psychological) or the potential for harm may be greater; and/or
- the culpability of the offender may be higher (the role of the offender within the group will be a relevant consideration).

13.4.5.3 Offence involved use or threat of use of a weapon

For these purposes, a 'weapon' can 'take many forms and may include a shod foot'. The use or production of a weapon is relevant:

- 'to the culpability of the offender where it indicates planning or intention to cause harm; and
- to the harm caused (both physical or psychological) or the potential for harm'.

Relevant considerations will include:

- 'the dangerousness of the weapon;
- whether the offender brought the weapon to the scene, or just used what was available on impulse;
- the context in which the weapon was threatened, used or produced'.

13.4.5.4 Planning of an offence

Evidence of planning 'normally indicates a higher level of intention and pre-meditation which increases the level of culpability'. Therefore, the 'greater the degree of planning the greater the culpability'.

13.4.5.5 Commission of the offence for financial gain

This factor is relevant where the offence 'is not one which by its nature is an acquisitive offence' but which 'has been committed wholly or in part for financial gain or the avoidance of cost'; this factor will increase the seriousness of the offence.

Where the offending is 'committed in a commercial context for financial gain or the avoidance of costs, this will normally indicate a higher level of culpability'. Examples include dealing in unlawful goods, failing to comply with regulatory requirements, or failing to obtain a necessary licence or permission in order to avoid costs. The guideline notes that this sort of offending 'can undermine legitimate businesses'. If a financial penalty is imposed, 'it should remove any economic benefit the offender has derived through the commission of the offence' (including costs that are avoided and any gain made as a direct result of the offending). Where a fine is imposed, 'the amount of economic benefit derived from the offence should normally be added to the fine ... it should not be cheaper to offend than to comply with the law'. When sentencing organisations, the fine 'must be sufficiently substantial to have a real economic impact which will bring home to both management and shareholders the need to comply with the law'.

13.4.5.6 High level of profit from the offence

The draft Guideline also notes that a high level of profit is likely to indicate 'high culpability in terms of planning and a high level of harm in terms of loss caused to victims or the undermining of legitimate businesses'.

13.4.5.7 Abuse of trust or dominant position

This factor is relevant where the relationship between the offender and victim(s) is one where the offender has 'a significant level of responsibility towards the victim(s) on which the victim(s) would be entitled to rely'. Examples given in the draft Guideline include 'relationships such as teacher and pupil, parent and child, professional adviser and client, or carer (whether paid or unpaid) and dependant', as well as '*ad hoc* situations such as a late-night taxi driver and a lone passenger'. However, it would 'not generally include a familial relationship without a significant level of responsibility'.

13.4.5.8 Gratuitous degradation of victim/maximising distress to victim

The Sentencing Council's draft General Guideline says that where an offender 'deliberately causes additional harm to a victim over and above that which is an essential element of the offence', this will increase the seriousness of the offence. The Guideline gives the example of posting images on social media designed to cause additional distress to the victim. Another example would be a burglary where the offender causes unnecessary damage.

13.4.5.9 Vulnerable victim

The draft General Guideline states that an offence 'is more serious if the victim is vulnerable because of personal circumstances such as (but not limited to) age, illness or disability (unless the vulnerability of the victim is an element of the offence)'. Vulnerability can also include 'the victim being isolated, incapacitated through drink or being in an unfamiliar situation'. Culpability will be increased if the offender 'targeted a victim because of an actual or perceived vulnerability'; the victim is 'made vulnerable by the actions of the offender (such as a victim who has been intimidated or isolated by the offender)'; or the offender 'persisted in the offending once it was obvious that the victim was vulnerable (for example continuing to attack an injured victim)'. The level of harm (physical, psychological or financial) is also likely to be increased if the victim is vulnerable.

13.4.5.10 Victim providing a public service or performing a public duty at the time of the offence

The draft General Guideline observes that 'people in public facing roles are more exposed to the possibility of harm and consequently more vulnerable' and/or 'the fact that someone is working for the public good merits the additional protection of the courts'.

13.4.5.11 Other(s) put at risk of harm by the offending

This involves consideration of both the likelihood of harm occurring and the extent of it if it does.

13.4.5.12 Offence committed in the presence of other(s) (especially children)

This reflects the psychological harm that may be caused to those who witnessed the offence. The draft Guideline also notes that the 'presence of one or more children may in some situations make the primary victim more vulnerable – for example an adult may be less able to resist the offender if concerned about the safety or welfare of children present'.

13.4.5.13 Actions after the event, including attempts to cover up/conceal evidence

Unless this conduct is the subject of separate charges, it makes the offence more serious.

13.4.5.14 Blame wrongly placed on other(s)

Where the investigation has been hindered and/or other(s) have suffered as a result of being wrongly blamed by the offender, this makes the offence more serious. The draft Guideline notes that this factor is not engaged where the offender 'has simply exercised his or her right not to assist the investigation or accept responsibility for the offending'.

13.4.5.15 Failure to respond to warnings or concerns expressed by others about the offender's behaviour

Where an offender 'had the benefit of warnings or advice about their conduct but has failed to heed it', this would make the offender more blameworthy. This is particularly so where the warning(s) or advice 'were of an official nature or from a professional source' and/or 'at the time of or shortly before the commission of the offence'.

13.4.5.16 Offence committed on licence or post-sentence supervision or while subject to court order(s)

An offender who is subject to licence or post-sentence supervision 'is under a particular obligation to desist from further offending'. It follows that commission of an offence while subject to a relevant court order makes the offence more serious (where it is not dealt with separately as a breach of that order). The draft Guideline cautions that care should be taken to avoid double counting matters that have already been taken into account when considering previous convictions (see above).

13.4.5.17 Location and/or timing of offence

The draft General Guideline states that, generally, an offence is not made more serious by its location and/or timing except in ways taken into account by other factors that are addressed in the Guideline (such as planning, vulnerable victim, offence committed in a domestic context, maximising distress to victim, others put at risk of harm by the offending, offence committed in the presence of others). Otherwise there is a risk of double counting. However, the Guideline does say that an offence may be more serious if it is committed in a place 'in which there is a particular need for discipline or safety such as prisons, courts, schools or hospitals'.

13.4.5.18 Established evidence of community/wider impact
This should serve to increase the sentence 'only where there is clear evidence of wider harm not already taken into account elsewhere'. A community impact statement (see later) assists the court in assessing the level of impact.

13.4.5.19 Prevalence
The draft General Guideline makes the point that the sentencing levels in the offence-specific guidelines take account of 'collective social harm'. Offenders should therefore 'normally be sentenced by straightforward application of the guidelines without aggravation for the fact that their activity contributed to a harmful social effect upon a neighbourhood or community'. The Guideline also makes the important point that it is 'not open to a sentencer to increase a sentence for prevalence in ordinary circumstances or in response to a personal view that there is "too much of this sort of thing going on in this area"'. For prevalence to be taken into account:

● First, there must be evidence provided to the court by a responsible body or by a senior police officer.

● Secondly, that evidence must be before the court in the specific case being considered with the relevant statements or reports having been made available to the Crown and defence in good time so that meaningful representations about that material can be made.

● Even if such material is provided, a sentencer will only be entitled to treat prevalence as an aggravating factor if satisfied
  ○ that the level of harm caused in a particular locality is significantly higher than that caused elsewhere (and thus already inherent in the guideline levels);
  ○ that the circumstances can properly be described as exceptional; and
  ○ that it is just and proportionate to increase the sentence for such a factor in the particular case being sentenced.

These points echo those made by the Court of Appeal in R v Oosthuizen [2005] EWCA Crim 1978; [2006] 1 Cr App R (S) 73 (per Rose LJ, at [15] and [16]). Prevalence was also considered by the Court of Appeal in R v Bondzie [2016] EWCA Crim 552; [2016] 1 WLR 3004, where the court emphasised the importance of evidence to show that an offence is particularly prevalent in a given area, and that increasing the sentence on that basis should be exceptional. Treacy LJ (at [10] and [11]) said:

> Sentencing levels set in guidelines such as the Drugs Guideline take account of collective social harm. In the case of drugs supply this will cover the detrimental impact of drug dealing activities upon communities. Accordingly, offenders should normally be sentenced by straightforward application of the guidelines without aggravation for the fact that their activity contributes to a harmful social effect upon a neighbourhood or community. It is not open to the judge to increase sentence for prevalence in ordinary circumstances or in response to his own personal view that there is 'too much of this sort of thing going on in this area'.
>
> Firstly, there must be evidence provided to the court by a responsible body or by a senior police officer. Secondly, that evidence must be before the court in the specific case being considered with the relevant statements or reports having been made available to the Crown and defence in good time so that meaningful representations about that material can be made. Even if such material is provided, a judge will only be entitled to treat prevalence as an aggravating factor if (a) he is satisfied that the level of harm caused in a particular locality is significantly higher than that caused elsewhere (and thus already inherent in the guideline levels); (b) that the circumstances can properly be described as exceptional and (c) that it is

just and proportionate to increase sentence for such a factor in the particular case before him. It is clear therefore, that a court should be hesitant before aggravating a sentence by reason of prevalence. Judges will be only too well aware of the types of harm which are caused by drug dealing and will not be assisted by statements of the obvious. Only if the evidence placed before the court demonstrates a level of harm which clearly exceeds the well understood consequences of drug dealing by a significant margin should courts be prepared to reflect this in sentence. If judges do so, they must clearly state when sentencing that they are doing so.

His Lordship added (at [19]):

If the Crown intends to invite the court to consider that matter, it must expressly say so at the hearing, identifying the materials upon which it relies as evidence and referring the judge to the relevant guideline. If a judge of his or her own motion is contemplating prevalence as a factor, he or she should clearly identify that as a matter to be addressed in submissions to the court. Any sentence imposed should then identify if prevalence has been a factor and provide reasoning so that the parties, and possibly this court, may understand how it has influenced the sentencing decision.

13.5 Thresholds

A custodial or community sentence can be passed only if the offence is sufficiently serious to justify such a sentence.

13.5.1 Custody threshold

Section 152(2) of the Criminal Justice Act 2003 provides:

The court must not pass a custodial sentence unless it is of the opinion that the offence, or the combination of the offence and one or more offences associated with it, was so serious that neither a fine alone nor a community sentence can be justified for the offence.

This is subject to the rider contained in s.152(3), that:

Nothing in subs.(2) prevents the court from passing a custodial sentence on the offender if –
(a) he fails to express his willingness to comply with a requirement which is proposed by the court to be included in a community order and which requires an expression of such willingness; or
(b) he fails to comply with an order under s.161(2) (pre-sentence drug testing).

The Sentencing Council Guideline on the Imposition of Custodial Sentences notes that the 'clear intention of the threshold test is to reserve prison as a punishment for the most serious offences'.

The classic test for interpreting the custody threshold (as set out in earlier legislation) was *R v Bradbourn* (1985) 7 Cr App R(S) 180, where Lawton LJ (at p.183) said that the phrase 'so serious that a non-custodial sentence cannot be justified' (which was then the statutory test) meant:

the kind of offence which ... would make right-thinking members of the public, knowing all the facts, feel that justice had not been done by the passing of any sentence other than a custodial one.

However, in R v *Howells* [1999] 1 WLR 307, Lord Bingham CJ (at p.311) said that this test is unhelpful, since the sentencing court has no means of ascertaining the views of right-thinking members of the public and inevitably attributes to such right-thinking members its own views. When applying this test, the sentencing court is doing little more than reflect its own opinion whether justice would or would not be done and be seen to be done by the passing of a non-custodial sentence. Thus, the test is saying little more than 'a custodial sentence is justified if the court thinks it is justified'. His Lordship then went on to offer some general guidance on determining which side of the line a particular case may fall. His comments (at pp.311–2) are worth quoting at length:

> [I]n approaching cases which are on or near the custody threshold courts will usually find it helpful to begin by considering the nature and extent of the defendant's criminal intention and the nature and extent of any injury or damage caused to the victim. Other things being equal, an offence which is deliberate and premeditated will usually be more serious than one which is spontaneous and unpremeditated or which involves an excessive response to provocation; an offence which inflicts personal injury or mental trauma, particularly if permanent, will usually be more serious than one which inflicts financial loss only. In considering the seriousness of any offence the court may take into account any previous convictions of the offender or any failure to respond to previous sentences ... and must treat it as an aggravating factor if the offence was committed while the offender was on bail ...
>
> In deciding whether to impose a custodial sentence in borderline cases the sentencing court will ordinarily take account of matters relating to the offender. (a) The court will have regard to an offender's admission of responsibility for the offence, particularly if reflected in a plea of guilty tendered at the earliest opportunity and accompanied by hard evidence of genuine remorse, as shown (for example) by an expression of regret to the victim and an offer of compensation. Attention is drawn to s.48 of the Criminal Justice and Public Order Act 1994. (b) Where offending has been fuelled by addiction to drink or drugs, the court will be inclined to look more favourably on an offender who has already demonstrated (by taking practical steps to that end) a genuine, self-motivated determination to address his addiction. (c) Youth and immaturity, while affording no defence, will often justify a less rigorous penalty than would be appropriate for an adult. (d) Some measure of leniency will ordinarily be extended to offenders of previous good character, the more so if there is evidence of positive good character (such as a solid employment record or faithful discharge of family duties) as opposed to a mere absence of previous convictions. It will sometimes be appropriate to take account of family responsibilities, or physical or mental disability. (e) While the court will never impose a custodial sentence unless satisfied that it is necessary to do so, there will be even greater reluctance to impose a custodial sentence on an offender who has never before served such a sentence.

Section 166(1) of the 2003 Act provides that nothing in s.152 'prevents a court from mitigating an offender's sentence by taking into account any such matters as, in the opinion of the court, are relevant in mitigation of sentence'. Moreover, s.166(2) provides that s.152(2):

> does not prevent a court, after taking into account such matters, from passing a community sentence even though it is of the opinion that the offence, or the combination of the offence and one or more offences associated with it, was so serious that a community sentence could not normally be justified for the offence.

It follows that, even if the court decides that an offence is sufficiently serious to justify the imposition of a custodial sentence, the court is not prevented from imposing a non-custodial sentence in the light of mitigating circumstances. The Sentencing Council Guideline on the Imposition of Custodial Sentences says that:

passing the custody threshold does not mean that a custodial sentence should be deemed inevitable. Custody should not be imposed where a community order could provide sufficient restriction on an offender's liberty (by way of punishment) while addressing the rehabilitation of the offender to prevent future crime.

The Guideline goes on to says that:

For offenders on the cusp of custody, imprisonment should not be imposed where there would be an impact on dependants which would make a custodial sentence disproportionate to achieving the aims of sentencing.

Where the offender is convicted of two or more offences, the court should consider the offences together and should decide whether the combination of offences is such that a custodial sentence is justified. In R v Oliver and Little [1993] 1 WLR 177, the Court of Appeal considered what should be done where an offender is convicted of a number of offences, some of which merit a custodial sentence and some of which do not. It was held that, once an offender has qualified for a custodial sentence, the court is not precluded from passing, on the same occasion, custodial sentences for offences that did not themselves satisfy the statutory requirements. However, it would usually be inappropriate for consecutive sentences to be passed for offences that did not themselves satisfy the requirements relating to custody (and so those sentences should be concurrent with the sentences for the offences which do merit custody, thereby not adding to the total period of custody to be served).

For a discussion of the effectiveness of the custody threshold, see Julian V. Roberts and Lyndon Harris, *Reconceptualising the custody threshold in England and Wales* (2017) 28 Criminal Law Forum 477–499.

13.5.2 Community sentence threshold

Section 148(1) of the 2003 Act says:

A court must not pass a community sentence on an offender unless it is of the opinion that the offence, or the combination of the offence and one or more offences associated with it, was serious enough to warrant such a sentence.

Section 148(2) goes on:

Where a court passes a community sentence –
(a) the particular requirement or requirements forming part of the community order ... comprised in the sentence must be such as, in the opinion of the court, is, or taken together are, the most suitable for the offender; and
(b) the restrictions on liberty imposed by the order must be such as in the opinion of the court are commensurate with the seriousness of the offence, or the combination of the offence and one or more offences associated with it.

13.6 Reduction in sentencing for pleading guilty

Section 144(1) of the 2003 Act says:

In determining what sentence to pass on an offender who has pleaded guilty to an offence in proceedings before that or another court, a court must take into account –

(a) the stage in the proceedings for the offence at which the offender indicated his intention to plead guilty; and

(b) the circumstances in which this indication was given.

The statute is otherwise silent on what approach a court ought to take where an offender pleads guilty. In 2017, the Sentencing Council issued a revised Definitive Guideline entitled 'Reduction in Sentence for a Guilty Plea'.

The rationale for the reduction in sentence where the offender pleads guilty is set out in Part B of the Guideline. This notes that, although

> a guilty person is entitled not to admit the offence and to put the prosecution to proof of its case, an acceptance of guilt (a) normally reduces the impact of the crime upon victims; (b) saves victims and witnesses from having to testify; and (c) is in the public interest in that it saves public time and money on investigations and trials.

The Guideline adds that a guilty plea 'produces greater benefits the earlier the plea is indicated'.

The rationale for this reduction in sentence was also considered by the Court of Appeal in R v Caley [2012] EWCA Crim 2821; [2013] 2 Cr App R (S) 47. Hughes LJ ([5]–[6]) said:

> In order of importance, plainly the first is the benefit for victims and witnesses. The impact of crime on its victims can be enormous or slight, but whether it is large or small the knowledge that a defendant has accepted his guilt and that punishment will follow normally reduces that impact substantially and thus brings significant benefit to the victim. It is generally worse for the victim when the offender, although guilty, is defiant. The same applies to the impact on those who may have to give evidence; they include, but are not confined to, the victim. A few may relish it, or think that they will, but for most the process is normally stressful and often unavoidably uncomfortable. Moreover the anticipation may often be painful, sometimes even more than the actuality. For both victims and witnesses the benefit from a plea of guilty remains even when it comes late, but generally speaking the later it is the less the benefit.
>
> The second major reason for the practice is a more pragmatic one but it is nevertheless vital in the public interest. The expenditure in public time and money on trials and on preparation for trials is considerable. The case must be thoroughly prepared so that the exacting standard of proof rightly required in a criminal case can be met. Further investigation is likely to be necessary, as may the assembly of a good deal more evidence, lay and expert. Such steps are necessary, but expensive. They are avoided or much reduced by an admission of guilt. The public's limited resources can then be concentrated on those cases where a trial will really be necessary, and such cases will not be delayed, often with accused persons in custody. At present something of the order of 75 per cent of all Crown Court cases result in pleas of guilty; if in all those cases the defendants were out of defiance or otherwise to insist on each detail of the case being proved to the hilt the administration of criminal justice would be in danger of collapse.

13.6.1 The amount of the reduction

Part D of the Guideline states that 'the maximum level of reduction in sentence for a guilty plea is one-third'. Where a guilty plea is indicated 'at the first stage of proceedings' a reduction of one-third should usually be made. The Guideline says that the first stage will 'normally be the first hearing at which a plea or indication of plea is sought and recorded by the court'. If the guilty plea is indicated 'after the first stage of proceedings', the maximum reduction is reduced to one quarter, with a sliding scale of reduction thereafter in which the reduction should be decreased from one-quarter to a maximum of one-tenth on the first day of trial, 'having regard to the time when the guilty plea is first indicated to the court relative to the progress of the case and the trial date ... The reduction should normally be decreased further, even to zero, if the guilty plea is entered during the course of the trial'.

The appendices to the Guideline illustrate how these reductions are to be applied:

- *Summary offences*: one-third reduction if the defendant pleads guilty when the plea is taken (thereafter, sliding scale from one-quarter to a maximum of one-tenth on day of trial);
- *Either-way offences*: one-third reduction if the defendant pleads guilty at the 'plea before venue' hearing (one-quarter if the defendant indicates a not guilty plea at the 'plea before venue' hearing but then pleads guilty at the first Crown Court hearing; thereafter, a sliding scale down to a maximum of one-tenth on day of trial);
- *Indictable-only offences*: one-third reduction if the defendant indicates a guilty plea in the magistrates' court and pleads guilty at the first hearing in the Crown Court; if the defendant pleads guilty at the first hearing in the Crown Court but did not indicate a guilty plea in the magistrates' court, the maximum reduction is one-quarter (thereafter, a sliding scale down to a maximum of one-tenth on day of trial).

It is clear from this that the timing of the plea is crucial to determining the amount of the reduction in sentence. The current version of the Guideline defines more clearly than previous versions when a plea must be entered in order to attract the maximum one-third discount (earlier versions referring to the defendant's 'first reasonable opportunity'). Two points are particularly worth emphasising:

- If the offence is triable either way, the defendant must plead guilty at the 'plea before venue' hearing in the magistrates' court. If the defendant indicates a not guilty plea at the 'plea before venue' hearing but then pleads guilty at the next hearing (which will be in the Crown Court if the magistrates decline jurisdiction or the defendant elects trial on indictment), the maximum reduction is reduced to one-quarter.
- If the offence is triable only on indictment, the defendant has no opportunity to enter a formal plea in the magistrates' court (because a magistrates' court cannot try an indictable-only offence); however, to obtain the maximum one-third reduction in sentence, a defendant has to indicate to the magistrates' court an intention to plead guilty (and then enter a guilty plea at the first opportunity in the Crown Court, which will usually be the Plea and Trial Preparation Hearing). It is for this reason r.9.7(5) of the Criminal Procedure Rules requires the magistrates' court, when sending the defendant to the Crown Court for trial for an indictable-only offence, to ask whether the defendant intends to plead guilty in the Crown Court and, if the answer is 'yes', make arrangements for the Crown Court to take the defendant's plea as soon as possible.

It should be noted that the reduction in sentence applies only to the 'punitive' elements of the sentence (for example, the length of a custodial sentence, the number of hours unpaid work in a community order, or the amount of the fine). It does not apply to the rehabilitative elements of a sentence, and it does not have any impact on ancillary orders, such as compensation or disqualification from driving.

Moreover, Part E1 of the Guideline states that the reduction in sentence for a guilty plea 'can be taken into account by imposing one type of sentence rather than another' (for example, by reducing a custodial sentence to a community sentence, or by reducing a community sentence to a fine); in such cases, 'there should normally be no further reduction on account of the guilty plea'. However, where the less severe type of sentence 'is justified by other factors, the appropriate reduction for the plea should be applied in the normal way'.

Part F of the Guideline deals with what are described as 'exceptions'. The first such exception is where the sentencing court is satisfied that there were 'particular circumstances which significantly reduced the defendant's ability to understand what was alleged or otherwise made it unreasonable to expect the defendant to indicate a guilty plea sooner than was done'; in such cases, a reduction of one-third should be made even though the guilty plea was indicated after the first hearing where the defendant had an opportunity to indicate a plea. This exception will rarely be applicable. The Guideline requires sentencers to 'distinguish between cases in which it is necessary to receive advice and/or have sight of evidence in order to understand whether the defendant is in fact and law guilty of the offence(s) charged, and cases in which a defendant merely delays guilty plea(s) in order to assess the strength of the prosecution evidence and the prospects of conviction or acquittal'.

In R v Caley [2012] EWCA Crim 2821; [2013] 2 Cr App R (S) 47, Hughes LJ (at [14]) said:

> There will certainly be cases where a defendant genuinely does not know whether he is guilty or not and needs advice and/or sight of the evidence in order to decide. We do not attempt to define them ... They might however include cases where even if the facts are known there is a need for legal advice as to whether an offence is constituted by them, or cases where a defendant genuinely has no recollection of events. There may be other cases in which a defendant cannot reasonably be expected to make any admission until he and his advisers have seen at least some of the evidence. Such cases aside, however, whilst it is perfectly proper for a defendant to require advice from his lawyers on the strength of the evidence (just as he is perfectly entitled to insist on putting the Crown to proof at trial), he does not require it in order to know whether he is guilty or not; he requires it in order to assess the prospects of conviction or acquittal, which is different. Moreover, even though a defendant may need advice on which charge he ought to plead guilty to, there is often no reason why uncertainty about this should inhibit him from admitting, if it is true, what acts he did. If he does so, normally the public benefits to which we have referred will flow.

Part F3 of the Guideline addresses cases where the defendant is convicted of a 'lesser or different offence from that originally charged'. Where the defendant had earlier made 'an unequivocal indication of a guilty plea to this lesser or different offence to the prosecution and the court, the court should give the level of reduction that is appropriate to the stage in the proceedings at which this indication of plea (to the lesser or different offence) was made'. In the Crown Court, where the offered plea is a permissible alternative on the indictment as charged (under s.6(1) of the Criminal Law Act 1967), the defendant will not be treated as having made an unequivocal indication unless a guilty plea has been entered (and so it is the timing of the actual plea that determines the reduction in sentence).

3.6.1.1 Relationship between guilty plea and remorse

The Guideline states that the 'guilty plea should be considered by the court to be independent of the offender's personal mitigation'; it follows that factors such as 'admissions at interview, co-operation with the investigation and demonstrations of remorse should not be taken into account in determining the level of reduction. Rather, they should be considered separately and prior to any guilty plea reduction, as potential mitigating factors'. Thus, the reduction in sentence for pleading guilty should be applied after other mitigation has been taken account of.

However, in R v Barney [2007] EWCA Crim 3181; [2008] 2 Cr App R (S) 37, the Court of Appeal (considering an earlier version of the Guideline) said that the question of remorse cannot be entirely divorced from the question of a defendant's guilty plea. Where an entirely fictitious story was told to the police, that is a matter which the court is entitled to take into account when deciding upon the credit to be given for a subsequent guilty plea. A remorseful plea of guilty will not necessarily result in a discount of greater than one-third, although there are some circumstances in which clear remorse might be taken into account as an additional factor. A reduction in the credit due for a guilty plea on the basis of lack of remorse might not in itself be appropriate; however, where a defendant went out of his way to seek to avoid responsibility (for example, denying responsibility in the defence case statement), that can be taken into account in the context of both remorse and the plea of guilty (per Cooke J, at [19] and [21]). In R v *Caley* [2012] EWCA Crim 2821; [2013] 2 Cr App R (S) 47, Hughes LJ (at [7] said:

> . . . [A] plea of guilty may of course be an indication of remorse for the offence, but it may not be and the two things are not the same. A defendant may indeed regret his offence, and, beyond that, it may be clear that he wishes to avoid doing it again. Equally, however, he may plead guilty not because he regrets committing the crime but simply because he does not see a way of avoiding the consequences. The benefits which we have described which come from a defendant who is guilty admitting that he is so remain present if it is a case of the latter type. Moreover, it accords with elementary instincts of justice to recognise the difference between two defendants, one of whom is defiant and requires the public to prove every dot and comma of the case against him and the other of whom accepts his guilt.

His Lordship noted that an early admission of guilt to the police is not required in order to obtain the maximum one-third reduction. However, he went on to observe (at [13]):

> It does not of course follow that it is irrelevant to sentence if a defendant frankly admits in police interview what he did. Far from it. The defendant who does so will have additional mitigation which should normally be recognised in sentencing. Its impact on sentence will of course vary according to circumstances. At one end of the scale, the defendant who volunteers an admission when the police could not have brought the allegation home (and occasionally when they did not even know about it) usually has a great deal of mitigation. So has the defendant who, by admitting what he did, spares others who would otherwise have come under suspicion. At the other end of the scale, the defendant who is confronted with evidence which is in practice unanswerable has little, although some, mitigation. The right way for courts to deal with admissions in interview is not, however, by treating them as essential in every case to according the maximum one-third reduction for guilty plea. Rather, the variable circumstances of such admissions are best dealt with not by percentage adjustments prescribed in advance but by recognising them as a factor tending towards downwards adjustment to the sentence passed, to be assessed in the ordinary way by the judge along with other aggravating and mitigating factors, but before adjustment for plea of guilty.

3.6.1.2 Where the prosecution case is overwhelming

The previous (2007) version of the Guideline provided for a maximum reduction of only 20% where the evidence against the offender was overwhelming. However, as Lord Judge said in R v *Wilson* [2012] EWCA Crim 386; [2012] 2 Cr App R (S) 77 (at [29]), even in an overwhelming case, the guilty plea has a distinct public benefit; the earlier that it is indicated, the better for everyone. His Lordship went on (at [32]) to refer to 'the value to the victims of crime and the administration of justice of an early indication that the defendant does not require the issues to be tried'. Similarly, in R v *Caley* [2012] EWCA Crim 2821; [2013] 2 Cr App R (S) 47, Hughes LJ (at [24]) said that the 'various public benefits which underlie the practice of reducing sentence for plea of guilty apply just as much to overwhelming cases as to less strong ones'. In a change to the practice required by the previous version of the Guideline, the present version states that the benefits of guilty pleas 'apply regardless of the strength of the evidence against an offender. The strength of the evidence should not be taken into account when determining the level of reduction'. It follows that there should be no reduction in the amount of the discount on the basis that the evidence against the defendant was overwhelming.

13.7 Procedure following a plea of guilty

Rule 24.11(3) of the Criminal Procedure Rules states that, where the defendant pleads guilty or is found guilty in the magistrates' court, the prosecutor must summarise the prosecution case, if the sentencing court has not heard evidence; provide information relevant to sentence, including any statement of the effect of the offence on the victim, the victim's family or others; where it is likely to assist the court, identify any other matter relevant to sentence, including any sentencing guidelines, or guideline cases, aggravating and mitigating features affecting the defendant's culpability and the harm which the offence caused, was intended to cause or might foreseeably have caused.

Rule 25.16(3) applies where the defendant pleads guilty or is found guilty in the Crown Court. It is in very similar terms to the equivalent provision for magistrates' courts, and requires the prosecutor to summarise the prosecution case, if the sentencing court has not heard evidence; provide information relevant to sentence, including any previous conviction of the defendant, and the circumstances where relevant; any statement of the effect of the offence on the victim, the victim's family or others; and identify any other matter relevant to sentence, including any sentencing guidelines, or guideline cases; aggravating and mitigating features affecting the defendant's culpability and the harm which the offence caused, was intended to cause or might foreseeably have caused.

It follows that, where the defendant pleads guilty, the first step is for the court to ascertain the facts of the case. The prosecution will therefore summarise the facts of the offence so that the court is able to form a view of how serious the offence was. The prosecutor will also draw the court's attention to the defendant's antecedents (that is, personal circumstances), including any previous convictions.

All the allegations that are made by the prosecution should be based on admissible evidence and should be apparent from the written witness statements that have been disclosed to the defence. In R v Hobstaff (1993) 14 Cr App R(S) 605, for example, the Court of Appeal criticised prosecuting counsel for making allegations about the effect of the offence on the victim because he used 'colourful and highly emotive language' and made allegations which were not contained in the witness statements which had been supplied to the defence.

3.7.1 Basis of plea agreements

Paragraph B.6 of Criminal Practice Direction VII, states that a defendant

> may put forward a plea of guilty without accepting all of the facts as alleged by the prosecution. The basis of plea offered may seek to limit the facts or the extent of the offending for which the defendant is to be sentenced.

Paragraph B.7 goes on to say that agreements between the prosecution and defence on the factual basis upon which the defendant is to be sentenced are subject to approval by the court:

> The prosecution may reach an agreement with the defendant as to the factual basis on which the defendant will plead guilty, often known as an 'agreed basis of plea'. It is always subject to the approval of the court, which will consider whether it adequately and appropriately reflects the evidence as disclosed on the papers, whether it is fair and whether it is in the interests of justice.

In R v *Cairns* [2013] EWCA Crim 467; [2013] 2 Cr App R (S) 73, Leveson LJ referred (at [5]) to the Attorney-General's Guidelines on the Acceptance of Pleas and the Prosecutor's Role in the Sentencing Exercise (the current version of which was issued in 2012). He summarised the relevant principles as follows:

(i) A basis of plea must not be agreed on a misleading or untrue set of facts and must take proper account of the victim's interests; in cases involving multiple defendants, the bases of plea for each defendant must be factually consistent with each other ...

(ii) The written basis of plea must be scrutinised by the prosecution with great care. If a defendant seeks to mitigate on the basis of assertions of fact outside the prosecutor's knowledge (for example as to his state of mind), the judge should be invited not to accept this version unless given on oath and tested in cross examination ... If evidence is not given in this way, then the judge might draw such inferences as he thought fit from that fact.

(iii) The prosecution advocate must ensure that the defence advocate is aware of the basis on which the plea is accepted and the way in which the case will be opened ... Where a basis of plea is agreed, having been reduced into writing and signed by advocates for both sides, it should be submitted to the judge prior to the opening. It should not contain matters that are in dispute ... If it is not agreed, the basis of plea should be set out in writing identifying what is in issue; if the court decides that the dispute is material to sentence, it may direct further representations or evidence in accordance with the principles set out in Newton (1982) 77 Cr App R 13.

(iv) Both sides must ensure that the judge is aware of any discrepancy between the basis of plea and the prosecution case that could potentially have a significant effect on sentence so that consideration can be given to holding a Newton hearing. Even where the basis of plea is agreed between the prosecution and the defence, the judge is not bound by such agreement ... But if the judge is minded not to accept the basis of plea in a case where that may affect sentence, he should say so.

The procedure to be followed where the defendant pleads guilty, but disputes the basis of offending alleged by the prosecution and agreement as to that has not been reached, is set out in para.B.11 of the Practice Direction:

(a) The defendant's basis of plea must be set out in writing, identifying what is in dispute and must be signed by the defendant;

(b) The prosecution must respond in writing setting out their alternative contentions and indicating whether or not they submit that a Newton hearing [see below] is necessary;

(c) The court may invite the parties to make representations about whether the dispute is material to sentence; and

(d) If the court decides that it is a material dispute, the court will invite such further representations or evidence as it may require and resolve the dispute in accordance with the principles set out in R v Newton.

13.7.2 The *Newton* hearing

In cases where the defendant pleads guilty but does so on a factual basis which is different from the prosecution version of what took place, the conflict must be resolved in accordance with the rules laid down by the Court of Appeal in R v *Newton* (1983) 77 Cr App R 13.

In *Newton*, the defendant was charged with buggery of his wife. He claimed that she consented to this (at that time not a defence, but relevant to sentence) but the prosecution alleged that she had not consented. The judge wrongly accepted the prosecution version without hearing evidence on the issue of consent. The Court of Appeal held that if, on a plea of guilty, there is a substantial conflict between the prosecution and the defence (that is, there is sharp divergence between the prosecution version of the facts and the defence version of the facts), the judge or magistrates must either:

- accept the defence version and sentence accordingly; or
- hear evidence on what happened and then make a finding of fact as to what happened, and sentence accordingly.

In other words, where there is a substantial divergence between the two stories (that is, a divergence which will have a material effect on the sentence imposed), the judge or magistrates can only reject the defence version after hearing evidence on what happened.

In the Crown Court, if the judge hears evidence, then he sits alone (that is, a jury is not empanelled for the *Newton* hearing). The parties are given the opportunity to call such evidence as they wish and to cross-examine witnesses called by the other side.

An example of a situation where the principles set out in *Newton* apply may be found in the facts of R v McFarlane (1995) 16 Cr App R(S) 315. The defendant was charged with assault occasioning actual bodily harm. The prosecution case was that he had jabbed his wife in the face with a fork and repeatedly punched her about the face. The defendant pleaded guilty but claimed that he had not jabbed her in the face with a fork and that he had slapped her (and had not punched her).

As we have seen, a *Newton* hearing in the Crown Court takes the form of the judge hearing evidence and deciding issues of the fact. However, in R v Newton, it was suggested that there may be cases where the difference between the versions put forward by the prosecution and the defence ought to be resolved by use of a jury. This can be done only where the difference in versions amounts in effect to an allegation that the defendant committed an additional offence. For example, in a robbery case, if the offender admits threatening the use of violence but denies brandishing a weapon, this dispute should be resolved by adding a count alleging possession of an offensive weapon (s.1 of the Prevention of Crime Act 1953). Indeed, the *Newton* hearing should not be used in a way that effectively defeats the defendant's right to be tried by a jury for an allegation which amounts to an additional offence. For example, in R v Eubank [2001] EWCA Crim 891; [2002] 1 Cr App R(S) 4, the defendant was charged with robbery. The prosecution alleged that he was carrying a firearm in the course of the robbery. The defendant pleaded guilty to robbery but denied carrying a firearm. The judge held a *Newton* hearing and decided that the defendant was indeed carrying a firearm. The Court of Appeal said that the judge had been wrong to resolve the question through a *Newton* hearing. The allegation that the defendant had a firearm amounted to a separate and additional offence, on which the defendant was entitled to the verdict of a jury, and so that allegation should have been reflected by a separate count on the indictment (per Lord Woolf CJ, at [9]).

Another example of where it would have been appropriate to empanel a jury comes from the case of R v Gandy (1989) 11 Cr App R(S) 564. The defendant pleaded guilty to a charge of violent disorder. The prosecution alleged that, during the course of the incident, the defendant threw a glass, causing serious injury to the victim. The defendant denied that this was the case. The judge held a *Newton* hearing, but the Court of Appeal said (obiter) that it would have been more appropriate to add a count alleging wounding with intent (s.18 of the Offences Against the Person Act 1861) or a count alleging unlawful wounding (s.20 of the Offences Against the Person Act 1861); this would have enabled a jury to determine whether the defendant threw the glass.

This method of resolving the difference between the two versions of events should be used only where the difference amounts, in substance, to an allegation that the defendant committed an additional offence (and one that is triable in the Crown Court). In R v *Dowdall* (1992) 13 Cr App R (S) 441, for example, the defendant was charged with stealing a pension book from a bag carried by a woman in a supermarket. He offered to plead guilty to theft on the basis that he had found the book and subsequently dishonestly appropriated it, but he denied that he had taken the book from the victim's bag (which would have been a more serious offence, given the closer proximity to the victim). The judge allowed the prosecution to amend the indictment so that it contained a count alleging theft by finding and an alternative count alleging theft from the woman's bag. The Court of Appeal said that the judge erred in allowing the prosecution to amend the indictment in this way. He should have accepted the defendant's plea of guilty and should then have held a *Newton* hearing (without empanelling a jury) to determine the circumstances in which the defendant stole the pension book.

In the magistrates' court, where the dispute amounts to an allegation that the defendant committed an additional offence, the proper procedure is for this additional offence to be the subject of a new charge, which is then tried by the magistrates in the usual way.

Where there is a difference between the version of the facts put forward by the prosecution and that put forward by the defence, it is not necessary for the court to determine which view of the facts is correct if the difference would not materially affect the sentence. If the difference will not materially affect the sentence, the court should simply proceed on the basis of the defendant's version (R v *Hall* (1984) 6 Cr App R (S) 321).

Likewise, it is not necessary for the court to conduct a *Newton* hearing if the defendant's account amounts to extraneous mitigation which does not contradict the prosecution case (R v *Broderick* (1994) 15 Cr App R (S) 476). Moreover, as Judge LJ said in R v *Underwood* [2004] EWCA Crim 2256; [2005] 1 Cr App R 13, at [10]:

> Generally speaking, matters of mitigation are not normally dealt with by way of a *Newton* hearing. It is, of course, always open to the court to allow a defendant to give evidence of matters of mitigation which are within his own knowledge. From time to time, for example, defendants involved in drug cases will assert that they were acting under some form of duress, not amounting in law to a defence. If there is nothing to support such a contention, the judge is entitled to invite the advocate for the defendant to call his client rather than depend on the unsupported assertions of the advocate.

3.7.2.1 Procedure for Newton hearings

Rule 24.11(5) of the Criminal Procedure Rules states that where the defendant pleads guilty in a magistrates' court but wants to be sentenced on a different basis to that disclosed by the prosecution case, the defendant must set out that basis in writing, identifying what is in dispute; the court may invite the parties to make representations about whether the dispute is material to sentence; and, if the court decides that it is a material dispute, the court must invite such further representations or evidence as it may require, and then decide the dispute.

Rule 25.16(4) applies where the defendant pleads guilty in the Crown Court. It provides that the court may give directions for determining the facts on the basis of which sentence must be passed if the defendant wants to be sentenced on a basis agreed with the prosecutor or, in the absence of such agreement, the defendant wants to be sentenced on the basis of facts different from those disclosed by the prosecution case.

Paragraph B.8 of Criminal Practice Direction VII refers to the guidance on *Newton* hearings given by the Court of Appeal in R v *Underwood* [2004] EWCA Crim 2256; [2005] 1 Cr App R 13, where Judge LJ (at [3]–[9]) gave the following guidance:

The starting point has to be the defendant's instructions. His advocate will appreciate whether any significant facts about the prosecution evidence are disputed and the factual basis on which the defendant intends to plead guilty. If the resolution of the facts in dispute may matter to the sentencing decision, the responsibility for taking any initiative and alerting the prosecutor to the areas of dispute rests with the defence. The Crown should not be taken by surprise, and if it is suddenly faced with a proposed basis of plea of guilty where important facts are disputed, it should, if necessary, take time for proper reflection and consultation to consider its position and the interests of justice. In any event, whatever view may be formed by the Crown on any proposed basis of plea, it is deemed to be conditional on the judge's acceptance of it.

The Crown may accept and agree the defendant's account of the disputed facts. If so, the agreement should be reduced to writing and signed by both advocates. It should then be made available to the judge before the start of the Crown's opening, and, if possible, before he is invited to approve the acceptance of any plea or pleas. If, however, a plea has already been accepted and approved, then it should be available before the sentencing hearing begins. If the agreed basis of plea is not signed by the advocates for both sides, the judge is entitled to ignore it; similarly, if the document is not legible. The Crown may reject the defendant's version. If so, the areas of dispute should be identified in writing and the document should focus the court's attention on the precise fact or facts which are in dispute.

The third, and most difficult, situation arises when the Crown may lack the evidence positively to dispute the defendant's account. In many cases an issue raised by the defence is outside the knowledge of the prosecution. The prosecution's position may well be that it had no evidence to contradict the defence assertions. That does not mean that the truth of matters outside its own knowledge should be agreed. In these circumstances, particularly if the facts relied on by the defendant arise from his personal knowledge and depend on his own account of the facts, the Crown should not normally agree the defendant's account unless it is supported by other material. There is, therefore, an important distinction between assertions about the facts which the Crown is prepared to agree, and its possible agreement to facts about which, in truth, the prosecution is ignorant. Neither the prosecution nor the judge is bound to agree facts merely because, in the word currently in vogue, the prosecution cannot 'gainsay' the defendant's account. Again, the court should be notified at the outset in writing of the points in issue and the Crown's responses. We need not address those cases where the Crown occupies a position which straddles two, or even all three, of these alternatives.

After submissions from the advocates the judge should decide how to proceed. If not already decided, he will address the question whether he should approve the Crown's acceptance of pleas. Then he will address the proposed basis of plea. We emphasise that, whether or not the basis of plea is 'agreed', the judge is not bound by any such agreement and is entitled of his own motion to insist that any evidence relevant to the facts in dispute should be called before him. No doubt, before doing so, he will examine any agreement reached by the advocates, paying appropriate regard to it, and any reasons which the Crown, in particular, may advance to justify him proceeding immediately to sentence. At the risk of stating the obvious, the judge is responsible for the sentencing decision and he may therefore order a Newton hearing to ascertain the truth about disputed facts.

The prosecuting advocate should assist the judge by calling any appropriate evidence and testing the evidence advanced by the defence. The defence advocate should similarly call any relevant evidence and, in particular, where the issue arises from facts which are within the exclusive knowledge of the defendant and the defendant is willing to give evidence in support of his case, be prepared to call him. If he is not, and subject to any explanation which may be proffered, the judge may draw such inferences as he thinks fit from that fact. An adjournment for these purposes is often unnecessary. If the plea is tendered late when the case is due to be tried the relevant witnesses for the Crown are likely to be available. The Newton hearing should proceed immediately. In every case, or virtually so, the defendant will be present. It may be sufficient for the judge's purpose to hear the defendant. If so, again, unless it is impracticable for some exceptional reason, the hearing should proceed immediately.

The judge must then make up his mind about the facts in dispute. He may, of course, reject evidence called by the prosecution. It is sometimes overlooked that he may equally reject assertions advanced by the defendant, or his witnesses, even if the Crown does not offer positive contradictory evidence.

The judge must, of course, direct himself in accordance with ordinary principles, such as, for example, the burden and standard of proof. In short, his self-directions should reflect the relevant directions he would have given to the jury. Having reached his conclusions, he should explain them in a judgment.

These principles were helpfully summarised (and their importance emphasised) by Hallett LJ in R v Marsh [2018] EWCA Crim 986; [2018] 2 Cr App R (S) 28 (at [3]–[4]):

Where there is any dispute as to the factual basis for sentencing that may have a significant impact upon the nature or length of any sentence imposed, the dispute should be resolved, if necessary by holding a Newton hearing. If a defendant decides to plead guilty but does not submit a basis of plea, the defence advocate should ensure the prosecutor is aware of any differences in the case as presented by the prosecution and the defendant's instructions as to be advanced in mitigation, so that the prosecutor is not taken by surprise.

If a basis of plea is tendered, the prosecutor should analyse carefully if it is accepted or challenged. It is not sufficient for the prosecutor to use expressions such as they do not gainsay the defendant's account or for the prosecutor to leave it to the judge to decide what to accept without the benefit of their submissions. If it is accepted it should be signed by both advocates. The judge should not accept a basis of plea that runs counter to the evidence as presented and in the judge's mind wrongly minimises the defendant's role or conduct. She/he should inform the defence of any issues that arise so that the defence advocate can make any submissions or a Newton hearing can be held. A judge should not make findings of fact based on evidence called in a trial conducted without the defendant present or represented which run counter to the mitigation or a basis of plea without informing the defence of their intention to do so, so that the defence can make submissions. Finally, where a Definitive Guideline exists, both defenders and prosecutors should take care to select the correct guideline and address the judge on the appropriate categorization.

At the conclusion of a Newton hearing, 'in order to meet the requirements of the defendant and the wider public, the judge should provide a reasoned decision as to his findings of fact and thereafter, following mitigation, proceed to sentence' (R v Cairns [2013] EWCA Crim 467; [2013] 2 Cr App R (S) 73, per Leveson LJ, at [7]).

13.7.2.2 Standard of proof in a Newton hearing

The judge, when making findings of fact in a Newton hearing, must approach questions of fact which have to be decided in accordance with the criminal burden and standard of proof, so the judge must be satisfied so that he is sure that the prosecution version is correct before sentencing on that basis (R v Kerrigan (1993) 14 Cr App R(S) 179).

In R v Gandy (1989) 11 Cr App R(S) 564, it was stressed by the Court of Appeal that where the judge holds a Newton hearing, the rules of evidence must be followed strictly and the judge must direct himself in the same terms as he would direct a jury. In that case, for example, the Court of Appeal rejected the finding of fact made by the judge that it was the defendant that had caused injury to the victim because the judge had not taken proper account of the weaknesses in the identification evidence against the accused (cf. R v Turnbull [1977] QB 224).

13.7.2.3 Effect of *Newton* hearing on guilty plea discount

It should be borne in mind that if there is a *Newton* hearing and the court rules against the accused (in other words, having heard evidence, the court accepts the prosecution version), the accused will lose some (though not all) of the credit that he would otherwise have received for pleading guilty (see, for example, R v Webster [2004] EWCA Crim 417; [2004] 2 Cr App R (S) 77).

Part F2 of the Sentencing Council Guideline states that where an offender's version of events is rejected at a *Newton* hearing, 'the reduction which would have been available at the stage of proceedings the plea was indicated should normally be halved'. Where witnesses are called during such a hearing, as will usually be the case, 'it may be appropriate further to decrease the reduction' (the Guideline does not go into further detail as the extent of that decrease).

Judge LJ summarised the position in *Underwood* (at [11]):

> The final matter for guidance is whether the defendant should lose the mitigation available to him for his guilty plea if, having contested facts alleged by the prosecution, the issues are resolved against him. The principles are clear. If the issues at the Newton hearing are wholly resolved in the defendant's favour, the credit due to him should not be reduced. If for example, however, the defendant is disbelieved, or obliges the prosecution to call evidence from the victim, who is then subjected to a cross-examination, which, because it is entirely unfounded, causes unnecessary and inappropriate distress, or if the defendant conveys to the judge that he has no insight into the consequences of his offence and no genuine remorse for it, these are all matters which may lead the judge to reduce the discount which the defendant would otherwise have received for his guilty plea, particularly if that plea is tendered at a very late stage. Accordingly, there may even be exceptional cases in which the normal entitlement to credit for a plea of guilty is wholly dissipated by the Newton hearing.

In R v Caley [2012] EWCA Crim 2821; [2013] 2 Cr App R (S) 47, Hughes LJ said (at [26]–[27]):

> ... If despite a plea to the indictment the defendant insists on a version of events which calls for a trial of the issue before the judge some witnesses may well have to give evidence and even if they do not court time will be taken up and further preparation by the Crown will often be necessary. Of course, if the Crown cannot prove its version, the defendant's reduction for plea of guilty will be unaffected. But if the defendant fails, the converse follows. It is of no little importance to the administration of justice that where bases of plea which will affect sentence are tendered, judges should decide the facts. It is particularly important that unrealistic bases of plea should receive no incentive.
>
> [The extent of the reduction] will depend ... on all the circumstances of the case, including the extent of the issue determined, on whether lay witnesses have to give evidence and on the extra public time and effort that has been involved. Some cases involve little more than an assertion in mitigation which the judge is not minded to accept at face value, so that the defendant is given an opportunity to give evidence about it, often (sensibly) there and then. In that case, the reduction ought normally to be less than it would have been if the (false) assertion had not been made, but significant reduction for plea of guilty will, we anticipate, normally survive. Other cases may be ones where something akin to a full trial has to take place, with full preparation by the Crown, lay witnesses having to be called and considerable court time taken up. In such a case, the reduction for plea of guilty which survives is likely, we suggest, to be very small, and may be none at all. In between there may be a considerable range of situations. These must be left to the informed judgment of the sentencing judge.

13.7.2.4 Exceptional cases where *Newton* does not have to be applied

Paragraph B.10 of Criminal Practice Direction VII says that a judge is not entitled to reject a defendant's basis of plea without a *Newton* hearing 'unless it is determined by the court that the basis is manifestly false and as such does not merit examination by way of the calling of evidence'.

Thus, a *Newton* hearing need not be held where the defendant's story is manifestly false or implausible. See, for example, R v *Hawkins* (1985) 7 Cr App R(S) 351, where the Court of Appeal said that the story told by the defendant was 'so manifestly false that the judge was entitled to reject it' without further ado (per Lord Lane CJ, at p.353).

In such cases, the court can accept the prosecution versions of events without having first heard evidence to support that version. In *Underwood*, Judge LJ said (at [10(f)]) that the judge:

> is entitled to decline to hear evidence about disputed facts if the case advanced on the defendant's behalf is, for good reason, to be regarded as absurd or obviously untenable. If so, however, he should explain why he has reached this conclusion.

The judge is also entitled to reject the defendant's basis of plea 'where the defendant declines the opportunity to engage in the process of the *Newton* hearing whether by giving evidence on his own behalf or otherwise' (Criminal Practice Direction VII, para.B.10).

13.7.2.5 Appeals in *Newton* cases

In R v *Ahmed* (1985) 80 Cr App R 295 (followed in R v *Wood* (1992) 13 Cr App R (S) 207), the Court of Appeal said that it would not interfere with the judge's findings of fact in a *Newton* hearing unless no reasonable jury could have reached the conclusion reached by the judge (per Parker LJ, p.297).

In appropriate cases, the Court of Appeal may conduct a *Newton* hearing itself if one did not take place in the Crown Court (see R v *Guppy* [1995] 16 Cr App R(S) 25). However, if the judge wrongly fails to conduct a *Newton* hearing, the Court of Appeal will usually allow an appeal against sentence and will impose the sentence which would be appropriate on the basis that the defendant's version of events is the correct one (R v *Mohun* (1993) 14 Cr App R(S) 5), effectively giving the benefit of the doubt to the defendant.

13.8 Procedure following conviction after a 'not guilty' plea

Where the defendant was convicted following a plea of not guilty, the facts of the offence will have emerged during the evidence. However, the prosecution may still have to summarise the facts of the case where there has been an adjournment after conviction, as will usually be the case where a pre-sentence report has to be prepared. In the Crown Court, it is usually the judge who presided over the trial who passes sentence and it is likely that he will use his note of the evidence to refresh his memory, and so will not need the prosecution to remind him of the facts in great detail. In magistrates' courts, however, it is very common for a bench other than the bench that convicted the defendant to pass sentence, so the bench that passes sentence will need a complete summary of the facts from the prosecution.

In R v *McGlade* (1990) 12 Cr App R (S) 105, Lord Taylor CJ (at p.109) said:

> There is clear authority that if the verdict of a jury leads inexorably to one version of the facts being found and only one version, the learned judge is bound to sentence upon that basis. But if the verdict of a jury leaves open some important issue which may affect sentence, then

the learned judge, having heard all the evidence himself in the course of the trial, is free and, indeed, it is his duty to come to a conclusion, if he can, upon where the truth lies.

This approach was followed in R v Cairns [2013] EWCA Crim 467; [2013] 2 Cr App R (S) 73, where Leveson LJ (at [8]) said:

After conviction following a trial, the judge is bound to honour the verdicts of the jury but, provided he does so, is entitled to form his own view of the facts in the light of the evidence.

His Lordship added (at [9]) that this was not to say 'that a Newton hearing is never appropriate after a trial. If an issue not relevant to guilt but relevant to sentence has not been canvassed in the trial, a further hearing may be necessary'.

In R v King [2017] EWCA Crim 128 [2017] 4 WLR 95, the Court of Appeal considered the approach to basis for sentence to be adopted in cases where more than one interpretation of the jury's verdict was possible. The court held (at [31]) as follows:

In our view the correct approach by the judge, after a trial, to the determination of the factual basis upon which to pass sentence, is clear. If there is only one possible interpretation of a jury's verdict(s) then the judge must sentence on that basis. When there is more than one possible interpretation, then the judge must make up his own mind, to the criminal standard, as to the factual basis upon which to pass sentence. If there is more than one possible interpretation, and he is not sure of any of them, then (in accordance with basic fairness) he is obliged to pass sentence on the basis of the interpretation (whether in whole or in relevant part) most favourable to the defendant.

13.9 Pre-sentence reports

As well as considering the prosecution summary of the facts (if given) and the defendant's antecedents, the court will often consider a pre-sentence report. In the case of offenders who have attained the age of 18, pre-sentence reports are compiled by probation officers. For offenders who are under 13, reports are prepared by local authority social workers. In the case of young offenders who have attained the age of 13, reports are usually prepared by a social worker, but the report may be prepared by a probation officer if, for example, the probation service was already having dealings with a member of the offender's family.

The court is not bound to accept the conclusions in a pre-sentence report. So, for example, if the report says that the offender is suitable for a community order, the court does not have to accept that view.

13.9.1 Circumstances where a pre-sentence report is required

Section 156(1) of the Criminal Justice Act 2003 provides that, before forming an opinion about the appropriateness of a community sentence or the appropriateness of a custodial sentence, the court 'must take into account all such information as is available to it about the circumstances of the offence ... [and any] offences associated with it, including any aggravating or mitigating factors'; also, in forming an opinion about the suitability of the imposition of specific require-ments as part of a community sentence, the court may take into account any information about the offender which is before it.

By virtue of s.156(3), the court is required to request a pre-sentence report before deciding:

- that the community or custody threshold has been crossed;
- what is the shortest term of a custodial sentence that is commensurate with the seriousness of the offence;
- whether the restrictions on liberty in a community order are commensurate with the seriousness of the offence; and
- whether the requirements of a community order are suitable for the offender.

It follows that a pre-sentence report should not normally be requested where the court considers that it is likely to be appropriate to impose a fine.

Under s.156(4), the court need not obtain and consider a pre-sentence report if, in the circumstances of the case, the court is of the opinion that it is 'unnecessary' to obtain one.

Where, however, the offender is under the age of 18, the court cannot dispense with a pre-sentence report unless (a) there exists a previous pre-sentence report obtained in respect of the offender, and (b) the court has had regard to the information contained in that report or, if there is more than one such report, the most recent report (s.156(5)).

Section 156(6) provides that no custodial sentence or community sentence is invalidated by the failure of a court to obtain and consider a pre-sentence report as required by s.156. However, if the sentencing court did not obtain a pre-sentencing report in a case where one was required under s.156, the court hearing the appeal should obtain a pre-sentence report unless that court is of the opinion (a) that the sentencing court was justified in forming an opinion that it was unnecessary to obtain a pre-sentence report, or (b) that, although the court below was not justified in forming that opinion, in the circumstances of the case at the time it is before the appeal court, it is unnecessary to obtain a pre-sentence report (s.156(7)). If the offender is under 18, the appeal court can only dispense with a pre-sentence report if (a) there exists a previous pre-sentence report obtained in respect of the offender, and (b) the court has had regard to the information contained in that report, or, if there is more than one such report, the most recent report (s.156(8)).

A pre-sentence report should contain:

- basic facts about the offender and the sources used to prepare the report;
- an offence analysis;
- an assessment of the offender;
- an assessment of the risk of harm to the public and the likelihood of reoffending;
- a sentencing proposal.

Under s.158(1A) of the Criminal Justice Act 2003, the court may accept a pre-sentence report given orally in open court. However, a pre-sentence report that relates to an offender aged under 18, and which is required before the court passes a custodial sentence, must be in writing (s.158(1B)).

Under s.157 of the 2003 Act, where the offender is (or appears to be) mentally disordered, the court must obtain and consider a medical report before passing a custodial sentence unless (under subs.(2)) the court is of the opinion that it is unnecessary to do so. The procedure for commissioning a medical report for sentencing purposes is set in r.28.8 of the Criminal Procedure Rules. In particular, the court must identify each issue in respect of which it requires expert medical opinion and specify the nature of the expertise likely to be required for giving such opinion; the court must also set (and enforce) a timetable for the production of the report.

13.9.2 Disclosure of the pre-sentence report

Disclosure of the pre-sentence report is governed by s.159 of the Criminal Justice Act 2003. The defence advocate invariably has sight of a copy of the pre-sentence report if one has been prepared. It is good practice to ask the defendant if he has seen a copy of the report. If he has not, then he should be asked to read through it and check its accuracy (or the advocate should summarise its contents). The report is normally based on a single interview between the defendant and the writer of the report, and there is the potential for errors to creep in. In any event, s.159(2) requires the pre-sentence report to be disclosed to the offender or to his legal representative.

Section 159(2)(c) also requires the report to be disclosed to the prosecutor. Section 159(5) stipulates that the prosecutor can use information gleaned from the report only for the purpose of deciding whether to make representations to the court about the content of the report and for making any such representations. The disclosure of the report to the prosecutor under this provision means that prosecutors have a chance to check that any factual information contained in the report agrees with information contained in the prosecution file. Any representations made by the prosecutor are likely to be confined to drawing the attention of the court to any factual inaccuracies in the report.

Under s.159(2)(b) of the 2003 Act, if the offender is under 18, a copy of the report must also be given to a parent or guardian (if present in court); this is subject to the proviso in s.159 (3) that, if the offender is aged under 18 and it appears to the court that the disclosure to the offender or to his parent or guardian of any information contained in the report would be likely to create a risk of significant harm to the offender, a complete copy of the report need not be given to the offender or to the parent or guardian. Where the offender is under 18 and is in local authority care, a copy of the report goes to the local authority (s.159(6)).

13.9.3 Adjournments prior to sentence

Section 10(3) of the Magistrates' Courts Act 1980 empowers a magistrates' court to adjourn before passing sentence in order to enable inquiries to be made as to the most suitable method of dealing with the offender. Under s.10(3), adjournments between conviction and sentence should be for no more than four weeks at a time if the offender is on bail (note that the presumption in favour of bail created by s.4 of the Bail Act 1976 applies to such an offender) and for no more than three weeks at a time if the offender is in custody. The Crown Court has inherent jurisdiction to adjourn and there is no statutory limit on the length of the adjournment.

13.9.3.1 Keeping sentencing options open

When the court adjourns the case prior to passing sentence, great care must be exercised when the court explains to the defendant what is happening. In R v Gillam (1980) 2 Cr App R(S) 267, the judge adjourned the case so that a report could be prepared to assess whether the defendant was suitable for what was then known as community service (unpaid work under a community order). The circumstances were such that the defendant was led to believe that, if the report was favourable, he would receive community service rather than a custodial sentence. In the event, the report was favourable but a custodial sentence was passed nonetheless. The Court of Appeal said that the judge should have imposed a non-custodial sentence. Watkins LJ (at p.269) said that when a judge in such circumstances purposely postpones sentence so that an alternative to imprisonment can be examined and that alternative is found to be a satisfactory one in all respects, the court ought to adopt the alternative, otherwise a feeling of injustice is aroused. Similarly, in R v Howard (1989) 11 Cr App R(S) 583, the court adjourned for a pre-sentence report and the defendant was told that the court was minded to deal with the case by means of a community order. A custodial sentence was subsequently imposed, and this sentence was quashed by the Court of Appeal.

Lord Bingham CJ in R v Nottingham Magistrates' Court [2000] Cr App R (S) 167 (at p.169) expressed the position thus:

> If a court at a preliminary stage of the sentencing process gives to a defendant any indication as to the sentence which will or will not be thereafter passed upon him, in terms sufficiently unqualified to found a legitimate expectation in the mind of the defendant that any court which later passes sentence upon him will act in accordance with the indication given, and if on a later occasion a court, without reasons which justify departure from the earlier indication, and whether or not it is aware of that indication, passes a sentence inconsistent with, and more severe than, the sentence indicated, the court will ordinarily feel obliged, however reluctantly, to adjust the sentence passed so as to bring it into line with that indicated.

This principle applies only if there was something 'in the nature of a promise, express or implied, that, if a particular proposal is recommended, it will be adopted' (R v Moss (1983) 5 Cr App R(S) 209, per Croom-Johnson LJ, at p.213). Thus, if the court makes it clear that it is not committing itself to a non-custodial sentence even if the pre-sentence report recommends a non-custodial sentence, no legitimate sense of injustice is created if a custodial sentence is passed, even if the court rejects a recommendation for a non-custodial sentence contained in the report (R v Horton (1985) 7 Cr App R(S) 299).

However, the expectation of a non-custodial sentence must be a *legitimate* one. In Nicholas v Chester Magistrates' Court [2009] EWHC 1504 (Admin); (2009) 173 JP 542, Wilkie J (at [10]) made the point that:

> no judicial review would lie on the basis of legitimate expectation if the legitimate expectation was founded on a decision of a bench which was so unreasonable as to be perverse or such that no reasonable bench properly directing itself could have reached.

13.10 Victim Personal Statements

A very important factor when determining sentence is the impact of the offence on the victim. Victims of crime are offered the chance to make a victim personal statement ('VPS'). Paragraph F.1 of Criminal Practice Direction VII says that this statement 'gives victims a formal opportunity to say how a crime has affected them ... The court will take the statement into account when determining sentence'. That paragraph goes on to observe that, in some circumstances, 'it may be appropriate for relatives of a victim to make a VPS, for example where the victim has died as a result of the relevant criminal conduct'.

Paragraph F.3 refers to guidance given by the Court of Appeal in R v Perkins [2013] EWCA Crim 323; [2013] 2 Cr App R (S) 72, where Lord Judge CJ said (at [9]):

> (a) The decision whether to make a statement must be made by the victims personally. They must be provided with information which makes it clear that they are entitled to make a statement, but ... no pressure, either way, should be brought to bear on their decision. They are entitled to make statements, and they are equally entitled not to do so. They should be informed of their right, and allowed to exercise it as they wish: in particular the perception should not be allowed to emerge that if they choose not to do so the court may misunderstand or minimise the harm caused by the crime.

(b)   When the decision whether or not to make a statement is being made, it should be clearly understood that the victim's opinion about the type and level of sentence should not be included ... If necessary, victims must be assisted to appreciate that the court is required to pass the appropriate sentence, in accordance with decisions of this Court, and definitive guidelines issued by the ... Sentencing Council, and make a judgment based on all the facts of the case, including both the aggravating and the mitigating features.

(c)   The statement constitutes evidence. That is the basis on which it is admitted. It must therefore be treated as evidence. It must be in a formal witness statement, served on the defendant's legal advisers in time for the defendant's instructions to be taken, and for any objection to the use of the statement, or part of it, if necessary, to be prepared. ...

(d)   Just because the statement is intended to inform the sentencing court of specific features of the consequences of the offence on the victim, responsibility for presenting admissible evidence remains with the prosecution.

(e)   It follows that the statement may be challenged, in cross-examination, and it may give rise to disclosure obligations, and indeed ... may be used, after conviction, to deploy an argument that the credibility of the victim is open to question.

Paragraph F.3(b) of the Practice Direction emphasises that the VPS must be in 'proper form, that is a witness statement made under s.9 of the Criminal Justice Act 1967'. That paragraph also says:

Except where inferences can properly be drawn from the nature of or circumstances surrounding the offence, a sentencing court must not make assumptions unsupported by evidence about the effects of an offence on the victim. The maker of a VPS may be cross-examined on its content.

Paragraph 3.F(c) goes on to say:

At the discretion of the court, the VPS may also be read aloud or played in open court, in whole or in part, or it may be summarised. If the VPS is to be read aloud, the court should also determine who should do so. In making these decisions, the court should take account of the victim's preferences, and follow them unless there is good reason not to do so; examples of this include the inadmissibility of the content or the potentially harmful consequences for the victim or others. Court hearings should not be adjourned solely to allow the victim to attend court to read the VPS.

It must also be underlined that the court is only concerned with the impact of the offence on the victim, not with the victim's views on how severe, or lenient, the sentence should be. Paragraph 3.F(e) says:

The court must pass what it judges to be the appropriate sentence having regard to the circumstances of the offence and of the offender, taking into account, so far as the court considers it appropriate, the impact on the victim. The opinions of the victim or the victim's close relatives as to what the sentence should be are therefore not relevant, unlike the consequences of the offence on them. Victims should be advised of this. If, despite the advice, opinions as to sentence are included in the statement, the court should pay no attention to them.

13.10.1 Community Impact Statements

Paragraph H.1 of Criminal Practice Direction VII says that a 'community impact statement', the contents of which may be summarised or read out in open court, may be prepared by the police to 'make the court aware of particular crime trends in the local area and the impact of these on the local community'.

13.10.2 Impact Statement for Business

Paragraph I.1 of Criminal Practice Direction VII says that, 'if the victim, or one of the victims, is a business or enterprise (including charities but excluding public sector bodies), of any size, a nominated representative may make an Impact Statement for Business ('ISB')'. This gives a 'formal opportunity for the court to be informed how a crime has affected a business'. The supply of an ISB 'does not prevent individual employees from making a VPS about the impact of the same crime on them as individuals. Indeed, the ISB should be about the impact on the business exclusively, and the impact on any individual included within a VPS'.

13.11 The plea in mitigation

A plea in mitigation usually comprises a speech by the advocate appearing for the defence. If the defendant is unrepresented, he will be asked if there is anything he wishes to say before sentence is passed.

The plea in mitigation by the defence will usually address the seriousness of the offence, and then draw the attention of the court to any mitigating factors relating to the offender.

Occasionally, witnesses will be called to show the previous good character of the offender or to explain why he acted out of character by committing an offence.

The decision on the sentence to be passed will take account of any relevant guidelines issued by the Sentencing Council (or guideline judgments of the Court of Appeal if no guideline has been issued by the Sentencing Council), and so the defence advocate will have to make use of those resources when preparing the plea in mitigation.

In R v Tongue and Doyle [2007] EWCA Crim 561, the Court (at [13]) noted that, once relevant guidelines have been issued by the Sentencing Council, it should be the exception rather than the rule for advocates to cite previous cases (that is, cases which pre-date the guideline in question).

13.11.1 Factors reducing seriousness or reflecting personal mitigation

The Sentencing Council's draft General Guideline identifies a number of factors that may serve to reduce the sentence imposed on the offender.

13.11.1.1 No previous convictions or no relevant/recent convictions

The Guideline states that 'first time offenders generally represent a lower risk of re-offending. Re-offending rates for first offenders are significantly lower than rates for repeat offenders. In addition, first offenders are normally regarded as less blameworthy than offenders who have committed the same crime several times already'. First-time offenders are therefore treated more leniently (unless the crime is a particularly serious one).

The Guideline gives the following additional guidance:

● Where there are previous offences but these are old and/or are for offending of a different nature, the sentence will normally be reduced to reflect that the new offence is not part of a pattern of offending and there is therefore a lower likelihood of reoffending.
● When assessing whether a previous conviction is 'recent' the court should consider the time gap since the previous conviction and the reason for it.
● Previous convictions are likely to be 'relevant' when they share characteristics with the current offence (examples of such characteristics include, but are not limited to: dishonesty, violence, abuse of position or trust, use or possession of weapons, disobedience of court orders). In general, the more serious the previous offending the longer it will retain relevance.

13.11.1.2 Good character and/or exemplary conduct

The phrase 'previous good character' is sometimes used to connote merely the absence of previous convictions. However, to have 'positive' good character, going beyond a mere absence of previous convictions, can be very strong mitigation (and may, as the draft General Guideline points out, even apply where the offender has previous convictions). As the Guideline states, evidence 'that an offender has demonstrated positive good character through, for example, charitable works may reduce the sentence'.

For example, in R v Clark (Joan) (1999) The Times, 27 January, the defendant engaged in benefit fraud to the value of some £18,000 over a period of six years (a very serious offence, almost certain to carry a lengthy prison sentence). However, there was a moving tribute from the nephews and nieces she had brought up following the death of their mother, and her parish priest gave evidence of a number of local community and charitable activities with which she had been involved. The Court of Appeal held (perhaps a little surprisingly) that the judge should have placed greater weight on her positive good character (that is, good character going beyond the legal sense of an absence of convictions); the sentence of six months' imprisonment was reduced to seven days, enabling her immediate release from custody.

It should be noted, however, that this factor is less likely to be relevant if the offence is a very serious one. Moreover, if an offender has used his/her good character or status to facilitate or conceal the offending, this is likely to be treated as an *aggravating* factor.

13.11.1.3 Remorse

For remorse to be accepted as mitigation, the court will need to be satisfied that the offender is genuinely remorseful for the offending behaviour. It follows that, in a plea in mitigation, something has to be said about what the defendant has done to demonstrate remorse. This might be (for example) voluntary payment of compensation, or sending a letter of apology to the victim.

The draft Guideline cautions that lack of remorse should never be treated as an aggravating factor.

13.11.1.4 Self-reporting

Where an offender has self-reported to the authorities, particularly in circumstances where the offence may otherwise have gone undetected, this should serve to reduce the sentence (in addition to the subsequent application of the guilty plea reduction).

13.11.1.5 Cooperation with the investigation/early admissions

The draft General Guideline notes that 'assisting or cooperating with the investigation and/or making pre-court admissions may ease the effect on victims and witnesses and save valuable police time justifying a reduction in sentence' (again this is separate from any guilty plea reduction).

13.11.1.6 Little or no planning

Where an offender has committed the offence with little or no prior thought or planning, this will generally indicate a lower level of culpability and so justify a reduction in sentence. However, the draft Guideline notes that 'impulsive acts of unprovoked violence or other types of offending may indicate a propensity to behave in a manner that would not normally justify a reduction in sentence'.

13.11.1.7 Lesser or subordinate role

Acting as part of a group or gang may make an offence more serious; however, if the offender's role was a minor one, this may indicate lower culpability and so justify a reduction in sentence.

13.11.1.8 Involvement through coercion, intimidation or exploitation

This reduces the culpability of the offender and so justifies a reduction in sentence. The draft General Guideline makes the following additional points:

- This factor may be of particular relevance where the offender has been the victim of domestic abuse, trafficking or modern slavery, but may also apply in other contexts.
- Courts should be alert to factors that suggest that an offender may have been the subject of coercion, intimidation or exploitation which the offender may find difficult to articulate, and where appropriate ask for this to be addressed in a PSR.
- This factor may indicate that the offender is vulnerable and would find it more difficult to cope with custody or to complete a community order.

13.11.1.9 Limited awareness or understanding of the offence

The Guideline notes that the culpability of an offender who was acting alone may be reduced if he did not appreciate the significance of the offence; where an offender is acting with others, his culpability may be reduced if he did not appreciate the extent of the overall offending.

13.11.1.10 Little or no financial gain

The Guideline says that 'where an offence (which is not one which by its nature is an acquisitive offence) is committed in a context where financial gain could arise, the culpability of the offender may be reduced where it can be shown that the offender did not seek to gain financially from the conduct and did not in fact do so'.

13.11.1.11 Activity originally legitimate

Where the offending arose from an activity which was originally legitimate, but became unlawful (for example, because of a change in the offender's circumstances or a change in regulations), this may indicate lower culpability and so justify a reduction in sentence.

13.11.1.12 Age and/or lack of maturity

The draft Guideline notes that age and/or lack of maturity can affect both the offender's responsibility (and therefore culpability) for the offence and also the effect of the sentence on the offender. This is considered in more detail in Chapter 15, in the context of young offenders.

13.11.1.13 Sole or primary carer for dependent relatives

The court will consider the effect of the sentence on people other than the offender. The draft General Guideline notes that this factor is

> particularly relevant where an offender is on the cusp of custody or where the suitability of a community order is being considered. For offenders on the cusp of custody, imprisonment

should not be imposed where there would be an impact on dependants which would make a custodial sentence disproportionate to achieving the aims of sentencing. Where custody is unavoidable consideration of the impact on dependants may be relevant to the length of the sentence imposed. For more serious offences where a substantial period of custody is appropriate, this factor will carry less weight.

In R v Kazeem [2014] EWCA Crim 1107, Hickinbottom J considered the relevance of the effect on others of imposing a custodial sentence on an offender. He said (at [11]):

When an offender commits a crime … it is only too often the case that others suffer more than the perpetrator. Those others frequently include parents and children, for whom the offender has care. It is right that sentencers take such responsibilities into account when fixing the appropriate sentence. But where the offending is serious … the extent to which the court can appropriately mitigate the sentence as a result of such factors may be limited …

13.11.1.14 Physical disability or serious medical condition

Physical disability or serious medical conditions requiring urgent, intensive or long-term treatment may affect the impact of a sentence on the offender (in effect, making the sentence more onerous) and, on that basis, may justify a reduction in sentence.

13.11.1.15 Mental disorder or learning disability

The draft General Guideline makes the important point that mental disorders and learning disabilities 'are different things, although an individual may suffer from both. A learning disability is a permanent condition developing in childhood, whereas mental illness (or a mental health problem) can develop at any time, and is not necessarily permanent; people can get better and resolve mental health problems with help and treatment'.

For the purposes of sentencing, this includes a wide range of offenders, including those with:

- an intellectual impairment (low IQ);
- a cognitive impairment such as (but not limited to) dyslexia, attention deficit hyperactivity disorder (ADHD);
- an autistic spectrum disorder (ASD) including Asperger's syndrome;
- a personality disorder;
- offenders with a mental illness.
- a combination of these conditions.

The Guideline emphasises that courts 'should be alert to the fact that not all mental disorders or learning disabilities are visible or obvious'.

A mental disorder or learning disability can affect both the offender's responsibility for the offence and the impact of the sentence on the offender.

In such cases, the court will be assisted by a pre-sentence report and, where appropriate, medical reports in assessing the degree to which a mental disorder or learning disability has reduced the offender's responsibility for the offence, and also any effect of the mental disorder or learning disability on the impact of the sentence on the offender (for example, making it more difficult for the offender to cope with custody or comply with a community order).

So far as culpability is concerned, the condition may have had an 'impact on the offender's ability to understand the consequences of their actions, to limit impulsivity and/or to exercise self-control'. A relevant factor is 'the degree to which a mental disorder or learning disability has been exacerbated by the actions of the offender (for example by the voluntary abuse of drugs or alcohol or by voluntarily failing to follow medical advice)'. In considering the voluntariness of the offender's actions, the court should consider 'the extent to which a mental disorder or learning disability has an impact on the offender's ability to exercise self-control or to engage with medical services'.

13.11.1.16 Determination to address addiction or offending behaviour

Where offending is driven by (or closely associated with drug or alcohol abuse), for example 'stealing to feed a habit, or committing acts of disorder or violence whilst drunk', a commitment to address the underlying issue may justify a reduction in sentence, particularly where the court is considering whether to impose a sentence that focuses on rehabilitation. A pre-sentence report is like to assist the court in making this assessment.

13.11.2 Assisting the authorities

Where an accomplice pleads guilty and gives evidence for the prosecution against his erstwhile co-defendants, substantial credit should be given, particularly where that person's evidence leads to the conviction of a co-defendant or induces a co-defendant to plead guilty. In R v A (*Informer: Reduction of Sentence*) [1999] 1 Cr App R(S) 52, Lord Bingham CJ (at p.56) said:

> Where defendants co-operate with the prosecuting authorities, not only by pleading guilty but by testifying or expressing willingness to testify, or making a witness statement which incriminates a co-defendant, they will ordinarily earn an enhanced discount of their sentences, particularly where such conduct leads to the conviction of a co-defendant or induces a co-defendant to plead guilty.
>
> It has been the long-standing practice of the courts to recognise by a further discount of sentence the help given, and expected to be given, to the authorities in the investigation, detection, suppression and prosecution of serious crime ... The extent of the discount will ordinarily depend on the value of the help given and expected to be given ... If the information given is accurate, particularised, useful in practice, and hitherto unknown to the authorities, enabling serious criminal activity to be stopped and serious criminals brought to book, the discount may be substantial ... Where, by supplying valuable information to the authorities, a defendant exposes himself or his family to personal jeopardy, it will ordinarily be recognised in the sentence passed.

Section 73 of the Serious Organised Crime and Police Act 2005 ('SOCPA') applies where the defendant pleads guilty and, pursuant to a written agreement made with the prosecution, has 'assisted or offered to assist the investigator or prosecutor in relation to that or any other offence'. Under s.73(2), when determining what sentence to pass on the defendant, the court 'may take into account the extent and nature of the assistance given or offered'. In R v P [2007] EWCA Crim 2290; [2008] 2 Cr App R (S) 5, Sir Igor Judge P noted (at [27]) that the essential feature of this statutory framework is that 'the offender must publicly admit the full extent of his own criminality and agree to participate in a formalised process'. His Lordship added (at [28]) that 'the process is not confined to offenders who provide assistance in relation to crimes in which they were participants, or accessories, or with which they were otherwise linked'. Moreover, the common law principles have not been abolished: 'there will be occasions when a defendant has provided assistance to the police which does not fall within (these) arrangements, and in particular the written agreement. He is not thereby deprived of whatever consequent benefit he should receive' (at [34]). Concerning the sentence to be imposed on an offender who has entered into an agreement under the Act, his Lordship said (at [39] and [40]):

> The first factor in any sentencing decision is the criminality of the defendant, weight being given to such mitigating and aggregating features as there may be. Thereafter, the quality and quantity of the material provided by the defendant in the investigation and subsequent prosecution of crime falls to be considered. Addressing this issue, particular value should be attached to those cases where the defendant provides evidence in the form of a witness statement or is prepared to give evidence at any subsequent trial, and does so, with added force where the information either produces convictions for the most serious offences, including terrorism and murder, or prevents them, or which leads to disruption to or indeed the break-up of major criminal gangs. Considerations like these then have to be put in the context of the nature and extent of the personal risks to and potential consequences faced by the defendant and the members of his family. In most cases the greater the nature of the criminality revealed by the defendant, the greater the consequent risks ... [T]he discount for the assistance provided by the defendant should be assessed first, against all other relevant considerations, and the notional sentence so achieved should be further discounted for the guilty plea ...
>
> The SOCPA procedure requires the defendant to reveal the whole of his previous criminal activities. This will almost inevitably mean that he will admit, and plead guilty to offences which would never otherwise have been attributed to him, and may indeed have been unknown to the police. In order for the process to work as intended, sentencing for offences which fall into this category should usually be approached with these realities in mind and, so far as s.73 agreements are concerned, should normally lead to the imposition of concurrent sentences ...

His Lordship added (at [41]) that it would only be in the 'most exceptional case' that the appropriate level of reduction would exceed three-quarters of the total sentence which would otherwise be passed; the 'normal level' should be a reduction of somewhere between one-half and two-thirds of that sentence.

It should be emphasised that the sentence to be imposed in such a case is a matter for the court, and not something that can be agreed between the prosecution and the defence. In R v Dougall [2010] EWCA Crim 1048; [2011] 1 Cr App R (S) 37, Lord Judge CJ (at [19]) made it clear that, in this jurisdiction, 'a plea agreement or bargain between the prosecution and the defence in which they agree what the sentence should be, or present what is in effect an agreed package for the court's acquiescence is contrary to principle', adding (at [21]) that it is equally clear that no such agreement is in contemplation in the 2005 Act. His Lordship emphasised (at [23]) that 'agreements between the prosecution and the defence about the sentence to be imposed on a defendant are not countenanced'.

13.11.3 Qualities of a good plea in mitigation

In appropriate cases, a plea in mitigation should try to explain why the offender has turned to crime. For example, it may well be that a person with no previous convictions suddenly starts committing offences at a time when suffering stress at work or as a result of a family break-up. A related argument is that, if the source of the stress has been removed, the risk of reoffending is negligible.

Following interviews with the judges, Jacobson and Hough, in *Mitigation: The Role of Personal Factors in Sentencing* (Prison Reform Trust, 2007) were able to produce a checklist setting out the attributes of a good plea in mitigation (p.46):

Realistic and informed

- Realism is about acknowledging and dealing with the bad features of the case straight away, before moving on to the other aspects.
- A good plea should be understated, should acknowledge the downsides of a case, and then 'marshal in a logical and coherent way' the positive issues.
- Realism is also about providing 'the hooks on which to hang a sentence' that is considerably more lenient than one would have thought, by providing a 'realistic, intellectual framework to justify the sentence'.
- The good advocates are those who 'give you pause for thought, lead you by the hand and persuade you that you don't have to send him to prison, and that it would be wrong to do so: not for emotional but for intellectual reasons'.

Creative

- A good plea 'draws your attention to matters you have not previously considered, or lays appropriate emphasis on matters that you have not thought important'.
- Good pleas are those that 'really go for it': there is a 'real art' in persuading someone to do something that is more lenient than he would otherwise do.
- Under the pressure of a long court list, 'skilful mitigation makes the task of identifying those unusual features or novel features [of a case] that much easier'. This is a matter of 'giving some life to the sort of formulaic mitigation that most practitioners can do in their sleep'.
- If mitigation is to have an impact, it needs to contain something 'slightly out of the ordinary [that] sounds genuine', and must engage the interest of the judge.

Structured

- A good advocate will 'enumerate in a logical order' the main points of the case, without adopting a 'hectoring manner'.
- A good plea is 'relevant, concise, well-informed and realistic'.
- A good plea has 'tercity [sic], lack of repetition, clarity and relevance to the nature of the offence'.
- A good plea is organised, succinct, in bullet points.
- Attractive presentation counts, and there is no need for 'hours of oratory'.

13.12 Sentencing only for offences of which defendant stands convicted or has admitted

An offender should be sentenced only for offences to which he has admitted or of which he has been found guilty. For example, if the offender is charged with an indictment containing a count alleging wounding with intent (s.18 of the Offences Against the Person Act 1861) and an alternative count alleging unlawful wounding (s.20), and the jury acquits the offender of the s.18 offence but convicts him of the s.20 offence, the judge must ensure that the sentence reflects the fact that the offender is guilty only of the lesser offence. This is so even if the judge disagrees with the verdict of the jury. The same applies where the prosecution agree to accept a plea of guilty to a lesser offence and the more serious offence is left on the file or the prosecution offer no evidence in respect of it (see R v Stubbs (1988) 10 Cr App R (S) 97).

Moreover, the judge must not sentence the offender on the basis that he has committed similar offences on other occasions, even if the circumstances of the offence of which the defendant has been convicted (or even admissions made by the defendant to the police) suggest that the offence of which the defendant has been convicted is part of a course of criminal conduct (R v *Ayensu* (1982) 4 Cr App R(S) 248; R v *Reeves* (1983) 5 Cr App R (S) 292).

In R v *Perkins* (1994) 15 Cr App R(S) 402, the defendant was accused of breaching a notice under planning legislation preventing him from tipping waste on to certain land. The charge alleged a breach of the notice on one particular day. However, the judge imposed a fine on the basis not of one incident, but on the basis that breaches of the notice had been taking place over an extensive period of several months. The Court of Appeal said that since the basis of the appellant's conviction was a single breach of the notice, that should be the basis of the sentence. The appellant had not admitted other breaches of the notice and so should have been sentenced only for the offence of which he had actually been convicted.

13.12.1 Offences taken into consideration ('TICs')

It is very common for an offender to ask for offences with which he is not charged to be 'taken into consideration' when he is sentenced for the offences with which he is charged and to which he pleads guilty. These other offences are often known as 'TICs'.

Suppose that a person is arrested for an offence and, when interviewed by the police, admits committing a large number of similar offences. In such a case, the defendant is usually charged with a number of the offences that he has admitted committing. The prosecution will also draw up a list containing the other offences which the offender has admitted to the police. Before the sentencing hearing, the offender is asked to sign the list to confirm that he wishes those offences to be taken into consideration. Any offences which he subsequently denies should be deleted from the list. When the prosecution summarise the facts of the case, they will refer to the list of TICs and the court will ask the offender to confirm that he wishes the offences to be taken into consideration.

The offender does not stand convicted of offences that are taken into consideration. This means that the maximum sentence which the court may impose is fixed by the offences to which the offender has pleaded guilty or of which he has been found guilty.

It follows from this that no separate penalty can be imposed in respect of an offence which has been taken into consideration. However, TICs are regarded as 'associated offences' under s.161(1) (b) of the Powers of Criminal Courts (Sentencing) Act 2000 and so the presence of TICs may result in an increase in the sentence imposed for the offences of which the defendant stands convicted.

Because the offender does not stand convicted of offences that have been taken into consideration, the doctrine of *autrefois convict* does not apply to those offences (R v *Nicholson* (1948) 32 Cr App R 98). Thus, in theory, the offender could subsequently be prosecuted for offences that have been taken into consideration. However, such action would be taken only in exceptional circumstances as it would be likely to amount to an abuse of process.

There is no statutory basis for the practice of taking offences into consideration. However, it enables the police to close their files on the offences that have been dealt with in this way (which has a good effect on their 'clear-up rate'). As far as the offender is concerned, although the existence of TICs may result in an increased sentence, the defendant is able to 'wipe the slate clean' (which is a good indicator of remorse), and the increase in sentence will almost certainly be considerably less than the sentence which would have been passed had the offences been prosecuted separately.

In R v Miles [2006] EWCA Crim 256, the Court of Appeal made some observations about TICS. Sir Igor Judge P (at [10]–[11]), said:

[T]he sentence is intended to reflect a defendant's overall criminality. Offences cannot be taken into consideration without the express agreement of the offender. That is an essential prerequisite. ... If they are to be taken into account (and the court is not obliged to take them into account) they have relevance to the overall criminality. When assessing the significance of TICs ... the court is likely to attach weight to the demonstrable fact that the offender has assisted the police, particularly if they are enabled to clear up offences which might not otherwise be brought to justice. It is also true that cooperative behaviour of that kind will often provide its own very early indication of guilt, and usually means that no further proceedings at all need be started. They may also serve to demonstrate a genuine determination by the offender ... to wipe the slate clean, so that when he emerges from whatever sentence is imposed on him, he can put his past completely behind him, without having worry or [be concerned] that offences may be revealed [with the result] that he is then returned to court.

... In some cases the offences taken into consideration will end up by adding nothing or nothing very much to the sentence which the court would otherwise impose. On the other hand, offences taken into consideration may aggravate the sentence and lead to a substantial increase in it. For example, the offences may show a pattern of criminal activity which suggests careful planning or deliberate rather than casual involvement in a crime. They may show an offence or offences committed on bail, after an earlier arrest. They may show a return to crime immediately after the offender has been before the court and given a chance that, by committing the crime, he has immediately rejected. There are many situations where similar issues may arise. One advantage to the defendant, of course, is that if once an offence is taken into consideration, there is no likely risk of any further prosecution for it. If, on the other hand, it is not, that risk remains. In short, offences taken into consideration are indeed taken into consideration. They are not ignored or expunged or disregarded.

The Sentencing Council has issued a definitive Guideline on TICs:

When sentencing an offender who requests offences to be taken into consideration (TICs), courts should pass a total sentence which reflects *all* the offending behaviour. The sentence must be just and proportionate and must not exceed the statutory maximum for the conviction offence.

The court has discretion as to whether or not to take TICs into account. In exercising its discretion the court should take into account that TICs are capable of reflecting the offender's overall criminality. The court is likely to consider that the fact that the offender has assisted the police (particularly if the offences would not otherwise have been detected) and avoided the need for further proceedings demonstrates a genuine determination by the offender to 'wipe the slate clean'.

It is generally undesirable for TICs to be accepted in the following circumstances:

- where the TIC is likely to attract a greater sentence than the conviction offence;
- where it is in the public interest that the TIC should be the subject of a separate charge;
- where the offender would avoid a prohibition, ancillary order or similar consequence which it would have been desirable to impose on conviction. For example:
  - where the TIC attracts mandatory disqualification or endorsement and the offence(s) for which the defendant is to be sentenced do not;

- where the TIC constitutes a breach of an earlier sentence;
- where the TIC is a specified offence for the purposes of s.224 of the Criminal Justice Act 2003 [dangerous offenders], but the conviction offence is non-specified; or
- where the TIC is not founded on the same facts or evidence or part of a series of offences of the same or similar character (unless the court is satisfied that it is in the interests of justice to do so).

The Guideline goes on to make it clear that a magistrates' court 'cannot take into consideration an indictable-only offence'. However, the Crown court 'can take into account summary only offences provided the TICs are founded on the same facts or evidence as the indictable charge, or are part of a series of offences of the same or similar character as the indictable conviction offence'.

The Guideline adds that the sentence imposed on the offender 'should, in most circumstances, be increased to reflect the fact that other offences have been taken into consideration'. The court should:

(1)   Determine the sentencing starting point for the conviction offence, referring to the relevant definitive sentencing guidelines. No regard should be had to the presence of TICs at this stage.

(2)   Consider whether there are any aggravating or mitigating factors that justify an upward or downward adjustment from the starting point. The presence of TICs should generally be treated as an aggravating feature that justifies an upward adjustment from the starting point. Where there is a large number of TICs, it may be appropriate to move outside the category range, although this must be considered in the context of the case and subject to the principle of totality. The court is limited to the statutory maximum for the conviction offence.

(3)   Continue through the sentencing process including:
- consider whether the frank admission of a number of offences is an indication of a defendant's remorse or determination and/or demonstration of steps taken to address addiction or offending behaviour;
- any reduction for a guilty plea should be applied to the overall sentence;
- the principle of totality;
- when considering ancillary orders these can be considered in relation to any or all of the TICs, specifically:
  - compensation orders – in the magistrate's court the total compensation cannot exceed the limit for the conviction offence;
  - restitution orders.

13.12.2 'Specimen' or 'sample' counts

A 'specimen' (or 'sample') count is where the defendant is charged with one or more offences occurring on specific occasions, but the prosecution allege that such conduct was representative of other criminal conduct of the same kind on other occasions which are not the subject of specific charges. Take, for example, the case of a defendant who uses a stolen credit card on 20 occasions: if the indictment contains three counts relating to the use of the card, those three counts would be sample counts.

In a number of cases, such as R v Huchison [1972] 1 WLR 398, R v McKenzie (1984) 6 Cr App R(S) 99 and R v Burfoot (1990–91) 12 Cr App R(S) 252, the Court of Appeal has made it clear that the offender should only be sentenced on the basis that the counts of which he stands convicted are sample counts, illustrative of an overall course of conduct (rather than being sentenced on the basis that he had only committed the offences of which he stands convicted), if he *accepts* that the convictions represent an overall course of conduct. For example, in R v *Clark* [1996] 2 Cr App R(S) 351, the appellant was convicted of a single count of indecent assault. This single count was said by the prosecution to reflect a series of offences committed over a two-year period. However, the appellant did not admit committing any offence. The judge passed sentence on the basis that the defendant had committed a series of offences. The Court of Appeal said that, having been convicted on a single count particularising a single act and not having admitted any offence beyond that, the appellant could only be sentenced on the basis of that single act.

In R v *Kidd*; R v *Canavan* [1998] 1 WLR 604, Lord Bingham CJ (at p.607) reiterated that a defendant is not to be convicted of any offence with which he is charged unless and until his guilt is proved. Such guilt may be proved by his own admission or (on indictment) by the verdict of a jury. He may be sentenced only for an offence proved against him (by admission or verdict) or which he has admitted and asked the court to take into consideration when passing sentence.

His Lordship therefore thought it 'inconsistent with principle that a defendant should be sentenced for offences neither admitted nor proved by verdict' (p.608). If the prosecution wish other incidents to be taken account of, those other incidents must be the subject of individual charges (or TICs). In R v T [1999] 1 Cr App R(S) 419, Alliott J said (at p.422) that, 'if the prosecution want to rely on a continuous course of conduct, they have to give more instances of that course of conduct in distinct counts in the indictment..

In R v *Smith*; R v *Tovey* [2005] EWCA Crim 530; [2005] 2 Cr App R (S) 100, Lord Woolf CJ (at [21]–[22]) said that, where an offender pleads guilty and admits that his plea embraces a wider course of conduct than that specifically charged, that is the equivalent of an informal invitation to the court to take into consideration the other offences, and a sentencing judge can properly proceed to pass sentence on the wider basis admitted. The court added (at [30]) that, where the evidence of the prosecution and defence does not raise different issues in respect of all the acts said to be part of the same activity, it is perfectly acceptable to charge the defendant with the single activity representing more than one act, provided that there is no unfairness caused to the defendant. The court approved *Barton* v DPP [2001] EWHC Admin 223; (2001) 165 JP 779, where there were 94 takings from a cash register over a period of a year; the Divisional Court concluded that it was permissible to charge the whole course of conduct as a continuous offence because the defendant had no specific explanation for the individual takings and put forward the same defence for all the takings (and so there was no discernible prejudice or unfairness to the defendant). The court in *Smith* added that, in preparing the indictment, the prosecution should always have in mind, in a situation of multiple offending, the need to provide the sentencing judge with sufficient examples (and no more) of the offending to enable the judge to impose a sentence which properly reflects the offender's criminal behaviour (at [33]). It is also important to draft the counts that are included in the indictment so as to establish the period during which the offending occurred ([34]).

In R v *Hartley* [2011] EWCA Crim 1299; [2012] 1 Cr App R (S) 28, the defendant was charged with two counts of sexual abuse. The prosecution had alleged that the offending took place over two years and in two distinct phases, and clearly intended the two counts to be specimen charges, but there was no evidence that the defendant had ever assented to them being treated as such. Hughes LJ at [22], said:

[T]he problem of which this case is an example can normally be dealt with by the framing of an indictment which does not contain an enormous number of counts but does contain sufficient to enable the judge to pass sentence on a basis which sufficiently represents what really happened ... Ordinarily we would suggest where there is simply a complaint of a course of conduct over a period of months, often years, more than a single count for each period is usually appropriate, although one per year may well suffice if the alleged period is extended.

In R v A [2015] EWCA Crim 177; [2015] 2 Cr App R (S) 12, the Court of Appeal gave guidance on how to approach drafting the indictment where multiple offending is alleged (for example, in a case involving sexual offences). Fulford LJ (at [45]) noted that there are three possibilities open to the prosecution:

- To include a count or counts in the indictment alleging a course of conduct (r.10.2(2) of the Criminal Procedure Rules provides that: 'More than one incident of the commission of the offence may be included in a count if those incidents taken together amount to a course of conduct having regard to the time, place or purpose of commission').
- To request that the judge resorts to ss.17–19 of the Domestic Violence (Crime and Victims) Act 2004, which enables the judge in particular circumstances to try the outstanding allegations following conviction (after trial by jury) on sample counts; or
- to include sufficient counts to enable the judge to impose a sentence which sufficiently represents what happened, although care is needed not to overload the indictment.

Fulford LJ went on (at [46]) to note that alleging a course of conduct, under r.10.2(2), may mean that 'the extent, seriousness and timespan of the defendant's offending is unclear from the jury's verdict'. His Lordship went on to say (at [47]):

> In our judgment, the central answer to this problem is to be identified in the purpose underpinning multiple counts: it is to enable the prosecution to reflect the defendant's alleged criminality when the offences are so similar and numerous that it is inappropriate to indict each occasion, or a large number of different occasions, in separate charges. This provision allows the prosecution to reflect the offending in these circumstances in a single count rather than a number of specimen counts. However, when the prosecution fails to specify a sufficient minimum number of occasions within the multiple incident count or counts, they are not making proper use of this procedure. In cases of sustained abuse, it will often be unhelpful to draft the count as representing, potentially, no more than two incidents. Indeed, in this case, if there had been a multiple incident count alleging, for example, 'on not less than five occasions' with an alternative of one or more specimen counts relating to single incidents for the jury to consider if they were unsure the offending had occurred on multiple occasions, the judge would have had a solid basis for under-standing the ambit of the jury's verdict and he would been able to pass an appropriate sentence. Therefore, the prosecution needs to ensure that there are one or more sufficiently broad course of conduct counts, or a mix of individual counts and course of conduct counts, such that the judge will be able to sentence the defendant appropriately on the basis of his criminality as revealed by the counts on which he is convicted. In most cases it will be unnecessary for the counts to be numerous, but they should be sufficient in number to enable the judge to reflect the seriousness of the offending by reference to the central factors in the case: e.g. the number of victims, the nature of the offending and the length of time over which it extended. Therefore, in drafting the indictment, a balance needs to be struck between including sufficient counts to give the court adequate sentencing powers and unduly burdening the indictment ... [T]he indictment must be drafted in such a way as to leave no room for misinterpretation of a guilty verdict and regard must be had to the possible views reached by the jury and to the position of the judge, so as to enable realistic sentencing.

13.13 Reasons for sentencing decisions

Section 174 of the Criminal Justice Act 2003 requires the court to give reasons for, and to explain the effect of, the sentence being passed. Under s.174(2), the court must state 'in open court, in ordinary language and in general terms, the court's reasons for deciding on the sentence'. Under subs.(3), the court must explain to the offender in ordinary language:

(a) the effect of the sentence;

(b) the effects of non-compliance with any order that the offender is required to comply with and that forms part of the sentence,

(c) any power of the court to vary or review any order that forms part of the sentence; and

(d) the effects of failure to pay a fine, if the sentence consists of or includes a fine.

In particular, under subs.(6), the court must identify any Sentencing Council guidelines that are relevant to the offender's case and explain how the court discharged its duty to follow those guidelines. Where the court was satisfied that it would be contrary to the interests of justice to follow the guidelines, it must state why.

Where, as a result of taking account of the fact that the offender pleaded guilty, the court imposes a punishment which is less severe than the punishment it would otherwise have imposed, the court must state that fact (subs.(7)).

In *Attorney-General's References (Nos 115 and 116 of 2007)* [2008] EWCA Crim 795, the Court of Appeal emphasised the importance of explaining any departure from the sentencing guidelines.

13.14 Sentencing in the absence of the defendant

Section 11 of the Magistrates' Courts Act 1980 empowers a magistrates' court to try a defendant in his absence in certain circumstances. This power extends to sentencing a defendant who has been convicted in his absence. However, the power to sentence a defendant in his absence is subject to two restrictions:

- a person may not be sentenced to a custodial sentence in his absence (s.11(3)), subject to the rider that if a custodial sentence is imposed is imposed in the absence of the offender, he must be brought before the court before being taken to begin serving his sentence, and the sentence is not to be regarded as taking effect until he is brought before the court (s.11 (3A)); and
- a person may not have any disqualification imposed on him in his absence (s.11(4)). This applies to any disqualification and so would include, for example, the most common disqualification, namely, disqualification from driving but would also include, for example, disqualification from keeping an animal.

However, by virtue of s.11(5), these restrictions apply only where the proceedings were commenced by the laying of an information or by the issue of a written charge and requisition (and so do not apply to cases where the accused was arrested and charged).

Where the defendant was tried in his absence under s.11, the court has the power to issue a warrant for the defendant's arrest under s.13(1) if the offence is an imprisonable one (s.13(3)(a)) or if the court is minded to impose a disqualification on him (s.13(3)(b)).

Where the defendant has pleaded guilty by post under s.12 of the Magistrates' Courts Act 1980, the court will have to adjourn the case if it is minded to impose a custodial sentence or to make an order involving disqualification. There is no power to issue an arrest warrant against the defendant unless the court has adjourned once and the defendant fails to appear on the occasion of the adjourned hearing.

13.15 Deferring sentence

Section 1 of the Powers of Criminal Courts (Sentencing) Act 2000 empowers the Crown Court and magistrates' courts to defer passing sentence on an offender. Under s.1(4), the maximum period of deferment is six months. The purpose of the deferment (under s.1(1)) is to enable the court, when passing sentence, to have regard to the defendant's 'conduct after conviction (including, where appropriate, the making by him of reparation for his offence)' or 'any change in his circumstances'.

Under s.1(3), sentence may be deferred only if:

(a) the offender consents;

(b) the offender undertakes to comply with any requirements as to his conduct during the period of the deferment that the court considers it appropriate to impose; and

(c) the court is satisfied, having regard to the nature of the offence and the character and circumstances of the offender, that it would be in the interests of justice to exercise the power.

Section 1ZA of the 2000 Act enables the court to include restorative justice requirements when deferring sentence. A restorative justice requirement is defined by subs.(2) as an activity:

(a) where the participants consist of, or include, the offender and one or more of the victims;

(b) which aims to maximise the offender's awareness of the impact of the offending concerned on the victims; and

(c) which gives an opportunity to a victim or victims to talk about, or by other means express experience of, the offending and its impact.

For these purposes, 'victim' means 'a victim of, or other person affected by, the offending concerned'.

The court may deal with the offender before the end of the period of deferment if satisfied that he has failed to comply with one or more requirements imposed under s.1(3)(b) (s.1B(1)(b)), or if, during that period, he is convicted of any offence (s.1C(1)). Where the offender has reoffended during the period of deferment, the court which sentences him for the later offence may also deal with him for the offence(s) for which sentence has been deferred (s.1C(3)); however, this power cannot be exercised by a magistrates' court if the court which deferred sentence was the Crown Court (s.1C(3)(a)), and if the Crown Court passes sentence in respect of an offence where sentence was deferred by a magistrates' court, it cannot pass a sentence which could not have been passed by the magistrates' court had they not deferred sentence (s.1C(3)(b)).

Under s.1D(2), when the court deals with the offender at the end of the period of deferment (or earlier if he does not comply with the requirements or commits another offence), it can deal with him in any way in which it could have done had sentence not been deferred (including, where the offence is triable either way and the court which deferred sentence was a magistrates' court, committing him to the Crown Court for sentence).

Given the comparatively short period of deferment, it may well be that the offender is charged with a further offence allegedly committed during the period of the deferment but the offender has not been convicted of that offence before the date when the court passes sentence in respect of the original offence. In such a case, the allegation of a later offence should be ignored by the court dealing with the offence for which sentence was deferred. It is only where the offender has been convicted of an offence committed during the period of deferment that account can be taken of the later offence when sentence is passed for the offence in respect for which sentence was deferred. An unproved allegation of a further offence should be disregarded (R v *Aquilina* (1989) 11 Cr App R(S) 431).

R v *George* [1984] 1 WLR 1082 was decided at a time when the statutory provisions relating to deferral of sentence were slightly different, but most of the comments made by Lord Lane CJ (at pp.1084–5) about deferring sentence remain valid:

> The power is not to be used as an easy way out for a court which is unable to make up its mind about the correct sentence … Experience has shown that great care should be exercised by the court when using this power …
>
> The consent of the defendant must of course be obtained to the making of the order. The court should make it clear to the defendant what the particular purposes are which the court has in mind under s.1(1) of the Act of 1973 and what conduct is expected of him during deferment … It is essential that the deferring court should make a careful note of the purposes for which the sentence is being deferred and what steps, if any, it expects the defendant to take during the period of deferment. Ideally the defendant himself should be given notice in writing of what he is expected to do or refrain from doing, so that there can be no doubt in his mind what is expected of him.
>
> Thus the task of the court which comes to deal with the offender at the expiration of the period of deferment is as follows. First the purpose of the deferment and any requirement imposed by the deferring court must be ascertained. Secondly the court must determine if the defendant has substantially conformed or attempted to conform with the proper expectations of the deferring court, whether with regard to finding a job or as the case may be. If he has, then the defendant may legitimately expect that an immediate custodial sentence will not be imposed. If he has not, then the court should be careful to state with precision in what respects he has failed.

It will always be a requirement that the offender does not commit any further offences, but merely refraining from committing further offences will not be enough. Requirements that may be imposed when sentence is deferred are at the discretion of the court, but may include (for example) making a real effort to find work (R v *George*).

In R v *Hazard* [2014] EWCA Crim 1124, the Court of Appeal highlighted the need to take care when setting out the court's expectations of the offender when sentence is deferred. The Court quashed an immediate custodial sentence imposed after a period of deferment, saying that the defendant was entitled to conclude from the fact of deferment there was a legitimate expectation that an immediate custodial sentence would not be imposed if he responded well during the period of deferment. Moreover, the judge when imposing the custodial sentence had failed to explain in what way the defendant had failed to meet the court's expectations.

13.16 The responsibility of the advocates

Sentencing law has grown increasingly complex over the years. The relevant provisions are contained in a number of different statutes, and many of the provisions are far from straightforward. Moreover, there are many provisions that are on the statute book but not yet in force. Furthermore, when provisions are amended by subsequent legislation, the amendments are often piecemeal. It is unsurprising that a number of sentences are vitiated by legal errors. The ever-increasing complexity of sentencing legislation underlines the importance of the work being done by the Law Commission to codify sentencing legislation.

The Court of Appeal has, on several occasions, emphasised the importance of vigilance on the part of the advocates to ensure that the court passes a lawful sentence. For example, in R v Cain [2006] EWCA Crim 3233; [2007] 2 Cr App Rep (S) 135, Lord Phillips CJ (at [1]) said:

> It is of course the duty of a judge to impose a lawful sentence, but sentencing has become a complex matter and a judge will often not see the papers very long before the hearing ... In these circumstances a judge relies on the advocates to assist him with sentencing ...

His Lordship went on (at [2]) to emphasise that this duty is owed by both defence and prosecution advocates.

In R v Maxwell [2017] EWCA Crim 1233; [2018] 1 Cr App R 5, where a number of sentencing errors had been made, Treacy LJ (at [46]) observed:

> The problems arise from the complexity of modern sentencing legislation, but that phenomenon is well known and all involved in the Crown Court should therefore be alert to the need for care in technical matters. Sentencing judges who have the primary responsibility for getting things right are often burdened with long sentencing lists. They have a right to expect appropriate assistance from the advocates before them.

13.17 Restorative Justice

We have seen that 'Restorative Justice' can be a feature of community sentencing and may also take place when sentence is deferred. However, Restorative Justice can also be used as an alternative to criminal proceedings, or alongside a more traditional sentence (for example, while the offender is serving a custodial sentence).

The website of the Restorative Justice Council says this about Restorative Justice in the context of criminal justice:

> In criminal justice, restorative practice is widely known as restorative justice. Restorative justice gives victims the chance to meet or communicate with their offenders to explain the real impact of the crime – it empowers victims by giving them a voice.
>
> It also holds offenders to account for what they have done and helps them to take responsibility and make amends. Government research demonstrates that restorative justice provides an 85% victim satisfaction rate, and a 14% reduction in the frequency of reoffending.
>
> Restorative justice is about victims and offenders communicating within a controlled environment to talk about the harm that has been caused and finding a way to repair that harm.
>
> For offenders, the experience can be incredibly challenging as it confronts them with the personal impact of their crime. For victims, meeting the person who has harmed them can be a huge step in moving forward and recovering from the crime.
>
> Restorative justice conferences, where a victim meets their offender, are led by a facilitator who supports and prepares the people taking part and makes sure that the process is safe. Sometimes, when a face to face meeting is not the best way forward, the facilitator will arrange for the victim and offender to communicate via letters, recorded interviews or video.
>
> For any kind of communication to take place, the offender must have admitted to the crime, and both victim and offender must be willing to participate.
>
> Restorative justice can be used for any type of crime and at any stage of the criminal justice system, including alongside a prison sentence.

The Ministry of Justice has produced a series of action plans to encourage the use of Restorative Justice. These action plans define Restorative Justice as:

> the process that brings those harmed by crime, and those responsible for the harm, into communication, enabling everyone affected by a particular incident to play a part in repairing the harm and finding a positive way forward.

This definition emphasises that the 'fundamental element is the dialogue between the victim and the offender'. Reference is also made to John Braithwaite's definition of *Restorative Justice in Restorative Justice and De-Professionalization*, The Good Society (2004) vol. 13, No.1, p.28:

> Restorative justice is a process where all the stakeholders affected by an injustice have an opportunity to discuss how they have been affected by the injustice and to decide what should be done to repair the harm. With crime, restorative justice is about the idea that because crime hurts, justice should heal. It follows that conversations with those who have been hurt and with those who have afflicted the harm must be central to the process.

The Ministry of Justice action plans go on to describe the benefits of Restorative Justice ('RJ'), saying that it:

> offers victims an opportunity to be heard and to have a say in the resolution of offences, including agreeing rehabilitative or reparative activity for the offender. It can provide a means of closure and enable the victim to move on. RJ also provides an opportunity for offenders to face the consequences of their actions, recognise the impact that it has had upon others and where possible make amends. In this way, RJ has the potential to help rehabilitate offenders and enable them to stop offending. It has the potential to motivate them to change and become responsible, law-abiding and productive members of society.

The guidance issued by the Ministry of Justice in 2014 (para.1.21) in respect of the power to defer sentence in order to allow a Restorative Justice intervention to take place, say that a Restorative Justice can include:

- '*A victim-offender conference* (sometimes called a face-to-face meeting or RJ conference): Involves a trained facilitator, the victim(s), the offender(s) and supporters, usually family members. Professionals, such as social workers may also be involved. Such meetings might well conclude with an agreement for further steps to be taken, such as some sort of reparation but this is not mandatory. On some occasions it may be necessary and appropriate to consider live video or audio/telephone as a means of bringing parties together;
- *A community conference*: Involves members of the community which has been affected by a particular crime and all or some of the offenders. This is facilitated in the same way as a RJ conference but it differs in that it can involve more people.
- *Indirect communication* (sometimes called 'shuttle RJ'): Involves a trained facilitator carefully passing messages back and forth between the victim, offender and supporters, who do not meet. This can also be by recorded video, audio/telephone or written correspondence. This approach can lead to a face-to-face meeting at a later stage.

Paragraph 2.1 of the guidance says that a Restorative Justice activity is only suitable (in the context of deferring sentence) where:

- there is an identifiable victim or victims. In relation to cases with a corporate victim there must be someone who has been personally harmed or affected;
- the offender accepts responsibility and has made a guilty plea at any point in proceedings; and
- the victim, offender and any other participants all consent to take part in a RJ activity.

If Restorative Justice is taking place instead of criminal proceedings, an admission of guilt by the perpetrator would be needed in order for a Restorative Justice intervention to take place.

The Ministry of Justice guidance adds (at para.2.2) that a Restorative Justice activity may be suitable for any offence, adding that current evidence 'suggests that the greater the harm experienced the more effective Restorative Justice can be. Restorative Justice is most effective with more serious offences, particularly violent and acquisitive crime'. However, the guidance cautions that it should not normally be used in cases of domestic violence (due to the risk of ongoing harm to the victim) and for hate crime and sexual offences, unless a victim of such offence requests a Restorative Justice activity and suitably experienced and skilled facilitators are available.

A pre-sentence Restorative Justice activity 'may be suitable irrespective of the type of sentence which may be under consideration, and is not limited to cases close to the community sentence or custodial threshold' (para.2.3).

For a detailed discussion of the definition of Restorative Justice, and its key elements, see Katherine Doolin, *But What Does It Mean? Seeking Definitional Clarity in Restorative Justice* (2007) Journal of Criminal Law vol.71, 427–40.

For an analysis of the role of Restorative Justice within the Criminal Justice System, see Joanna Shapland et al, *Situating restorative justice within criminal justice* (2006) Theoretical Criminology 505–32, and Gwen Robinson & Joanna Shapland, *Reducing recidivism: a task for restorative justice?* (2008) British Journal of Criminology vol. 48(3), 337–58.

For a discussion of some of the potential limitations of Restorative Justice, see Gerry Johnstone, *Restorative justice for victims: inherent limits?* (2017) Restorative Justice 382–95.

Chapter 14

Sentencing Adult Offenders

Chapter Contents

In this chapter we examine the sentences that may be imposed on offenders who have attained the age of 18.

14.1 Custodial sentences

Where, at the date of conviction, the offender is aged 18–20 inclusive, the custodial sentence that is available is 'detention in a young offender institution'; where the offender has attained the age of 21, the custodial sentence that is available is imprisonment. Detention in a young offender institution is dealt with in Chapter 15.

14.2 Imprisonment

As we saw in the previous chapter, a custodial sentence can be passed only if the seriousness of the offence merits it (s.152 of the Criminal Justice Act 2003).

Prison overcrowding has led the courts to emphasise the importance of alternatives to custody in appropriate cases. In *Attorney-General's Reference* (No 11 of 2006) [2006] EWCA Crim 856; [2006] 2 Cr App R (S) 108, for example, Lord Phillips CJ (at [20]) observed that, when prisons are overcrowded, 'the result is to hinder or prevent the valuable work of rehabilitation that a prison should normally provide' and so, where the sentencer's decision is 'on the cusp . . . there is a real issue as to whether a community sentence can be justified rather than a custodial sentence'. Similarly, in R v Seed [2007] EWCA Crim 254; [2007] 2 Cr App R (S) 69, Lord Phillips CJ (at [5]) said that, when considering the length of a custodial sentence, 'the court should properly bear in mind that the prison regime is likely to be more punitive as a result of prison overcrowding'. His Lordship added (at [6]–[7]):

> Unless imprisonment is necessary for the protection of the public, the court should always give consideration to the question of whether the aims of rehabilitation and thus the reduction of crime cannot better be achieved by a fine or community sentence rather than by imprisonment and whether punishment cannot adequately be achieved by such a sentence . . . [W]here the offender has the means, a heavy fine can often be an adequate and appropriate punishment. If so, the 2003 Act requires a fine to be imposed rather than a community sentence.
>
> Particular care should be exercised before imposing a custodial sentence on a first offender. Association with seasoned criminals may make re-offending more likely rather than deter it, particularly where the offender is young. A clean record can be important personal mitigation and may make a custodial sentence inappropriate, notwithstanding that the custodial threshold is crossed.

14.2.1 Length of sentence

If the case is sufficiently serious to justify the imposition of a custodial sentence, the next question is how long that sentence should be. Section 153 of the Criminal Justice Act 2003 provides that, except in cases where there are mandatory minimum sentences, 'the custodial sentence must be for the shortest term (not exceeding the permitted maximum) that in the opinion of the court is commensurate with the seriousness of the offence, or the combination of the offence and one or more offences associated with it'.

In R v Bibi [1980] 1 WLR 1193, Lord Lane CJ (p.1195) said that a custodial sentence should be 'as short as possible, consistent only with the duty to protect the interests of the public and to punish and deter the criminal'. A similar point was made by Rose LJ in R v *Ollerenshaw* [1999] 1 Cr App R(S) 65 (at p.67):

> When a court is considering imposing a comparatively short period of custody, that is of about 12 months or less, it should generally ask itself, particularly where the defendant has not previously been sentenced to custody, whether an even shorter period might be equally effective in protecting the interests of the public, and punishing and deterring the criminal. For example, there will be cases where, for these purposes, six months may be just as effective as nine, or two months may be just as effective as four.

This point may be of particular relevance where the offender has been remanded in custody prior to conviction and/or sentence; it may well be possible to mitigate on the basis that the period already spent behind bars on remand is sufficient punishment.

Guidance on length of sentence for specific offences can be found in definitive guidelines issued by the Sentencing Council and (for offences in respect of which such guidelines have not yet been issued) in guideline judgments of the Court of Appeal.

14.2.2 Concurrent and consecutive sentences

Where an offender is convicted of more than one offence, a separate sentence will usually be imposed for each offence. In the case of custodial sentences, the terms may be concurrent or consecutive. Sentences are concurrent if they are to be served simultaneously (for example, a sentence of nine months on count 1 and three months concurrent on count 2 means that the offender receives a total sentence of nine months); sentences are consecutive if they have to be served one after the other (for example a sentence of nine months on count 1 and three months consecutive on count 2 means that the offender receives a total sentence of 12 months). If the court fails to specify whether sentences are concurrent or consecutive, they are deemed to be concurrent.

It is possible to have a mixture of consecutive and concurrent sentences. For example, an offender could be sentenced to six months on count 1, nine months consecutive on count 2 and three months concurrent on count 3. The total sentence would be 15 months.

Courts must have regard to the total length of sentence passed, particularly where consecutive sentences have been imposed, to ensure that the sentence properly reflects the overall seriousness of the behaviour. Thus, where an offender is being sentenced to imprisonment for a number of offences, the court should ensure that the total sentence is commensurate with the overall seriousness of the offender's crimes. This is known as the principle of 'totality', a principle expressly preserved by s.166(3)(b) of the Criminal Justice Act 2003.

The Sentencing Council has issued a Definitive Guideline on Totality. The guideline states that the total sentence must reflect 'all the offending behaviour' the court is dealing with and must also be 'just and proportionate'. This is so 'whether the sentences are structured as concurrent or consecutive'.

The Guideline says that concurrent sentences will ordinarily be appropriate where:

- *offences arise out of the same incident or facts* (for example, a single incident of dangerous driving resulting in injuries to multiple victims; robbery with a weapon where the weapon offence is ancillary to the robbery and is not distinct and independent of it; fraud and associated forgery; separate counts of supplying different types of drugs of the same class as part of the same transaction); or
- *there is a series of offences of the same or similar kind, especially when committed against the same person* (for example, repetitive small thefts from the same person, such as by an employee; repetitive benefit frauds of the same kind, committed in each payment period).

The Guideline goes on to say that, where concurrent sentences are to be passed, 'the sentence should reflect the overall criminality involved. The sentence should be appropriately aggravated by the presence of the associated offences'. This means that 'concurrent sentences will ordinarily be longer than a single sentence for a single offence'. This is because the seriousness of an offence is increased if there are associated offences.

To give an example, it may be that the appropriate sentence for an offence committed in isolation would be six months. However, there are associated offences which make the 'main' offence more serious, and justify an increase to (say) nine months. The sentences for the associated offences run concurrently, but the existence of those associated offences is reflected in a higher sentence for the main offence.

Next, the guideline states that *consecutive* sentences will ordinarily be appropriate where:

- *offences arise out of unrelated facts or incidents* (for example, where the offender commits a theft on one occasion and a common assault against a different victim on a separate occasion; an attempt to pervert the course of justice in respect of another offence also charged; a Bail Act offence; offences that are unrelated because, while they were committed simultaneously, they are distinct and there is an aggravating element that requires separate recognition (such as an assault on a constable committed to try to evade arrest for another offence also charged, or threats to kill in the course of a sexual assault)); or
- *offences that are of the same or similar kind but where the overall criminality will not sufficiently be reflected by concurrent sentences* (for example, where offences committed against different people, such as repeated thefts involving several different shops; where offences of domestic violence or sexual offences are committed against the same individual).

The Guideline adds that, where consecutive sentences are to be passed, the court should 'add up the sentences for each offence and consider if the aggregate length is just and proportionate. If the aggregate length is not just and proportionate the court should consider how to reach a just and proportionate sentence'. That might be achieved (for example) by reducing all the sentences proportionately; identifying a main offence and reducing the sentence for the other offences proportionately; making the sentences for some of the offences run concurrently rather than consecutively; imposing no separate penalty for some offences.

Terms of imprisonment may be ordered to run consecutively even if the total sentence is greater than the maximum which could have been imposed for one of the offences. For example, in R v *Backwell* [2003] EWCA Crim 3213, the defendant pleaded guilty to seven offences of sexual assault, for which the statutory maximum (for a single offence) was 10 years' imprisonment. The judge passed six sentences of six years to run concurrently for six of the offences, and a further six years to run consecutively for the seventh offence (making a total of 12 years). The Court of Appeal upheld this sentence, holding that it was not wrong in principle even though it exceeded the statutory maximum for a single offence.

14.2.3 Effect of time spent on remand

Under s.240ZA(3) of the 2003 Act, time spent remanded in custody counts as time served as part of the sentence:

> The number of days for which the offender was remanded in custody in connection with the offence or a related offence is to count as time served by the offender as part of the sentence.

Under s.240A, where the offender was on bail subject to a curfew condition (requiring him to remain at one or more specified places for a total of not less than nine hours in any given day) and an electronic monitoring condition, then the court must direct that the 'credit period' (that is, half of the number of days on which the offender was subject to those bail conditions) is to count as time served by the offender as part of the sentence.

14.2.4 Release from custody

Under s.244 of the CJA 2003, a fixed-term prisoner (i.e., one serving a determinate sentence) must be released on licence after serving half of his sentence. This release is subject to 'standard' and 'prescribed' conditions (and so, in effect, the second half of the sentence is 'served in the community'). Under s.249, the licence remains in force for the remainder of the sentence (i.e., the second half). Section 250 provides for conditions to be prescribed. The Criminal Justice (Sentencing) (Licence Conditions) Order 2015 (SI 2015/337) sets out conditions which may be set as part of licences upon release from prison. The standard conditions (in para.3) are to:

- be of good behaviour and not behave in a way which undermines the purpose of the licence period;
- not commit any offence;
- keep in touch with the supervising officer in accordance with instructions given by the supervising officer;
- receive visits from the supervising officer in accordance with instructions given by the supervising officer;
- reside permanently at an address approved by the supervising officer and obtain the prior permission of the supervising officer for any stay of one or more nights at a different address;
- not undertake work, or a particular type of work, unless it is approved by the supervising officer and notify the supervising officer in advance of any proposal to undertake work or a particular type of work;
- not travel outside the United Kingdom except with the prior permission of the supervising officer.

Paragraph 7 makes provision for additional conditions, including:

- residence at a specified place;
- restriction of residency;
- making or maintaining contact with a person;
- participation in, or co-operation with, a programme or set of activities;
- possession, ownership, control or inspection of specified items or documents;
- disclosure of information;
- a curfew arrangement;
- freedom of movement;
- supervision in the community by the supervising officer, or other responsible officer, or organisation;
- restriction of specified conduct or specified acts.

Section 254(1) of the Criminal Justice Act 2003 empowers the Secretary of State to revoke a prisoner's licence and thereby to recall the prisoner to prison.

By virtue of s.256AA of the CJA 2003, where a sentence of less than two years is imposed, the offender must comply with 'supervision requirements' during the 'supervision period', which begins with the expiry of the sentence, and ends 12 months after the offender has served the requisite custodial period (i.e., 12 months after the half-way point of the sentence). Section 256AA(2) requires offenders to comply with requirements during this supervision period. The purpose of such supervision is the rehabilitation of the offender (subs.(5)). Section 256AB sets out requirements that may be specified during the supervision period:

- to be of good behaviour and not behave in a way that undermines the rehabilitative purpose of the supervision period;
- not to commit any offences;
- to keep in touch with the supervisor;
- to receive visits from the supervisor;
- to reside permanently at an address approved by the supervisor and to obtain prior permission for any stay of one or more nights a different address;
- not to undertake work, or a particular type of work, unless it is approved by the supervisor, and to notify the supervisor of any proposal to undertake work;
- not to travel outside the British Islands except with prior permission of the supervisor or to comply with a legal obligation (for example, deportation or extradition);
- to participate in activities in accordance with instructions given by the supervisor (including a rehabilitation activity requirement);
- a drug testing requirement;
- a drug appointment requirement, to attend appointment to address the offender's dependency on, or propensity to misuse, controlled drugs.

Section 256AC deals with breach of supervision requirements imposed under s.256AA. The court may issue a summons for the offender to appear or a warrant for the offender's arrest. Section 256AC(4) sets out the sanctions available to the court where it is proved to the satisfaction of the court that the offender has, without reasonable excuse, failed to comply with a requirement during the supervision period: committal to prison for a period not exceeding 14 days; a fine not exceeding level 3 on the standard scale; a 'supervision default order' imposing either an unpaid work requirement or a curfew requirement.

The fact of early release should not be taken into account when deciding what sentence to impose (R v Round [2009] EWCA Crim 2667; [2010] 2 Cr App R (S) 45). One reason for this is that sentencing guidelines are produced in the knowledge that a prisoner will be released in accordance with the early release provisions. The Sentencing Council Guideline on the Imposition of Custodial Sentences says that, in considering what is the shortest term commensurate with the seriousness of the offence, the court must not consider any licence or post-sentence supervision requirements which may subsequently be imposed upon the offender's release.

14.3 Suspended sentences

Section 189(1) of the Criminal Justice Act 2003 provides that where a court passes a sentence of imprisonment for a term of least 14 days but not more than two years, it may make an order that the sentence of imprisonment is not to take effect unless, during the period specified in the order (the 'operational period') the offender commits another offence (whether or not punishable with imprisonment). Under subs. (2), where two or more sentences imposed on the same occasion are to be served consecutively, the sentences may be suspended only if the aggregate of the terms of those sentences does not exceed two years.

Under subs.(1A), the order may also provide that the offender must comply, during the period specified in the order (the 'supervision period') with one or more requirements permitted by s.190(1). These are the same requirements that can be imposed under a community order (considered later in this chapter).

Under subs.(3), the supervision period (if any) and the operational period must each be between six months and two years, beginning with the date of the order. The supervision period must not end later than the operational period (subs.(4)).

Section 189(6) provides that a suspended sentence is to be treated as a sentence of imprisonment. It follows that the custody threshold (s.152) must be crossed before the court can impose a suspended sentence. The Sentencing Council Guideline on the Imposition of Custodial Sentences makes it clear that a suspended sentence is a custodial sentence. A suspended sentence must *not* be imposed 'as a more severe form of community order ... Sentencers should be clear that they would impose an immediate custodial sentence if the power to suspend were not available. If not, a non-custodial sentence should be imposed'.

The Guideline goes on to give examples of factors which would indicate that it is not appropriate to suspend a custodial sentence:

- Offender presents a risk/danger to the public
- Appropriate punishment can only be achieved by immediate custody
- History of poor compliance with court orders

Factors indicating that it may be appropriate to suspend a custodial sentence include:

- Realistic prospect of rehabilitation
- Strong personal mitigation
- Immediate custody will result in significant harmful impact upon others.

The Guideline also cautions against imposing excessive requirements in a suspended sentence order, saying that, to 'ensure that the overall terms of the suspended sentence are commensurate with offence seriousness, care must be taken to ensure requirements imposed are not excessive. A court wishing to impose onerous or intensive requirements should reconsider whether a community sentence might be more appropriate'.

14.3.1 Breach of suspended sentence of imprisonment

Schedule 12 to the Act provides for the revocation or amendment of suspended sentence orders, and sets out the effect of further convictions.

Paragraph 8(2) sets out the powers of the court where either:

- it is proved to the satisfaction of the court that the offender has failed without reasonable excuse to comply with any of the community requirements of the suspended sentence order; or
- the offender is convicted of an offence that was committed during the operational period of the suspended sentence.

The court must do one of the following:

- order that the suspended term is to take effect with its original term unaltered (i.e. the offender has to serve the whole of the suspended sentence);
- order that the sentence is to take effect but for a lesser term (i.e. the offender has to serve only part of the suspended sentence);

- order the offender to pay a fine of an amount up to £2,500;
- extend the operational period (to a maximum of two years from date of original sentence);
- (where the suspended sentence order imposed one or more community requirements) amend the order by
  - imposing more onerous community requirements; or
  - extending the supervision period (to a maximum of two years from date of original sentence).

By virtue of para.8(3), the court must order that the suspended sentence is to take effect (sometimes known as 'activating' the suspended sentence), either in whole or in part, 'unless it is of the opinion that it would be unjust to do so in view of all the circumstances'.

In particular, under subs.(4), where the offender has committed an offence during the operational period, the court should consider the facts of the subsequent offence; where the offender has failed to comply with any community requirements under the order, the court should consider the extent to which he has complied with those requirements.

By virtue of para.8(6) if a magistrates' court is dealing with an offender wo is in breach of a suspended sentence order made by the Crown Court, the magistrates' court may commit the offender (in custody or on bail) to the Crown Court to be dealt with. Paragraph 11(1) provides that, where the offender has failed to comply with requirements under a suspended sentence order, the Crown Court may deal with the breach (whether the order was imposed by the Crown Court or a magistrates' court), and that a magistrates' court may deal with breach of a suspended sentence order made by that or any other magistrates' court. Under para.11(2), where an offender is convicted by a magistrates' court of an offence committed during the operational period of a suspended sentence passed by the Crown Court, the magistrates may commit him (in custody or on bail) to the Crown Court, otherwise they must give written notice of the conviction to the Crown Court. In the latter case, para.12 enables the Crown Court to issue a summons requiring the offender to appear before the court, or to issue a warrant for his arrest.

It should be noted that the commission of a further offence amounts to a breach of a suspended sentence only if it is committed during the operational period of the suspended sentence. It follows from this that the defendant will be in breach of the suspended sentence even if he is convicted of the later offence after the expiry of the operational period, provided that the offence was committed during the operational period.

14.3.1.1 Dealing with breaches of suspended sentences

The Sentencing Council's Guideline for Breach Offences includes guidance on breach of suspended sentence orders. It states that the court dealing with the breach 'should remember that the court imposing the original sentence determined that a custodial sentence was appropriate in the original case'. In determining whether activation of the suspended sentence would be 'unjust', the court may consider all factors including:

- any strong personal mitigation;
- whether there is a realistic prospect of rehabilitation;
- whether immediate custody will result in significant impact on others.

The guidance also emphasises that only 'new and exceptional factors/circumstances not present at the time the suspended sentence order was imposed should be taken into account'.

It notes that, where the offender has been convicted of a further offence committed during operational period of order, the 'facts/nature of the new offence is the primary consideration in assessing the action to be taken on the breach', though in some cases 'the prior level of compliance is also relevant'. The Guideline gives detailed guidance on the approach the court should take in such cases:

- Where the breach involves commission of multiple and/or more serious new offence(s), there should be full activation of the original custodial term;
- Where the breach involves a new offence that is similar in type and gravity to the offence for which the suspended sentence order was imposed, and there has been:
  - no or a low level of compliance with the suspended sentence order, there should be full activation of the original custodial term;
  - medium or high level of compliance with the suspended sentence order, the court should activate sentence but apply an appropriate reduction to the original custodial term, taking into consideration any unpaid work or curfew requirements that have been completed.
- Where the breach involves a new offence that is less serious than the original offence, but which requires a custodial sentence, and there has been:
  - no or a low level of compliance with the suspended sentence order, there should be full activation of the original custodial term;
  - medium or high level of compliance with the suspended sentence order, the court should activate sentence but apply an appropriate reduction to the original custodial term, taking into consideration any unpaid work or curfew requirements that have been completed.
- Where the breach involves a new offence which does not require a custodial sentence, either:
  - activate the suspended sentence but apply a reduction to the original custodial term, taking into consideration any unpaid work or curfew requirements that have been completed, or
  - impose more onerous requirement(s) and/or extend the supervision period and/or extend the operational period and/or impose a fine.

It should be noted that the fact that the later offence is of a different type from the offence for which the suspended sentence was imposed does not prevent the court from activating the suspended sentence.

However, the fact that the 'breach offence' is not sufficiently serious to warrant a custodial sentence provides a very strong argument against bringing the suspended sentence into operation. In R v Stewart (1984) 6 Cr App R (S) 166, it was said that the appropriate method of dealing with such cases is to look first at the 'breach offence', to determine whether it is sufficiently serious to warrant a custodial sentence; if it is not, that is a 'strong circumstance' for not bringing the suspended sentence into operation (per Beldam J, at p.169).

Another argument in favour of leniency is that the later offence was committed when the operational period of the suspended sentence had almost expired.

Where the breach takes the form of failure to comply with a community requirement during the supervision period of the order, the 'predominant factor in determining whether activation is unjust relates to the level of compliance with the suspended sentence order'. The Guideline continues:

The court must take into account the extent to which the offender has complied with the suspended sentence order when imposing a sentence.

In assessing the level of compliance with the order the court should consider:

(i) the overall attitude and engagement with the order as well as the proportion of elements completed;

(ii)   the impact of any completed or partially completed requirements on the offender's behaviour; and

(iii) the proximity of breach to imposition of order; and

(iv)   evidence of circumstances or offender characteristics, such as disability, mental health issues or learning difficulties which have impeded offender's compliance with the order.

The Guideline then gives specific guidance:

- If the breach involves no or a low level of compliance, there should be full activation of the original custodial term.
- If there has been a medium level of compliance, the court should activate the suspended sentence but apply a reduction to the original custodial term, taking into consideration any unpaid work or curfew requirements completed.
- If there has been a high level of compliance, the court should either
  - ○   activate the suspended sentence but apply a reduction to the original custodial term, taking into consideration any unpaid work or curfew requirements completed, or
  - ○   impose more onerous requirement(s) and/or extend the supervision period and/or extend the operational period and/or impose a fine.

In R v Finn [2012] EWCA Crim 881; [2012] 2 Cr App R (S) 96, the court had to consider to what extent, if at all, a defendant should obtain credit against the imposition of a suspended sentence because he has complied with some parts of the original order. Coulson J said (at [12]) that the judge had not erred in principle in concluding that it was not unjust to impose the suspended sentence in full:

A suspended sentence order must be complied with in full; non-compliance risks activation of the suspended sentence in full. In those circumstances, a defendant … who does not comply with the terms of the suspended sentence order, only has himself to blame if non-compliance leads to activation of the suspended sentence in full.

14.4 Life sentences

Most prison sentences are 'determinate' (i.e. for a fixed term). However, in some circumstances the court can impose an indeterminate sentence.

14.4.1 Mandatory life sentences

Murder is punishable with imprisonment for life; such a sentence is mandatory. Section 269 of the Criminal Justice Act 2003 governs the determination of the minimum term in relation to mandatory life sentences. Under s.269(2), a court passing a mandatory life sentence must make an order specifying a period of time the prisoner must serve before the Parole Board can consider release on licence. Under subs.(3), the minimum term is to be such as the court considers appropriate, taking into account the seriousness of the offence(s).

However, under s.269(4), where the offender was aged 21 or over at the time of the offence, and the court takes the view that the offence is so serious that the offender ought to spend the rest of his life in prison, no order is made under subs.(2). This is sometimes known as a 'whole life order'.

When considering the seriousness of the offence, the court has to have regard to the principles set out in sch.21.

14.4.2 Discretionary life sentences

There are several offences (such as manslaughter, rape, inflicting grievous bodily harm with intent, and robbery) which may result in a life sentence. When imposing a discretionary life sentence, the trial judge is empowered to specify a minimum length of time which the offender should serve before release on licence is considered by the Parole Board (s.82A of the Powers of Criminal Courts (Sentencing) Act 2000).

Guidance on discretionary life sentences was given in R v *Whittaker* [1997] 1 Cr App R (S) 261. Lord Bingham CJ (at p.264) said that there were two preconditions:

> The first is that the offender should have been convicted of a very serious offence. If he (or she) has not, then there can be no question of imposing a life sentence. But the second condition is that there should be good grounds for believing that the offender may remain a serious danger to the public for a period which cannot be reliably estimated at the date of sentence. By 'serious danger' the Court has in mind particularly serious offences of violence and serious offences of a sexual nature.

14.4.3 Life sentence for 'second listed offence'

Section 224A of the 2003 Act makes provision for a life sentence for a 'second listed offence'. A number of conditions have to be satisfied:

- a person aged 18 or over is convicted of an offence listed in Part 1 of Sch.15B;
- the court would otherwise impose a custodial sentence of 10 years or more (the 'sentence condition').
- at the time the present offence was committed, the offender had been convicted of an offence listed in Sch.15B and, for that previous offence, either a life sentence where the offender was not eligible for release during the first five years of the sentence, or a sentence of imprisonment for 10 years or more, had been imposed on the offender (the 'previous offence condition').

Where those conditions are met, the court must impose a sentence of imprisonment for life unless it is of the opinion that there are particular circumstances which relate to the offence, to the previous offence, or to the offender, and which would make it 'unjust to do so in all the circumstances'.

In *Attorney General's Reference* (No. 27 of 2013) [2014] EWCA Crim 334; [2014] 1 WLR 4209, Lord Thomas CJ (at [8]) observed that:

> (i) For a life sentence to be imposed under s.224A there is no requirement of a finding that the offender is dangerous within the meaning of the CJA 2003, although it is likely that in most such cases he will be. It follows that the fact that an offender is not dangerous is not something that of itself would make it unjust to pass a life sentence under this section.
>
> ...
>
> (iii) Section 224A could lead in cases that may be rare to the imposition of a life sentence in respect of an offence which does not carry life as a maximum.

14.4.4 Life sentences for serious offences

Section 225 of the Criminal Justice Act 2003 applies where:

- a person aged 18 or over is convicted of a serious offence (i.e. a specified violent offence or a specified sexual offence, listed in Sch.15); and

- the offence is punishable with imprisonment for life, and
- the court 'is of the opinion that there is a significant risk to members of the public of serious harm occasioned by the commission by him of further specified offences'; and
- the court considers that the seriousness of the offence (and any associated offences) is such as to justify the imposition of a sentence of imprisonment for life.

In those circumstances, the court must impose a sentence of life imprisonment (or custody for life where the offender is aged 18–20 at the date of conviction).

Section 226 makes similar provision ('detention for life') for offenders under the age of 18.

In *Attorney General's Reference (No. 27 of 2013)* [2014] EWCA Crim 334; [2014] 1 WLR 4209, Lord Judge (at [10]) noted that where the sentencing judge is satisfied 'in the exercise of his judgment' that an offender is dangerous and that the conditions in s.225 are met, 'there is no discretion. He must pass a life sentence'. His Lordship went on to say (at [22]) that:

> [T]he question in s.225(2)(b) as to whether the seriousness of the offence (or of the offence and one or more offences associated with it) is such as to justify a life sentence requires consideration of: (i) The seriousness of the offence itself, on its own or with other offences associated with it in accordance with the provisions of s.143(1). This is always a matter for the judgment of the court. (ii) The defendant's previous convictions (in accordance with s.143 (2)). (iii) The level of danger to the public posed by the defendant and whether there is a reliable estimate of the length of time he will remain a danger. (iv) The available alternative sentences.

14.4.4 Release of life prisoners

Release on licence of life prisoners is considered by the Parole Board. Under s.28(5) of the Crime (Sentences) Act 1997, a prisoner who has served the minimum period specified by the court must be released if the Parole Board so directs. Under subs.(6), the Parole Board can give a direction under subs.(5) only if it is 'satisfied that it is no longer necessary for the protection of the public that the prisoner should be confined'. If the Board does not decide to release the prisoner, he can require his case to be considered every two years (s.28(7)(b)).

14.5 Dangerous offenders

The 'dangerous offender' provisions apply only to certain offences. Under s.224 of the Criminal Justice Act 2003, a 'specified offence' means a violent offence specified in Part 1 of Sch.15 or a sexual offence specified in Part 2 of that schedule. A 'serious offence' means a violent or sexual offence specified in Sch.15 which is punishable with life imprisonment or a determinate sentence of at least 10 years' imprisonment. The phrase 'serious harm' means death or serious personal injury, whether physical or psychological (s.224(3)).

14.5.1 Extended sentences for violent or sexual offences

Section 226A of the 2003 Act makes provision for 'extended sentences' for offenders who have attained the age of 18 and who have been convicted of certain violent or sexual offences. It applies where a number of conditions are met:

- a person aged 18 or over is convicted of a specified offence;
- the court considers that there is a 'significant risk to members of the public of serious harm occasioned by the commission by the offender of further specified offences';
- the court is not required by s.224A or s.225 (see above) to impose a sentence of imprisonment for life; and
- either:
  - at the time the offence was committed, the offender had been convicted of an offence listed in Sch.15B; or
  - if the court were to impose an extended sentence of imprisonment, the term that it would specify as the appropriate custodial term would be at least four years.

Where these conditions are met, the court may impose an extended sentence of imprisonment on the offender.

An extended sentence comprises (a) the appropriate custodial term (that is, the term of imprisonment which would otherwise have been imposed), and (b) a further period (the 'extension period') for which the offender is to be subject to licence.

The extension period must be a period of such length as the court considers necessary for the purpose of protecting members of the public from serious harm occasioned by the commission by the offender of further specified offences, but cannot exceed five years in the case of a specified violent offence or eight years in the case of a specified sexual offence.

Section 226B makes similar provision for offenders under the age of 18.

Early release is not automatic in the case of a prisoner who is serving an extended sentence. Under s.246A of the 2003 Act, a prisoner who is serving an extended sentence may be released by the Parole Board after serving the requisite custodial period, namely two-thirds of the appropriate custodial term). The Secretary of State must refer the case to the Parole Board when the two-thirds point of the 'appropriate custodial term' (i.e. the sentence passed by the court) has been reached; the Board can direct the release of the prisoner only if satisfied that it is no longer necessary for the protection of the public that he should be confined. The prisoner, if not already released, is released automatically at the end of the appropriate custodial term.

In *Attorney General's Reference* (No. 27 of 2013) [2014] EWCA Crim 334; [2014] 1 WLR 4209, Lord Judge (at [25]) said that:

> It should not be overlooked that s.226A(4) makes the imposition of this sentence discretionary ... [E]ven where there is a finding of dangerousness, an ordinary determinate sentence is sometimes appropriate ... Where a life sentence is not justified an extended sentence will usually, but not always, be appropriate. The option of a determinate sentence should not be forgotten.

Lord Thomas went on to give guidance on the approach that a court should take when considering whether to impose a sentence under the dangerous offender provisions of the Criminal Justice Act 2003 (at [43]):

(i) Consider the question of dangerousness. If the offender is not dangerous and s.224A does not apply, a determinate sentence should be passed. If the offender is not dangerous and the conditions in s.224A are satisfied then (subject to subs.(2)(a)(b)), a life sentence must be imposed.

(ii) If the offender is dangerous, consider whether the seriousness of the offence and offences associated with it justify a life sentence. Seriousness is to be considered ...

(iii) If a life sentence is justified then the judge must pass a life sentence in accordance with s.225. If s.224A also applies, the judge should record that fact in open court.

(iv) If a life sentence is not justified, then the sentencing judge should consider whether s.224A applies. If it does then (subject to the terms of s.224A) a life sentence must be imposed.

(v) If s.224A does not apply the judge should then consider the provisions of s.226A. Before passing an extended sentence, the judge should consider a determinate sentence.

14.5.2 Assessing dangerousness

Section 229(2) provides that the court must take into account all such information as is available to it about the nature and circumstances of the offence, and may take into account any information about any pattern of behaviour of which the offence forms part, and any information about the offender which is before it.

Detailed guidance was given in R v Lang [2005] EWCA Crim 2864; [2006] 1 WLR 2509. Rose LJ (at [7]) said that significant risk to members of the public from serious harm by the commission of further specified offences requires significant risk to be shown in relation to two matters: the commission of further specified, but not necessarily serious, offences; and the causing thereby of serious harm to members of the public. His Lordship went to give further guidance (at [17]):

(i) The risk identified must be significant. This is a higher threshold than mere possibility of occurrence and in our view can be taken to mean ... 'noteworthy, of considerable amount ... or importance'.

(ii) In assessing the risk of further offences being committed, the sentencer should take into account the nature and circumstances of the current offence; the offender's history of offending including not just the kind of offence but its circumstances and the sentence passed, details of which the prosecution must have available and whether the offending demonstrates any pattern; social and economic factors in relation to the offender including accommodation, employability, education, associates, relationships and drug or alcohol abuse and the offender's thinking, attitude towards offending and supervision and emotional state. Information in relation to these matters will most readily, though not exclusively, come from antecedents and pre-sentence probation and medical reports ... The sentencer will be guided, but not bound by, the assessment of risk in such reports. A sentencer who contemplates differing from the assessment in such a report should give both counsel the opportunity of addressing the point.

(iii) ... Sentencers must ... guard against assuming there is a significant risk of serious harm merely because the foreseen specified offence is serious. A pre-sentence report should usually be obtained before any sentence is passed which is based on significant risk of serious harm. In a small number of cases, where the circumstances of the current offence or the history of the offender suggest mental abnormality on his part, a medical report may be necessary before risk can properly be assessed.

(iv) If the foreseen specified offence is not serious, there will be comparatively few cases in which a risk of serious harm will properly be regarded as significant ... Repetitive violent or sexual offending at a relatively low level without serious harm does not of itself give rise to a significant risk of serious harm in the future. There may, in such cases, be some risk of future victims being more adversely affected than past victims but this, of itself, does not give rise to significant risk of serious harm ...

14.5.3 Special custodial sentences for certain offenders of particular concern

Section 236A of the Criminal Justice Act 2003 makes provision for 'special custodial sentences for certain offenders of particular concern'. It applies where (i) a person is convicted of an offence listed in Sch.18A to the Act (which includes a number of terrorism-related and sexual offences); (ii) the offender was aged 18 or over when the offence was committed, and (iii) the court does not impose a sentence of life imprisonment for life or an extended sentence under s.226A. Where those conditions are satisfied, if the court imposes a sentence of imprisonment for the offence, the term of the sentence must be equal to the aggregate of the appropriate custodial term and a further period of one year for which the offender is to be subject to a licence. By virtue of subs.(4), the term of a sentence of imprisonment imposed under s.236A must not exceed the maximum term permitted for the offence. The offender is eligible for release by the Parole Board after serving half the custodial term (and must be released at the end of the custodial term).

In R v Fruen [2016] EWCA Crim 561; [2016] 1 WLR 4432, Treacy LJ (at [9]) said that:

> It is clear to us that the purpose of the new legislation was to ensure that such persons were subject to licence for a period after release even though, by definition, they had not been found to be dangerous by the sentencing judge. The effect, therefore, is not dissimilar to a modified form of extended sentence imposed under s.226A, although one important point of difference is that the case must be considered by the Parole Board once the offender under s.236A has served half rather than two thirds of the custodial term.

14.6 Mandatory sentences

For some offences, a minimum sentence has been prescribed by statute.

14.6.1 Third Class A drug trafficking offence

Section 110 of the Powers of Criminal Courts (Sentencing) Act 2000 applies where an offender is convicted of a Class A drug-trafficking offence and, at the time when that offence was committed, he had been convicted (on separate occasions) of two other Class A drug-trafficking offences. In such a case, a custodial sentence of at least seven years must be imposed unless the court takes the view that there are particular circumstances which relate to any of the offences or to the offender and which would make it 'unjust' in all the circumstances to impose the minimum sentence. In R v Marland [2018] EWCA Crim 1770, Simon LJ (at [31]) said that, 'One way of testing whether a sentence will be unjust in the particular circumstances will be whether the sentence under s.110 is markably more severe than the sentence which would be passed applying the Sentencing Council guidelines for the offence. But this has to be measured against the deterrent element which underlies s.110'.

14.6.2 Minimum sentence for a third domestic burglary

Section 111 of the 2000 Act prescribes a minimum sentence of three years for conviction of a third domestic burglary (that is, burglary of a dwelling), again unless there are particular circumstances relating to any of the offences or to the offender which would make it unjust in all the circumstances.to impose the minimum sentence.

14.6.3 Minimum sentence for certain firearms offences

Section 51A of the Firearms Act 1968 prescribes minimum sentences for certain firearms offences under the Firearms Act 1968. Under s.51A(5), the minimum sentence for a person aged 18 or over at the time of the offence is five years (three years where the offender was under 18 at the time of the offence). Section 51A(2) provides that the court must impose a custodial sentence for a term of at least the required minimum unless it is of the opinion that there are 'exceptional circumstances relating to the offence or to the offender which justify its not doing so'.

14.6.4 Violent Crime Reduction Act 2006

Section 29 of the Violent Crime Reduction Act 2006 sets minimum sentences for offences under s.28 of that Act (using someone to mind dangerous weapons). Where the offender is aged 18 or over at the date of conviction, the minimum sentence is five years; where the offender is aged under 18, the minimum sentence is three years (s.29(4) and (6) respectively). In both instances, the court may refrain from imposing the minimum sentence if it is of the opinion that there are exceptional circumstances relating to the offence or to the offender which justify its not doing so.

14.6.5 Discount for guilty plea

Where ss.110 or 111 of the Powers of Criminal Courts (Sentencing) Act 2000 are applicable, the court can still give credit for a guilty plea under s.144 of the Criminal Justice Act 2003. However, the amount of discount is limited by s.144(2) of the 2003 Act, which provides that in such a case, the court can take account of a guilty plea by passing a sentence which is not less than 80 per cent of what would otherwise be the minimum sentence prescribed by the 2000 Act.

For s.110, the sentence cannot be reduced below five years and 219 days; for s.111, two years and 146 days. In R v Goodale [2013] EWCA Crim 1144; [2014] 1 Cr App R (S) 37, it was pointed out that, in the case of such fixed minimum sentences, it is not uncommon to see sentences recorded in days so that the necessary precision is achieved.

Similar provision is not made for the other mandatory minimum sentences discussed above.

14.7 Custodial sentencing powers of magistrates' courts

The sentence which may be imposed by a magistrates' court often depends on whether the offence is summary or triable either way.

14.7.1 Summary offences

The statute creating a summary offence will indicate whether or not the offence is punishable with imprisonment. The maximum sentence is six months or that prescribed by the statute which creates the offence, whichever is less (s.78(1) of the Powers of Criminal Courts (Sentencing) Act 2000). If the statute creating the offence expressly overrides the limit of six months, then the statute creating the offence prevails (s.78(2)).

14.7.2 Either-way offences

The maximum sentence for an offence which is triable either way because it is listed in Sch.1 to the Magistrates' Courts Act 1980 is six months' imprisonment (s.32(1) of the 1980 Act).

Where the offence is triable either way because the statute creating it gives alternative penalties for summary conviction and conviction on indictment, the maximum penalty is six months' imprisonment or the term specified in the statute creating the offence, whichever is the lesser (s.78(1) of the Powers of Criminal Courts (Sentencing) Act 2000). If the statute creating the offence expressly overrides the six-month limit, the statute creating the offence prevails (s.78(2)).

14.7.3 Consecutive terms of imprisonment

Section 133(1) of the Magistrates' Courts Act 1980 empowers a magistrates' court to order custodial sentences to run consecutively. However, the maximum aggregate sentence which may be imposed is six months (s.133(1)) unless the court is dealing with the offender for two or more either-way offences, in which case the maximum aggregate sentence is 12 months (s.133(2)).

Thus, if an offender is convicted of three summary offences each of which is punishable with three months' imprisonment, the maximum aggregate term is six months. The magistrates could, for example, impose a sentence of three months on each offence but one of the terms would have to be concurrent, so that the total does not exceed six months; alternatively, they could impose a sentence of two months on each to run consecutively. If the offender is being dealt with for one either-way offence and a number of summary offences, the maximum aggregate sentence remains six months. It is only where the court is dealing with an offender for at least two either-way offences that a total of up to 12 months' custody may be imposed.

It should be noted that where a magistrates' court activates a suspended sentence (which it can only do if that sentence was imposed by a magistrates' court), the provisions of s.133 do not apply; the effect of this is that, while the sentence(s) for the present offence(s) must not exceed the limit set by s.133, the suspended sentence may be activated even if doing so has the effect of imposing a total term in excess of the limit set by s.133 (R v Chamberlain (1992) 13 Cr App R(S) 525).

14.8 Community sentences

The Sentencing Council Guideline on the Imposition of Community Order says that:

> Community orders can fulfil all of the purposes of sentencing. In particular, they can have the effect of restricting the offender's liberty while providing punishment in the community, rehabilitation for the offender, and/or ensuring that the offender engages in reparative activities.

The Criminal Justice Act 2003 gives the court what might be described as a 'pick-and-mix' menu to enable it to construct a community order that is appropriate to the particular offender. Section 177(1) of the Act provides that where a person aged 16 or over is convicted of an offence, the court may make a 'community order' imposing on him any one or more of a list of requirements (considered below).

Under s.177(5), the community order must specify an end date, not more than three years after the date of the order, by which all the requirements in it must have been complied with.

Under s.148, the offence must be serious enough to warrant a community sentence, and the restrictions on liberty imposed by the order must be commensurate with the seriousness of the offence.

It may well be that an offender who ultimately receives a community sentence was remanded in custody prior to conviction and/or sentence. Section 149(1) of the 2003 Act provides that, in such a case, when determining the restrictions on liberty to be imposed under the order, the court may have regard to any period for which the offender has been remanded in custody in connection with the offence or any related offence.

Section 177(2A) stipulates that, where the court makes a community order, the court must include in the order 'at least one requirement imposed for the purpose of punishment' and/or impose a fine for the offence in respect of which the community order is made. However, under subs.(2B), this requirement does not apply if there are exceptional circumstances relating to the offence or to the offender which would make it unjust in all the circumstances for the court to comply with that requirement. The statute does not identify which requirements are to be regarded as punitive for this purpose, and the guidance from the Sentencing Council simply says that it is a matter for the court to decide which requirements amount to a punishment in each case.

The requirements which may be imposed are listed in s.177:

- an unpaid work requirement (defined by s.199),
- a rehabilitation activity requirement (defined by s.200A),
- a prohibited activity requirement (defined by s.203),
- a curfew requirement (defined by s.204),
- an exclusion requirement (defined by s.205),
- a residence requirement (defined by s.206),
- a foreign travel prohibition requirement (defined by s.206A),
- a mental health treatment requirement (defined by s.207),
- a drug rehabilitation requirement (defined by s.209),
- an alcohol treatment requirement (defined by s.212),
- (where the offender is aged under 25) an attendance centre requirement (defined by s.214).

14.8.1 Unpaid work requirement

Under an unpaid work requirement, the offender works (under supervision) for the specified number of hours on local community projects.

The number of hours work to be carried out must be specified in the order and must be between 40 and 300 (s.199(2)).

Under s.199(3), the court may not impose an unpaid work requirement unless it is satisfied (for example, through the pre-sentence report) that the offender is a 'suitable person to perform work under such a requirement'.

Where the court imposes an unpaid work requirement in respect of two or more offences, it may direct that the hours of work imposed for one offence are to be concurrent with, or additional to, the hours specified for another offence. However, the total number of hours must not exceed 300 (s.199(5)).

Section 200(2) stipulates that the unpaid work should normally be performed within 12 months. However, under subs.(3), a community order imposing an unpaid work requirement remains in force (unless revoked) until the offender has completed the number of hours specified in the order.

14.8.2 Rehabilitation activity requirement

Section 200A(1) defines a 'rehabilitation activity requirement' ('RAR') as a requirement that, during the period for which the community order remains in force, the offender 'must comply with any instructions given by the responsible officer to attend appointments or participate in activities or both'.

The order must specify the maximum number of days for which the offender may be instructed to participate in activities (subs.(2)). Under subs.(3), any 'instructions given by the responsible officer must be given with a view to promoting the offender's rehabilitation; but this does not prevent the responsible officer giving instructions with a view to other purposes in addition to rehabilitation'. The instructions can include a requirement that the offender must attend appointments with the responsible officer (usually a probation officer) or with someone else (subs.(4)). Under subs.(7), the activities that responsible officers may instruct offenders to participate in include activities forming an accredited programme and activities whose purpose is reparative, such as restorative justice activities. For these purposes, an activity is a restorative justice activity if:

(a) the participants consist of, or include, the offender and one or more of the victims,

(b) the aim of the activity is to maximise the offender's awareness of the impact of the offending concerned on the victims, and

(c) the activity gives a victim or victims an opportunity to talk about, or by other means express experience of, the offending and its impact. (subs.(8)).

The term 'victim' includes any person affected by, the offending (subs.(9)).

The Sentencing Council Guideline notes that the court does not prescribe the activities to be included (it merely specifies the maximum number of activity days the offender must complete). The responsible officer will decide the activities to be undertaken. The Guideline stipulates that, 'where appropriate this requirement should be made in addition to, and not in place of, other requirements. Sentencers should ensure the activity length of a RAR is suitable and proportionate'.

14.8.3 Programme requirement

This requires the offender to participate in a programme (that is, a systematic set of activities) on the number of days specified in the order.

14.8.4 Prohibited activity requirement

This is a requirement that the offender must refrain from participating in the activities specified in the order either on specified days or for a specified period.

14.8.5 Curfew requirement

This is a requirement that the offender must remain, for the periods specified in the order, at a place specified in the order.

Under s.204(2), the court may specify different places or different periods for different days. However, the period of curfew must be between two and 16 hours in any day to which the order applies. A curfew requirement can be imposed for a maximum period of 12 months (s.204(3)).

Section 204(6) stipulates that, before imposing a curfew requirement, the court must obtain and consider information about the place proposed to be specified in the order (including information as to the attitude of persons likely to be affected by the enforced presence there of the offender).

A curfew order is similar in effect to house arrest. The offender has to stay at the specified address (usually at their home) for the curfew period. A tag, worn on the ankle or wrist, notifies monitoring services if the offender is absent during the curfew hours.

14.8.6 Exclusion requirement

This prohibits the offender from entering a place or area specified in the order for a period specified in the order.

The maximum duration of such a requirement is two years (subs.(2)). The exclusion can be limited to particular periods, and may specify different places for different periods or days (subs.(3)).

14.8.7 Residence requirement

This is a requirement that, during the period specified in the order, the offender must reside at the place specified in the order.

Under subs.(3), before imposing a residence requirement, the court must consider the home surroundings of the offender.

Subsection (4) stipulates that the court may not specify a hostel or similar institution as the place where an offender must reside unless a probation officer so recommends.

14.8.8 Foreign travel prohibition requirement

This is a requirement that prohibits the offender from travelling, on the day(s) or period specified in the order, overseas (either generally or to specified countries). This requirement cannot last for more than 12 months.

14.8.9 Mental health treatment requirement

This is a requirement that the offender must submit, during the period(s) specified in the order, to treatment by or under the direction of a registered medical practitioner or psychologist with a view to the improvement of the offender's mental condition. Under subs.(2), the treatment required may be as an in-patient or as an out-patient.

Under subs.(3), the court must be satisfied that the mental condition of the offender requires, and may be susceptible to, treatment (but is not such as to warrant the making of a hospital order or guardianship order under the Mental Health Act 1983), and that the offender has expressed willingness to comply with such a requirement.

14.8.10 Drug rehabilitation requirement

This is a requirement that, for the period specified in the order, the offender must submit to treatment with a view to the reduction or elimination of dependency on, or propensity to misuse, drugs.

Under subs.(2), the court must be satisfied that the offender is dependent on (or has a propensity to misuse) drugs, and that this dependency or propensity is such as requires, and may be susceptible to, treatment. Moreover, the offender must express willingness to comply with the requirement before it can be imposed.

14.8.11 Alcohol treatment requirement

This is a requirement that the offender must submit, during the period specified in the order, to treatment with a view to the reduction or elimination of dependency on alcohol.

Under subs.(2), the court may only impose an alcohol treatment requirement if it is satisfied that the offender is dependent on alcohol and that dependency is such as requires, and may be susceptible to, treatment. Such a requirement may only be imposed if the offender expresses willingness to comply with it (subs.(3)).

14.8.12 Attendance centre requirement

An 'attendance centre' is a place at which offenders under the age of 25 'may be required to attend and be given under supervision appropriate occupation or instruction' (s.221(2)).

Section 214(1) provides that the court may impose a requirement that the offender must attend an attendance centre for the number of hours specified in the order. Subsection (2) states that the aggregate number of hours for which the offender may be required to attend an attendance centre must not be less than 12 or more than 36. Under subs.(6), an offender may not be required to attend an attendance centre on more than one occasion on any one day, or for more than three hours on any occasion.

14.8.13 Electronic monitoring requirement

This requirement, for the electronic monitoring of the whereabouts of the offender, may be imposed in order to monitor the offender's compliance with other requirements imposed by the community order, or as a free-standing requirement.

14.8.14 Restrictions on community orders

Section 217 requires the court to ensure, as far as practicable, that any requirement imposed under a community order avoids 'any conflict with the offender's religious beliefs or with the requirements of any other relevant order to which he may be subject', and also avoids 'any interference with the times, if any, at which he normally works or attends any educational establishment'.

14.9 Breach of community orders

Part 2 of Sch.8 to the 2003 Act deals with breach of community orders.

Under para.5(1), if the responsible officer is of the opinion that the offender has failed without reasonable excuse to comply with any of the requirements of a community order, the officer must give the offender a warning unless either he has been given a warning in the previous 12 months or the officer refers the case back to the court. Under para.5(2), the warning must inform the offender that, if he again fails to comply with any requirement of the order during the next 12 months, he will be liable to be brought before a court.

By virtue of para.6(1), if the responsible officer has given a warning under para.5 and, within the next 12 months, the responsible officer is of the opinion that the offender has again failed without reasonable excuse to comply with any of the requirements of the order, the officer must refer the offender to an enforcement officer so that offender can be brought back to court. A probation officer has no discretion to give a second warning; if there is a second breach, the matter must be referred to the court (*West Yorkshire Probation Board v Robinson & Tinker* [2009] EWHC 2517 (Admin); (2010) 174 JP 13).

Under para.7(2), a justice of the peace may issue a summons requiring the attendance of the offender, or (if the allegation of breach is in writing and substantiated on oath) a warrant for the offender's arrest, if it appears that the offender has failed to comply with any of the requirements of a community order. Under para.7(4), if the offender fails to appear in answer to the summons, the magistrates' court may issue a warrant for his arrest. Paragraph 7(2) makes it clear that this power only applies if the community order is still in force (thus preventing enforcement proceedings being commenced after the order has expired).

Paragraph 8 confers the same powers on the Crown Court where it has made a community order which does not include a direction that a failure to comply with the requirements be dealt with by the magistrates' court.

Paragraph 9(1) provides that if it is proved to the satisfaction of the magistrates' court that the offender has failed without reasonable excuse to comply with any of the requirements of the community order, the court must deal with him in one of the following ways:

- by amending the terms of the community order so as to impose more onerous requirements;
- ordering the offender to pay a fine of an amount not exceeding £2,500;
- where the community order was made by a magistrates' court, by dealing with the offender, for the offence in respect of which the order was made, in any way in which the court could deal with him if he had just been convicted by it of the offence (that is, revoking the order and resentencing the offender);
- where the community order was made by a magistrates' court, the offence in respect of which the order was made was not an offence punishable by imprisonment, and the offender has wilfully and persistently failed to comply with the requirements of the order, imposing a sentence of imprisonment for a term not exceeding six months (this empowers the court to impose a custodial sentence, even though the original offence was not imprisonable, but only if the offender has 'wilfully and persistently' failed to comply with the requirements of the community order).

When dealing with the non-compliance, the court must take into account the extent to which the offender has complied with the order (para.9(2)).

An offender who is resentenced can appeal to the Crown Court against the new sentence (para.9(8)).

Where the order was made by the Crown Court (and that court directed that failures to comply should be dealt with by the magistrates' court), the magistrates' court dealing with the breach can (instead of dealing with the offender themselves) commit him, in custody or on bail, to be dealt with by the Crown Court (para.9(6)).

Paragraph 10 sets out how the Crown Court must deal with failure to comply with a community order (whether the Crown Court is dealing with the case under para.8 or para.9). The options open to the Crown Court are the same as those available to the magistrates' court.

The Sentencing Council Guideline on Breach Offences includes guidance on breach of community orders. It states that:

> The court must take into account the extent to which the offender has complied with the requirements of the community order when imposing a penalty.
>
> In assessing the level of compliance with the order the court should consider:
>
> (i) the overall attitude and engagement with the order as well as the proportion of elements completed;
>
> (ii) the impact of any completed or partially completed requirements on the offender's behaviour;
>
> (iii) the proximity of breach to imposition of order; and
>
> (iv) evidence of circumstances or offender characteristics, such as disability, mental health issues or learning difficulties which have impeded offender's compliance with the order.

In *West Yorkshire Probation Board v Boulter* [2005] EWHC 2342; [2006] 1 WLR 232, it was held that a breach of a community order has to be proved to the criminal standard (namely, beyond reasonable doubt).

The fact that an appeal against sentence has been lodged does not prevent enforcement of the community order. The order takes effect when it is imposed and it remains in full force and effect until and unless it is quashed on appeal or revoked or amended by order of the court (*West Midlands Probation Board v Sutton Coldfield Magistrates' Court* [2008] EWHC 15 (Admin); [2008] 1 WLR 918 (per Dyson LJ, at [13]).

14.9.1 Commission of further offences

Being convicted of an offence during the currency of a community order does not constitute a breach of the order. However, because a further conviction may lead to the conclusion that the community order is not working, Part 5 of Sch.8 deals with the powers of the court in relation to a community order where the offender is convicted of a further offence.

Paragraph 21 provides that where an offender in respect of whom a community order made by a magistrates' court is in force, is convicted of an offence by a magistrates' court, and it appears to the court that it would be in the interests of justice to do so (having regard to circumstances that have arisen since the community order was made), the magistrates' court may either (a) revoke the order, or (b) revoke the order and deal with the offender, for the offence in respect of which the order was made, in any way which he could have been dealt with for that offence by the court which made the order. If the offender is resentenced, the court must take into account the extent to which he complied with the order (para.21(3)), and the offender has a right of appeal to the Crown Court (para.21(4)).

If the magistrates' court is dealing with the later offence but the community order was made in the Crown Court, the magistrates may commit the offender (in custody or on bail) to appear at the Crown Court (para.22(1)).

Paragraph 23 confers the same power to revoke, or to revoke and resentence, on the Crown Court where the offender is convicted by the Crown Court of an offence committed during the currency of a community order (or where the offender is committed to the Crown Court under para.22). If the Crown Court resentences the offender for an offence where the original sentence was passed by a magistrates' court, the Crown Court's sentencing powers are limited to those of a magistrates' court.

14.10 Fines

A fine may be imposed for any offence except one that carries mandatory life imprisonment.

14.10.1 Crown Court fines

Section 163 of the Criminal Justice Act 2003 empowers the Crown Court, when sentencing an offender who has been convicted following trial on indictment, to impose a fine on the offender instead of, or in addition to, dealing with him in any other way. This power also applies when the offender was convicted by a magistrates' court but committed for sentence under s.3 of the Powers of Criminal Courts (Sentencing) Act 2000, since the powers of the Crown Court following such a committal are the same as if the offender had been convicted on indictment.

There is no statutory limit on the amount of a fine imposed by the Crown Court. Note, however, that where a Crown Court is dealing with an offence following committal under s.6 of the 2000 Act, the Crown Court cannot exceed the amount of the fine that the magistrates could have imposed.

14.10.2 Magistrates' courts fines

The maximum fine for a summary offence is that prescribed by the statute that creates the offence. Most enactments refer to a level on 'the standard scale' of fines, rather than to a specific sum of money. Under s.37(2) of the Criminal Justice Act 1982, the standard scale has five levels:

Level of current maximum fine (per offence):

1: £200
2: £500
3: £1,000
4: £2,500
5: Any amount

Where a magistrates' court convicts a person of an either-way offence, the court may impose a fine of any amount (s.85 of the Legal Aid, Sentencing and Punishment of Offenders Act 2012).

The Legal Aid, Sentencing and Punishment of Offenders Act 2012 (Fines on Summary Conviction) Regulations 2015 (SI 2015 No. 664) makes specific provision for maximum fines for a large number of specified offences. For example, a maximum fine of £20,000 is prescribed for the offences listed in sch.2. The effect is that an either-way offence is punishable with a fine of any amount unless specific provision is made for that offence in this Statutory Instrument.

14.10.3 Fixing the amount of the fine

Section 164 of the CJA 2003 sets out the process for fixing the amount of a fine:

(1) Before fixing the amount of any fine to be imposed on an offender who is an individual, a court must inquire into his financial circumstances.

(2) The amount of any fine fixed by a court must be such as, in the opinion of the court, reflects the seriousness of the offence.

(3) In fixing the amount of any fine to be imposed on an offender (whether an individual or other person), a court must take into account the circumstances of the case including, among other things, the financial circumstances of the offender so far as they are known, or appear, to the court.

(4) Subsection (3) applies whether taking into account the financial circumstances of the offender has the effect of increasing or reducing the amount of the fine.

Thus, the court first fixes an amount related to the seriousness of the offence (taking account of any aggravating features, and any relevant mitigating circumstances) and then considers whether that amount should be increased or reduced as a result of the offender's means.

In R v Warden [1996] 2 Cr App R(S) 269, it was held that in determining the amount of a fine in a case where the offender has been remanded in custody in connection with the offence, some credit should be given for the time spent on remand.

If the offender does not have the means to pay a fine which adequately reflects the seriousness of the offence but the offence is not sufficiently serious to justify a custodial sentence, it is wrong in principle to impose a custodial sentence (R v Reeves (1972) 56 Cr App R 366). On the other hand, if the seriousness of the offence does justify a custodial sentence, the offender should not escape custody merely because he has the means to pay a large fine (R v Markwick (1953) 37 Cr App R 125).

In R v F Howe & Son Ltd [1999] 2 Cr App R (S) 37, the Court of Appeal gave guidance on fines where the defendant is a company: the fine needs to be large enough to bring home the seriousness of the offending to the managers and to the shareholders (per Scott Baker J, at p.44). In *R v Balfour Beatty Rail Infrastructure Services Ltd* [2006] EWCA Crim 1586; [2007] 1 Cr App R(S) 65, the court accepted that a fine does not have to stand in any specific relationship with the turnover or net profit of the defendant; each case must be dealt with according to its own circumstances. The company's resources and the effect of a fine on its business are important (per Lord Phillips CJ, at [22]–[23]).

In *R v Sellafield Limited and Network Rail Infrastructure* [2014] EWCA Crim 49, the Court of Appeal again considered the approach to be taken when imposing a fine on a large company. Lord Thomas CJ (at [5]) said:

> Where a fine is to be imposed a court will therefore first consider the seriousness of the offence and then the financial circumstances of the offender. The fact that the defendant to a criminal charge is a company with a turnover in excess of £1 billion makes no difference to that basic approach.

His Lordship went on, at [6]:

> The fine must be fixed to meet the statutory purposes with the objective of ensuring that the message is brought home to the directors and members of the company (usually the shareholders).

A fine may be imposed at the same time as a compensation order. However, s.130(12) of the Powers of Criminal Courts (Sentencing) Act 2000 provides that if an offender has insufficient means to pay both a fine and a compensation order, the compensation order takes priority; thus, in such a case, the fine will be reduced or a different sentence altogether imposed.

Section 162 of the Criminal Justice Act 2003 empowers a court to make a 'financial circumstances order' requiring the offender to provide a statement of his assets and other financial circumstances within the period specified in the order. Failure to provide a statement is an offence, under subs.(4). It is also an offence, under subs.(5), to make a statement which is known to be false, or recklessly to furnish a statement which is false, or knowingly to fail to disclose a material fact. See Table 14.1.

Under s.164(5), where the offender has failed to comply with an order under s.162, or has otherwise failed to co-operate with the court in its inquiry into his financial circumstances, and 'the court considers that it has insufficient information to make a proper determination of the financial circumstances of the offender, it may make such determination as it thinks fit'.

14.10.3.1 Fine bands in magistrates' courts

In the Sentencing Council's Magistrates' Court Sentencing Guideline, fines are expressed as one of six fine bands (A, B, C, D, E or F), subject to the maximum fine that may be imposed (if applicable). See Table 14.1.

14.10.4 Enforcement of fines

Where a fine is imposed, payment is due immediately. However, where the offender does not have the means to pay the fine forthwith, the magistrates are empowered to allow time for payment or to order payment by instalments (s.75(1) of the Magistrates' Courts Act 1980). Where payment by instalments is ordered, the total fine should usually be one that the offender will be able to pay off within 12 months.

Enforcement of fines is carried out by the offender's local magistrates' court. If the offender fails to pay the fine or fails to pay the instalments as ordered, the magistrates' court can issue a

Table 14.1 Assessing fines in magistrates' courts

Band	Starting point	Category range
A	50% of relevant weekly income	25–75% of relevant weekly income
B	100% of relevant weekly income	75–125% of relevant weekly income
C	150% of relevant weekly income	125–175% of relevant weekly income
D	250% of relevant weekly income	200–300% of relevant weekly income
E	400% of relevant weekly income	300–500% of relevant weekly income
F	600% of relevant weekly income	500–700% of relevant weekly income

summons requiring the offender to attend court or the court can issue a warrant for the offender's arrest (s.83 of the Magistrates' Courts Act 1980). At the hearing, the court will investigate the offender's means (and the offender can be required to produce evidence of income and out-goings).

Under s.85(1) of the Magistrates' Courts Act 1980, where a fine has been imposed by a magistrates' court, the court may at any time remit the whole or any part of the fine, but only 'if it thinks it just to do so having regard to a change of circumstances'. Under subs.(2), where the court remits the whole or part of the fine after a term of imprisonment has been fixed (as will always be the case with Crown Court fines), it must also reduce the term by a proportionate amount (or remit the whole term if the whole fine is cancelled). It should be noted that the power to remit is restricted to fines; there is no equivalent power in respect of compensation orders (s.85(4)).

Assuming that the fine is not remitted, the court has at its disposal a wide array of enforcement mechanisms to ensure that fines are paid, including:

- A 'warrant of control' authorising seizure and sale of goods owned by the offender under s.62 of the Tribunals, Courts and Enforcement Act 2007 (s.82(4A)(d) of the Magistrates' Courts Act 1980).).
- An 'attachment of earnings order', so that money is deducted from the offender's wages (Attachment of Earnings Act 1971).
- An order for deduction of money from the offender's income support, universal credit, state pension credit, job-seeker's allowance or employment and support allowance (Fines (Deductions from Income Support) Regulations 1992 (SI 1992/2182)).
- An attendance centre order, but only if the offender is under the age of 25 (s.82(4A)(e) of the Magistrates' Courts Act 1980).
- Under s.35 of the Crime Sentences Act 1997, where a court has the power to commit an offender to prison in default of payment of a fine (see later), the court may instead order the offender to comply with an unpaid work or curfew requirement.
- Under s.40 of the Crime (Sentences) Act 1997, instead of committing an offender to custody in default of payment of a sum, the court may disqualify the offender from driving for a period of up to 12 months.
- Imprisonment, but only if either (i) the offence for which the fine was imposed is imprisonable, and the offender has sufficient means to pay forthwith, or (ii) the court is satisfied that the offender's failure to pay the fine is due to 'wilful refusal' or 'culpable neglect' and the court has considered or tried all other methods of enforcement but it appears to the court that they are inappropriate or have been unsuccessful (s.82(4) of the Magistrates' Courts Act 1980).

Schedule 5 to the Courts Act 2003 puts in place an additional set of powers to aid the enforcement of fines to complement the other mechanisms for enforcement. For example, there is provision for fines to be increased in the event of non-payment (para.42A). The Act also enables the offender's vehicle to be clamped, and then sold, if a fine remains unpaid (para.38(1)(d)). Schedule 6 enables the court to allow an offender over the age of 18 to discharge a fine by means of unpaid work (under a 'work order').

14.11 Discharges

Section 12(1) of the Powers of Criminal Courts (Sentencing) Act 2000 provides that, where a court has convicted a person of an offence but is of the opinion, having regard to the nature of the offence and the character of the offender, that it is 'inexpedient to inflict punishment', the court may either:

- discharge the offender absolutely; or
- discharge the offender subject to a condition that he does not commit a further offence during the period (of up to three years) specified in the order.

Under s.14(1), a conditional or absolute discharge only counts as a conviction for certain purposes. It follows that where an offence is dealt with by way of a discharge, conviction for that offence cannot amount to a breach of an earlier order.

14.11.1 Absolute discharge

The effect of an absolute discharge is that, apart from the fact that a conviction is recorded against the offender, no penalty is imposed.

An absolute discharge is appropriate where the court decides that it would be wrong to take any action against the accused. For example, an absolute discharge may be ordered if the defendant is convicted of a very trivial offence or if the circumstances of the commission of the offence show little or no blame on the part of the defendant. In R v O'Toole (1971) 55 Cr App R 206, for example, an ambulance driver who collided with another vehicle while answering a 999 call received an absolute discharge.

14.11.2 Conditional discharge

The only condition of a conditional discharge is that the offender does not commit another offence during the period of the conditional discharge. No other condition may be imposed. An offender who commits another offence during the period of the conditional discharge is liable to be sentenced for the original offence as well as for the subsequent offence.

Since a discharge is only to be imposed where it is inexpedient to inflict punishment (s.12(1) of the 2000 Act), it would be wrong in principle to combine a discharge with any other sentence for the same offence (see, for example, R v Sanck (1990) 12 Cr App R(S) 155, where it was held that a conditional discharge cannot be combined with a fine for the same offence).

Section 12(7) of the 2000 Act, however, enables the court to make an order for costs and/or compensation even if it discharges the offender. Moreover, an offender may also be disqualified (for example, from driving) even though he has been discharged.

14.11.2.1 Breach of conditional discharge

If the offender commits an offence during the period of a conditional discharge, the court dealing with the breach may deal with the offender in any way in which the offender could have been dealt with when the conditional discharge was ordered (s.13(6) of the Powers of Criminal Courts (Sentencing) Act 2000).

If an offender is convicted by a magistrates of an offence committed during the period of a conditional discharge imposed by another magistrates' court, the convicting court may, with the consent of the court which made the order, deal with him, for the offence for which the order was made, in any way in which the court could deal with him if it had just convicted him of that offence (s.13(8)).

Where a person who is subject to a conditional discharge is convicted by the Crown Court of an offence committed during the period of that conditional discharge, the Crown Court may resentence for the original offence whether the conditional discharge was imposed by the Crown Court or by a magistrates' court. If the order was made by a magistrates' court, the powers of the Crown Court are limited to those of a magistrates' court if it resentences the offender for the original offence (s.13(7)). A magistrates' court which convicts someone of an offence committed during the currency of a conditional discharge imposed by the Crown Court cannot resentence the offender for the original offence but may commit the offender (in custody or on bail) to the Crown Court to be dealt with for the breach (s.13(5)).

14.12 Compensation orders

Section 130(1)(a) of the Powers of Criminal Courts (Sentencing) Act 2000 empowers a court which has convicted someone of an offence to require that person 'to pay compensation for any personal injury, loss or damage resulting from that offence or any other offence which is taken into consideration by the court in determining sentence'.

Under s.130(2A), court must consider making a compensation order in any case where s.130 empowers it to do so; under subs. (3), the court has to give reasons if it does not make a compensation order in such a case.

Under s.130(4), a compensation order should be for 'such amount as the court considers appropriate, having regard to any evidence and to any representations that are made by or on behalf of the accused or the prosecutor'. The amount of the damage should be proved if it is not agreed between the parties.

In R v Donovan (1981) 3 Cr App R(S) 192, at p.193, Eveleigh LJ said that compensation orders are designed for simple and straightforward cases 'where the amount of the compensation can be readily and easily ascertained'.

In R v Stapylton [2012] EWCA Crim 728; [2013] 1 Cr App R (S) 12, Cranston J (at [12]) summarised the key principles:

- The court has no jurisdiction to make a compensation order where there are real issues as to whether those to benefit have suffered any, and if so, what loss.
- Compensation orders are for straightforward cases, and so a court should not embark on a detailed inquiry as to the extent of any injury, loss or damage.
- Compensation orders must not be made unless there is a realistic possibility of compliance.

Similarly, in R v White [1996] 2 Cr App R(S) 58, at p. 60, Owen J said that a compensation order 'should only be made where there is no question of a difficult or complex issue as to liability'.

Some causal connection between the offence and the personal injury, loss or damage must be established before compensation can be ordered, but the offence need not be the sole cause of the injury, loss or damage (R v Corbett (1993) 14 Cr App R(S) 101, per Tuckey J, at p.102).

Section 131(1) of the 2000 Act sets a limit of £5,000 compensation for an offence where the order is made by a magistrates' court and the offender is under the age of 18. Where the offender is appearing in a magistrates' court and has attained the age of 18, or is appearing in the Crown Court, there is no limit on the amount of the compensation order that can be made in respect of the offence(s) for which he is being dealt with.

Section 130(11) of the 2000 Act requires the court to take account of the offender's means in deciding whether to make a compensation order and, if so, the amount of the order.

14.13 Surcharges

Sections 161A(1) of the Criminal Justice Act 2003 provides that, when a court is sentencing an offender for one or more offences, it must also order him to pay a 'surcharge' unless the court considers that it would be appropriate to make a compensation order, but the offender has insufficient means to pay both the surcharge and appropriate compensation, in which case the court must reduce the surcharge accordingly, if necessary to nil (subs.(3)). This provision does not apply if the court grants an absolute discharge (subs.(4)(a)).

By virtue of the Criminal Justice Act 2003 (Surcharge) Order 2012 (SI 2012/1696), the surcharge depends on the sentence imposed. For offenders over the age of 18, it is as follows:

- Conditional discharge: £20.
- Fine: 10 per cent of the value of the fine, rounded up or down to the nearest pound but must be no less than £20 and no more than £120.
- Community order: £85.
- Suspended sentence (six months or less): £115.
- Suspended sentence (more than six months): £140.
- Imprisonment/detention in a young offender institution imposed by the Crown Court for up to six months: £115.
- Imprisonment/detention in a young offender institution imposed by the Crown Court for more than six months up to 24 months: £140.
- Imprisonment/detention in a young offender institution for more than 24 months: £170.
- Life sentence: £170.

14.14 Other orders that may be made following conviction

In this section, we look at some of the ancillary orders that can be made after conviction.

14.14.1 Endorsement of driving licences and disqualification from driving

Under s.34(1) of the Road Traffic Offenders Act 1988, where a person who has been convicted of a road traffic offence involving obligatory disqualification, the court must order that he be disqualified from driving for at least 12 months unless the court finds that there are 'special reasons' for not doing so or for imposing a shorter period of disqualification. A 'special reason' must be connected with the commission of the offence itself; mitigation which is personal to the offender is not a special reason (*Whittall v Kirby* [1947] KB 194). Other road traffic offences carry discretionary disqualification (see Sch.1 to the Road Traffic Offenders Act 1988). In such cases, the punishment of disqualification should generally be restricted to cases involving bad driving, persistent motoring offences, or the use of vehicles for the purposes of crime (per Morland J in R v *Callister* [1993] RTR 70).

Many road traffic offences carry a number of penalty points which have to be endorsed on the offender's driving licence in the event of conviction. The number of points to be endorsed is set out in Sch.1 to the Road Traffic Offenders Act 1988; sometimes, the number is fixed; sometimes there is a range, with a minimum and a maximum number specified.

Under s.35 of the Road Traffic Offenders Act 1988, where a person is convicted of an offence which carries discretionary disqualification and mandatory endorsement and the number of penalty points on the offender's driving licence (including those imposed for the present offence) is 12 or more, the court must disqualify the offender from driving for at least six months (if it is the driver's first disqualification) or 12 months (if it is the driver's second) or two years (if the driver has already been disqualified twice), unless the court takes the view that there are grounds for not doing so or for disqualifying for a shorter period. Penalty points are taken into account if they were imposed within the last three years (s.29(2)). This is known as a 'totting up' disqualification.

When the court is deciding whether there is mitigation to justify not disqualifying the offender (or for shortening the disqualification), s.35(4) states that the court cannot take account of (a) any circumstances that are alleged to make the offence or any of the offences not a serious one, (b) hardship, other than exceptional hardship, or (c) any circumstances which, within the three years immediately preceding the conviction, have been taken into account in deciding not to disqualify or to impose a shorter period of disqualification.

Additionally, s.146 of the Powers of Criminal Courts (Sentencing) Act 2000 provides that, in addition to, or instead of, dealing with an offender in any other way, a court may disqualify the offender from holding or obtaining a driving licence for such period as it thinks fit. Thus, the penalty of disqualification from driving can be imposed for any offence, not just driving offences. In R v *Cliff* [2004] EWCA Crim 3139; [2005] 2 Cr App R (S) 22, the court said that it is not necessary for the offence to be connected to the use of the motor car: the section provides an additional punishment available to the court. However, the court added that there must be a sufficient reason for the disqualification.

14.14.2 Forfeiture

Section 143 of the Powers of Criminal Courts (Sentencing) Act 2000 empowers the Crown Court or a magistrates' court to make a forfeiture order (sometimes called a 'deprivation order') in two situations:

- Under s.143(1), in respect of property which has been lawfully seized from the offender, or which was in his possession at the time when he was apprehended for the offence. This power only applies if the property was used for the purpose of committing (or facilitating the commission of) an offence, or was intended by him to be used for that purpose.
- Under s.143(2), where the offender has been convicted of an offence which consists of unlawful possession of property which has lawfully been seized from him (or which was in his possession at the time he was apprehended for the offence).

In deciding whether or not to make a forfeiture order, the court must have regard to the value of the property and to the likely financial and other effects of the order on the offender (s.143 (5)). Under s.143(6) and (7), an offender convicted of an imprisonable offence under the Road Traffic Act 1988 may have their car seized.

There are several specific statutory powers to make forfeiture orders, including s.27 of the Misuse of Drugs Act 1971 (forfeiture, and destruction where appropriate, of property related to drugs offences, where it is shown that the property is related to the offence of which the offender has been convicted); s.52 of the Firearms Act 1968 (firearms and ammunition); and s.1(2) of the Prevention of Crime Act 1953 (offensive weapons).

14.14.3 Confiscation orders

Section 6 of the Proceeds of Crime Act 2002 provides that, where an offender is being sentenced in the Crown Court (having been convicted there or committed for sentence from a magistrates' court), the court may (at the request of the prosecution or of its own motion) proceed to decide whether the defendant has a criminal lifestyle and, if so, whether the offender has benefited from 'general criminal conduct'.

If the court decides that the offender does not have a criminal lifestyle, it must decide whether the offender has benefited from 'particular criminal conduct', namely the offence(s) of which the offender has been convicted.

An offender can have a criminal lifestyle in three ways (s.75):

- the offence of which the offender has been convicted is specified in Sch.2; or
- the offence constitutes 'conduct forming part of a course of criminal activity' (that is, the offender has been convicted of three or more other offences and has benefited from them, or the offender has two or more separate previous convictions during last the last six years and has benefited from them); or
- the present offence was committed over a period of at least six months and the offender has benefited from it.

For these purposes, an offence is disregarded unless the offender obtained benefit of more than £5,000 from it.

The next stage is for the court to decide the value of the benefit which the offender has derived from the criminal lifestyle.

In deciding whether (and by how much) an offender has benefited from criminal conduct, the court is required to make certain assumptions (contained in s.10):

- Any property transferred to the offender in the six years prior to the commencement of the present proceedings (i.e. property acquired during that period) was obtained as a result of general criminal conduct.
- Any property held by the offender at any time after the date of conviction (in effect, property currently owned by the offender) was obtained as a result of general criminal conduct.
- Any expenditure incurred by the offender in the previous six years was met from property obtained by the offender as a result of general criminal conduct.
- The offender holds all property free of any other interests in it.

By virtue of s.10(6), the court must not make a required assumption in relation to particular property or expenditure if either:

- the assumption is shown (on the balance of probabilities) to be incorrect; or
- there would be a serious risk of injustice if the assumption were made.

The practical effect is that the offender has to show (on the balance of probabilities) that the assets to which the assumptions apply are not the proceeds of crime.

Having quantified the value of the offender's benefit from criminal conduct (the 'recoverable amount'), the court must go on to decide the 'available amount' (that is, the value of the offender's current assets). If the offender shows that the 'available amount' is less than the total benefit from criminal conduct, the confiscation order will be for the available amount. It should be noted, however, that if the value of the offender's assets subsequently increases (and the confiscation order was for less than the total value of the offender's benefit from criminal conduct), the prosecution can apply (under s.22) for an increase in the amount of the confiscation order.

Under s.38 of the Act, the court will impose a term of imprisonment in default (which will not start to run until the offender has served any prison sentence imposed for offence(s) which led to the confiscation order being made); serving a sentence in default does 'not prevent the confiscation order from continuing to have effect so far as any other method of enforcement is concerned' (so the offender still owes the money).

14.14.4 Criminal Behaviour Orders

Section 22(2) of the Anti-social Behaviour, Crime and Policing Act 2014 provides that the court may make a criminal behaviour order against someone who has been convicted of an offence if two conditions are met:

- 'The court is satisfied, beyond reasonable doubt, that the offender has engaged in behaviour that caused or was likely to cause harassment, alarm or distress to any person'; and
- 'The court considers that making the order will help in preventing the offender from engaging in such behaviour'.

Subs.(5) defines a criminal behaviour order as an order which, for the purpose of preventing the offender from engaging in such behaviour, prohibits the offender from doing anything described in the order, and/or requires the offender to do anything described in the order.

A criminal behaviour order must be made in addition to a sentence imposed in respect of the offence or a conditional discharge (subs.(6)) and can be made only on the application of the prosecution (subs.(7)).

In R v Khan [2018] EWCA Crim 1472; [2018] 2 Cr App R (S) 53, Bean LJ (at [14]) said that:

As with any order of a criminal court which has characteristics of an injunction, it is essential that the guidance given by this court in R v Boness [2005] EWCA Crim 2395 at [19]–[23] in relation to anti-social behaviour orders [which have since been abolished] should be borne in mind [when making a criminal behaviour order]. The terms of the order must be precise and capable of being understood by the offender. The findings of fact giving rise to the making of the order must be recorded. The order must be explained to the offender. The exact terms of the order must be pronounced in open court and the written order must accurately reflect the order as pronounced'.

His Lordship added (at [15]):

Because an order must be precise and capable of being understood by the offender, a court should ask itself before making an order 'are the terms of this order clear so that the offender will know precisely what it is that he is prohibited from doing?' Prohibitions should be reasonable and proportionate; realistic and practical; and be in terms which make it easy to determine and prosecute a breach. Exclusion zones should be clearly delineated (generally with the use of clearly marked maps …) and individuals whom the defendant is prohibited from contacting or associating with should be clearly identified.

14.14.5 Registration of sex offenders

Sections 80–92 of the Sexual Offences Act 2003 require those convicted of specified sexual offences (listed in Sch.3 to the Act), within three days of the conviction, to notify certain personal details (including name (and any aliases), home address and any other addresses at which the offender regularly resides or stays) to the police (s.83). Any changes to this information must be notified to the police (s.84). This process is commonly known as being put on the 'sex offenders register'.

14.15 Bind overs

A magistrates' court can bind a person over 'to keep the peace'. One source of the power of justices of the peace to bind over to keep the peace may be found in the Justices of the Peace Act 1361. The Crown Court, as a court of record, also has the power 'to bind over to keep the peace, and power to bind over to be of good behaviour, a person who or whose case is before the court' (s.1(7) of the Justices of the Peace Act 1968).

The effect of such an order is that the offender promises to pay a specified sum of money in the event of misbehaving during the period specified by the court. When exercising its power to bind over, the court must fix the period during which the bind over is to last (i.e. the period during which misbehaviour will result in forfeiture of the recognisance) and must also fix the amount to be forfeited if the person breaches the order.

Generally, binding over to keep the peace is warranted only where there is evidence of likely personal danger to others involving violence or the threat of violence (see *Emohare v Thames Magistrates' Court* [2009] EWHC 689 (Admin); (2009) 173 JP 303).

Criminal Practice Direction VII, para.J.1, refers to two decisions of the European Court of Human Rights: *Steel v United Kingdom* (1999) 28 EHRR 603 and *Hashman and Harrup v* United Kingdom (2000) 30 EHRR 241. The Practice Direction goes on to give guidance in the light of these decisions (at paras J.2 and J.3):

> Before imposing a binding over order, the court must be satisfied so that it is sure that a breach of the peace involving violence, or an imminent threat of violence, has occurred or that there is a real risk of violence in the future. Such violence may be perpetrated by the individual who will be subject to the order or by a third party as a natural consequence of the individual's conduct.
>
> In light of the judgment in Hashman, courts should no longer bind an individual over 'to be of good behaviour'. Rather than binding an individual over to 'keep the peace' in general terms, the court should identify the specific conduct or activity from which the individual must refrain.

Moreover, the court must be 'satisfied so that it is sure of the matters complained of before a binding over order may be imposed (para.J.8).

When fixing the amount of the recognisance, the court 'should have regard to the individual's financial resources and should hear representations from the individual or his legal representatives regarding finances' (para.J.11).

It should be noted that a conviction is not a precondition for being bound over. In *Veater v G* [1981] 1 WLR 567, Lord Lane CJ said (at p.574) that the power to bind over is 'exercisable not by reason of any offence having been committed, but as a measure of preventive justice, that is to say, where the person's conduct is such as to lead the justice to suspect that there may be a breach of the peace, or that he may misbehave'. It follows that a defendant who has been acquitted may be bound over R v *Inner London Crown Court Ex p. Benjamin* (1987) 85 Cr App R 267); the same applies where the prosecution are unable to proceed (R v *Lincoln Crown Court ex p Jude* [1998] 1 WLR 24).

Chapter 15

Sentencing Young Offenders

Chapter Contents

In this chapter, we examine the sentences that may be imposed on offenders who, at the date of conviction, are under the age of 18.

15.1 Sentencing young offenders

Section 142A of the Criminal Justice Act 2003, which (at the time of writing) is not in force, sets out the purposes of sentencing where a court is dealing with an offender under the age of 18.

Under subs.(2), the court must have regard to (a) the principal aim of the youth justice system, which is to prevent offending (or re-offending) by persons aged under 18 (see s.37(1) of the Crime and Disorder Act 1998); and (b) the welfare of the offender (in accordance with s.44 of the Children and Young Persons Act 1933); and the purposes of sentencing that are set out in subs.(3), namely: (i) the punishment of offenders; (ii) the reform and rehabilitation of offenders; (iii) the protection of the public; and (iv) the making of reparation by offenders to persons affected by their offences. These purposes are the same as those for adult offenders save for the omission of the reduction of crime (including its reduction by deterrence).

Even though s.142A is not in force, the court of course still has to comply with s.37(1) of the Crime and Disorder Act 1998) and s.44 of the Children and Young Persons Act 1933. If s.142A were to be brought into force, the main effect would be to remove deterrence as a legitimate sentencing objective when dealing with young offenders.

In June 2017, a new Sentencing Council Guideline came into effect, entitled *Overarching Principles – Sentencing Children and Young People*. Paragraph 1.2 states that:

> While the seriousness of the offence will be the starting point, the approach to sentencing should be individualistic and focused on the child or young person, as opposed to offence focused. For a child or young person the sentence should focus on rehabilitation where possible. A court should also consider the effect the sentence is likely to have on the child or young person (both positive and negative) as well as any underlying factors contributing to the offending behaviour.

Paragraph 1.4 goes on to say that:

> It is important to avoid 'criminalising' children and young people unnecessarily; the primary purpose of the youth justice system is to encourage children and young people to take responsibility for their own actions and promote re-integration into society rather than to punish. Restorative justice disposals may be of particular value for children and young people as they can encourage them to take responsibility for their actions and understand the impact their offence may have had on others.

Paragraph 1.5 makes the point that children and young people 'are not fully developed and they have not attained full maturity', and that this 'can impact on their decision making and risk taking behaviour'. It is therefore important to consider

> the extent to which the child or young person has been acting impulsively and whether their conduct has been affected by inexperience, emotional volatility or negative influences. They may not fully appreciate the effect their actions can have on other people and may not be capable of fully understanding the distress and pain they cause to the victims of their crimes'.

Moreover, they are also 'likely to be susceptible to peer pressure and other external influences and changes taking place during adolescence can lead to experimentation, resulting in criminal behaviour'. It should also be emphasised, when considering a child or young person's age, that 'their emotional and developmental age is of at least equal importance to their chronological age (if not greater)'.

This may impact on the choice of sentence. Paragraph 1.6 says:

> For these reasons, children and young people are likely to benefit from being given an opportunity to address their behaviour and may be receptive to changing their conduct. They should, if possible, be given the opportunity to learn from their mistakes without undue penalisation or stigma, especially as a court sanction might have a significant effect on the prospects and opportunities of the child or young person and hinder their re-integration into society.

The Guideline goes to make two further general points about young offenders to be borne in mind by sentencers (paras 1.7 and 1.8):

> Offending by a child or young person is often a phase which passes fairly rapidly and so the sentence should not result in the alienation of the child or young person from society if that can be avoided.
>
>   The impact of punishment is likely to be felt more heavily by a child or young person in comparison to an adult as any sentence will seem longer due to their young age. In addition, penal interventions may interfere with a child or young person's education and this should be considered by a court at sentencing.

For an analysis of this Sentencing Council Guideline, see Nigel Stone, *Sentencing children: overarching principles revisited* (2017) Youth Justice 171–80.

15.1.1 Welfare

As we have seen, the court is required to have regard to the welfare of the child or young person. The Sentencing Council Guideline notes that this statutory obligation 'includes the obligation to secure proper provision for education and training, to remove the child or young person from undesirable surroundings where appropriate and the need to choose the best option for the child or young person taking account of the circumstances of the offence' (para.1.11).

Paragraph 12 sets out a number of matters to which the court should be alert:

- any mental health problems or learning difficulties/disabilities;
- any experiences of brain injury or traumatic life experience (including exposure to drug and alcohol abuse) and the developmental impact this may have had;
- any speech and language difficulties and the effect this may have on the ability of the child or young person (or any accompanying adult) to communicate with the court, to understand the sanction imposed or to fulfil the obligations resulting from that sanction;
- the vulnerability of children and young people to self-harm, particularly within a custodial environment; and
- the effect on children and young people of experiences of loss and neglect and/or abuse.

The court should also take account of the 'reasons why, on some occasions, a child or young person may conduct themselves inappropriately in court (e.g. due to nervousness, a lack of understanding of the system, a belief that they will be discriminated against, peer pressure to behave in a certain way because of others present, a lack of maturity etc.)' (para.1.15). Put another way, conduct that might be regarded as disrespectful to the court or inconsistent with remorse should not necessarily count against the child or young person.

The Guideline encourages sentencers to contextualise the offending. For example, para.1.16 makes the point that:

> Evidence shows that looked after children and young people are over-represented in the criminal justice system. When dealing with a child or young person who is looked after the court should also bear in mind the additional complex vulnerabilities that are likely to be present in their background.

Similarly, para.1.18 makes the very important point that:

> There is also evidence to suggest that black and minority ethnic children and young people are over-represented in the youth justice system. The factors contributing to this are complex. One factor is that a significant proportion of looked after children and young people are from a black and minority ethnic background. A further factor may be the experience of such children and young people in terms of discrimination and negative experiences of authority.

Paragraph 1.20 adds that:

> When considering a child or young person who may be particularly vulnerable, sentencers should consider which available disposal is best able to support the child or young person and which disposals could potentially exacerbate any underlying issues. This is particularly important when considering custodial sentences as there are concerns about the effect on vulnerable children and young people of being in closed conditions, with significant risks of self-harm, including suicide.

This section of the Guideline concludes with the point that these principles 'do not undermine the fact that the sentence should reflect the seriousness of the offence'. Nonetheless, the clear message from the Guideline is that custody should be avoided unless there is no realistic alternative, and that the court should endeavour to pass a sentence that will help the child/young person get his/her life back on track.

Section 4 of the Guideline addresses 'determining the sentence'. Paragraph 4.1 says that the 'key elements' to consider are:

- the principal aim of the youth justice system (to prevent re-offending by children and young people);
- the welfare of the child or young person;
- the age of the child or young person (chronological, developmental and emotional);
- the seriousness of the offence;
- the likelihood of further offences being committed; and
- the extent of harm likely to result from those further offences.

Paragraph 4.5 addresses the question of culpability, which includes consideration of the awareness that the child/young person had of his/her actions and the possible consequences of those actions:

> There is an expectation that in general a child or young person will be dealt with less severely than an adult offender. In part, this is because children and young people are

unlikely to have the same experience and capacity as an adult to understand the effect of their actions on other people or to appreciate the pain and distress caused and because a child or young person may be less able to resist temptation, especially where peer pressure is exerted. Children and young people are inherently more vulnerable than adults due to their age and the court will need to consider any mental health problems and/or learning disabilities they may have, as well as their emotional and developmental age. Any external factors that may have affected the child or young person's behaviour should be taken into account.

Paragraph 4.10 goes on to say that:

the developmental and emotional age of the child or young person should always be considered and it is of at least equal importance as their chronological age. It is important to consider whether the child or young person has the necessary maturity to appreciate fully the consequences of their conduct, the extent to which the child or young person has been acting on an impulsive basis and whether their conduct has been affected by inexperience, emotional volatility or negative influences.

15.2 Custodial sentences

There are three types of custodial sentence which apply to offenders who have not attained the age of 21:

- a 'detention and training order', under s.100 of the Act (offenders under 18);
- long-term detention under s.91 of the Act (offenders under 18 convicted of 'grave' crimes);
- 'detention in a young offender institution', under s.96 of the Powers of Criminal Courts (Sentencing) Act 2000 (18–20 year olds).

Unless there is an offence-specific Sentencing Guideline that applies to young offenders, the court has to take as its starting point the offence-specific guidelines applicable to adult offenders, subject of course to the guidance contained in the Sentencing Council Guideline on Sentencing Children and Young People. That Guideline says (at paras 6.46 and 6.47):

When considering the relevant adult guideline, the court may feel it appropriate to apply a sentence broadly within the region of half to two thirds of the adult sentence for those aged 15 – 17 and allow a greater reduction for those aged under 15. This is only a rough guide and must not be applied mechanistically. In most cases when considering the appropriate reduction from the adult sentence the emotional and developmental age and maturity of the child or young person is of at least equal importance as their chronological age.

The individual factors relating to the offence and the child or young person are of the greatest importance ad may present good reason to impose a sentence outside of this range. The court should bear in mind the negative effects a short custodial sentence can have; short sentences disrupt education and/or training and family relationships and support which are crucial stabilising factors to prevent re-offending.

There is an expectation that custodial sentences will be particularly rare if the offender is aged 14 or under. If custody is imposed, 'it should be for a shorter length of time than that which a young person aged 15–17 would receive if found guilty of the same offence' (para.6.48).

The Guideline urges extreme caution before imposing a custodial sentence on a child or young person, saying (at para.6.49):

> The welfare of the child or young person must be considered when imposing any sentence but is especially important when a custodial sentence is being considered. A custodial sentence could have a significant effect on the prospects and opportunities of the child or young person and a child or young person is likely to be more susceptible than an adult to the contaminating influences that can be expected within a custodial setting. There is a high reconviction rate for children and young people that have had custodial sentences and there have been many studies profiling the effect on vulnerable children and young people, particularly the risk of self-harm and suicide and so it is of utmost importance that custody is a last resort.

15.2.1 Detention and Training Orders (DTOs

Section 100 of the Powers of Criminal Courts (Sentencing) Act 2000 provides for the making of a 'detention and training order' where an offender between the ages of 12 and 17 is convicted of an offence which (in the case of an adult offender) is punishable with imprisonment.

A DTO is a custodial sentence and may be imposed only if the offence is so serious that neither a fine alone, nor a community sentence, can be justified (s.152(2) of the Criminal Justice Act 2003, which applies to all custodial sentences).

Where the offender has not attained the age of 15 at the date of conviction (i.e. is aged 12–14), a DTO may be imposed only if he is a 'persistent offender' (s.100(2)(a)). The term 'persistent offender' is (rather surprisingly) not defined in the legislation.

In R v Charlton [2001] 1 Cr App R(S) 120, the offender had been held to be a persistent offender solely on the basis of the offences currently before the court (three counts of burglary and two allowing himself to be carried in a motor vehicle which had been taken without consent). The Divisional Court held that the sentencing court was entitled to regard the offender as a persistent offender on the basis of the offences currently before the court. In R v G(TT) [2004] EWCA Crim 3086, McCombe J (at [10]) noted that formal cautions can be considered, along with convictions, in deciding whether or not an offender is persistent in his/her offending, and indeed that the provisions can apply in the case of a previously unconvicted offender who embarks upon a brief, but nonetheless persistent, spree of offending. Similarly, in R v B (A Juvenile) [2001] 1 Cr App R(S) 113, Turner J (at [14]) said that it is 'not necessary, as counsel sought to argue, that before a person should be categorised as a persistent offender he should have been committing a string of offences either of the same or a similar character, or that his failure to address his offending behaviour arose by his failure to comply with previous orders of a relevant court'.

The Sentencing Council Guideline summarises the position thus (at paras 6.5–6.9):

> ... In general, it is expected that the child or young person would have had previous contact with authority as a result of criminal behaviour. This includes previous findings of guilt as well as admissions of guilt such as restorative justice disposals and conditional cautions.
>
> A child or young person who has committed one previous offence cannot reasonably be classed as a persistent offender, and a child or young person who has committed two or more previous offences should not necessarily be assumed to be one. To determine if the behaviour is persistent the nature of the previous offences and the lapse of time between the offences would need to be considered.
>
> If there have been three findings of guilt in the past 12 months for imprisonable offences of a comparable nature (or the child or young person has been made the subject of orders as

detailed above in relation to an imprisonable offence) then the court could certainly justify classing the child or young person as a persistent offender.

When a child or young person is being sentenced in a single appearance for a series of separate, comparable offences committed over a short space of time then the court could justifiably consider the child or young person to be a persistent offender, despite the fact that there may be no previous findings of guilt. In these cases the court should consider whether the child or young person has had prior opportunity to address their offending behaviour before imposing one of the optional sentences available for persistent offenders only; if the court determines that the child or young person has not had an opportunity to address their behaviour and believes that an alternative sentence has a reasonable prospect of preventing re-offending then this alternative sentence should be imposed.

The court may also wish to consider any evidence of a reduction in the level of offending when taking into account previous offending behaviour. Children and young people may be unlikely to desist from committing crime in a clear cut manner but there may be changes in patterns of criminal behaviour (e.g. committing fewer and/or less serious offences or there being longer lengths of time between offences) that indicate that the child or young person is attempting to desist from crime.

Even if the court does consider the child/young person to be a persistent offender, this should not inevitably lead to a custodial sentence. The court must bear in mind that custodial sentences 'must be a last resort for all children and young people and there is an expectation that they will be particularly rare for children and young people aged 14 or under' (para.6.10).

Where the offender is aged 10 or 11 at the date of conviction, a DTO cannot be imposed unless and until the Secretary of State extends such orders to offenders of this age group (this had not happened at the time of writing) and the court is of the opinion that only a custodial sentence would be adequate to protect the public from further offending by the offender (s.100(2)(b)).

15.2.1.1 Duration of a detention and training order

Section 100(3) defines a DTO as a sentence comprising 'a period of detention and training followed by a period of supervision'. The total length of a DTO 'shall be 4, 6, 8, 10, 12, 18 or 24 months' (s.101(1)). However, the term of a DTO must not exceed the maximum term of imprisonment that the Crown Court could impose on an adult offender for that offence (s.101 (2)). Where the offender is convicted of more than one offence, the court may impose consecutive DTOs (s.101(3)), but the total term imposed must not exceed 24 months (s.101 (4)). Under s.101(8), in determining the length of a DTO, the court must take account of any period for which the offender has been remanded in custody (on bail subject to a qualifying curfew condition and an electronic monitoring condition) in connection with the offence.

In R (A) v The Governor of Huntercombe Young Offenders' Institute [2006] EWHC 2544 (Admin); (2007) 171 JP 65, the court noted that it is not open to a court to impose a detention and training order of a duration other than one of those specified in s.101(1).

Section 102(2) provides that the period of detention under a DTO is to be one-half of the total term of the order.

The length of a DTO cannot exceed the maximum sentence that may be passed in respect of the particular offence. In Pye v Leeds Youth Court [2006] EWHC 2527, for example, the offence carried a maximum sentence of three months, so the court quashed a four-month DTO, holding that where the maximum sentence for the offence is less than four months, it is not possible to impose a DTO (which cannot be for less than four months).

The reduction in sentence for pleading guilty (see Chapter 13) applies to DTOs as much as to any other custodial sentence. The Sentencing Council Guideline notes (at para.5.9) that if the reduction in sentence for a guilty plea results in a sentence that falls between two prescribed periods the court must impose (4, 6, 8, 10, 12, 18 or 24 months), 'the court must impose the lesser of those two periods. This may result in a reduction greater than a third, in order that the full reduction is given and a lawful sentence imposed'.

15.2.1.2 Supervision under a DTO

Section 103(1) provides that the period of supervision under a DTO begins with the offender's release from custody and lasts until the expiry of the total term of the order. During the period of supervision, the offender is under the supervision of a probation officer, or a member of a youth offending team (s.103(3)). The offender receives a notice setting out any requirements with which he must comply during the period of supervision (s.103(6)(b)).

Section 104 provides that failure to comply with such requirements will lead to the issue of a summons requiring the offender to appear before the youth court (if the allegation of breach is in writing and substantiated on oath, an arrest warrant may be issued instead). If breach of the requirement(s) is proven, the court may (under s.104(3)):

- order the detention of the offender for a period of three months, or the length of time from the date the breach was committed until the end of the order (whichever is shorter);
- impose an additional period of supervision for the same period;
- impose a fine of up to £1,000; or
- take no action.

Under s.104(3C), the court may impose a period of supervision or detention for breach even after the term of the DTO has finished.

Even if the offender has attained the age of 18 proceedings for breach of the supervision requirements must be dealt with in the youth court.

15.2.1.3 Commission of further offences during the supervision period of a DTO

Section 105 applies where a person is convicted of an imprisonable offence committed after release from detention but before the expiry of the term of the DTO (that is, during the period of supervision). The court that convicts him of the later offence may (as well as dealing with him for the later offence) order his detention for a period equal in length to the period between the date of the commission of the later offence and the date when the original DTO would have expired.

15.3 Detention under s.91 of the Powers of Criminal Courts (Sentencing) Act 2000

Once an offender has attained the age of 18, the courts can impose the same length of custody (by way of detention in a young offender institution if under the age of 21) that they could in the case of an adult (by way of imprisonment). However, in the case of an offender who is under 18 at the date of conviction, the usual custodial sentence (the detention and training order) is limited to a total of 24 months (of which only half is served in custody). Plainly, this would not be adequate punishment where an offender under the age of 18 has committed a really serious offence. Section 91 of the 2000 Act provides for long-term detention where the offence is punishable (in the case of an adult offender) with 14 years' imprisonment or more. It also applies to a number of offences under the Sexual Offences Act 2003 (including sexual assault, under s.3) and under the Firearms Act 1968.

Under s.91(3), a sentence of detention under s.91 may be imposed only if the court is of the opinion that neither a Youth Rehabilitation Order ('YRO') (see below) nor a DTO is suitable.

The maximum sentence that can be imposed under s.91 is the same as the maximum sentence of imprisonment which can be imposed on an adult offender for that offence (s.91(3)). If the offence carries life imprisonment in the case of an adult, detention for life can be ordered under s. 91.

15.4 Detention in a young offender institution

Section 96 of the Powers of Criminal Courts (Sentencing) Act 2000 provides that where an offender who has attained the age of 18 but is under 21 is convicted of an offence which is punishable with imprisonment in the case of an offender who has attained the age of 21, the court may impose a sentence of 'detention in a young offender institution'. Because this is a custodial sentence, it can be imposed only if the offence crosses the custody threshold in s.152(2) of the Criminal Justice Act 2003 ('CJA 2003').

The Criminal Justice and Court Services Act 2000 abolishes the sentence of the detention in a young offender institution. However, this repealing provision had not been brought into force at the time of writing. When this sentence is abolished, a court imposing a custodial sentence on a defendant aged 18 or over at the time of sentence will impose a sentence of imprisonment (as it would in the case of an offender who has attained the age of 21).

Under s.189(1) of the CJA 2003, a sentence of detention in a young offender institution may be suspended in the same way that a sentence of imprisonment can.

The maximum period of detention is the same as the maximum sentence of imprisonment in the case of an offender who has attained the age of 21 (s.97(1) of the 2000 Act). Section 97 (4) allows the court to impose consecutive sentences of detention in the same way that consecutive sentences of imprisonment can be imposed on an offender who has attained the age of 21.

15.5 Life sentences

Section 90 of the Powers of Criminal Courts (Sentencing) Act 2000 requires the court to detain the offender 'during Her Majesty's pleasure' (effectively a life sentence) if convicted of murder (or any other offence the sentence for which is fixed by law as life imprisonment) and he was under 18 at the time the offence was committed.

Where a person aged between 18 and 21 is convicted of murder, s.93 of the 2000 Act requires the court to pass a sentence of 'custody for life'. Section 94 of the 2000 Act provides that where an offender aged 18–20 is convicted of an offence which carries discretionary life imprisonment in the case of an adult offender, the Crown Court may impose custody for life. These provisions will be repealed when imprisonment becomes available in the case of offenders who have attained the age of 18 (and so a sentence of life imprisonment will be possible).

15.6 Youth rehabilitation orders (YROs)

Section 1 and Sch.1 of the Criminal Justice and Immigration Act 2008 create 'youth rehabilitation orders', a generic community order for children and young people which mirrors the generic community order for adults established by the Criminal Justice Act 2003.

Section 1(6) makes it clear that the power to impose a YRO is subject to s.148 of the Criminal Justice Act 2003, and so a YRO may be imposed only if the seriousness of the offence merits it, and the restrictions on liberty imposed by the order must be commensurate with the seriousness of the offence.

A range of requirements (the details of which is set out in Sch.1 to the Act) can be imposed under a YRO. Those listed in s.1(1) of the Act are:

- an activity requirement;
- a supervision requirement;
- if the offender is aged 16 or 17 at the time of the conviction, an unpaid work requirement;
- a programme requirement;
- an attendance centre requirement;
- a prohibited activity requirement;
- a curfew requirement;
- an exclusion requirement;
- a residence requirement;
- a local authority residence requirement;
- a mental health treatment requirement;
- a drug treatment requirement;
- a drug testing requirement;
- an intoxicating substance treatment requirement; and
- an education requirement.

Under s.1(2), a YRO may also impose an electronic monitoring requirement.
Section 1(3) goes on to provide that a YRO may be:

- a YRO with intensive supervision and surveillance; or
- a YRO with fostering.

The Sentencing Council Guideline (at para.6.26) cautions against imposing excessive requirements in a YRO: 'The court should take care to ensure that the requirements imposed are not too onerous so as to make breach of the order almost inevitable'.
Paragraphs 6.30 and 6.31 go on to say that:

> If a child or young person is assessed as presenting a high risk of re-offending or of causing serious harm but the offence that was committed is of relatively low seriousness then the appropriate requirements are likely to be primarily rehabilitative or for the protection of the public.
>
> Likewise, if a child or young person is assessed as presenting a low risk of re-offending or of causing serious harm but the offence was of relatively high seriousness then the appropriate requirements are likely to be primarily punitive.

15.6.1 Activity requirement

Paragraph 6 of Sch.1 says that this is a requirement that the offender must participate, on a specified number of days, in activities specified in the order (this can include participation in residential exercises).

The total number of days specified in the order must not exceed 90 days (para.6(2)). Participation in a residential exercise is limited to a period of seven days (para.7(3)).

Specified activities may consist of or include 'an activity whose purpose is that of reparation, such as an activity involving contact between an offender and persons affected by the offences in respect of which the order was made' (para.8(2)).

15.6.2 Supervision requirement

Paragraph 9 of Sch.1 defines this as a requirement that, during the period for which the order remains in force, the offender must attend appointments with the responsible officer, at such times and places as may be determined by the responsible officer.

15.6.3 Unpaid work requirement

This requirement (under para.10 of Sch.1) may be imposed only if the offender is aged 16 or 17 at the date of conviction. The total number of hours' unpaid work must be not less than 40, and not more than 240 (para.10(2)). The court may not impose an unpaid work requirement unless it is satisfied that the offender is a suitable person to perform work under such a requirement, and that appropriate work is available in the area where the offender resides (para.10(3).

The unpaid work must be performed during the period of 12 months from the making of the order (para.10(6)). However, unless it is revoked, the order remains in force until the offender has completed the specified number of hours (para.10(7)).

15.6.4 Programme requirement

This is a requirement that 'the offender must participate in a systematic set of activities ("a programme") specified in the order at a place or places so specified on such number of days as may be so specified' (para.11(1) of Sch.1). A programme requirement may also require the offender to reside at any place specified in the order, for any period so specified, if it is necessary for the offender to reside there for that period in order to participate in the programme (para.11(2)).

15.6.5 Attendance centre requirement

This requires the offender to attend an attendance centre for a specified number of hours (para.12 (1) of Sch.1). Paragraph 12(2) stipulates that the aggregate number of hours for which the offender may be required to attend an attendance centre varies according to age:

- if the offender is aged 16 or over at the time of conviction: not less than 12, and not more than 36 hours;
- if the offender is aged 14 or 15 at the time of conviction: not less than 12, and not more than 24 hours;
- if the offender is aged under 14 at the time of conviction: not more than 12 hours.

The offender may not be required to attend an attendance centre on more than one occasion on any day, or for more than three hours on any single occasion (para.12(6)).

At the attendance centre. the offender is required to 'engage in occupation, or receive instruction, under the supervision of and in accordance with instructions given by ... the officer in charge of the centre' (para.12(7)).

15.6.6 Prohibited activity requirement

This requires the offender to refrain from participating in activities specified in the order, on a day or days so specified, or during a period so specified (para.13(1) of Sch.1).

15.6.7 Curfew requirement

This requires the offender to remain, for periods specified in the order, at a place specified in the order (para.14(1) of Sch.1).

The curfew requirement may specify different places or different periods for different days, but may not specify periods which amount to less than two hours or more than 16 hours in any one day (para.14(2)). Moreover, the curfew requirement may not specify periods which fall outside the period of 12 months beginning with the day on which the requirement first takes effect (para.14(3)).

15.6.8 Exclusion requirement

This prohibits the offender from entering a place or area specified in the order for a period specified in the order (para.15(1) of Sch.1). The period specified must not be more than three months (para.15(2)).

The requirement may provide for the prohibition to operate only during the periods specified in the order, and may specify different places for different periods or days (para.15(3)).

15.6.9 Residence requirement

This is a requirement that, during the period specified in the order, the offender must reside with an individual specified in the order, or at a place specified in the order (para.16(1) of Sch.1). The latter type of residence requirement may not be included unless the offender is aged 16 or over at the time of conviction (para.16(4)).

15.6.10 Local authority residence requirement

This is a requirement that, during the period specified in the order, the offender must reside in accommodation provided by a local authority (para.17(1) of Sch.1). The order may also stipulate that the offender is not to reside with a person specified in the order (para.17(2)).

The court may include a local authority residence requirement in a YRO only if satisfied that 'the behaviour which constituted the offence was due to a significant extent to the circumstances in which the offender was living', and that 'the imposition of that requirement will assist in the offender's rehabilitation' (para.17(3)).

The period for which the offender must reside in local authority accommodation must be no longer than six months, and must not include any period after the offender has reached the age of 18 (para.17(6)).

15.6.11 Mental health treatment requirement

This is a requirement that the offender must submit, during the period(s) specified in the order, to treatment by a registered medical practitioner psychologist, with a view to the improvement of the offender's mental condition (para.20(1) of Sch.1). The treatment may be as an in-patient or as an out-patient (para.20(2)).

The court may include a mental health treatment requirement only if satisfied that the offender's mental condition is such as requires, and may be susceptible to, treatment, but is not such as to warrant the making of a hospital order or guardianship order under the Mental Health Act 1983; moreover, the offender must have expressed willingness to comply with the requirement (para.20(3)).

15.6.12 Drug treatment requirement

This is a requirement that the offender must submit, during the period(s) specified in the order, to treatment with a view to the reduction or elimination of dependency on, or propensity to misuse, drugs (para.22(1) of Sch.1). The court may include a drug treatment requirement only if it is satisfied that the offender is dependent on, or has a propensity to misuse, drugs, and that this dependency or propensity is such as requires, and may be susceptible to, treatment (para.22(2)).

Under para.23, the court may also include a drug-testing requirement, which requires the offender to provide samples for analysis.

15.6.13 Intoxicating substance treatment requirement

This is a requirement that the offender must submit, during the period(s) specified in the order, to treatment with a view to the reduction or elimination of dependency on or propensity to misuse intoxicating substances (para.24(1) of Sch.1). For this purpose, 'intoxicating substances' means alcohol or any other substance or product (other than a drug) which is capable of being inhaled or otherwise used for the purpose of causing intoxication (para.24(5)).

This requirement can be included only if the court is satisfied that the offender is dependent on, or has a propensity to misuse, intoxicating substances, and that this dependency or propensity is such as requires, and may be susceptible to, treatment (para.24(2)).

15.6.14 Education requirement

This is a requirement that the offender must comply, during the period(s) specified in the order, with approved education arrangements (para.25(1) of Sch.1), namely arrangements for the offender's education made by the offender's parent or guardian, and approved by the local education authority for the area in which the offender resides (para.25(2)).

Such a requirement can be included only if the court is satisfied that the inclusion of the education requirement is 'necessary for securing the good conduct of the offender or for preventing the commission of further offences' (para.25(4)).

An education requirement must not include any period after the offender has ceased to be of compulsory school age (para.25(5)).

15.6.15 Electronic monitoring requirement

Under s.1(2)(a) of the Criminal Justice and Immigration Act 2008, a YRO may include an electronic monitoring requirement in addition to other requirements. Under s.1(2)(b), and para.2 of Sch.1, where the order imposes a curfew requirement or imposes an exclusion requirement, the order must also impose an electronic monitoring requirement unless (in the particular circumstances of the case) the court considers it inappropriate for the order to do so. These provisions are subject to the general restrictions on electronic monitoring contained in para.26 of Sch.1.

15.6.16 Intensive supervision and surveillance

Section 1(3)(a) of the Act makes provision for a YRO 'with intensive supervision and surveillance'.

Under s.1(4), this can be done only if the offence for which the offender is being dealt with is punishable with imprisonment, and the court is of the opinion that the offence was so serious that a custodial sentence would otherwise be appropriate. If the offender is under the age of 15 at the time of conviction, the court must also be of the opinion that he/she is a persistent offender.

Under para.3(2) of Sch.1, if the court makes a YRO with intensive supervision and surveillance which imposes an activity requirement, it may specify in relation to that requirement a number of days, which must be more than 90 but not more than 180. Such an activity requirement is known as 'an extended activity requirement'. A YRO which imposes an extended activity requirement must also impose a supervision requirement and a curfew requirement, together with an electronic monitoring requirement (para.3(4)).

15.6.17 Fostering requirement

Section 1(3)(b) of the Criminal Justice and Immigration Act 2008 makes provision for a fostering requirement. The requirements set out in s.1(4) (see above) have to be satisfied. The court also has to be satisfied that, under para.4(2) of Sch.1, 'the behaviour which constituted the offence was due to a significant extent to the circumstances in which the offender was living', and that the imposition of a fostering requirement 'would assist in the offender's rehabilitation'.

A YRO which imposes a fostering requirement must also impose a supervision requirement (para.4(4)).

Paragraph 18(1) of Sch.1 defines a 'fostering requirement' as a requirement that, for a period specified in the order, the offender must reside with a local authority foster parent. This requirement must last for no more than 12 months and must not include any period after the offender has reached the age of 18 (para.18(2)).

A YRO with intensive supervision and surveillance may not impose a fostering requirement (para.5 of Sch.1), and so the two are mutually exclusive.

The Sentencing Council Guideline notes that 'an intensive supervision and surveillance requirement and a fostering requirement are both community alternatives to custody' (para.6.32). The offence must cross the custody threshold before one of these requirements can be imposed (para.6.33).

15.6.18 Duration of YRO

Paragraph 32(1) of Sch.1 stipulates that a YRO must specify a date, not more than three years after the date on which the order takes effect, by which all the requirements in it must have been complied with. Where the order imposes two or more different requirements, different dates may be specified (para.32(2)).

The minimum duration of a YRO with intensive supervision and surveillance is six months (para.32(3)).

15.6.19 Breach of YRO

Breach of a requirement under a YRO is governed by Part 2 of Sch.2 to the Criminal Justice and Immigration Act 2008.

Under para.3, if the responsible officer is of the opinion that the offender has failed without reasonable excuse to comply with a YRO, he must give the offender a warning or refer the matter back to the court.

Under para.4(1), if the responsible officer has given a first warning to the offender, and during the following 12 months has given a second warning to the offender, and during the period of 12 months following the date of the first warning the offender has again failed without reasonable excuse to comply with the order, the responsible officer must refer the matter back to the court. Paragraph 4(1) thus envisages two warnings before the case is referred back to the court.

The responsible officer may refrain from referring the matter back to the court if there are exceptional circumstances which justify not doing so (para.4(2)).

If the offender has not received a warning but fails without reasonable excuse to comply with the order, the responsible officer may refer the matter back to the court without going through the warning procedure (para.4(3)). This might be appropriate where, for example, the breach is a very serious one or it is clear that the offender has no intention of complying with the order.

Where the offender is referred back to the court, this is done by the responsible officer laying an information, and the court then issuing a summons requiring the attendance of the offender, or issuing an arrest warrant if the information is in writing and on oath (para.5).

If the original order was made by the Crown Court and did not contain a direction that further proceedings relating to the order should take place in a youth court or other magistrates' court, the offender will have to appear before the Crown Court. Otherwise, if he is under 18, he will have to appear before the youth court for the area where he resides or, if he has attained that age, his local magistrates' court (para.5).

Under para.6(2), where an offender appears before a youth court or other magistrates' court, and it is proved to the satisfaction of the court that the offender has failed without reasonable excuse to comply with the YRO, the court may:

- impose a fine (up to £2,500);
- amend the terms of the YRO so as to impose any requirement which could have been included in the order when it was made, whether in addition to, or in substitution for, any requirement(s) already imposed by the order;
- revoke the YRO and resentence the offender for the original offence in any way in which the court could have dealt with him at the time; or
- take no action.

When dealing with the offender, the court must take into account the extent to which he/she has complied with the YRO (para.6(4)).

Paragraph 6(8) stipulates that the court may not, if it is imposing additional requirements, impose an extended activity requirement, or a fostering requirement, if the order does not already impose such a requirement.

Where the court resentences the offender for the original offence, and he has 'wilfully and persistently failed to comply' with a YRO, the court may impose a YRO with intensive supervision and surveillance under para.6(13) whether or not the offence is an imprisonable one and whether or not it crosses the custody threshold (and so the restrictions in s.1(4)(a) and (b) do not apply). If the offender breaches a YRO with intensive supervision and surveillance, and the offence for which it was imposed was punishable with imprisonment, the court dealing with the breach may impose a custodial sentence even if the original offence did not cross the custody threshold (para.6(14)). If the offender breaches a YRO with intensive supervision and surveillance and the original offence was not punishable with imprisonment, the court dealing with the breach may impose a four-month DTO (para.6(15)).

Under para.7, where the YRO was made by the Crown Court and contains a direction that further proceedings should take place in a youth court or other magistrates' court, the youth court (or magistrates' court) may, instead of dealing with the offender themselves, commit him (in custody or on bail) to be dealt with by the Crown Court.

Under para.8, where the offender appears before the Crown Court (either because the order was made by the Crown Court and did not contain a direction that breaches are to be dealt with by magistrates, or because the magistrates have committed the offender to the Crown Court to be dealt with), and it is proved to the satisfaction of that court that the offender has failed without reasonable excuse to comply with the YRO, the Crown Court has the same options as the magistrates (see above).

The Sentencing Council Guideline emphasises that the 'primary objective when sentencing for breach of a YRO is to ensure that the child or young person completes the requirements imposed by the court'.

15.6.20 Commission of subsequent offences

Paragraphs 18 and 19 of Sch.2 deal with the situation where a YRO is in force in respect of an offender, and he/she is convicted of a further offence.

Where the offender is convicted of the further offence by a youth court or other magistrates' court ('the convicting court') and the YRO was made by a youth court or other magistrates' court, or was made by the Crown Court but contains a direction that further proceedings should be dealt with by a youth court or other magistrates' court, the convicting court may revoke the order (para.18(3)) and, if it does so, may also resentence the offender for the original offence (para.18(4)).

The convicting court may not revoke the order and resentence unless it considers that it would be in the interests of justice to do so, having regard to circumstances which have arisen since the YRO was made (para.18(5)). When resentencing, the sentencing court must take into account the extent to which the offender has complied with the order (para.18(6)).

If the YRO was made by the Crown Court and contains a direction that further proceedings should be dealt with by magistrates, the convicting court may (instead of dealing with the offender themselves) commit him/her (in custody or on bail) to the Crown Court to be dealt with (para.18(8) and (9)).

Where the YRO was made by the Crown court and does not contain a direction that further proceedings should be dealt with by magistrates, the convicting court may commit the offender (in custody or on bail) to the Crown Court (para.18(10) and (11)).

Under para.19, where a YRO is in force in respect of an offender, and that offender is convicted by the Crown Court of an offence (or has been committed to the Crown Court to be dealt with), the Crown Court may revoke the order and may also resentence the offender for the original offence. The Crown Court must not revoke the order or resentence unless it considers that it would be in the interests of justice to do so, having regard to circumstances which have arisen since the YRO was made (para.19(4)). When resentencing the offender, the Crown Court must take into account the extent to which the offender has complied with the order (para.19(5)).

15.7 Reparation orders

Under s.73(1) of the Powers of Criminal Courts (Sentencing) Act 2000, a reparation order may be made where a person aged under 18 has been convicted of an offence. The order requires the offender to make the form of reparation specified in the order (but not payment of compensation) either to the victim of the offence or someone otherwise affected by it (in either case, the person must be named in the order) or to the community at large.

A reparation order cannot require the offender to work for more than a total of 24 hours or to make reparation to any person without the consent of that person (s.74(1)). The form of reparation ordered must be commensurate with the seriousness of the offence(s) for which the offender is being dealt with (s.74(2)). The reparation has to be made under the supervision of a probation officer, a social worker or a member of a youth offending team ('YOT'), and has to be made within three months of the making of the order (s.74(8)).

Before making a reparation order, the court must obtain and consider a pre-sentence report indicating the type of work that is suitable for the offender and the attitude of the victim(s) to the requirements proposed to be included in the order (s.73(5)).

Section 73(8) requires the court to give reasons if it does not make a reparation order in any case where it has power to make such an order.

A reparation order cannot be made at the same time as a custodial sentence, a YRO or a referral order (s.73(4)).

15.8 Referral orders

A referral order may be either compulsory or discretionary. Under s.16(2) of the Powers of Criminal Courts (Sentencing) Act 2000, a referral order is mandatory where:

- a youth court or adult magistrates' court is dealing with an offender under the age of 18;
- the court is not minded to impose a custodial sentence, or to make a hospital order under the Mental Health Act 1983, or to grant an absolute or conditional discharge; and
- the conditions in s.17(1) are satisfied, namely:
  - the offence is punishable with imprisonment;
  - the offender pleaded guilty to the offence and to any connected offence; and
  - the offender has no previous convictions.

Under s.16(2), the court may also make a referral order if the conditions set out in s.17(2) are satisfied, namely:

- the compulsory referral conditions are not satisfied in relation to the offence;
- the offender pleaded guilty to the offence or, if the offender is being dealt with for the offence and for any connected offence, he has pleaded guilty to at least one of those offences.

Under s.18(1), the referral order requires the offender to attend meetings with a 'youth offender panel' (established by a 'youth offending team'). The offender enters into a youth offender contract (under s.23) for a period specified by the court (which must not be fewer than three nor more than 12 months).

Where the offender is under 16 when the referral order is made, a parent or guardian is required to attend the meetings of the youth offender panel established for their child, unless (and to the extent that) it would be unreasonable so to require (s.20).

If the offender fails to attend a panel meeting, he/she may be referred back to the court (s.22(2)).

At the first meeting of the youth offender panel established for the offender, the panel seeks to reach agreement with the offender on 'a programme of behaviour the aim (or principal aim) of which is the prevention of reoffending by the offender' (s.23(1)).

Under s.23(2), the terms of the programme may include any of the following:

- making financial or other reparation to a victim of, or person otherwise affected by, the offence(s);
- attending mediation sessions with any such victim or other person;
- carrying out unpaid work or service in or for the community;
- being at home at specified times;
- attendance at a school or other educational establishment or at a place of work;
- participation in specified activities ('such as those designed to address offending behaviour, those offering education or training or those assisting with the rehabilitation of persons dependent on, or having a propensity to misuse, alcohol or drugs');
- presenting him/herself to specified persons at specified times and places;
- staying away from specified places or persons (or both);
- enabling the offender's compliance with the programme to be supervised and recorded.

The programme is reduced into writing and is signed by the offender and a member of the panel (ss.23(5) and (6)).

Section 27 deals with the final meeting, which is held when the compliance period of the contract is due to expire. At the final meeting, the panel reviews the offender's compliance with the contract and decides whether he has satisfactorily completed the contract (s.27(2)). If the panel decides that the offender has complied with the contract, this decision has the effect of discharging the referral order (s.27(3)). Otherwise, the panel refers the offender back to the court (s.27(4)).

It should be noted that it possible for a child/young person to receive a referral order despite having received one on a previous occasion. The Sentencing Council Guideline (at para.6.20) says that:

> bearing in mind that the principal aim of the youth justice system is to prevent children and young people offending, second or subsequent referral orders should be considered in those cases where:
>
> (a) the offence is not serious enough for a YRO but the child or young person does appear to require some intervention OR
> (b) the offence is serious enough for a YRO but it is felt that a referral order would be the best way to prevent further offending (as an example, this may be because the child or young person has responded well in the past to such an order and the offence now before the court is dissimilar to that for which a referral order was previously imposed).

15.9 Fines

Under s.135(1) of the Powers of Criminal Courts (Sentencing) Act 2000, the maximum fine which may be imposed by a youth court or an adult magistrates' court on an offender who has not attained the age of 18 is £1,000. Where the offender has not attained the age of 14, the fine is limited to a maximum of £250 (subs.(2)). There is, however, no limit on the fine which may be imposed by the Crown Court.

Under s.137(1) of the Powers of Criminal Courts (Sentencing) Act 2000, where the offender is under 16, the court must order that any fine (or compensation order) be paid by the parent or guardian of the offender unless either the parent or guardian cannot be found, or it would be unreasonable to order the parent or guardian to pay the fine. Where the offender has attained the age of 16, the court has a power (not a duty) to order the parent or guardian to pay the fine (subs.(3)).

Where a parent or guardian is ordered to pay the fine, it is the means of the parent or guardian (not those of the young offender) which are taken into account in fixing the amount of the fine (s.138). Accordingly, s.136 empowers the court to make a 'financial circumstances order' requiring the parent or guardian to provide a statement of means.

15.10 Surcharge

By virtue of the Criminal Justice Act 2003 (Surcharge) Order 2012 (SI 2012/1696), the victim surcharge for offenders under the age of 18 is:

Conditional discharge: £15
Fine: £20
YRO: £20
Referral order: £20
Custodial sentence: £30

15.11 Bind over: parental recognisance

Section 150 of the Powers of Criminal Courts (Sentencing) Act 2000 empowers the Crown Court, a youth court or a magistrates' court to order the parent or guardian of an offender who has not attained the age of 18 to enter into a recognisance to 'take proper care of the offender and to exercise proper control over him' (s.150(2)). The effect of such an order is that the parent or guardian promises to pay a sum specified by the court, which must not exceed £1,000 (subs.(3)), if they fail to comply with the terms of the order. Such an order can be made only if the court is satisfied that it is desirable to do so in the interests of preventing the offender from committing further offences (s.150(1)(a)).

Under s.150, if the child or young person is aged under 16 then the court has a duty to make a parental bind over, if it would be desirable in the interest of preventing the commission of further offences; where the young person is aged 16 or 17, the court has a discretionary power to do so. If the court chooses not to impose a parental bind over or parenting order it must state in open court its reasons for not doing so. (s.150(1)(b)).

The Sentencing Council Guideline notes that, in most circumstances. a parenting order (under s.8 of the Crime and Disorder Act 1998) is likely to be more appropriate than a parental bind over (para.3.3).

15.12 Relevant age for determining age of offender

In R v Danga [1992] QB 476, the Court of Appeal ruled that the sentence to be imposed is determined according to the offender's age at the date of conviction, not at the date when sentence is passed. Thus, an offender who is 20 when convicted, but 21 at the date of sentence, would be sentenced to detention in a young offender institution, not to imprisonment. For example, in Aldis v DPP [2002] EWHC 403 (Admin); [2002] 2 Cr App R(S) 88, it was held that a defendant could receive a DTO even though he had attained the age of 18 prior to the sentencing hearing.

In R v Ghafoor [2002] EWCA Crim 1857; [2003] 1 Cr App R(S) 84, the offender was 17 at the date of the offence but, by the time he pleaded guilty, he had reached the age of 18. Since he had passed his 18th birthday before he pleaded guilty, the court was able to pass a sentence of up to a maximum of 10 years' detention in a young offender institution, whereas if he had pleaded guilty when he was still only 17, the maximum available custodial sentence would have been a term of 24 months' DTO. The Court of Appeal replaced a sentence of four and a half years' detention in a young offender institution with a sentence of 18 months. Dyson LJ (at [31]–[33]) said that, where a defendant crosses a relevant age threshold between the date of the commission of the offence and the date of conviction:

> The starting point is the sentence that the defendant would have been likely to receive if he had been sentenced at the date of the commission of the offence ... It should be noted that the 'starting point' is not the maximum sentence that could lawfully have been imposed, but the sentence that the offender would have been likely to receive.
>
> [T]the sentence that would have been passed at the date of the commission of the offence is a 'powerful factor'. It is the starting point, and other factors may have to be considered. But ... there have to be good reasons for departing from the starting point ...
>
> ... It will rarely be necessary for a court even to consider passing a sentence that is more severe than the maximum that it would have had jurisdiction to pass at the date of commission of the offence.

In R v Yarow [2013] EWCA Crim 1175; [2014] 1 Cr App R (S) 39, Elias LJ (at [9]) reiterated that regard should be had to the sentence that would have been appropriate had the offender been sentenced at the date the offence was committed, and that this sentence is 'a powerful factor, albeit not the sole determining one', in deciding what the sentence should be.

Paragraph 6.1 of the Sentencing Council Guideline notes that there will be occasions when an increase in the age of a child/young person will result in the maximum sentence on the date of the finding of guilt being greater than that available on the date on which the offence was committed (primarily turning 12, 15 or 18 years old). Paragraph 6.3 goes on to say:

> When any significant age threshold is passed it will rarely be appropriate that a more severe sentence than the maximum that the court could have imposed at the time the offence was committed should be imposed. However, a sentence at or close to that maximum may be appropriate.

15.13 Powers of an adult magistrates' court

There are some circumstances in which a juvenile may be tried and sentenced by an adult magistrates' court (see Chapter 6). However, the range of sentences available to the adult court is very limited. Under s.8(7) and (8) of the Powers of Criminal Courts (Sentencing) Act 2000, an adult magistrates' court may:

- make a referral order;
- order an absolute or conditional discharge;
- impose a fine;
- order the parents of the juvenile to enter into a recognisance to take proper care of, and to exercise proper control over, him.

The court may also make ancillary orders, such as compensation and disqualification from driving or from holding a driving licence.

15.14 Powers of youth court and Crown Court

As regards non-custodial sentences, the powers of the youth court and the Crown Court are identical.

15.15 Summary: sentences available according to age

Table 15.1 Sentences available according to age

Sentence	10–11	12–14	15–17
Referral order	✓	✓	✓
Absolute/conditional discharge	✓	✓	✓
Fine 10–13: max £250 14–17: max £1,000	✓	✓	✓
Youth rehabilitation order (YRO)	✓	✓	✓
YRO with intensive supervision and surveillance or fostering	✗	✓ If persistent offender	✓
Detention and training order (DTO)	✗	✓ If persistent offender	✓
Detention under s. 91 PCC(S)A 2000 (if 'grave' crime)	✓	✓	✓

Index

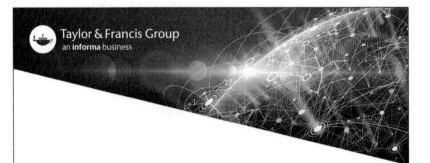